S0-BMY-405

975.8
St4a

21469

DATE DUE			
Dec 6 '8C			
GAYLORD M-2			PRINTED IN U.S.A.

WITHDRAWN
COLLEGE LIBRARY

AMERICAN HISTORY
SINCE 1865

HARPER'S HISTORICAL SERIES

Under the Editorship of

GUY STANTON FORD

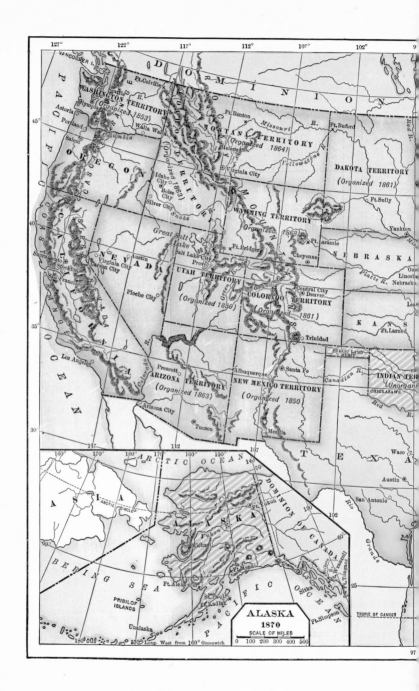

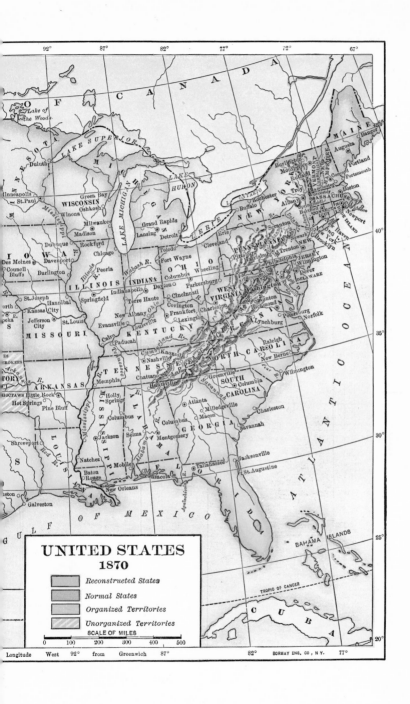

AMERICAN
HISTORY
SINCE 1865

by

GEORGE M. STEPHENSON

Professor of History
University of Minnesota

CARL A. RUDISILL
LIBRARY
LENOIR RHYNE COLLEGE

HARPER & BROTHERS PUBLISHERS
NEW YORK   LONDON

AMERICAN HISTORY SINCE 1865

Copyright, 1939, by Harper & Brothers
Printed in the United States of America

All rights in this book are reserved.
No part of this book may be reproduced in any
manner whatsoever without written permission.
For information address
Harper & Brothers

FIRST EDITION

L-N

973.8
St4a

21469
mai '46

CONTENTS

ILLUSTRATIONS

MAPS

EDITOR'S FOREWORD

YOU CANNOT READ THIS VOLUME WITHOUT LEARNING ABOUT American History from 1865 to the last "Fireside Chat" of Franklin Roosevelt. That is not its sole, perhaps not its chief, merit. No one can read this vigorous and scholarly review of the last seventy-five years of our national history without being compelled to think. This compulsion arises in part out of a treatment that illuminates neglected phases of our recent history and raises familiar topics to new importance. The longer perspective of seventy-five years supplied by this book helps the student and reader to understand the forces that are playing upon a nation still in the making. The recurring and emerging problems of this western democracy are visible to the discerning reader even while he is carried along by the unbroken story of the years. The sturdy navigator of your historical craft believes that if you, his readers, are to carry on where he leaves off you will do it better if you know the shoals and rocks and conflicting currents behind you and presumably ahead of you. The implication of such a treatment is that you have the courage and forward-looking mind that belong to my colleague, the author of this book.

Often when I have written the editorial forewords to the Harper histories I have had to resist doing the unconventional thing of talking about the author rather than commenting on the book. This book, or rather this author, has tested my wavering adherence to editorial conventions more than any other. Perhaps it is because we had some of the same teachers in American history, notably one, Frederick Jackson Turner. Perhaps it is because we are both Middle Westerners slightly watered down by Atlantic seaboard associations. Perhaps it is the differences rather than the likenesses. When the son of the best of immigrant stock talks about America it becomes my America. I am more certain of it because to his native discrimination and sound judgment the author has added research into many divergent factors in American history. I am just naturally interested in a scholar who masters the problem of the nation's public land policy, sweeps over the story of the peopling of a continent by the greatest mass *Völkerwanderung* in history, writes the story of the wars of Lutheran synods in America so that they become as interesting and significant as the doctrinal feuds that fill the early history of New England and overflow into the history of America. All this while he has so far suppressed, but not permanently, I hope, a desire to write a real history of baseball. But all this verges on what I have firmly foresworn.

If those who read or study this volume get as much pleasure and stimulation out of it as did the editor, I can assure the publishers that the only thing "in the red" will be the covers.

GUY STANTON FORD

AMERICAN HISTORY
SINCE 1865

CHAPTER I

A PRESIDENT WITHOUT A PARTY

A CIVIL WAR OF UNPRECEDENTED MAGNITUDE HAD GIVEN A RE-
publican form of government the severest test possible. Under the
stress of a conflict that was to test whether or not a "nation, conceived in liberty, and dedicated to the proposition that all men are
created equal" could long endure, the people of the North were
willing to intrust almost despotic power to the government. During
four years of civil strife the country was fortunate in having an
administration that in a most remarkable way personified the spirit
of the American people. From a small-town lawyer at the time
of his nomination by the Republican national convention in May,
1860, Abraham Lincoln grew to the stature of preeminence among
Presidents of the United States. He was a man the people were
willing to trust. Endowed with a native shrewdness and sense of
humor, a patriot and friend of humanity, he was perhaps the most
consummate politician who has ever occupied the office of President—calculating, moving with the current, feeling his way, ready
to temporize and to compromise. Events controlled him, as he
himself said.

A more untimely death than that of Abraham Lincoln, on April
15, 1865, is not recorded in the annals of the country. On April
9, according to the terms of surrender agreed upon at Appomattox, the tattered remnants of the gallant army commanded by
Robert E. Lee laid down their arms. The ramparts of the Confederate States of America were crumbling.

On the day of Lee's surrender, Lincoln returned to Washington
from a visit to Richmond, the capital of the Confederacy, heartened by the fortunate turn of events but weighed down by the
appalling task of reconstructing a divided nation. His death was
a calamity, a dire visitation on the South no less than on the North.

1

One searches in vain in his state papers and speeches for expressions of vindictiveness toward the South. In its lofty spirit of forgiveness and fatalistic submission to the judgments of a just and righteous God, Lincoln's Second Inaugural Address reads like a book of the New Testament. American Slavery he regarded as a scourge for which both North and South were responsible.

On the occasion of his last cabinet meeting on April 14, he expressed the hope that there would be no persecution, no bloody work, after the war was over. "No one need expect me to take any part in hanging or killing these men, even the worst of them," he said. "Frighten them out of the country, open the gates, let down the bars, scare them off. Enough lives have been sacrificed. We must extinguish our resentments if we expect harmony and union. There is too much of a desire on the part of some of our very good friends to be masters, to interfere with and dictate to those states, to treat the people not as fellow citizens; there is too little respect for their rights. I do not sympathize in these feelings."

It was in this spirit that President Lincoln had already outlined and begun the process of reconstructing the nation when he was shot down by the pistol of an assassin. In spite of ominous indications of impatience and hostility on the part of members of Congress and influential citizens with the policy the President proposed to pursue, he and he alone might have carried it to a reasonable degree of consummation, if it was humanly possible to temper the passions of the victors and save the self-respect of the vanquished. Just as cautiously as he had coped with the problem of the emancipation of the slaves, so did he temper his words and actions in preparing to bind up the nation's wounds. With a keen penetration into the constitutional aspects of a civil war, he proposed to cut through technicalities that served only to befog the vital issue of a speedy return to peace and union. As to whether the seceded states were in or out of the Union, he did not regard the question as material. He considered the question "bad as a basis of controversy, and good for nothing at all—a merely pernicious abstraction." He believed it possible to restore the states to their proper relation without deciding or even considering whether they had ever been out of the Union.

The wise and conciliatory Lincoln was succeeded by a man who was sadly lacking in those qualities that made the Great Emancipator a leader of men. Andrew Johnson, who was the vice-presidential candidate with Lincoln on the Union ticket in 1864, had electrified the North by his ringing speech in the United States Senate on December 18, 1860, in which he excoriated secession and avowed that the battle between the North and the South ought to be fought "inside of the Union, and upon the battlements of the Constitution itself." He denied that the election of a sectional President like Lincoln justified secession; and he made no distinction between a group of individuals in a state defying the laws of the federal government, and all the people in a state bent on the same purpose. He admitted that the federal government had no power to coerce a state, but he argued that it could clamp down on individuals within the boundaries of a state.

Coming from a Senator representing a slave state, Johnson's speech brought him scores upon scores of letters from both sections. In the South he was denounced as a "black-hearted wretch" who had betrayed his own section and state, whereas in the North he was extolled as a patriot who dared to face his southern colleagues who openly defended the right of a state to secede.

It is difficult for the historian to do justice to Andrew Johnson. His contemporaries in both sections of the country misunderstood him. Born amid surroundings perhaps even more humble than those that attended the youth of Lincoln, Johnson presented an accurate summary of his life when, in 1852, he wrote to a friend as follows: "When I calmly review my whole public life and consider the limited means I had in the beginning, as to education, money relations, and a fierce and wealthy opposition to contend with at every step of my advance, I feel bound to confess that I am more than grateful to friends for accomplishing what I have."

This "mechanic statesman," as he was called, was born in Raleigh, North Carolina, in 1808. When he was ten years of age he was apprenticed to a tailor, an occupation he continued to follow until he became a successful politician. At the age of eighteen he migrated to Greeneville, Tennessee, where in the course of years he became the personification and idol of East Tennessee. In spite of meager facilities for improving his mind—his wife taught him to read—he arose successively to the positions of alderman, mayor, member of the legislature, Congressman, governor, and United States Senator. He admired another Tennesseean, Andrew Jackson, for his unfaltering devotion to the Union; and, like "Old Hickory," he espoused the cause of the common man against the special privileges of wealth and birth. A man of great moral and physical courage, he waged unceasing warfare against the slave-holding aristocracy in behalf of the small farmer and laborer, whose interests were similar to those of his constituents in East Tennessee. Early in his career as a Congressman he advocated a homestead law on the ground that this legislation would build up the great middle class, populate the rural districts, strengthen the bonds of the Union, and create a better voting population.

Johnson's espousal of the homestead measure brought him notice in the newspapers of the North and West, and in 1860 his name was even mentioned in connection with the Democratic nomination for the Presidency. It was his courageous Union speech, delivered after the election of Lincoln and only two days before the convention in South Carolina unanimously passed an ordinance of secession, that brought applause and praise from lovers of the Union. After portions of Tennessee had been reclaimed by the military forces for the federal government in 1862, Lincoln appointed him military governor of the state. In discharging the duties of this position he showed superb courage and commendable ability.

This record made it a stroke of policy for the Republicans to nominate Johnson for the Vice-Presidency in order to emphasize the Union character of their party and to recognize the part the War Democrats had played in supporting the prosecution of the war against disunion. It could not be foreseen that the untimely death of Lincoln would automatically elevate to the Presidency a southern man, a Jacksonian Democrat, who had little in common with the dominant element of the Union Republican party, except opposition to secession and hostility toward the slaveholding aristocracy.

President Johnson understood that in every southern state there was a considerable element in the population that had opposed secession and had taken up arms against the federal government only after Lincoln had issued a call to arms to suppress resistance to federal authority. His own unswerving attachment to the Union and his knowledge that in East Tennessee the Union element was strong perhaps deceived him into thinking that reconstruction was a simpler process than it proved to be. His ear was not sensitive to public opinion; and even if it had been, his uncompromising nature would have prevented him from making concessions to his critics and adversaries in both North and South.

It is futile to discuss the merits of Johnson's reconstruction policy—to argue that it was wiser than the one that eventually prevailed—because the temper of both sections was such that wisdom and reason and perspective yielded to the passions of the victors and to the natural reluctance of the vanquished to admit defeat. To say that Johnson's plan for the restoration of the Union was practically identical with Lincoln's is to leave out of account the fact that Lincoln had begun his second term with the indorsement of the people and had safely steered the ship of state through an unprecedented sectional storm, whereas Johnson was an untried man and a Southerner. It was easy for propagandists, unscrupulous as well as idealistic, to cast suspicion on a man whose record showed him to have been opposed to abolitionist sentiments and to have stated that John Brown's raid on Harper's Ferry was the logical outcome of abolitionist teachings. His courage, patriotism, devotion to principle and duty, and integrity were buried under a barrage of propaganda that besmirched his character. He was said to be a drunkard, a libertine, an ignoramus, a southern sympathizer, and even a traitor.

In approaching the era of reconstruction it must be remembered that neither Lincoln nor Johnson could levy on the experience of the past. No other Presidents had faced the problems of secession or reconstruction. Both men yielded not one jot or tittle to others in their veneration for the Constitution; but Lincoln differed from Johnson in that he believed that within broad limits expediency should guide him in restoring peace to the country, in bringing the states into their proper relations to the federal government, and in guarding against the recurrence of civil war. Johnson, on the other hand, was doctrinaire in his constant appeal to the letter of the Constitution, and waved aside expediency in arguing the constitutional aspects of proposed legislation.

Johnson held with Lincoln that secession was impossible, and he clung to the theory that war was waged not against the states but against the insurgents personally. His problem, to state it simply, was to find the loyal citizens of the eleven so-called seceded states and to intrust to them the task of setting up loyal governments. The people of the South, however, insisted that the war had been fought over the question of state rights—not over slavery. Now that the war had resulted in victory for the North, they maintained that the question of whether or not a state had a right to secede had been answered in the negative. The major question having been settled, they argued that it remained only for the state to resume its proper place in the Union and for its citizens to take the oath of loyalty to the federal government.

In the North, however, there were powerful leaders who believed that the people of the states "lately in rebellion" could not be trusted and that certain well-defined conditions should be laid down to prevent the recurrence of war, to safeguard the rights of the whites—"Lincoln hirelings," they were called locally—who had risked life and property by remaining loyal to the federal government, and to protect the Negroes in their newly won freedom.

Senator Charles Sumner of Massachusetts set forth the view that by enacting ordinances of secession the states had committed treason against the United States and had thereby forfeited their rights and privileges under the Constitution. He developed the argument that the states had ceased to exist and had relapsed into territories, and that Congress therefore had the right to legislate for them in the more or less arbitrary fashion that it did for other territories.

Perhaps a more logical theory than Sumner's "state suicide theory" was expounded by Thaddeus Stevens, a member of Congress from Pennsylvania. This able and vindictive Pennsylvanian argued that the secessionists had no claim to the protection of the Constitution because they had attempted to destroy it. By violently

breaking the bonds of Union, they had placed themselves outside
the pale of the Constitution. It followed, according to Stevens,
that the states were in effect conquered provinces. "They are dead
as to all national and political action, and will remain so until
the government shall breathe into them the breath of life anew
and permit them to occupy their former position," he said. "In
other words, they are not out of the Union, but are only dead
carcasses lying within the Union."

Sumner and Stevens were in agreement that the people of the
southern states need not be consulted, since they were not to be
trusted; and they also believed that in the interest of safety and
justice Congress and not the President ought to cope with the
problem of reconstruction.

Both Lincoln and Johnson, however, took the position that the
task of reconstruction properly belonged to the chief executive by
virtue of the power vested in him to enforce the laws and to grant
pardons. Before the end of the war, on December 8, 1863, in an
amnesty proclamation Lincoln offered full pardon to persons who
had, directly or by implication, participated in the existing rebellion, provided that they took the oath of allegiance to the government of the United States. For the time being, certain persons
whose record and position made it dangerous to grant full pardon
were excluded from this offer. When a number of persons in
each state constituting not less than one-tenth of the votes cast in
the presidential election of 1860 had taken the oath of allegiance,
a loyal government could be set up.

When Johnson succeeded Lincoln in April, 1865, reconstruction
along the lines suggested in the amnesty proclamation had proceeded so far in Tennessee, Louisiana, and Arkansas that governors, members of legislatures, Congressmen, and Senators had
been elected.

In the earliest stages of Lincolnian reconstruction Congress was
disposed to concur; but opposition to the President's liberal terms
developed, and by the summer of 1864 Congress had formulated
its own plan in the so-called Wade-Davis bill. This bill foreshadowed the harsh terms of what eventually became the congressional plan of reconstruction. Lincoln, however, disposed of the

Wade-Davis bill by a pocket veto and in an explanatory proclamation of July 8, 1864, stated that, although he was reluctant to give his approval to a legislative enactment that committed him to an inflexible plan of reconstruction, he was willing to proceed along the lines suggested in the bill if the loyal people of any state preferred it to his own plan. It is evident therefore that, had Lincoln lived, his plan of reconstruction would have encountered powerful opposition within his own party.

When Andrew Johnson took the oath of office, the nation was in mourning for its martyred chief, the rebellion had been crushed, and Congress had adjourned over a month previously, not to convene until December, 1865, unless called into extraordinary session. The new President's antecedents and experiences certainly foreboded revenge upon the South; and his utterances and acts during the first days of his incumbency seemed to assure the radicals who disliked Lincoln's policy that a man after their own hearts was in the White House. Senator Grimes of Iowa, who three years later was to earn the hatred of the radicals because of his unwillingness to vote for Johnson's removal from office, wrote to his wife on the day following Lincoln's assassination that he was full of forebodings about Johnson. "He is loyal enough," he wrote, "but he is a man of low instincts, vindictive, violent, and of bad habits. His course will depend much upon the hands he falls into at the outset."

Johnson immediately issued a proclamation offering rewards for the arrest of certain prominent leaders of the Confederacy as accomplices in the assassination of Lincoln. Other men of influence, like General Grant, subscribed to the belief that the assassination was a Confederate conspiracy. After a short period of indecision, however, Johnson disappointed the radicals and made it plain that he intended to pursue a policy that coincided in the main with that of his predecessor.

Why did Johnson change? As in the case of most men charged with heavy duties, responsibility sobered him. Moreover, constitutionally he sympathized with the southern view of reconstruction, and he had Lincoln's magnanimous example before him.

Accordingly, on May 29, 1865, Johnson issued an amnesty proclamation which, though somewhat harsher in its terms than

Lincoln's of December, 1863, embodied the essentials of his predecessor's proclamation. This was followed by successive proclamations appointing provisional governors for seven states. The provisional governors were clothed with power to prescribe rules and
regulations for electing delegates to conventions for the purpose
of amending their constitutions and of restoring the states to their
proper relations to the federal government. During the summer
the President also recognized and sustained the loyal governments
of Virginia, Tennessee, Louisiana, and Arkansas which had been
set up under the Lincoln Administration.

The conventions made such changes in the constitutions as the
new order demanded, invalidated the ordinances of secession, abolished slavery, and, with one exception, repudiated the debts that
had been incurred by waging war against the federal government.
Then followed elections for state officers, including members of
the legislature. With but one exception, the legislatures ratified
the Thirteenth Amendment abolishing slavery, which had been
passed by Congress on January 31, 1865. When Congress convened on December 4, 1865, Representatives and Senators elected
by the reconstructed states appeared to take their seats.

It is important to remember that these fundamental changes
had been effected through the instrumentality of the President,
without his having called Congress into extraordinary session. For
this procedure Johnson was severely criticized by powerful men
within his own party; and historians like Rhodes have pronounced it a fatal mistake on Johnson's part. On the other hand,
in justification of Johnson it has been pointed out that shortly
before his assassination Lincoln stated to his cabinet that he regarded it providential that the rebellion had been crushed just at
the time Congress had adjourned: that there would be none of the
disturbing elements of that body to embarrass him. "If we are
wise and discreet we shall reanimate the states and get their governments in successful operation, with order prevailing and the
Union reestablished before Congress comes together in December,"
he said.

This may have been wisdom for Lincoln, but hardly for Johnson, though the bitterness on both sides was such that it may be

doubted whether or not the states reconstructed under Lincoln would have been readmitted without serious modifications imposed by Congress. Historical parallels are dangerous, but the experience of Woodrow Wilson seems to prove that even a President with the prestige of having led the country through a successful war and having been acclaimed as the savior of mankind can be thwarted in his purpose to deal magnanimously with the vanquished by a hostile Congress and a population warped in its judgment by the resources of the press and other agents of propaganda. Though far removed from the scenes of battle, the visible scars of war, in the form of saddened homes, crippled men, thwarted ambitions, and heavy taxes, together with the selfishness of partisan politics, inevitably embitter the victors.

The course of events in the Johnsonian reconstructed states did not make Johnson's path smoother. In every one of these states there were men who gave vent to ill-advised and intemperate utterances. They denounced the government of the United States and the outcome of the war and declared that the South was defeated but not conquered. Men and women showed their resentment over the presence of blue-clad soldiers by disrespectful remarks and conduct. It was only natural that a proud people should smart under the suffering of a war that produced Sherman's march to the sea and that brought to thousands the loss of business and social station. Throughout the South were signs of ruin in devastated fields, dismantled railways, and cities laid in ashes. But it was also natural for people in the North to resent aspersions on their own section. Moreover, the fact that the southern states were falling into the control of former "rebels" seemed to indicate to some that they were not honestly coming back into the Union, that the oaths of loyalty were merely nominal. It was presuming a great deal of human nature to expect that the North would welcome the election to the United States Senate of the former vice-president of the Confederate States of America, Alexander H. Stephens of Georgia. Did his election, as well as that of former Confederates to important positions, augur well for the treatment that would be accorded men who had risked their lives and fortunes by remaining loyal to the Union—men who had been stigmatized as "Lincoln hirelings" and "scalawags"?

Despite the fact that the Johnsonian governments, with but one exception, had ratified the Thirteenth Amendment, the actions of their legislatures with respect to the colored people nullified whatever advantage had been gained by it. Laws—so-called "black codes"—were enacted which required the freedmen to register, to be in the employ of white persons, and to refrain from attending public meetings after sunset. Negroes were not permitted to preach without permits, and physical chastisement could be administered by employers. In short, the civil rights of the freedmen were severely restricted.

These "black codes" were justified in the South on the ground that it was unsafe to allow a race suddenly released from bondage privileges ordinarily enjoyed by white citizens. It is true that the Negroes showed a disposition to enjoy their newly won freedom, that they held meetings to celebrate their emancipation, that some of them deserted plantations, and that there was petty thievery. These extraordinary conditions probably demanded the aid of the federal government to adjust the relations between the races. In any event, there were individuals in the North who saw in the regulations by the Johnsonian legislatures a disposition to retain the Negroes in bondage in defiance of the Thirteenth Amendment. And if slavery was the cause of the Civil War, as was generally believed in the North, it behooved the federal government to safeguard the fruits of victory. Moreover, conditions in the South opened the flood gates of propaganda to picture Andrew Jackson, a southern man and a Democrat, as a traitor.

During the seven months that intervened between the assassination of Lincoln and the assembling of Congress on December 4, 1865, the increasing bad temper of the Republican leaders was obvious; and hardly had the sound of the gavel of the clerk of the House of Representatives died out before the assault on the President's policy was launched. In the Senate, Charles Sumner, the humanitarian, and in the House, Thaddeus Stevens, the embittered septuagenarian, were in the saddle. The proceedings were "cut and dried." In the House, the clerk, acting in obedience to the Republican caucus, omitted from the preliminary rôle of members the names of members from the Johnsonian reconstructed states. The Democrats made a vigorous protest, alleging that according to this procedure the President of the United States was an alien because he was a citizen of Tennessee, one of the states whose Representatives were denied admission. But the parliamentary steam-roller was put into operation to crush attempts at delay and debate.

Then, as another slap at Johnson, Stevens introduced a resolution to provide for a Joint Committee on Reconstruction to consist of nine Representatives and six Senators, which should inquire into the conditions of the southern states—all this before Congress had accorded the usual courtesy to the President of listening to the reading of his message. The resolution was carried by an overwhelming vote.

Johnson's message proved to be a disappointment to his enemies. It was an admirable document, couched in dignified language, setting forth what had been accomplished in the direction of reconstruction and discoursing on the proper relations between the states and the federal government under the Constitution. In the words of the *New York Times*, "Probably no executive document was ever awaited with greater interest than the message transmitted to Congress yesterday. It is safe to say that none ever gave greater satisfaction when received."

But Congress was in no mood to be conciliated. Within a few days the Senate, at the suggestion of Sumner, called for documents in the possession of the President relating to conditions in the South, the purpose being to get before the country the report of General Carl Schurz, who at the instance of Johnson had made a tour of investigation. Sumner knew beforehand that Schurz's report was hostile to the President's policy; but Johnson attempted to checkmate his purpose by coupling with the Schurz report another written by General Grant, who had reported that the "mass of the thinking people of the South accept the present situation of affairs in good faith." In a brief message transmitting these documents the President expressed the opinion that "the aspect of affairs is more promising than, in view of all the circumstances, could well have been expected."

Sumner pronounced the President's statement a "whitewashing message" and compared it with President Pierce's message on affairs in Kansas, thereby coupling Johnson's name with that of a President who was looked upon a tool of the slaveholding aristocracy.

These skirmishes were preliminary to the battles that were to be fought over major items of legislation. The first battle was waged over the Freedmen's Bureau Bill. On March 3, 1865, Lincoln had approved a bill designed to assist freedmen in getting a start in life by establishing a bureau to have supervision and management over all abandoned lands and to have control of matters pertaining to freedmen. Through the bureau Negroes could obtain clothing, provisions, fuel, and shelter, as well as lands that had been confiscated or abandoned. The task of assisting them to obtain an education was also included. This law was to remain in force for the duration of the war and one year thereafter. Under the new bill passed by Congress the bureau was to continue for two years and was further charged with the duty of protecting legal and certain civil rights of the Negroes. It was expected that Johnson would sign the bill; but on February 19, 1866, he vetoed it because in his judgment it was unconstitutional and inexpedient. At the conclusion of the reading of the veto message there were hisses and cheers in the Senate gallery. The following day the bill failed to pass the Senate over the veto, eight Republicans voting with the Democrats to sustain the President.

Unfortunately, the President followed up his victory with a speech from the portico of the White House on Washington's Birthday, in which he incautiously gave his enemies an opening to get under his guard by indulging in personalities. From that time on Andrew Johnson was a defeated man. All the power of a hostile press and the resources of political generalship were employed to discredit a President who was as courageous and honest as he was inept in playing the game of politics as it was played by the radicals in Washington.

On the next major item of legislation on the radical program the President's veto was overridden. This was the Civil Rights Bill, which provided that all persons of African descent born in the United States were citizens thereof, and that there was to be no discrimination in civil rights or immunities among the inhabitants of any state or territory on account of race, color, or previous condition of servitude. In the debates on the bill the question was not merely whether the measure was just and wise, but whether Congress under the Constitution had the power to pass laws for the ordinary administration of justice in the states. The author of the bill, Senator Lyman Trumbull of Illinois, who was also the author of the Freedmen's Bureau Bill, argued that under the Thirteenth Amendment Congress had the power to legislate with the purpose of securing freedom to all people in the United States. On March 27 the President vetoed the bill because, in addition to constitutional scruples, he doubted the expediency of conferring citizenship on Negroes. The bill was promptly passed over the veto, as were all subsequent bills of importance, sometimes without even waiting for the formality of reading the veto message.

The exchange of shots between the White House and the Capitol was a prelude to a battle to be waged on a much wider front, namely, the congressional elections which were to determine whether the people of the respective states would return a majority to Congress sufficient to override presidential vetoes. After the veto of the Civil Rights Bill the issue between the radicals and the President was clearly joined; and it was made even sharper when the Joint Committee on Reconstruction made its report in April, 1866.

The committee was not unanimous as to the status of the seceded states; but it was agreed that the states were out of their natural relations to the Union and that it was necessary for Congress to take charge. Of the eleven states, only Tennessee was ready for admission, the committee reported. Congress must be convinced, the report continued, that the constitutions and laws of the other ten were in harmony with the Constitution of the United States, and that there was sufficient guarantee that peace would be maintained.

In order to bring this about, the committee formulated the

Fourteenth Amendment, which, as finally adopted, contained the following provisions : All persons born or naturalized in the United States are citizens of the United States and of the state wherein they reside. No state shall make or enforce any law which shall abridge the privileges of citizens of the United States; nor shall any state deprive any person of life, liberty, or property without due process of law. The second section provides that if a state denies the right of suffrage to male inhabitants twenty-one years of age or over, the basis of representation shall be proportionately reduced. The third section provides that no person who had taken part in the rebellion and had previously sworn to support the Constitution of the United States as a national or state officer should be a Senator or Representative in Congress or hold any office under the United States or any state, unless relieved of that disability by a two-thirds vote of each house of Congress. By the fourth section the Confederate debt was repudiated.

It should be noted that this amendment, which was ratified on July 28, 1868, did not extend suffrage to Negroes; it merely provided that if a state chose to deny them the right to vote, it would take the consequences in the form of reduced representation. By excluding prominent citizens from active citizenship at a time when friendly cooperation was desirable, reconciliation between the two sections was retarded. This section gave rise to debates when the question of granting pardons to individuals in this class was before Congress; and as a result old wounds were kept open. It furnished opportunities for radicals to hurl charges of disloyalty, which were replied to in kind by Senators and Representatives from the South. The "bloody shirt" continued to wave for many years.

Tennessee promptly ratified the Fourteenth Amendment and was admitted on July 24, 1866; but many things were to transpire before the ten remaining "erring sisters" were permitted to resume their places in the Union.

The events of the summer and autumn of 1866—the "critical year"—threw the balance in favor of the opponents of the President's policy. The fact that the legislatures of the Johnsonian states refused to ratify the Fourteenth Amendment was used to prove that the states were not willing to come back honestly. A serious race riot in New Orleans on July 30 was used to the same purpose. Indicative of the widening breach between the President and Congress was the resignation of three members of the cabinet, and the National Union convention at Philadelphia on August 14, called for the purpose of uniting the supporters of the President's policy. During the last days of August Johnson left the capital on a speaking tour to appeal to the electorate to indorse his policy.

The President's "swing around the circle" made him even more unpopular in the North. For one thing, the country did not approve of the then unusual spectacle of a President making a series of stump speeches; but Johnson's manner of speaking was even more unfortunate. He had been trained in campaigning in the rough-and-tumble school of Tennessee politics; and hostile audiences and carefully timed heckling baited him into replying in kind. He not only charged his opponents with treason but he singled out individuals for special castigation. It may be true that Johnson was no less intemperate than his adversaries, but his conduct was incompatible with the fine traditions of his office. The truth is that neither the President nor his adversaries could take pride in their respective performances. The radicals were more clever than the President in obscuring the issues at stake.

The results of the election indicated that the voters in the North did not wish to surrender to the South what they conceived to be the fruits of victory, and that the voters in the South did not want to be disfranchised, nor did they relish the prospect of losing a considerable number of Representatives in Congress, as provided in a section of the pending Fourteenth Amendment. Johnson's plan of reconstruction was doomed when the voters elected a majority of radical Republicans to Congress—sufficient to override vetoes.

When Congress convened in December, 1866, the radicals could congratulate themselves that their constituents had given them a mandate to heat the furnace for the "rebels" and to destroy the ten Johnsonian states, which they proceeded to do by passing over the veto the first Reconstruction Act on March 2, 1867. This act divided the ten "rebel" states into five military districts,

each of which was in charge of an army officer who was instructed to enroll the entire male population twenty-one years of
age or over. In each state a convention was to be called to formulate a new constitution to be submitted to the voters for approval.
After having adopted a constitution and having ratified the
Fourteenth Amendment, a state might be admitted into the Union,
subject to the approval of Congress.

In order to keep a tight rein on Johnson and to avoid such an
interval as existed between the assassination of Lincoln and the
assembling of Congress, the expiring Congress, which adjourned
on March 4, 1867, adopted a resolution convening Congress in
extraordinary session at once.

During March and July the new Congress enacted—over the
veto, of course—supplementary laws which prescribed in detail
the procedure to be followed in reconstructing the states. Pointing
his remarks to the gist of these acts, the historian Rhodes writes:
"No law so unjust in its policy, so direful in its results had passed
the American Congress since the Kansas-Nebraska Act of 1854."

Congressional reconstruction soon got under way. In several
states a majority of Negroes appeared on the registration lists of
voters enrolled under the auspices of military commanders; and
the delegates elected to the constitutional conventions were made
up of Negroes and men who were low in the social scale—former
Confederates having been excluded from active citizenship by
the Reconstruction Acts. The conventions enfranchised Negroes
and disfranchised "rebels." By June, 1868, seven states had ratified the Fourteenth Amendment and were admitted; and by March,
1870, the remaining three were admitted, with radicals in control
of every state.

In the struggle between the President and Congress the opponents of congressional reconstruction appealed to the courts to
stay the hand of the radicals. In the case of Mississippi *v.* Andrew
Johnson (1867) the United States Supreme Court decided that the
President could not be restrained by injunction from carrying
into effect an act of Congress alleged to be unconstitutional, whereupon Georgia filed a suit to restrain Secretary of War Stanton,
but the decision went against the state. In the case of *ex parte*

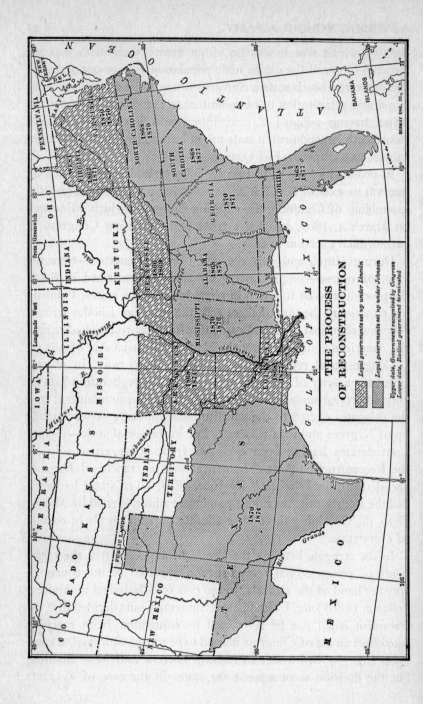

THE PROCESS
OF RECONSTRUCTION

Loyal governments set up under Lincoln

Loyal governments set up under Johnson

Upper date, Government recognized by Congress
Lower date, Radical government terminated

McCardle it appeared that the court could not avoid expressing condemnation of the military government of Mississippi without ignominiously reversing itself in the case of *ex parte* Milligan (1868); but Congress came to the rescue of the justices by repealing the law that gave the court jurisdiction over the case (March 27, 1868).

It is a tribute to the integrity and sagacity of Johnson that in the heat of partisanship he performed his duties in connection with the enforcement of laws, which his veto messages had pronounced unwise and unconstitutional, in such a manner that for over a year a congressional committee appointed for that purpose could find no grounds for impeaching him. On February 24, 1868, however, the House of Representatives, by a large majority, adopted an impeachment resolution. This action was precipitated by the President's alleged violation of the Tenure of Office Act (1867) by removing from office Secretary of War Stanton.

This act provided that members of the cabinet should hold office during the term of the President by whom they had been appointed, and that they could not be removed without the consent of the Senate. It was enacted in order to prevent Johnson from removing Stanton, who was not in sympathy with the President's policy and whose position clothed him with authority in connection with the administration of the Reconstruction Acts. Stanton's position in the cabinet was obnoxious to Johnson because of his flagrant disloyalty to his chief. Upon Stanton's refusal to resign, Johnson suspended him from office and appointed General Grant *ad interim* secretary, it having been agreed upon between Johnson and Grant that it was the President's purpose to test the constitutionality of the Tenure of Office Act. When the Senate refused to concur in Stanton's removal, Grant resigned, much to the disgust of Johnson, who charged that Grant had played him false. The President, however, refused to yield and appointed General Lorenzo Thomas, with instructions to eject Stanton from office. Stanton arrested Thomas; but Congress, not wishing to have the validity of the Tenure of Office Act tested in the courts, ordered Thomas to be released. It preferred to bring charges of high crimes and misdemeanors against Johnson and have the case tried in the Senate.

The able counsel for the President maintained that he was not guilty of intentional violation of the act—that he had the right to test its constitutionality—and further that he had not violated it, in view of the fact that Stanton had been appointed by Lincoln and therefore did not come within the scope of the law. After weeks of taking testimony and hearing arguments of counsel, at noon on May 18, 1868, every Senator was in his seat, the galleries were crowded with spectators, and intense silence reigned in the Senate chamber.

It was a matter of common knowledge that thirty-five Senators would vote for conviction and eighteen for acquittal. The one Senator whose vote was uncertain was Ross of Kansas. If he voted "Guilty," Andrew Johnson would be convicted; if he voted "Not guilty," the President would be acquitted. All eyes were fixed upon the hitherto undistinguished Senator when Chief Justice Chase, the presiding officer, addressed him as follows: "Mr. Senator Ross, how say you? Is the respondent, Andrew Johnson, President of the United States, guilty or not guilty of a high misdemeanor, as charged in this article?" Senator Ross arose and voted "Not guilty." Thirty-five Senators voted for conviction, and nineteen for acquittal—one vote less than the necessary two-thirds for conviction. Of the nineteen, twelve were Democrats and seven were Republicans. This act of courage on the part of the seven Republican Senators proved to be fatal to their public careers. It also permitted Johnson to serve out his term until March 4, 1869, when he was succeeded by General Grant, who by surrendering the office of Secretary of War to Stanton had won the gratitude and favor of the Republican leaders. But the nineteen Senators, some consciously and some unconsciously, played for the verdict of history—and won. Historians are in unanimous agreement that the verdict of May, 1868, was just. But Johnson retired, a discredited man and a man without a party.

March 4, 1875, was a day of triumph for the old fighter from Tennessee, for on that day he was sworn in as a Senator from Tennessee—the only former President to be accorded that distinction. He returned to the Senate to find himself in the group of men who had left no stone unturned to drive him from public life. These same men grasped his hand as he stood by his desk bedecked with flowers placed there by admirers. Even newspapers, which but a few short years before had joined the hue and cry against the "usurper" and "traitor," spoke kindly of the man. Visitors to Greeneville, Tennessee, are shown Andrew Johnson's tailor shop, inclosed in a brick building, and are directed to his monument which stands on a high eminence in a cemetery just outside the mountain city, which marks the resting place of the seventeenth President of the United States.

CHAPTER II

RADICAL RECONSTRUCTION AND ITS UNDOING

SIMULTANEOUSLY WITH THE COLLAPSE OF THE IMPEACHMENT proceedings, the politicians were preparing for the approaching presidential campaign of 1868. Eight of the states "lately in rebellion" would be eligible to cast their electoral votes. The Republican party was prepared to "go to the country" for approval of what had been done to reconstruct the southern states, and the Democratic party had no alternative but to nominate a candidate and adopt a platform that joined the issue.

The Republican national convention nominated General Ulysses S. Grant, whose record was acceptable to the Republican leaders. He had emerged from the Civil War as a successful general; and, although he had not committed himself squarely on the paramount issue, it was generally understood that he was in sympathy with radical reconstruction. At any rate, his quarrel with Johnson had made it plain that he was not in sympathy with the President's policy.

The Republican platform asked approval of what had been done in reconstruction, but the plank on Negro suffrage was an achievement worthy of the most expert political carpenter. "The guarantee by Congress of equal suffrage to all loyal men in the South was demanded by every consideration of public safety, of gratitude, and of justice, and must be maintained; while the question of suffrage in all loyal states properly belongs to the people of those states." The platform deplored the untimely death of Lincoln and regretted the accession of Johnson, "who has acted treacherously to the people who elected him . . . and has been justly impeached for high crimes and misdemeanors, and properly pronounced guilty thereof by thirty-five Senators."

The Democratic platform declared that the war was over and that the questions that had brought the war were settled. It demanded the immediate restoration to all states of their rights in the Union, amnesty for all past political offenses, and the regulation of the franchise in the states by their citizens. Johnson was gratefully remembered for having resisted the aggressions of Congress upon the constitutional rights of the states. In nominating Horatio Seymour of New York, the Democrats furnished the Republicans with the opportunity of contrasting the patriotism of Grant with the alleged disloyalty of Seymour, who as governor of New York, it was charged, had failed to cooperate wholeheartedly with the Lincoln administration in prosecuting the war.

Grant's 214 electoral votes against 80 for Seymour was a decisive victory for Republican reconstruction; but it was not a guarantee that Republican ascendancy would be maintained in the South, where the activity of the Freedmen's Bureau and the Loyal League, together with the presence of the federal army, gave rise to the suspicion that many Republican ballots were of the hothouse variety. In spite of the disfranchisement of many whites, it was already evident that they would stand together against the Negroes and that intimidation might coerce the Negroes to vote Democratic or not vote at all. If one of the objectives of radical reconstruction was to maintain Republican supremacy, it behooved the leaders of the party to devise a better safeguard for Negro suffrage than the negative policy of the Fourteenth Amendment.

Accordingly, in February, 1869, in the session of Congress that followed the election, the Fifteenth Amendment was passed, and by March 30, 1870, it was ratified by twenty-nine of the thirty-seven states. Thereafter it was unconstitutional to deny the right of suffrage to citizens on account of race, color, or previous condition of servitude. According to the interpretation of the Supreme Court in the cases of United States *v.* Reese and United States *v.* Cruikshank (1876), the right of suffrage is not a necessary attribute of citizenship, but exemption from discrimination in the exercise of that right is a necessary attribute; the right to vote comes from the states, subject to exemption from discrimination as stated in the amendment. The Fifteenth Amendment, therefore, does not confer the right of suffrage upon anyone; it merely prohibits states from giving preference to one citizen over another by reason of race, color, or previous condition of servitude.

On the day of Grant's inauguration, March 4, 1869, Virginia, Mississippi, and Texas were still "out of the Union," and they were denied admission until they had ratified the Fifteenth Amendment. By the end of March, the following year, their Representatives and Senators were seated, and one phase of reconstruction was completed; but the presence of federal troops in the South during the eight years of Grant's administration was a reminder that the readmission of the states was but one stage in the process of acquiring home rule.

By virtue of the fact that a considerable number of men who had risen to leadership in the South before the close of the Civil War had been disfranchised by the Fourteenth Amendment, the government of those states fell into the control of carpetbaggers, scalawags, and Negroes. "Carpetbaggers" was the name applied to northern men who migrated to the South after the war; and the whites who had remained loyal to the federal government or who had taken the oath of loyalty after the war were in derision called "scalawags."

The state governments under carpetbag rule were scandalous. The expenses of government increased alarmingly, salaries and offices multiplied, taxes were in many instances ruinous, and officials were unspeakably corrupt. Railways were projected, charters were secured through bribery, and bonds for railways that were never built or whose property was worth little or nothing were guaranteed by the states. As a result of this orgy of corruption, extravagance, and inefficiency, the states were saddled with heavy debts, which in some cases were repudiated after the carpetbag régime was overthrown. Millions are still held abroad, in spite of efforts to effect settlements—a circumstance that has sometimes complicated the efforts on the part of the government of the United States to adjudicate financial difficulties of its own citizens and to adjust the payment of "war debts" following the World War.

In retrospect the years from 1868 to 1876 seemed like a nightmare to the people of the South. As late as the opening years of the twentieth century, a Senator from South Carolina, Benjamin R. Tillman, confessed that bitterness surged up when he thought of the reconstruction period. "It comes up in such a volume of animosity and recollection of the degradation to which my people were subjected from 1868 to 1876 under the horde of carpet-baggers and thieves and scoundrels and ignorant Negroes that I hardly know how to contain myself," he said.

The ratification of the Thirteenth Amendment marked the end of slavery and the beginning of an appalling racial problem. The immediate emancipation of millions of Negroes was one of the "fundamental and astounding" results of the Civil War. It goes without saying that neither whites nor blacks were ready for it, as mankind never is prepared for events of catastrophic proportions. Neither fanatical haters of the Negro race nor doctrinaire humanitarians were competent to cope with the problem.

It will be recalled that Johnson's veto in February, 1866, prevented the efforts of Congress to continue the Freedmen's Bureau; but within a few months another bill with the same purpose was passed over the veto. Without ignoring many things that have been said to the contrary, it seems to be a fact that the bureau did good work in assisting Negroes to bridge the transition from bondage to freedom.

Friends of the Negroes in the North were anxious to extend to them the advantages of education. An educated Negro was thought to be the best safeguard against radical Southerners, in view of the fact that it had been the policy of his master to keep him in ignorance in order to shield him from exposure to abolitionist and other literature which would make him dissatisfied with his lot. Speaking generally, after the war the enlightened people of the South were not opposed to Negro education, but they did object most decidedly to what was taught by teachers who came down from the North, many of whom had no fundamental understanding of the Negro and his problems. Some of the teachers were not only poorly qualified but rough and rude. Partly, but not wholly, as a result of this situation, the cause of education among the freedmen suffered. Indeed, congressional reconstruction, which for a time fastened upon the states the most corrupt and incompetent governments they had ever known, retarded a brighter and better day for the Negro.

One reaction to Negro and carpetbag rule was the Ku Klux Klan. The origin of this organization is somewhat shrouded in mystery, but it is another example of the spontaneous rising of a people when conditions are considered intolerable. Societies under various names sprang up in all parts of the South to protect their members from what were conceived to be dangerous and intolerable conditions.

The Ku Klux Klan was organized in Tennessee in the fall of 1865 by Confederate soldiers who craved amusement in the form of fantastic costumes, ritual, and fellowship. It occurred to some of its members that the society had possibilities of terrorizing Negroes during the witching hours of the night. The superstitious and simple black folk were made to believe that the hooded beings were souls of departed Confederate soldiers who could work miracles, such as taking their bodies apart, rattling their bones, and drinking pailfuls of water.

Through intimidation and terrorism the Ku Klux Klan and the Knights of the White Camelia assisted in restoring white rule in the South, in spite of laws passed against them by the carpetbag governments. And President Grant on April 20, 1871, approved the Force Act, which gave the President authority to declare the southern states in rebellion and to suspend the writ of habeas corpus. The jurisdiction of the federal courts was extended to Ku Klux cases. It was, however, difficult to convict members of the Klan, partly because juries were intimidated and partly because Klansmen sat on juries.

In the summer of 1871 Congress appointed a committee to investigate the Ku Klux disturbances. The testimony taken by this committee and its recommendations are published in several bulky volumes known as the Report of the Ku Klux Committee. Much interesting information is contained in these volumes, but the material must be used with critical discernment because, in the nature of the case, many witnesses, both black and white, were unreliable and frightened by fear of consequences if certain testimony were offered. It is the judgment of the historian Rhodes that the report of the Democratic minority was nearer right than was the report of the Republican majority. The Democrats admitted that outrages had been perpetrated, but denied that the better element among the whites approved of them. Rhodes points out that the keystone of the Republican reconstruction policy was Negro suffrage, which had resulted in the worst government ever known in the United States. The Republicans could not ignore all the evil; some of it they palliated. The Democrats, on the other hand, dealt with realities and showed that the operations of the Klan had been sporadic. They made no apology for them. After 1872 the outrages for the most part ceased.

Laws and constitutional provisions that are not deeply rooted in customs and traditions and do not reflect existing social and political thought are doomed to eventual repeal or circumvention. The Ku Klux Klan was a sign that the intolerable conditions which had come into existence partly through the election to office of incompetent and corrupt men could not continue indefinitely. The Republican carpetbag governments were born of the extraordinary conditions that usually follow in the wake of upheaval and transition; and they were sustained by the power of the federal government conspicuously revealed by the presence of the army. It was inevitable, however, that with the subsidence of the war animosity and with the enactment of the Amnesty Act of 1872, which removed civil disabilities from all, except certain members of Congress, officers in the judicial, military, and naval service of the United States, heads of departments, and foreign ministers who joined the Confederacy, the normal political influence of the whites would assert itself.

Another factor that hastened the restoration of white rule was the perpetration of fraud at the polls. Intimidation, dishonesty in counting votes, stuffing ballot boxes, and gerrymandering were by no means unknown in the South and elsewhere before the advent of Negro suffrage; but these methods were eagerly seized upon in the South. In the "tidal wave of 1874," when the Democrats swept the country, Alabama, Arkansas, and Texas went into the Democratic column; and by the summer of 1875 only four recon-

structed states—North Carolina, South Carolina, Florida, and
Mississippi—remained under Republican control.

By that time the undoing of Republican reconstruction was in
the offing: the Fourteenth and Fifteenth Amendments were breaking down. The Fourteenth Amendment defined citizenship and
prohibited the abridgment of the rights and privileges of citizens
of the United States; the Fifteenth Amendment prohibited discrimination in the matter of suffrage on account of race, color, or
previous condition of servitude.

It would be a great mistake to assume that in the North the
Fifteenth Amendment was hailed with unanimous enthusiasm.
In some states, like Pennsylvania, for example, it created serious
situations for politicians in both parties. The constitution of Pennsylvania provided that all white male citizens of the state, properly
qualified, should enjoy the right of suffrage; and in accordance
with that provision the Republican State of Pennsylvania denied
to Negroes the right to vote. After the ratification of the Fifteenth
Amendment a considerable number of Republicans were averse to
increasing the number of illiterate voters; and in particular localities, embracing the slum districts of Philadelphia and the mining
districts, there was serious objection to Negro suffrage from the
Irish and the foreign elements generally. The immigrants were in
active competition with Negroes as hewers of wood and drawers
of water. It will be remembered that the suffrage plank in the
Republican national platform of 1868 was a masterly "straddle"
pointed to similar conditions in several northern states, including
Ohio and New York.

The interpretation of the Fourteenth Amendment by the United
States Supreme Court was not encouraging to the radicals. Laws
had been enacted to give Negroes equal rights with whites in
railway cars and waiting rooms, in theaters, and in other public
places. These laws were enforced until the court declared them to
be unconstitutional.

In the Slaughter House cases of 1873 the court was called to
pass upon the validity of a Louisiana statute which the plaintiffs
in error alleged was in violation of the Thirteenth and Fourteenth
Amendments, in that the law created an involuntary servitude,

abridged the privileges and immunities of citizens of the United States, denied to citizens equal protection of the laws, and deprived them of property without due process of law.

The court held that a person may be a citizen of the United States without regard to citizenship of a state. It specifically stated that the Fourteenth Amendment had overturned the Dred Scott decision by making all persons born or naturalized in the United States, and subject to the jurisdiction thereof, citizens of the United States and of the state wherein they reside. The court further declared that the language of the amendment made a clear distinction between citizenship of the United States and citizenship of a state; that is, a person must reside in a state to make him a citizen of it, but to be a citizen of the United States it is only necessary that he should be born or naturalized in the United States. After making this distinction, the court went on to say that the amendment speaks only of privileges and immunities of citizens of the United States, and does not speak of those of citizens of the several states. "It is a little remarkable," said the court, "if this clause was intended as a protection to the citizen of a state against the legislative power of his own state, that the word citizen of the state should be left out when it is so carefully used, and used in contradistinction to citizens of the United States, in the very sentence which precedes it." There is a difference between privileges and immunities belonging to a citizen of the United States as such and those belonging to a citizen of a state as such. "The latter must rest for their security and protection where they have heretofore rested."

The Fourteenth Amendment, then, did not transfer from the states to the federal government the security and protection of all civil rights. The court excused itself from defining the privileges and immunities of citizens of the United States which no state can abridge, "until some case involving those privileges may make it necessary to do so."

Ten years later, in 1883, the court held that the Fourteenth Amendment did not give Congress power to protect colored persons in equal enjoyment with white persons of the privileges of hotels, passenger trains, barber shops, and the like. The states

could, and did, enact laws segregating the races under the police
power. The so-called reconstruction amendments, then, gave the
Negro equality before the law, but did not compel states to give him
equal social privileges, although in the matter of public education
and accommodations on passenger trains, and the like, the courts
held that states and corporations are under obligations to furnish
instruction and service on a par with those enjoyed by other
citizens. In such matters, however, existing conditions in the
South, including "Jim Crow laws," illustrate the wide gulf between reality and theory.

With the withdrawal of federal troops from the South following the inauguration of President Hayes, the South was free to
deal with racial problems without serious threats of interference
from the federal government. It remained to find a means of cir-
cumventing the Fifteenth Amendment without resorting to flagrant
fraud and intimidation. The whites would rest easier if Negroes
could be deprived of the right to vote under the forms of legality.
The grandfather clauses and the white primaries furnished the
answer, though not without the unfavorable scrutiny of the Supreme Court.

It was found that property and educational qualifications and
vagrancy clauses would disfranchise a considerable number of
Negroes. Unfortunately, these disabilities were not peculiar to one
race, and, therefore, all too many whites would be disfranchised.
In order to provide loopholes for whites whose records were not
clear, it was provided by state constitutional enactments that
property and educational tests would not apply to persons who
themselves or whose fathers or grandfathers, had served in the
Confederate army or had voted prior to a certain date, usually
January, 1867, shortly before the first Reconstruction Act became effective. Beginning in 1890 these so-called grandfather
clauses were incorporated in the constitutions of southern states.
In 1915, however, the Supreme Court declared the Oklahoma
grandfather clause contrary to the federal Constitution.

When the direct primary came into vogue in the early years of
the twentieth century, certain southern states made use of it to
assure the supremacy of the white race by enacting laws excluding

Negroes from voting in Democratic primary elections. By reason of the fact that nomination for office on the Democratic ticket assured election, the real contest between rival candidates took place in the primary election, not in the election that followed. In 1927 Oliver Wendell Holmes, the liberal and well-beloved justice of the Supreme Court, celebrated his eighty-sixth birthday by reading the unanimous opinion of the court that the Texas law barring Negroes from Democratic primaries was unconstitutional. The court held that the Fourteenth Amendment not only gave citizenship to persons of color but also denied to any state the power to withhold from them equal protection of the laws. In the previous primary election in Texas considerably more than 700,-000 votes were cast in the Democratic primary, but only about 100,000 at the regular election. To claim that exclusion from the primary was not disfranchisement was a mere trick of rhetoric.

The South has been chary of giving its approval to any law that might furnish a pretext for federal interference in elections. For this reason there was considerable opposition to amendments providing for the direct election of Senators and conferring suffrage upon women. In 1911, seeing the shadow of a force bill over a resolution submitting to the states an amendment providing for the direct election of Senators, several southern Senators opposed it on the ground that it called for federal control of the election of Senators. The primary in the South was virtually the direct election of Senators by white voters; and thus by their votes against the proposed constitutional amendment, the Senators in effect voted against the method of electing Senators which their states had put into effect without constitutional warrant.

The establishment of white rule meant the establishment of Democratic rule. The basis for the "Solid South" was the determination of the white voters to concentrate their strength in one political party, thereby assuring control of their governments even in states like South Carolina, for example, where the Negroes were in the majority.

With the exception of occasional rumblings of dissent from certain "liberal" elements in the North and campaign thunder when conditions made it advantageous to raise the issue, there has been little effective criticism directed against the South for its treatment of the colored population. Southern fire eaters, like Senator Cole Blease of South Carolina and Senator James K. Vardaman of Mississippi, drew the fire of some northern newspapers during the first two decades of the present century by their intemperate utterances on the racial problem. Vardaman openly advocated the repeal of the Fourteenth and Fifteenth Amendments, and Blease hotly declared that his state did not propose to allow Negroes to vote despite decisions of the courts.

As the years after reconstruction marched on, the people of the North were increasingly concerned with the immigration of Chinese, Japanese, and people from southern and eastern Europe, to say nothing about the steadily increasing migration of Negroes to the North and the existence of "black belts" in cities like Chicago and Detroit.

Able leaders of the Negro race like Booker T. Washington and Robert Mouton gave themselves to prepare for a better understanding between the races. They recognized the wide gulf between them and faced conditions as they were, much as they may have deplored them. Washington advised his people to cease, for the time being, agitating for the suffrage; and he urged them to aspire to better things by contributing to the cultural, social, and economic development of their own race. The increasing number of Negro physicians, attorneys, merchants, and teachers, and, not least, the educational institution at Tuskegee, bear witness to his zeal and ability.

The "Solid South," however, is an enduring heritage of the Civil War and reconstruction. It was not until the presidential election of 1928 that there were signs that portended a serious break in the ranks of the solid Democratic states. The bloc of southern Democratic Senators and Representatives in Congress made both Democratic and Republican parties more sectional than would otherwise have been the case. The Republican party in the South has been merely a skeleton of federal officeholders to be manipulated in Republican national conventions to the detriment of the party and of the nation.

However, since the unhappy days of war and reconstruction

there has been a gradual growth of a better feeling between the sections. The Tillmans, the Vardamans, and the Bleases have given their section notoriety; but the southern spirit has also been voiced by such public men as L. Q. C. Lamar, John B. Gordon, John Sharp Williams, Hilary A. Herbert, Henry W. Grady, and others.

Forty-five years after the close of the Civil War, the Hamilton Club, one of Chicago's leading Republican organizations, discontinued its annual celebration of Appomattox Day, out of deference to the feelings of Southerners residing in Chicago. In July, 1913, the thinned ranks of the gray-clad veterans who fifty years before had fought at Gettysburg under Lee, charged over the terrain that had been watered by the blood of Pickett's men, to be received with hearty cheers and handclasps by blue-clad veterans waiting for them on Cemetery Ridge. Symbolic of a reunited nation was the spectacle of Senator Knute Nelson of Minnesota, a veteran of the Union army, and Senator John H. Bankhead of Alabama, a veteran of the Confederate army, marching arm-in-arm in a patriotic parade in Washington, at the head of which was President Woodrow Wilson, a Virginian and a Democrat. Lee's statue, clothed in Confederate uniform, stands in Statuary Hall in the National Capitol.

Republican Presidents since Hayes have relegated the racial problem to the states where the Negro resides. It remains to be seen whether or not time, with its healings and a higher culture for both races, will bring a solution of one of the most distressing problems that was ever presented to a self-governing people.

CHAPTER III

WAVING THE BLOODY SHIRT

THE ELECTION OF GRANT IN 1868 WAS ACCOMPLISHED WITHOUT serious opposition. His popularity as a successful general, the unpopularity of his opponent, the sectional hostility toward the former Confederate States of America, the disfranchisement of former "rebels," and the enfranchisement of the freedmen spelled victory for the Republicans. Notwithstanding two notable achievements of the Grant administration—the payment of the national debt according to the spirit of the contract and the pending settlement of long-standing grievances against Great Britain—the outlook for Republican success in the election of 1872, with Grant at the head of the ticket, was not hopeful.

The growth of the Republican party was in no slight degree due to the stress of the Civil War and to the split in the Democratic party. In the election of 1864, in order to attract the votes of men of all parties who believed in the preservation of the Union, the Republican party called itself the Union party and nominated for the Vice-Presidency Andrew Johnson, a War Democrat and a Southerner. After the close of the Civil War and during the heated battles fought over reconstruction in Johnson's and Grant's administrations, many War Democrats deserted the Republican fold and returned to the Democratic party.

The North was beginning to question seriously the wisdom of radical reconstruction, to ask if it was wise and just to disfranchise former Confederates and to maintain federal troops in the South to enforce the Force Act and the Ku Klux Act. Grant entered the White House with a political naïveté that was astounding to the seasoned politicians who worked with him. He was a man of little intellectual force and almost no imagination. His political experience had been meager. Before he was thrown into the political turmoil that followed the war, he had been indifferent to the political battles that raged around conditions and events that produced the Compromise of 1850, the Kansas-Nebraska Act, the Dred Scott decision, the Lincoln-Douglas debates, and the secession of eleven states. His record at West Point was worse than mediocre, and he had left the army under a cloud that hung over his head even after he had electrified the North by his victories at Forts Henry and Donelson, Vicksburg, and Chattanooga. As President he was slow to learn that civil and military authority were two distinct prerogatives. It was even said that he had removed the headquarters of the army to the White House. He had incurred the ill will and enmity of such able and powerful Republicans as Sumner of Massachusetts, Trumbull of Illinois, Schurz of Missouri, and Fenton of New York.

During Grant's administration the Republican party fell into the hands of selfish and unscrupulous interests. The extraordinary conditions that prevailed during the Civil War furnished opportunities for individuals and corporations to wax fat off the government and the public; and with the wealth and power they had achieved they debauched legislators and public officials to a degree unknown before. In spite of the enactment of the Homestead Act in 1862 by a Republican Congress, lavish grants of lands to railways continued; and it was suspected and known that these corporations, already unpopular because of practices inimical to the best interests of the public, were corrupting legislatures and Congress. Grant's appointments proved him to be a poor judge of men; and civil service reformers demanded a President who would clean the Augean stables and keep them clean.

In short, by the close of 1871 Grant was confronted by a formidable movement of liberals and independents looking to the rehabilitation of the Republican party by dethroning its present leaders. Believing that Grant was the greatest obstacle to reform, these men bent their efforts to prevent his renomination. In the summer of 1870, James W. Grimes of Iowa wrote to Lyman Trumbull: "It looks at this distance as though the Republican party was 'going to the dogs'—which, I think, is as it

should be. Like all parties that have an undisturbed power for
a long time, it has become corrupt, and I believe that it is today
the most corrupt and debauched political party that has ever
existed."

The Liberal Republican movement took tangible form in Missouri. That state had been the scene of a fierce struggle between
secessionists and Union men. The state refused to secede, but
many Missourians espoused the Confederate cause and enlisted
in the army. After the Union men had secured control of the
state, they enacted most severe laws against their adversaries.
These laws were enforced for some years after the war, but in
time the more level-headed Republicans came to see that political
proscription for past offenses was unwise and unsafe. One of
the leaders who was in favor of wiping the slate clean was Carl
Schurz, who immediately after the collapse of the Confederacy
had made a tour of the South and had recommended to President Johnson a reconstruction policy much harsher in its terms
than the one the President proposed to follow. Schurz, a German
emigrant of that remarkable group known as the "Forty-eighters,"
settled in Wisconsin before the Civil War and exercised a commanding influence in leading his countrymen into the Republican
party and to the support of Lincoln's administration. After the
war he moved to Missouri and immediately became a leader of
the powerful German element in that state. In 1869 he was elected
to the United States Senate, where he was unsparing in his
criticism of Grant. He denied that opposition to Grant's reconstruction policy and to his renomination implied disloyalty to
the Republican party.

In 1870 the Republican party in Missouri split, and the liberal
faction nominated a full state ticket and adopted a platform
that declared that political disabilities should be removed. The
old-line wing favored restoration of political rights "as soon as
it could be done with safety." The Democrats made no nomina-
tions and indorsed the Liberal Republican candidates, which resulted in a sweeping victory.

The events in Missouri attracted the attention of the country. Naturally Grant and his supporters took alarm and sought

to discipline the Liberals by depriving them of the patronage. These tactics, however, drove them out of the party; and when it became clear that the nomination of Grant could not be prevented, they launched out on a campaign to unite liberals in both parties in a new party.

The movement spread rapidly. It captured several of the most influential periodicals and newspapers in the country: the *Springfield* (Massachusetts) *Republican*, a model of journalism under Samuel Bowles; the *Chicago Tribune*, under the leadership of Horace White; the *Cincinnati Commercial*, under Murat Halstead; the *New York Tribune*, edited by Horace Greeley and Whitelaw Reid; the *New York Post*, distinguished by the pen of William Cullen Bryant; the *Louisville Courier Journal*, "Marse" Henry Watterson's paper; and the *Nation*, under E. L. Godkin.

When the Liberal Republican convention met at Cincinnati in May, 1872, the most likely candidates for the presidential nomination were Charles Francis Adams, who had the prestige of a successful minister to Great Britain during the trying years of the Civil War, Lyman Trumbull and David Davis, both of Illinois. The prospects of these men, however, were wrecked by jealousies and intrigues; and through the instrumentality of a "deal" Horace Greeley was nominated for the Presidency and B. Gratz Brown of Missouri for the Vice-Presidency.

The hope for a Liberal Republican victory rested on the success of attracting a large number of Democrats; but in Greeley the Liberals had a candidate who for a generation had poured out his most stinging invective against them. Moreover, it would have been impossible for the most skillful campaigners to convince the electorate that Greeley was a tariff reformer; no amount of oratory could have explained away columns of editorials in the *New York Tribune* extolling a protective tariff. Furthermore, as editor of his widely read paper, Greeley had antagonized the Catholic Church under the aggressive leadership of Archbishop Hughes. For years the *Tribune* had been an exponent of "isms"; and one of the editor's pet reforms ran directly counter to the idea of personal liberty cherished by the Germans whom Schurz hoped to attract to the Liberal Republican standard, namely, prohibition. Unfortunately, from the list of Greeley's reforms which included Fourierism, vegetarianism, and agrarianism, civil service reform was conspicuously absent. And after the methods by which Greeley's nomination had been accomplished became known, the Liberal Republicans could hardly consistently appeal to civil service reformers, who knew that the Cincinnati convention had been manipulated according to the orthodox standards of professional politicians.

Notwithstanding, the Democrats indorsed Greeley and Brown, and for a time it appeared that the Republicans might have a battle on their hands; but before the campaign drew to a close the more sincere reformers either lapsed into lukewarm support or withdrew their support, although Schurz, after a delay of some weeks, announced that he would stay within the fold on the ground that almost any candidate was preferable to Grant. However, "Anything to beat Grant" was not an effective campaign slogan. After an unexciting campaign, Grant was overwhelmingly elected. Greeley died before the electoral votes were counted.

That a movement conceived in noble impulses and enthusiasm should have ended ingloriously was a calamity for the country. There is reason for believing that either Adams or Davis could have been elected because they would have held the support of powerful newspapers and the sincerely liberal voters. In any event, the election returns and the inception of the Liberal Republican movement showed that radical reconstruction was growing unpopular in the North and that the states "lately in rebellion" were slipping away from carpetbag and Negro control.

History must record that the country would have been fortunate if the fame of Grant might have rested solely on his illustrious career as a general, and Greeley's fame on his triumphs in the field of journalism.

Grant's second term brought the country to what Professor Dunning calls "The Nadir of National Disgrace." In addition to what was known about conditions in the southern states, the public was astounded by the revelation of unspeakable corruption that permeated the federal government itself and even tarnished the name of a member of the cabinet. Secretary of War Belknap was impeached by the House of Representatives for malfeasance in office, and he escaped conviction only by tendering his resignation and thereby raising in the minds of a sufficient number of Senators doubts as to the jurisdiction of that body. It was angrily charged that Belknap had escaped just punishment by raising an obstacle that might not have been insuperable but for the sympathy of the President.

The systematic plundering of the federal treasury by the "whiskey ring" also brought Grant into public light as a man of poor judgment and credulity. The members of the ring who appropriated to themselves large sums that ought to have been paid into the treasury as excises on whiskey were shown to have been on friendly terms with the President's private secretary and even with Grant himself. A former Speaker of the House, James G. Blaine, was involved in a scandal in connection with transactions of railway companies. When brought into the light of day, the details of another scandal brought sleepless nights to several prominent members of Congress. Oakes Ames, a member of the House from Massachusetts, was a leader of a group of financiers who as stockholders in the Union Pacific Railway Company awarded to themselves as stockholders in the Crédit Mobilier very favorable contracts to build a considerable portion of the mileage of the road. By a judicious distribution of Crédit Mobilier stock among members of Congress "where it would do the most good," they were free to proceed with their plans to loot the railroad.

In the midst of these and other unsavory revelations, not only did Grant fail to rise to the heights of righteous indignation by demanding the punishment of the men who had been false to their trust, but he acted in a manner that boded no good for the men who had sought them out.

The so-called "tidal wave of 1874," which brought a Democratic majority in the House of Representatives, precipitated an assault on "Grantism" which could be used for partisan purposes in the coming presidential campaign.

The year 1876 opened in gloom for the Republicans. For the first time since the Civil War the Democrats were in control of the House and the Republican majority in the Senate was threatened. Moreover, the country was in the dark as to the probable Republican nominee for the Presidency. Grant still had a large following, but there was formidable opposition to a third term and his name was anathema to reformers and independents. Grant would probably have accepted the nomination. He had written a letter in which he stated that he did not desire the nomination any more than he had desired it in 1868 and that he "would not accept a nomination if it were tendered, unless it should come under such circumstances as to make it an imperative duty."

This was the signal for attacks upon the President. The Democratic House of Representatives in 1875 adopted by an overwhelming majority a resolution declaring that any attempt to depart from the precedent established by Washington and other Presidents "would be unwise, unpatriotic, and fraught with peril to our free institutions." The Ohio Republican convention in 1874 resolved that the observance of Washington's example was an essential rule of unwritten Republican law.

Blaine's chances for the nomination appeared to be the best, but his unfortunate connection with the railroad scandals and the enmity of powerful men within his party proved to be his undoing at the convention. The Liberal Republicans were still to be reckoned with. In May, 1876, at a conference of leaders they drew up an address to the American people in which it was stated that they would not support a candidate controlled by the element opposed to reform. Blaine led on the first six ballots, but on the seventh Rutherford B. Hayes of Ohio came to the front and was subsequently nominated. The platform denounced the treasonable character of the Democratic party, mildly rebuked the spoils system, declared in favor of a protective tariff, and equivocated on the question of the resumption of specie payments.

The Democrats nominated Samuel J. Tilden of New York over several aspirants. Tilden presented an unusually brilliant record which recommended him to men interested in the restoration of good government. As governor of New York he effected the fall of "Boss" Tweed by fearlessly exposing his shameless corruption. The keynote of the Democratic platform was "reform": reform of the civil service, reform of taxation, reform of the tariff, reform of the currency, and retrenchment. Tilden's speech of acceptance also featured reform, but was ambiguous on finance. Hayes, on the other hand, was refreshingly clear and frank in discussing the financial question. In fact, his record as governor of Ohio and his sterling character were strong campaign assets.

Hayes was an acceptable candidate to the Liberal Republicans. Schurz, always a harsh taskmaster, wrote to Charles Francis Adams, Jr.: "Unless I am very much mistaken, the Cincinnati convention has nominated our man without knowing it. He is a man of more than average ability and decidedly unspoiled as a politician."

In the conduct of the campaign considerable ability was displayed by both sides. Hayes was somewhat handicapped by his campaign manager, Zachariah Chandler; but this was offset by Tammany's support of Tilden and by the fact that the vice-presidential candidate, Thomas H. Hendricks, was a soft-money man, and for that reason was disliked by the Liberal Republicans and the Germans. The Republicans attracted attention from their party's record by waving the "bloody shirt." Blaine and Garfield had prepared the way for these tactics by baiting on the floor of Congress southern members, whose indignant speeches were in black and white on the pages of the *Congressional Record.*

In the early weeks of the campaign the tide was running strongly in favor of Tilden. The country seemed to take favorably to the Democratic cry that a change was needed and that a party controlled by such men as Chandler, Roscoe Conkling, Simon Cameron, and Oliver P. Morton should be dethroned.

On the day after election the newspapers conceded the election of Tilden. On the face of the returns he had 203 electoral votes against 166 for Hayes. On second thought, however, the Republican papers charged fraud in South Carolina, Louisiana, and Florida. If the nineteen electoral votes of these states could be transferred from Tilden to Hayes, the Republican candidate would have 185 votes, one more than Tilden and a bare majority. In other words, in order to win, Hayes had to have every one of the nineteen disputed votes. In Oregon one electoral vote was in doubt on a technicality, the elector in question being a federal officeholder, though the popular vote of the state was Republican without a doubt.

In disputed elections it is customary to count only honest votes and to throw out dishonest ones, or else declare the whole election fraudulent and order a new election. The Twelfth Amendment of the Constitution merely provides that "the president of the Senate shall, in the presence of the Senate and House of Representatives, open all the certificates, and the votes shall then be counted." In the election of 1876, however, two sets of certificates were returned from each of the three states whose votes were in dispute. Should the Senate decide which returns were to be accepted, or should the matter be decided by the House? Should Congress go behind the returns and investigate conditions in the three states? The whole affair was complicated by the circumstances that the Senate was Republican and the House Democratic.

In the weeks intervening between election and the convening of Congress in December, the country was in a feverish state. Partisanship ran high. President Grant kept a level head and was a steadying influence. Each house appointed committees to find a way out of the imbroglio, to devise a scheme to reduce partisanship to a minimum. It was finally decided that the rule that had governed previous elections should be set aside for this election and an electoral commission should be appointed. Congress was to meet in joint session, and the president of the Senate was to open the returns from the states. If no objection was voiced, the vote of a state was to be counted. In the case of only one return, if it was objected to, both houses had to concur separately in order to throw it out. If two reports from a state were pre-

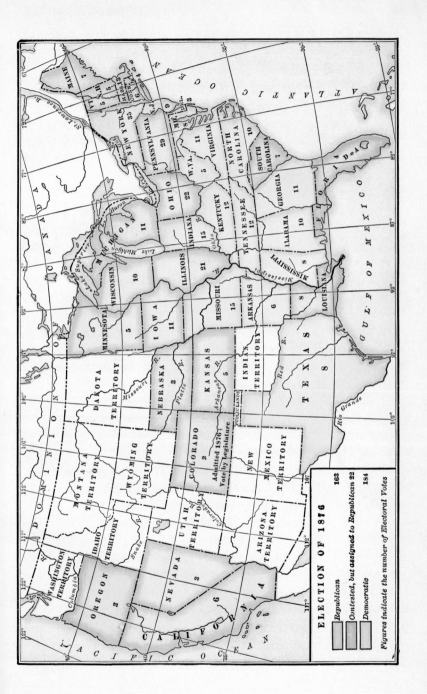

ELECTION OF 1876

Republican   163

Contested, but *assigned to Republican* 22

Democratic   184

Figures indicate the number of Electoral Votes

sented, the electoral commission was to decide. The commission was composed of five Representatives, five Senators, and five Justices of the Supreme Court, with the tacit understanding that three Representatives, two Senators, and two Justices would be Democrats; and three Senators, two Representatives, and two Justices would be Republicans. The four justices were to choose a fifth from their number, and it was also tacitly understood that he would be David Davis of Illinois, an independent. Unfortunately, just as the scheme was about to be put into effect Davis was elected to the Senate by the Democratic legislature of Illinois. For this reason he refused to serve, and Justice Bradley, a Republican, became the fifteenth member of the commission, making the composition of the body eight Republicans and seven Democrats.

Although on minor issues there were deviations from partisanship, on all major points the commission decided in favor of Hayes by a vote of eight to seven. It was by that vote that the electoral votes from each of the three disputed states were awarded to the Republican candidate. Who was really elected is as much in doubt today as it was in 1877; but there is no doubt that fraud was practiced on both sides. A biographer of Hayes defends the decision of the commission, but a biographer of Tilden affirms that he has the unique distinction of being the first President-elect to be feloniously excluded from the chief magistracy.

In perspective, the disputed election of 1876 appears as an incident in the long period of readjustment following the Civil War. The conflict between parties and races in three southern states manifested itself in fraud and violence, which might have plunged the country into civil strife. It put constitutional government to a terrible strain. The fact that Hayes' title to the Presidency was clouded hampered the effectiveness of his administration and made it weak in certain essentials; but this very weakness contributed to bringing to an end the national aspects of reconstruction. When the new President withdrew federal troops from the South, the Republican governments in Louisiana and South Carolina collapsed, thus happily terminating the dangerous situation of having two rival governments in those states. The South was now solidly Democratic.

For the next twenty years the balance between the parties in presidential elections was slight. From 1876 to 1892, including the contests of those years, the Democrats won a majority in the electoral college only twice, but the Republican candidates had a majority of popular votes in only a single election, that of 1880, when Garfield had a nominal majority over Hancock.

CHAPTER IV

POST-BELLUM DIPLOMACY AND FINANCE

AT THE CLOSE OF THE CIVIL WAR THE DEPARTMENT OF STATE was called upon to settle difficult controversies of long standing with the two leading powers of the world, Great Britain and France. It was fortunate that the American Secretary of State was William H. Seward, who, after a rather bad start in the first months of the Lincoln administration, proved himself to be a match for the skilled diplomatists of the Old World and the equal of the politicians in his own country. He had the advantage of knowing that the success of the federal government in suppressing the greatest rebellion in modern times had demonstrated to the skeptical statesmen of Europe that a democracy that had elevated to the highest office such an unconventional man as Abraham Lincoln had enduring qualities.

Four years of Civil War had accumulated a long list of grievances against Great Britain—some real and some imaginary. Although Her Majesty's government was entirely within its rights in recognizing the belligerency of the Confederate States of America, it seemed to Charles Francis Adams, the American minister at the Court of St. James's, and to the American people that it had been done with unseemly haste. Moreover, it was not until after the Battle of Gettysburg and the surrender of Vicksburg that threats of recognition of the independence of the Confederacy were finally removed. The *"Trent* affair" of 1861 was remembered as another example of the unfriendly attitude of the British government, in spite of the fact that the Lincoln government had disavowed the act of Captain Wilkes. The most serious grievance, however, was what has gone down in history as the *"Alabama* claims."

At the beginning of the war the Confederate government sent

agents abroad to purchase military supplies and ships for the navy. A special agent was commissioned to make contracts with commercial firms in order to obtain money to build blockade runners. Under the provisions of the Foreign Enlistment Act the British government had made it illegal to build and equip warships in British shipyards for belligerent governments. In order to accomplish the purposes of their missions, therefore, the agents were obliged to disguise the ships contracted for, nor could Confederate crews be taken on board within the three-mile limit.

The most famous Confederate cruiser was the *Alabama*. While the ship was under construction in the Laird Brothers' shipyard, Charles Francis Adams was diligent in collecting evidence that she was intended for the Confederacy; but in spite of his vigilance and his protests that the British government was permitting a naval expedition to be fitted out against the United States, the cruiser sailed for the Azores, where she was christened the *Alabama* and began her spectacular depredations on American commerce under the command of Captain Semmes, until she was sunk off the coast of France by the *Kearsarge*.

After the war the unresponsiveness of the British to suggestions from Secretary Seward that the claims of American citizens against the British government caused by Confederate cruisers built in Great Britain ought to be satisfied created a bellicose feeling in the United States. "Twisting the British lion's tail" has always been politically profitable; and at this time the situation was especially complicated by the activity of the Fenian Brotherhood, an organization composed of Americans of Irish birth and descent, which took as its motto "Ireland—Free and Independent." A number of Irish who had been naturalized, or claimed to have been naturalized, in the United States went to Ireland to cooperate with their brethren in the cause of Irish independence. When some of them were arrested by British authorities, a great commotion was set up in the United States by persons who protested the seizure of American citizens. The difficulties of the American government were further increased by Fenian raids across the Canadian border. The efforts of the government to live up to its obligations to a neighboring power with which it was at peace were held up by the Fenians and their sympathizers as evidence of pro-British sympathy.

In England, on the other hand, there was a noticeable shifting toward a more friendly attitude toward the United States. This was due in part to the dangerous diplomatic situation in Europe following the Seven Weeks' War and to the exigencies of colonial wars in which Her Majesty's government was engaged.

In 1868 Charles Francis Adams resigned and was succeeded at the Court of St. James's by Reverdy Johnson, whose efforts to effect a settlement resulted in the Johnson-Clarendon Convention. This treaty, however, was rejected by the Senate in April, 1869, by a vote of 54 to 1, because it did not specifically commit the British government to an acknowledgment of its responsibility with respect to the sailing of the *Alabama*.

The debate on the ratification of the treaty attracted the attention of the public in both countries by the sensational speech of Charles Sumner, chairman of the Senate Committee on Foreign Relations. Sumner asserted that individual losses suffered by the depredations of the *Alabama* were trifling compared with national losses, in which he included such items as the loss of carrying trade, injury to the shipbuilding industry, and the increased expenditures necessitated by the prolongation of the war caused by the failure of the British government to prevent the *Alabama* from sailing. The Senator maintained that the United States had indirect claims amounting to over two billion dollars against Great Britain for "raising hell generally," as the popular mind phrased it. He generously conceded that he did not desire the liquidation of these claims in money; if Great Britain would cede Canada, it would be accepted as an entirely satisfactory settlement.

Sumner's speech did not pour oil on the troubled diplomatic waters, but, taken together with other threats and other possible developments, it probably convinced British statesmen of the seriousness of the situation.

In his first annual message of December, 1869, Grant made no mention of the *Alabama* claims, but a year later he suggested that the government should take over the claims of its citizens against Great Britain. This was a threat that could not be ignored; but Hamilton Fish, Grant's able Secretary of State, made it plain to Sumner that the administration was not in sympathy with his extreme position. Sumner as chairman of the Senate Committee on Foreign Relations wielded a powerful influence; but his opposition to Grant's proposed annexation of Santo Domingo and to Fish's reasonable attitude toward the *Alabama* claims resulted in his removal from the chairmanship of the committee. Thus one heavy obstacle to Fish's policy was removed.

In the meantime Sir John Rose, representing the British government, and Secretary Fish were making progress in the direction of a satisfactory settlement. The upshot of their negotiations was the appointment by their respective governments of commissioners who drew up the Treaty of Washington which was ratified by the United States on May 24, 1871. In this treaty— one of the most remarkable in diplomatic annals—the British government expressed regret over the escape, "under whatever circumstances, of the *Alabama* and other vessels from British ports, and for the depredations committed by those vessels," thereby conceding the main contention put forth by the United States. A tribunal to consist of five members to be appointed respectively by the President of the United States, the queen of Great Britain, the emperor of Brazil, the king of Italy, and the president of the Swiss Confederation was to arbitrate claims presented by the United States. This generous concession on the part of Great Britain is partly explained by the exigencies of the Franco-German War. If Britain were drawn into war, she might have cause to regret a policy that permitted the *Alabama* to be built for a belligerent power.

The tribunal began its sittings at Geneva on December 15, 1871. The American case was ably handled, but at one stage the proceedings were almost wrecked by the presentation of claims for indirect damages, contrary to a tacit understanding. So great was the indignation in Great Britain that for a time it appeared that the British government would withdraw. However, at the suggestion of Charles Francis Adams, who represented the United

States on the tribunal, the claims were withdrawn; and in September, 1872, the United States was awarded the sum of $15,-500,000 in gold.

This was a diplomatic triumph for the Grant administration. "Grant needed all the glory he could get out of the Treaty of Washington and the Geneva Tribunal to atone for the faults of his first administration," says the historian Rhodes. He also says that the hero of the Geneva Tribunal was Charles Francis Adams.

A second major diplomatic problem that grew out of the Civil War was the French episode in Mexico. Following the war between the United States and Mexico there was a succession of unstable governments in the latter country until a "reform" government was set up by Benito Juarez, a full-blooded Indian, who issued a decree separating church and state, nationalizing all church property, and prohibiting monastic orders. In 1861 the new government suspended payments on foreign loans. The United States formally recognized the Juarez government in 1860; but when the War of Secession claimed the energies of the federal government, the Emperor Napoleon III of France took advantage of the opportunity to intervene and set up a Clerical Latin Empire in Mexico.

In the summer of 1863 the City of Mexico was captured by French troops, and placards were posted calling for a monarchy. A year later Maximilian of Austria was proclaimed emperor. As early as the spring of 1862 Secretary Seward informed Napoleon that the interference of European powers was contrary to the interests of the governments of the Western Hemisphere; and in April, 1864, the House of Representatives resolved that they were "unwilling, by silence, to leave the nations of the world under the impression that they are indifferent spectators of the deplorable events now transpiring in the Republic of Mexico; and they therefore think fit to declare that it does not accord with the policy of the United States to acknowledge a monarchial government, erected on the ruins of any republican government in America, under the auspices of any European power."

In reply to representations from the American Secretary of

State, the French emperor gave assurance that he had no intention of personal aggrandizement. Seward pretended to accept the assurance at face value and also refused to recognize the Maximilian government. President Lincoln was not seriously concerned over the situation, believing that the empire was doomed soon "to tumble to pieces." It was "a pasteboard concern on which we won't waste a man or a dollar."

When the Civil War ended, the United States had over a million trained men and a large navy and was in a position to use language that could not for long be ignored by Napoleon, whose own position on the French throne was becoming increasingly precarious. Finally, after having expressed concern over the continued presence of the French army, Seward in February, 1866, inquired when he might be informed of its withdrawal. Not wishing to risk a war with the United States, Napoleon complied with the virtual ultimatum, and before the summer of 1867 Maximilian was left to his fate. The archduke of the ill-fated House of Hapsburg was captured and sentenced to death; and in spite of the efforts of the United States to save his life, he faced a firing squad on the morning of June 19, 1867. Lincoln's prophecy had been fulfilled. Juarez was restored to the presidency, and in 1873 his comprehensive program of reform was incorporated into the constitution. Seward's policy won the gratitude of the Mexican people. The United States sent a minister to congratulate the people of the neighboring republic on the happy outcome.

Democracy in Mexico, however, consisted merely in paying homage to its forms; and within a few years Porfirio Diaz established a military dictatorship which lasted until 1910, when the United States was again called upon to deal with a situation that threatened to provoke foreign intervention. From 1876 to 1910, however, the relations between the United States and Mexico were on the whole calm and cordial.

Secretary Seward was an ardent expansionist, but an unfavorable Senate defeated his efforts to purchase the Danish West Indies and to annex Santo Domingo. Curiously enough, in 1867 he was successful in obtaining the ratification of a treaty for the purchase of Alaska, a Russian possession about which little or nothing was known in the United States. Many Americans, looking upon the territory as merely a waste of ice and snow, opposed the expenditure of $7,200,000 in order to obtain it. "Seward's folly," as it was called, did not become wisdom until many years later—after it had paid for itself many times over by the discovery and exploitation of mineral deposits.

The problem of adjusting the expenditures and revenues of the government to a peace-time basis was no less pressing than that of restoring eleven states to their proper relations to the federal government. From 1861 to 1865 the government borrowed a considerable part of the wealth of the country and embarked on a system of taxation such as the world had never seen. Heavy taxation drew from the pockets of the people purchasing power, and the flotation of large loans and the issuance of inconvertible notes diverted money into different channels. When the government took the momentous step of issuing legal tender notes in 1862 and a year later suspended their convertibility, it bequeathed to the post-war generation a series of problems that agitated business men, farmers, wage earners, and politicians. For the first time since the beginning of the century the people were saddled with a public debt that staggered the imagination.

The financial problems attendant on the cessation of war may be grouped in three categories: (1) funding the public debt; (2) readjustment of taxation; (3) resumption of specie payments.

Johnson's Secretary of the Treasury was Hugh McCulloch, an able man who was constantly hampered, as was Secretary Seward, in pursuing a consistent policy by the quarrel between the President and Congress. McCulloch favored the early retirement of the legal tender notes, popularly called greenbacks. He regarded them as temporary expedients to tide the country over the difficult period of war. His policy met the powerful opposition of men who believed that the country needed all the currency then in circulation and that sudden contraction of the circulating medium would bring low prices and business depression.

Despite this, Congress enacted the Funding Act of April 12,

1866, which, among other items, provided for the gradual retirement of the greenbacks; but in April, 1868, further contraction was suspended by large majorities in both houses. There
was, however, a considerable element that was not satisfied with
a negative policy and demanded that the currency should be expanded by issuing more greenbacks. The Greenbackers, who were
more numerous in the West, argued that since the bondholder
had paid for his securities in depreciated currency, he ought not
to insist that the government repay him in gold, which had a
much greater purchasing power than paper money. The western
farmer who had borrowed depreciated money could not see the
justice of paying his mortgage in gold. He thought the greenbacks were the poor man's money. He raised the cry "One currency for the capitalist and for the debtor," or "One currency
for the bondholder and for the plowholder."

Some students of financial history have concluded that the
soundest policy would have been to take steps for the resumption of specie payments and at the same time to adopt a new
monetary unit which recognized existing conditions. In other
words, a new gold dollar worth about seventy-five per cent of
the old dollar ought to have been coined. The ideal of the hard-
money men was finally realized in 1879, when the greenbacks
were pulled up to the value of one hundred cents in gold; but
the goal was reached at the cost of falling prices, which retarded
industrial development and ruined men who in good faith had
purchased property at its valuation in depreciated currency. Republican leaders, however, accepted the views of the extreme business interests of the East and, with a setback here and there, carried through a legislative program which brought the resumption
of specie payments at the opening of the year 1879. Before and
after that date, however, a greenback party under various names
advocated inflation, although neither of the old parties was free
of men who spoke the language of the Greenbacker. By virtue
of the fact that the power of the business interests was largely
concentrated in the Republican party, the Greenbackers found
a more congenial atmosphere in the Democratic household.

The inauguration of Grant (1869) was shortly followed by

a congressional enactment pledging the faith of the United States to the payment, in coin or its equivalent, of all obligations of the United States, unless the contract stipulated otherwise. This act enabled the Grant administration to refund bonds with favorable interest rates and dates of retirement, thus shaping the character of the public debt for the next quarter of a century. The use of the term "coin" instead of "gold," however, gave aid and comfort to the advocates of the free coinage of silver.

In the first year of Grant's second term the country was plunged into one of the most serious depressions in its history. The panic of 1873 was precipitated by the failure of the banking house of Jay Cooke and Company, but, like all periods of prolonged depression, it grew out of a combination of events and conditions. Fluctuations in the value of money led to speculation in money, which necessitated large profits and high rates of interest, accompanied by luxury and extravagance in the life of the people. Extensive railway building, of which the Union Pacific was but one example, involved sinking capital into projects far beyond what was immediately productive. The Bessemer process of steel manufacturing which was introduced during the Civil War greatly decreased the cost of manufacture and attracted a large volume of capital in that field of activity. The opening of great areas in the West, coupled with the opening of the Suez Canal, depressed the price of wheat. Hundreds of millions of dollars' worth of government bonds were held in Europe; and when these obligations commenced to be paid in gold instead of in bonds, an unfavorable balance of trade was caused by the drainage of gold from the country. The extraordinary developments in Europe accompanying and growing out of the Franco-German War made the depression world wide.

The deplorable condition of the country brought forth a plethora of suggestions for curing the malady. The Greenbackers claimed that the cause of the trouble was the scarcity of money. They demanded an increase in the volume of greenbacks. In April, 1874, Congress passed a bill for the permanent increase of greenbacks to four hundred million dollars. President Grant, in the face of strong pressure to the contrary, vetoed the bill on the ground that it was incompatible with national obligations to creditors and to previous enactments of Congress. In his annual message of December, following the "tidal wave of 1874," Grant discoursed on the necessity of returning to a specie basis, and recommended the accumulation of a gold reserve in the treasury to redeem the legal tender notes.

Under the stress of a business depression and a decisive Democratic victory in the congressional elections, Congress under the leadership of John Sherman, George F. Edmunds, and Carl Schurz passed the Resumption Act of 1875. This law provided that the fractional currency, popularly called "shinplasters," should be retired in favor of subsidiary coins, that the amount of greenbacks should ultimately be reduced to three hundred million dollars, that they should be redeemed in "coin," and that the date for the resumption of specie payments should be January 1, 1879. The Secretary of the Treasury was authorized to use the surplus in the treasury and, if necessary, to sell bonds in order to accumulate a gold reserve.

This measure was essentially a compromise. The word "redeem" was vague, and the date for the resumption of specie payments was remote. It was left an open question whether or not greenbacks should be reissued after the three-hundred-million mark was reached. Moreover, the treasury could not sell bonds directly for greenbacks, but had to sell bonds for coin. Since the greenbacks had driven coin out of circulation, the government had to depend on financial concerns, instead of selling bonds directly to the people. This gave rise to the charge that the government was closely allied with big business.

Before the date fixed for resumption was reached, many battles were fought on the hustings between the inflationists and the resumptionists. The issue came prominently before the country in the gubernatorial campaign of 1875 in Ohio, where inflation was so popular that it was known as the "Ohio idea." The Republicans adopted a platform declaring in favor of resumption and nominated Hayes, who took a firm stand for "sound money." The Democrats espoused the "Ohio idea." The anti-Greenbackers realized that the struggle was crucial; if the Democrats with their inflationist platform won the victory, the greenback cause might sweep the Middle West. Accordingly, the Republicans moved their big oratorical guns up to the line of battle. John Sherman and Carl Schurz made a smashing assault on the "sophism" that money ought to be made "equal to the wants of trade." The Republicans won, and their victory was important in committing their party to the support of the Resumption Act. It also made Hayes an "available" candidate in the presidential election of the following year.

As it turned out, the task of carrying out the provisions of the Resumption Act fell to Hayes' Secretary of the Treasury, John Sherman, who had had an important part in framing it. In spite of obstacles along the road, he pursued a policy that led straight to resumption. His rulings and actions became precedents for future secretaries. By establishing intimate and cordial relations with large financial interests, he secured their confidence and cooperation. His difficulties were augmented by the increasing business depression, which gave color to the allegation that the operations of the treasury were to blame. Savage railway strikes, industrial unrest, and falling prices handicapped an administration already suffering from lack of confidence on the part of many in Hayes' title to the Presidency. He was faced with a Democratic majority in the House of Representatives, and after the election of 1878 the Republicans lost control of the Senate.

The silver question, which agitated the country until the issue appeared to have been settled by the presidential election of 1896, was projected into Congress during the Hayes administration. The depreciated greenbacks had driven both gold and silver out of circulation, and in 1873 the silver dollar was dropped from the list of coins without serious opposition, because the metal was worth more in bullion than in coin. That is, the silver miner received more for his commodity by selling it on the open market than by bringing it to the mint. After 1873, however, there was a sharp decline in the value of silver, largely caused by the discovery and development of new silver mines in the West. As a result it was charged that the act of 1873 was a conspiracy of eastern bankers and legislators to demonetize silver, and it became the "crime of '73."

In 1877 Richard P. Bland of Missouri, who had been an Idaho miner, introduced in the House of Representatives a bill providing for the free coinage of silver. While the bill was pending, Congress passed a resolution declaring that the bonds of the United States were payable in the silver dollars of the Bland bill. This resolution affected adversely the credit of the government at the time Sherman was converting bonds to lower interest rates. Sherman used every possible means to defeat the Bland bill, but it passed the House by a vote of 163 to 34. The vote was sectional and not according to party lines. There were prominent Republicans as well as Democrats voting in the affirmative and in the negative. In the Senate the bill was amended and became the Bland-Allison Bill. The free coinage was eliminated in favor of a provision that required the government to purchase and coin not less than two million dollars' worth of silver or more than four million dollars' worth of silver per month. The silver dollars were to be legal tender for all public and private debts. Despite Hayes' veto, the bill became a law in 1878.

Efforts to repeal the Resumption Act failed, but by the Bland-Allison Act the retirement of greenbacks was stopped. This act became effective when there were over some 346 million dollars' worth in circulation, which is the present amount.

Sherman fixed the amount of the gold reserve for the redemption of greenbacks at not less than 100 million dollars. In the middle of December, 1878, gold sold at par in New York; and when the date fixed for the resumption of specie payments came— January 1, 1879—greenbacks were exchanged for gold at par.

With the restoration of the gold standard, business began to boom and applications for United States bonds came from all over the world. The increasing revenue that poured into the treasury and the demonstrated ability of the government to shoulder unprecedented financial obligations of war enhanced the credit of the government; and during the next decade statesmen were faced with the problem of a surplus in the treasury.

CHAPTER V

THE POST-WAR GENERATION

IN. 1876 THE CENTENNIAL OF THE DECLARATION OF INDEPEND-
ence was celebrated at a great exposition in Philadelphia when
the pall of great depression lay over the country. Thousands were
obliged to forego the pleasure of visiting the Quaker City because
of disasters that had overtaken their fortunes and business enterprises; but it was fortunate that the exposition was not delayed
until the following year, when industrial strife swept over the
land from ocean to ocean and when trunk-line railways were for
a time in possession of mobs which crippled and even stopped
traffic. The large number of unemployed, thousands near the margin of starvation, and the widening gulf between capital and labor
brought to the people a realization of the fact that the stupendous
development of the country and prosperity could bring tears and
sorrow as well as happiness and well-being.

Miracles wrought by inventors were spread before the eyes
of visitors to the Centennial Exposition; but they were only hints
of what men and women in the next half-century were to witness on highways and streets, on water and in the air, and in
their own homes. On city streets the slowly moving horse cars
and the jerky cable cars would soon give way to vehicles driven
by motors connected with overhead trolleys. The telephone in a
small way brought messages into business houses and into homes
of the wealthy. Incandescent and arc lights had not yet displaced
candles, kerosene lamps, and gas jets. A machine called a phono-
graph made squeaky noises resembling the human voice and musical instruments. Photographs were mingled with tintypes in the
family album which occupied a conspicuous place alongside the
family Bible on the parlor table. The chain-driven safety bicycle
had not yet driven out of locomotion the crazy velocipede, with

its front wheel of huge diameter setting a fast pace for the tiny wheel that tagged along.

City streets were poorly paved, if paved at all, and only a few of them were made hideous by the noises of elevated railways. Congested traffic of omnibuses, wagons, and cabs was somewhat relieved by bridges, but it was not until 1883 that engineering science had completed the Brooklyn suspension bridge. Municipalities had not solved the problem of disposing of waste elimination; it remained for the decades of the eighties and nineties to devise sewage systems that not only made cities and homes more comfortable and attractive but also reduced the number of cases of sickness, especially typhoid fever and cholera. Great fires that laid large sections of Chicago and Boston in ashes in the early seventies, and lesser conflagrations which in the aggregate entailed heavy property losses were caused in part by inadequate water systems and inefficient apparatus for fighting fire.

In the country life was primitive in contrast with that in rural communities of the twentieth century. Families rode to church and to the county seat in wagons or platform buggies over roads that were bumpy and, in the spring, almost bottomless. Impassable roads often made it necessary to walk or ride horseback to the village for mail. It was not until the nineties that farmers who lived in favored communities knew the convenience of the rural free delivery; and many post offices received mail only two or three times a week. During the winter season snow blockades deprived towns of mail for weeks at a time, and mail trains were sometimes from ten to eighteen hours late.

By the middle of the eighties the whistle of the locomotive was familiar except to people living in the most remote localities; but to most rural residents a "train ride" was an event worth telling the neighbors about. The traveling salesman who visited the country merchant was an object of envy to the young man whose hands were calloused by toil on the homestead. The city clothes and free and easy ways of the "drummer" were in striking contrast with the attire and manner of the farmer's son. The general store was the broadcasting booth of important events and petty gossip, for only the farmer whose position entitled

Edwin Levick

A Horse Car

Brown Brothers

him to be called "squire" could afford the luxury of a daily paper. His neighbors had to be content with "big news" found in the "boiler plate" inside the local paper or with such items as might be found in the farm journal. The Jewish peddler with his pack strapped on his back was a welcome visitor to the farm; and for the privilege of staying over night he would usually present from his assortment of linens, mouth organs, combs, and other notions an article to the housewife.

The farmer harvested his grain with a self-binder, cut his hay with either a McCormick, Deering, or Champion mower, and raked it with a self-rake. The plowman "followed" the plow, though his more fortunate neighbor perhaps rode a sulky plow. His grain was threshed by a separator run by a steam traction engine, which in this period displaced horse power. The windmill was conspicuous on many western farms, but many hired hands and boys were still obliged to put their hands to the pump to draw water for the livestock. The cornplanter came to be a necessity; and the hayfork that elevated hay into the mow was a great improvement over the pitchfork. About the only conveniences that relieved the drudgery of the farmer's wife were the sewing machine and the hand-driven washing machine and wringer.

Threshing time brought extraordinary duties for men and women and excitement for the boys, who were thrilled by the unusual sight of a steam engine—whistle and all. Neighbors "swapped" threshing and in anticipation of long tables laden with choice victuals for hungry threshing hands, the men butchered a hog or sheep and the women vied with their sisters to bake pies and other "fancy" dishes. In the late fall or early winter neighbors "helped out" in laying up a supply of meat and in making cheese. Auction sales, which were usually held in the fall, brought to farms neighbors and strangers who spent the day inspecting livestock, implements, and household goods, and laughing at the sallies of wit and humor from the auctioneers.

The farm was still in a sense an economic unit. The farmer brought grist to the mill; butchered, prepared, and preserved meat for the family's use; raised sugar cane and cooked his own sorghum, repaired harness and even boots and shoes for the family. Women sewed their own clothing, and the spinning wheel and the loom had by no means disappeared from the equipment of the farm. The women baked bread, churned butter, canned fruit, and made soap. Prepared breakfast foods, "store" cookies, baker's bread, fruits canned in tins, and meat from packing houses were luxuries on the farm until the closing years of the century. There were a goodly number of organs and melodeons in country homes, but pianos were found only in exceptional cases.

The American home celebrated in story and song was seen at its best in the second half of the nineteenth century. The family photograph taken in the eighties portrays the father and mother seated at the extreme ends, with members of a large family ranging in age from the twenties to the baby in arms. The family library was small; and perhaps the literature that was read the most diligently was the Bible and the almanacs published by patent medicine firms like Ayers, Jaynes, and Hostetters, although in the North *Uncle Tom's Cabin* was still read aloud in the family circle. The oldest daughter perhaps wept over Edna Lyall's *Lena Rivers* and Louisa M. Alcott's novels, or reveled in the popular novels of the Reverend E. P. Roe, the "best sellers" of the seventies and eighties. Youths thought themselves fortunate if the family budget permitted a subscription to the *Youth's Companion*; and if the mother subscribed to the *Ladies' Home Journal*, the advertisements and Palmer Cox's Brownies interested both young and old.

Although compulsory-attendance school laws began to be enacted by the states in the decade of the seventies, their enforcement was lax. In country and city the public schools were simple. Comparatively few youths enjoyed the advantages of a high school education, and still fewer went to college. The high school itself was a new thing in this period. The "brightest" boys and girls might spend a winter term or two in a business college or a private academy. The population of college and university campuses was meager compared with that of the second decade of the twentieth century. Cities and county seats boasted of large public school buildings, but there were no consolidated schools.

The typical country school building was a one-room structure, poorly equipped and furnished, and usually set in surroundings equally unattractive. In the spring and fall terms the scholars were recruited from the younger members of families, because after a boy or girl reached the age of fourteen or fifteen, or even less, his services were required on the farmstead. In the winter the older son was perhaps even permitted to come late to school in order to allow him to "do the chores." When a class was called to recite, the scholars took seats on long benches at the front of the school. In the estimation of the school population, the best scholars excelled in spelling and arithmetic. It was a noteworthy achievement to "spell down" the whole school. The teachers of the post-bellum generation knew little or nothing of teachers' institutes and "I.Q.'s," and it was a solemn occasion for the scholars and a trying time for the teacher when the county superintendent paid one of his rare visits. There is, however, much to be said for an educational system or lack of system, that made wide use of the McGuffey readers. To be able "to do cube root" was the height of mathematical achievement. The penmanship of scholars who made use of the "copy book" may not compare favorably with that of later generations, but the maxims and mottoes that were laboriously written were worth perhaps more than any formal exercise in the art of writing.

Life was simple in the quarter-century following the Civil War. In the horse and buggy age the county seat seemed far away; and the state capital was too remote for the ordinary mortal to think of visiting it. What little news was printed in the local paper about what transpired in Washington seemed unreal to the man and woman, boy and girl, whose horizon was limited by the boundaries of the county. The metropolitan dailies maintained Washington correspondents, but the space devoted to the proceedings of Congress and to the activity of the President was meager. Horace Greeley's *Weekly Tribune* was still the Bible of a host of readers. The "political rally" was a torchlight procession, followed by the singing of campaign songs and by one or

ECLECTIC EDUCATIONAL SERIES.

McGUFFEY'S

NEW

THIRD ECLECTIC READER:

FOR YOUNG LEARNERS.

By WM. H. McGUFFEY, LL. D.

VAN ANTWERP, BRAGG & CO.,

137 WALNUT STREET,   28 BOND STREET,
CINCINNATI.   NEW YORK.

McGUFFEY'S THIRD READER—TITLE PAGE

more addresses delivered by spellbinders who exhorted their hearers to "vote her straight and let her go, Gallagher!"

Amusements were few and simple. Instead of moving picture theaters with bright lights and flaming posters, towns of a thousand population or more had an "opera house," which was usually shunned by pietistic churchgoers; but those whose consciences and pocketbooks permitted it were thrilled by lurid melodrama. Regularly *Uncle Tom's Cabin,* which resembled something that suggested Mrs. Stowe's book, played a one-night stand. The greatest thrill that came to the boy of the eighties and nineties was the circus. For weeks he had gazed with awe at posters portraying beasts of the jungle and trapeze performers that covered one or more sides of the livery stable. And when one of the larger "greatest show on earth"—Barnum and Bailey's, Ringling Brothers, Forepaugh and Sells, or "Buffalo Bill's Wild West and Congress of Rough Riders" arrived at the county seat, he was lined up with hundreds on the sidewalks of Main Street to witness the street parade that preceded the afternoon performance. Fathers and mothers who would have regarded with horror the idea of attending a theater gladly paid their quarters and fifty-cent pieces to the noisy ticket-seller, who called "Hurry, hurry, hurry" at the entrance to the big tent.

In the fall families rode over dusty roads to the county fair, which offered entertainment in the form of horse-racing, balloon ascensions, sideshows, fireworks, and perhaps a baseball game. After having found a "hitching post" for the team of horses and partaken of a generous lunch prepared by the housewife, the family had time to gossip with acquaintances and inspect the modest exhibits before going to the grandstand to see the races.

Although the post-war generation showed increasing interest in outdoor sports, it was not until near the close of the century that athletic contests attracted hundreds and thousands. Before the Civil War baseball was confined largely to the East, probably because with the growing industrialization of the country factories became nuclei of compact settlements. Cities had commons and sand lots where men and boys congregated on Sundays; and better facilities for travel and clusters of cities and villages made it comparatively easy for teams from neighboring communities to "cross bats," as the phrase used to run. The Civil War was instrumental in infecting soldiers from every state with the "baseball bug"; players from New York, Boston, and other eastern cities taught "Yanks" and "Rebs" the fine points of the game; and it seems to be a fact that Union and Confederate soldiers not only swapped tobacco, stories, and newspapers but also occasionally engaged in friendly rivalry on the baseball field.

Baseball was played largely by amateurs, but the germs of professionalism were seen as early as 1869, when a professional club calling itself the Cincinnati Red Stockings was organized. This was followed in 1871 by the organization of the National Association of Professional Baseball Players, the purpose of which was partly to eliminate evils that had grown up with the game: gambling, bribing players, foul language used by players, drinking by spectators, and the like. The answer to this critical situation was the organization in 1876 of the National Association of Professional Baseball Clubs, which through many vicissitudes has had an enduring existence.

Although professional baseball in the eighties and nineties was more respectable than it had been, in many circles it was not considered good form to attend professional games; and Sunday ball was frowned upon and even prohibited in such large cities as Boston, Philadelphia, and Cleveland. Huge and palatial grandstands, electric score boards, almost perfect playing fields, and fabulous salaries paid to players were developments of the twentieth century. Baseball parks in minor leagues were poorly equipped; and in the country youths and young men were hardly aware of the existence of professional clubs and knew nothing about the standings of the clubs in pennant races. Compared with later years the space devoted to baseball in newspapers was small. Schoolboys played "two, three, or four old cat" and "chose up sides," but in the country poor means of communication made it difficult to assemble teams; and cities and towns had not yet embarked on programs of development that included playgrounds for baseball, tennis, golf, and football. Croquet, which could be played on lawns, was a popular pastime. Roller skating rinks,

Brown Brothers

CIRCUS DAY

foot-racing, and bowling alleys provided amusements and recreation for young and old. More educational were Lyceums and Chautauquas.

University and college students played football, but Harvard, Yale, and Princeton dominated the sport. Walter Camp of Yale, who selected the members of the mythical All-American team, rarely deigned to look west of the Hudson River. The funds of the athletic departments of colleges and universities—even of the large universities in the Middle West—were too meager to permit the employment of high-salaried coaching staffs, the purchase of expensive equipment, or the playing of intersectional games. The mammoth stadiums that dwarf the other structures on campuses today had not in the nineteenth century become the "main tent."

Despite the simplicity and crudeness in this century in comparison with the following, the development of American life was steady and wholesome. American youth was devoid of ambitions that later were taken for granted, but faith and optimism radiated alike from farms, villages, and cities. A vast continent was bestowing its favors on mankind: cities were springing up like magic; Uncle Sam was rich enough to give every man a farm; forests were falling before the axe; and the bowels of the earth were being turned inside out to produce metals. Water power, steam, and electricity raised the standard of living; the railroad, the machine, and the printing press had by 1890 obliterated the frontier line recorded in successive censuses and had widened the horizons of the mind. Money had not yet made it possible to build and maintain schools and libraries that brought the advantages of a secondary education to almost every boy and girl, but there was a seriousness and genuineness in the body of the population.

Colleges, academies, high schools, and theological seminaries sprang up in all parts of the country, and churches and Sunday schools grew in number and attendance. Great religious revivals swept over the land, and religious leaders were burning with zeal to bring the gospel not only to their countrymen but also to the heathen in Asia, Africa, and the South Sea Islands. Moreover,

Amerikanska Maskiner.

ELFWING & C:o,
STOCKHOLM,
Agenter för

Adriance Platt & Co, Poughkeepsie, New York,
Wheeler Mellick & Co, Albany, New York,
Brown & Sharpe, M'f'g Co, Providence, R. I.,
Duryea & Co, New York,
American Diamond Drill Co, New York,
Walker Brothers, Minneapolis, Minn.,
New England, Machine Co, Fitchburg, Mass.,
Ruston Proctor & Co, Sheaf Iron Work, Lincoln, England,
Charles Churchill & Co., London,

upptaga ordres på alla slags Maskiner och Maskindelar.

Vexlar på Amerika

säljas fortfarande af undertecknad, till billigaste priser, och ombesörjes penningars remitterande till alla platser i Amerika.

Det belopp, för hvilket vexel begäres, bör skickas i rekommenderadt bref eller postremissvexel, med tydlig adress på den person, till hvilken penningarna skola skickas, då jag genast sänder honom en **Prima** vexel samt till afsändaren en **Seconda** af samma innehåll, jemte redovisning för omvexlingen. — Äfven utfärdar jag, om så önskas, **vexlar i svenskt mynt**, betalbara i Amerika.

Amerikanska Emigrant-Kompaniets vexlar inlöses af mig fortfarande.

G. W. Schröder,
Vexelör.
Göteborg, N:o 8 Norra Hamngatan.

AMERIKA.

Hamburg-Amerikanska Ångfartygs-Aktiebolaget befordrar passagerare från **Göteborg, Stockholm, Kalmar** och **Malmö** till de flesta städer och jernvägsstationer i Förenta Staterna medelst dess ytterst snabbgående och beqvämt inredda första klassens passagerare, hvilka reguliert afgå från **Hamburg** till **New-York** hvarje **Onsdag** samt till **New-Orleans** en gång i månaden under Februari, Mars, April, September, Oktober och November.

Biljetter säljas å nedanstående kontor, der äfven erforderliga upplysningar meddelas.

Hamburg-Amerikanska Ångfartygs-Aktiebolaget.

Stockholm. Kontor, Köpmangatan N:o 7.
Kalmar. Kontor, N:o 32, hörnet af Södra Långgatan och Larmgatan.
Malmö. Kontor, S. Wallgatan N:o 34.
Göteborg. Kontor, Skeppsbron N:o 1.

Till AMERIKA!

befordrar **FREDERICK NELSON** med ***„National-Liniens“*** utmärkt väl inredda ångare fortfarande passagerare hvarje Fredag beqvämt, snabbt och billigt.

Mynt och **Vexlar på Amerika** säljas till dagens kurs.

Göteborg i Mars 1873.

Frederick Nelson.

Till New-York och Boston

äfvensom alla öfriga större platser i

Amerika

Genast från seglationens början, hvarje Fredag lägenhet med ***Cunard-Liniens Kongl. Postångfartyg.*** Passagerarebiljetter och närmare upplysningar erhållas å Ångbåtsbolagets kontor i Göteborg, Sillgatan N:o 47.

S. SÖRENSEN.
Bolagets Agent för Sverige.

NATIONAL-LINIEN.

The National Steam Ship Company. (Limited)
befordrar genom undertecknad fortfarande hvarje Fredag utvandrare till alla delar af Amerika med dess stora, snabbgående och beqvämt inredda första klassens jernångare.

Närmare underrättelser lemnas af mig eller mina ombud i landsorten.
Vexlar och Amerikanskt mynt säljas till billigaste priser.

Göteborg i Februari 1873.

B. B. PETERSON.
Kontor, 44 Sillgatan.

Filialkontor i **Stockholm** och **Malmö.**
A. V. Hallberg. 6 Skeppar Carlsgränd
Olof Svensson. Vid Hamnen.

INMAN-LINIEN

befordrar fortfarande emigranter till Amerika med sina utmärkta *Kongl. Postångskepp,* de största och mest snabbgående i hela verlden; ha från 3,000 till 5,000 tons drägtighet och ända till 5,000 hästars machinkraft samt tillryggalägga resan mellan England och Amerika på 7 till 9 dagar.

☞ **Frederick Nelson** i Chicago emottager personligen alla emigranter, som blifvit befordrade på Inman-Linien; men befattar sig icke på vilkor med andra bolags passagerare.

John Odell.
firma **WILLIAM INMAN.**
Göteborg, Franska Tomten.

Allan-Linien.

Kort sjöväg till Förenta Staterna och Canada.

Montreal Ocean Steam Ship Companys Kongliga Postångare:

Sardinian,	*Circassian,*	*Polynesian,*	*Sarmatian,*
Scandinavian,	*Prussian,*	*Austrian,*	*Nestorian,*
Moravian	*Peruvian,*	*Hibernian,*	*Nova Scotian,*
North American	*Caspian,*	*Corinthian,*	*Manitoban,*
Canadian,	*St. David,*	*St. Andrew,*	*St. Patrick,*

afgå från ***Liverpool*** till ***Portland*** (vintertiden) och ***Quebec*** (sommartiden) hvarje Torsdag, medtagande post, passagerare och gods.

Detta är den mest fördelaktiga vägen till Canada och de vestra Förenta Staterna. Kortaste sjöväg och hastig jernvägsbefordran.

Till ***Halifax, Norfolk*** och ***Baltimore*** afgå ***Hibernian*** den 25 Februari, ***Nestorian*** den 11 Mars och såvidare, hvarannan Tisdag.

Detta är den mest direkta vägen till de södra och mellersta staterna, äfvensom till kolonien New-Sweden i staten Maine.

Hvarje ångare medför examinerad läkare. Nödig medicin utlemnas gratis. För qvinliga passagerarnes uppassning finnas fruntimmer anställda.

Jernvägsbiljetter till nästan alla delar af Amerika försäljas.

Passageprisen äro de billigaste.

Närmare underrättelser meddelas af undertecknad, bolagets Generalagent för Sverige.

Karl Möllersvärd.
Adress: Göteborg.

Nytt svenskt settlement

MINNESOTA.

Vid Lake Superior & Mississippi-jernbanan, som sammanbinder Mississippifloden vid S:t Paul med de stora insjöarne vid Duluth i staten Minnesota, anlägges nu ett nytt svenskt settlement i en vacker och fruktbar dal, som genomskäres af Kettlefloden, och blott en half till två svenska mil från jernvägen.

Kompaniet eger öfver en million tunnland jord längs med banan, men största delen deraf är bevuxt med tallskogar och är olämpligt för jordbruk, deremot den jord, som utbjudes åt jordbrukare är af utmärkt beskaffenhet, bestående dels af naturliga ängar, dels af högländt mark, bevuxt med löfskog såsom ek, lönn, asp, alm, ask m. m. och är alldeles stenfri. För de, som äro vana vid skogsmark erbjuder dessa trakter bättre förmåner än någon annan plats i Amerika.

Minnesota är, enligt sammanstämmande omdömen från många olika håll, det landskap i Amerika, hvilket för närvarande erbjuder åt utvandraren från Skandinavien de största fördelarne; ty denna unionsstat har ett herrligt klimat, som särdeles väl passar för nordbon, och dess rikedom på fruktbar jord, som kan erhållas till billigt pris, är betydlig. Dertill kommer en naturskönhet, hvilken verkar att den, som en gång skådat dessa herrliga trakter, känner sig oemotståndligt fästad vid dem.

Emigrationen från Sverige och Norge har också hittills hufvudsakligen dragit sig åt detta håll, och ingen annan af de amerikanska unionsstaterna eger ett större antal skandinavisk befolkning.

Under de sista åtta åren hafva 2,000 (engelska) mil jernvägar blifvit byggda i Minnesota; ibland dessa jernvägar är den ofvannämnde Lake Superior & Mississippi-vägen af mycket stor betydelse, enär den sammanbinder verldens största inlandseglationsleder, öfver hvilka flere hundra fartyg och ångare föra vesterns mineralier, timmer, spannmål och boskap till alla delar af den stora amerikanska verldsdelen och äfven till Europa.

Det är detta jernvägskompani, och för hvilket jag är agent, som gör stora uppoffringar för att få sitt land, längs med banan, befolkadt af de omtyckte svenskarne. — I de settlement omkring North Branch och Rush City, som jag förlidet år beskref i några svenska tidningar, är nu det mesta landet upptaget, hvarför vi nu börjat anlägga ett nytt settlement längre upp åt banan i närheten af stationen Hinckley, och erbjuda följande vilkor till alla, som der bosätta sig under loppet af nästkommande år, nemligen:

1. Godt land till ett pris af 8 till 10 riksdaler svenskt ($2\frac{1}{2}$ till 3 dollar) pr acre, på kredit med 8 års amortering.
2. Fria bostäder i rymliga och beqväma hus tillhörande kompaniet, under loppet af ett par månader, tills köparen hinner bygga ett eget hus.
3. Kompaniet uppför åt hvarje familj, som det önskar, ett beqvämt boningshus på det land, som familjen utväljer, och säljer huset med landet till kostnadspris på samma vilkor som jorden.
4. Kompaniet **skänker** jord till kyrka, prestboställe och skola åt hvarje kommun.
5. Genom en anordning, gjord af kompaniet, kunna alla kolonister, som vilja resa med ångbåt öfver Huron- och Superiorsjöarne till Duluth, erhålla en nedsättning i biljettpris af cirka 25 rdr pr hel biljett — i så fall böra de köpa biljett från Göteborg eller Köpenhamn endast till **Sarnia**, som kostar ungefär 156 rdr, derifrån med ångbåt till Duluth omkring 25 à 30 rdr. Resan härifrån till Sarnia kan ske med hvilken linie som helst.
6. Kompaniet transporterar **fritt** hvarje kolonist med familj och bagage från Duluth eller S:t Paul till settlementet.
7. Kompaniet förbinder sig att taga famnved vid jernbanan, efter gällande priser, i betalning för jord och hus af sådana, som bosätta sig på dess skogsland, och på detta sätt önska göra sina afbetalningar.
8. Kompaniet garanterar stadigt vinterarbete, till gällande pris, i sina skogar eller vid banan, åt alla, som köpa land af detsamma. — N.B. Under sommartiden kan hvar och en med lätthet erhålla arbetsförtjenst hvar som helst i Minnesota mot en dagspenning af cirka 2 à $2\frac{1}{2}$ dollar (7 à 8 rdr) pr dag.

Dessa jernvägsland erbjuda det mest helsosamma klimat, bördig jordmån, utmärkt vatten, land till billigt pris, skolor, der undervisningen meddelas gratis, god afsättningsort, goda arbetsförtjenster samt utmärkt tillgång på jagt och fiske. Svenska kyrkor och skolor äro redan der inrättade. Inom dessa områden finnes stor tillgång på timmer och jorden kan användas både för spanmålsproduktion, får- och boskapsafvel samt mejerihandtering.

Kompaniets skogsland säljes i huru stora områden som helst till personer, som önska drifva skogshandtering. Afverkningsrätt till större eller mindre delar af kompaniets skogar kan äfven erhållas till billigt pris.

Jag ämnar sjelf resa öfver till dessa settlement i slutet af nästkommande Maj månad, och skall med nöje biträda såväl under resan som vid framkomsten, alla som önska bosätta sig inom något af settlementen vid denna jernväg. Det bör märkas att ifall dessa land ej falla inflyttaren i smaken, så finnes tillräckligt „prairie“ (slätt) land i närheten, och att jag ej säljer något land eller tager emot några handpenningar här, utan får hvar och en först vid framkomsten och efter att hafva besett trakten, bestämma för sig sjelf.

Personer, som ämna sig till andra orter i Amerika, kunna äfven, ifall de så önska, få ressällskap med mig.
Vidare upplysning såväl om land som om resan lemnas då man adresserar sig till undertecknad.

Christianstad i Mars 1873.

H. MATTSON,
f. d. öfverste i Förenta Staternas Armee.

Hem i Nya Verlden.

Svenska Kolonierna

Iowa och Nebraska.

Redan för trenne år sedan grundlades i dessa stater flera svenska kolonier eller settlementen utaf

Burlington och Missouri River Jernvägsbolag

på land tillhörande detta bolag, skänkt utaf Förenta Staternas regering.

De förnämsta af dessa kolonier äro i Iowa: **Stanton** och **Red Oak, Junction**; i Nebraska: **Alma, Swedburgh** och **Edinburgh** (Sanders Co.) Vid städerna **Crete, Dorchester, Exeter Fairmount, Grafton, Harward, Juniata, Kenosaw** och **Lowell** samt tvenne större kolonier i **York Co.**, och två i **Clay Co.**

Dessa koloniers framsteg och tillväxt ha icke ett motstycke i hela den stora vesterns utveckling. Ända upp till 200 familjer ha samtidigt bosatt sig på en plats. Ifrån Unionens alla olika stater ha tillströmmat stora sällskaper af kolonister, såväl som större partier ifrån Europa. Allesamman instämma uti de högsta loford öfver jordens egenskaper, klimatets sundhet, den allmänna välmågan och framtida utsigter. Många resande igenom denna trakt påstå, att de aldrig någonsin sett ett jordbrukslandskap så vackert.

Aftonbladets resande korrespondent i Amerika, Hr H. Nisbeth, gjorde under förra årets lopp en tur igenom alla dessa kolonier, hvarom han skrifvit fullständiga korrespondenser. I en af dessa artiklar säger han att „de (kolonisterna) berömde enstämmigt jordens godhet. Gödsling behöfde icke förekomma på 15 till 18 år, och afkastningen var i allmänhet från 20 ända upp till 34 bushels hvete pr acre.“

„Skogstillgången var visserligen sparsam, men deremot var det godt om kol, som endast kostade 15 cents pr bushel. Vattnet var godt och vintrarne icke strängare än att boskapen kunde gå ute hela året om.“

Säkert är, att ingen trakt i Amerika har gjort så stora och hastiga framsteg i folkökning och välmåga, som just denna, sedan den blef tillgänglig genom anläggandet af ofvannämnde jernväg.

Orsaken till detta är att finna uti de ojemförligt större naturförmåner denna trakt har att bjuda på framför andra, hvadan ock tilltänkte utvandrare till vestern hasta dit i stora skaror.

Ännu återstår till salu öfver en million acres af detta bördiga land, som försäljes till verkliga nybyggare på lång kredit, nämligen 10 år. De första två åren betalas endast intresse å köpesumman. Priset å jorden är lågt, varierande ifrån 4 dollars till högre priser, allt efter läge och beskaffenhet.

Fyra större kolonisationspartier kommer under årets lopp att afgå härifrån dit till hvilka alla som så åstunda kunna ansluta sig. Annars kan resan ske lika godt egenhändigt, då man lägger noga märke till att vid inköp af biljetter, som sker hos någon af de lagligt authoriserade emigrantagenterna, densamma lyder **„via Burlington.“** Se noga efter att detta påskrifves, ty annars kan möjligen resan förlängas ifrån 6 till 24 timmar. Biljetter bör köpas till **Lincoln, Nebraska**, hvarest bolaget har sitt hufvud-kontor till försäljning af Nebraska land, samt hvarest äfven förenta staterna har sitt landkontor, ifall man föredrager att köpa af regeringen eller uttaga „homestead“ d. v. s. fritt land. Jernvägsbolaget har äfven i Lincoln uppfört ett stort och rymligt emigranthem, hvarest, landköpare kunna med sina familjer logera fritt, tills de hinna bereda egna hem på sitt land.

Innan afresa sker bör man efterskrifva eller personligen afhemta hos, bolagets ombud i Göteborg, ett rekommendationsbref till föreståndarne i Amerika, som bereder för innehafvarne alla de fördelar bolaget är i stånd att lemna.

Närmare upplysningar lemnas gratis då man tillskrifver eller personligen besöker undertecknade.

En tryckt upplaga af väl utförda och naturtrogna vyer öfver landet sändes, om man innesluter 12 öre för postporto.

Georg S. Harris,
Land-Kommissionär.
Burlington, Iowa eller Lincoln, Nebraska.

Joseph E. Osborn,
Ombudsman.
Norra Hamngatan N:o 8, Göteborg.

PAGE OF ADVERTISEMENTS IN THE "NEW WORLD," A PAPER PUBLISHED IN GOTHENBURG, SWEDEN, MARCH 6, 1873

Baptists, Methodists, Congregationalists, and Mormons vied with one another to send messengers to compete with priests and pastors of the established churches in the countries of Europe, whose doctrine and policy were vastly different from the ecclesiastical organizations that had sprung up in a land free from the trammels of an Old World civilization. American missionaries to countries like England, Germany, Sweden, Denmark, and Norway not only preached the gospel as interpreted by their respective denominations but also advertised America as a land of freedom and opportunity for men and women hemmed in by the conventions and restrictions of the Old World. Sunday schools patterned after those in the United States were set up in parish after parish, and Sunday school papers filled with stories about the wonderful land in the West were distributed to children, many of whom were later to seek their fortunes in the land of their dreams.

In the decade preceding the election of Lincoln, 2,598,214 immigrants came to the United States, mainly from Great Britain, Ireland, Germany, Norway, Sweden, and the Netherlands; but this number was only the vanguard of the mighty host that deserted the Old World in favor of the great republic in the West, known to emigrants as the "Dollar Land," the "Land of Canaan," and the "Saga Land."

After the panic of 1857 and the outbreak of the Civil War, immigration declined; but when the victory of the North appeared to be certain, the stream of humanity began to assume the huge volume that in the seventh decade deposited on American shores over five million immigrants. This number was exceeded only in the two decades from 1901 to 1920, when the respective arrivals were 8,795,386 and 5,735,811. The migration of over thirty-seven millions of people from 1820 to 1930 is the greatest movement of population in history.

Prior to the middle of the decade of the eighties, the overwhelming majority of immigrants came from the countries of northern and western Europe, the so-called old immigration, composed mainly of people of Teutonic stock and in more recent years designated as the Nordic race. This great exodus which began in earnest before the Civil War was the product of complex forces operating over a long period of time, so complicated, in fact, that in a work of this character only the most fundamental elements can be set forth.

It is obvious that millions of people would not have cast loose from the old moorings of their native parishes without having reached the conviction that America furnished opportunities denied them in Europe; and it is equally obvious that their longings for a better existence in the New World could not have been satisfied without adequate means of transportation—cheap and rapid. The steamship and the railroad, together with inventions that revolutionized manufacturing and agriculture, not only brought tremendous adjustments in the lives of individuals in Europe and America but also for purposes of communication brought London, Paris, Berlin, Stockholm, Oslo, Copenhagen, and Rotterdam closer to New York in 1880 than the time required to bridge the distance between London and Paris in 1800. Some idea of the meaning of the revolution in transportation is conveyed by the fact that rate wars between steamship companies and between railway companies made it possible at one time in the seventies for an immigrant to purchase for twenty-one dollars a ticket that entitled him to transportation from Stockholm to Chicago. This is, of course, an exceptional instance; but in the eighties and nineties thousands of immigrants purchased for thirty-five dollars tickets that entitled them to transportation from European ports to Chicago or Minneapolis.

With the development of rail transportation in Europe, railway stations were cluttered with baggage belonging to excited emigrants jostling each other to board special trains to take them to ports of embarkation, from which they set out on the greatest adventure of their lives. Upon arrival at New York, Boston, or Montreal, the immigrants were hustled to special trains to carry them to the interior, usually to Chicago, the greatest railway center in the world, which was the clearing house of immigration. With thousands of immigrants pouring into the city, Chicago was a paradise for runners, sharks, and agents, representing wildcat organizations and speaking the language of their victims. It requires little imagination to see myriads of these jackals grabbing baggage, "spieling" for disreputable hotels, cheating at exchange, and selling tickets to false destinations. Similar conditions existed in New York, which until the opening of Ellis Island in 1892 could offer no better accommodations to the newcomers than Castle Garden, although through the agencies of churches and other philanthropic societies assistance was given to homesick, tired, and discouraged men, women, and children.

At the close of the Civil War this traffic in human flesh had become highly systematized, with agents operating on both sides of the Atlantic. A host of emigration agencies, like the American Emigrant Company and the Great European-American Emigration Land Company, for example, were engaged in many activities, such as selling steamship and railway tickets, maintaining exchange bureaus and employment agencies, and promoting colonies for the purpose of selling land. These agencies established offices in the principal European and American cities; subagents distributed literature, made house-to-house canvasses, organized emigration societies, and delivered addresses which painted glowing pictures of America and dark pictures of Europe. Papers subsidized or owned by these corporations were established, and their pages blazed forth huge advertisements of land companies, railway companies, and agencies of every stripe.

The stakes in the emigration game were big, and neither the United States nor the countries of Europe had laws giving adequate protection to men, women, and children who were at the mercy of unscrupulous men who fattened on the gullibility and inexperience of persons to whom everything outside of their native parishes was strange. In cities like Liverpool, Glasgow, Gothenburg, and Hamburg the immigrants were packed into unspeakable hotels infested with vermin and disreputable agents. In England *en route* from Scandinavian countries and Germany, the emigrants were herded like cattle into railway cars and starved in hotels. Conditions in the steerage were worse, if that was possible. On arrival at New York they were met by a mob of runners who shouted, "Come with me, countrymen!" Having run this gauntlet, they were placed aboard a train for Chicago. One immigrant in 1869 wrote that this journey via the Erie Railroad took four days and four nights. From New York to Cleveland his party rode in regular emigrant cars, but at Cleveland they were packed into box cars. Some of the cars jolted so much that it was impossible to sit or lie down. The plight of mothers with small children can more easily be imagined than described. On arrival at Chicago another army of runners was ready for action.

One of the worst swindles perpetrated on the emigrants was selling them tickets to the southern states, with a promise of lucrative employment or the prospect of purchasing land. Agents were said to be on the ground ready to assist them in the process of getting settled. Some of these colonies existed only on attractively drawn maps distributed by agents or printed in foreign language newspapers; other proposed colonies were remote from other settlements, without transportation facilities, without water, and without good soil.

In 1871 a government inspector reported as follows: "If Europe were to present us with 300,000 cattle per year, ample agencies would be employed to secure their proper protection and distribution, but thus far the general government has done but little to diminish the numerous hardships of an emigrant's position. All legislation having for its purpose the good of the poor and the lowly, will necessarily be opposed by those who make money off their ignorance and helplessness."

Despite the hardships of the voyage and the discouraging welcome that awaited them when they set foot on American soil, the immigrants wrote letters to friends and relatives back home which radiated the optimism that characterized America in the nineteenth century. The unprecedented development of the country—industrial expansion, railway construction, the opening of new territories, cheap and fertile land, the enactment of the Homestead Law in 1862—furnished opportunities undreamed of to these hard-working, frugal, and peaceful strangers from another continent.

One of the highly prized advantages America offered was the opportunity to rise from the lowest stratum of society. The immigrant found a land where the man whose hands were calloused by toil was looked upon as just as useful to society as the man with a white collar. The man who chafed under the cramped social conventions of Europe could not conceal his joy at finding a country where custom and tradition counted for little and where manual labor did not carry with it a social stigma. "Freedom and equality are the fundamental principles of the Constitution of the United States," wrote an immigrant in Iowa in 1846. "There is no such thing as class distinction here, no counts, barons, lords, or lordly estates. . . . Every one lives in the unrestricted enjoyment of personal liberty."

The American frontier reacted not only upon the older sections of the United States but upon Europe as well. The revolutionary economic, social, religious, and political readjustments that rocked Europe in the nineteenth century did not take form in the United States; and to millions of immigrants and prospective immigrants the western republic was the "Land of Canaan"—a land flowing with milk and honey. It was a land where it was possible for them to write about cities springing up like magic, high wages, and large farms, whose owners counted their livestock by the scores and their chickens by the hundreds. The "America letters" contain the surprising information that the laborer and the farmer ate meat and wheat bread every day, syrup at every meal, and eggs and milk as often as desired.

It is true that many immigrants wrote that they did not know what hard work was until they set their hands to the plow or the shovel in the United States, but there was a certain pride in the admission. It was probably the American optimism that sustained their spirits. They saw everything in the light of a future in which a farm plus a bank account was the ultimate goal. This feeling of independence and self-confidence was also heightened by the vast distances of America—its large farms, billowing prairies, and budding cities. Moreover, the immigrant was not conscious of living under the surveillance of the government as he had been in his native land. He could move from community to community and from state to state without entangling himself in yards of red tape. By contrast he was hardly conscious of living under a government, and the system of taxation fooled him into thinking that there were no taxes at all.

The immigrants, whether Catholic, Protestant, or Jew, could write with equal truth as a Swedish immigrant wrote: "The American does not bother about the religious beliefs of his fellow men. It is the individual's own affair to worship God according to the dictates of his conscience, without interference from prelates clothed with power to prescribe what one must believe in order to obtain salvation." The immigrants quickly sensed the difference in spirit and method of Christianity in the old country and in the new. The same leveling process of the frontier that obliterated class distinctions and produced the self-made man in politics and business also produced the democratic, warmhearted, pietistic, uncultured, and plain-spoken man in the pulpit.

For the most part, the immigrants were free to work out their own salvation—religious, economic, and social. They established their own newspapers, churches, educational institutions, and societies; and soon the United States took on that polyglot appearance unknown in any other country. Some of the immigrant stocks attempted to set up and maintain Lutheran and Catholic parochial schools in competition with the public schools; but the Lutherans were not very successful, although the Catholics made steady progress in building up their own educational system.

The immigrants who came from Germany, Norway, Sweden, Denmark, and the Netherlands in the three decades following the Civil War maintained their native languages as spoken languages into the twentieth century, but the prediction that dialects would grow up in foreign communities has not been realized. Few of them spoke grammatical German, Norwegian, Swedish, Danish, or Dutch; they spoke the dialect of their native provinces; and soon almost everybody spoke a ludicrous combination of English and native dialect that was unintelligible to Americans as well as to recent arrivals from Europe. These humble folk brought with them little of the culture of their native lands. In their first years in America they were engaged in a ceaseless struggle with poverty and strange conditions. Their leaders, whether pastors or politicians, were largely recruited from the ranks and had little or no appreciation of the literature and history of the land that gave them birth. The foreign language was inadequate for the transaction of everyday affairs because it had no equivalents for many typically American things.

The children of immigrants learned to speak the language of their parents in the home, in the Sunday school, and in the parochial school, but the magic of the "melting pot" could not be denied. The invasion of the language of the adopted country through the medium of the public school, the ubiquitous newspaper, and associates on the farm and in the factory could not be repelled. There are traces of the influence of the speech of immigrants in the language of the country today; but the propagandists who strove to perpetuate the language of the immigrants fought a losing battle. According to the census of 1930, only 869,865 of the 13,366,407 foreign-born whites did not have a working command of English; and only a very small percentage of the old immigrants were unable to speak English.

The great bulk of immigrants who sought their fortunes in the United States in the nineteenth century were conservative along political, social, and religious lines. They found America a Utopia, in contrast with Europe; and the opportunities that they struck in the adopted country made them satisfied and grateful. Radical agitators found foreign language communities sterile soil for sowing their doctrines of discontent, except in certain industrial centers where unsavory working and living conditions were notorious. The influence of foreign-language newspapers and pastors of foreign-language churches was overwhelmingly on the side of conservatism. It is true that politicians appealed to the racial pride and clannishness of immigrant stocks—sometimes successfully—but by and large the naturalized voters followed the channels cut by the native-born.

The post-war generation, whether native-born or foreign-born, had unbounded faith in the destiny of America. The country had successfully emerged from a great Civil War which threatened to disprove the stability of a republican form of government and brought in its wake financial, economic, and social disorder, but this was forgotten in the midst of material prosperity such as the world had never seen. The feverish activity of the post-war generation was translated into the language itself. Brevity, short cuts, striking phrases, culminating in the terse, screaming headlines on the first page of newspapers at the time of the Spanish-American War, reflected the nervous, hectic life of the people.

In the midst of material wealth, the heedless exploitation of natural resources, the creation of huge personal fortunes built on sharp practices and ruthless competition, the operations of hard-headed captains of industry, and shameful corruption in government, there were idealism and faith. Crusaders for political and social righteousness, as well as high-powered evangelists who stormed and exhorted in American revivalist fashion and preached sermons heavily charged with the "law," attracted multitudes in the cities of the East and on the prairies of the West. America was strong, vigorous, and unafraid. In spite of a certain boastfulness, America did not yet know its strength—nor did Europe.

CHAPTER VI

INDIANS, COWBOYS AND RAILROADS

WITH THE ACQUISITION OF THE TERRITORY KNOWN AS THE Gadsden Purchase in 1853, the boundaries of continental United States took final form, with the exception of certain boundary adjustments; and it was not until the purchase of Alaska in 1867 that the expansionist tendencies of the American people brought new territory under the jurisdiction of the United States.

The Civil War and the arid region slowed up the march of population across the continent; but within thirty years after the surrender of Lee nine states were admitted into the union, constituting one-fifth of the total number of states. From 1907 to 1912 the three remaining territories—Oklahoma, Arizona, and New Mexico—were admitted to statehood. The progress of settlement from the Atlantic seaboard to the Mississippi River was peaceful, orderly, and gradual compared with the settlement from the Mississippi to the Pacific coast. East of the Mississippi the greatest obstacle to the determination of the pioneers to conquer the wilderness was the Indians. Before the Civil War settlement had penetrated across the Mississippi; and five states—California (1850), Minnesota (1858), Oregon (1859), Kansas (1861), and Nevada (1864)—had been admitted before the Confederacy collapsed. In 1860 the total population of Montana, Idaho, Wyoming, Colorado, New Mexico, Arizona, Utah, Nevada, Washington, Oregon, and California was 619,000; and by 1870 the population of this far-western region had increased to 990,000.

It was in the Great Plains that a new type of American was created—the cowboy, picturesque and quick on the trigger. A brilliant student who has studied the history of the Great Plains, Walter Prescott Webb, asserts that "the Great Plains offered such a contrast to the region east of the ninety-eighth meridian . . .

as to bring about a marked change in the ways of pioneering and living." In contrasting the civilization of the Great Plains with that of the eastern timberland, he sees what he calls an institutional *fault* running from middle Texas to Illinois or Dakota, roughly following the ninety-eighth meridian. "Practically every institution that was carried across it was either broken and remade or else greatly altered," he says. "East of the Mississippi civilization stood on three legs—land, water, and timber; west of the Mississippi not one but two of these legs were withdrawn—water and timber—and civilization was left on only one leg—land."

Instead of felling trees, rolling logs, and raising log cabins, the pioneers who settled in Kansas and Nebraska in the seventies and eighties made sod houses or dugouts their humble dwellings until such time as the railroads and their economic status made it possible to erect buildings. Some of them experienced vicissitudes and hardships that convinced them that their venture was a mistake. Not only were they made penniless by the hard times that followed the panics of 1873 and 1893, but the hot winds that blew in the southern portion of the Great Plains sometimes destroyed their growing crops and made it impossible for them to feed their livestock. And in the northern plains—in the Dakotas—the blizzards were equally terrifying and devastating to human and animal life.

But the indomitable pioneer spirit could not be daunted by wind and weather. The farmers who settled the Great Plains, like their predecessors east of the Mississippi, wrote optimistic letters to friends and relatives in the old states and in Norway, Sweden, Denmark, and Germany. Missionaries forded streams, slept in the open, stayed overnight in dugouts and sod houses, organized congregations, and established schools, academies, and colleges. Letters and reports printed in newspapers stimulated the organization of land and colonization societies, and cheap railroad rates brought homeseekers. By the beginning of 1870 the Burlington and Missouri River Railroad was completed as far as Council Bluffs, Iowa, and the land department of the railroad launched an extensive advertising campaign in the newspapers of the country as well as in the countries of Europe. Similar activities were

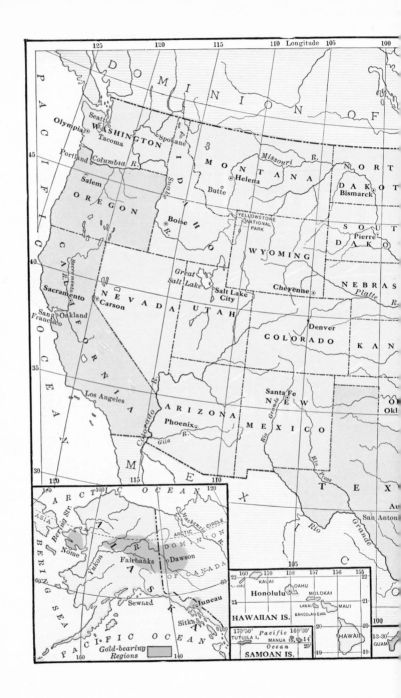

DOMINION OF

PACIFIC

125   120   115   110 Longitude 105   100

WASHINGTON
Olympia·   Seattle
                  Tacoma·   Spokane·

45   Portland Columbia R.

IDAHO

MONTANA   Missouri R.   NORT

Salem·   Helena·   DAKOT
OREGON   Butte·   Bismarck·

                  Boise·   SOU
                  R.   DAKO
                        YELLOWSTONE
                        NATIONAL
                        PARK   WYOMING   Pierre·

40   Great
                        Salt Lake   Cheyenne· NEBRAS
Sacramento·   NEVADA   Salt Lake   Platte R.
                  ·Carson   City   UTAH

San ·Oakland   Denver·
Francisco   COLORADO   KAN

35   Denver

                        R.
Los Angeles·   ARIZONA   NEW   Santa Fe·   Okl

                  Colorado   Phoenix·   MEXICO
30   Gila   Rio Pecos   TEX
120   115   110

CALIFORNIA

PACIFIC   OCEAN

MEXICO

San Antoni

Au

ARCTIC   OCEAN
ASIA   Bering Str.   Mackenzie
Nome·   ARCTIC CIRCLE
              YUKON R.   DOMINION
BERING   Fairbanks· ·Dawson
SEA   60°   ALASKA   OF CANADA   60
              Seward·
                        Juneau·
              Sitka·
PACIFIC   OCEAN
        Gold-bearing
        Regions
160   140

160   159   158   157   156   155
22   OAHU
     KAUAI   22
     ·NIIHAU   Honolulu· MOLOKAI
21   LANAI   MAUI   21
                  KAHOOLAWE
HAWAIIAN IS.   100

170°50' Pacific 169°30'
TUTUILA I.   MANUA IS. 14   HAWAII   13-30'
              Ocean   20'   GUAM
19   19
SAMOAN IS.

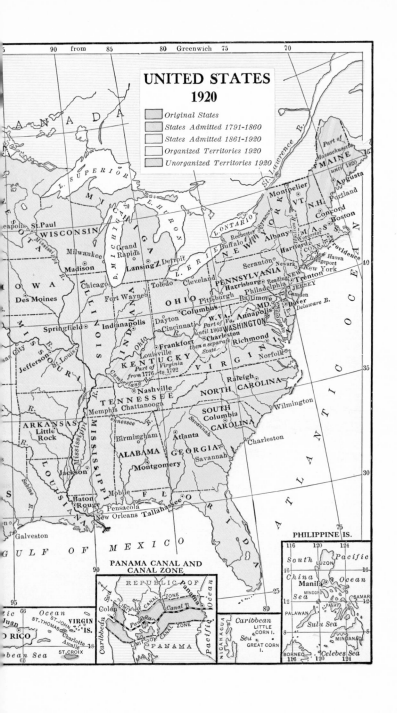

UNITED STATES
1920

Original States
States Admitted 1791–1860
States Admitted 1861–1920
Organized Territories 1920
Unorganized Territories 1920

PANAMA CANAL AND
CANAL ZONE

PHILIPPINE IS.

conducted by the Union Pacific Land Department and by the Kansas Pacific Railroad. Moreover, the new states emulated the example of their older sisters, like Iowa, Wisconsin, and Minnesota, and established boards of immigration charged with the duty of employing agents and publishing propaganda literature.

The following eulogy of the Homestead Law, written in 1887 by a cultured Swedish Lutheran clergyman who took a homestead claim in Kansas in the late sixties, probably clothes the inarticulate thoughts of many a pioneer:

A finer law has never been enacted on earth. Where is the country that can boast of such an affectionate and charitable law for the poor? This is the brightest star in the whole galaxy of the Stars and Stripes. When I think of all the settlements I have visited, when I see all the pleasant homes I have visited, which my countrymen have built under toil and difficulties but with the divine reward of having their own homes, my heart leaps with joy, especially when I see it all in the light of history and know that only a few centuries ago all the workingmen in the world's most civilized continent, Europe, were slaves. In America, every workingman can, if he will, become a nobleman, baron, and count.

The Indian problem during the Civil War and reconstruction periods resolved itself into the question of what disposition was to be made of the Red Men, with the advance of railways and the establishment of mining camps. The problem of subduing the Plains Indians was exceedingly difficult partly because they were mounted, partly because of their ferocity and cruelty, and partly because of the nature of the country in which they roamed. "There is evidence to show that in their fights with the Plains Indians white men learned to save one bullet for themselves," writes Walter Prescott Webb.

During the Civil War the government had been forced to send military expeditions against the Indians, who could see the approaching end of the freedom that had been theirs. The most serious trouble was the Sioux outbreak in Minnesota in 1862. The Indians paid dearly for the lives they had taken and the property they had destroyed. Their lands were confiscated, and the Sioux fled toward the Black Hills. The Sioux war continued for some time, and at the same time the Comanches, the Arapahoes, and the Apaches were active in the Southwest. Late in 1866 the Sioux destroyed the entire force commanded by Captain W. J. Fetterman at Fort Philip Kearney, an event that aroused a storm of revenge against the Indians and indignation against the government for its alleged mismanagement of Indian affairs.

In the meantime, General William T. Sherman was put in command of the Department of Missouri, and it was proposed to make two great reservations in the West. The northern reservation was to be north of Nebraska, west of the Missouri River, east of the Rocky Mountains, and south of Canada. The southern reservation was called Indian Territory and included the territory of the present State of Oklahoma.

In 1868 the Sioux accepted a treaty which gave them a northern reservation which included what became the western end of South Dakota, north to the forty-sixth parallel and thence to the Missouri River.

Within a short time hostilities broke out anew because of dissatisfaction with the treaty. The Indians feared, among other things, that they were in danger of losing their chief means of livelihood, the buffalo, which had roamed the plains in uncounted numbers. General Philip H. Sheridan operated against the Indians and succeeded in rounding them up, so that by 1869 the worst of the troubles with the Plains Indians was over. That year Congress created a Board of Civilian Indian Commissioners to cooperate with the Indian Department in caring for and civilizing these wards of the nation.

In 1871 Congress took a further step in the direction of a more enlightened policy by enacting a law that prohibited the making of any Indian treaty in the future. Thereafter Congress—not the Senate—was to have the power of making agreements with the Indians. President Grant pursued a benevolent policy; and when his successor, President Hayes, appointed Carl Schurz Secretary of the Interior, the Indians had in a responsible position a man of integrity, good judgment, and sterling honesty. By the Dawes Act of 1887 provision was made for granting citizenship to the Indians and for dividing their reservations into tracts under individual ownership and not held in communal ownership, although the government continued to watch over the transition in order to protect the Indians against unscrupulous individuals. To this end the Dawes Act was modified in 1906 by the Burke Act, which allowed greater latitude to the Secretary of the Interior in individual cases.

With the coming of gold diggers into the Black Hills of South Dakota, the Sioux under the leadership of Sitting Bull donned their war paint; and in 1876 occurred the massacre of General Custer's forces in a battle on the Little Big Horn. The renewed war ended as all wars between the redskins and the whites ended: the Indians were crushed and Sitting Bull fled to Canada. He returned in the early eighties to witness the steady settlement by whites on lands he had called his own. The incipient outbreak of the Indians under their great leader was crushed by prompt action on the part of army officers and Indian agents and by the death of the chief. The Indians had met the fate of inferior peoples and weak nations in a chapter of the history of mankind which has sometimes been called the expansion of people of European blood. There was no room for Indian tribes in a country crisscrossed by railroads and defended by an army equipped with high-powered rifles and Gatling guns.

The rise and fall of the "Cattle Kingdom" is a spectacular chapter in the history of the Great Plains. The great public domain in the West from 1866 to 1886 produced a type of American familiar to Americans of today through "Wild West" magazines, cowboy songs broadcast over national hookups, traveling rodeos, moving picture productions, Buffalo Bill shows, and Frederick Remington's pictures.

The "Cattle Kingdom" was a man's country, in which men on horseback reigned and ruled. It was a country of men, horses, and cattle. Like the habiliments of the cowboy, which were adapted to the character of his work, the cow country became what it was because of conditions peculiar to it. The man in the "Cattle Kingdom" who could not ride a horse was either a young man who had not been there long enough to be initiated into the fraternity of roughriders, or a tenderfoot from the East who had come to have a look.

Just as the railroad made possible the settlement of territory that would otherwise have remained a wilderness, so did the "iron horse" create and destroy within a generation that phase of civilization known as the "Cattle Kingdom." The cattle-grazing industry moved westward with the march of settlement; but the "ranch" as understood after the Civil War applied to the semi-arid portion of the Great Plains and included parts or all of western Texas, Oklahoma, Kansas, Nebraska, the Dakotas, Montana, Wyoming, Nevada, Utah, Colorado, and New Mexico. The "range" was simply the range land, which brought out the ranch in its peculiar form—the central point, the ranch house surrounded by a great expanse. The ranchman was a cattle-raiser on a large scale, who employed cowboys to attend to his livestock.

Cattle-raising on a large scale had its origin in Texas when the Texans found that they could drive their cattle to the miners in the Rocky Mountains, some fifteen hundred miles away, and to the railroads which would transport them to the East. This operation began even before the advent of the Pacific railroads, when the buffalo herds and Indians were obstacles; but by the time the cattle industry reached its flourishing period, from 1876 to 1885, the buffalo herds had been well-nigh exterminated and the Indians had been pretty well rounded up. It was not until 1866 that the "long drive" from Texas brought a considerable number of cattle into the feeding areas of Kansas, Missouri, and Iowa. From that time on a steady procession of cattle moved from the south to populate the Cattle Kingdom of the Great American Desert. "To all those who saw that long line of Texas cattle come up over a rise in the prairie, nostrils wide for the smell of water, dust-caked and gaunt, so ready to break from the nervous control of the riders strung out along the flanks of the herd, there came the feeling that in this spectacle there was something elemental, something resistless, something perfectly in keeping with the unconquered land about them," writes Ernest S. Osgood.

In the early years of the Cattle Kingdom the cattle belonging to a certain ranch could roam as far as water and grass would permit; but with the increase in the number of ranches cattle bearing the brands of different ranches could and did mingle. Out of this situation developed the round-up, in which all the ranchmen interested participated. There were two annual round-ups: in the spring, when the calves were branded; and in the fall, when the summer calves and cattle that had been missed in the spring were branded.

The history of the Cattle Kingdom includes a consideration not only of the conditions and forces that created it but also the developments that destroyed it. The same railroads that made it possible for the ranchman to ship his cattle to market broke down the possibility of a grazing reserve. The railroads sold the lands that had been granted to them by the government in small lots to homesteaders. In spite of obstacles that had at one time seemed insuperable—the lack of timber and water—the blind American optimism brought homesteaders into the region of the Great Plains. They inclosed their farms with barbed wire fences. There could be neither truce nor compromise between the open range and barbed wire. Moreover, the cattle men were at war among themselves; and, though cattle-growers' associations were formed in order to eliminate overcrowding of the range and flooding of the market, it was difficult to reach agreements and still more difficult to enforce them. Moreover, the Texas fever and the hoof and mouth disease spread infection among other herds and brought laws prohibiting the driving of cattle across state boundaries. The profits of the business in boom years resulted in overcrowding the range and placing cattle at the mercy of drought.

By the middle of the eighties cattle prices slumped heavily, and cattle were thrown on the market in order that the cattle men might get something out of the crash. After the collapse of 1885 the business of cattle-raising entered a new phase; the open range was about to yield to a more orderly method of raising cattle. With the disappearance of the last American frontier also disappeared the cow country that was contemporaneous with it.

A study of the decennial railroad maps showing the progress of construction in the United States from 1860 to 1900 illustrates the tremendous development of the country from the Atlantic

to the Pacific. East of the Mississippi River settlement preceded
the railroads, but west of it, speaking in general terms, the process
was reversed. West of the ninety-eighth meridian the railroad
promoters became the pioneers; railroads were built in unoccupied regions with the expectation that settlement would follow.
East of the Mississippi trunk-line railroads connecting the seaboard with Chicago or St. Louis were created by consolidating
existing roads. Men of outstanding ability—and also of doubtful morals—like William H. Vanderbilt, Daniel Drew, Jay Gould,
James Fisk, J. Edgar Thomson, Alexander J. Cassatt, and J.
Pierpont Morgan, by sharp practices, unscrupulous stock manipulations, and genius and foresight, succeeded in consolidating railway mileage into great systems like the New York Central, the
Erie, the Pennsylvania, and the Baltimore and Ohio. The fact
that the lines composing these systems were built after towns and
cities had grown up explains the character of the railroad map—
a closely woven network of lines built to carry traffic furnished by
industries that gave employment to dwellers in these cities and
towns.

The western railroads were built primarily to connect the principal cities of the Middle West with the Pacific coast. They
struck boldly across the Great Plains to attain their objectives,
so far as the topography of the country permitted. Moreover, if
the roads were to be built across a vast expanse of territory with
a sparse population or no population at all, capital would have
to be attracted through the instrumentality of subsidies furnished
/by the federal government. It would be years before the railroads
would be able to pay dividends out of revenues derived from
traffic. In 1850 the federal government embarked on a system of
land grants to encourage railroad construction, and the total
acreage of these grants in succeeding years down to the close of
the seventies is staggering.

With the discovery of gold in California in 1848, fortune
hunters found their way in increasing numbers to the Golden
State; and in 1850 the state was admitted into the Union. Although the idea of a Pacific railroad was an old one, in the decade
preceding the Civil War it was urged as a necessity to bind the

nation together. The competition between certain cities like Chicago and St. Louis for the terminal of the proposed road, and
sectional rivalry and jealousy, however, made it impossible to
agree on a route. Should it be a Southern Pacific or a Central
Pacific or a Northern Pacific railroad?

It was not until eleven southern states had seceded that the
Pacific Railway Act was signed by the President of the United
States in 1862. This act provided for the construction of the
Union Pacific starting from the East, and the Central Pacific
starting from the Pacific coast, and continuing until the two roads
should meet. The roads were promised alternate sections of land
on each side of the right of way, amounting to ten square miles
for each mile of road. In addition to this inducement, the federal
government granted first-mortgage loans for each mile, the amount
varying with the nature of the country through which the road
was constructed.

No capital was attracted under the terms of this act, however;
and in 1864 it was amended by doubling the land grant and allowing the roads to borrow private capital on first-mortgage bonds
equal to the amount borrowed from the government on second-
mortgage bonds. The amount the roads were permitted to borrow
per mile varied according to the nature of the country, as in the
previous act. Twice the amount that could be borrowed on the
road constructed on the plains could be borrowed on the miles
between the mountain ranges, and three times the first amount on
the road that ran through the mountains. The point of junction
fixed by the act was ultimately abandoned; and this precipitated
a race between the roads to see which one could construct the
greater mileage and thus obtain larger government subsidies.

In the process of construction many difficulties came up, including various forms of fraud and graft, the most flagrant being
the profits taken by the Crédit Mobilier, a construction company
made up of directors of the Union Pacific, who were in the fortunate position of combining in themselves buyer and seller. Not
only did these circumstances increase the cost of constructing the
roads but they also saddled them with financial difficulties to
plague them in the future. For example, in 1897-98 the Union

Pacific was a bankrupt road as the result of methods that made individuals rich and also wrecked properties. In the end, the government, in the inferior position of a second-mortgage holder, was compelled to agree to a settlement that was far from equitable. It remained for a financial wizard, Edward H. Harriman, to take over a bankrupt property at a bargain price and rehabilitate it.

Notwithstanding unsavory developments, the completion of a Pacific railway in May, 1869, was a notable achievement. A motley crowd of laborers, including Chinese, was attracted to the temporary camps which were moved from time to time as miles of rails lengthened. "Hell on wheels" was the name applied to one of the camps by a journalist who was an interested spectator. In addition to problems of construction and of commissary supplies for the army of men, the Indians remained a menace, although among the laborers were veterans of the Civil War who knew how to respond to commands of officers who had likewise seen service in that war.

The decade from 1860 to 1870 saw the construction of some twenty-two thousand miles of railroad; and from 1865 to 1873 the total increase in mileage in the West alone was over twenty-two thousand, and in the East over twelve thousand. By the middle of the eighties shippers had the choice of seven different routes to the Rocky Mountains and five different lines across the continental divide. Besides land grants totaling millions of acres, railroads received millions of dollars donated by towns and counties in order to obtain terminals and railroad facilities. Moreover, by means of logrolling and bribery, promoters obtained concessions from Congress and state legislatures. Some projected roads were never built, and investors were in consequence heavy losers. Farmers who had furnished teams and labor had nothing to show for their efforts to contribute to the development of their communities.

One of the major causes of the panic of 1873 was the unprecedented construction of railroads, especially in the West, where vast amounts of capital were tied up in enterprises that yielded no adequate returns on the investment. The panic was precipitated by the failure of the financial house of Jay Cooke and Company of Philadelphia, which was unequal to the strain of financing the Northern Pacific Railway. Jay Cooke had been remarkably successful in financing government loans during the Civil War, but he failed to carry the Northern Pacific to completion. Within six months after Jay Cooke and Company closed their doors, the road was thrown into receivership; and it was more than ten years before the project was completed.

In the meantime another promoter had started in a small way to rehabilitate a bankrupt road which eventually expanded into the Great Northern Railway and became a competitor of the Northern Pacific. This man was James J. Hill of St. Paul, who in 1870 was driving dog sleds and some thirteen years later traveled over the same region on his own railway. In spite of objections that a railroad could not be constructed and made to pay across the country south of the Canadian border, a region containing vast stretches of seemingly worthless land, Hill's road opened traffic through to the Pacific coast in 1893, the year of another devastating panic. His achievement is even more impressive and suggestive of his leonine daring when one considers that it was accomplished without government subsidies and land grants.

Naturally Hill was primarily interested in obtaining dividends from his investment, but one of the by-products of his self-interest was the inauguration of systematic efforts to attract settlers to develop the country through which his road ran. Extensive advertising in foreign-language newspapers published in Europe and in the United States and the employment of agents who knew the tricks of the trade brought thousands of Scandinavian farmers to Minnesota and the Northwest, who looked upon "Yim" Hill as their benefactor. Indeed, throughout the last quarter of the nineteenth century and beyond into the present century the influence of railroads in promoting settlement was a constant factor. The Northern Pacific, the Union Pacific, the Kansas Pacific, the Burlington and Missouri, and other railroads established land and emigration companies and engaged in propaganda in a big way. And homeseekers' excursions—one fare plus two dollars, with a thirty-day limit—spurred many ambitious men to look for better clover in other parts of the country. Simultaneously with the expansion of transportation by rail occurred the decline of transportation by water. The heavy traffic on the Mississippi River, which continued through the eighties, gradually gave way to the railroads; and with the passing of the steamboat ended a picturesque chapter in American history. Even as late as the closing years of the nineteenth century the residents of St. Paul, Dubuque, Clinton, Davenport, Rock Island, Burlington, St. Louis, and other cities along the Mississippi were privileged to see huge rafts of logs floating down the Father of Waters destined for sawmills operating in flourishing industrial centers. And the arrival of the steamboat with its motley passengers and decks cluttered with freight, including household gear belonging to settlers, farm implements, livestock and grain, was a frequent occurrence.

In spite of the Civil War, steamboating on the Mississippi and its tributaries was at its height from about 1855 to 1865; but the havoc wrought by the railroads is strikingly revealed by the fact that in 1880 there were thirteen railroad bridges spanning the river between St. Paul and St. Louis. By that time the main highways of transportation were not the natural lines of communication running north and south, but the trunk-line railroads running east and west.

Thus a combination of events had by the close of the nineteenth century given the lie to the prediction of Senator Thomas H. Benton of Missouri, who in 1830 said that it was insanity to think that railways could compete with natural waterways; that the natural course of transportation could not be changed. He said that the idea of sending the products of the West across the Alleghenies was the conception of insanity itself. No railroads or canals would carry them, even if they did it gratis. One transshipment, he said, would exceed the cost of transportation to New Orleans, to say nothing of the upstream work of getting to the canal or railway. Besides, he continued, such an unnatural reversal of the course of trade would be injurious to the western cities and fatal to the steamboats of the West. The Senator declared that the people of the West were not going to abandon the Mississippi—their sea—for the comforts of scaling the Allegheny

Mountains with hogsheads of tobacco, barrels of whiskey, pork and flour, bales of hemp, and coops of chickens on their backs.

The upper Mississippi almost ceased to be an avenue of transportation not only because of competition furnished by limited passenger trains and fast freights, but also because the demands of civilization—great cities and improved farms—denuded Michigan, Wisconsin, and Minnesota of their magnificent forests. After 1900 large rafts towed by stern-wheelers with powerful engines were no more. In 1873 the number of rafts passing the bridge at Rock Island was estimated at 680, indicating the activity of lumberjacks in the northern woods; but within three decades the lumber industry was in the process of shifting to the Pacific Northwest and to the Southwest. By 1910 the great sawmills in Minneapolis were silent, and the smaller plants along the St. Croix were mere shadows of their former greatness.

CHAPTER VII

DISCONTENT ON FARMS

IN THE MIDST OF PROSPERITY BUILT ON EXPANDING INDUSTRY, increasing railway construction and traffic, the exploitation of mines and forests, and expanding acreage of improved farms, there were also poverty and discontent. Among the heritages bequeathed to the post-war generation were a heavy public debt, heavy taxes, a fluctuating and unsound currency, and corruption in public office. Nevertheless, America was the land of opportunity not only to her own sons and daughters but also to hundreds of thousands who left friends and relatives in Europe to seek fortune in "God's country."

It was the very optimism and "go-ahead" spirit of the people, however, that sometimes spelled hard times and ruin for some of them; and others who toiled and saved with reasonable success saw the ruthlessness and selfishness of individuals and corporations who took thought for the morrow neither of the nation nor of the individuals and families they exploited. Notwithstanding the fact that during the twenty-five years following the close of the Civil War the well-being of the American people exceeded that of any country in the world, farmers and laborers had serious grievances.

The gist of the farmer's complaint was not that he was poor or suffering, but that others who labored and deserved less received the greater share of the profits of his produce. This was also to a degree the complaint of organized labor.

Some of the conditions of which the farmer complained could be traced to the Civil War. He complained not only of heavy taxes but also of their inequality. The exigencies of war fastened upon the country the highest tariff up to that time; and although it would not be true to say that the western farmer was opposed to a protective tariff, it is true to say that he was of the opinion that the existing tariff was framed largely in the interest of the industrial East. He was likewise dissatisfied with the circulating medium. In his opinion money was not plentiful enough, and he was disposed to place the major portion of the blame for this on the banking and financial interests. He objected to the rapid retirement of the greenbacks and to the demonetization of silver. The "crime of '73," he thought, had been committed by certain financial interests to their own advantage and to the disadvantage of the farmer.

The opening of new areas for the cultivation of wheat and corn made possible by the extension of railroads into unoccupied territory, and the invention of new-fangled farm machinery augmented those crops and contributed to declining prices, especially in comparison with the high prices that had prevailed during the Civil War. The situation that confronted the cotton farmer in the South was much the same.

The fabulous stories about great opportunities in the West—the same stories with variations that fired the imagination of peasants in Europe—precipitated a rush of population into that region. Most of the pioneers were men of small means who took preemption or homestead claims or purchased land from railroads and land companies. In order to purchase farm implements and to stock their farms and build houses and barns, they borrowed money from banks and loan companies. Many of these loans were made through agents of eastern capitalists who exacted large commissions and high rates of interest. The optimism of some pioneers caused them to purchase land for speculative purposes; and when prices fell, land values also declined and debtors were inevitably caught.

The farmer was also discontented with the middleman. He contended that he was the producer and that the commission men, the men who bought his grain and livestock, were parasites who exacted unreasonable commissions and profits.

The intelligent farmer knew that corruption and inefficiency reached into Congress, legislatures, and offices of chief executives of states. He had read about the Crédit Mobilier, the whiskey ring, and other instances of flagrant fraud. Moreover, he saw that the farmer was not properly represented in lawmaking bodies and that legislators did not know his needs and problems, or, if they did, their votes and speeches did not reveal sympathy with the man who followed the plow.

Another disturbing factor to the farmer and his wife was the increasing tendency of their sons and daughters to desert the farm in favor of the city in the belief that the chances for success were better than in the country. The city was growing at the expense of the farm. In contrast with the social intercourse, entertainment, and intellectual satisfaction offered by the city, the boy and girl on the farm were oppressed by isolation, solitude, and hard and endless work. The rural telephone and the rural free delivery of mail were advantages denied until the closing years of the nineteenth century.

Notwithstanding the enactment of the Morrill Act of 1862, which provided that each state should be allotted 30,000 acres of public land for each Senator and Representative in Congress for the establishment of at least one college for the purpose of providing instruction in agriculture and the mechanic arts, it was some years before the ideal embodied in the law was realized in satisfying measure. The farmer complained that the curricula of schools and colleges were barren of courses that would make for a richer and more satisfying career on the farm. The portrayal of ludicrous hayseeds on the stage and in comic periodicals, and quips from the pens of paragraphers who featured Farmer Corntassel, not only lowered the estimation of farm life in the minds of people who in their own way were as "green" as was the farmer, but also made the boy and girl on the farm look up to the city "dude" as a superior being. On his first visit to the city the farmer was supposed to blow out the gas, to crane his neck at tall buildings, to ask foolish questions of the railroad conductor, and to buy gold bricks from the "sharper."

The chief ground of discontent, however, was the railroad. Farmers took stock in railroads in order to encourage the development of their communities and to give them a voice in the management of the company—as they thought. But when through the

machinations of high finance or the effects of hard times railroads
went into receiverships, the farmers met the fate of small investors and lost their investments. They knew that some of these
things would not have happened but for the awarding of contracts
to construct railroads at enormous prices, as in the case of the
Pacific roads, and the watering of stocks to the point beyond
which the earnings failed to pay dividends. Neither did they like
the uncivility of the station agent and the conductor and brake-
man, whose uncouth conduct reflected the unaccommodating road
that employed them.

Not only did the railroads discriminate against stations that had
no competing lines, but they granted favors to large shippers to
the detriment of the farmer. In the absence of laws and regulations that were later imposed by state and federal governments,
the railroads charged what the traffic would bear; and when certain states did establish railroad commissions, the officials refused
to recognize their authority and hid behind the claim that rates
could not be lowered without crippling the financial integrity of
the company. The railroad officials contended that it was through
their foresight and risk that roads had been built into unoccupied and sparsely settled regions, thereby making it possible for
farmers to get land; that the farmers had no understanding of the
technique of operating a railroad; that the companies were private
corporations; and that if the farmers were dissatisfied with the
service provided, they could patronize some other transportation
agency or join with their dissatisfied associates to construct a
road that would meet their requirements.

In the light of history it appears that, in common with his
contemporaries, the western farmer was too optimistic; that he
did encourage railroad construction; that he did not fully understand the principle of credit; and that he was not duly appreciative
of what the railroad had done for him. But it is equally true that
the farmer had a right to insist that when the financial pinch
came, the capitalist ought to take his medicine as well as the
farmer.

The discontent of the farmer took concrete form in organizations designed to stimulate a more abundant life and to furnish

more effective means through which his wants could be made known to legislators and railroad magnates.

The most important farmers' movement in the sixties and seventies began as a non-political organization in 1867. This order took the name Patrons of Husbandry, but it was more commonly known as the Grange. The inception of the Granger movement is found in the decision of President Johnson to send a clerk in the Bureau of Agriculture to the South to obtain information with reference to agricultural conditions. The emissary was Oliver Hudson Kelley, a New Englander who had settled on a farm in Minnesota before taking up his duties in Washington. From his observations on the plight of the southern farmers he conceived the ideal of agricultural societies organized on the principles of the Masons. Kelley and his associates were interested in educating the farmers to make them better tillers of the soil rather than to mobilize them for political action. Moreover, it was a "coeducational" enterprise, in that women were admitted to the order.

It proved to be slow and discouraging work to organize the conservative and inexperienced rural population into a militant body; and for the first four years Kelley had difficulty in raising enough money to pay the printer and to purchase postage stamps, not to mention remuneration for his own services. The order met with opposition from a certain type of clergyman who believed that secret organizations were of the devil; that the principles and spirit of Christianity could not flourish in an order in which unbelievers were privileged to mingle with believers. This attitude was pronounced among the Lutheran Scandinavians and Germans, and some synods and conferences went so far as to adopt resolutions condemning the Patrons of Husbandry. The United Brethren and certain Presbyterian synods took similar action. However, Kelley's persistence was rewarded by the organization of local, state, and national granges, with headquarters in Washington.

By the close of the year 1870 the granges were confined almost exclusively to Minnesota, Iowa, Wisconsin, Illinois, and Indiana. In 1872, however, the order got under way in earnest, and by the close of 1873 it had penetrated all but four states, with its strength centered largely in the Middle West. Besides the granges, there were other farmers' clubs which were identified or in sympathy with the grangers, and it is probable that these clubs, rather than the granges proper, started the agitation against the railroads. Out of these organizations grew political movements sponsored by farmers and known variously as Anti-Monopoly, Reform, Independent, or Farmers' parties.

These instruments of political action sometimes functioned as independent parties, and sometimes fused with one or more parties, usually with the Democratic party which during the reconstruction period played the rôle of an opposition party to the dominant Republican party, although many members of the farmers' clubs did not feel at home in Democratic company because of their Republican traditions and because of the stigma of disloyalty that attached itself to the Democratic name. In some instances the farmers contented themselves by holding mass meetings and interrogating candidates for legislatures on matters pertaining to railroads and agriculture.

These methods bore fruit in several states in the form of legislation designed to curb the piratical practices of railroads. In Illinois, for example, the legislature in 1871 enacted a law denying the right of a railroad to discriminate between a long haul and a short haul, and establishing a maximum rate. The Supreme Court of Illinois in 1873, however, declared this law unconstitutional and took the position that the state could prevent only unjust discrimination. This aroused the ire of the farmers, who descended on Springfield in such numbers that the legislature passed even more stringent laws for the regulation of railroads. In the elections of that year a judge who had declared the law unconstitutional was defeated for reelection. Criticism directed at the judiciary has always been considered lese majesty by a certain type of conservative; and this action by the Illinois farmers was most disturbing. Similar legislation in states like Wisconsin, Minnesota, and Iowa was denounced by eastern investors as socialistic and confiscatory.

Many leaders of the revolting farmers were novices in politics and were no match for the wealth and resourcefulness of the railroads, who made their influence felt in legislative bodies and either prevented the enactment of laws directed against them or else succeeded in having such laws repealed or amended. In its immediate results the Granger movement was a political failure, but the agitation for certain reforms set in motion by it was carried into succeeding decades and bore fruit in federal and state laws. The social and educational aspects of the movement cannot be overlooked. Although cooperative stores and other enterprises designed to eliminate the middlemen did not function satisfactorily, the cooperative idea lingered on and rose to greater success in the years to come.

The most important immediate result of the Granger movement was the establishment of the right of a state to control its public transportation companies. The so-called granger laws established maximum passenger fares, prohibited unjust discrimination in freight rates, and created railroad commissions clothed with power to enforce these laws and to investigate the business of transportation.

The railroads appealed to the courts in order to protect themselves against these laws. These cases were appealed to the Supreme Court of the United States, and are known as the "granger cases." The court upheld the right of a state to regulate a business that is public in nature. In the case of Munn v. Illinois (1876) a warehouse was declared to be a common carrier and subject to regulation by the state. The efforts of the railroads to hide behind their charters were met by the decision of the court that they did not limit the power of the state to regulate rates. With reference to the contention that state laws applicable to rates charged within a state infringed upon the powers of Congress under the clause pertaining to interstate commerce, the court denied that there was infringement so long as Congress had not legislated on the subject. In a later case the court held that regulation of rates by a state did not apply to interstate commerce; and in 1890 the court invalidated a Minnesota law because it denied judicial hearing to the reasonableness of rates.

In conclusion, the granger cases established the legal right of a state to regulate railroads, although the courts exercised the right to decide the reasonableness of such legislation. The right that the law gives, however, was not always respected by the railroads. By liberal use of money, by bestowal of favors of one kind or another, including passes, upon members of legislatures, by secret rebates camouflaged by various devices, they were able to circumvent the will of the people.

The collapse of the Granger movement as an expression of political power and as an experiment in cooperation and social welfare was partly due to the novelty of it in American life, partly to the hard times of the seventies which threw thousands of miles of railway into receivership, and partly to the superiority of its foes in political strategy and business acumen. As an expression of the yearning of farmers and their families for improvement in material, intellectual, and spiritual realms, it was a prelude to achievements, some of them far in the future.

Although the Granger and the Greenback movements are separate and different, the conditions that gave rise to them are similar and related. We have seen that the country emerged from the Civil War with a heavy debt and a large number of greenbacks, and that the Secretary of the Treasury embarked on a policy of converting them into interest-bearing bonds and of substituting for them national banknotes. This policy raised strong opposition, especially from the debtor farmers in the West who were of the opinion that a contracting currency lowered prices and raised interest rates, whereas an expanding currency raised prices and lowered interest rates. In other words, they were possessed of the idea that the quantity of money fixed the rate of interest. They argued that since the value of gold and silver was dependent on demand and supply, so also was the value of greenbacks dependent on demand and supply. Moreover, since the greenbacks represented purchasing power, they argued that the destruction or retirement of a greenback destroyed that amount of wealth. By increasing the supply of greenbacks, money would be cheaper and interest rates would be lower.

It will be recalled that after the "tidal wave of 1874," the Republicans in Congress passed the Resumption Act of 1875, which provided for the resumption of specie payments on January 1, 1879. The Republican party thereby pledged itself to what its

leaders were pleased to call "sound money." By virtue of this fact
the inflationists looked with greater favor on the Democratic
party; but Democratic platforms and many Democratic speakers
were equivocal on the money question. In consequence, the Greenbackers pinned their hopes for a satisfactory solution of this
important problem on third parties. In 1872 the Labor Reform
party resolved that it was the duty of the government to establish
a just standard of distribution of capital and labor by providing
a national circulating medium based on the faith and resources of
the nation, "issued directly to the people without the intervention
of any system of banking corporations."

The hard times following the panic of 1873 and the financial
legislation of Congress gave birth to the Independent Greenback
platform of 1876, which demanded the immediate and unconditional repeal of the Resumption Act, and called upon "all patriotic men" to organize in every congressional district with a view
to stopping "the present suicidal and destructive policy of contraction." Peter Cooper, the presidential candidate of this party,
which had its strength in the West, polled only 81,000 votes.

The widespread unrest of the following year played into the
hands of "calamity orators," and in the elections of 1878 the
Greenback Labor party candidates polled about a million votes.
Fifteen Greenbackers were elected to Congress, of whom James
B. Weaver of Iowa was the most prominent. Weaver's oratorical
ability, his integrity, and his devotion to principle won for him
the presidential nomination of the Greenback Labor party in
1880. In spite of his unprecedented speaking tour, his vote was
disappointingly small, probably because the smiling prosperity
that followed in the wake of the resumption of specie payments
gave the lie to the contention of the inflationists that prices could
not rise under a system of specie payments. In the next presidential election Benjamin F. Butler, the Greenback candidate,
made an even worse showing. This was the last presidential campaign in which a party calling itself "greenback" made an appeal
to the electorate, although the currency question continued to
plague both major parties, and third parties espoused the principles that had been written into greenback platforms.

The Greenback party met the fate that has usually overtaken so-called third parties; but such radical proposals as a graduated income tax, the regulation of interstate commerce, opposition to land grants to railroads, and immigration restriction, which the major parties fought shy of, were kept before the country by a small minority of voters who did not believe that they were throwing away their votes by voting for candidates who obviously had little or no chance of election. Moreover, by fusing with one of the major parties or by indorsing candidates nominated by major parties, third parties have sometimes exercised greater influence than the cold election statistics suggest.

The Greenback movement may be regarded as an interlude between the demise of the Granger movement as a political factor and the rise of the Farmers' Alliance. In fact, there is an "apostolic succession" of agrarian movements, with leaders of earlier movements taking the initiative in creating new organizations to meet problems that came with changing conditions. The career of Ignatius Donnelly of Minnesota is illustrative of this. Beginning his career in Pennsylvania before the Civil War as a Democrat, he moved to Minnesota and threw his fortunes with the idealistic Republican party. Then his independent and erratic course swerved from the Republican path, and he became successively a Granger, a Greenbacker, a Farmers' Alliance man, and a Populist; and at every stage of his political pilgrimage his remarkable oratory aroused farmers to gird themselves against the iniquities of capitalists, merchants, bankers, and railroads. Temperamentally he was unfitted to bend his back to the burden of party discipline; he was an apostle of discontent ready to espouse the cause of the farmer and the laborer.

The culmination of agrarian unrest came in the late eighties and the early nineties. After the decline of the Patrons of Husbandry, the outcry of the farmers against what was going on was voiced through various orders, the most important of which was the Farmers' Alliance. Sporadic movements looking to the organization of farmers sprang up in both the northern and southern states, independent in origin but with the identical purpose of improving conditions on the farm; and by the close of the eighties there were such organizations as the National Farmers' Alliance and Co-operative Union of America in the South and the National Farmers' Alliance and Industrial Union in the North, a Negro Farmers' Alliance, the National Agricultural Wheel, besides mutual benefit associations. Although efforts to bring about a union of the northern and southern alliances were largely unfruitful, the leaders of these respective organizations and of others were in agreement in diagnosing the maladies that beset the rural population and in prescribing remedies.

In addition to establishing cooperative elevators and stores in order to eliminate the middleman, Alliance organizers and newspapers demanded pure food legislation to protect the husbandman against competition with impure and adulterated food, monetary reform, tariff revision, an income tax, revision of tax laws, modification of patent laws, taxation of evidences of debt, abolition of alien landholding, restoration to the government of lands granted to railroads and held for a rise in values, government loans on land, federal regulation or government ownership of railroads and telegraph lines, postal savings banks, and the secret ballot.

In subsequent chapters we shall consider such important developments as the growth of monopolies and trusts, railroad abuses, and the incompetent and dishonest grading, warehousing, and shipping of grain as factors that produced the Populist party and profoundly influenced political campaigns. Let it suffice here to say that the nucleus of the Farmers' Alliance movement was the demand for better transportation rates and greater efficiency and honesty in handling staple crops. The farmer felt, and with good reason, that others who deserved less received a disproportionate share of the profits of his produce. Some of the grievances of which he complained were incident to the hardships of pioneer farming, such as crop failures, distance from market, high interest rates, and over-optimistic faith in the future.

As a party of protest and agitation, the Alliance served a useful purpose in awakening the country to the radical changes in industrial and social relations that had been effected by the substitution of machinery for manual labor and the railroad for the oxcart and the stagecoach. The remedies proposed by the Alliance sprang out of American traditions and experience and not out of Europe, where nothing short of revolution could strike off the shackles of a stratified society. European socialism had no attraction for the Alliance men. On the contrary, they aimed their shafts at organized capital in the form of corporations that exercised governmental functions or wielded power dangerous to the welfare of the public and the individual. They avowed that Congress had the right to legislate upon matters of national interest, despite the contentions of conservatives that such legislation was not contemplated by the framers of the Constitution, that it was "class legislation," that it was socialistic, that it was un-American. Nevertheless, the future was with the Alliance men, and their activity gave sleepless nights to Republican and Democratic Congressmen, Senators, and members of legislatures, and returned a number of them to private life.

CHAPTER VIII

DISCONTENT IN CITIES

CONTEMPORANEOUSLY WITH THE EFFORTS OF FARMERS TO achieve a "more abundant life" through cooperation, organization, and political action, there arose leaders among those who toiled in factories and on railroads who sought to obtain shorter hours, higher wages, and better working conditions. Just as the farmers who saw the necessity of organization were in the minority, so also were the laborers in the cities who affiliated with labor organizations in the minority. Throughout the years American labor as an organized entity has exercised far less influence than has organized labor in Europe. Unions have never claimed more than 15 per cent of American laborers; but in Germany, England, and Australia the percentage has risen as high as 75, 65, and 60 per cent, respectively. The highest membership ever attained in the United States before 1900 was about one million, and in 1920 the number rose to five million.

The fact that from 1820 to 1920 over thirty million Europeans deserted their native lands in favor of the United States is in itself proof that opportunities in the New World were better than in the Old. The fabulous resources of the United States, its abundance of forests and metals, its rivers and lakes swarming with fish, the restless ambition of its people, its epoch-making inventions in manufacturing, in transportation, and in farming, all conspired to give the farmer and laborer opportunities undreamed of in Europe. The self-respect of the Americans was contagious, and in a remarkably short time the immigrants caught the contagion. The "go-ahead" spirit of America was commented on in thousands of letters that crossed the Atlantic.

The fact that thousands of immigrants overcame the handicap of a strange environment, with a foreign language and unfamiliar methods and customs, and after a few years of drudgery became homeowners and sent their children to high schools and colleges, bears eloquent testimony to the material prosperity of America. And returned emigrants who visited their native parishes, dressed in ready-made clothes and displaying gold watches and jingling money in their pockets, fired the ambitions of their cousins who thought of America in terms of silk dresses in contrast with the calico dresses that satisfied the wants of the stay-at-homes. The so-called upper classes looked with disdain upon this display of finery, but the sons and daughters of farmers and laborers dreamed of the day when they, too, might return to arouse envy. Millions of dollars in the aggregate crossed the Atlantic in sealed envelopes and made it possible to purchase steamship tickets preliminary to obtaining employment in the mines of Pennsylvania, in the factories of New England, on the streets with pick and shovel, and in the homes of well-to-do farmers, merchants, bankers, and professional men.

The wife of the American laborer set a table adorned with a white table cloth, silver cutlery, and victuals that were missing from the tables of the peasants and laborers in Europe. "America letters" written by housewives who had not yet learned the language of the adopted country boasted of wheat bread, milk, eggs, meat, and fruit. After a few years they boasted that their children were attending public school; and the acme of happiness was reached when they could write that their oldest sons had graduated from high school and had obtained employment in a store or office. It even happened that mothers could announce that sons had been elected to the legislature, to Congress, and to the governorship of a state.

If the United States in the second half of the nineteenth century was a land of great possibilities, it was also a land of great contrasts. Here could be seen extremes of wealth and poverty, of rectitude and dishonesty, of temperance and debauchery, of piety and puritanism and agnosticism and license, of ruthless exploitation and humanitarianism.

The great body of wage earners was conservative along social and political lines. America was not fertile soil for sowing seeds

CARL A. RUDISILL
LIBRARY
LENOIR RHYNE COLLEGE

of radicalism. The fact that from 1860 to 1908 the Republican party was victorious in all but two presidential elections bears witness to the fundamental conservatism of farmers and laborers as a class. Although organized labor exerted influence on political parties and on legislation, it was exercised by supporting or by withholding support from one or the other major parties, depending on conditions peculiar to each campaign. Leaders of organized labor were chary of laying themselves open to the charge of fostering class hatred and class legislation by joining organizations against which such charges could be made.

The dual nature of government in the United States may in part explain the strategy of labor; it was necessary to exert pressure not only on Congress but on the legislatures of many states as well. Moreover, varying conditions in sections and regions in a country as large as the United States complicated the problems of labor leaders as well as of political leaders. Periodic depressions which swept over the country made it difficult to pursue a sustained policy. During times of depression membership in unions declined sharply. The leaders of union labor struggled with the same difficulty that plagued the leaders of the farmers—unwillingness or inability to take a long-range view of public policy. They expected immediate results.

The increasing industrialization of the country built up huge aggregations of capital, with superior resources and means for influencing public opinion and legislative bodies and sowing discord in the ranks of labor. This explains in part the savage character of certain strikes, which by their ruthlessness brought discredit on the cause of labor. The press was overwhelmingly on the side of capital in most of the fundamentals at stake.

The formative period of organized labor was interrupted by the panic of 1857 and by the Civil War. With the return of the soldiers to productive life and the development of great corporations, agitation and organization began anew; and in 1866 delegates from labor organizations of all kinds met at Baltimore to organize the National Labor Union. This organization held annual conventions, and in 1872 placed a presidential ticket in the field. This venture into politics brought dissension and wrecked the organization. "It was a typical American politico-reform organization," says a student of American labor, "led by labor leaders without organizations, politicians without parties, women without husbands, and cranks, visionaries, and agitators without jobs."

Out of discouragement and defeat emerged the Knights of Labor, which took its inception in a local secret society in Philadelphia in 1869, under the leadership of Uriah S. Stephens, a garment cutter. The growth of this order was slow, but the hard times of the seventies played into the hands of agitators who exposed the abuses of corporations, including the railroads. One unusual aspect of the Knights of Labor was its membership, which included not only wage earners but also farmers, small business men, lawyers, clergymen, physicians, and politicians. Negroes as well as whites were eligible to membership. Unlike the American Federation of Labor which succeeded it, membership in the Knights of Labor was direct, and not indirect through affiliated independent trades unions.

From 1877 to 1886 the Knights of Labor dominated the labor movement, but the order was bitterly attacked by radicals who ridiculed its vague objectives and its policy of admitting to membership individuals whose interests clashed with men and women who toiled in factories. Moreover, the secrecy of the order was objectionable to Roman Catholics and Lutherans, as well as to adherents of certain other faiths. During the nineteenth century and even later, labor had to reckon with the conservative influence of the Catholic and Lutheran churches. For example, Cardinal Gibbons of Baltimore used his powerful position and influence to oppose socialism, the direct election of Senators, the initiative, referendum, and the recall. In general, the religious press of the nineteenth century pulled in the direction of conservatism.

The immigrant invasion that followed hard upon the close of the Civil War also retarded the progress of organized labor. Speaking generally, labor unions opposed unrestricted immigration on the ground that the immigrants lowered the standard of living by their willingness to work long hours for low wages, and also on the ground that their strange languages, foreign customs,

and unfamiliarity with the ways of the country made it difficult
to enlist them in a common cause. Enemies of labor unions capitalized mutual distrust rooted in old-world backgrounds.

With the exception of a federal law of 1862 prohibiting the
immigration of Chinese coolies, the policy of state and federal
governments during the twenty years after the outbreak of the
Civil War was to encourage immigration. In 1864 President
Lincoln approved a law that legalized contracts by which immigrants pledged the wages of their labor for a term not to exceed
twelve months, to repay the expenses of their journey to the
United States. Undoubtedly this bill had back of it considerable
pressure from employers of labor; and it is significant that shortly
after it became a law the American Emigrant Company was
organized. This corporation imported laborers upon orders from
employers, who advanced the expenses of the immigrants and
paid a commission to the company.

This law was repealed in 1868, but there was no lack of
encouragement of immigration in the form of propaganda by
steamship and railroad companies and immigration commissions
established by several states, including the carpetbag states of the
South. By the Burlingame Treaty of 1868 with China, emigrants
from the Celestial Kingdom were admitted on favorable terms;
and the Republican platform of that year placed the party on
record in favor of encouraging immigration. The Committee on
Foreign Affairs of the House of Representatives reported favorably on the passage of a bill for that purpose, and boldly stated:
"In harmony, then, with the spirit of the age, and having in view
the growth, prosperity, greatness, and power of our land, as also
the general good of mankind, let us throw open wide the doors
of this republic, and invite the earnest and honest people of all
nations to come."

In October, 1870, a convention called by governors of several
states met at Indianapolis to devise means of promoting immigration; and the following years the federal government published
a *Special Report on Immigration* by Edward Young, of which
several thousand copies, some of them in translation, were distributed in Europe.

It was not until 1882 that Congress passed the first general immigration law, which was not restrictive but regulative in that it proposed to exclude convicts and persons of unsound physical and mental health. In 1885, partly in response to pressure from the Knights of Labor, which at the time had about reached the peak of its membership and influence, Congress made it unlawful to prepay the transportation or in any way assist or encourage the importation of aliens under a contract to perform labor or service of any kind, except skilled workmen in a new industry when labor could not otherwise be obtained. This law, however, was honored more in the breach than in the observance by steamship companies, emigration companies, and employers of labor. In some cases immigrants were recruited and their expenses were paid merely on their verbal promise to work in a factory for a stipulated time.

At the third annual general assembly of the Knights of Labor in 1879, Uriah S. Stephens was succeeded as grand master workman by Terence V. Powderly, and this office he held for thirteen years. Powderly was an idealist whose chief source of power was his oratorical talents. He pinned his hope for a better day on land reform. By reserving the public lands for settlers, he believed that more would be done for labor than by enacting an eight-hour working day. He was also an ardent temperance advocate, but not a prohibitionist. Education and agitation were his weapons. He was opposed to strikes and was very inept in conducting them.

Under Powderly's leadership the membership of the Knights of Labor mounted to 702,000 in 1886, the peak year; but the decline in influence and membership was almost as sudden as its rise. The waning power and eventual disappearance of the Knights of Labor were the result of a confluence of circumstances and events which shattered Powderly's dream of labor solidarity. Powderly was not the Moses to lead labor into the Promised Land. The panic of 1857 and the Civil War almost completely disrupted the labor movement that appeared to be marching toward success in the forties and fifties; the depression of the seventies, savage strikes and lockouts, the power of corporate wealth, the American tradition of individualism, the opposition of government and churches, and unrestricted immigration blocked the way toward effective organization in the last quarter of the century.

In spite of Powderly's opposition to the strike as an instrument of labor, it was this form of conflict between capital and labor that did as much as any single thing to discredit the labor movement.

In 1877, when the country was in the trough of the depression, industry and commerce were for the first time confronted with a nation-wide uprising of workers. It was in that year that the railroads were the objects of bitter attacks from the Grangers and from labor. The depression that threw thousands of miles of railroad into receiverships emphasized the mismanagement and corruption of the men who had built them.

Following reductions of wages on several railroads, the decision of the Baltimore and Ohio to cut wages over a dollar a day by 10 per cent precipitated a strike in July, 1877. Firemen and brakemen complained that the reduced wages would bring them to the extremity of supporting their families and paying expenses on their runs on an income of from five to six dollars per week.

In the early stages of the strike public sympathy was with the strikers; and when the governors of West Virginia and Maryland called out the militia, the temper of strikers and their sympathizers was such that the executives called upon President Hayes for federal troops. The strike spread rapidly to the Pennsylvania, the Erie, the New York Central, and to several roads as far west as Chicago and St. Louis; and workers in several cities went out on sympathetic strikes. The riot in Pittsburgh was so serious that for a time it was feared that law and order would entirely break down. For the first time the country was threatened with a general strike. The prompt and ruthless use of state and federal troops, and the threat of President Hayes to declare martial law, coupled with the savage attacks on the strikers by the newspapers, shattered the morale of the strikers after two weeks of heavy property damage and serious loss of life.

The newspapers referred to the strikers as hoodlums, looters, communists, loafers, incendiaries, and felons, and demanded a stronger and more efficient military force to cope with similar situations that might arise in the future. The Reverend Henry Ward Beecher, the greatest pulpit orator of his time, in a sermon preached in New York declared that "God has intended the great to be great, and the little to be little. . . . Persons have the right to work when or where they please, as long as they please, and for what they please." He looked upon the importation of communistic and similar European notions as abominations and rejected as "un-American" the idea that the government should take care of the welfare of its subjects and provide them with labor.

Labor was confronted with a movement on the part of employers to suppress all forms of concerted action. Picketing was condemned as an assault on the right of private property and freedom of contract; and the courts were appealed to in order to safeguard what were considered these essentials of American democracy.

If the torrent of abuse that rushed upon strikers from editors, ministers, lawyers, business men, and capitalists in 1877 was bitter, it was mild compared with what gushed forth after the Haymarket riot in 1886. So terrific was the indictment that public opinion was lashed into such a fury that even elementary safeguards against injustice were ignored in the courtroom where the victims of public indignation were on trial. It is not an overstatement to say that the Haymarket affair left a mark that was not rubbed out for a generation and affected the outcome of political campaigns from ocean to ocean. Anarchism and socialism were identified in the public mind; and distinctions that for safety and orderly progress ought to have been drawn were obscured by responsible members of society. The great body of American labor was conservative and law-abiding; but after the Haymarket affair it was impossible for many people to differentiate between "radicalism" and progress.

In 1886 Chicago was the arena of a little industrial war; and as a result of the act of a single individual that city and the entire country forgot about the causes of the conflict and condemned in intemperate fashion the alleged behavior of the warriors enlisted on one side of the conflict. For weeks and months the country was hysterical.

In 1882 the peak of immigration from Europe before 1900 was reached; and Chicago, as we have seen, was the clearing house of immigration. Into that polyglot city drifted thousands of foreigners, the overwhelming majority of whom were law-abiding and industrious. There was, however, in this motley horde an element that recruited the numbers of the less responsible members of society. There was also a small sprinkling of radicals who agitated and preached their doctrines through the medium of foreign-language publications. Some of them called upon their "comrades" to make war on an industrial system that enabled the few to exploit the many. "Alien agitators" have been unpopular and feared in every country—and the United States has not been exceptional in that respect. In 1886 there were a number of strikes in Chicago fomented by leaders who demanded an eight-hour day. The successful strikes against the Wabash, the Missouri, Kansas, and Texas, and the Missouri Pacific, militant boycotts against employers hostile to union labor, and widespread unemployment in 1886 recruited the membership of the Knights of Labor to the highest figure in its history. These events were indicative of the self-consciousness of wage earners.

Threatened with a determined and united body of laborers in the strike which began on May 1, 1886, the Chicago employers were equally determined and united to reject their demands. The police force of the city was directed by men who had antagonized labor by their ruthless methods of dispersing strikers. On the day before the Haymarket affair, police fired deliberately into retreating strikers and wounded many. These strikers had attacked and heckled strike breakers at the McCormick Harvester Works, where the employees had been locked out in reply to their demand that the company cease discriminating against men who had participated in an earlier strike. This called forth a summons to workingmen to arm themselves and appear in full force at a mass meeting to be held at the Haymarket on the evening of

May 4. Mayor Carter H. Harrison gave permission to hold the meeting and was himself present.

The meeting was orderly, and the mayor left for home in the belief that no trouble would come. Within a few minutes, however, a detachment of police appeared and ordered the meeting to disperse, whereupon a bomb was thrown, killing seven police and wounding many others. The perpetrator of the crime was never found, nor were any of his associates; but it appears that it was the work of a madman or of a man who sought revenge for past offenses by the police. It was the general opinion, however, that an uprising of anarchists had been planned. The Chicago newspapers were joined by the press of the country in a campaign to fan the fury of the populace against men who had spoken and written against the structure of society and had called for revenge on the police "bloodhounds." The police contributed to the hysteria by raiding homes, printing offices, and meeting halls, and by taking into custody everybody suspected of sympathy with radicalism. Anything that remotely suggested evidence of an "anarchist" plot was played up by the newspapers.

A grand jury speedily returned indictments against eight men who had been active in the International; and the police and prosecuting attorney adopted the theory that by their words the defendants had provoked the killing of the police. It is the conviction of a judge, Samuel P. McConnell, who was well acquainted with Mayor Harrison, Governors Ogelsby and Altgeld, the prosecuting attorney, the trial judge, and slightly with two of the defendants, that the principal assistant to the prosecuting attorney was a man without a conscience and that the judge, however honest, was clearly incompetent. "Every principle and precedent of Anglo-Saxon law was outraged by the rulings of Judge Gary," he wrote. He believed also that, in view of the state of public opinion and the rulings of the judge, any jury would have found the defendants guilty. He had a low opinion of the ability of the defense lawyers. If the men had been tried separately, not one would have been convicted, he believed.

It developed that the men were on trial for their ideas about property, and the prosecution was permitted to read into the record incendiary articles culled from radical publications. In order to make a graphic presentation of the effects of such printed material, the police were permitted to exhibit before the jury infernal machines designed for the purpose of destroying lives and property. In his plea to the jury, the prosecuting attorney concluded as follows: "Law is upon trial. Anarchy is on trial. These men have been selected, picked out by the grand jury and indicted because they were leaders. They are no more guilty than the thousands who follow them. Gentlemen of the jury, convict these men, make examples of them, hang them and you save our institutions, our society."

It was a foregone conclusion that the jury would return a verdict of guilty. Seven of the defendants were sentenced to hang, and one was sentenced to fifteen years' imprisonment. The Supreme Court of Illinois sustained the verdict of the lower court, although it found that legal errors had been committed. Governor Ogelsby commuted the sentences of two men to life imprisonment, one committed suicide, and four were hanged.

If these men were hounded to the gallows and to the penitentiary by the newspapers, the campaign was not abated after the sentences had been executed, notwithstanding the fact that reporters who had worked on the Haymarket case from the beginning of the strike in the McCormick Harvester Works down to the hanging of the defendants believed in their innocence.

In spite of the fact that prominent men in many walks of life had signed petitions in behalf of the convicted men, and after the execution of some of them had petitioned the governor to pardon the men within the walls of the penitentiary, the fury of the press was loosed on a governor who, seven years after the fatal bombing, exercised the power vested in him to right the wrong—in so far as it could be righted. So unrestrained was the press that the public gained the impression that the governor had opened the gates of the penitentiary for the promiscuous liberation of desperate criminals.

John P. Altgeld, the first Democratic governor of Illinois after the Civil War, was to millions of Americans during the closing years of the nineteenth century the symbol of anarchy and lawlessness. In hundreds of cartoons his features were distorted to portray the incendiary fiend who would apply the torch to all that was sacred in American civilization. As his biographer points out, Altgeld had pardoned the anarchists, therefore he himself was an anarchist, and any cause which he championed was anarchistic. In subsequent political campaigns the Republicans played up the alleged companionship of the Democratic party with revolution. At the time Altgeld was known to the laboring classes as their friend and the friend of the poor, and by a small number of persons who ministered to these classes he was recognized as the prophet of a new social democracy. History remembers him as one of the most courageous pioneer crusaders against the abuses of an industrial society.

Altgeld's offense was not primarily that of having granted pardons to the anarchists, which many had urged him to bestow. He had done the unpardonable thing of having examined the court record and of having reached the conclusion that the men had been unjustly convicted. In his pardon message the governor showed that much of the evidence presented at the trial was fabrication; that the jury had been packed; that the judge had been prejudiced; and that police officials had deliberately planned to have fictitious conspiracies formed in order that they might have the glory of discovering them.

The Haymarket affair was a blow from which organized labor was slow to recover. This incident, together with a confluence of unfavorable omens, including the Pullman strike of 1894, discredited efforts of liberals to adjust the pending conflict between labor and capital. Conservatives were aroused to what they believed to be the menace of radicalism and revolution. Although Powderly had consistently rejected any form of association with socialism and radicalism, and the leaders of the Knights of Labor gave neither aid nor comfort to the eight indicted and convicted "anarchists," the riot was used to discredit the order, which had just suffered defeat in a strike on the Gould Southwestern railroad system. After 1886 the Knights of Labor declined in membership and influence; and by the middle of the nineties, although in existence, the order was largely a memory. A new leader displaced Powderly and sought to lead labor into the Promised Land over routes untried by him.

Samuel Gompers, who was born in a London tenement, came with his family to the United States in 1863. As a young man earning his living as a cigarmaker, he witnessed and experienced the hardships of laborers during the depression of the seventies. His indomitable will and energy elevated him from leadership in the movement to organize the cigarmakers' union, to the presidency of the American Federation of Labor in 1886, the year it was organized. This office he held, with the exception of one year, until the year of his death, 1924. Gompers proceeded along lines that were better suited to the conditions of his time than were those of the Knights of Labor—or at least they were generally so regarded.

Gompers impressed on the American Federation of Labor the idea that there should be a single union for each trade or industry. He rejected the idea of company unions and of dual membership in unions. Unlike the Knights of Labor, the American Federation of Labor closed its membership to farmers, business men, and clergymen, and admitted only skilled laborers. Gompers eschewed direct political action in the form of a labor party; his aim was to make labor immune from governmental interference by achieving the right to bargain collectively with capital. He would have nothing to do with Powderly's program of cooperative stores, factories, and the like. He sought better wages, better hours, and better working conditions by entering into trade agreements in order to obtain uniform shop rules in an entire industry. The union label in trades where it could be used—like clothing, tobacco, and printing—was also a "moral weapon."

In spite of incipient revolts against his essentially conservative leadership attempted by Socialists, Syndicalists, I.W.W.'s, and others less radical, Gompers was remarkably successful in holding to his policy. He was able to do this partly, if not largely, by the peculiar organization of the American Federation of Labor.

The American Federation of Labor is not a single union; it is composed of sovereign trade unions, each of which elects delegates to the assembly of the Federation. Thus individuals are not members of the Federation; they are members of a single union which is represented in the Federation according to the relative strength of its membership. The character of the organization makes it difficult for insurgency to make itself felt. Radicalism might capture a union, but the votes of delegates from that union would be neutralized or overwhelmed by the votes of delegates from other unions. It has happened that an insurgent union has been expelled from the Federation because of irreconcilable differences between its delegates and what they were pleased to call the "machine." The exclusion of unskilled labor from membership in the American Federation of Labor has also reduced the danger from radicalism in its membership.

From 1885 to 1895 several labor organizations were born and later grew into national unions which affiliated with the American Federation of Labor. From the closing years of the nineteenth century the growth of membership in labor unions was marked and steady, though fluctuating with the ups and downs of industry. The American Federation of Labor, though not without powerful enemies both within and without the ranks of labor, escaped criticism from ecclesiastical organizations which objected to the secret character of the Knights of Labor, and also from individuals and corporations which shied off from unions organized along less conservative lines.

CHAPTER IX

POLITICS, 1876-1884

WE HAVE SEEN THAT THE ELECTION OF HAYES WAS ATTENDED by unusual circumstances and that in the opinion of many he was not entitled to the Presidency. This circumstance alone was a serious handicap for the administration, but it was still further hampered by factional discord within the Republican party. Blaine, who had aspired to the presidential nomination in 1876, did not approve of Hayes' conciliatory southern policy, nor did he like some of the President's appointments. Hayes himself did not hold a high opinion of the political ethics of the attractive Senator from Maine. Moreover, the President was not in the good graces of such powerful Republican leaders as Roscoe Conkling of New York, Zachariah Chandler of Michigan, and J. Donald Cameron of Pennsylvania. The Democratic opposition to Hayes was formidable because during the four years of his administration that party had a majority in the House of Representatives and during the last two years in the Senate also.

Hayes had the same qualities that characterized the other middle-western Presidents after the Civil War—not brilliant, but more independent. The stamina of his independence was tested by the appointment of Carl Schurz as Secretary of the Interior. Schurz, it will be recalled, was one of the most prominent leaders of the Liberal Republican movement; and his name was anathema to men like Blaine who believed that party regularity was a first principle. During the campaign of 1876 and between election and inauguration Hayes communicated frequently with Schurz; and their correspondence shows that the President leaned heavily on the advice of the prominent German-American in preparing his inaugural address. The President's correspondence and diary also prove that he was sincerely devoted to the purpose of giving the country a clean and nonpartisan administration. In the opinion of Senator George F. Hoar of Massachusetts, himself a man of high principles and fidelity to duty, Hayes carried out the principles of civil service reform more faultlessly than any President down to Theodore Roosevelt.

In his letter of acceptance and inaugural address Hayes took high ground in favor of civil service reform, and in an executive order issued in June, 1877, stated that no officer should be required or permitted to take part in the management of political organizations, conventions, and election campaigns, and that no assessments for political purposes should be allowed. This order pleased neither Democrats nor Republicans. When the President removed Chester A. Arthur, a notorious machine politician, from the post of collector of customs in New York, the Senate, under Conkling's whip, rejected the nomination of his successor. But the President refused to yield, and at the next session of the Senate the appointment of another man to the position was confirmed in spite of Conkling's opposition. When Hayes left the White House, however, civil service reform was far from reality. In the campaign of 1880 both parties levied "voluntary contributions" from state and federal officeholders.

Hayes' cabinet was on the whole composed of able men, but it was unpopular with Republican members of both houses. It was said that only four of them were Republicans; that two, Schurz and William M. Evarts, the Secretary of State, were disorganizers, doctrinaires, and liberals; and that the Postmaster-general, David M. Key, was an ex-Confederate and a Democrat.

The Democratic strength in Congress not only made it difficult for the President to carry out his policies, but he was obliged to make use of the veto in order to prevent the enactment of legislation designed to embarrass him still further. Not having the two-thirds majority necessary to override the veto, the Democrats resorted to the use of "riders" in order to compel the President to approve bills that were obnoxious to him. Hayes protested against coupling bills that had little or no relation with each other; and in one instance his veto of an appropriation bill carrying a "rider" necessitated the calling of a special session of Congress.

The resumption of specie payments and the Bland-Allison Act
—both of which fell within the Hayes administration—have been
discussed in a previous chapter. Both measures incurred the ire
of the Greenbackers and the advocates of the free coinage of
silver.

It was fortunate for the Republican party that in the campaign of 1880 it had a powerful argument for the continuation
of its control of the executive department—prosperity. If prosperity had not returned, it would have been easy for the Democrats to argue that the depression had been prolonged by the
resumption policy of the Republican administration.

Hayes' independent course was probably due in part to his resignation to a single term in the White House. In his letter of
acceptance and inaugural address he had recommended an amendment to the Constitution limiting the President to a single term
and extending it to six years.

At the beginning of the year 1880 it seemed probable that the
Republicans would nominate Grant for the Presidency. His
vociferous reception in San Francisco in September, 1879, upon
his return from a triumphant tour around the world, and his
flattering receptions along the route of his journey across the
continent to his home in New York convinced the politicians who
longed for the fleshpots of the Grant régime that his election was
certain. The former President's fortunes were in the hands of
men schooled in all the arts of political strategy—men like
Conkling, Cameron, and John A. Logan of Illinois, who were out
of sympathy with the Hayes administration. These men argued
that there was every reason to expect that the Democrats would
carry the Solid South by fair means or foul, and that Grant,
who knew how to deal with the "southern brigadiers" in Congress, was needed to pursue a vigorous southern policy. At first
Grant posed as a "receptive candidate," but financial embarrassment and family ambition converted him into an active candidate.

The hope of defeating Grant's nomination depended on the
success of the anti-Grant forces in uniting on a candidate who had
a popular appeal. Blaine, who was not enthusiastic over the prospect of waging a political campaign in his own behalf, was the

strongest of the available candidates, with John Sherman of Ohio, Elihu B. Washburne of Illinois, and George F. Edmunds of Vermont also in the running. It was Grant against the field. There was little or no harmony between the Blaine and the Sherman forces, but they worked together to defeat Grant.

Cameron succeeded in overcoming the Blaine men in the Pennsylvania Republican convention; Grant was indorsed and the unit rule was adopted. Likewise in the New York convention Conkling "put his man over" and got the unit rule adopted, although in somewhat ambiguous words. Logan also delivered his state, but his manipulation of the convention was so high-handed that several delegates revolted. By adopting the unit rule, by which the vote of each state would be determined by the will of the majority in each delegation, the Grant leaders hoped to obtain united action in the national convention.

Both the Grant forces and their opponents understood that the outcome of the national convention would depend to a considerable degree upon the temporary organization. This precipitated a contest between them for the control of the Republican National Committee. The Grant men planned to manipulate things so that the temporary chairman of the convention would be a man of their own choice and would enforce the unit rule. Under the leadership of James A. Garfield, a delegate from Ohio who was pledged to Sherman, the anti-Grant men served notice that they would not submit to "steam-roller" methods; and, after some "trading" between the leaders, George F. Hoar, who was neither for nor against Grant, was elected temporary chairman and later permanent chairman.

When the convention voted down the unit rule, the stock of the Grant men slumped. This action made it impossible for Grant to get the nomination on the first ballot, as his supporters had hoped. Conkling's nominating speech was one of the most eloquent ever delivered in a political convention, and down to the thirty-sixth ballot the Grant phalanx held firm; but on that ballot enough delegates pledged to Blaine and Sherman deserted their candidates to nominate Garfield.

Garfield was not a "dark horse." He had been in public life

for many years, and long before the convention met he had been
mentioned as a possible nominee. His conduct at the convention
inspired confidence. In a brief sensible speech he had persuaded
Conkling to withdraw a resolution designed to browbeat the delegates, and his speech nominating Sherman was a brilliant effort,
in spite of the fact that it left the impression on some that the
speaker was not loyal to Sherman. When the delegates commenced
to vote for him, Garfield protested that he was not a candidate,
but Chairman Hoar cut him off for fear that he would say
something that would make it impossible for him to accept the
nomination.

The Republican candidate was a man of wide acquaintance and
good judgment; and his nomination, however disappointing to
some, proved to be fairly popular. The nomination of Chester A.
Arthur of New York for the Vice-Presidency spread dismay in
the ranks of independents and reformers. It was hard to believe
that this exponent of New York machine politics, this henchman
of Conkling, this collector of customs who had been removed
from office by Hayes, had been named as Garfield's running mate.

The Republican platform was not a strong document. The platform committee was silent on civil service reform; and when it
was moved on the floor of the convention that such a plank be
adopted, a certain Flanagan of Texas arose and said: "What are
we here for? I mean that members of the Republican party are
entitled to office, and if we are victorious, we will have office."
Nevertheless, a plank indorsing Hayes' civil service policy was
adopted.

Before the opening of the Democratic national convention at
Cincinnati, it seemed to many people that Tilden ought to be the
nominee not only because of his commendable record but also as
a "vindication" of his "election" in 1876. However, the delegates
construed a letter written by him to mean that he did not desire
the honor, and the nomination went to General Winfield Scott
Hancock of Pennsylvania, a man of fine presence and high character, with a good war record, as well as a record as a commanding
officer in the South during reconstruction that commended him
to the people of that section. Hancock did not prove to be an

effective campaigner, though one of his sayings became famous: "The tariff is a local issue."

The platform adopted at Cincinnati was not outstanding. It denounced Hayes for his alleged failure to reform the civil service; it demanded gold and silver money and paper currency convertible into coin on demand; it advocated a tariff for revenue only, "home rule," and the exclusion of Chinese immigrants.

In the absence of clear-cut issues between the major parties, the campaign was tinged with personal attacks on Garfield, who was alleged to have been involved in the notorious Crédit Mobilier affair. On the Pacific coast, where the anti-Chinese feeling was strong, a forged letter which represented Garfield as deprecating the agitation against the Chinese was circulated. Whatever may have been the effect of the letter, only one Republican elector out of nine in California and Nevada was chosen.

For a while Conkling sulked in his tent, but later in the campaign both he and Grant took the stump. The fact that shortly before Conkling became active in his behalf Garfield had attended a conference of old-line Republican leaders brought forth the charge that Garfield had "sold out" to this element in the party. Garfield's reputation for honesty, however, was his strongest asset.

The election returns were not encouraging to the Republicans, in spite of the fact that Garfield carried every northern state with the exception of California, New Jersey, and Nevada. His electoral vote was 214, to 155 for Hancock. Garfield's popular vote exceeded that of Hancock by slightly less than ten thousand. Weaver, the Greenback candidate, polled about three hundred thousand. The South was now solid.

The divided character of the Republican party was brought into public light shortly after Garfield's inauguration, when the new President boldly challenged one of the most powerful leaders of the Stalwart wing of the party. Senator Conkling and Vice-President Arthur were infuriated when Garfield submitted to the Senate the name of William H. Robertson, an irreconcilable enemy of the Senator from New York, for the post of collector of customs in New York. After weeks of intensive and vain efforts to defeat the confirmation of Robertson, Conkling and his colleague,

Thomas C. Platt, resigned their seats in the Senate, in the firm expectation that the legislature would vindicate them by returning them to the Senate. To their great mortification—and to the amusement of the country—the legislature failed to reelect them and thereby inflicted a heavy blow to the prestige of both Conkling and Arthur.

The unseen hand of fate, however, intervened to terminate the unseemly and undignified quarrel among politicians, when on July 2, 1881, a demented man assassinated President Garfield in the railway station in Washington. "I am a Stalwart of the Stalwarts. . . . Arthur is President now," were the words of the assassin. For weeks—until Garfield's death on September 19—the country was without a President; and when Arthur took the oath of office, the country feared the worst with a machine politician in the White House. It was expected that the Stalwarts would be restored to their high command and that the Half-breeds would be driven out.

The responsibility and dignity of his high office, however, brought out the best qualities of the new President; and, although the members of Garfield's cabinet, with a single exception, resigned within a few months, Arthur did not prove himself to be vindictively partisan. Surprisingly enough, civil service reform found a friend in the new President; and the enactment of the Pendleton Law in 1883 was made possible by his sympathetic attitude. The tragic death of Garfield at the hand of a disappointed office-seeker and the defeat of the Republicans in the elections of 1882 were also factors.

The bill was reported by Senator George H. Pendleton of Ohio, a Democrat, but more Democrats than Republicans voted against the final passage. In both houses there was considerable dodging on the part of members of both parties. The act authorized the President to appoint three commissioners who should classify all government employees into grades. Competitive examinations for applicants for offices were devised, and assessments on office-holders for political purposes were prohibited. Honorably discharged soldiers and sailors were given preference over other competitors. The President was given large discretionary power in the enforcement of the act. For example, he might transfer to the merit or classified list as many or as few of the positions within his appointive power as he saw fit.

Arthur's appointments to the Civil Service Commission were commendable, and his efforts to put the law into successful operation were sincere and effective. The Pendleton Act, however, was only a conservative beginning of civil service reform, which succeeding Presidents have furthered according to the exigencies of the political situations that have confronted them or in proportion to their own inclinations. The prohibition of assessments for campaign purposes was nullified in practice by tapping the resources of corporations and wealthy individuals, who expected due appreciation for their generous contributions.

We have seen that in the campaign of 1880 both major parties pledged themselves to the enactment of a law prohibiting Chinese immigration. The mounting numbers of immigrants from Europe in the late seventies and eighties aroused labor to the menace of competition with men and women who were accustomed to a low standard of living. Acting in response to pressure from the Knights of Labor and other organizations, Congress in 1882 excluded foreign convicts (except those convicted of political offenses), lunatics, and persons likely to become public charges; and in 1885 it was made unlawful to prepay the transportation or in any way to assist or encourage the importation of aliens under contract to perform service or labor of any kind, except skilled workmen in a new industry when they could not otherwise be obtained. This law was defective, however, in that machinery for its enforcement was not set up, nor did it provide for inspection and deportation. By an act of 1887 the Secretary of the Treasury was clothed with power to deport contract laborers.

In the case of the Chinese it was proposed not only to regulate immigration, as in the case of emigration from Europe, but to exclude them entirely.

The migration of Chinese to the United States began with the discovery of gold in California in 1848, when these peaceful and industrious strangers were welcomed because they were willing to perform menial tasks in a community where everybody else was engaged in mining gold. In 1862 Congress prohibited the importation of Chinese coolies, but in spite of the law many were brought in to do the rough construction work on the Pacific railways. After the completion of the roads in 1869, however, laborers from the eastern states flocked to the Golden State, and friction between them and the Chinese developed to the point where the legislature enacted anti-Chinese laws. The Burlingame Treaty of 1868 indicates that the anti-Chinese sentiment had not as yet spread to other parts of the country. By this treaty Chinese subjects residing in the United States were granted the same rights and privileges as those enjoyed by citizens of the most favored nations, although the right of naturalization was denied to them.

In California the fury against the Chinese was fanned by a demagogue named Denis Kearney. In 1877 on a large sand lot on the west side of San Francisco this spellbinder delivered a series of intemperate speeches which invariably ended with the words: "And whatever happens, the Chinese must go." The newspapers took up the hue and cry, and shortly what had been a problem peculiar to the Pacific coast arrested the attention of the nation.

In the early weeks of 1879 a Democratic House of Representatives and a Senate with a bare Republican majority abrogated the Burlingame Treaty. This bill was supported by western and southern Representatives and Senators and was generally opposed by Republicans. President Hayes returned the bill without his approval, giving as his reasons that it would undo the progress that had been made in the direction of opening China to American civilization and that it would wound the pride of a polite and sensitive people. He conceded that the discontent of the people on the Pacific coast with the workings of Chinese immigration demanded the serious attention of the American people, but he denied the power of Congress to abrogate a treaty. The President also expressed the fear that the immediate abrogation of the treaty would endanger the welfare of American merchants and missionaries in China and of Chinese residents in the United States.

In order to effect an amicable settlement of the problem, under the auspices of the Hayes administration a new treaty with China was negotiated and ratified in 1880. The Chinese government conceded to the United States the right to regulate, limit, or suspend Chinese immigration whenever it was deemed necessary, but in no case was immigration to be prohibited. The treaty specified that the limitation or suspension should be reasonable and applicable only to Chinese coming as laborers.

Legislation under the terms of this treaty was postponed until the Arthur administration, when, in 1882, Chinese immigration was suspended for twenty years. The President vetoed the bill because he believed a twenty-year suspension of immigration was an unreasonable interpretation of the treaty. He suggested a shorter period, and Congress reduced it to ten years.

This law, as it proved, established the permanent exclusion of the Chinese. Subsequent legislation extended exclusion indefinitely and tightened up the restrictions by requiring Chinese residents to take out registration certificates, in order to reduce the number of illegal immigrants; and in 1904 the insular possessions of the United States were included within the scope of the law.

In spite of protests from the Chinese government and opposition from prominent Americans, this legislation was sustained by the Supreme Court. In a test case brought by a Chinaman in 1883 the court held that, although the act contravened the treaties of 1868 and 1880, it was not on that account invalid, because a treaty can be repealed or modified at the pleasure of Congress.

One of the legacies of the Civil War was the highest tariff in the history of the country down to that time. The high duties on imports had come into existence largely through the need for revenue to finance the war. As excise duties were increased from time to time, it was also necessary to raise the duties on imports. After the collapse of the Confederacy, however, it was agreed that the heavy burden of taxation should be lightened, and within a few years excises were lowered and ultimately removed on all commodities except tobacco and liquors.

It is probable that few people expected that the high tariff duties would be allowed to remain; and even prominent Republicans stated that it would be folly for the protectionists to insist on the high duties then in existence. The dissatisfaction with the tariff in the West as expressed by the Grangers and other agrarians, and the restlessness in all parts of the country over high taxes, seemed to indicate an early revision of the tariff; but several efforts to that end were defeated or clipped by the maneuvers of astute leaders and by the lobbying of protectionists. Downward revision was defeated by referring bills to conference committees in which under the cloak of secrecy bargains were struck; by the failure at a critical time to muster a two-thirds vote to suspend the rules necessary to the consideration of a bill; and by minor and unimportant reductions on articles not produced in the United States. But the protectionists not only defeated attempts to reduce the tariff; they succeeded in actually raising duties on certain commodities by transferring them from one schedule to another and by combining specific and *ad valorem* duties. In some instances the interests directly concerned framed the schedules.

In the campaign of 1880 the tariff was an issue, although a minor one. The Democratic platform declared for a tariff for revenue only, and the Republicans contented themselves by avowing "that the duties levied for the purpose of revenue should so discriminate as to favor American labor." While it would not be true to say that in the eighties the Democratic party adhered closely to the tariff-for-revenue doctrine and that the Republican party was the party of protection, it is true to say that by reason of the fact that the Republican party had been in undisputed control of Congress from 1865 and had not disturbed the tariff, corporations and monopolies believed that their fortunes were safer in Republican hands, especially in the circumstance that the rural South had a heavy influence in the Democratic party. In accordance with the principle that the business of the opposition is to oppose, the Democratic party formally espoused the principle of downward tariff revision. Moreover, the accumulation of a surplus in the treasury furnished an argument in favor of reducing the revenue by lowering the duties on imports.

In 1882 Congress provided for the appointment of a Tariff Commission, which was to report its findings at the next session of Congress. Arthur appointed to this commission a majority who were advocates of high protection, and the president was none other than the secretary of the Wool Manufacturers' Association. In December, 1882, Arthur recommended a reduction of duties as a means of reducing the surplus in the treasury, after he had defeated a raid on the treasury by vetoing a "pork barrel" appropriation bill. The Tariff Commission recommended reductions on many articles, and Arthur commended to Congress a careful consideration of the report.

The Senate framed a bill based in the main on the report of the commission and tacked it onto a House bill reducing excises. The amended bill was referred to a conference committee from which it emerged with the lower duties of the Senate bill either eliminated or revised upward. This bill passed both houses by a strict party vote, but on a number of schedules the Democrats, especially those from manufacturing states, voted with the Republican protectionists. The tendency of the "mongrel tariff of 1883" was to lower duties on the cheaper grades of textiles and to raise them on the better grades. The tariff on lumber was continued—in the face of the fact that the forests in the Northwest were disappearing before the axe.

Two more efforts to revise the tariff downward were made in the eighties—the Morrison Bill in 1884 and the Mills Bill in 1888 —but without success. It was not until Cleveland's epochal message of 1887, which was altogether devoted to tariff revision, that the tariff issue was joined and became the paramount issue in the campaign of 1888. From that time down into the nineties "free trade" and "protection" were household words, with the Democrats, for want of a more potent issue, attributing to Republican protection most of the ills that beset the country, and the Republicans singing hosannas to their idol as the author of prosperity. There were apostates in both parties, much to the discomfiture of Republican and Democratic Presidents.

In perspective it appears that the Republicans and the Democrats were fighting sham battles over issues that had ceased to be vital. The election of Grover Cleveland in 1884 and the organization of the Farmers' Alliance, followed by the birth of the Populist party in 1891, were symptoms of widespread dissatisfaction.

CHAPTER X

DEMOCRATIC VICTORY AND DEFEAT, *1884-1888*

THE CAMPAIGN OF 1884 HAS GONE DOWN IN HISTORY AS A NO-table political contest not only because for the first time since 1856 a Democratic President was elected but also because of the orgy of mud-slinging that characterized the conduct of the campaign. By 1884 the flight of time had softened the animosities of the reconstruction period. The fading memories of the Civil War were revived when in 1885 General McClellan and General Grant passed away, and also in the following year when Winfield S. Hancock, Horatio Seymour, and Samuel J. Tilden died. Neither candidate of the major parties in 1884 had been prominent during the years of the Civil War. Another noteworthy feature of this campaign was the bolting of the independent Republicans in favor of the Democratic candidate, which has caused the contest to be remembered as the "Mugwump campaign."

The fight between the Stalwart and Half-breed factions within the Republican party, and the outcome of the congressional elections of 1882 and of certain state elections in the Arthur adminis-tration, boded no good for the Republicans in the impending presidential election. Between the Stalwarts—that is, the regular Republicans—and the insurgent Half-breeds there had developed serious differences. In 1882 Robert Pattison, the Democratic can-didate for governor, carried the rock-ribbed Republican State of Pennsylvania on a platform of retrenchment and reform; and in the same year Grover Cleveland was elected governor of New York over Charles J. Folger, the Republican machine candidate, in a campaign that revealed the feud between the Stalwarts and the Half-breeds and indicated that the Republicans would have a fight on their hands to keep the state in the Republican column two years hence.

With Arthur eliminated because of his part in the factional fight within the party, as well as his failure to make a popular appeal, the men most prominently mentioned for the Republican nomination were Blaine, John Sherman, George F. Edmunds, and General William T. Sherman. Senator Edmunds had received considerable publicity in connection with the anti-polygamy law of 1882 and was entirely satisfactory to the independents. General Sherman was played up as a man who was not objectionable to either faction and was urged by Blaine to become a candidate, but he was opposed by people who did not want a "father confessor in the White House," his wife being a Roman Catholic. Sherman was not ambitious politically, but, even if he had been, he would not have exposed his wife's religion to public criticism. Blaine, notwithstanding his unfortunate connection with railroad scandals, his unsatisfactory civil service record, and the fierce opposition to his nomination from the independents, was nominated in a frenzy of enthusiasm. His nomination was practically assured when the Logan delegates went over to him. The nomination of John A. Logan for the Vice-Presidency was not a source of strength to the ticket. The rough and contentious Illinoisan, whose stock in trade was hostility toward the South and who sneered at civil service reform, was placed on the ticket to attract the "G.A.R. boys."

The two likely candidates for the Democratic nomination were Grover Cleveland and Thomas F. Bayard of Delaware, both of whom were acceptable to the independents. Cleveland had the advantage of being a resident of New York and of having won the enmity of Tammany Hall. When the Democrats nominated him, they presented to the country a courageous, blunt, plain-spoken man, who could also be stubborn and obtuse. He had made a good record as governor of New York, but he neither had a large acquaintance nor was he a forceful and logical speaker.

The independent Republicans, or the Mugwumps, as they were called, did not hesitate for one moment in making a choice between Blaine and Cleveland. All other issues, including the tariff

and the currency, faded into insignificance in their reading of
Blaine's record. With them the issue was honesty in government.
Schurz, who was one of the most effective Mugwumps, summoned all the irony, invective, and logic of which he was master
to prove that Blaine was unfit to occupy the high office of President, that the American people would stultify themselves by
electing the writer of the notorious Mulligan letters.

Blaine felt keenly the loss of support from such prominent
men as Schurz. Not being able to conciliate them, the Republicans hurled at them such epithets as "pharisees," "saints," "dudes,"
and "gentle hermits."

Cleveland's public record was short and good and immune to
attacks from the opposition. For this reason the Republicans
resorted to an attack upon his private life. When an irresponsible
Buffalo, New York, newspaper revealed that Cleveland was the
father of an illegitimate son, Republican newspapers and speakers
seized upon the story to attract attention from Blaine's public
record. The dismay and doubts of some of Cleveland's supporters
were soon dispelled when the Democratic candidate in reply to a
friend said: "Whatever you do, tell the truth." And when the
truth stripped the story of its sensational features, and even
raised doubts as to the chief indictment, Cleveland not only won
back the confidence of the wavering, but also probably added to
his reputation for truthfulness and integrity. For example, Lyman Abbott, the editor of the *Christian Union*, published the facts
of the scandal, and, after weighing them, announced that future
issues would be closed to a discussion of them.

In every presidential campaign there are a variety of "issues"
that appeal to a variety of voters; and one of the perplexing
problems that confronts the student of history is to levy an accurate assessment of values in the maze of false and true issues
that may or may not have deceived the voters. In other words,
what were the "decisive" issues or what was the "decisive" issue
in the campaign of 1884, a campaign remarkable in several
respects and not least because the Republicans went down to defeat? The election of 1884 was one in a succession of elections—
1876, 1880, 1884, 1888—in which victory was won by the nar-

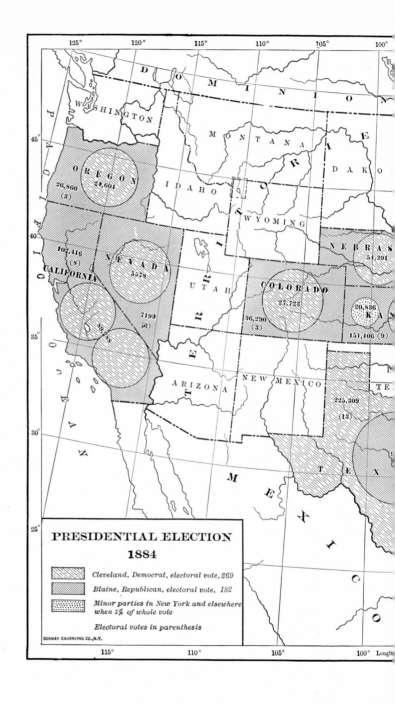

PRESIDENTIAL ELECTION
1884

Cleveland, Democrat, electoral vote, *269*

Blaine, Republican, electoral vote, *182*

Minor parties in New York and elsewhere
when 5% of whole vote

Electoral votes in parenthesis

BORMAY ENGRAVING CO.,N.Y.

rowest of margins. In fact, the popular votes of the defeated candidates in 1876 and in 1888 exceeded those of the candidates who had a majority in the electoral college. In 1884 the election hinged upon the electoral vote of New York, where Cleveland had a plurality of only 1,149 out of a total vote of 1,167,169; and out of the total nation-wide popular vote of 10,000,000, Cleveland's plurality was less than 25,000.

The defection of the Mugwumps was a heavy blow to Blaine; but it must not be forgotten that in spite of devastating attacks on Blaine's public character, such men of independent judgment as Senator Hoar and a host of clergymen preferred him to Cleveland. Perhaps the factional fight in the Republican camp in New York weighed more heavily. When asked to make a speech for Blaine, Conkling, who was not overscrupulous in the employment of political methods, replied: "Thank you, but you know I do not engage in criminal practice." The feud between Conkling and Blaine was of long standing. The New York Senator never forgot Blaine's reference to his "turkey-gobbler strut."

The part that religion plays in politics is elusive, and it is as easy to overlook it as it is to overemphasize it. Sometimes it is purely local and sometimes it assumes nation-wide importance, as in the elections of 1916 and 1928. As contrasted with the Democratic party, the Republican party showed a nativistic and puritanical tinge, a heritage from the years of Know-nothingism before the Civil War. Normally the bulk of Catholic voters preferred the Democratic party; but in 1884 Blaine stood a good chance of cutting in on it. Cleveland was not on friendly terms with Tammany Hall, and as governor of New York he had vetoed the Catholic Protectory Bill. Blaine, on the other hand, although a member of the Presbyterian church, was the son of a Catholic mother and the brother of a Mother Superior in a convent. This advantage was lost by the indiscreet remarks of the Reverend Samuel D. Burchard, whom Blaine described—unfortunately too late—as "an ass in the shape of a preacher."

The incident referred to occurred on October 29, when Blaine was present at a gathering of several hundred Protestant clergymen in the parlor of a New York hotel. Burchard, one of the speakers, in the course of his remarks pledging support to Blaine expressed himself as follows: "We are Republicans, and don't propose to leave our party and identify ourselves with the party whose antecedents have been rum, Romanism, and rebellion." That Blaine should have allowed this slur on his mother's religion to go unrebuked has been explained in various ways; but the Democrats were quick to make political capital of the clergyman's indiscretion and the candidate's obtuseness or poor hearing. The following Sunday an army of distributors was stationed at the doors of Catholic churches throughout the land armed with handbills displaying Burchard's words. It was easy for some Democratic politicians to put Burchard's words into Blaine's own mouth.

The unfortunate associations of certain men of wealth, whose reputations were not too good, with Blaine's cause also furnished an opportunity to besmirch his character. On the evening of the same day that Burchard's unfortunate speech was made, Blaine attended a meeting of millionaires who had assembled for the purpose of raising money to defray the expenses of the Republican campaign. Headlines in Democratic papers referred to the affair as "Belshazzar's Feast" and "The Boodle Banquet." With idle factories and many men in want, it was poor advertising for Blaine to have been seen in the company of Jay Gould and men of that stripe.

Cleveland was stronger than his party. He had not been in office many months before Republicans were saying: "Cleveland is a good man in bad company." By his forthrightness and vigorous actions in emergencies and crises, he won the respect and admiration of political adversaries, but he also made powerful enemies within his own party. His narrow victory in 1884 and his sweeping victory in 1892 are explained by the sins of the Republican party rather than by his own popularity or by the achievements of his party.

Independents expected great things from the new administration, but so did the Democratic spoilsmen who had subsisted for so many years on the bitter fruits of defeat. The President knew that he was under heavy obligation to the Mugwumps—men who had refused to support Blaine because they wanted good government; but some of them, like Schurz, were dogmatic and unreasonable and made no allowance for the tremendous pressure of political exigencies. The impatient criticism of the civil service reformers irritated Cleveland into replying in kind; and his efforts to carry out the spirit of the Pendleton Act made him unpopular with leaders of his own party.

In spite of the handicap of a rather vacillating Civil Service Commission, and department heads who were either lukewarm or hostile to reform, Cleveland's administration marked real progress in improving the Civil Service; and men who came into personal contact with the President testified as to his high purposes. Fourth-class postmasters were largely replaced by Democrats, but the classified list was extended. In cases where tenures expired, some Republicans were reappointed, but more often they were replaced by Democrats.

In the matter of pensions Cleveland's courage was submitted to the severest test possible, and it was not found wanting. The country took pride in the liberal treatment the government had accorded veterans of the Civil War; but at the time Cleveland took office pensions had degenerated into an unworthy scramble for political power and a drain on the public in behalf of unscrupulous men. The Pension Bureau was administered in an extravagant manner, and men who had never smelled powder were awarded pensions through the efforts of cheap politicians and the chicanery of pension attorneys. In 1875, when the outlay for pensions amounted to twenty-nine million dollars, Garfield asserted that expenditures for this purpose had reached its maximum; but within a few years an Arrears of Pensions Act was passed (1879).

This law gave to each pensioner back pay from the time his disability had been incurred, with the result that expenditures almost doubled. When the Pension Bureau rejected applications, private pension bills were introduced, with scant opportunities for members of Congress to vote according to the merits of the applicants. At the cost of valuable time and painstaking research, Cleveland made a study of private pension bills and vetoed one after the other, giving his reasons in detail in his veto messages.

In 1887 he vetoed the Dependent Pension Bill, which granted a pension of twelve dollars a month to every honorably discharged veteran of the war who had served three months and was dependent on his own labor or on the support of others. It also provided relief to the dependent parents of all deceased veterans.

For this guardianship of a public trust Cleveland was bitterly assailed by the former service men, who were united in the G.A.R. The Grand Army of the Republic was established in 1868 as a non-political organization, but during the eighties and nineties no candidate for public office could escape interrogation by its members in the matter of pensions. The presence of ex-Confederates in Cleveland's cabinet brought charges that the President was friendly to Confederates and hostile to the men who wore the blue. While the feeling against the President was riding high, he committed a colossal political blunder—characteristic of the bluntness or obtuseness of the man. He approved an order returning the battle flags, including Confederate flags, stored with the War Department.

The "rebel flag order" was denounced by men of every shade of political affiliation, and it was pointed out that the President had exceeded his authority. Cleveland looked into the matter and came to the decision that he had exceeded his authority, and the order was annulled. So bitter was the feeling that the President thought it the part of prudence to reconsider acceptance of the invitation to attend the G.A.R. encampment at St. Louis, because he feared that the dignity of his office would be insulted.

It remained for one of Cleveland's successors—Theodore Roosevelt, who was on better terms with the newspapers—to execute the "rebel flag order" and win the applause of the country. Cleveland had the misfortune to have the newspaper reporters against him, and he took no pains to cultivate their good will. In any event, during the campaign of 1888 the Republicans sang songs about Cleveland's vetoes of pension bills.

The death of Vice-President Hendricks in 1885, about two weeks before the assembling of Congress, not only left the Senate without a duly appointed presiding officer, but by reason of the fact that there was no president *pro tempore* of the Senate, there was no one to succeed the President in the event of his death. A similar situation had existed in 1881 after the death of Garfield. By the Presidential Succession Act approved in January, 1886, the order of succession was fixed by making the members of the cabinet eligible in the order of the establishment of their respective departments.

Though Cleveland's administration is not barren of constructive legislation, the time called for a leader in the White House with intuition enough to discern the signs of the times. Cleveland was not only woefully lacking in diplomacy, but he had little imagination. Moreover, during the last two years of his term the House was Democratic and the Senate was Republican and the antiquated rules of procedure in the lower body made it exceedingly difficult to transact business. The influence of wealth and big business caused the Senate to be referred to as the "House of Lords." The unpopularity of the railroad magnates, however, registered itself in the enactment of the Interstate Commerce Act, which was approved by the President on February 7, 1887.

In spite of hostility toward land grants to railroads and demands for railroad regulation as expressed by the Grange, the Farmers' Alliance, and organized labor, the interest of the people in transportation problems was tardy. In the rush of settlement to the West and the development of the country, people were willing to pay liberally for improvements in transportation; but with the approaching end of free land and the growth of monopolies, there was an increasing tendency to take stock of the resources of the country.

The seventies and eighties brought intense competition between railroads for traffic. The railroads represented the investment of a vast amount of capital. With the necessity of laying more and better tracks and the construction of larger and better terminals, coupled with periods of business stagnation, the law of diminishing returns began to operate; and this brought the incentive to obtain additional traffic by reducing rates and by granting rebates.

These years saw the steady diminution of freight rates, especially on bulky commodities shipped between competitive points. Between local and non-competitive points rates remained relatively high, partly, if not largely, because of rate wars which slashed rates below the cost of transportation. These losses to the railroads were ultimately paid by the public in one form or another. Certain cities were favored by the roads, and others suffered accordingly. Moreover, personal discrimination worked not only to the disadvantage of business and the public but also to the railroads. The roads were at the mercy of large shippers who played one road off against the other. No man trusted his neighbor because he thought he was getting better rates.

In 1885 Charles Francis Adams, the president of the Union Pacific Railway, testified before the Cullom Committee of the Senate that he was powerless to remedy the abuses practiced on his road. He could issue orders to cease irregular practices, he said, but his freight and passenger agents were judged by their ability to produce results and felt themselves obliged to meet competition by granting special favors. In a hearing conducted in 1879 by the State of Pennsylvania, Alexander J. Cassatt of the Pennsylvania System admitted that his road had become the creature of the Standard Oil Company. Investigations of the steel industry revealed similar conditions. Even after the turn of the century the Carnegie Steel Company threatened to build its own railroad to the Atlantic seaboard if the existing railroads refused to grant rebates. In fact, the success of great industries, like the Standard Oil Company, the United States Steel Corporation, the meat-packing industry, and the lumber syndicates, was due not entirely to business efficiency but also to sharp practices which forced the "little man" to the wall or compelled him to sell out, sometimes on ruinous terms. A concrete example of the working of rebates by which railroads contributed to building up monopolies is furnished by the Standard Oil Company, which is discussed in the following chapter.

One inevitable reaction to ruinous competition was the resort of the railroads to pooling agreements by which each road that entered the combination retained a percentage of its freight receipts and threw the remainder into a common fund to be divided pro rata. One of the most important pooling agreements was made in 1885.

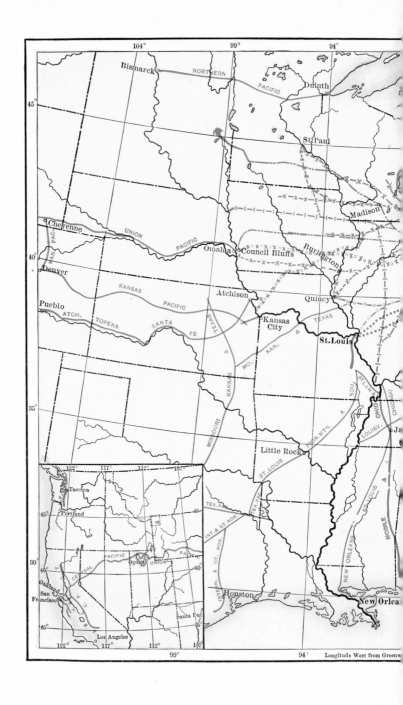

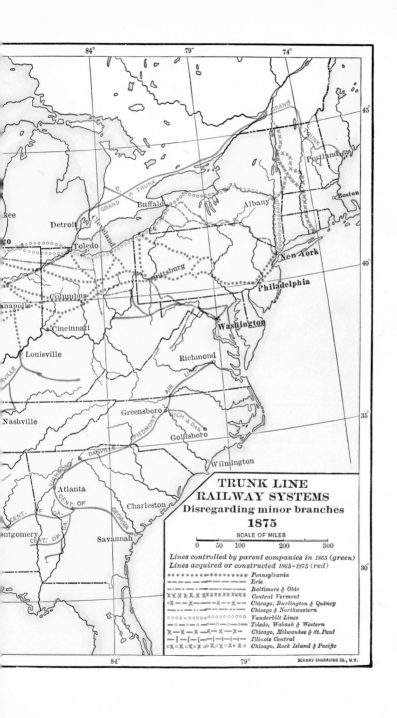

TRUNK LINE
RAILWAY SYSTEMS
Disregarding minor branches
1875

SCALE OF MILES

0   50   100   200   300

Lines controlled by parent companies in 1865 (green)
Lines acquired or constructed 1865-1875 (red)

••••••••••••••	Pennsylvania
————————	Erie
— — — — — — —	Baltimore & Ohio
XXXXXXXXXXXXXX	Central Vermont
-X— X—— —X—X—	Chicago, Burlington & Quincy
— — — — — — —	Chicago & Northwestern
ooooooooooooooo	Vanderbilt Lines
o—o—o—o—o—o—o	Toledo, Wabash & Western
X—X—X—X—X—X—	Chicago, Milwaukee & St. Paul
—l—l—l—l—l—l—	Illinois Central
oX oX oX oX oX oX o	Chicago, Rock Island & Pacific

BORMAY ENGRAVING CO., N.Y.

The attempt to remedy these practices took the form of the Interstate Commerce Act of 1887, a very conservative beginning which emerged out of a report prepared by a Senate committee which had been appointed for that purpose. The original purpose was to frame a law to place the control of railroads in the Interstate Commerce Commission but as a result of a powerful lobby of the railroad interests, the bill signed by President Cleveland was so emasculated as to leave the Commission almost powerless to remedy even the most fundamental abuses.

The act was intended to restore competition by making it illegal for a carrier to enter into any agreement with other lines for the pooling of freight traffic or for the division of any portion of the earnings of a carrier from competitive traffic. The act also prohibited discriminations and made it illegal to charge more for a short haul than for a long haul over the same line. The railroads were required to file their tariffs with the Commission. The Commission was composed of five members who were charged with the duties of investigating abuses and of levying fines for illegal acts, but their orders did not have the binding force of court decrees.

In spite of the fact that unjust discriminations continued, pools were formed, and passes were issued to legislators, judges, officials, clergymen, and others "where it would do good," the enactment of the law was in itself important and significant. It is the first federal control commission—a precedent for what has been done since. However, the act was erroneous in principle in that it assumed that competition must be maintained at all costs. Only slowly did it dawn that competition was not only unnecessary but in many ways an evil. Railroad transportation is in large degree a natural monopoly; the element of competition is wanting except between terminal points and between trunk lines. The development of sleeping car companies, express companies, and fast freight lines which ran through cars over several roads was a form of combination wholly desirable.

The tendency after 1865 was toward the accumulation of railroad interests in the hands of a few. Moreover, the paralleling of roads was of no advantage to the public, but rather repre-

sented a great waste of money. Another remarkable feature of
railroad development was the extent to which railroad corporations were engaged in business outside the legitimate service of
transportation—how they controlled the coal business, the oil
business, and the lumber trade. The tremendous power of these
corporations made it impossible to enact legislation designed to
curb their political activity. The influence exercised by such railroad magnates as James J. Hill and Edward H. Harriman, for
example, on governors, legislatures, and Congress, not to mention railroad commissions, is beyond computation. As stated by
a politician in a western state who sought to find a remedy for
the refusal of a railroad corporation to pay its fair share of
taxes: "It would seem that a bill that is not backed by the railroad lobby stands no show in our legislature."

Charles Francis Adams of the Union Pacific Railway stated
the gist of the problem in the following words:

Irresponsible and secret combinations among railways always have
existed, and, so long as the railroad system continues as it now is, they
unquestionably always will exist. No law can make two corporations,
any more than two individuals, actively undersell each other in any
market, if they do not wish to do so. But they can only cease doing
so by agreeing, in public or private, on a price below which neither
will sell. If they cannot do this publicly, they will assuredly do it
secretly. . . . Against this practice, the moment it begins to assume
any character of responsibility or permanence, statutes innumerable
have been aimed, and clauses strictly interdicting it have of late been
incorporated into several state constitutions. The experience of the last
few years, if it has proved nothing else, has conclusively demonstrated
how utterly impotent and futile such enactments and provisions necessarily are.

The experience of the Interstate Commerce Commission during the first years of its existence substantiated the statement
of the railroad president. State commissions were equally impotent, the courts in some instances setting aside their orders.
The Interstate Commerce Commission repeatedly asked Congress for increased power. In its report for December 1, 1895,
the Commission stated: "The Commission is not a court and

has no means of its own for enforcing its order. . . . If a carrier can simply ignore the findings of the Commission and wait for a new trial in the courts . . . the delay alone substantially defeats the remedy. . . . Until such a result is practically made possible, the work of the Commission, in its most valuable aspects, must be more or less a disappointment."

The depression that followed the panic of 1893 worked havoc with the railroads, and an era of receiverships followed. As markets became stagnant, traffic fell to a low ebb. In their anxiety to pay dividends on their stocks and interest on their bonds, railroads resorted to giving rebates; and with the growth of industrial combinations as business recovered, the railroads found themselves at the mercy of large shippers. The Interstate Commerce Commission was powerless. The integration of railroad corporations, and the consolidation of great systems during the opening years of the twentieth century, however, offered relief. By purchasing a sufficient amount of stock in competing lines in order to obtain a voice in their management, a community of interest was established. In that way several systems were so interlocked that they could resist the demands for rebates from giant trusts like the Standard Oil Company and the United States Steel Corporation.

During the era of "trust-busting" under the dynamic personality of Theodore Roosevelt, the government and the public frowned on combinations, as the dissolution of the Northern Securities Company in 1904 bears witness. Roosevelt's administration brought the Elkins Act of 1903 and the Hepburn Act of 1906. The former act prohibited secret rebates and discriminations, and made the corporation as well as the official giving the rebate punishable by a fine of not less than $1,000 nor more than $20,000 for each offense. By the Hepburn Act the Interstate Commerce Commission was authorized to prescribe just and reasonable maximum rates, and a penalty of $5,000 a day was fixed for the violation of any order to that effect. The Commission was further authorized to prescribe the forms of accounts, records, and memoranda kept by carriers. In 1908 passes except to employees and clergymen were forbidden. In 1910 the power of the Commission was further augmented by authorizing it to take the initiative in fixing rates. Pending an investigation as to the fairness of new rates, it could also postpone the effective date of such proposed changes. Other items of legislation looking to adequate regulation and control were added from time to time.

Another measure that enacted a plank of the Populist platform of 1892 was the Automatic Coupler Act of 1893, which required railroads to adopt the use of safety appliances in the coupling of freight cars. In 1894 only 27 per cent of the freight cars were equipped with automatic couplers, with the result that there was appalling loss of life and limb among brakemen using the old link and pin coupling. Moreover, the poor construction of many roads, inefficient management, undermanned trains, long hours, and the absence of block signals contributed to heavy loss of life and injury among trainmen and passengers. According to the report of the Interstate Commerce Commission for 1894, during the preceding year one out of every one hundred and fifty-six employees was killed, and one out of every twelve injured. It was five times as safe to be a railroad employee in Great Britain so far as life was concerned. The wages of railroad employees in the United States during the same year were somewhat higher than in England; but if allowance is made for idleness, the difference was very small. Engineers received $3.61 per day; conductors, $3.04; firemen, $2.03; switchmen, flagmen, and watchmen, $1.75.

When the Interstate Commerce Bill was before Congress, it seems that no one had the express companies in mind; and when the Commission ruled that they came within the scope of the act, the companies declined to furnish information. They took a similar attitude toward the state commissions. Although there were several companies, it was generally understood that they were closely connected, stockholders in one company having shares in the other. The compilers of the Census of 1880 tried to get information about their capital, owners, watered stock, length of lines in miles, amounts paid to railroads, expenditures, salaries, and the like, but only two companies responded.

There was virtually no competition between express companies, or between them and the railroads. Railroad magnates were large stockholders in express companies, and the contracts between the railroads and the express companies precluded competition between them. The Interstate Commerce Commission urged Congress to enact necessary legislation and pointed to the immense business transacted by express companies and the necessity of compelling them to give the public good service and reasonable rates. It was not until the passage of the Hepburn Act in 1906 that Congress responded.

In fixing maximum rates, the Interstate Commerce Commission and the state commissions recognized that an express company differs in many particulars from a railroad company. In determining the reasonableness of rates, little reference could be had to the value of the property employed, because the main object of express service is expedition and safety; and rates could not be so low as to attract business that might properly go by freight. Inquiry was made, therefore, into the character of the business, the amount of capital required for its conduct, the hazard involved, and the profits which a company was making on its present rates. In the words of the Commission, "a system must be. developed by which express rates (rates applicable to an expedited railroad service, plus additional terminal services) shall conform to the standards to which railroads have in great measure conformed and which the law enjoins."

During the year 1910 a large number of commercial bodies representing nearly every city and section in the United States appealed to the Interstate Commerce Commission to make a thorough investigation of express rates and practices, and asked for relief from certain abuses. The enactment of the parcels post law in 1912 was perhaps the most effective answer to this request. It has been said that "Boss" Platt and the four great express companies, in which he was a stockholder, are the reasons why there was no parcels post until 1912.

In 1910 the Interstate Commerce Act was amended by giving to the Commission jurisdiction over telegraph, cable, and wireless companies.

To return to the politics of the Cleveland administration, it has been said that it was accidental that the tariff was the paramount issue in the campaign of 1888. It was Cleveland's disregard of advice from certain independents and free traders in devoting his annual message of 1887 to tariff revision that largely determined the character of the coming presidential campaign. In this important message, Cleveland coined a famous phrase: "It is a condition which confronts us, not a theory." He deprecated the bandying of the epithets "free trade" and "protection," and in bold language called to the attention of Congress a state of affairs which demanded immediate consideration, namely, the great excess of receipts over the expenditures of government which had built up an unwieldy surplus in the treasury. The government, he said, had purchased available bonds and had considered various solutions, among them being the refunding of the debt at a lower rate of interest and paying the bondholders the difference. The proposed expedient of depositing the surplus in banks would, in the judgment of the President, bring about an unnatural relation between the government and business. He also believed that if the government purchased bonds on the open market, it would cause the national banks to sell their bonds at a premium and retire bank notes which were secured by bonds deposited with the Treasurer of the United States.

These expedients were brushed aside in favor of a more practical solution: the reduction of the tariff. The President said that high taxes enabled business to profit unduly and placed an unnecessary burden on the consumer. While admitting that someone had to suffer for the common good, he recommended that the tariff schedules should be revised so as not to disturb business. One suggestion in the message was singled out for special condemnation by the President's opponents, namely, the removal of duties on raw material, including wool. The wool-growers, he said, were a relatively unimportant element in the agricultural population.

The first session of the Fiftieth Congress, which convened on December 5, 1887, and remained in session until October, 1888, was up to that time the longest in congressional history. In the Senate there were 39 Republicans and 37 Democrats, but in the

House the Democrats were in undisputed control. It was inevitable that the efforts of the Democrats to carry out the recommendations in the President's message would take the form of a battle between them and the Republicans as a prelude to the more important battle on a wider front for the possession of the White House and the control of Congress.

The Democrats in the House wrote their idea of tariff revision in the bill introduced by Roger Q. Mills of Texas, and passed it with only four Democratic votes in the negative. The Republican Senate, however, formulated its own measure, and neither bill, nor a modified version, came to the President for his approval or disapproval. The two bills were understood to represent the positions of the respective parties on tariff legislation.

Republican stump speakers eagerly seized upon Cleveland's message and the Mills Bill, and, by taking up for special consideration certain schedules in various parts of the country, sought to demonstrate the dire results that would follow its enactment into law. They charged that Cleveland's tariff policy, as well as his foreign policy, was pro-British. To emphasize this, a letter written by the British minister to the United States, Sir Lionel Sackville-West, was made public. This so-called "Murchison letter" was addressed to a man who represented himself as a naturalized citizen of British birth and sought advice as to how he should vote in the coming election. The British minister advised his correspondent, who proved to be a newspaper man, to vote for Cleveland. The letter was turned over to the Republican politicians, as was intended, who withheld it from publication until the closing days of the campaign. Some Republican papers ran the letter in several issues in leaded type alongside the British crown. These tactics were designed to alienate Irish voters from Cleveland. Secretary of State Bayard cabled the British Foreign Office that Sackville-West's usefulness had ended.

What gave rise to the incident was the pending settlement of disputes growing out of rights claimed by American fishermen in British North American waters, which offered Cleveland's adversaries the opportunity to charge him with a lack of courage in upholding American rights. The President's critics were struck

dumb when he sent his famous "retaliation message" to Congress
on August 23, 1888, and asked legislation to empower him to
"subserve the interests of our people and maintain the high
standard and becoming pride of American citizenship." The
"Murchison letter" was published to counteract the effect of this
"patriotic" message.

Cleveland's defeat in 1888, after his election in 1884, made it
convenient for the triumphant Republicans to interpret their victory as an indorsement of their tariff policy. Undoubtedly the
Republican assault on the Mills Bill was effective, but to attribute
the Republican victory solely to the tariff is too simple.

Cleveland had alienated prominent Democrats by his obstinancy
and forthrightness, and his vetoes of the Dependent Pension Bill
and private pension bills had disappointed the "G.A.R. boys,"
whether they were Democrats or Republicans. He was not on
good terms with the Democratic candidate for governor of New
York, David B. Hill, who made no secret of his dislike for Cleveland, nor did the President conceal his dislike for Hill. If Cleveland had carried the thirty-six electoral votes of New York, he
would have won. As it was, his popular vote over the country
exceeded that of his opponent by over one hundred thousand.
Cleveland's campaign manager was not the equal of the director
of the Republican campaign, Matthew S. Quay of Pennsylvania,
who drew on a huge fund from a "barrel" filled by individuals
and corporations who knew the advantages of a protective tariff.
Quay and his lieutenants were none too scrupulous in the use they
made of this money.

In nominating Benjamin Harrison of Indiana the Republicans
presented a candidate whose public record was unblemished by
major errors. His nomination was made possible by Blaine's
positive refusal to allow his name to come before the convention.
The Republican candidate was a grandson of President William
Henry Harrison, the hero of Tippecanoe. Benjamin Harrison
had served with gallantry during the Civil War, had won the
respect of his associates as a very able lawyer, and had served
one term in the Senate. He was a forceful and logical speaker,
and absolutely without the arts of the demagogue. He was as

unimaginative as Cleveland, but it was not until the politicians had to deal with him in the White House that they were frozen by his austerity. Senator Cullom of Illinois, who knew every President from Lincoln to Wilson, pronounced Harrison the most unattractive man who ever sat in the White House. A member of the House of Representatives who was laid up with a heavy cold was chided by his colleagues for risking an interview with Harrison without wearing an overcoat and earmuffs. The new President was a deeply religious man and it was the sneer in Washington that "they opened oysters with prayer at the White House."

With an unpopular President surrounded by men whose ears were deaf to the rumblings of a political revolution, the achievements of the Harrison administration were buried in an avalanche of defeat in 1892.

CHAPTER XI

THE REPUBLICANS IN CONTROL

WITH NEITHER PARTY IN SIMULTANEOUS CONTROL OF THE PRESidency, the Senate, and the House for more than two periods—1889-91 (Republican) and 1893-95 (Democratic)—during the sixteen years from 1881 to 1897, the problem of leaders in both parties was to frame legislation that would strike a compromise between the East, West, and South. In the brief period of two years (1889-91) when the Republican party was in control of both branches of the government, legislation was enacted that was destined to have far-reaching effects and to have the immediate consequence of overwhelming Republican defeats in 1890 and 1892.

The House of Representatives that convened in December, 1889, was presided over by Thomas Brackett Reed of Maine, a leader of men and a great speaker, whose mastery of sarcasm and famous parliamentary ruling whipped the minority and the unruly majority into line and enabled him to jam legislation through. When the Democratic members tried to lock the wheels of legislation by refusing to answer roll calls, Reed counted them present for the purposes of a quorum. The Democrats stormed and raved, but the "Czar" was adamant. When the Democrats sought to slow up the progress of bills by dilatory motions, the speaker refused to entertain them.

For some years liberals and radicals had castigated the Senate as the citadel of reaction and had stigmatized it by such names as "millionaires' club" and "House of Lords." A coterie of able Republican Senators, sometimes by strategy and sometimes by coercion, marshaled their Republican colleagues—and they were not without aid and comfort, when it was needed, from certain Democratic Senators. The Republican strategists were Nelson W.

Aldrich of Rhode Island, Eugene Hale of Maine, Orville H. Platt of Connecticut, John C. Spooner of Wisconsin, and William B. Allison of Iowa. The influence of corporate wealth was personified in Leland Stanford, a Senator from California, one of the builders of the Central Pacific, who represented the railroad interests. In fact, railroads practically controlled the politics of states like California, Nebraska, and Wyoming.

In the eighties letters written by Collis P. Huntington, who was associated with Stanford and others in building the Central Pacific and later was the dominating personality in the Southern Pacific, were made public and revealed him as an active, cynical, and powerful railroad lobbyist. Senator Allison, chairman of the Committee on Appropriations from 1881 to 1908 and a member of the Committee on Finance—though sitting for agricultural Iowa —was a faithful servant of corporate wealth. One of his colleagues, himself in the good graces of the New York Central, said of him: "He could grant to an adversary an amendment with such grace and deference to superior judgment that the flattered enemy accepted a few suggestions from the master as a tribute to his talents. The post-mortem revealed his mistake." Senator Spooner, an exceedingly able man, bore the title of "chief of the corporation lobbyists." Quay was thoroughly trained and disciplined in the school of Pennsylvania politics. He never lost touch with the Standard Oil Company. After Harrison's election, Quay, his campaign manager, said in the presence of Alexander J. McClure, a Philadelphia newspaper man, that Harrison would never know how close a number of men were compelled to approach the gates of the penitentiary to make him President. Some of these men cared nothing for Harrison and bent their efforts to prevent his renomination in 1892.

Harrison's cabinet was not strong from the standpoint either of administrative ability or of political influence. Blaine, the Secretary of State, was the outstanding personality, and Harrison appointed him not because he desired to profit by his ability and experience but rather because the administration needed the support of Blaine's large personal following. For four years many Republicans lamented that the man from Maine was not in the

White House instead of the hard-working, conscientious, and austere Hoosier.

The Republican platform had committed the administration to the extension of the civil service, and Harrison endeavored with some success to redeem the pledge by extending the classified list and by appointing Theodore Roosevelt to the Civil Service Commission. The strenuous New Yorker was very vigorous in defending the work of the Commission. Harrison's inaugural address, however, gave comfort to party men by its assertion that party service ought to be rewarded. In the case of fourth-class postmasters, wholesale removals followed.

The Republican platform denounced the "hostile spirit" shown by Cleveland in his numerous vetoes for pension relief, and declared that "in the presence of an overflowing treasury it would be a public scandal" to fail to extend legislation so as to provide against the possibility that any man who wore the federal uniform might become an inmate of an almshouse or dependent upon private charity. Congress passed the Dependent Pension Bill; and Harrison's commissioner of pensions, "Corporal" James Tanner, not only increased the number of persons on the pension rolls but also raised disability ratings and ordered the payment of thousands of dollars in back pensions.

After the Democrats had obtained a majority in the House in 1892, the speaker appointed a select committee to investigate the administration of Tanner's successor, Green B. Raum, who was declared to be incompetent and corrupt. The conclusions of the committee, however, must be discounted because it is evident that the report was written to supply ammunition for use in the impending presidential campaign.

With the Republicans in control of the government, certain leaders conceived that it would be opportune to reduce the strength of the South by enacting a "Force bill" to enforce the Fourteenth and Fifteenth Amendments. This item on the legislative program, however, was defeated by logrolling and the lukewarm or hostile attitude of a number of Republicans who had no desire to call back the darkness of carpetbag rule. The obstructionist tactics

of southern Senators, who threatened to delay or defeat the pending tariff bill, were also effective.

The McKinley Tariff Act of 1890 was the direct result of
Cleveland's tariff message of 1887. By their attacks on the Mills
Bill the Republicans had maneuvered themselves into a position
where party consistency and political exigencies compelled them
to pass a tariff that measured up to their assertions that high
duties and high prices were advantageous to the country—to
farmers, wage earners, and capitalists alike. However, in view of
serious defections from Republican ranks into the Farmers' Alliance and dissatisfaction with Republican protection expressed in
Republican platforms adopted in western states, it was good strategy for the leaders in Congress to call the McKinley Bill a "bill
to reduce the revenue and equalize the duties on imports."

Moreover, the admission of North and South Dakota, Washington, Montana, Idaho, and Wyoming—the "omnibus states"—
in 1889 and 1890 greatly complicated the problem of framing
financial and tariff legislation that would command a majority in
Congress. There was a majority in both houses in favor of a
high protective tariff; but in the Senate the advocates of the free
coinage of silver, whose strength had been augmented by the admission of the "omnibus states," were powerful enough to hold up
the consideration of the McKinley Tariff Bill until the House,
which was opposed to free coinage, gave evidence of its willingness to yield something substantial to the Silver cause.

After 1880 the price of silver had declined sharply and the per
capita circulation of money had decreased. This, together with
the prevailing low prices and the consequent inability of western
farmers to reduce the mortgages on their farms, was believed by
many to be caused by the shrinkage of gold and the corner of
that commodity by the "gold bugs." It will be recalled that in
1878 a House free coinage bill was amended in the Senate and
became the Bland-Allison Act which provided only for limited
coinage. In the years following the enactment of this measure the
feeling grew, especially in the West, that gold as a sole standard
was not found in sufficient quantities to maintain the proper ratio

between the amount of money and the wealth of the country. For this reason the bimetallists in both parties advocated the free and unlimited coinage of silver.

Harrison's Secretary of the Treasury was William Windom, a man of confused ideas on finance, but a clever politician. He was not willing to recommend a free coinage bill, but he did propose that the treasury should buy at the market price as much silver as the mine owners chose to offer, paying for it in treasury notes redeemable in such quantities of silver as were equal to the face value of the notes, or in gold at the option of the government. In other words, the Secretary proposed to reduce silver to the level of other commodities to be left with the government as security.

The House caucus framed and the Republican majority passed a bill limiting the issue of such treasury notes to $4,500,000 monthly. The Senate promptly substituted for it a free coinage bill and also turned down the McKinley Tariff Bill on the calendar as a notification to the House that it would have to make larger concessions to the Silverites. The trans-Missouri Senators voted for the free coinage bill. The House having refused to accept the Senate substitute, both bills went to a conference committee from which they emerged greatly modified. This bill, known as the Sherman Silver Purchase Bill of 1890, was duly passed and signed by President Harrison. It required the treasury to purchase not more than 4,500,000 ounces of silver per month—instead of $4,500,000 worth—to be paid for in legal tender bills and to be redeemed in gold or silver at the discretion of the Secretary of the Treasury. The bill also contained a provision, suggested by Senator John Sherman, pledging the government to maintain the two metals on a parity. Obviously this was a compromise measure phrased in ambiguous words.

The enactment of the Sherman Silver Purchase Law was the beginning of a serious embarrassment for the government. It speedily raised the question of whether or not the government would be able to maintain the two metals on a parity, with silver declining in value and the treasury every month purchasing it and issuing legal tender notes against it. Would the gold reserve of

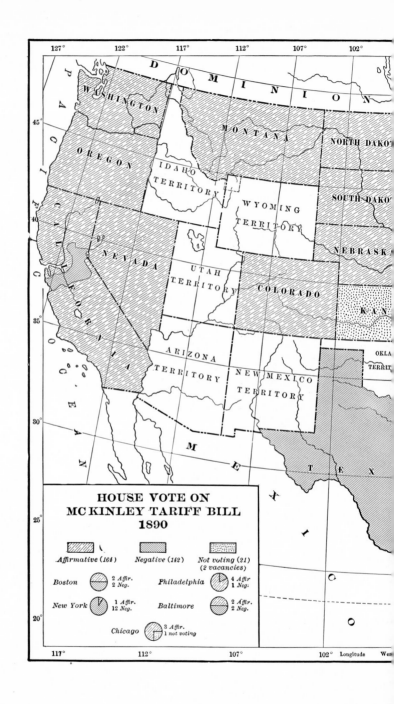

HOUSE VOTE ON
MCKINLEY TARIFF BILL
1890

Affirmative (164)   Negative (142)   Not voting (21)
(2 vacancies)

Boston   2 Affir.   Philadelphia   4 Affir.
          2 Neg.   1 Neg.

New York 1 Affir.   Baltimore   2 Affir.
          12 Neg.   2 Neg.

Chicago   3 Affir.
          1 not voting

$100,000,000 maintained for the purpose of redeeming green-backs be equal to the additional strain of redeeming the silver certificates? The surplus in the treasury was melting away under the assaults of an extravagant Congress, and the McKinley Tariff Act was designed to reduce the revenue. How long could the day of reckoning be postponed?

The silver compromise removed the chief obstacle to the journey of the McKinley Tariff Bill to the White House. It raised the duties on a large number of articles and removed many from the free list, some of which were necessities of life. It greatly reduced the revenue by removing duties on raw sugar; but in order to placate the sugar refiners, it retained duties on refined sugar. By granting bounties to sugar growers, it reduced the surplus in the treasury. The House Bill had no provision for reciprocity; but at the insistence of Secretary Blaine, and with an eye on the uneasy West, reciprocity became a part of the act in the form of a Senate amendment. The President was empowered to impose by proclamation duties on sugar, molasses, tea, coffee, and hides, if he considered that any country exporting those commodities to the United States imposed duties on agricultural or other products of the United States.

The effect of the McKinley Tariff was immediately felt in the form of higher prices on commodities that entered every household; and the fact that the bill had been jammed through the House by the autocratic rule of "Czar" Reed brought home to the people that Congress was not representing them. The congressional elections of 1890 came just at the time when indignation was running high; and Republican Congressmen returned to their districts to face the angry blasts of public opinion. A novel form of electioneering was employed by the Democrats. Well-dressed peddlers, smoking good cigars and driving sleek horses, supposedly selling tinware, went around in many districts. They were not concerned with selling tinware; their purpose was to advertise the high cost of their articles as a result of the McKinley Tariff.

The Republican majority in the House was swept away in favor of a huge Democratic majority; and in the Senate the Republican majority was reduced from fourteen to six. Even the author of the bill, William McKinley of Ohio, was defeated, though this was in part due to a gerrymander which had been made to favor his Democratic opponent.

Unquestionably the McKinley Tariff was an important factor in the downfall of the Republicans, but in some states the Farmers' Alliance movement was the immediate cause. The election was not a clean-cut victory for free trade or for a tariff for revenue. This is shown in some states where the Democratic vote fell off more than the Republican, in spite of the fact that the Alliance membership was largely recruited among Republicans. There were deeper causes of discontent than the McKinley Tariff, and the Alliance movement was but one symptom of that discontent. When dissatisfaction is abroad, it is the party in power that usually suffers; and in 1890 it happened to be the Republican party, which also had many sins on its register.

One of the most popular words in the political lexicon of the eighties was "trust," and it continued to be the text of political speeches far beyond 1900. The trust became the symbol of a monopolistic monster that devoured huge profits wrung from the public. At his beck and call railroads granted rebates, which enabled him to undersell smaller competitors until bankruptcy forced them out of business or until they surrendered their establishments to the enemy, sometimes under most unfavorable terms.

The Standard Oil Company became the model for combinations of capital that came to be known as trusts. This trust was organized under the terms of an agreement by which stockholders of associated companies assigned their stock to a board of trustees and in return received trust certificates. The various associated companies retained their individual identities, but the trustees held the legal title to the stock and the voting rights that pertained to it. This trust functioned so successfully that the pattern was copied by industrial capitalists in many fields. The arrangement placed the control and administration of different concerns in the hands of one set of directors. It became a most effective method of creating a monopoly. In the words of a state legislative committee, a trust is a combination "to destroy competition and to restrain trade through the stockholders therein combining with other corpora-

tions or stockholders to form a joint-stock company of corporations, in effect renouncing the powers of such several corporations,
and placing all powers in the hands of trustees."

It was not only the dangers lurking in monopolistic control
that were complained of; it was the tremendous power exercised
by trusts in government, by the election to public office of men
directly interested in them, and by bribing members of Congress
and legislatures, governors, and judges. The influence of corporate
wealth in the Pennsylvania legislature was facetiously expressed
by a member as follows: "I move to adjourn if the Pennsylvania
Railroad has no more business for this body to transact."

A flagrant example of similar events was the election, in the
middle of the eighties, of Henry B. Payne to the United States
Senate by an Ohio legislature bribed by the Oil Trust. Payne's
election astonished the people of the state, who did not even know
that he was a candidate. Indignation was so strong that when a
new legislature was elected, it had a mandate to investigate the
senatorial election. A committee of the United States Senate, however, with two able members dissenting, refused to recommend
an investigation. By various devices, such as delays, appeals to
courts on technicalities, intimidation, destruction of records, and
the like, the parties guilty to such transactions escaped the consequences.

The Standard Oil Company was the most prominent, powerful,
and unscrupulous, but other trusts prominent in the public eye of
the eighties were the Diamond Match Company, the Sugar Trust,
and the Dressed Beef Combine.

One of the marvelous industries that developed after the Civil
War was the production, refining, and distribution of petroleum
oil. The existence of oil wells had been known before the Civil
War; but with the development of improved means of transportation and methods of refining, oil became an important commodity of commerce, prices advanced, and an era of wild speculation set in. Fortunes were made overnight. The very lavishness of
nature in the oil fields of Pennsylvania made it difficult to control
the industry, and cutthroat competition threatened to ruin the
men who had invested their money. Naturally, games in which

the stakes are high attract men who relish big undertakings. The man who for a long time personified the methods and achievements of the Standard Oil Company was John D. Rockefeller, who worked for a small salary as a clerk in Cleveland, Ohio, until he saw the possibilities of accumulating a fortune in oil.

In the course of years Rockefeller associated with himself men like Henry M. Flagler, John D. Archbold, and William Rockefeller, who proved apt lieutenants to their chief. By a combination of fortuitous circumstances, business acumen, ruthless methods, efficiency, and public lethargy, the Standard Oil Company grew to the proportions of a mammoth. The railroad magnates, who had their own code of ethics, speedily learned to dance to the tune piped by the Oil Trust.

This trust took its beginning when the South Improvement Company was organized in January, 1872. This company entered into an agreement with the Pennsylvania, the Erie, and the New York Central, by which it was to furnish an equitable division of traffic, in return for which the railroads were to pay secret rebates on all oil shipped. But that was not all. The railroads were to pay rebates to the South Improvement Company on all oil shipped by its competitors. In that way the South Improvement Company was supplied with information about the business of its competitors, even to the names of the firms with which the railroads transacted business.

When the terms of this agreement became known, the independent producers, faced with extinction, rose up in their wrath, and the State of Pennsylvania annulled the charter of the South Improvement Company. However, the so-called "oil war of 1872" gave at best only a check to the movement to crush out competition; and in 1882 refiners who controlled over 90 per cent of the oil production formed the Standard Oil Company. The ethics of this new organization rose no higher than those of the South Improvement Company. Rebates, strong-arm methods, bribery, espionage, and efficient methods in the production, refining, and distribution of oil—from well to lamp—summarize the reasons for the growth of this monopoly.

Legislative investigations of the Standard Oil Company, litigation, and the correspondence of John D. Archbold leave no one in doubt that the officials of this organization did not scruple about forcing men in high governmental positions to do their bidding, though much of what might have been revealed was undoubtedly covered up by evasive witnesses, technical objections raised by highly paid attorneys, and the destruction of incriminating documents.

The Dressed Beef Combine was another monopolistic venture that profited by the increasing complexities of life and had the advantage of handling one of the fundamental necessities. Transportation and refrigeration enabled captains of industry like Gustavus F. Swift, Philip D. Armour, Nelson Morris, George H. Hammond, A. A. Libby, and John Cudahy to make Chicago the "porkopolis" of the nation. The convergence of trunk-line railroads on Chicago, the construction of unusual facilities for handling livestock, and the invention and perfection of the refrigerator car conspired to make Chicago the center of the meat-packing industry. Swift and Armour, for example, saw the waste and expense of shipping cattle on the hoof to be slaughtered at numerous distributing points. The railroads, however, believing that they profited more by hauling livestock, fought the introduction of the refrigerator car and charged excessive rates on dressed meat. But the packers built and owned their own cars and, after getting some railroads to accept them, succeeded in persuading the others.

Keen competition brought improved methods, the elimination of waste, and the utilization of by-products. It also brought pressure on railroads to grant rebates and other concessions; and in the eighties it was suspected that the business was practically controlled by the "Big Four" in Chicago, who were in a "combine" to eliminate competition with respect to the seller of livestock and the retailer of dressed meat. Using the methods of the Standard Oil Company, they combined to destroy retailers who bought from independent packers by opening their own shops to undersell them. In this warfare the "combine" enlisted the cooperation of railroads who refused to furnish stock cars to the packers' competitors.

In the iron mines of Pennsylvania and in the great deposits of iron ore in the Lake Superior region of Minnesota the American people possess a natural resource unequaled in any other part of the world. By developing this great gift of nature, another genius in the person of Andrew Carnegie, a canny Scot, made a huge fortune and laid the foundation of one of the greatest corporations in the world. In 1889, about twenty-five years after Carnegie had begun to apply his organizing ability to the manufacture of steel, the United States replaced Great Britain as the greatest steel-producing country.

Carnegie attributed his phenomenal success to his good fortune in enlisting the services of men of outstanding ability who, like himself, had an optimistic faith in the future of the country and by anticipating favorable opportunities excelled competitors in adopting improved machinery. The Carnegie Steel Company was not a trust in the sense of the Standard Oil Company or of the Diamond Match Company; but the immense aggregation of capital it represented, with its ramifications into railroads and allied industries, brought it into the public eye at the time when trusts, combines, and corporations were subjects of investigations.

The abuses of big business have tended to obscure the advantages of large organizations. They contributed to the development of the country, just as the individualistic, exploitive pioneer opened and developed the West. By pushing products into the markets of the world, large-scale production furnished employment to millions and reduced the prices of many necessities. The buccaneering seventies and eighties produced pirates who looted the timber resources and wasted the oil and mineral reserves of the nation, just as the pioneer farmers not infrequently took no thought of the morrow and destroyed the beauties of nature. The exploitive era was conducive to the operations of individuals who saw few values in life that could not be translated into profits—values that were questioned by some of their contemporaries and liberally discounted by later generations.

The leonine daring, optimism, and organizing ability of these captains of industry and "promoters" challenge admiration, if not always respect. Many of them were good men, judged by the standards of their time. It is true that they gave out of their abundance, for the thousands and the millions of Rockefeller, Carnegie, Morgan, McCormick, Deering, Duke, Vanderbilt, and even of Daniel Drew built and endowed libraries, universities, theological seminaries, art galleries, and other institutions that promoted the welfare and cultural enrichment of life.

Radicals and liberals saw the disastrous consequences to the public of watered stocks, legal monopolies, and combinations of capital, and advocated as the only method of breaking their hold government regulation and even government ownership and control of railroads and telegraph companies. The agitation of the Farmers' Alliance and the Knights of Labor bore fruit in anti-trust laws passed by legislatures, mainly in western states. These measures, which on the whole proved to be ineffectual, furnished valid evidence even to old-line Republicans and Democrats that western "insurgency" was a factor to be reckoned with: that party loyalty was below par.

In 1888 the Senate appointed a committee to investigate the trusts. The report of this committee contains hundreds of pages of testimony, much of it furnished by members of the Oil Trust. In his inaugural address President Harrison stated that if the "great corporations would more scrupulously observe their legal limitations and duties, they would have less cause to complain of the unlawful limitations of their rights or of violent interference with their operations." And in his annual message of 1889 he recommended that Congress give earnest attention to the question of how far the restraint of those "combinations of capital commonly called 'trusts' is a matter of federal jurisdiction." He said that if these organizations crushed out healthy competition and monopolized the production or sale of articles of general necessity, they should be made the subject of prohibitory and even penal legislation.

On June 2, 1890, Harrison signed what came to be known as the Sherman Anti-Trust Act, one of the most important items in the legislative annals of the country and paradoxically almost without effect in accomplishing the purpose for which the public thought it was intended. Though the act bears the name of John

Sherman, its authorship has been variously claimed and attributed; but it appears that the final draft was largely the work of Senator George F. Edmunds of Vermont, although, of course, other members of the Judiciary Committee had a part in framing it.

The essential provisions of the act outlawed contracts, combinations in the form of trusts, or conspiracy in restraint of trade or commerce among the several states or with foreign nations; and persons guilty of such practices were deemed guilty of misdemeanors. Persons injured in business or property by such misdemeanors might sue to recover three times the amount of the damages sustained. The title of the bill reads as follows: "A bill to protect trade and commerce against unlawful restraints and monopolies."

The public soon became aware of the futility of the law when the courts rendered decisions in cases that arose under it and when the trusts metamorphosed into new forms of organization cleverly devised by their executives and legal advisers. The Standard Oil Company emerged stronger than ever in 1899 as a holding company chartered under the laws of New Jersey. The Sugar Trust became a consolidated corporation. After ruinous competition, rival tobacco companies under the leadership of James B. Duke, joined in 1890 in the American Tobacco Company; and for the next five or six years the public was treated to the elevated spectacle of rival combinations buying extensive newspaper space to advertise "Battle-ax Plug: forty big chews for ten cents," "Quantity and Quality," and other brands of chewing tobacco, until in 1898 the manufacturers of plug tobacco formed the Continental Tobacco Company under the presidency of Duke.

This corporation and the American Tobacco Company were controlled by the same interests. The trust then entered the retail trade by establishing the United Cigar Stores Company; and in 1901 the Consolidated Tobacco Company was formed as a holding company in control of the American and Continental Companies. Following a Supreme Court decision ordering the dissolution of a railroad holding company in 1904, the three companies then merged under the name of the American Tobacco Company. Finally, in 1911, the Supreme Court ordered the dissolution of this "combination in restraint of trade." Since that time there have been several rival manufacturers of cigars, cigarettes, chewing tobacco, and snuff.

The history of the steel industry furnishes another example of the ineffectiveness of the Sherman Act. Ten years after the law had been approved, the steel industry was threatened with a war to the hilt between a dozen "trusts," the most formidable of which was the Carnegie Steel Company. In 1901, under the driving power of J. Pierpont Morgan, the United States Steel Corporation was chartered under the laws of New Jersey, a state that became known as the "mother of trusts." To write about the wide and multifarious interests of the some two hundred subsidiaries of the United States Steel Corporation would require a volume in itself. Let it suffice to say that this giant draws its sustenance from the rich ore deposits on the Mesabi Range in Minnesota, where huge steam shovels bite off the surface of loose earth before they proceed to load the ore onto railroad cars that roll down to the docks at Duluth to discharge their freight into the fleet of ore boats that churn the waters of the Great Lakes on their way to the furnaces in Cleveland, Chicago, Gary, and Ashtabula.

In addition to this richest of all iron deposits, the corporation owns reserves in Michigan and Alabama, to say nothing about coal reserves in Kentucky, West Virginia, Illinois, and Pennsylvania. The corporation has land holdings equal to the combined area of Massachusetts, Vermont, and Rhode Island; it owns railroads to the extent of thousands of miles; it owns a fleet of boats that dock at its own ports. Yet in 1920 the Supreme Court exonerated this corporation from the charge of being a monopoly in restraint of trade.

There will be occasion later to refer to these and other industrial mammoths. We leave the subject at this point by observing that from first to last the "trusts" carried off victory after victory in legal battles waged before judges and justices, with an occasional defeat that carried not much more significance than the surrender of a corporal's guard in the World War.

It was the irony of fate that a legislative weapon that was

forged to stop the onslaughts of a monster that threatened to strangle labor should have been turned against it. The Grangers and the Alliance men and the Knights of Labor and the men in the American Federation of Labor who had cried out against the menacing tentacles of the octopus were speedily disillusioned. Under the guise of the Sherman Act in the early nineties, federal injunctions and judicial constitutionality became instruments to break strikes and hamper labor organizations. After 1890 the injunction was used with increasing frequency to command a party or parties to a suit to refrain from action adjudged by the court to be criminal. The question as to the issuance of an injunction is decided by a judge or judges without a trial by jury.

Although there is some evidence to the contrary, it appears that when the Sherman Anti-Trust Bill was pending, neither members of Congress nor the public expected that the law would be used against labor. The name by which it was popularly known—"The Anti-Trust Law"—would indicate that. However, it is the judgment of a distinguished student of law, Professor Felix Frankfurter of the Harvard Law School, that students of the Sherman Act agree "that it has been one of the strongest influences counteracting trade unionism in the United States." Samuel Gompers, president of the American Federation of Labor, testified that he and his associates had several conferences with members of Congress while the bill was pending and received assurances that the law was intended to punish illegal trusts and not labor unions.

Although Senator Edmunds, on the floor of the Senate, and some years later in a magazine article, stated that it was the intent of the law to apply to labor unions, a study of the debates on the bill has convinced competent scholars that it was not so understood by other Senators, in spite of the fact that a proposed amendment expressly exempting labor unions was omitted when the final draft was reported out of the Committee on the Judiciary, to which it had been recommitted. Several Senators expressed themselves as opposed to the bill if it could be interpreted to include the Farmers' Alliance and labor organizations. Senator Sherman was most positive in stating that such organizations were not business combinations and that it was not the purpose of the bill to interfere with them. It is true that there have always been individuals and interests that have looked askance at combinations of farmers and laborers; but in 1890 the wrath of the public was directed against monopolistic combinations of capital. By passing the Sherman Act, Congress undoubtedly intended to translate this wrath into effectiveness, or at least to give the impression that it intended to do so.

The courts, however, decided otherwise, as is evidenced by the fact that from 1890 to March, 1897, the Supreme Court rendered twelve decisions against labor unions under the Sherman Act and only one decision pertaining to "trusts." Moreover, the application of the law has been extended to include activities of labor organizations that were not considered illegal when the bill was debated. Whereas in 1920, thirty years after the enactment of the Sherman Law, the Supreme Court by a four to three decision gave the United States Steel Corporation a clean bill of health, seven years later in the Bedford Stone case, with two justices dissenting, the court ordered the issuance of an injunction against a union which one of the dissenting justices declared had been innocent of trespass, breach of contract, picketing, violence, intimidation, and boycotting. The case arose out of the refusal of members of a union to handle the products of quarries where non-union men were employed.

Down to the administration of Theodore Roosevelt the Sherman Anti-Trust Act as a weapon against trusts was allowed to rust. Harrison, Cleveland, McKinley, and their Attorneys-General made little or no effort to test the effectiveness of the statute. In his report for 1893, the Attorney-General avowed that "it would not be useful, even if it were possible, to ascertain the precise purposes of the framers of the statute." He argued that "since all ownership of property is a monopoly . . . any literal application of the provisions of the statute is out of the question."

A fitting conclusion to this chapter is a quotation from a stimulating book by Herbert Croly, *The Promise of American Life*:[1]

---

[1] From Herbert Croly, *The Promise of American Life*. By permission of The Macmillan Company, publishers.

They have corporations in Europe, but they have nothing corresponding to the American corporation lawyer. The ablest American lawyers have been retained by the special interests. In some cases they have been retained to perform tasks which must have been repugnant to honest men; but that is not the most serious aspect of the situation. The retainer which the American legal profession has accepted from the corporations inevitably increases its natural tendency to a blind conservatism; and its influence has been used not for the purpose of extricating the large corporations from their dubious and dangerous legal situation, but for the purpose of keeping them entangled in its meshes. At a time when the public interest needs a candid reconsideration of the basis and the purpose of the American legal system, they have either opposed or contributed little to the essential work, and in adopting this course they have betrayed the interests of their more profitable clients—the large corporations themselves—whose one chance of perpetuation depends upon political and legal reconstruction. . . . If there is any thoroughgoing reorganization needed, it will be brought about in spite of the opposition of the legal profession. They occupy in relation to the modern economic and political problem a position similar to that of the Constitutional Unionists previous to the Civil War. Those estimable gentlemen believed devoutly that the Constitution, which created the problem of slavery and provoked the anti-slavery agitation, was adequate to its solution. In the same spirit learned lawyers now affirm that the existing problems can easily be solved, if only American public opinion remain faithful to the Constitution. But it may be that the Constitution, as well as the system of local political government built up around the federal Constitution, is itself partly responsible for some of the existing abuses, evils, and problems; and if so, the American lawyer may be useful, as he was before the Civil War, in evading our difficulties; but he will not be very useful in settling them. He may try to settle them by decisions of the Supreme Court; but such decisions . . . would merely excite a crisis, which they were intended to allay, and strengthen the hands of the more radical critics of the existing political system.

This penetrating observation was written in 1909, when the Progressive movement as typified in Theodore Roosevelt, Robert M. La Follette, and William J. Bryan was riding high, when "trust-busting" was a topic of everyday conversation, and when it appeared that the American people were determined to be masters in their own right; but it applies with even greater emphasis to the years from 1921 to 1929, when the golden calf was worshiped as never before. Moreover, Croly's attitude is exactly that of liberals from the eighties on through the years, who were concerned lest an inflexible system based on a written constitution might bring disaster. It is a graceful statement of the blunt meaning of a radical satirist who said: "If you can't serve God and mammon, hire a lawyer to prove that God is unconstitutional."

CHAPTER XII

THE GATHERING STORM

IF ONE MAY JUDGE BY THE RESPECTIVE PLATFORMS ADOPTED IN 1892 by the Republican and Democratic national conventions, the delegates were oblivious to the impending political tornado. These documents "denounced," "called attention to," "viewed with alarm," and "favored" according to the orthodox pattern of previous platforms. At the Minneapolis convention the Republicans renominated Benjamin Harrison and indorsed his administration, in spite of the fact that for two years an anti-Harrison faction under the leadership of Matthew S. Quay, Thomas C. Platt, Russell A. Alger, Thomas B. Reed, and Don Cameron had fought to prevent it. The country over, thousands expressed a preference for James G. Blaine.

From the beginning of Harrison's administration the relations between the President and the Secretary of State were cool, not to say strained. Harrison was aware of his own unpopularity and of the popularity of Blaine; and it is probable that he would have been satisfied with one term had it not been for the tactics of his adversaries.

On June 4, three days before the opening of the Republican convention, Blaine startled the country by resigning the state portfolio; and Harrison accepted the resignation in a curt formal communication. The reason or reasons that impelled the Secretary to take this unusual and ill-advised action have puzzled his biographers. One conjecture that seems valid is that Blaine's failing health made it possible for Harrison's adversaries to overrule his better judgment. In any event, Harrison's control of the patronage, and Blaine's tardy resignation, assured the President's renomination, in spite of an excess of oratorical eulogies of the man from Maine.

From his retirement Cleveland had watched with dismay the enactment by a Republican Congress of the Dependent Pension Law, the McKinley Tariff, and the Sherman Silver Purchase Act. With equal dismay he had seen the increasing strength of the element in favor of the free coinage of silver within the Democratic party. The danger to the Democratic party from the radicals within the fold, and the disgust within the Republican party with the Harrison administration, caused many conservatives to turn to Cleveland as the Democratic standard bearer who could give the country conservative leadership. Within the Democratic party, however, Cleveland was opposed by Tammany Hall and by Senator David B. Hill, who also aspired to the Presidency. In spite of what at the time appeared to be another colossal blunder, the former President was nominated on the first ballot at the Chicago convention.

Cleveland's supposed error consisted in addressing a letter to a gathering of business men called to voice opposition to the free coinage of silver. The letter was dated February 10, 1891, more than a year before the meeting of the Democratic convention. Cleveland was advised not to attend the meeting because it would hurt his chances in the West, where the free-coinage sentiment was strong. With characteristic courage, he wrote a letter in which he flatly condemned the free-coinage proposition. His adversaries were full of glee, and Hill launched a campaign for delegates pledged to himself. The Hill boom was quickly deflated, however, notwithstanding efforts to stampede the convention by pressing into service the powerful oratorical talents of W. Bourke Cockran.

In the campaign the Democrats and the Republicans pressed the tariff issue to the fore and sought to smother the silver question by silence. They also ignored the existence of the People's, or Populist, party, which had been launched in May, 1891, at a great mass convention at Cincinnati. The Populist party was the political expression of the Farmers' Alliance movement. At the Omaha convention the party nominated James B. Weaver of Iowa on a platform that denounced the old parties for agreeing to "drown the outcries of a plundered people with the uproar of a sham battle over the tariff, so that capitalists, corporations, national banks, rings, trusts, watered stock, the demonetization of silver, and the oppressions of the usurers may all be lost sight of." The platform included planks calling for government ownership of railroads, telegraph, and telephone lines, free coinage of silver, a graduated income tax, postal savings banks, parcels post, and the reclamation by the government of certain lands granted to railroads and lands owned by aliens.

Although the newspapers and Republican and Democratic spellbinders either ignored or ridiculed the Populists, the voters were aware of their existence. General Weaver said that he counted his hearers not by the thousands but by the acres. In Colorado, Idaho, Kansas, North Dakota, Nevada, and Wyoming the Democrats named no electoral ticket and voted for the Populist candidate.

The results of the election were startling. Cleveland was overwhelmingly elected, with 277 electoral votes against 145 for Harrison. The Populists showed phenomenal strength in the West by polling over one million popular votes and winning the twenty-two electoral votes from Colorado, Idaho, Kansas, and Nevada.

The first smashing defeat suffered by the Republicans in a presidential election since the election of the first Republican President in 1860 was the result of the confluence of events and conditions, among them being the personal unpopularity of Harrison and the lethargy of prominent Republicans; but the fundamental cause was deep-seated unrest. A discontented West and a restless labor world registered themselves in an unprecedentedly large third-party vote and a large Democratic vote as a protest against the party in power.

No sooner had Cleveland taken the oath of office on March 4, 1893, than he encountered bitter opposition within his own party. The slim Democratic majority in the Senate was largely dominated by men who had long disliked Cleveland's independence; but in the House the Democrats had a heavy majority.

On the surface the country appeared to be enjoying prosperity during the four years of Harrison's administration; but prosperity had the usual effect of stimulating speculation. By 1890 the inevitable reaction had set in, and cautious men had begun to sell securities and to restrict credits. Business failures were numerous. Unfavorable conditions were accentuated by the generous appropriations of the Republican Congress—designed to reduce the surplus—and by the operation of the McKinley Tariff which seriously reduced the revenue, as was intended.

At the close of Cleveland's first term in 1889, there was a cash balance in the treasury of nearly three hundred million dollars, of which almost two hundred million was gold. In 1891, after the second year of Harrison's administration, the cash balance had dropped by more than one hundred million, and the balance in gold was less than one hundred twenty million. In 1893 Harrison left to Cleveland $100,982,410 in gold, and this amount had been kept up only by the heroic efforts of the Secretary of the Treasury. In fact, plates had already been engraved for bonds to be issued in order to prevent the gold reserve from falling below the one hundred million reserve for the redemption of greenbacks.

To make matters worse, by the Sherman Silver Purchase Act of 1890 the government had embarked on a policy of purchasing a certain amount of silver each month, to be paid for in silver certificates and to be maintained on a parity with gold. Thus with a diminishing gold reserve the outstanding notes against it were increased with the passing of each month; and with the declining value of silver doubts were raised as to the ability of the government to redeem the greenbacks and the silver bullion certificates in gold.

This was the state of affairs when Cleveland took office. The country was on the rim of a panic, which had been averted in the previous administration by a shortage of wheat in Europe and a bumper crop in the United States, thereby converting Europe from an exporter of wheat to an importer. This had the effect of bringing gold to the United States.

Nerves were still more unsettled by a rumor telegraphed from Washington that when the gold reserve fell below the one-hundred-million mark, the treasury notes of the Silver Purchase Act would no longer be redeemed in gold. The panicky feeling was temporarily dispelled by a prompt statement from Cleveland that gold payments would be maintained under all circumstances. Business failures increased, however, and by June, 1893, the country was in the throes of a panic. The perilous condition of the gold reserve impelled the President to call a special session of Congress to repeal the Silver Purchase Act. Congress convened on August 7, and within three weeks the House of Representatives passed a bill that complied with the President's request, with the Democrats badly divided and the Republicans overwhelmingly in favor.

In the Senate, however, an acrimonious debate delayed the final passage of the bill until October 30. Silver Democrats and Silver Republicans, mainly from the West and the South, introduced free-coinage bills, and other Democrats held out for patronage which Cleveland granted, greatly to the dissatisfaction of civil service reformers.

The repeal of the Silver Purchase Act did not remove the danger to the gold reserve. The depressed state of business and agriculture dried up fruitful sources of revenue, and gold went into hiding where hoarders thought it would be safe. During January and February, 1894, the Secretary of the Treasury resorted to the sale of bonds for gold; but with greenbacks and silver certificates presented for redemption and again placed in circulation, an endless chain was created, until the drain on the gold reserve again became serious.

With the refusal of Congress to extricate the government from the dilemma, Cleveland took action that called down upon him the wrath of the bimetallists. The government entered into a contract with a syndicate of bankers who undertook to maintain the gold reserve during the period stipulated in the contract. The bankers agreed to obtain from Europe at least one-half of the gold to be paid for government bonds and, to the extent of their ability, to protect the treasury against withdrawals of gold pending the complete performance of the contract. What made this pill extremely bitter to the bimetallists was the fact that the bankers received a premium on the bonds. This convinced them that the President was the tool of Wall Street. In 1896, after the termination of the contract, another bond issue was deemed necessary.

Cleveland's supporters credited him with having saved the country from bankruptcy; but many of the bimetallists indorsed the sentiment of Governor Altgeld of Illinois, who said in 1895: "To laud Clevelandism on Jefferson's birthday is to sing a Te Deum in honor of Judas Iscariot on Christmas morning."

The division in the Democratic party was again evident when Congress set itself to the task of redeeming one of the pledges of the campaign by replacing the unpopular McKinley Tariff by another measure. At the regular session which convened in December, 1893, the House passed the Wilson Tariff Bill by a vote of 204 to 140. The bill was framed under the guidance of William L. Wilson of West Virginia, who with ability of high order steered it to final passage. It provided substantial but conservative reductions on manufactured commodities and placed many raw materials on the free list. In response to pressure from the West, where Populism was a factor to be reckoned with, a tax of 2 per cent on incomes above $4,000 was included—a decidedly radical innovation. Opponents referred to an income tax as un-American, a "monarchial" form of taxation, a tax on thrift. Moreover, so the argument ran, it would give officials the right to pry into the private affairs of all business men.

The Senate stripped the House tariff bill of its raiment, and it became the Wilson-Gorman Tariff of 1894. A group of Democratic Senators who represented special interests was responsible for some six hundred amendments. The man who was chiefly responsible for thwarting the wishes of the President to place raw materials, such as coal, iron ore, and sugar, on the free list was Arthur Pue Gorman of Maryland, whose solicitude for the coal and iron interests was well known. Senator Hill of New York, Cleveland's rival for the nomination in 1892, was opposed to a "Populistic income-tax feature being placed in the bill." Hill's colleague, Edward Murphy, looked out for the shirt and collar manufacturers of Troy. The two Senators from Louisiana voted in terms of the sugar interests of their state. Other Democratic Senators were encouraged in their assaults on the Wilson bill by such Republican Senators as Aldrich of Rhode Island, Allison of Iowa, and Hoar of Massachusetts. After weeks of debate on the floor of the Senate, and deals and conferences behind the closed doors of cloak and committee rooms, the only important commodities that remained on the free list were wool and copper, and rates were generally revised upward.

Cleveland's efforts to obtain a bill that represented genuine downward revision were largely futile, partly because of personal hostility toward him, partly on account of animosities that had been aroused during the debates on the repeal of the Silver Purchase Act, and partly on account of the President's inept handling of the situation. At one stage the President consented to the publication of a letter addressed to Representative Wilson in which he stigmatized the abandonment of the principles of the House bill as "party perfidy and party dishonor." This sharp reproof rallied Senators to the defense of the well-known dignity of the Senate; and Gorman, in a blistering speech, impugned the honesty of the President. Gorman's defense was that the Democratic majority was so slim that the House bill could not pass; that after weeks of patient conferences amendments were agreed upon to assure a majority in favor of a bill that improved upon the existing McKinley Tariff.

The House refused to agree to the Senate amendments, and both bills went to a conference committee, the graveyard of many good intentions; and when a bill was reported by the conference committee, it retained substantially the Senate amendments, but with the income tax provision intact. This is the "free trade" bill which the Republicans in the campaign of 1896 and in subsequent campaigns blamed for the panic of 1893, despite the fact that it was enacted more than a year after the country felt the acute pinch of hard times. In order to attract the attention of the voters from the legislation of the Republican Congress of 1890, it was good strategy to attribute the panic to the lack of confidence on the part of business in the anticipated Democratic tinkering with the tariff.

The Senate had administered a crushing defeat to the President; and for a time he wavered between two possible courses of action: whether he should exercise the veto or whether he should allow the bill to become a law without his signature. He chose the latter alternative because he believed that, with all its inconsistencies and crudities, it was better than the McKinley Tariff. However, he publicly denounced those who had stolen the "livery of Democratic tariff reform" and had worn it "in the service of Republican protection." "The trusts and combinations—*the communism of pelf*—whose machinations have prevented us from reaching the success we deserved, should not be forgotten nor forgiven," he said.

The events of the first two years of his administration showed that Cleveland had lost the leadership of his party and that the Democratic party, as well as the Republican party, was in the hands of the interests—that the government was dominated by a bipartisan machine.

The fiasco of "scientific" tariff revision and hard times brought overwhelming defeat to the Democrats in the elections of 1894. The Democratic majority in the House of Representatives was transformed into a hopeless minority. The political map of 1892 shows only sixteen Republican states; the map of 1894 shows thirty-one. The verdict of 1894, however, was rather one of condemnation of the Democratic party than approval of the Republican. Election statistics can be as misleading as other statistics. From 1884 to 1896 politics were topsy-turvy, and events played into the hands of what the complacent elements of the population were pleased to call "calamity orators."

Cleveland was strangely indifferent or obtuse to the demands of the Populistic West; and what little comfort that section could draw from the Wilson-Gorman Tariff was taken away when the Supreme Court by a five to four decision on April 4, 1895, declared the income tax provision unconstitutional. One justice who had previously thought the tax constitutional switched over to what became the majority. The court held that it was a direct tax and therefore in violation of that provision of the Constitution which states that "No capitation or other direct tax shall be laid, unless in proportion to the census or enumeration hereinbefore directed to be taken." The dissenting opinion was vigorous, but an income tax had to wait for a constitutional amendment.

This court decision strengthened the conviction of those who believed that the government was in the firm grip of the interests, especially in view of the fact that the income tax had been the target of attacks from the large daily papers which were thought to be mouthpieces of intrenched wealth, and from Representatives and Senators from the industrial East. The Supreme Court, which had recovered from the unpopularity cast upon it by the Dred Scott decision, once more drew the fire of men and women who sought legislation that would promote the general welfare. They complained of the inequitable distribution of wealth and a system of taxation that emphasized the inequalities. Moreover, the deficit in the federal treasury, which the revenue from the income tax was expected to fill, grew larger than ever.

At a time when the price of wheat, oats, and corn was below the cost of production, and the farmer had difficulty in meeting the interest, to say nothing about the principal, on the mortgage on his homestead, and the public lands had ceased to function as a safety valve, he listened to the Farmers' Alliance and the Populist orators who told him that the old pioneer individualism belonged to a past generation and that the only recourse was to turn to legislation. Mrs. Mary E. Lease told the Kansas farmers that they needed "to raise less corn and more *Hell*." Her ringing words went home to farmers who had lost their farms by mortgage foreclosures: "Kansas suffers from two great robbers, the Santa Fe Railroad and the loan companies. The common people are robbed to enrich their masters. . . . We want money, land, and transportation. We want the abolition of National banks, and we want the power to make loans direct from the government. We want the accursed foreclosure system wiped out. Land equal to a tract thirty miles wide and ninety miles long has been foreclosed and bought in by loan companies of Kansas in a year."

Among the chief grievances of the western farmer was the method by which his grain was transported, warehoused, and graded. He complained of high freight rates and was justly suspicious of the men who bought or handled his grain. He had information that departments of grain inspection were corrupt and that inspection was conducted in the interest of buyers and against the interests of shippers and producers. Legislative committees had found that grading had not been uniform, that inspectors had been careless and incompetent, that weighing of grain at terminals had been done in a loose manner, and that farmers had suffered heavy losses by shipping unclean grain and by loading clean grain into dirty cars.

The wheat farmers in the Northwest were at the mercy of line elevator companies, whose large capital resources enabled them to control the market of a large area and also to control terminal elevators. The owners of line elevators often had financial interest in the railroads over which they shipped grain and were thereby able to obtain better rates than independent elevators or elevators cooperatively owned. Having driven competitors out of business, they fixed prices to suit themselves and reaped large profits by mixing good grain with that of inferior grade.

The "roller process" made it possible to grind hard spring wheat at the Falls of St. Anthony in Minneapolis; and by 1882 this thriving Minnesota city had become the flour-milling center of the country, partly because of water power, partly by reason of favorable transportation rates, and partly because the city was situated in a great wheat-raising region. By 1870 Iowa, Illinois, Ohio, Indiana, and Wisconsin had become the leading wheat-growing states, with Minnesota seventh in the list. With the flocking into Minnesota of Scandinavian and German farmers and the opening of the rich Red River Valley, production of wheat mounted. It was a crop peculiarly suited to pioneer farming. However, crop failures, high rates of transportation, hardships of pioneer life, and the depressed price of wheat made the Northwest a recruiting ground for Alliance and Populist orators and organizers. The farmer toiled early and late, but there was little profit for him in his labor. He complained of this, but he complained still more because the products of his labor added to the colossal possessions of a small class of people.

The West had grown too rapidly; it had been too easy to borrow money; the optimism of the pioneer had brought into cultivation lands that were unsuitable for cultivation. Farms in the semi-arid belt of Kansas, Nebraska, Montana, and the Dakotas were the first to go under the hammers of sheriffs.

In the South the plight of the farmers was such that they elected
men like Benjamin R. Tillman, a Democrat, governor of South
Carolina in 1890 and in 1892, and Thomas E. Watson of Georgia,
a Populist, to Congress in 1890. Tillman told the farmers that
they were the dupes of lawyers and merchants; and as governor
he inaugurated reforms in taxation, education, representation,
and the sale of intoxicating liquor—all in the interest of the
small farmers whose problems he himself had faced. This champion of agrarian reform promised the people that if they could
elect him to the United States Senate, he would stick his pitchfork into Cleveland's "old ribs." When his ambition was gratified,
his maiden speech in that dignified body was an uncouth attack
on the President. The fiery, red-headed Watson, carrying aloft
the banner of Populism, waged a crusade in bloody and fraudulent
political contests. His relentless leadership of the revolting southern farmers won for him the vice-presidential nomination on the
Populist ticket in 1896.

In the East the impression was abroad that the Populist ranks
were filled exclusively by the ne'er-do-wells of the community—
the unthrifty and the riffraff. Theodore Roosevelt, a New Yorker
and a Harvard graduate of aristocratic birth, who many years
in the future was destined to denounce the "silk stockings" of
Boston's Back Bay and to champion the cause of Lincoln's "plain
people," wrote an article for the September, 1896, *Review of Reviews,* in which he delivered himself of the following:

Senator Tillman, the great Populist or Democratic orator from
South Carolina, possesses an untrammeled tongue which doubtless Mr.
Watson really envies, and moreover, Mr. Tillman's brother has been
frequently elected to Congress upon the issue that he never wore either
an overcoat or an undershirt, an issue which any Populist statesman
finds readily comprehensible. . . .

Altogether Mr. Watson, with his sincerity, his frankness, his extreme suspiciousness, and his uncouth hatred of anything he cannot
understand and of all the elegancies and decencies of civilized life, is
an interesting personage. . . . Mr. Watson would at a blow destroy
all banks and bankers, with a cheerful, albeit vague, belief that thereby
he was in some abstruse way benefiting the people at large. And he

would do this with the simple sincerity and faith of an African savage who tries to benefit his tribe by a sufficiency of human sacrifices.

A more sympathetic observer, Henry Demarest Lloyd, in the same periodical wrote about the Populist national convention at St. Louis in 1896:

The Populist gathering of this year lacked the drill and distinction and wealth of the Republican convention held the month before in the same building. . . . Every one commented on the number of gray heads—heads many of them grown white in previous independent party movements. The delegates were poor men. One of the "smart" reporters of the cosmopolitan press dilated with the wit of the boulevardier upon finding some of them sitting with their shoes off,—to rest their feet and save their shoes, as they confessed to him. Perhaps even his merry pen would have withheld its shafts if he had realized that these delegates had probably had to walk many weary miles to get to the convention, and that they had done their duty at such sacrifice only for conscience sake. Cases are well known of delegates who walked because too poor to pay their railroad fare. It was one day discovered that certain members of one of the most important delegations were actually suffering for food. They had had no regular sleeping place, having had to save what money they had for nickel meals at the lunch counter.

It is true that the Populist movement attracted to itself cranks, extremists, and individuals whose eccentricities drew the fire of cartoonists and paragraphers and whose deadly earnestness alarmed individuals whose conservatism and defense of property rights was no less extreme. But Senator Peffer's long beard does not obscure the fact that among the Populist leaders who advocated a series of reforms that have since been written into law and even into constitutions—such as the income tax and direct election of Senators—were men like James B. Weaver, Eugene V. Debs, William V. Allen, Henry Demarest Lloyd, Marion Butler, and John Lind. And there was a host of men and women who did not call themselves Populists but were nevertheless in sympathy with their crusade against special privilege and for reforms in government.

When discontent is rife, the less responsible and less level-headed members of society sow their seeds of revolt and disorder. Widespread unemployment from 1893 to 1896 recruited the ranks of vagrants and tramps who begged from door to door. Factories were idle, and in cities trolley cars were almost empty of passengers. Cities sought to cope with poverty by organizing relief committees in which charitable organizations, religious bodies, mercantile associations, boards of trade, labor unions, philanthropic individuals, and police cooperated to raise money to provide employment and to alleviate want and suffering. Free soup houses were set up,. and in some cities the managers of these institutions sold tickets to merchants and others, who gave them to vagrants instead of giving them money. Other cities by popular subscription or by appropriations voted by city councils made it possible for men to obtain work grading streets and removing snow from sidewalks. A simple mode of life in both country and city and the heritage of the pioneer spirit opened homes to friends and relatives until favorable agricultural and industrial conditions furnished means of self-support.

Conditions peculiar to the Middle West and the Pacific coast produced remarkable mobilizations of men who were victims of the depressed state of the country which in the early months of 1894 converged on the capital of the nation. These "industrial armies" and the crusaders of the "Commonweal of Christ" were numerous; but the man whose name figured most prominently in the newspapers of the time was "General" Jacob S. Coxey of Massillon, Ohio, a successful business man of some means who believed that the government ought to take direct action in the emergency. As a Greenbacker and Populist, he advocated that the federal government should issue $500,000,000 in legal tender irredeemable paper money to finance the building of roads, and that state and local governments should issue non-interest-bearing bonds to be deposited with the Secretary of the Treasury, also for the purpose of financing internal improvement projects. The crusading armies, however, were not creations of an individual or of a small group of individuals. They originated in sporadic movements of protest and demonstration.

The armies were not composed exclusively of miscellaneous

ragamuffins. There was a religious fervor in their ranks, manifested by carrying banners proclaiming "peace on earth," by singing hymns, and by the evangelistic exhortations of their leaders. The camps that were pitched along the lines of march were policed, discipline was enforced, and drunkards were expelled. Coxey was a religious enthusiast; and Carl Browne of California, who exercised a strong influence over him, was a fanatic who pinned his faith on some sort of reincarnation that would bring to earth the kingdom of heaven in which even members of Congress would do the will of God.

The leaders of the respective armies had high hopes for the success of their undertaking. They expected that, once under way, their armies would be swelled by thousands of recruits. Coxey's army started from Massillon, Ohio; Lewis C. Frye's from Los Angeles, California; and "General" Charles T. Kelley's from San Francisco. Other groups took their points of departure from the Pacific Northwest, and still others from New England. A swarm of newspaper reporters accompanied the large battalions, and the public read reams of "copy" about their reception along the way, the stealing of railroad trains, the issuance of court injunctions, sympathetic and unsympathetic governors and politicians, the consternation in some communities at the approach of the "tramps," and public contributions, sometimes for the purpose of getting rid of them and sometimes out of sympathy. Very few of the crusaders had the stamina to continue the march to Washington; and those who did reach the goal found an unsympathetic Congress. Coxey and a handful of his men were arrested and arraigned before a police magistrate, charged with walking on the grass and carrying banners on the Capitol grounds.

The spectacular protest staged by the "Coxeyites" was not nearly so serious as the manifestation of bad blood between capital and labor. One of the most savage conflicts occurred in 1892 in the steel works at Homestead, Pennsylvania. It is said to have contributed to the defeat of Benjamin Harrison, and it was capitalized by the Democrats as an example of the unfavorable operation of the McKinley Tariff.

The conflict had its origin in the decision of the Carnegie Steel

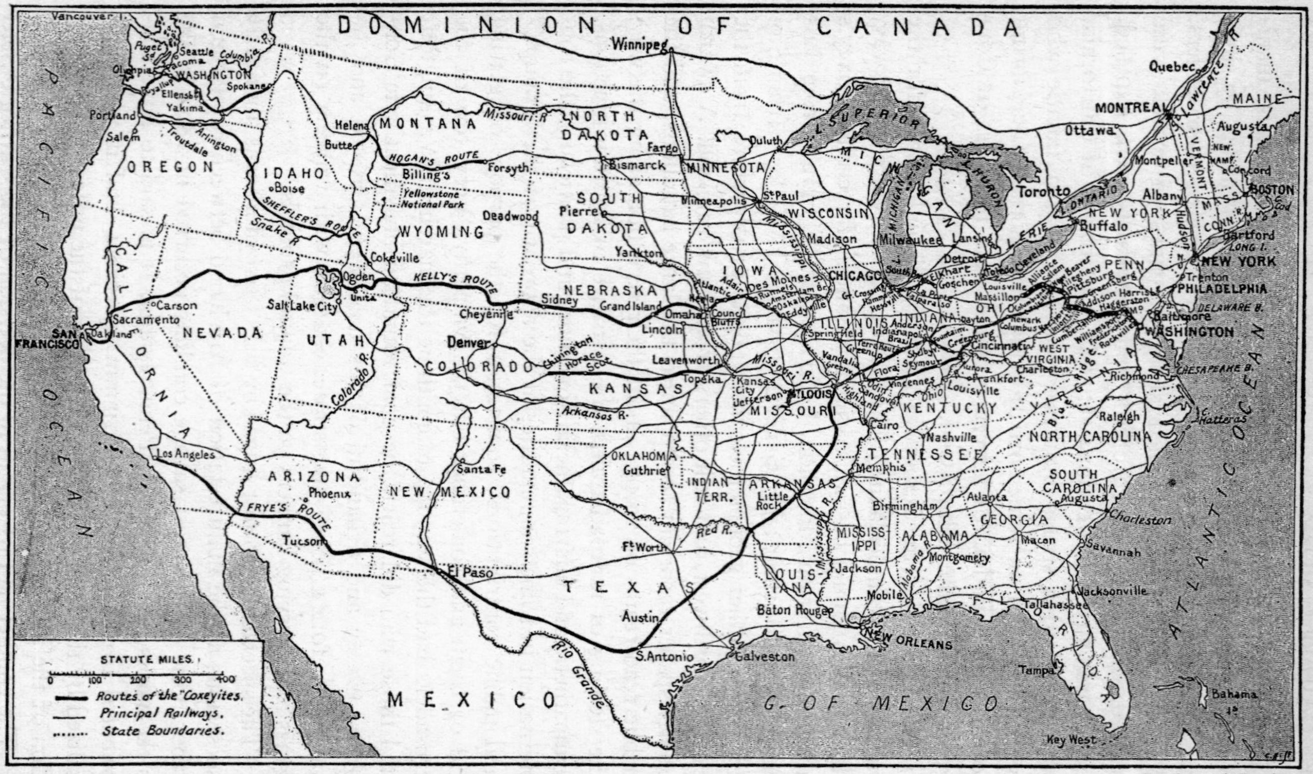

Review of Reviews

Company to cut wages and in its refusal to negotiate with the Amalgamated Association of Iron and Steel Workers. A congressional committee which investigated the affair concluded that if Henry Clay Frick, who wielded the managing authority of the Carnegie Company, had shown a disposition to deal with the Amalgamated Association, the trouble would have been avoided. Instead, the entire force was locked out. What infuriated the workmen was the effort of Frick to enlist the services of Pinkerton detectives in order to employ "scabs" to take the places of the locked-out workmen. A battle between the Pinkertons and the steel workers resulted in loss of life on both sides and the calling out of the militia. Although juries refused to convict the men indicted for murder, the Amalgamated Association sustained such an overwhelming defeat that the cause of unionism in the steel industry was set back for years.

A more serious conflict occurred in Chicago two years later, in 1894, and, coming at the time of Coxey's army, alarmed the country as it has seldom been alarmed. Conservatives feared that anarchy was raising its ugly head, and labor had reason to believe that blind reaction threatened to crush out all its efforts to contend for what it conceived to be its rights. To the student of history this labor war furnishes a striking example of how contemporary opinion with reference to events can be reversed by the verdict of another generation. For more than a generation, however, the Pullman strike lingered in the social memory, and the men who played the principal parts in it received misplaced praise and condemnation.

For the second time in the history of the country federal troops were called out to quell violence in an industrial dispute; but Cleveland, unlike Hayes, did not wait for a request from the state authorities but on his own initiative took action that brought sharp reproof from the governor of Illinois. Cleveland acted with his usual vigor and courage and received the approval and plaudits of the country, but the verdict of history is that the President was grossly misinformed by certain individuals and badly advised by his Attorney-General. The hero who emerges after years of research and reflection is Governor John P. Altgeld, whose coura-

geous pardoning of the "anarchists" of the Haymarket affair
made him a target for as devastating an attack as any individual
in America has ever endured. Under the leadership of the Chicago
newspapers, Altgeld's honesty, courage, and humanitarianism were
buried under a barrage of propaganda, misrepresentation, and
falsehood almost unparalleled. The man who rightfully should
have borne the brunt of indignation, George M. Pullman, at the
time escaped almost unscathed.

The town of Pullman, just south of Chicago, founded in 1880
as the site of the Pullman Palace Car Company, was advertised
as a model town, but even such a defender of property rights as
Mark Hanna made remarks about it that were unprintable. In
this city of factories, parks, and homes, the Pullman Company
was both landlord and employer for more than five thousand workers who manufactured and repaired cars that ran on the rails of
three-fourths of the railroad mileage of the country. The depression in the winter of 1893-94 furnished the pretext for the Pullman Company to cut wages on an average of 35 to 40 per cent,
notwithstanding the fact that there was no reduction in the salaries
of officers, managers, and superintendents, and no reductions in
rents. The company continued to pay high dividends on an exaggerated capitalization.

Competent investigators found that not only did George M.
Pullman have the hard-bitten nineteenth-century attitude of the
self-made man toward labor unions, but also that his company
ground its employees down to the very margin of subsistence.
After the company had deducted rents on its own houses, some
of the employees received checks that were unbelievably small.
After futile negotiations and threats of a lockout, the Pullman
employees struck in May, 1894.

The opposing forces were the American Railway Union on the
one side and the General Managers' Association on the other. The
railroads entering Chicago had previously organized themselves
into the General Managers' Association, and this organization
immediately prepared to do battle in behalf of the Pullman Company. In June, 1893, the American Railway Union had been organized, with Eugene V. Debs as president. This was an organi-

zation of the "industrial" type, whose goal was to bring within its fold all railroad employees of the country. It proved its efficiency by winning a surprise strike on the Great Northern Railway in the spring of 1894. The Pullman employees were members of the A.R.U. and appealed to the organization for a sympathetic strike. When the A.R.U. responded by ordering a boycott of Pullman cars, Debs took charge.

The strikers were anxious to avert violence and destruction of property, but, as events fell out, Chicago was highly inflammable. Its population was drawn from many countries and from all corners of the United States—some of them had been stranded there after the World's Columbian Exposition of 1893. The Civic Federation of Chicago and other organizations made efforts to bring the Pullman Company to arbitrate, but Pullman was unyielding.

The boycott of Pullman cars was amazingly effective. Not only in Chicago but in several other large cities railroad men refused to couple or haul them. Traffic was at a standstill. In cutting out Pullman cars, however, the mail service was crippled, and the federal government took a hand. The railroad strikes of 1877 had shown that federal troops were far more effective in quelling strikes than were the militia. Regulars were better disciplined and more impersonal, whereas in some instances the militia men showed sympathy with the strikers.

When President Cleveland learned of the obstruction of the mails, the serious tie-up of freight service, and acts of violence, which the newspapers erroneously attributed exclusively to the strikers, he acted on the advice of his Attorney-General, Richard Olney of Massachusetts.

Cleveland's brilliant biographer, Allan Nevins, is unsparing in criticism of Olney, whose long career as a railroad attorney, he says, necessarily affected his attitude toward the Chicago situation. Olney's solution was to obtain an injunction forbidding attempts to interfere with the mails; and then, if the injunction was not obeyed, to employ federal troops. To accomplish his purpose, on the advice of the General Managers' Association he appointed a railroad attorney as special counsel to the federal attorney in Chicago, who, acting under Olney's instructions, secured a sweeping injunction against Debs and his men. Then, prompted by misleading dispatches from a federal marshal supported by federal judges, federal troops were ordered to the city.

The presence of troops irritated the strikers, but subsequent investigations proved that the violence that followed was the work of hoodlums and deputies paid by the General Managers' Association, with strikers taking little part. A reign of terror ensued, with the usual rumors in such situations striking terror in the hearts of both innocent and guilty. Debs and six others were convicted of contempt of court for violating the injunction. They later served prison terms, only to be released in the closing weeks of 1895 to receive one of the most remarkable demonstrations in the history of Chicago.

During the excitement Governor Altgeld wired Cleveland that the facts in the situation had not been correctly presented to him and that he had violated a fundamental principle of constitutional government by sending federal troops without consulting the governor of the state. This protest was unheard in the hubbub raised by the press, which ignored the issue and cried "anarchy." Cleveland's reply also ignored the issue, but struck a responsive chord in the public.

The significance of the Pullman strike is not found in the surrender of the strikers to superior force and to an unsympathetic public; it is found in the unprecedented use of the injunction and the sweeping and far-reaching character of the court order. It opened the door for the use of the injunction as a most effective instrument for breaking strikes. In upholding the legality of the injunction and the conviction of Debs for contempt of court, the Supreme Court in a unanimous decision interpreted the Interstate Commerce Act and the Sherman Anti-Trust Act in such a way as to make it possible by court order to prevent strikes, picketing, and boycotting.

After the termination of the strike, Cleveland appointed a commission of investigation. The commission condemned the Pullman Company and the General Managers' Association and exonerated the American Railway Union from the charge of provoking vio-

Harper's Weekly, 1894

THE GREAT RAILWAY STRIKES

The first meat train leaving the Chicago stockyards under escort of United States Cavalry, July 10, 1894

lence; but its recommendation for compulsory arbitration of disputes between employers and employees was almost unnoticed. The Pullman strike was not forgotten in the presidential campaign of 1896, however, and it was turned to good use by Republican campaign managers in their efforts to pin the stigma of anarchism on Bryan, whose kindly and benevolent face was made to appear a mask for "Altgeldism," anarchism, and repudiation.

In the eyes of social reformers like Jane Addams the "Debs rebellion" revealed the distinct cleavage in society; but while the savage conflict disturbed the complacency of political economists and public leaders, it did not shake their faith in the essential soundness of the structure of a society that had grown up within the short span of a few years. Debs was branded by them as a "menace"; and some of them attributed his infamous rôle and that of other labor leaders to the heavy immigration which brought with it lawless hordes who were incapable of understanding and appreciating American institutions. They deplored the agitation against big business; they deprecated any infringement by the government on the domain of private industry and private property; and they looked upon the trusts as a natural and desirable evolution.

However, the effect of a generation of efforts to extend and improve the public school system, and the influence of universities under the leadership of great educators—like Charles W. Eliot of Harvard, for example—who gave free reign to the spirit of research and inquiry, showed itself in the rise of leaders of advanced thought with respect to social and economic problems.

For example, Professor Richard T. Ely, director of the School of Economics, Political Science, and History of the University of Wisconsin, and author of a little book, *French and German Socialism,* contributed an article to the *Forum* for October, 1894, shortly after the collapse of the Pullman strike, which brought an investigation of his teaching by a committee of the Board of Regents. Although the professor was cleared of charges of teaching socialism and anarchism, newspaper editors expressed the opinion that men who taught socialism had no place on the faculties of state universities. Conservatives maintained that states could not sanction propaganda "directed against the political and social principles embodied in the Constitution." In his magazine article Ely weighed the arguments for and against socialism, but he also delivered himself of the opinion that "Socialism is indeed a philosophy of society supported by many very able men. I have held and still hold that the study of socialism is most useful." Ely's exoneration, written by Senator Vilas in words now on a bronze tablet in Bascom Hall, furnishes another example to successive generations of students, of how contemporary opinions are nullified by time and intelligence.

The breaking down of pioneer individualism reacted on the minds of men who wrote more or less popular books which laid bare the injustices of the social order, and suggested remedies. Among the most popular books were Henry George's *Progress and Poverty*, first published in 1879, and Edward Bellamy's *Looking Backward*, first published in 1888.

Henry George, "the prophet of San Francisco," had drained the dregs of poverty. It was not only the pleasing style that made his book a "best seller," but also the righteous fervor of its exposition of the reasons for increasing poverty in a country rich beyond parallel in resources and accumulating wealth. The president of the newly founded American Economic Association would not insult his readers by discussing George's remedy—the single tax, a project "steeped in infamy." Notwithstanding this pontifical pronunciamento, *Progress and Poverty* was speedily translated into a dozen languages.

In *Looking Backward* Bellamy set forth utopian socialism with such charm and conviction that the sales of the book speedily mounted to a million copies. His disciples organized Bellamy Clubs which accepted the book as almost inspired. In retrospect from the year 2000 A.D., Bellamy explained how the utopian state had evolved from huge monopolies built up on the process of manufacturing by machinery: how small enterprises had been stifled by steam and electricity. In Bellamy's state the stagecoach had forever passed away, and its citizens were unable to understand how the people of the closing decades of the nineteenth century could tolerate the wastefulness of the "profits system." They

asked how there "could . . . be a more conclusive demonstration
of the imbecility of the system of private enterprise as a method
for enriching a nation than the fact, that in an age of such general
poverty and want of everything, capitalists had to throttle one
another . . . to invest their capital, and workmen rioted and
burned because they could find no work to do?" In other words,
Bellamy attempted to show how pioneer individualism made possible the competitive system, which in turn brought monopolies
that stifled competition, and this in turn was followed by the socialist state.

Thorstein Veblen's biting attack on business in his *Theory of
the Leisure Class* was not published until 1899, but already Bellamy had pictured a form of society in which no leisure class of
property existed. And in 1894 Henry Demarest Lloyd, a former
editor of the *Chicago Tribune*, in *Wealth against Commonwealth*
had marshaled a whole army of facts to reveal in all its nakedness
the iniquities of the Standard Oil Company and its brother monopolies in throttling free enterprise and in bribing legislatures and
Congress. Of good family and wealth, Lloyd early enlisted in the
cause of municipal reform, took part in overthrowing the in-
iquitous Tweed ring in New York, and devoted his time to writing books and articles on social and economic questions. He
espoused the cause of workingmen. At the time of the strike of
the coal miners in Spring Valley, Illinois, in 1888, he characterized
the contracts which the miners were forced to sign as "slavery in
yearly installments." "Where the self-interest of society is made
the standard," he said, "the lowest must rise up to the average. The
one pulls down, the other up. . . . Bad kings make bad reigns,
but monarchy is bad because it is arbitrary power, and that,
whether it be political or industrial, makes even good men bad."

In a terrific chapter on "The Old Self-Interest" he wrote : "What
we call cheapness shows itself to be unnatural fortunes for a very
few, monstrous luxury for them and proportionate deprivation
for the people, judges debauched, trustees dishonored, Congress
and State legislatures insulted and defied, when not seduced, multitudes of honest men ruined and driven to despair, the common
carrier made a mere instrument for the creation of a new baronage,

an example set to hundreds of would-be commercial Caesars, to repeat this rapine in other industries and call it 'business,' a process set up in operation all over the United States for the progressive extinction of the independence of the laboring men, and all business men except the very rich, and their reduction to a state of vassalage to lords or squires in each department of trade and industry."

To Populists and others who read the works of Henry George, Edward Bellamy, and Henry Demarest Lloyd, the words of Ignatius Donnelly at the Populist convention of 1892 rang true when he predicted an alliance between the major parties to protect the interests which the Populists loathed. In 1896 the stage was set for an "educational campaign" such as the country had never before witnessed. It was a struggle in which the West and the South, in alliance with labor, asserted their rights against the money power of the East. Already, prominent Democrats and Republicans in the West had served notice that with them loyalty to party was secondary to what they conceived to be the interests of their sections.

CHAPTER XIII

THE BATTLE OF THE STANDARDS

ONE OF THE MANY REMARKABLE FEATURES OF THE PRESIDENTIAL campaign of 1896 is the fact that after depending for many years on third parties—Grangers, Greenbackers, and Populists—western ideals captured a major political party. In the South the Populists had been "boring from within" the Democratic party, and in several states Populism and Democracy were synonymous; in the campaign of 1892 the Democrats in six western states named no electoral ticket and indorsed the Populist candidates; but in 1896 not only did Populist ideals capture the Democratic national convention but the Populist convention indorsed the Democratic candidate for the Presidency.

That the Democratic candidate was a Nebraskan, an exuberant Westerner in whom the American spirit found eloquent expression, is significant. Under his leadership the Populistic West girded itself for a supreme struggle against the conservative East. William Jennings Bryan's brilliant talents as a speaker and debater had already attracted the attention of his colleagues in the House of Representatives when, in his zeal for the free coinage of silver, he joined with many Democrats in opposing the repeal of the Sherman Silver Purchase Act in the special session called by Cleveland in 1893. Under his magnetic leadership reformers in all parties enlisted for a battle in behalf of those measures they deemed essential to bring prosperity to the great middle class, the "yeomanry of the nation." His picture hung prominently in the parlors of mortgaged homesteads whose owners believed that the single gold standard spelled ruin for them.

The election of 1896 hinged on the currency question. Voters wore either "silver bugs" or "gold bugs" on the lapels of their coats to advertise their preferences for the rival candidates. "Sixteen to one" was an inspiration to some and a synonym for ruin to others. The country was flooded with literature expounding the principles of monetary policy, and neighbors gathered in homes to listen to "experts" discourse on the merits of the money planks of the respective platforms. This battle of the standards has gone down in history as an "educational campaign." It was a class struggle, with the debtors in the rural West and South arrayed against the East. The great mass of the advocates of the free and unlimited coinage of silver were the farmer debtor class and men whose sympathies were with this class. They ascribed the fall in the prices of agricultural products to the scarcity of gold and to the cornering of that commodity by the financiers of the East. Allied with this "honest" debtor class were those who wanted cheap money and an abundance of it, and the silver mine owners in the West who expected a rise in the market value of silver with the triumph of free coinage.

There was a school of economists who argued that with the limited supply of gold the price of that metal would steadily increase and prices of other commodities would correspondingly decrease. They could see no other solution of the problem than the establishment of a standard of value in the form of a combination of metals. The great objection to this, however, was the large output of silver. For this reason some economists favored an international agreement by which the production of silver would be limited and the price of the metal stabilized.

In 1894 W. H. Harvey published a book entitled *Coin's Financial School* and dedicated it "to those trying to locate the seat of the disease that threatens the life of the nation." According to Harvey's admirers, the book was "to the people of the present day what Tom Paine's *Common Sense* was to the Colonies" in that "it mercilessly scourges the money changers in the Temple of the Republic."

The opening statements of the first chapter of this book in paper covers which sold for twenty-five cents reminded the reader of the distracted state of the country, with very few marketable things above the cost of production, with tens of thousands out of employment, with the gold reserve sinking, with huge debts hanging over the country, with taxes assuming the importance of a mortgage, with hungry and half-starved men marching toward Washington, with riots and strikes prevailing throughout the land, and with Wall Street looking in vain for an excuse to account for the failure of prosperity to return since the repeal of the Silver Purchase Act.

In *Coin's Financial School* a fictitious young financier living in Chicago sought to instruct the nation in the principles of money. In reply to questions put in the mouths of merchants, bankers, journalists, railroad magnates, economists, and others, whose real names were given, Coin discoursed on the iniquity of the "crime of '73," the ratio between gold and silver, and the "fallacy" of gold monometallism. The book was profusely illustrated with graphs, charts, statistics, and pictures. The depressed price of farm products was illustrated by a farmer dining in a first-class Chicago restaurant. Resting on the floor beside him were sacks containing four bushels of corn and a like amount of wheat, which represented what it cost the farmer to order a meal. Another drawing contrasted the prosperous condition of the workingman under bimetallism in 1872 with his condition of poverty in 1894 after the repeal of the Silver Purchase Act. Still another picture represented debts in the form of a sponge soaking up the money of the West.

The heavy sales of *Coin's Financial School* provoked replies from leading newspapers and called forth similar popular publications to counteract its undeniably strong influence. For example, in 1894 the Sound Currency Committee of the Reform Club began to publish a semi-monthly pamphlet entitled *Sound Currency*, each number of which contained a special discussion of some "sound currency question." The issue for May 1, 1895, was dignified by an article by Horace White, a recognized student of money and banking. The article was entitled "Coin's Financial Fool" and attacked Coin's reasoning and conclusions. After examining the structure of the book, White reached the following conclusion: "The question may be asked how the book came to have so much popularity and such large circulation. The answer is easy —it is due to the pictures. These, it must be admitted, are very

SECOND EDITION.   100 THOUSAND

A Book that will create a profound impression throughout the United States.   **25 Cents.**

—Chicago Times.

It mercilessly scourges the money changers in the Temple of the Republic.

—New York Recorder.

This book is to the people of the present day, what Tom Payne's Common Sense was to the Colonies.

—Chicago Searchlight.

PUBLISHERS :

COIN PUBLISHING COMPANY,

115 MONROE STREET,

CHICAGO.

COIN'S FINANCIAL SERIES, Issued Quarterly. Price, $1.00 per Year. Vol. 1. No. 3, June, 1894

Entered at the Postoffice, Chicago, as second-class mail matter.

FOR SALE BY ALL NEWSDEALERS.

COIN'S FINANCIAL SCHOOL—OUTSIDE COVER

clever, although of unequal merit. Without them not five hundred copies of such a senseless book could have been sold or given away. But what a gloomy fate would be ours if the destiny of the Republic lay in the hands of any skillful designer of comic almanacs!"

The problem that faced the leaders in 1896 was how to keep the eastern and western wings of the Democratic and Republican parties together, in view of the strength of the free silver elements in the West and the opposition to them in the East. It was fortunate for the Republican party that it had in the person of Marcus A. Hanna of Ohio one of the ablest strategists in the long list of able Republican field marshals. Hanna was a typical business man who believed that the salvation of the country depended on the supremacy of the Republican party. In the eighties he became a power in Ohio politics, not least in his home city of Cleveland. His vast business interests and ingratiating personality attracted a wide personal acquaintance. This remarkable man formed a strong personal attachment to William McKinley.

In 1896 William McKinley was well known as the author of the tariff of 1890, the highest protective tariff down to that time. In the Democratic landslide of 1890, McKinley was defeated for reelection to Congress; but in 1891 he was elected governor of Ohio and two years later was triumphantly reelected. His personal character was above reproach, but he was a man of no pronounced or independent convictions. Speaker Cannon once said of President McKinley that he kept his ear so close to the ground that it got full of grasshoppers; and Theodore Roosevelt, his running mate in 1900, said that he "had no more backbone than a chocolate éclair."

During McKinley's tenure as governor of Ohio, corporations and public utility companies took heavy toll on the public, with no visible signs of disapproval from the chief executive. In 1893 McKinley became bankrupt through no fault of his own: he had indorsed some paper for a man who failed in business. Through Hanna's efforts a number of men prominent in big business, including Andrew Carnegie and Henry C. Frick, steel magnates, contributed an amount sufficient to liquidate the governor's debts.

Hanna had two things very dear to his heart. He wanted to make McKinley President of the United States and himself a United States Senator—and he accomplished both. In 1895 Hanna retired from business in order to devote his time to the first objective. He rented a house in Thomasville, Georgia, where McKinley as his house guest made the acquaintance of, and consulted with, prominent Republican politicians. In the process of grooming his friend for the presidential race, Hanna put the soft pedal on the money question and played him up as a protectionist and the "advance agent of prosperity." He also kept him from committing himself publicly on vital issues. This strategy was devised in order to avoid antagonizing either the eastern or the western wing of the Republican party, for McKinley's record on the currency was vulnerable. In 1878 he had voted for the free coinage of silver and for the Bland-Allison Act; in 1890 he had favored the Sherman Silver Purchase Act; and in 1893, by his fortunate absence from Congress, he had escaped going on record on the repeal of the Silver Purchase Act.

When the Republican national convention assembled at St. Louis on June 15, 1896, Hanna's pre-convention campaign speedily brought results. McKinley's nomination was a foregone conclusion; but Hanna had manipulated affairs to obtain his nomination with the least possible friction over the money plank. McKinley had already committed himself to a gold standard plank before the convention met; but Hanna saw the advantage of playing his hand in such a way that the "gold bugs" would think they had forced it. In other words, he wished to leave the impression that he had made a concession to them. McKinley was nominated on the first ballot, and Hanna was made chairman of the national committee. The platform pledged the party to maintain the existing gold standard until an international agreement with the leading commercial nations of the world should provide for the free and unlimited coinage of silver.

The Silver Republicans under the leadership of Henry M. Teller of Colorado presented a substitute plank demanding the free and unlimited coinage of silver at the ratio of 16 to 1, but it was rejected by an overwhelming vote. This precipitated a bolt by the Silverites, led by Teller, Dubois of Idaho, Pettigrew of South Dakota, and Cannon of Utah. This action by the Republican convention consolidated the advocates of free coinage in the Democratic party, and, as it proved, made the election turn upon the money question.

In the meantime the agitation of Silverites like William J. Bryan of Nebraska, Richard P. Bland of Missouri, Horace Boies of Iowa, and John W. Daniel of Virginia had played up Cleveland's alleged treachery and had marshaled their forces in a solid phalanx. But the Democrats lacked a magnetic leader. The old leaders were entirely discredited. When the delegates to the Democratic national convention assembled at Chicago on July 12, it was noticeable that there was a large number among them who were about to be initiated into the devious ways of political conventions. "Hayseeds," some of the spectators called them. In the extraordinary excitement and hubbub, there was an unusual display of oratory. Tillman of South Carolina aspired to the nomination for the Presidency, but he spoiled whatever chances he may have had by pacing the platform like an enraged bull. So agitated was he in denouncing Cleveland and all his works that portions of his speech were unintelligible. Governor Altgeld, Cleveland's archenemy, was there to render heroic service to the silver cause.

The old-line Democrats were in control of the National Committee, and they intended to have David B. Hill elected temporary chairman of the convention. Hill was far from friendly to Cleveland; and although he was not in the good graces of the Populistic element in the Democrat party, he did not represent the extreme eastern opposition to it. The Free Silverites were in no mood for compromise, however, and carried their fight to the convention. By a heavy majority they elected their candidate for the temporary chairmanship, John W. Daniel, an ardent Free Silverite. The convention then overruled the National Committee by seating contesting silver delegates, among them being the delegation from Nebraska, of which Bryan was a member. As it turned out, by making the eloquent Nebraskan a member of the convention the way was paved for his brilliant speech which won for him the nomination for the Presidency.

Bryan had been present as a newspaper correspondent at the
Republican national convention and had been aroused by the victory of the "gold bugs." At the Democratic convention he was
delegated to answer the speeches of the gold delegates, who could
not be heard in the tumult raised by the restless and resentful
crowd; his effort has been remembered as one of the most remarkable speeches of all time. When he took the platform, there was
such a stillness that his very first words penetrated to the most
distant parts of the great Coliseum. It was the speech not of a
demagogue but of a young, exuberant Westerner, supremely confident in himself and in the righteousness of his cause. Under the
spell of the moment, Bryan rose to the heights of oratory; but his
effort was not extemporaneous, as many believed at the time. For
years he had delivered before popular audiences the substance of
this epoch-making speech, and for weeks he had rehearsed it for
the occasion he had hoped for. It was not only that the address
expressed the feeling of a great assembly—there were some fifteen
thousand people in the Coliseum—but the thirty-six-year-old
speaker possessed a voice of singular resonance and carrying
power. He was already known as "the silver-tongued orator of
the Platte."

Compared with the logical speech of Senator Hill which preceded it, Bryan's "Cross of Gold" oration was lacking in analytical power; it was an emotional appeal in behalf of the masses that
was far more effective in routing the gold advocates than any
dextrous marshaling of facts and statistics would have been.
Beginning with the assertion that "the humblest citizen in all the
land, when clad in the armor of a righteous cause, is stronger
than all the whole hosts of error they can bring," he pictured the
Silverites as crusaders as inspired as were those who followed Peter
the Hermit.

In reply to the charge of eastern delegates that the free silver
advocates would disturb their business interests, Bryan formulated a new definition of a business man. "The man who is employed for wages is as much a business man as his employer. The
attorney in a country town is as much a business man as the
corporation counsel in a great metropolis. The merchant at the

crossroads store is as much a business man as the merchant of New York. The farmer . . . is as much a business man as the man who goes upon the Board of Trade and bets upon the price of grain. The miners . . . are as much business men as the few financial magnates who in a back room corner the money of the world." He eulogized the pioneers "away out there" as deserving of the consideration of those who lived on the Atlantic coast. The country needed an Andrew Jackson to stand against the encroachments of aggrandized wealth, he said.

Turning to opponents who criticized those who criticized the Supreme Court, Bryan called attention to the dissenting opinions of the court. He denied that the income tax was unconstitutional. "It did not become unconstitutional until one judge changed his mind, and we cannot be expected to know when a judge will change his mind." Defending the proposal to make the money issue paramount to the tariff, he said: "If protection has slain its thousands the gold standard has slain its tens of thousands." Paying his respects to the Republican nominee, William McKinley, he asserted that the man who used to boast that he looked like Napoleon shuddered at the thought that he was nominated on the anniversary of the Battle of Waterloo.

There are two ideas of government. There are those who believe that if you just legislate to make the well-to-do prosperous their prosperity will leak through on those below. The Democratic idea has been that if you legislate to make the masses prosperous their prosperity will find its way up and through every class and rest upon it.

In a peroration that bade defiance to the defenders of the gold standard, Bryan concluded as follows: "You shall not press down upon the brow of labor this crown of thorns. You shall not crucify mankind upon a cross of gold."

Then followed a scene such as no political convention has ever witnessed. Pandemonium broke loose. Bryan was carried on the shoulders of members of the frenzied Nebraska delegation. When order was restored, the plank demanding "the free and unlimited coinage of silver at the present legal ratio of 16 to 1, without waiting for the aid or consent of any other nation" was adopted, and the convention adjourned for the day. Bryan could probably have been nominated that very day, but he is reported to have said: "If my boom will not last until tomorrow, it certainly would wilt before election day."

Up to the time Bryan delivered his speech, the names most prominently mentioned for the presidential nomination were Horace Boies, Richard P. Bland, and Henry M. Teller, the last of whom had bolted the Republican party. Bland led on the first three ballots, but Bryan made steady gains until he was nominated on the fifth. The gold delegates, some two hundred in number and mostly from the East, refused to vote for any candidate to run on the "radical" platform, thus foreshadowing the bolt of the Gold Democrats, just as the Silver Republicans had turned their backs on their party.

By adopting a free silver plank, the Democratic party repudiated a Democratic administration; but, taken as a whole, the entire platform was a sweeping indictment of Cleveland. It condemned his policy of selling bonds to replenish the gold reserve; it denounced his dispatch of federal troops to Chicago at the time of the Pullman strike; it expressed disapproval of "government by injunction"; it used plain language in referring to the Supreme Court. All in all, the Democratic convention stole the Populist planks and incorporated them into the platform, and it nominated a candidate whose habitat was the domain of Populism. Populism from the lips of the "boy orator of the Platte" was more terrifying to Republicans than any volume of oratory from Populist spellbinders.

The nomination of Bryan on a Populist platform was the signal for the fusion of Democrats, Populists, and Silver Republicans in several western states; but the triumph of fusion was effected at the Populist national convention which convened at St. Louis on July 22. Here the party met the fate of all third-party movements—the party which had made such an auspicious beginning as the instrument of agrarian reform. The delegates to the convention of 1896 were divided between those who, despite the metamorphosis of the Democrats into Populists, desired to "keep to the middle of the road" by nominating an independent ticket, and those who believed that the cause of Populism could triumph only by fusing with the Democrats. In other words, by indorsing the Democratic ticket, the Populist party would lose its identity; by naming a separate ticket, the silver forces would be divided, with the advantage swinging toward the Republicans.

The main strength of the Mid-Road Populists was in certain states in the Northwest and especially in the South. The election of Tillman to the governorship of South Carolina in 1890 was a symptom of the revolt of the small farmers in the back country against the aristocratic element, but Tillman and his followers hated the lowly Negroes as cordially as they hated the aristocratic whites. But in certain states, like North Carolina, for example, where the Negroes were not in the majority as they were in the neighboring state, Populism rode on a rising wave of indignation against the old oligarchy in which Negroes and whites enlisted in a common cause. So bitter was the feeling between the Populists, who represented the masses, and the Democrats, who represented the classes, that elections assumed the character of guerilla warfare in which men shot to kill. Thomas E. Watson's campaigns in Georgia, for example, were bloody battles. Negro and white delegates from the South pleaded with the Populist national convention not to take action that would place them at the mercy of the old-line Democrats.

The election of Marion Butler of North Carolina as temporary chairman and of William V. Allen of Kansas as permanent chairman was a victory for fusion and a triumph for the delegates who believed that the Populists could not afford to take any action that would work to the advantage of the "money power." As a concession to the Mid-Roaders, however, the convention reversed the usual order of procedure by nominating Watson for the Vice-Presidency before indorsing Bryan. In that way the Populists maintained a shadow of independence and avoided indorsing the Democratic vice-presidential candidate, Arthur Sewall of Maine, who was the president of a bank, a wealthy employer of labor, and a director in several corporations. But the outcome of the convention was a disappointment to many Populists who regarded free silver as only one of many reforms for which they had contended. The combined ticket was called in derision "Popocratic."

The gold delegates to the Democratic convention, some of whom had been unseated in favor of silver delegates, were infuriated at the triumph of Populism, and even before the convention adjourned there were threats of bolting. Some leading Democrats openly declared that they would support McKinley; but in the West, where McKinley and "McKinleyism" were unpopular, there was a demand for an independent Gold Democratic ticket. After preliminary conferences extending over several weeks, Gold Democrats assembled in convention at Indianapolis on September 2 and nominated John M. Palmer of Illinois for the Presidency and Simon B. Buckner of Kentucky for the Vice-Presidency on a platform indorsing the Cleveland administration and the gold standard. A few of the leading Democratic newspapers supported Palmer, but the great majority flew the McKinley banner. The most the Gold Democrats could hope for was to divert enough votes from Bryan to elect McKinley.

The Silver Republicans, or the National Silver party, as they were officially designated, were in convention at St. Louis at the same time the Populists were in session, but there seems to have been little cooperation between the two bodies. The former convention indorsed Bryan and Sewall.

The fusion of the Democratic and Populist parties was both an advantage and a disadvantage to the Republicans. The Republicans had expected that the paramount issue of the campaign would be the tariff, but the nomination of Bryan on a free silver platform upset their plans. By repudiating Cleveland and all his works, the Democrats relieved themselves of the disagreeable duty of defending the party in power, which the Republicans had expected to blame for the hard times and to offer a Republican protective tariff as a cure-all. But the Bryanites were even more vehement than the Republicans in denouncing Cleveland, and left the Republicans no alternative but to meet the free silver issue squarely. The Republicans were fortunate in attracting to their support low tariff men like Carl Schurz, who abhorred McKinleyism but feared Bryan's free silver "heresy" even more. They were "sound money" men first of all, and McKinley supporters not from choice but from necessity. In the early weeks of the campaign, however, the bolt of the Silver Republicans appeared to be more serious than that of the Gold Democrats.

The association of the Bryan Democracy with Populism and "Altgeldism" gave the Republicans the opportunity to launch a campaign of vituperation and abuse almost unparalleled. Mark Hanna, McKinley's campaign manager, with money contributed by corporations (the Standard Oil Company contributed $250,-000), launched a campaign in which the press and pulpit joined to caricature Bryan as an apostle of "repudiation," "anarchy," and "atheism." He was a "lunatic," "a mouthy, slobbering demagogue, whose patriotism is all in his jawbone," and his platform was "made in hell." When he appeared at New Haven, Yale students showed their disapproval by attempting to disturb the meeting. When Bryan was able to make himself heard, he retorted by saying that he had been so used to talking to young men who had earned their own living that he hardly knew what language to use to address himself to those who desired to be known not as creators of wealth but as distributors of wealth which somebody else had created. "I am not speaking now to the sons who are sent to college on the proceeds of ill-gotten gains," he said.

Bryan's personal part in the campaign was unprecedented. He was untiring in his efforts; every place of importance in doubtful states was visited. He traveled about eighteen thousand miles. His speeches were entirely devoid of personalities. The immense throngs that gathered to hear the evangelistic candidate alarmed the Republicans; and it appears that if the election had been held in August, Bryan would have been elected.

However, time played into the hands of the forces combined against him. All the resources of the financial interests were brought into action through the efforts of Chairman Hanna and Cornelius N. Bliss, the treasurer of the Republican National Committee. James J. Hill assisted Hanna in raising money in Wall Street. Bryan's heaviest contributors were the silver mine owners, but their resources were meager against the financial power of bankers, industrialists, and railroad magnates. Certain doubtful states in the West, like Iowa, were literally shingled over with money. In Nebraska, for example, Democrats admitted that they were paid twenty-five dollars a day for wearing McKinley buttons. Debtors seeking renewals of loans were told that if Bryan was elected, all notes would have to be paid when due; and notices were posted on factory doors that unless McKinley was elected, factories would remain closed. The press reported spectacular incidents where creditors known to favor free silver were paid large sums in silver dollars as a foretaste of what would happen if Bryan triumphed. Farmers, laborers, merchants, teachers, and others would be paid in "fifty-cent dollars"; and insurance companies' mortgagees would pay in depreciated silver dollars according to the 16 to 1 ratio—so it was said.

Lurid cartoons pictured the shade of Abraham Lincoln warning Bryan against leading an army bearing banners of repudiation, anarchy, socialism, confiscation, and riot to effect national destruction. Bryan, the assassin, holding the dagger of repudiation in one hand and in the other a poster reading "Down with the courts" stood beside the dead body of the credit of the United States in the form of a fair lady. The sinister figure of anarchy with the features of Altgeld lurked behind the smiling Bryan. Another cartoon suggested a motto for the fifty-cent dollar: "In God we trust. With Bryan we bust."

A Republican poster which was displayed from coast to coast represented Bryan standing in front of the United States Mint and McKinley standing in the foreground of factories with smoking chimneys, with the latter saying to his audience: "I do not know what you think about it, but I believe it is a good deal better to open the mills of the United States to the labor of America than to open up the mints of the United States to the silver of the world." Never before had posters and cartoons figured so prominently in a political campaign. In almost every town farmers driving up "Main Street" passed under two American flags, each one of which had sewed on to it a "McKinley and Hobart" or a "Bryan and Sewall" banner.

The Democrats retorted in kind to the Mark Hanna campaign. McKinley was said to be the puppet of Mark Hanna; and a Re-

REPUBLICAN POSTER USED TO ILLUSTRATE A SENTIMENT IN ONE OF
MCKINLEY'S SPEECHES

publican "Hurrah for McKinley!" was often echoed by a Democratic "Hurrah for Mark Hanna!" Homer Davenport's cartoons in the *New York Journal* gave the cue to cartoonists on the staffs of Democratic papers. Hanna was a coarse figure dressed in a suit of clothes figured with dollar signs. Sitting beside a picture of Lincoln on which was inscribed his famous statement about not being able to fool all of the people all of the time, Hanna remarks: "He didn't know his business."

McKinley's part in the campaign was dignified and effective. He remained at home to address visiting delegations from all parts of the country from his front porch. The visits of these delegations were carefully arranged. The Republican managers saw to it that no incidents similar to the Burchard affair in the campaign of 1884 would occur. The manuscripts of the spokesmen of the delegations and those of McKinley himself were carefully scrutinized beforehand.

McKinley had hoped to make the tariff the issue and to straddle the money question; but Bryan's tactics would not permit the evasion. He even "carried the war into Africa" by expounding the free silver doctrine in New England, although the Republicans alleged that the "Janus-faced" orator told the western farmers that prices would advance under free silver because the purchasing power of the present dollar was too great, and that he told the eastern workingmen that prices would not advance under free silver. He assured the wage earners, it was alleged, that free coinage would make the silver dollar worth as much as the gold dollar.

In the closing weeks of the campaign the Republican strategists succeeded in converting enough voters to assure McKinley's election by identifying the gold dollar with the "honest dollar." Bryan was honest in advocating free silver—and there was much truth in his arguments—but by playing up "repudiation," "free riots," "Altgeldism," and "anarchism," the Republicans convinced many that his remedy for the ills that beset the country was dishonest. To millions Bryan's remedy seemed sound; but where the Democratic candidate met his Waterloo was in the Middle West. He had to carry this section in order to obtain a majority in the electoral college—and in August it seemed probable that he would succeed—but he could not convince the conservative German, Norwegian, and Swedish voters who remained loyal to their old allegiance. In western states the Republicans skillfully played on the fears of voters that capital would shun them if it became known that their states were the abodes of "wild, long-haired Populists."

Nature herself took a hand in determining the outcome of the election. In August wheat sold on the Chicago Board of Trade for fifty-three cents a bushel—less than the cost of production to most farmers. In October the news of a partial failure of the wheat crop in India sent the Chicago price of wheat up to seventy-five cents and a few days before election up to about ninety-four cents. Bryan's managers quickly perceived the effect of this on the voters, and they declared that the "money power" was putting up the price before election in order to delude the farmers. Bryan had said, however, that under the gold standard the price of wheat could not go up; but there it was at the highest price for some years. The explanation failed to satisfy because, whatever the reason may have been, the fact remained that wheat was doing what Bryan had said was impossible.

Bryan's failure to carry the Middle West gave McKinley a majority of ninety-five in the electoral college, but Bryan polled 6,500,000 popular votes—nearly a million more than had been cast for a successful candidate in previous elections. McKinley's popular majority was about 600,000, but in certain states the vote was very close. In Minnesota, with its large German and Scandinavian population, however, McKinley's plurality was unexpectedly large—62,768. Bryan carried twenty-two states, but outside of the South they were sparsely populated western states. He did not carry the electoral vote of a single northern state east of the Missouri River; and on the Pacific coast, California and Oregon were in the Republican column. The agitation for cheap money was localized in the South and the Far West, including Kansas, Nebraska, and South Dakota.

The campaign of 1896 was "decisive" in the sense that for a generation the currency was a minor issue. The Republican party held undisputed sway until the election of a Democratic House of Representatives in 1910 and the election of Woodrow Wilson with a Democratic majority in both houses in 1912. But prosperity was tardy in returning, despite the psychological effect of the defeat of a party hostile to big business. By 1900, however, the hard times had been largely forgotten.

One favorable development was the discovery of gold fields in South Africa and in the Klondike in Alaska, which increased the

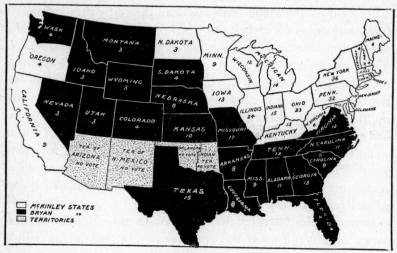

A GEOGRAPHICAL VIEW OF THE ELECTION RESULTS, 1896

output of gold. The shortage of the 1897 wheat crop in Europe and an unusually heavy crop in the United States weighed heavily in the balance. In August, 1897, wheat touched a dollar on the Chicago Board of Trade—the highest price since 1891. Gold commenced to flow into the United States, a precise reversal of the process during the previous six years. The industrial boom that brought the country to new heights of prosperity is the theme of later chapters.

The immediate fruit of the Republican victory was the enactment by Congress, in extraordinary session, of the Dingley Tariff of 1897. This tariff served the country for better or worse until 1909, when the Payne-Aldrich Tariff brought disaster to the Republican party. The Dingley Tariff provided higher duties on certain commodities than were contained in the McKinley Act, and in general rates were leveled up to the schedules of that law. Reciprocity, which had been left out of the Wilson-Gorman Tariff, was restored. As a revenue producer the Dingley Tariff was not a conspicuous success. Despite the "unscientific" character of the law, however, exports of American manufactured products steadily mounted, largely on account of Europe's remarkable economic recovery.

In spite of the victory for the gold standard in a campaign that had pushed the tariff aside in favor of money, the Republicans allowed the fiscal policy of the government to drift. In the Senate the Silver Republicans were strong enough to jeopardize the success of legislation directly in line with what appeared to be the wishes of the voters. It was not until March, 1900, on the eve of another presidential campaign, that Congress passed the Gold Standard Act.

This law increased the amount of the gold reserve from $100,-000,000 to $150,000,000 and set this fund aside for the specific purpose of redeeming United States notes. To relieve the strain on the treasury caused by the endless chain of 1893 and the years immediately following, it was further provided that notes redeemed from the gold reserve should be held in reserve until exchanged for gold. Moreover, the use of the gold reserve to meet a deficit in the treasury was forbidden. Doubts as to the power of the government to borrow money to protect the gold reserve were removed by expressly requiring that such action be taken.

The Gold Standard Act was a compromise. It established the gold standard by making the gold dollar of a certain weight the standard unit of value; but greenbacks, silver certificates, national bank notes, and silver dollars remained in circulation under such conditions as to complicate the gold standard policy.

CHAPTER XIV

FOREIGN AFFAIRS UNDER CLEVELAND AND HARRISON

FOR A PERIOD OF FIFTY YEARS AFTER THE CLOSE OF THE WAR with Mexico the United States remained at peace with the nations of the world. Aside from difficult problems of diplomacy that arose during the Civil War, which were amicably settled within less than ten years after the collapse of the Confederacy, the American people were hardly aware of the existence of a Department of State at Washington. After the ratification of the Thirteenth Amendment, they were free to bend their energies toward the settlement of the country without the disturbing factor of slavery extension.

The navy was allowed to dwindle into insignificance; and the existence of the army was made known not by the presence of uniformed men in various parts of the country but solely through newspaper dispatches about battles and skirmishes with the Indians and the strikes of 1877 and 1894. The regular army had been reduced to less than thirty thousand men, and the militia was more of an ornament than a weapon of defense. The Iowa schoolboy in 1890 who was brought up on the tradition of Patrick Henry, the War of 1812, and the *Monitor* and the *Merrimac* believed in the invincibility of the United States; but the possibility of the country becoming involved in a foreign war was so remote that the veterans of the Civil War who were given places of honor at Fourth of July celebrations seemed to be ghosts of a remote past. China and Japan were far-off lands, whose inhabitants ate rice with chopsticks and made firecrackers for his entertainment on "The Fourth." With a weak power on the southern boundary and a friendly possession of Great Britain to the north, there was not a single black cloud on the diplomatic horizon.

If the Iowa schoolboy was the son of immigrant parents, he was perhaps no more internationally-minded, except as he might have imbibed erroneous ideas about the land from which his parents had emigrated. Immigrants thought of Europe in terms of poverty, class distinctions, and injustice, and of the United States in terms of new opportunities. The children of immigrant parents were bilingual, but rarely were they what the twentieth century was pleased to call "hyphenated citizens." America worked its magic within less than a generation.

It may or may not be significant that in 1889 in the new American navy, in which people were beginning to take pride, there were 4,278 enlisted men of foreign birth, as against 3,668 natives. Of the four hundred sailors in the crew of the *Trenton* at the time of the terrible hurricane in the harbor of Apia, Samoa, all but forty were foreigners, mostly Scandinavians. The admiral reported that in the whole course of his naval experience he had never known a case of more perfect discipline than was exhibited on board the *Trenton.*

As the nineteenth century entered the last decade, the normal expansion of the American people had obliterated the frontier line, and manifest destiny was about to assume a new meaning. The American flag was about to be planted beyond the seas.

During Cleveland's first administration, partly on account of the surplus in the treasury, Congress appropriated money for the construction of ships that became the nucleus of the new navy. During Harrison's administration certain incidents, unimportant in themselves, brought a realization that in spite of protecting oceans the United States might be called to play some part in international affairs. And in 1898 it was proved that long-continued peace had dulled neither the patriotism nor the "fighting edge" of the people. In that year when Congress declared war on Spain, there was a relatively small and fairly well-equipped, though untried, navy, and an army of some twenty-five thousand enlisted men, commanded by officers who had been promoted solely on the basis of seniority and who were enmeshed in red tape such as only military men wind about themselves. The army was in a badly disorganized state and was scattered among posts from coast to coast. After orders for mobilization had been carried out, classmates at West Point renewed acquaintances that had lapsed for years.

The reckless language employed by members of Congress when foreign affairs were under consideration was indicative of provincialism and inexperience. With the exception of the all-important post at London, ministers plenipotentiary and consular officials were appointed to reward them for services to parties rather than to obtain men skilled in the game of diplomacy.

When in 1889 Harrison appointed Blaine Secretary of State, some people were uneasy because they believed him to be a jingo. It is certainly true that his foreign policy was vigorous, but it can hardly be said to have been jingoistic. It so happened that a series of events abroad and at home forced themselves upon the attention of the Department of State during the four years of Harrison's administration.

In Cleveland's first administration Secretary of State Bayard inherited a dispute with Great Britain over the rights claimed by American fishermen in British North American waters. In Arthur's administration Congress had abrogated the clauses pertaining to fishing in the Treaty of Washington of 1871. Early in 1888 Cleveland submitted to the Senate a new treaty with Great Britain, but it failed of ratification because of the opposition from New England Senators. This aroused the indignation of the President, and in August he sent his famous "retaliation message" to Congress in which he recommended immediate legislative action that would "subserve the interests of our people and maintain the high standard and becoming pride of American citizenship." A bill that embodied the President's recommendations passed the House with only four negative votes, but it was defeated in the Senate, at which it was aimed instead of Canada. The upshot of the affair was an arrangement which granted certain concessions to the Americans. In 1910 the Hague Tribunal adjudicated the controversy, chiefly upholding the Canadian contentions.

A more serious dispute between the two governments was concerned with the protection of fur seals in the Bering Sea. In order to prevent deep-sea sealing, which threatened to exterminate the valuable herds of seals, Blaine sought to get an international agreement to regulate seal hunting. Failing in this, and after long-drawn-out negotiations, he persuaded Great Britain to submit the question to arbitration in February, 1892. The court of arbitration rejected every claim advanced by the United States. It was not until 1911, when the threatened extermination of the herds was more serious, that a joint treaty was agreed to by the United States, Great Britain, Japan, and Russia, by which deep-sea sealing was prohibited and the nations interested were conceded the right to take seals on land.

An unpleasant incident that transpired in New Orleans in March, 1891, ruffled the relations between the United States and Italy and revealed the impracticability of the dual system of government in matters pertaining to the presence of immigrants in the United States. A local situation over which the federal government had no control involved the safety of subjects of a foreign government, which could make protests only through the channels of diplomacy. The chief of police in New Orleans was assassinated by Italian criminals. Thousands of citizens, indignant at what they conceived to be a miscarriage of justice, lynched eleven Italian prisoners. The Italian government issued a virtual ultimatum that the perpetrators of the "massacre" be brought to justice. In reply to the assurance of Blaine that the government would use all its power under the Constitution to protect citizens of foreign governments residing in the United States, the Italian government referred to the United States as a country where justice could not be obtained. Blaine had made it clear that the government of the United States was bound by treaty to protect citizens of Italy just as far as it could protect its own citizens. And in reply to the sharp note from Italy he made the equally sharp observation that it was a matter of indifference to him what people in Italy might think of American institutions. He could not change them, much less violate them. The United States had never taken orders from a foreign power, he said, and it did not propose to begin now.

After the Italian premier had mollified his words, it proved relatively easy to adjudicate the controversy. It developed that only three of the victims of the mob were Italian subjects, and the Italian government was entirely satisfied with the payment of an indemnity of $25,000 to the families of the slain men.

When Harrison became President, the relations between the United States and Germany were strained because of a peculiar situation that had developed in the Samoan Islands, twelve in number, about equal in area to Rhode Island, and situated on the route between the United States and Australia. By the middle of the century a foreign colony composed of Americans, English, and Germans had established itself in the islands. During Grant's administration Commander R. W. Meade of the United States navy made a treaty with the head chief of the natives, who ceded the port of Pago-Pago in Tutuila in return for promised protection by the United States. Meade's action was unauthorized, and the treaty was never ratified. By a treaty between the United States and the Samoan king which was ratified in 1878, the United States guaranteed the autonomy of the native government in return for the confirmation of the cession of Pago-Pago.

For a number of years the islands were torn with dissension and warfare between rival chiefs, rivalries between consuls, and the zeal and ambitions of missionaries. The presence of warships flying the flags of the United States, Great Britain, and Germany complicated matters, and peace hinged upon the discretion of the respective commanders. Shortly after Blaine became Secretary of State, Harrison appointed delegates to a conference to be held at Berlin to effect an amicable settlement of the imbroglio. Before the conference assembled, however, a terrible hurricane on March 16, 1889, swept the Samoan Islands, sank all the German warships and two American ships, and caused great loss of life. Under the sobering influence of this disaster, the Berlin conference worked out a scheme for a tripartite control of the islands, but it proved to be a clumsy and expensive arrangement. In 1899, after ten years, it was agreed that the United States should have Tutuila and a few small islands and that Great Britain should give up her claims to Germany in return for concessions else-where.

When Blaine became Secretary of State, a civil war was raging in Chile between the partisans of President José Balmaceda and the congressional oligarchy. In the war between the Balmacedists and the congressionalist faction, it was charged that the American minister, Patrick Egan, was a partisan of Balmaceda and that the American naval forces in the harbor of Santiago acted as spies for him, the greater part of the Chilean navy having gone over to the congressional party. Feeling against the United States ran high in Chile. In fact, the Chileans had harbored resentment against Blaine dating back to the administrations of Garfield and Arthur, when Blaine as Secretary of State interfered to preserve the territorial integrity of Peru against the designs of Chile.

Two or three incidents revealed the tense feeling. In May, 1891, a Chilean vessel, the *Itata*, left the port of San Diego, California, with a shipment of rifles which had been purchased in the United States for the rebels. Suspicious of her status, a federal deputy marshal had taken possession of the *Itata* and had forbidden her to leave port; but the vessel left with the marshal on board. An American cruiser was dispatched in pursuit, and the insurgents sent a cruiser to convoy the fleeing ship. What might happen if the American cruiser overtook the *Itata* in convoy of the Chilean warship kept the American public in suspense, until it was re-ported that the vessel had been delivered over to the American authorities.

In the meantime, the congressional party had gained a decisive victory over the Balmacedists, some of whom had fled to the American legation for protection. Egan refused to surrender the fugitives. Some weeks later matters were further complicated when drunken sailors from the American cruiser *Baltimore* on shore leave in Santiago were set upon by a mob, in which the police joined. Two Americans were killed and several wounded. Captain Winfield Scott Schley in command of the *Baltimore* re-ported to his government that the attack was unprovoked. A sharp note from the American government provoked an equally sharp note from the Chilean government. Weeks dragged on without a satisfactory settlement of the *Baltimore* affair, until in his annual message of December 9, 1891, President Harrison expressed the hope that a satisfactory response would be forthcoming from Chile. In the event of needless delay or an unsatisfactory response, the President promised to bring the matter to the attention of Congress "for such action as may be necessary."

Harrison's message precipitated a most extraordinary action on the part of the Chilean foreign minister. He made public a telegram in which he used most discourteous language with reference to the conduct of American officials, including Harrison. In the meantime, preparations for war were feverishly pushed in the United States. In the harbor of Santiago, Captain Robley D. Evans of the *Yorktown*, whose courage was matched only by his proficiency in the use of profanity, resented the irritating maneuvers and conduct of the Chilean navy in language that could not be misunderstood.

On January 21, 1892, Blaine sent an ultimatum to Chile demanding the withdrawal of the offensive expressions in the foreign minister's dispatch, and a suitable apology. Almost immediately a new foreign minister complied with the ultimatum and arranged a monetary settlement for the *Baltimore* incident.

Although Blaine was criticized for his alleged jingoism, and Harrison was accused of fostering the war spirit on the eve of a presidential campaign, it is difficult to see how these men could have handled the situation in different fashion, in view of the intemperate language of the Chilean notes. Moreover, the reaction of the public to the policy of the American government was unmistakable.

The Harrison administration was not so successful or so skillful in its attempts to annex the Hawaiian Islands. Blaine, it will be recalled, resigned the State portfolio in June, 1892, and he did not live to see the full results of a situation in the Hawaiian Islands which had begun to take form before he was succeeded by John W. Foster.

The Hawaiian Islands are situated two thousand miles southwest of San Francisco, on one of the important trade routes of the world. The island of Hawaii comprises about two-thirds of

the area of the entire group. Honolulu, the capital, is situated
on the island of Oahu. According to the Census of 1890, the
population was ninety thousand, of whom thirty-four thousand
were natives, fifteen thousand Chinese, twelve thousand Japanese,
eighty-six hundred Portuguese, and about twelve thousand of
European and American origin. The climate of the islands is
moderate and distinctly cooler than that of Cuba, though in the
same latitude.

By the close of the first quarter of the nineteenth century the
presence of whalers, traders, and missionaries bore witness to the
rival interests of Russia, Great Britain, France, and the United
States. During the second half of the century the wealth of the
Islands, in the form of sugar plantations, increased greatly. The
presence of Chinese, Japanese, and Portuguese is explained by
the importation of laborers to take the places of the alarmingly
decreasing native population.

Even before the Civil War the United States was interested in
the islands from the standpoint of trade; and after the acquisition of California interest increased to such an extent that there
was talk of annexation. In 1875 a reciprocity treaty between the
United States and Hawaii was ratified. This treaty not only boomed
the sugar industry but virtually made the islands an economic
colony. By a new treaty ratified in 1887, reciprocity was extended
and the United States was granted Pearl Harbor on the island
of Oahu for a coaling station for the navy. The wealthy sugar
planters, who were nearly all Americans, were aware that their
prosperity was dependent upon favorable trade concessions from
the United States; and knowing the uncertainty of tariff legislation as revealed in the Mills Bill and in the McKinley Tariff, this
influential element set about to accomplish the annexation of the
islands to the United States.

In 1890 political conditions in the islands were very unstable,
with a small and declining native population, with Orientals, English, Germans, and an American aristocracy, and with a corrupt
and extravagant native monarchy. By placing raw sugar on the
free list, the McKinley Tariff wiped out the advantage granted
to the Hawaiian planters in the reciprocity treaty. The death of

the native king in 1891, who was somewhat amenable to the wishes and demands of the American aristocracy, played into the hands of the annexationists, for his sister, Queen Liliuokalani, proved to be a sovereign of great independence and less wisdom. She set about changing the constitution and threatened measures hostile to the "foreigners." In January, 1893, some months after Blaine had left the Department of State, "Queen Lil," as she was called in the United States, was deposed and a provisional government was established under the protection of marines from the *Boston*, who had been conveniently landed at a critical moment at the request of John L. Stevens, the American minister to Hawaii. It is a matter of dispute whether or not the marines aided the revolutionists in deposing the queen. Be that as it may, the head of the provisional government, Sanford B. Dole, a son of American missionaries, dispatched commissioners to negotiate a treaty of annexation, which Harrison promptly submitted to the Senate for ratification. Unfortunately for the annexationists in both countries, the Harrison administration was within a few days of its termination when these events were transpiring; and when Cleveland became President on March 4, 1893, the Senate had not acted upon the treaty.

With his strong sense of justice, his scrupulous regard for the proprieties of international relations, and his jealous guardianship of national honor, Cleveland withdrew the treaty of annexation and dispatched James H. Blount to Hawaii to ascertain and report the facts in the case. In the meantime, through the instrumentality of Minister Stevens and at the request of the provisional government, the American flag had been raised and a protectorate had been proclaimed. Blount proved himself entirely worthy of the trust imposed on him by Cleveland. After painstaking investigation, he wrote a long report in which he showed how the annexationist movement had been inspired and furthered by the "sugar barons" who were in close communion with the Sugar Trust. He concluded that the revolutionary movement would not have been undertaken but for the assurances of Stevens and the landing of marines. "The American minister and the revolutionary leaders," he wrote, "had determined on annexation to the United States, and had agreed on the part each was to act to the very end."

Cleveland sustained the action of Blount in lowering the American flag and in terminating the protectorate; and in his message to Congress on December 18, 1893, he said that substantial wrong had been done. He did not mince words in referring to the "bargain" that had been struck under the auspices of the Harrison administration.

Cleveland's policy was disappointing to the advocates of expansion who wished to depart from the traditional isolation of their country; but it won high praise from men who believed that national honor was more sacred than the gratification of greed. Cleveland found, however, that the old Hawaiian monarchy could not be restored, and he was forced by necessity to recognize the Dole government. The Hawaiian pear was not quite ripe, and it did not ripen under the sun of Cleveland's administration.

With the inauguration of William McKinley on March 4, 1897, the annexationists took renewed hope. They did not know that between McKinley's election and inauguration he had given Carl Schurz assurance that the sugar planters would not lead him into their trap. Imagine Schurz's chagrin, after hearing from McKinley's own lips that there would be "no jingo nonsense" under his administration, when he learned that on June 16, 1897, three months after his inauguration, he had submitted to the Senate a treaty of annexation. The two-thirds majority necessary for ratification could not be mustered. A joint resolution, however, required only a bare majority, and on July 7, 1898, President McKinley signed such a resolution. On August 12 the Hawaiian Islands were formally annexed to the United States.

Stirring events in another island made possible this annexation in the Pacific. In April, 1898, the United States declared war on Spain; on May 1 Commodore Dewey electrified the country by destroying the Spanish fleet in Manila Bay; and Admiral Sampson tendered the American people a "Fourth of July present" in the form of the Spanish fleet submerged in the waters surrounding the island of Cuba. Under these conditions it was easy to prove that the possession of Hawaii was necessary to the defense of

American interests in the Pacific Ocean. Moreover, during the war with Spain the government of Hawaii extended every courtesy and aid to the American cause, making no pretense of neutrality. The people of the islands lavished hospitality on the expeditionary forces *en route* to the Philippine Islands. The Spanish-American War threw the balance in favor of annexation not only because with Dewey in Manila Bay it was deemed necessary to have a coaling station in the Pacific, but also because the cause of annexation rode high on the wave of nationalism and imperialism.

Of all the incidents and situations that suggested the possibility of armed conflict before the war with Spain, the most alarming was the dispute with Great Britain over the boundary of Venezuela. Cleveland's vigorous—and even impulsive—handling of this affair seems to belie his reputation for a sane and conciliatory foreign policy; but at the bottom of his Venezuelan policy was the same indignation over what he thought was an act of aggression on the part of a strong power against a weak nation. It is unfortunately true that Cleveland brought the United States and Great Britain uncomfortably close to war; but in the end the two governments agreed to submit their differences to arbitration, and abided by the findings of the arbitration board. Moreover, the Venezuelan affair brought the Monroe Doctrine into prominence, and Secretary of State Olney's exposition of it won the approval of the country, however much some people may have regretted the tone of his dispatches.

For many years Venezuela had tried to have the boundary between herself and British Guiana determined, but the British government refused to consider any settlement that involved territory west of a line drawn in 1841, by an engineer in the service of that government, Sir Robert Schomburgk, which was unsatisfactory to Venezuela. In his annual message of December, 1894, Cleveland called attention to the dispute between Venezuela and Great Britain regarding the boundary of British Guiana and expressed the wish that the British government would consent to arbitrate the question. The delay of the British government in responding to Cleveland's suggestion for arbitration exasperated the President; and in July, 1895, with Cleveland's approval, Secretary Olney dispatched a note to the British government in which it was plainly stated that both the honor and the interests of the United States were involved. The note went so far as to assert that the United States was practically sovereign in the Western Hemisphere and that its fiat was law upon those subjects to which it interposed. It also made the extraordinary announcement that three thousand miles of ocean made any permanent political union between a European and an American state unnatural and inexpedient.

In Lord Salisbury, the British prime minister, Secretary Olney found an opponent who was not easily overawed. The British statesman took his own good time in formulating a reply, which was not delivered to Olney until December 7, 1895. With an array of logic dressed in irritating phraseology, Salisbury rejected Olney's interpretation of the Monroe Doctrine and his demand for arbitration. Within ten days the President and his hot-tempered Secretary of State composed a message to Congress which inspired imperialistic and jingoistic editorials and prompted the Irish National Alliance to tender the services of one hundred thousand men. But the message also brought out the best in the other elements of the population, notably an address by Carl Schurz before the New York Chamber of Commerce in which he declared that all serious-minded Americans hoped for the continuance of the long-existing friendly relations between the United States and Great Britain. He praised the willingness of the Irish to fight for the United States; but as American citizens they should never forget that the republic had the right to expect of all adopted citizens, especially in questions of peace or war, the loyal and complete subordination of the interests of their native countries to the interests of the United States.

Cleveland and Olney weakened their case by proposing arbitration in phrases that breathed war. The concluding sentences of the message were uncalled for. After recommending an appropriation for the appointment of a commission to make the necessary investigation in order to find "what is the true divisional line between the Republic of Venezuela and British Guiana,"

Cleveland concluded as follows: "When such a report is made and accepted . . . it will be the duty of the United States to resist by every means in its power, as a wilful aggression upon its rights and interests, the appropriation by Great Britain of any lands . . . which we have determined of right belong to Venezuela. In making these recommendations I am fully alive to the full responsibility incurred, and keenly realize all the consequences that may follow."

Congress responded favorably to the message; and the President appointed a commission composed of distinguished men. Apparently aware of the fact that Great Britain had little or nothing to lose and conscious of the essential solidarity of the friendship between the two great English-speaking peoples, which expressions from prominent citizens in both countries confirmed, Lord Salisbury agreed to refer the dispute to an international tribunal, stipulating that lands held by British subjects for fifty years should be exempted from the territory in dispute. In 1899 the tribunal handed down a decision which in the main fixed "the true divisional line" identically with the Schomburgk boundary.

Cleveland's message brought home to responsible persons in both countries the calamity of a war between nations which, in spite of irritating conflicting interests, had remained at peace since 1815. To risk wholesale fratricide over a matter wholly insignificant to the proportions of the issue was repugnant to the consciences of men who took counsel with themselves. True, neither nation stood to gain any material advantage by resorting to war. In this instance self-interest obviously dictated peace, not war.

CHAPTER XV

THE WAR WITH SPAIN

THE MOST POPULAR HUMORIST OF HIS DAY, FINLEY P. DUNNE, known to newspaper readers as the creator of "Mister Dooley," gave the cue to the historian when he said that during the war between the two countries the United States was in a dream but Spain was in a trance. The people of the first country entered the war with the zeal of crusaders bent upon avenging the destruction of a battleship in the harbor of Havana and driving from the New World a power that was believed to have violated the rules of civilized warfare in the unholy cause of Spanish cruelty and tyranny. But a greater disillusionment was in store for the people of that country than that which came to the people of the other country who with resignation awaited inevitable defeat, unless in the providence of God or through the intervention of European governments a different outcome might be effected.

For the first time in history the United States transported troops across the sea to make war on an enemy nation, if exception be made of the Mexican War in which circumstances were wholly different; and the consequences of transporting expeditionary forces were wholly beyond what anybody at the beginning of the war even remotely anticipated. In some respects the disillusionment of the American people was speedy; in other respects it awaited the lapse of thirty or more years.

From a time antedating the ratification of the Constitution, the relations between the United States and Spain were strained over conflicting interests inherent in the possession by one power of territory coveted by another. The control of the mouth of the Mississippi and the possession of Louisiana, Florida, and Cuba by Spain were at one time or another obstacles to the expansionist tendencies of the American people, or at least to the am-

bitions of certain sectional interests. With respect to the seriousness of the designs of the slave power on Cuba, historians are
somewhat in disagreement; but the historian does know that by
virtue of its position, the island of Cuba was an obstacle to
the ambition of the United States to dominate the Caribbean Sea
and the Gulf of Mexico. So long as Cuba remained in the possession of a weak power like Spain, there was no great objection to having a foreign colony in proximity to the territory of
the United States, providing order was maintained and there
was no prospect that the island would be transferred to a first-
rate power.

During Grant's administration Spain succeeded in putting
down a rebellion in Cuba after a long and cruel war that enlisted the sympathy of the American people and imposed on
their government the task of preventing filibustering expeditions
and of protecting the rights of its citizens. Sharp notes were exchanged between the two governments; and one incident in particular—that of the *Virginius*—threatened to bring serious consequences.

In 1895 another Cuban rebellion broke out, and atrocities
were committed on both sides. President Cleveland endeavored
with remarkable success to maintain strict neutrality in the face
of strong pressure to intervene, and of the intense activities of
sympathizers with the insurgents to further their cause by filibustering and other activities. The Spanish government complained that the American government was not living up to its
obligations. The fact of the matter is that, considering the long
coast line of Cuba and the small American navy, the government
was surprisingly efficient. In 1896 the Democratic, Republican,
and Populist platforms expressed sympathy for the Cuban insurgents, and the last two declared that the United States ought
to intervene and establish peace and independence.

It was most unfortunate that with the inauguration of McKinley the Department of State was hampered by having at its head
the aging John Sherman, whose long and distinguished career
deserved a better fate than it received at the hands of McKinley
and Hanna. Hanna's biographer, Herbert Croly, denies that

either McKinley or Hanna did anything discreditable in appointing Sherman Secretary of State and thus paving the way for the appointment of Hanna to the Senate by the governor of Ohio. Sherman himself, says Croly, was a party to the plan to have Hanna succeed him after he had resigned his seat in the Senate. The biographer admits, however, that the appointment of Sherman was a mistake. He was seventy-four years old and had fulminated ignorantly—even surpassing some other Senators—against Spain. Some years later William R. Day, Assistant Secretary of State under Sherman, told President Taft that "Sherman's mind was infinitely worse than the public supposed it to have been." Day never dared leave him alone and always attended cabinet meetings with him. Sherman resigned on April 25, 1898, the day war was formally declared, but before that Day had discharged the duties of the Secretary.

The well-intentioned McKinley had no desire to lead the nation into war, but the ground swell of propaganda and political expediency unsteadied him. In the delightful volumes entitled *Taft and Roosevelt. The Intimate Letters of Archie Butt,* Major Butt relates a conversation he had in 1911 with H. H. Kohlsaat, a Chicago newspaper publisher, who told him that McKinley confided to him that "they were trying to force him into declaring war against Spain." The President broke down and wept, "his whole body was shaken with convulsive sobs." In the light of the impatience of Theodore Roosevelt and others with McKinley's tardiness in contracting the war fever, and in the light of the well-known kindliness of the President, the story has the ring of truthfulness.

Shortly before McKinley's inauguration General Campos, the governor-general of Cuba, a high-minded and chivalrous man, was succeeded by General Weyler, who was speedily designated in the American press as "Butcher Weyler." Weyler's strategy was to reduce the insurgents to submission by herding the peasants in the vicinity of fortified towns, thereby depriving them of the privilege of fighting in the ranks of the insurgent armies for a season and then returning to peaceful pursuits. That suffering and death resulted from the reconcentration policy of Weyler there can be no doubt; but it was to no avail that the Spanish authorities explained that the stories of Spanish atrocities published in the American papers were grossly exaggerated and that the insurgents were bloody and ruthless in their mode of warfare.

The American press featured stories of atrocities perpetrated on Cuban patriots. William Randolph Hearst, with more truth than the stories about Cuba that appeared in his *New York Journal*, appropriated to himself the credit for bringing on the Spanish-American War; but this dubious honor must be shared with Joseph Pulitzer, the publisher of the *New York World*, who met the challenge of this newcomer in the field of journalism by cutting the price of his paper to one cent and furnishing "yellow" competition that spurred the *Journal* to even greater heights—or depths—of sensationalism. But irresponsibility was unfortunately not confined to publishers competing for circulation; it found its way into the Senate Committee on Foreign Relations, to the floor of the Senate and House of Representatives in impassioned speeches, into the office of the Assistant Secretary of the Navy in the person of Theodore Roosevelt, and into the pulpit and the schoolroom. Another disturbing element was the activity of a junta in New York composed of naturalized citizens of Cuban birth. "Cuba libre" became a slogan.

In September, 1897, McKinley tendered the friendly offices of the United States to mediate between the Spanish government and the insurgents, but the offer was declined. The Spanish government recalled Weyler, however, and appointed as his successor the more humane General Blanco. It also promised to grant autonomy to Cuba as soon as conditions made it possible. It must not be forgotten that during these months of negotiations the Spanish government was very unstable, with the queen regent ruling in the name of the young Alfonso XIII. It is the Spanish nature to temporize and delay, but it would have been disastrous to the monarchy if the impression got abroad that it had failed to protect the national honor and territory of Spain under pressure from the "Yankees."

How successful the new Spanish policy in Cuba would have

proved and what course negotiations between the United States and Spain would have taken had it not been for two events of catastrophic proportions is a matter of pure surmise.

On January 25, 1898, the battleship *Maine*, one of the crack ships of the navy, steamed into the harbor of Havana—on a friendly visit. The conduct of Captain Sigsbee, his officers and men, and that of the Spanish officials in Havana was the acme of courtesy; but the sending of a warship flying the flag of a country whose people were notoriously hostile to Spain was an affront to the sensitive Spaniards, a sign of encouragement to the insurgents, and a hazard that seasoned diplomats would not have taken unless they desired to provoke war.

The mobilization of a large fleet, with steam up, at the Dry Tortugas, Florida, ready to sail at a moment's notice, was not unknown to Spain. The sending of the Spanish cruiser *Vizcaya* to New York Harbor to return the "friendly visit" of the *Maine* was regarded as an affront by the American press and necessitated extraordinary precautions on the part of the American government to prevent untoward incidents. It was even said that the visit of the cruiser occurred at a time when all American vessels able to cope with her were a long distance away.

While the *Maine* was riding at anchor, with extra sentries posted at night by order of her captain, deadly propaganda played its trump card. On February 9 Hearst's *New York Journal* printed a facsimile of a private letter written by Dupuy de Lome, the Spanish minister to the United States. This letter, which was stolen from the mails, was translated and printed in newspapers from coast to coast. The minister called McKinley a "common politician who tries to leave a door open behind himself while keeping on good terms with the jingoes of his party" and a "bidder for the admiration of the crowd." The letter also gave the impression that the Spanish government was acting in bad faith.

So experienced and accomplished a diplomat as Señor de Lome knew that his usefulness at Washington was over; and he anticipated the demand for his recall by immediately cabling his resignation. When his successor, Polo y Bernabe, presented his credentials to President McKinley on March 12, the *Maine* disaster and the appropriation, by the unanimous vote of Congress, of $50,000,000 for national defense had made his coming worse than useless. It inspired what at the time was said to be the shortest poem of the war:

> De Lome
> Went home
> Polo
> Also.

The most tragic event of the tragic year 1898 occurred between the hours of nine and ten o'clock on the night of February 15, when the *Maine* was blown up in the harbor of Havana, snuffing out the lives of 252 men and mortally wounding eight. The cause of the catastrophe has never been determined, or, if it has, it has never been made public, though several conjectures have been ventured. Both the American and Spanish governments impaneled courts of inquiry. The American court reached the verdict that the destruction of the vessel was caused by an external explosion, but was unable to fix responsibility; the Spanish court found no evidence of an external explosion.

On March 17, 1912, the wreck of the *Maine*, which for fourteen years had rested in the mud of Havana harbor, with portions of her superstructure visible, was towed out to sea and sunk in six hundred fathoms of water. What revelations, if any, were disclosed by the raising of the *Maine* have never been made public, although the official report leaves the impression that the explosion came from without.

During the weeks the court of inquiry sat, the public suspended judgment; but never before perhaps had the American people concentrated their thoughts and conversation on a single topic as they did during those hectic February and March days. Every day farmers came to town and waited for hours for the daily papers. All the while the yellow press blazed forth huge headlines, and the wildest speculations were presented as "facts." One rumor had it that the *Fern*, which had been dispatched to Havana, had met the same fate as the *Maine*. Both nations pressed feverish preparations for war; arsenals worked day and night.

With a weak and vacillating President, a Congress bent on war, and a disorganized Department of State in one country, and a tottering government in the other, it was to no avail that the level-headed American minister in Madrid, Stewart L. Woodford, from first to last labored to spare both countries the horrors of an unnecessary war. Woodford knew that the Spanish officials realized the hopelessness of conducting a successful war against the United States. His knowledge of the state of mind of the "dons" was wholly at variance with the belligerent cartoons in the Spanish press that were reproduced in the United States. But fighting for peace in 1898 was inglorious, notwithstanding the fact that a few men, even among the journalists, had the stamina to strike discordant notes. Even after the *Maine* disaster *Harper's Weekly* published steadying articles about "National Honor" by Carl Schurz.

Though there were exceptions, the European press was generally hostile to the United States. It was alleged that the American people were too corrupt to fight, that the composite population of the country would divide against itself, and that the navy was manned by hireling foreigners. In official circles in many countries there was a sullen and hostile attitude toward the "Yankees." This was especially true of France and Austria. Fortunately the United States had the good will of the British government, in spite of the recent Venezuela affair. Whatever prospect there may have been for joint action in behalf of Spain by the great powers, Britain's flat refusal to be a party to it was fatal. The innocuous character of the joint note presented to President McKinley on April 7 by the diplomatic representatives of Great Britain, France, Austria, Germany, Italy, and Russia is explained by the refusal of Sir Julian Pauncefote, the British ambassador, to agree to a stronger statement. In reply, McKinley expressed the appreciation of his own government for the "humanitarian and disinterested character of the communication now made on behalf of the powers named." He also expressed confidence that they would show equal appreciation for his own government's unselfish endeavors to fulfill a duty to humanity. In the words of a Hearst cartoonist, Uncle Sam said to the diplomats: "I speak only American, and I don't care for advice."

Pope Leo XIII offered his services as a mediator, but, to quote the editor of the *Review of Reviews*, "There were ample reasons why from the point of view of the government at Washington this was impossible." Protestant America would not be cheated out of a war by the head of the Roman Catholic Church. In a country where the anti-Catholic feeling was so strong that the formal unveiling of a statue of Père Marquette in Statuary Hall in the Capitol at Washington had to be abandoned in 1896, there could be no "dictation" from Rome.

All the while Minister Woodford labored heroically to make it possible for Spain to escape a war which her statesmen neither wanted nor could afford. At the last moment he sent a personal telegram to McKinley in which he pleaded that nothing be done to humiliate Spain. He was satisfied that the government was ready to go as fast and as far as it could go. The day before McKinley sent his message to Congress, the Spanish minister at Washington delivered a note to the Department of State which granted substantially what the United States had demanded. The following day, April 11, the President played right into the hands of the war party by submitting the whole question to the decision of Congress.

McKinley's message is a strange, halting, and diffuse document. After the President had read the document to the cabinet, Secretary of the Navy Long recorded the following comment in his diary: "I suppose it is the best he can do; yet it seems to me the narrative which he makes the basis of his conclusion leads to a very different result from that which he reaches. He is in a very trying situation. He has been robbed of sleep, overworked; and I fancy that I can see that his mind does not work as clearly and directly and as self-reliantly as it otherwise would."

In a concluding paragraph the message mentioned the reception of the latest Spanish proposals after the foregoing message had been prepared, but the details had not as yet been communicated to the President. McKinley asked authority to use the military and naval forces of the United States to terminate the war in Cuba and to establish a stable government. Though the court of inquiry did not assume to fix the responsibility for the destruction of the *Maine*, the event was to the President a "patent and impressive proof of a state of things in Cuba that is intolerable."

On April 19, 1898, Congress resolved that Cuba was free and independent, that the government of Spain should relinquish its authority over the island, that the President was empowered to use the military and naval forces, and that the United States had no intention to annex Cuba. The last resolution was added in the Senate in the form of an amendment introduced by Senator Teller and was accepted by the House of Representatives.

On the day war was declared Commodore George Dewey was in command of the Asiatic Squadron at Hongkong; Rear Admiral William T. Sampson, who had been promoted over a dozen senior officers, was in command of the North Atlantic Squadron at Key West; and Commodore Winfield Scott Schley was in command of the Flying Squadron at Hampton Roads. On April 23 President McKinley issued a call for 125,000 men. These men, together with the regular army, were expected to "Remember the *Maine*."

In the light of later events, the panic that swept over the Atlantic coast from fear of the Spanish fleet under the command of Admiral Cervera is ridiculously amusing. The Navy Department was deluged with urgent demands from cities and individuals that vessels be sent for their protection. Where was Cervera? Neither the public nor the navy found out until the last days of May—over a month after the war began. In the meantime startling news from another part of the world caused factory whistles to blow for hours.

In the early morning of May 1 Commodore Dewey's fleet steamed unmolested into the harbor of Manila Bay and at dawn his four protected cruisers and two gunboats engaged a Spanish fleet, so inferior in armament, ordnance, and man power as to be helpless. The strategy of the Spanish admiral consisted in taking a position "in the least water possible" to await destruction.

He did not have long to wait. Within a few hours the entire Spanish fleet was destroyed. The American casualties were eight wounded and one death from heat stroke. For this achievement of mingled "wisdom and daring," as John Hay put it, Dewey instantly found himself converted into one of the most lionized heroes in history, an emotion that unfortunately soon ran its course.

Dewey's feat of sinking the Spanish hulks gave tremendous prestige to the navy in the eyes of the American people; but it did much more than that. For the first time many Americans learned of the existence of the Philippine Islands, and they later learned that they were to become possessions of the United States. Within two months after Dewey's victory a distinguished editor wrote: "We may as well accept the fact, and simply make the task of managing the Philippines a part of the regular day's work. It will certainly be a most fortunate thing for the Philippines themselves. Any American who denies this statement is a subject either for pity or for indignation." Before many weeks an expeditionary force under the command of General Wesley Merritt sailed out of the Golden Gate bound for Manila, seven thousand miles away, there to cooperate with insurgents to drive "Spanish tyranny" from the Far East.

In the meantime Admiral Sampson's fleet was on the hunt for Cervera's fleet, but it could find no scent. The Spanish ships were reported as having been seen at various places, even at Cadiz. Cervera's objective was to elude the American squadrons and find a safe refuge. For him to engage either Admiral Sampson's or Commodore Schley's squadrons with his four armored cruisers and six torpedo boat destroyers was to invite the fate that had overtaken his brother admiral in Manila Bay. Three of Cervera's destroyers were useless, and the other three were far from being fighting machines. Spanish inefficiency had reduced the cruisers almost to the minimum of efficiency. The crews were poorly trained in gunnery and almost mutinous at the thought of the fate that awaited them; ammunition was lacking and poor in quality; and the supply of coal was equally poor and scanty.

As a dutiful and loyal subject, and for the honor of Spain,

however, Cervera under protest obeyed orders and sailed for the West Indies. Thinking that the "dons" might be in the harbor of San Juan, Puerto Rico, Admiral Sampson's squadron, with two monitors in tow and one battleship with badly leaking boilers, made slow progress to that port; but the prey was not there. After bombarding the shore batteries, the fleet steamed slowly away. Meanwhile Cervera had been seen at Martinique. Telegrams flew thick and fast, and dispatch boats churned the waters, until at last, on May 21, Sampson ordered Schley, who was on the way to Cienfuegos, Cuba, to proceed "with all despatch, but cautiously," to Santiago de Cuba, where reports indicated Cervera had gone.

Having ascertained that the "dons" were not at Cienfuegos, Schley moved slowly in the direction of Santiago, with his progress slowed up by a collier and mishaps to his ships. At Santiago Schley could find no traces of the Spanish ships. He was worried about his coal supply and did not think it possible to coal at sea from the collier. Instead of remaining at Santiago, he made a retrograde movement and on May 27 cabled that he regretted that he could not obey orders to remain at Santiago but was forced to return for coal to Key West, more than seven hundred miles away. Fortunately for Schley, he reconsidered and returned to Santiago, where on May 29 he saw one of Cervera's cruisers in plain sight in the harbor. The Spaniards had been there since May 19! The limping Spanish fleet had crossed the Atlantic, steamed into the Caribbean Sea, taken coal, and entered Santiago harbor without a shot having been fired at it from the superior American navy.

On June 1 Sampson's forces joined the Flying Squadron at Santiago, and for five weeks under a sweltering tropical sun the combined squadrons, with Sampson in command, bottled up the only naval force that Spain could spare. To make assurance doubly sure, under cover of darkness on June 3 Lieutenant Richmond Pearson Hobson and a gallant volunteer crew of seven men attempted to sink the collier *Merrimac* in the channel entrance to the harbor in such a way as to obstruct it. The collier was sunk, but not in a position to block the channel. However, a new hero broke into the headlines. His immense popularity lasted long enough to cause him to be overwhelmed by kisses from emotional women when he returned to the United States. For a few years he was in demand as a Chautauqua speaker; but in March, 1937, he died, a forgotten man. Fate was unkind to Spanish War heroes, with the conspicuous exception of Theodore Roosevelt, the picturesque Rough Rider.

With the assurance that the American navy was "as strong as Sampson and as Schley as a fox," as the popular phrase had it, the army was free to embark on the mission of driving the "cruel and treacherous" Spaniards out of Cuba, in spite of the approaching rainy season in the tropics. In an amusing, vigorous, and belligerent chapter entitled "The War of America the Unready" in his *Autobiography,* Theodore Roosevelt lays bare the inefficiency and demoralization of the staff, quartermaster, and commissary departments of the army. The regulars assembled at Tampa, Florida, while volunteer regiments poured into Camp George H. Thomas at Chickamauga Park, Georgia. The slogan "Remember the *Maine*" swamped recruiting offices; but clothing, rifles, ammunition, supplies, and transportation were lacking. The West Pointers were almost as helpless and bewildered as were the officers of the militia and the host of political lieutenants, colonels, and generals. For lack of proper sanitation, wholesome food, and suitable clothing, men died like flies of fever and dysentery.

After weeks of confusion at Tampa, the expeditionary forces of about 17,000 men under General William R. Shafter sailed for Santiago de Cuba on June 14, eight weeks after war had been declared. In the pell-mell of embarking, parts of a regiment got on one transport and other parts on another; one transport had guns and another locks for the guns. In the case of Colonel Leonard Wood's and Lieutenant-Colonel Theodore Roosevelt's Rough Riders, it was a matter of having the fleetest heels and the most resourceful officers or being left behind. The process of disembarking from the crowded and stifling transports at Daiquiri, eighteen miles east of Santiago, was equally helter-skelter, but fortunately the Spaniards offered no resistance.

The American army that advanced on General Toral's forces

(about 12,000 men) at Santiago was composed almost exclusively of regulars, with three volunteer regiments, the most famous of which was the Rough Riders, recruited from Oklahoma, Indian Territory, Arizona, and New Mexico, and from college men in the East. The Americans advanced through thickets and jungle, winning skirmish after skirmish with the enemy, who had the advantage of using smokeless powder, whereas the black puffs from the American lines furnished excellent targets. Officers and men learned many things during those hot and wet days, among them that the Spaniards had Mauser and Krag-Jorgenson rifles and knew how to use them. As the wounded and dead were brought back from the battle lines, this awful truth came to the ailing General Shafter and his staff. The approaching rainy season, increasing sickness, and Spanish resistance made it dubious if the City of Santiago could be taken. Indeed, the army was threatened with disaster. But on the morning of Sunday, July 3, the whole scene changed.

At nine o'clock that morning Admiral Sampson's flagship, the *New York*, had steamed eastward about seven miles for a conference with the dejected and sick General Shafter, after having hoisted the signal "Disregard movements of flagship," leaving Commodore Schley the senior officer. The night before it had been reported that the Spanish ships appeared to be getting up steam; but from all appearances the officers and men of the blockading fleet expected Sunday to furnish the same torrid monotony that for five weeks had been theirs. At nine-thirty-five o'clock Cervera's flagship was observed steaming out of the channel and heading for the open sea. Followed by the other ships of the fleet, the flagship turned to the west directly toward Schley's flagship, the *Brooklyn*, westernmost of the blockading ships and the fastest of them all. Sampson's plan, in the event of the appearance of the Spanish fleet, was for his ships to converge upon the mouth of the harbor; but the battle resolved itself into a chase. There was nothing for the American ships to do but to chase the fleeing Spaniards.

The Spanish admiral was under no illusions as to the outcome of a battle with the blockading fleet. He had been ordered by his superiors to save the honor of Spain by taking action that would relieve him of the ignominy of surrendering his fleet after the fall of Santiago, which seemed imminent on account of the shortage of food and ammunition.

With foul bottoms, inferior ammunition and fuel, wooden decks, and poor marksmanship, the Spanish ships, one by one, were sunk or beached. The last one gave up the fight at one-fifteen o'clock, after having led the chase for fifty miles. The American casualties mounted to the total of one killed. Admiral Sampson, who was never beyond sight of the chase, finally caught up with Schley after the last Spanish ship had been beached. In reply to the signal of the commodore: "We have gained a great victory," the admiral, disappointed over not having fired a shot from his speedy flagship, replied simply: "Report your losses." But to his government and to the public the admiral sent the following message: "The fleet under my command offers the nation as a Fourth of July present the whole of Cervera's fleet," which was ridiculed by the public and the press. For four years Sampson waited for public and official recognition of his heroic conduct in the Santiago chase, but in 1902 he died, a disappointed and embittered man. Schley, on the other hand, won the not entirely merited applause of the public, though not of the government.

Disappointed over the refusal of the navy to run the risk of entering the harbor of Santiago after the departure of the Spanish fleet, Shafter effected the surrender of General Toral by correspondence, rather than risking further losses by action. The city surrendered on July 16. General Nelson A. Miles landed an army in Puerto Rico without opposition and received an enthusiastic reception from the inhabitants. General Merritt was getting his campaign under way in the Philippines.

Under these circumstances Spanish honor had no more meaning, and the government sought the good offices of France to obtain a cessation of hostilities. Accordingly, on August 12 a protocol was signed by the French ambassador at Washington and Secretary of State Day. It was agreed that the representatives of the United States and Spain were to meet at Paris to negotiate a definitive treaty, it being understood that Spain would surrender her sovereignty over Cuba and Puerto Rico and that the status of the Philippine Islands would be left for further consideration.

During the sixteen weeks of war the newspapers and illustrated weeklies and monthlies spread a veritable feast before their readers. Only the very exceptional paper opposed the war and exposed the inefficiency and corruption in the conduct of the war. But after the termination of hostilities, political expediency, rivalry and jealousy between officers in the army and the navy, and the condition of the returning soldiers brought an amazing series of exposures.

A wave of indignation swept over the nation when the wretched condition of the returning soldiers became known. The men who had seen service in the Santiago campaign were transported to Montauk Point, on Long Island. Crowded on the transports were wounded and sick men who were without proper care from physicians and nurses—and even without good food and pure water. It became known that if the Spanish officers had known of the condition of the American army, it was doubtful if they would have capitulated. So serious was the situation that after the surrender a "round robin" was addressed to General Shafter by officers who demanded that the army be at once removed from Cuba; the malarial fevers had practically destroyed the efficiency of the army, and yellow fever threatened to become epidemic. Shafter cabled the Secretary of War that the immediate transportation of the army from Cuba was the only course left open for its preservation.

Unfortunately, inefficiency and inexperience took heavy toll not only among the regulars who saw service in Cuba, but also in the volunteer camps, where diseases, notably typhoid fever, caused by open sewers on either side of which soldiers lived and slept, laid many low. Moreover, contractors furnished shoddy uniforms and shoes of inferior quality; and the clothing and equipment the expeditionary forces took with them were more suitable for service in Alaska than in the tropics. When the men were brought to Montauk Point, they were dressed in light clothing unsuitable for that temperature.

The wrath of the public also descended on the packing houses for supplying what the newspapers called "embalmed beef." General Miles gave to the public his testimony and that of other officers that the tinned beef was unfit for consumption and that soldiers became seriously sick from eating it. The newspaper clamor was so loud that President McKinley was impelled to appoint a commission to investigate the conduct of the war. Before this body the commissary-general, Charles P. Eagan, delivered a diatribe against General Miles in defense of his own conduct. This had the effect of loosing even more bitter shafts against Eagan.

When the report of the investigating committee was made public on May 7, 1899, the storm was not allayed. The report stated that the charge that meat had been treated with chemicals was not established; it was the tropical weather and the injury to containers in transportation that had caused the meat to spoil. The press and the public pronounced the report a "whitewashing document." Hearst's *New York Journal*, having been deprived of sensationalism by the termination of the war, now turned its guns on the War Department and the McKinley administration. A cartoon by Davenport portrayed a tombstone bearing the epitaph: "Killed by Spaniards, two hundred. Killed by official negligence and incompetence, two thousand." Certain it is that in the years to come many went to early graves from diseases contracted during the few short weeks of war.

The amiable McKinley was spared the torrent of abuse in the press, except in the Democratic newspapers, even though he practically set aside the sentence of General Eagan by a court-martial for conduct unbecoming an officer and a gentleman; but the public had to have a scapegoat. The incompetent Secretary of War, Russell A. Alger, bore the brunt of the attack, until finally political expediency compelled McKinley to demand his resignation. His successor, Elihu Root, restored some of the prestige of the War Department and of the army by effecting a reorganization. By the act of February 14, 1903, a general staff was

created, with a chief of staff having supervision over both the
line and the staff. However, reorganization did not completely
abolish the jealousy between the line and staff officers which had
brought such disastrous results in the Spanish-American War.

It would seem that the record of the navy would have made
it immune to the fate that overtook the army, but not so. The
unfortunate absence of Rear Admiral Sampson from the scene
of action at Santiago gave the glory of victory to Commodore
Schley—in the public eye. The coolness between the admiral and
the commodore when they met after the exciting chase was pain-
fully obvious; and in Sampson's telegraphic report of the victory
of the fleet "under my command" Schley was not even mentioned,
notwithstanding the fact that his flagship, the *Brooklyn*, led the
chase and was in the thick of the fight from the firing of the
first gun to the last.

When the *Brooklyn* returned to Guantanamo Bay after the surrender of Santiago, her officers and men were indignantly surprised to find a "sinister whisper" going around the fleet that the
Brooklyn had been careful to keep at a safe distance from the
enemy. In other words, the commodore's flagship was accused of
being "gun shy." This, together with the claim of Schley and
his friends that he was in chief command and was entitled to
credit for the victory, caused bitter feeling between officers and
men in the navy and gave rise to the famous Sampson-Schley
controversy. Sampson's austerity of manner did not appeal to
the public and the press, whereas Schley fared much better. In
fact, he was the hero of the public, but the Navy Department
and most of the officers took the side of Sampson. The upshot
of the controversy was a request from Schley that a court of inquiry be called for the purpose of investigating his conduct during the war.

The court of inquiry, under the presidency of Admiral Dewey,
convened on September 12, 1901, and for over a month sat to
hear a mass of testimony which is published in two stout volumes.
The press, while still friendly to Schley, published extracts from
the testimony of witnesses; and for the first time the public
learned of the jealousy and inefficiency of officers, the poor marks-

manship of gunners, and the poor condition of many of the "crack" ships.

The chief indictments of Schley were his vacillation and dilatoriness in locating the Spanish fleet; his retrograde movement from Santiago without having used due diligence in establishing the location of the fleet in the harbor; his disobedience of Sampson's order to proceed from Cienfuegos to Santiago "with all despatch"; and the famous "loop" made by the *Brooklyn*. The judge advocate sought to show that Schley's conduct during the battle was not characterized by bravery and that he did not direct the conduct of the battle.

The most vulnerable spot in Schley's conduct of the battle was the *Brooklyn's* loop. As the Spanish flagship came out of the harbor, she made directly for the *Brooklyn* with the intention of ramming her. The *Brooklyn*, being the westernmost of the blockading ships, closed in to meet the oncoming Spanish ships. But when they turned westward, it was necessary for the *Brooklyn* to make a semicircle in order to join in the chase. The *Brooklyn's* captain ordered the ship to turn outward—away from the Spanish ships—forcing the *Texas* to back water to avoid a collision and making it necessary for the *Brooklyn* to fight at longer range. Schley testified that he approved the captain's order. It was this that gave rise to the rumor that the flagship was "gun shy."

The court of inquiry, with Admiral Dewey dissenting, rendered a report in general adverse to Schley. In a separate report Dewey exonerated Schley and held that he was in command and deserved credit for the victory. The two reports infuriated both Sampson and Schley. They appealed to higher authority. Curiously enough, it fell to the most popular hero of the war, President Theodore Roosevelt, to make the final report. Roosevelt was satisfied that the court did Schley substantial justice. He condemned the *Brooklyn's* loop as unnecessarily avoiding danger and even said that Sampson ought to have relieved Schley of his command on account of his conduct in attempting to locate the Spanish fleet. In his judgment, neither Sampson nor Schley could claim credit for the victory. "It was a captains' fight," he said.

Even the fiat of the President of the United States did not

quiet the controversy. On January 15, 1902, both houses of the legislature of Mississippi unanimously adopted a resolution declaring Schley to be the "rightful hero" of the battle of Santiago. Other legislatures passed similar resolutions. In January, 1904, a taxpayers' convention in Baltimore County, Maryland, placed a ban on any textbook that failed to give Schley credit for the victory.

McKinley's Secretary of the Treasury, Lyman J. Gage, added to his reputation by his administration of the war finances. By sending circulars and posters to almost every post office and national bank in the country, he sold two hundred million dollars' worth of bonds bearing interest at the rate of 2 per cent. So popular was the loan that it was oversubscribed, notwithstanding skeptics who doubted that bonds bearing such a low rate of interest could be floated at par. By giving small bidders the preference over banks and financial institutions, Gage hoped to and did succeed in appealing to the patriotism of the small investor. Within a few days the bonds went to a premium, and many who had bought them at par sold them to banks at a profit. Despite the depression and the financial embarrassment of the government during Cleveland's administration, the credit of the United States was thus placed on a par with that of the preferred nations of the world.

In spite of the brief duration of the war, it greatly increased the size of the nation's budget. The new colonial possessions and the campaigns to reduce the insurrectionists in the Philippine Islands made necessary larger appropriations for the army and navy. And in the years to come the veterans of the Spanish-American War and the Filipino insurrection joined with the "G.A.R. boys" in demanding larger and larger pensions.

CHAPTER XVI

THE OBLIGATIONS OF A COLONIAL EMPIRE

WHEN THE DELEGATES TO THE PEACE CONFERENCE ASSEMBLED at Paris on October 1, 1898, the Spaniards had laid down their arms; but that was only the beginning of far more serious problems. After having triumphed over Spain in Cuba, Puerto Rico, and the Philippine Islands at the expense of life, money, and the exposure of inefficiency and corruption in their own government, it was disconcerting to learn from the press and returning soldiers that the people of those remote islands did not show seemly gratitude for their deliverance from "Spanish tyranny." Some were so unkind as to say that if it had been known what a sorry lot the Cubans were, the United States would not have intervened in their behalf. What disposition was to be made of the conquered territory, however, did not rest with the American people. That was decided by the President of the United States, the peace commissioners, and the Senate.

By the terms of the protocol, the Spaniards had agreed to relinquish Cuba and Puerto Rico, but the disposition of the Philippines was not so simple. The situation that had developed in those far-off islands after Dewey's victory was much more complicated.

The Spanish delegates to the peace conference were resigned to the relinquishment of Cuba and Puerto Rico; but in the hope that their government would be relieved of the obligation of paying the principal and interest of the Cuban debt, they sought to persuade the American delegates to agree to the cession of the island to the United States. This arrangement would have left it to the government of the United States to dispose of Cuba as it saw fit, and it would also have transferred the debt to the United States. The Americans refused to agree to this. It was finally agreed that Spain would relinquish her sovereignty over Cuba and cede Puerto Rico to the United States. This cleared the way for grappling with the problem of the Philippines.

It will be recalled that after the annihilation of the Spanish fleet, Dewey was master of Manila Bay. Then followed the embarkation of an expeditionary force under General Merritt. When the American troops landed in the Philippines, they found an insurgent army under Emilio Aguinaldo bent on putting an end to Spanish rule. The American officers, however, declined to permit the insurgents to share the glory of capturing Manila, and friction between the two armies increased, until at the time of the assembling of the delegates at Paris, relations were so strained that a new war was imminent. Aguinaldo, who had been one of the leaders of the Filipino insurrection in 1896, had been induced to cease his activities by bribery and promises of reform. After Dewey's victory, with the encouragement and assistance of the American government Aguinaldo was brought back to the islands to resume his activity against the Spanish government. As it turned out, Aguinaldo and other insurgent leaders were no more pleased at the prospect of having the islands under the rule of the United States than under Spain.

Another development that complicated the problem was the extraordinary situation in the Far East. The Sino-Japanese War of 1894-95 was followed by a scramble among the European powers for territory and concessions in China. The prospect of an American colony in the Far East was as unexpected to the diplomats of Europe as it was to the people of the United States. Although the official attitude of the governments of Europe toward the United States was entirely regular, and in the case of Great Britain cordial, Europe looked with jealous eyes on the power and influence of the young republic of the Western Hemisphere. Germany was a late-comer in the scramble for colonies, and there can be little doubt that at the time of the Spanish-American War she looked with covetous eyes on the Philippines and other territory in the Far East.

In any event, in spite of the neutral position of the German government, the conduct of Otto von Diedrichs, the admiral in command of the German fleet in Manila Bay, aroused the enmity and suspicions of Dewey, the government in Washington, and the American people; and but for the unmistakably friendly attitude of the British fleet under the command of Captain Chichester, it is impossible to say what might have happened. Dewey resented not only the presence of a German fleet equal, if not superior, to his own, but especially the irritating attitude of its commander. Undoubtedly, the suspicion that Germany had designs on the Philippines, whether justified or not, was a factor that influenced the American government to demand the cession of the islands by Spain.

When the American peace commissioners left for Paris, the position of the McKinley administration with respect to the Philippines had not been formulated. Whitelaw Reid, William P. Frye, and Cushman K. Davis favored the acquisition of the entire archipelago, but William R. Day did not believe that the military situation justified his government in making the demand. He would retain only a naval station. George Gray, the only Democrat on the commission, opposed the acquisition of any territory in the islands. By the time the commissioners were ready to deal with the problem, McKinley had gone over to the imperialist camp and had instructed the delegation to insist on the retention of the entire archipelago. With his ear always to the ground, the President on his trip to the West in the early fall is said to have been convinced that sentiment was in favor of this policy. Undoubtedly, the extraordinary situation in the Far East, with the European powers ready to swoop down on available territory to enlarge and strengthen their colonial empires, was a factor in bringing the President and Secretary of State John Hay to that decision.

In reply to the demand for the cession of the Philippines, the Spanish commissioners objected that it was in violation of the terms of the protocol and unwarranted by the military situation. Realizing that the demand could not be justified on the ground of conquest, the United States finally agreed to pay $20,000,000 to Spain for the islands.

By the terms of the treaty submitted to the Senate on January

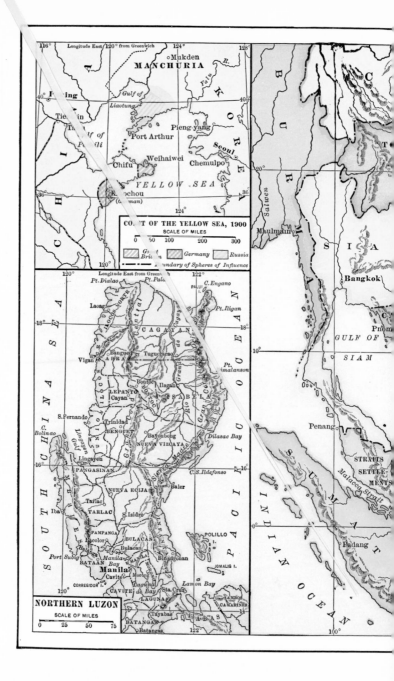

COAST OF THE YELLOW SEA, 1900

SCALE OF MILES

0   50   100   200   300

Great Britain   Germany   Russia

Boundary of Spheres of Influence

NORTHERN LUZON

SCALE OF MILES

0   25   50   75

I N A

Longitude East from Greenwich

Fu-chou

Chang-chou

Canton

Hongkong

Kwang-chou-wan
(French)

Hai-fong

Gulf of
Tongking HAINAN

Hue

SOUTH CHINA SEA

LUZON PHILIPPINE

Manila

ISLANDS

MINDORO

SAMAR

PANAY
Iloilo

CEBU

PALAWAN

NEGROS BOHOL

SULU SEA

MINDANAO

Zamboanga

Sandakan

Jolo

BRITISH
NORTH
BORNEO

Brunei

CELEBES

SARAWAK

SEA

Kuching

Menado

B O R N E O

CELEBES

EQUATOR

J A V A   S E A

PHILIPPINES
AND
EASTERN COAST OF ASIA
1900

SCALE OF MILES

0   50   100   200   300   400

United
States

Great
Britain

France

Netherlands

Japan

BORMAY ENG. CO., N. Y.

4, 1899, Spain relinquished her sovereignty over Cuba and ceded to the United States Puerto Rico, Guam (an island in the Ladrones), and the Philippine Islands. From that date until the ratification of the treaty on February 6, 1899, the Senate and the country debated the wisdom of establishing a colonial empire.

With newspapers publishing reports of tense relations between the American forces and the Filipino insurrectionists, mass meetings were held all over the country protesting the imperialistic policy of the administration. The most powerful single address against imperialism was William Graham Sumner's "The Conquest of the United States by Spain." The Yale professor of political economy presented a devastating analysis of the motives and inconsistencies of the imperialists. "The war with Spain was precipitated upon us headlong, without reflection or deliberation, and without any due formulation of public opinion," he said. In the flush of enthusiasm at the prospect of driving the Spaniards out of the Philippines as well as out of Cuba and Puerto Rico, there was great rejoicing when the expeditionary forces were ordered to embark for the Philippines; but after the Spaniards had laid down their arms, some of the volunteers thought that the purpose for which they had enlisted had been accomplished, and pressure was brought by officers, privates, and their relatives and friends on Congressmen and governors to have their regiments ordered to return home.

The opposition to the retention of Puerto Rico did not assume large proportions partly because of the proximity of the island to the United States and partly because it was believed, rightly or wrongly, that the Puerto Ricans were more suitable for American citizenship. But the remoteness of the Philippines and their large Oriental population, it was argued, made them unfit to be incorporated into the United States. In the words of Judson Harmon, Attorney-General under Cleveland, "Mere expansion is not growth, it is merely swelling; we may push across the seas, but we cannot grow there." The anti-imperialists also argued that for the United States to govern colonies as European governments governed them was in violation of the Declaration of Independence and the Constitution, as well as the spirit that animated the declaration of war against Spain.

Although the large business interests, speaking generally, had opposed the declaration of war against Spain because it was feared that hostilities would jeopardize the rapidly increasing export trade of the country and otherwise react unfavorably on the reviving prosperity, after Dewey's victory sentiment swung over in favor of retaining the Philippines as a means of enabling the United States to protect its trade in the Far East against the increasing encroachments of Europe.

The missionary zeal of the American churches also contributed to the imperialism of the McKinley administration. With great changes impending in China and the Far East, clergymen and laymen felt that the opportunities and responsibilities of Christian missions must not be overlooked or evaded. Protestant churches had heartily joined in the crusade against "Spanish cruelty and oppression," and it was not difficult to see the hand of God directing affairs to the end that the blessings of American Protestantism might be extended to Cuba, Puerto Rico, Hawaii, and the Philippines. Did not events portend that a higher power had decreed the end of the isolation of the United States? Voices from the churches did not fall on the deaf ears of William McKinley, himself a devout Methodist. He said that the answer to his prayers for divine guidance was that "there was nothing left for us to do but to take them all, and to educate the Filipinos, and uplift and civilize and Christianize them, and by God's grace do the very best we could by them as our fellow-men for whom Christ also died."

The debate on the ratification of the treaty in the Senate took a wide range, embracing constitutionality, expediency, national responsibility, patriotism, and the duty of supporting the President in the conduct of foreign affairs. The two-thirds majority necessary for the ratification of the treaty could not be recruited exclusively from the Republican members of the Senate. The opponents of ratification were all Democrats, with the exception of Hoar of Massachusetts and Hale of Maine. At the last moment, when it appeared that the treaty was doomed, two Democratic

Senators from the South went over to the Republican majority. Eleven Democrats joined with Republicans, Populists, Silverites, and Independents in voting for ratification. What turned the tide was the advice of Bryan to ratify the treaty in order to give formal recognition to the end of the war and to leave the status of the Philippines to be determined by the electorate in the next presidential election. Moreover, the news of the outbreak of hostilities between the American army and the Filipino insurrectionists raised the question of national honor. Should the American flag be lowered in the face of a hostile army?

The United States was thus committed to a colonial policy, entailing larger expenditures for the army and navy and responsibilities and problems undreamed of by an earlier generation. It is entirely possible that if the question of the retention of the Philippines had been submitted to a vote of the people, the verdict would have been against it. Be that as it may, a large element of the American people was never reconciled to the annexation of the islands; and the question of their retention never entirely dropped out of politics, even after 1934, when the islands were granted independence to be consummated after a "probationary" period of ten years. The experience of the United States in the Philippines adds further proof that it is sometimes easier to take military possession of territory than it is to relinquish it. American experience in Cuba furnishes similar evidence.

The ratification of the Treaty of Paris and subsequent legislation pertaining to the government and administration of the territory ceded to the United States gave rise to a number of cases which collectively are known as the "Insular Cases." They were decided by the Supreme Court in 1901. Without entering into the details of the laws and cases involved, it may be said that the effect of the decisions was to lay down or sustain three far-reaching principles. First, that the United States, being a sovereign nation, may acquire territory by war or by conquest. Second, that the acquisition of territory does not extend the laws of the United States to its inhabitants except by special congressional enactment. Third, that it falls within the power of Congress to govern such territory in a more or less arbitrary fashion.

The adoption of the Teller resolution left the United States no alternative but to withdraw its military forces from Cuba as soon as conditions permitted, although there was skepticism in the United States as well as in other countries as to whether or not the pledge would be honored. The immediate problem was to feed the starving Cubans and to minister to those who had been reduced to extremities of disease and misery during the long and devastating civil war. Under the efficient administration of Major General Leonard Wood, who served as governor-general from December, 1899, to May, 1902, Cuba's house was set in order. Not the least of the services rendered was the introduction of sanitary measures and the eradication of yellow fever, which had taken heavy toll of lives. Under the supervision of Walter Reed of the United States Army Yellow Fever Commission, experiments were conducted which determined that yellow fever was transmitted by the mosquito. With the method of transmission known, a war of extermination was waged so effectively on the mosquito that whereas in 1900 there were some fourteen hundred cases of yellow fever in Havana alone, in the following year there were only thirty-seven cases in the entire island.

A census preceded the assembling of a Cuban constitutional convention. After the convention had completed its work, an election was held and on May 20, 1902, the Republic of Cuba was launched on its stormy career, not without conditions having been imposed by the United States. By the Platt amendment to the annual army appropriation bill, which was approved by President McKinley on March 2, 1901, the United States signified its intention to leave the government to the control of the people of Cuba on condition that the constitution would contain certain provisions stipulated in the amendment. Cuba could never make a treaty that would impair its independence; the United States could intervene "for the preservation of Cuban independence, the maintenance of a government adequate for the protection of life, property, and individual liberty," and for discharging certain obligations imposed by the Treaty of Paris; Cuba should lease or sell lands to the United States for naval stations.

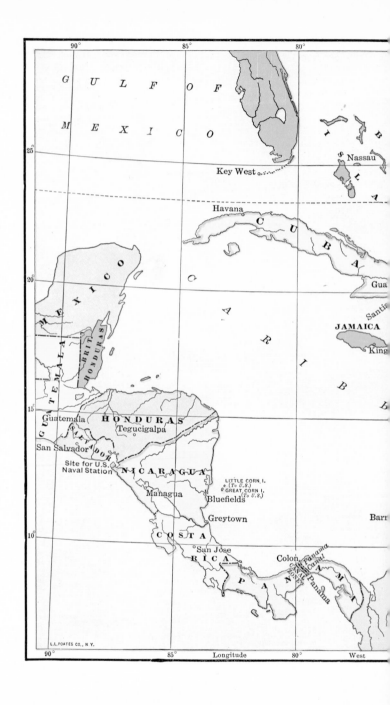

GULF OF

MEXICO

90°   85°   80°

25°

Key West

Nassau

Havana

CUBA

MEXICO

Gua

20°

JAMAICA

King

GUATEMALA

BRIT. HONDURAS

C

A

R

I

B

HONDURAS

Guatemala

Tegucigalpa

SALVADOR

San Salvador

15°

Site for U.S.
Naval Station

NICARAGUA

LITTLE CORN I.
(To U.S.)
GREAT CORN I.
(To U.S.)

Managua

Bluefields

Greytown

Barr

COSTA

San José

RICA

10°

Colon

Panama
Canal

CANAL

ZONE

Panama

PANAMA

L.L.POATES CO., N.Y.

90°   85°   80°

Longitude   West

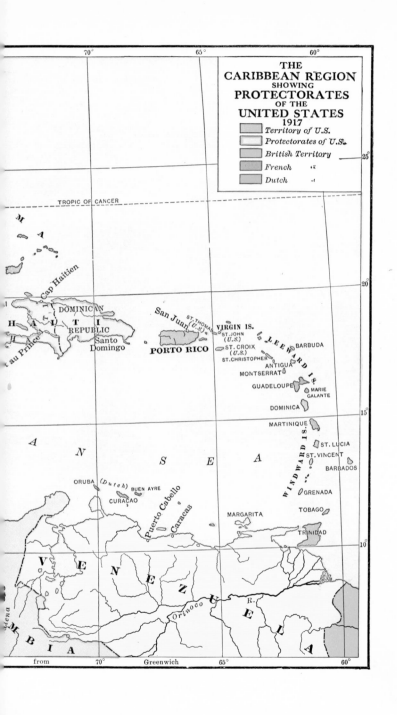

THE
CARIBBEAN REGION
SHOWING
PROTECTORATES
OF THE
UNITED STATES
1917

Territory of U.S.
Protectorates of U.S.
British Territory
French
Dutch

70°   65°   60°

25°

TROPIC OF CANCER

M A

Cap Haitien

DOMINICAN
H A I T I   REPUBLIC
au Prince   Santo
Domingo

San Juan   ST.THOMAS   VIRGIN IS.
                (U.S.)   ST.JOHN
PORTO RICO   (U.S.)
                ST. CROIX
                (U.S.)   BARBUDA
                ST.CHRISTOPHER   LEEWARD IS.
                        ANTIGUA
                MONTSERRAT
                GUADELOUPE   MARIE
                            GALANTE
                    DOMINICA

MARTINIQUE

A   N   S   E   A   ST. LUCIA
                        ST. VINCENT
                        WINDWARD IS.   BARBADOS

ORUBA (Dutch) BUEN AYRE   GRENADA
    CURAÇAO
        Puerto Cabello   TOBAGO
            Caracas   MARGARITA
                        TRINIDAD

V   E   N   E   Z   U   E   L   A

Orinoco   R.

MBIA

from   70°   Greenwich   65°   60°

20°

15°

10°

It was further stipulated that these provisions should be embodied in a treaty between the United States and Cuba.

The Cubans were disappointed because the United States had "tied a string" to its gift of independence, but the conditions of the Platt amendment were complied with. In September, 1906, the situation in Cuba had come to such a pass that President Roosevelt conceived it to be the duty of his government to intervene by sending an army and proclaiming martial law. It was not until January, 1909, that order was restored, life and property were safe and the government was again restored to the people. Once more the action of the United States gave the lie to those who had said that this country was in Cuba to stay.

The Cubans never appreciated the rôle of "big brother" played by the powerful American nation, nor did the other states of Latin America who feared the imperialistic ambitions of the North American colossus. In the summer following the inauguration of President Franklin D. Roosevelt on March 4, 1933, the president of Cuba was overthrown after a five-year period of disorder and economic depression. The American ambassador to Cuba sought to bring peace to the island by assuming the rôle of mediator between the factions; but the situation grew more tense, and there was much ill-feeling against the United States and the ambassador. Roosevelt could have justified intervention under the Platt amendment, but in harmony with his "good neighbor" policy he hesitated to take action that would be resented in Latin America. The upshot of the imbroglio was the ratification of a new treaty with Cuba on May 31, 1934, by which the Platt amendment was abrogated and certain commercial concessions were granted to Cuba.

For some months after Puerto Rico became a possession of the United States it was administered by the military authorities. The war had made it impossible for the Puerto Ricans to sell their coffee and sugar, and economic conditions were generally unfavorable. Three-fourths of the population could neither read nor write, and what schools there were did not function efficiently. The poorer people of the cities were crowded in miserable quarters, where they lived in filth, squalor, and immorality. Spanish rule in Puerto Rico had been no more efficient than in Cuba. The chief objectives of the American authorities were to establish government and to improve the condition of the people by introducing sanitation and establishing a system of schools.

By the Foraker Act of April 12, 1900, the inhabitants of the island were declared to be citizens of Puerto Rico. The government was vested in an executive, consisting of a governor and six heads of administrative departments, and a legislature of two houses, consisting of the executive council and a house of delegates. The judiciary was composed of a territorial court, a supreme court, and such inferior courts as the legislature might establish. The governor and members of the legislative council were appointed by the President of the United States, and the members of the house of delegates were elected by the people. The Foraker Act represented an effort to strike a balance in the legislature between the Americans and the natives, with the governor having the power of veto.

The Foraker Act, with minor modifications, remained the "organic act" until 1916, when the Puerto Ricans were made citizens of the United States and the legislature was converted into two houses, the members of each to be elected by the people. A resident commissioner who has no vote represents Puerto Rico in the Congress of the United States. Until the enactment of the Foraker Law, the high rates of the Dingley Tariff were enforced against Puerto Rico precisely as if the island had been foreign territory. The Foraker Act provided that until March 1, 1902, a duty of 15 per cent should be collected on commodities imported into the United States. This provision, which was upheld by the Supreme Court, was dictated by sugar growers of the United States, who feared competition with sugar imported duty free from the island. It was opposed by those who believed it to be inconsistent with the political relations between the United States and Puerto Rico.

Shortly after the passage of the joint resolution annexing the Hawaiian Islands, President McKinley appointed a commission of five men, Americans and Hawaiians, to consider questions essential to the government of the islands and their relations with the United States. The commission promptly reported its findings, but in the legislative jam Congress failed to pass an "organic act" until April 30, 1900. This law in general provided for a government closely similar to that of other territories. It extended to the islands the Constitution and laws of the United States and conferred American citizenship upon persons, including Chinese, who were citizens of Hawaii on August 12, 1898.

From the beginning the people of Hawaii dreamed about having their territory admitted into the sisterhood of states; and during Franklin D. Roosevelt's first term well-organized propaganda to that end was conducted in the United States. The American people, however, have taken little interest in their island possessions. Moreover, the fact that in 1930 the Japanese constituted about 38 per cent of the total population was a powerful factor operating against statehood. During the excitement that accompanied the law excluding Japanese from the United States in 1924, alarming reports were broadcast about the increase of the Japanese population in Hawaii. After 1900 the Japanese bugaboo lurked in many places.

The process of establishing government under American auspices in the Philippine Islands met with unexpected obstacles. When the Schurmann Commission appointed by President McKinley arrived in the Philippines in the early part of 1899, a military government had already been set up by General Elwell S. Otis, a Philippine Republic had been promulgated by the insurrectionists, and the rival forces were at war. The United States was thus confronted with the task of reducing a rebellion waged by a vastly larger population than that of Cuba in the rebellion against Spain. With startling suddenness the American authorities had occasion to regret the arrangement that had permitted Aguinaldo to depart from Hongkong in order to organize an insurrection against the Spaniards. After a series of battles in which the Americans were uniformly victorious, though not without serious casualties on both sides, the insurgents resorted to guerilla warfare which continued until the spring of 1902.

It was the irony of fate that the American officers felt themselves obliged to resort to methods of warfare that had been condemned when employed by the Spaniards in Cuba. In parts of the islands they adopted the reconcentration policy that had been inaugurated by "Butcher" Weyler in Cuba. The "water cure" was also used to obtain information about the location of rebels. A bamboo reed was inserted into the throat of the victim preliminary to pumping his body full of water.

It is not to be thought that the Americans only were guilty of cruel practices. As in the case of the Cuban insurrection, atrocities were committed on both sides; but the revelations of a Senate committee in 1902 were shocking and humiliating to the people of the United States. Such conduct, as well as the requirement of a literacy test for voters in Puerto Rico and Hawaii, brought taunts from southern Democrats that the Republicans had abandoned their solicitude for the Negro in the South as manifested in the Fifteenth Amendment and proposed bills for its enforcement.

Newspaper reports about conditions in the Philippines disillusioned those who had thought seriously of extending the blessings of territorial government preliminary to early statehood. After months of investigation, the Schurmann Commission reported that their lack of education and their political inexperience, combined with racial and linguistic diversities, made it inadvisable to impose on the Filipinos the burden of self-government. In March, 1900, a second commission headed by William H. Taft was charged with the duty of exercising legislative functions and of organizing civil government. A year later, in 1901, by the Spooner amendment to the army appropriation bill, the President of the United States was authorized to establish temporary civil government, and on July 4, 1901, Taft was inaugurated civil governor. The process of establishing civil government in the various provinces continued until, on the approval of the Philippine Government Act by President Roosevelt on July 1, 1902, congressional government succeeded arbitrary rule under the direction of the President.

By this act the Filipinos were declared to be citizens of the Philippine Islands and a legislative assembly of two houses was added. The upper house was the Philippine Commission and the lower chamber was elective under a greatly restricted franchise. In spite of his difficult assignment, Taft won the good will of the

Filipinos; and it was with considerable satisfaction that in 1907, in his capacity as Secretary of War, he went to the Philippines to open the first session of the assembly.

To Governor Taft also fell the disagreeable duty of ironing out the problem of the friar lands in the islands. Under Spanish rule some four hundred thousand acres of the best lands were held by friars of the Roman Catholic church and rented to tenants. During the insurrection the friars were driven out, but they transferred their lands in trust to corporations and individuals. The tenants, however, refused to pay rent. The settlement of the controversy necessitated the visit of Governor Taft to Rome; and in 1903 the American government purchased the lands for something over seven million dollars.

This was only one of several difficulties inherited from the Spanish régime. The difficult problem of the Roman Catholic church, which had incurred the hostility of powerful elements of the population, was settled tactfully and to the satisfaction of the papacy and the church authorities, if not always with the approval of the natives. The Spanish-American War, the Filipino insurrection, and the government of dependencies proved to be far more expensive and troublesome than anyone had anticipated when the adventure of war was so light-heartedly embarked upon in April, 1898.

In their platform of 1900 the Republicans promised that the Filipinos would be given self-government according to the measure of their welfare and American obligations. In denouncing the policy of the McKinley administration, the Democrats favored an immediate declaration of the nation's purpose to give the Filipinos, first, a stable form of government and, second, independence. There were, however, prominent men in both parties who were not satisfied with these declarations. There were imperialists and anti-imperialists among Republicans and Democrats alike. In successive campaigns the Democrats reiterated their purpose to grant independence to the Philippines; and when on March 4, 1913, the Democrats obtained control of the legislative and executive departments of the government, they proceeded to redeem their pledges. President Wilson appointed Francis Burton Harrison governor of

the Philippines. His appointment and administration raised hopes
for a larger measure of self-government and speedy independence.

On October 14, 1914, the House of Representatives passed the
Jones bill, which embodied the substance of these hopes; and in
the Senate the bill was amended to grant independence within not
more than four years and not less than two. The amendment,
however, failed to pass the House, the Republicans voting solidly
against it and about thirty Democrats, mostly Irish, joining them.
The Organic Act, without the so-called Clarke amendment, was
approved by President Wilson on August 29, 1916.

Progress toward a larger measure of self-government continued
until the return of the Republicans to power under Warren G.
Harding in 1921. He appointed General Leonard Wood governor-
general. His administration became very unpopular, so unpopular
in fact that both houses of the Philippine legislature fell into the
control of the party that demanded immediate independence. A
delegation even came to Washington to complain of the arbitrary
governor.

Events played into the hands of the nationalists. The islands
proved to be a poor investment, even though trade between them
and the United States increased to such an extent that they became
economically dependent on the "mother country." In 1934, for
example, the United States took 84 per cent of the exports and
furnished 66 per cent of the imports. This was one result of the
free trade between the United States and the Philippines which
was inaugurated in 1907. It was just this fact that contributed
mightily to the triumph of the anti-imperialists in the United
States. The farmers in the Middle West complained of the competition of Philippine products with the products of their own
farms; and when the depression that followed the World War was
further intensified by the debacle of agricultural products after the
crash of 1929, the way was paved for the consummation of Democratic promises under the auspices of Franklin D. Roosevelt. To
this must be added the desire of labor to prevent the immigration
of cheap labor from the islands and the influence of the sugar
interests who wished to stop the importation of sugar.

During the closing weeks of the Hoover administration, in January, 1933, the Hare-Hawes-Cutting Bill became a law over the President's veto. This act provided for a temporary protectorate over the Philippine Islands, the virtual exclusion of Filipino immigrants from the United States, and the imposition of duties on certain imports from the islands. The United States was to retain its naval and military establishments. The tariff and immigration provisions caused the Philippine legislature to reject this measure.

In a message of March 2, 1934, President Roosevelt recommended the elimination from the Hare-Hawes-Cutting Act of the provision for the retention of military posts and the amendment of the provision pertaining to naval bases. He also suggested that the time limit for the acceptance of the new proposal by the Philippine legislature be extended. These recommendations were written into the Tydings-McDuffie Act, which was approved on March 24, 1934. The Philippine legislature signified its approval on May 1, and a constitutional convention was held in July, 1935.

Under the provisions of the Tydings-McDuffie Act the President of the United States is represented by a high commissioner. During the first five years of the Commonwealth of the Philippine Islands, free trade between the two countries will continue, after which, during the remaining five years of the "probationary" period, duties will be levied by the Philippine government on all exports to the United States. After independence is attained, the regular duties will be levied on all imports of Philippine products into the United States.

Thus economic self-interest dictated a measure that had been under consideration for three decades; and the economic self-interest of the Philippines made independence a less welcome gift than if it had been tendered earlier. Legislation designed to protect the American farmer from competition with such products as cocoanut oil and copra threatens disaster to an important means of livelihood for a considerable element in the islands.

At a special convocation at the University of Notre Dame to celebrate the establishment of the Commonwealth of the Philippine Islands on December 9, 1935, at which President Roosevelt was present, Carlo Romulo, a distinguished Filipino publicist, made the principal address and expressed the gratitude of his people for

the generous policy of the American people and government. The
new republic was established on November 15, 1935, with the
inauguration of President Manuel Quezon. Previously, on May 15,
1935, the constitution had been adopted in a plebiscite. The Commonwealth of the Philippine Islands will be a final reality in
1944, with the approval and blessing of the American people,
unless the menacing situation in the Far East, which became
increasingly alarming after 1934, nullifies it, as seems likely.

In the years to come Americans can look back with pardonable
pride to the accomplishments during the years of the American
occupation of the Philippine Islands, the most important of which
is perhaps a system of elementary and secondary schools. Among
other achievements may be mentioned excellent roads, irrigation
projects, public health and sanitation, and security of life and
property, all of which have given the Filipinos a greater degree of
self-respect. In terms of dollars and cents the Philippines were a
poor investment for the American people; but translated into finer
values, the investment yielded rich returns to both peoples.

CHAPTER XVII

THE LIFE OF THE PEOPLE, 1900-1917

THE MATERIAL PROGRESS OF THE AMERICAN PEOPLE WAS INTER-
rupted by the depression that followed the panic of 1893, but at
the beginning of the twentieth century optimism was again in full
bloom. The Populist party lingered on until the election of 1904,
but the orators of that party were almost unheard after 1900.
Not that the American people had assumed an attitude of complacency; on the contrary, never before had the united forces of
wholesome reform won such a succession of victories over the
evils that threatened the material and moral stamina of the nation
as they did from 1900 to 1917. The "invisible government" was
on the defensive, in spite of its great power and many weapons.

The caustic pen of H. L. Mencken has written that from 1905
to 1929 was the heyday of Babbittry; but from 1900 down to the
World War, certainly, progressive ideas were in the ascendancy.
It is true that about 1905 the word "graft" became a synonym for
corruption, but never before had corruption in office, high and
low, been so mercilessly exposed by pulpit, press, and school. Never
had the daily press reflected more faithfully the idealism and
wholesomeness of the people, in spite of the increasing circulation
of sensational newspapers of the William Randolph Hearst type.
Never had the pages of fiction, whether in books or magazines,
been cleaner. The apostles of social justice, political integrity, and
peace and good will toward men were given respectful hearing on
the platform and on the printed page. True, in perspective it
appears that America was a fool's paradise; but the perspective
only magnifies the chaos, misery, and disillusionment of the years
of the World War and after.

In spite of the rising cost of living and the possible decline in
real wages, the industrious and thrifty farmer, laborer, and pro-

fessional man built, purchased, or rented better homes, purchased better furniture, read more and better literature, and sent their sons and daughters to high school and college. Immense sums were raised and contributed for primary, secondary, and higher education; great philanthropic foundations were established; impressive buildings were erected; the quality of teaching was improved; and the enrollment in high schools and colleges multiplied. Cities were beautified; parks and playgrounds were laid out and furnished recreation; public libraries were built and developed; hospitals and homes for unfortunates were increased and improved; churches multiplied and imposing edifices were erected. In spite of certain indications to the contrary, races and religions seemed to be drawing closer together. The "melting pot" was fusing the composite population into a new society, while millions of newcomers from strange shores were pouring in.

At the turn of the century a few automobile advertisements appeared with those of bicycles in the advertising sections of magazines. Fifteen years later the advertisements of the two-wheeled vehicle were as scarce as those of automobiles were numerous. Even before 1900 there were articles about the "horseless carriage" and predictions about its future usefulness in peace and war. "Flying machines" were also mentioned, but until the close of the first decade of the twentieth century these strange machines were seen only at state fairs or similar exhibitions.

The last decade of the nineteenth century was the day *par excellence* of the bicycle. In the Editor's Study of the January, 1896, *Harper's,* Charles Dudley Warner dubbed the year 1895 the "great bicycle year" and maintained that it would also be a landmark in the "progress" of women. When the "safety" bicycle first made its appearance, women were reluctant to mount the steed. It was even said that bicycling for women was vulgar; and when the "new woman" cyclist appeared in bifurcated skirts and high-topped shoes, staid and conservative people were horrified. In any event, bicycle-riding was incompatible with long skirts and heavy petticoats that swept floors and sidewalks and with huge hats adorned with ostrich plumes, bright feathers, and birds' wings. The absurdly long pointed shoes, "hard-boiled" bosom

Brown Brothers

In the Days of the Bicycle

Edwin Levick

The First Flight of Glenn H. Curtiss

Brown Brothers

shirts, and high stand-up collars worn by men pedaling bicycles looked just as ridiculous. The League of American Wheelmen, local bicycle clubs, and cycle paths gave occasion for exercise and informal activities.

During this period the railroads made great improvements in their roadbeds and equipment. Hundreds of millions of dollars were spent in laying heavier steel, straightening curves, laying double tracks, installing block signals and air brakes, displacing wooden coaches with those of steel construction, and building terminals and stations. Transcontinental and limited passenger trains were given attractive names like "The Empire State Limited," "The Twentieth Century Limited," "The Hummer," "The Golden State Limited," and "The Pioneer Limited." Passengers were invited to be "guests" of railroads on trains carrying observation cars, buffet cars, barber shops, maids, and valets. Headlines announcing train wrecks with heavy loss of life became less conspicuous, and by the end of the second decade of the century travel by rail had become the safest means of transportation.

Electric interurban cars furnished cheap, rapid, and frequent service; and from cities like Indianapolis, for example, radiated interurban lines in all directions. Between 1910 and 1920, however, privately owned automobiles did to the interurbans what high-speed automobiles, airplanes, and buses did to railroad passenger traffic after 1920.

The almost entire absence of paved highways and the poor quality of graveled roads made "touring" by automobile for a distance of fifty miles an all-day adventure in the Middle West until after the World War. And even for some years later, tourists were held up for days in Iowa by impassable roads. Iowa farmers assembled at church or in the county seat hurriedly gathered members of their families at the approach of threatening clouds that would not only "lay the dust" but would make driving hazardous.

The Ford automobile revolutionized life on the farm; and by 1917 this machine had come into such demand that some farmers actually offered to pay a bonus to dealers for early delivery of a "tin Lizzie" or a "road louse." Eight or ten years before, perhaps, the same farmers had paid a fare to ride around the county fair grounds in a one-seated electric. By 1917 there were few villages that could not boast of one or more filling stations and a garage.

The country town retained many of its nineteenth-century characteristics, but there were also many changes. Homes built by retired farmers were more attractive and modern, with bathrooms, central heating plants, pressure tanks and running water (if there was no municipal waterworks), and gas lights connected with a "lighting plant" on the premises (if there was no municipal plant). The general merchandise store was still prosperous, in spite of large mail-order houses like Sears, Roebuck, and Co., and Montgomery Ward & Co. The era of the chain stores had only begun.

Moving picture theaters invaded country towns in the second decade of the century, but, as in the large cities, this form of entertainment was largely of the ten-cent variety, showing such subjects as "The Pretty Dairy Maid or the Mad Man's Revenge," "Oscar's Elopement," and "The Stolen Sausage." In 1905 the Chicago moving picture theaters were on State Street in the form of a railroad observation car, with a "spieler" inviting passing pedestrians to take a trip through the Grand Canyon or some other scenic route.

In this period life grew richer and easier for the farmer and his wife. The rural telephone opened channels of conversation with neighbors; rural free delivery of mail brought the daily paper; the automobile brought church, school, courthouse, and market to his door; gas engines pumped water for livestock; tractors and self-feeding separators made plowing and threshing easier and faster; wires brought light, power for washing machines, and heat for irons; express service and local laundry agencies relieved housewives of the drudgery of "doing up" certain kinds of washing and ironing; prepared breakfast foods, baker's bread, canned fruits and vegetables could be purchased conveniently; dressed meat from packing houses eliminated "butchering" on the farm; the cream separator put an end to skimming milk; factory-made dresses and garments made the vocation of seamstress precarious; consolidated schools and school buses fore-

Library of Congress

PLOWING IN THE EIGHTEENTH AND NINETEENTH CENTURIES

Brown Brothers

shadowed the decline of the "little red schoolhouse"; refreshment in the form of ice cream soda could be had at the town restaurant or drug store.

The young man who smoked cigarettes was no longer regarded as a "no account," but it was not respectable for his sister to "light up" until the close of the third decade; and even after that school-teachers had to smoke on the sly. Local or county option or state-wide prohibition had removed saloons from many Main Streets; and no respectable woman would drink in public, except in certain foreign-born communities. Attendance at the county fair declined; lectures and concerts at the Chautauqua had greater attractions. Young men drove by automobile to see minor league baseball games, but it was not until the third decade that broadcasts of major league games came in over the loud speaker in the living room, in the barber shop, and still later in the beer parlor or "tavern." In 1905 the bank clerk, the clerk in the general store, and the farm hand who owned a rubber-tired top buggy were popular with the young ladies; fifteen years later even heroes returning from service in France stood little chance in competition with the young blade who drove an automobile.

In 1910 the "old settlers' picnic" was largely attended by retired farmers who lived on the rentals of their farms. Already mounting taxes reduced incomes, but their worries were minor compared with the heavy assessments for consolidated schools and improved roads twenty years later.

From 1900 to 1918 farm lands rose greatly in value. Farm lands in Iowa that sold for from seventy-five to one hundred dollars per acre in 1900 brought two hundred dollars or more in 1914, but it must be remembered that between those dates considerable money had been invested in tiling, woven wire fencing, barns, cattle sheds, and residences. Notwithstanding the prosperity of the Iowa farmer, the population of his state declined in the first decade of the century. Young men migrated to Minnesota, the Dakotas, the Southwest, and the Pacific Northwest, where farm lands could be purchased for less. Moreover, the trek of retired farmers to California had already begun.

The rising value of farm lands, the increasing acreage of land under cultivation, the declining rural population, and the growing numbers of tenant farmers foreshadowed the serious problems that beset the agricultural population after the World War: over-production, mortgages, high taxes, and labor shortage in certain regions. In 1890 the rural population was greatly in excess of the urban population, but the Census of 1920 reported a majority for

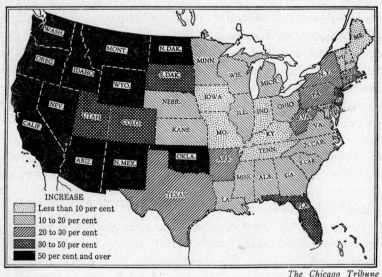

The Chicago Tribune

PERCENTAGE OF INCREASE IN TOTAL POPULATION BY STATES, 1900-10

the city dwellers. People had gravitated to the larger cities like Chicago, New York, Detroit, Cleveland, Boston, Minneapolis, St. Louis, and Cincinnati.

Farming in New England remained in a stagnant state; but among the eight million emigrants from Europe who arrived on American shores from 1900 to 1910, a number settled on abandoned farms to engage in truck farming—a profitable undertaking in view of the cheap land and the growing and prosperous industrial centers. The industrialization of New England attracted hundreds of thousands of French-Canadians and emigrants from the countries of southern and eastern Europe; and as early as the

eighties articles in periodicals and editorials in newspapers discoursed on the "transformation of New England." The school-
teacher from the Middle West who inquired of boys playing on
the streets of Salem the way to the House of the Seven Gables
was surprised to hear from their lips English with a pronounced
Polish, Italian, or Jewish accent.

In the South the chief crop was cotton. Fluctuating prices placed
heavy burdens on the cotton farmers and fastened mortgages on
their farms, so heavy that many of them met the fate that had
overtaken the farmers during the depression of the nineties. The
increasing production of cotton contributed to declining prices
in the same way that the increasing acreage of corn and wheat
land brought down the prices of those commodities. The invasion
of settlers into Texas and Oklahoma after 1900 made those states
leaders in cotton production. The boll weevil played havoc in the
Cotton Belt and caused heavy losses to farmers.

Another noticeable development in the South was the increase
in the number of white cotton farmers and the decrease in the
number of Negroes. These farmers were victims of the system of
share-cropping, which deprived them and their families of a decent standard of living and kept them in perpetual debt to landlords and financial agencies which exacted exorbitant commissions
and rates of interest. The plight of the share-croppers was one
of the most serious problems that confronted the country. And the
plight of their landlords added to the problem.

The increasing consumption of tobacco stimulated production.
Unlike the cotton planter, the tobacco planter in the South was
not seriously affected by the mounting production of his commodity in other countries. Tobacco requires intensive cultivation,
so intensive that a farmer and his family can husband only from
five to ten acres. Shortly after the Civil War, Virginia lost her
leadership in tobacco production to Kentucky, North Carolina, and
Tennessee. When the Kentucky planters in 1906 realized that
they were in the grip of the Tobacco Trust, an organization known
as "Night Riders" inaugurated a reign of terror by destroying
tobacco, regardless of property rights.

After 1900 the industrialization of the South took on such

AN ALLURING AND ARTISTIC FULL-PAGE ADVERTISEMENT OF BOCA RATON
(From A. M. Sakolski, *The Great American Land Bubble*, Harper & Brothers)

momentum that publicists wrote about the "New South." Unlike workers in the New England textile mills, however, the employees in the southern cotton mills were recruited not from the immigrant population but from tenant farmers and mountaineers. Reports in the foreign-language press of conditions in the milling centers of Virginia and North Carolina—low wages, long hours, unsanitary conditions, and child labor—kept immigration from flowing into the South, although the climate and the large Negro population were also factors.

The development of the steel industry in the Birmingham, Alabama, district; the exploitation of the timber resources in Arkansas, Louisiana, and Texas, following the exhaustion of the forests in the northern states; and the fabulous development of the oil fields in Texas, Oklahoma, Louisiana, and Arkansas, which shifted the great area of oil production from Pennsylvania, are among the striking events of the twentieth century. The Florida land boom, which reached its culmination 1925, was inflated by "development boards" and land and real estate mortgage companies, which propagandized the public through the daily press, magazines, and prominent citizens like Barron Collier, the advertising magnate, the Ringlings, circus operators, J. C. Penney, the merchant prince, and even William J. Bryan, the Great Commoner.

Great as were the changes in the mode of living in the rural districts, the twentieth century was preeminently the day of the city. The migration from farm to city and the increase of urban wealth at the expense of the country accelerated with the speed that suggests the transition from the horse and buggy to the automobile and from the automobile to the airplane. The growth of cities—some of them like Gary, Indiana, springing up like magic —brought serious problems; but for the well-to-do city dweller life grew richer.

Surface trolley lines, elevated railways, and subways furnished cheap and rapid transportation; department stores, telephones, and better methods of merchandising made shopping easier; streets were better paved and better lighted; residences, apartments, and public buildings became more attractive and convenient; public health was improved by sanitation and some progress toward socialized medicine; factories, stores, and office buildings were more attractive and better ventilated; public entertainment in the form of band concerts, symphony orchestras, and larger and finer and safer theaters was provided; many cities by zoning and city planning prevented the encroachments on residential sections by industries, saloons, and "nuisances"; the automobile was driving from the city the evil-smelling livery stable and the old-fashioned street sweeper; the milk man delivered butter in cartons and milk and cream in bottles, instead of sounding a gong to summon the housewife with a crock or pail; dairy lunches and cafeterias were cleaner, more attractive, and more efficient than the nineteenth-century restaurant; drinking fountains displaced the common cup; cuspidors and signs "Don't spit on the floor" were less in evidence in public buildings; the paper towel was a great improvement over the unspeakable "public towel."

Suburban trains, and automobiles later, enabled the laborer, clerk, and professional man and woman to enjoy the Saturday half-holiday and Sunday in the open, away from the noise, dust, and smoke of the city; and the amusement park, with its merry-go-round, roller coaster, bowling alleys, refectory, and band concert, provided less expensive entertainment. Tennis courts and golf courses grew more and more popular and were ceasing to be forms of recreation exclusively for the wealthy. Colleges, universities, high schools, and grade schools provided gymnasiums and athletic fields and added physical education to their curricula.

From 1900 to 1917 baseball was the most popular form of public entertainment and became highly commercialized, not entirely to the advantage of the sport. Mammoth grandstands were constructed, playing fields were improved almost to perfection, and rowdyism by players and spectators was reduced. The players were more restrained in language and conduct, and in most parks the sale of intoxicating liquor, including beer, was prohibited.

The Spanish-American War and unfavorable business conditions caused the National League, which had ruled baseball since 1876, to drop four clubs and return to an eight-club circuit in 1899. This action paved the way for a baseball war in which the stakes were high. In 1900 Byron Bancroft Johnson, who had

Brown Brothers

BROAD STREET, NEW YORK, IN 1893

Brown Bro

BROAD STREET, NEW YORK, IN 1933

made a success of running the Western League, organized a rival
major circuit which he called the American League. While Johnson's craft was confidently sailing onward, the National League
was foundering on the rocks of syndicated baseball, an experiment
similar to "chain store baseball," originated by the St. Louis
Cardinals after the World War, with the important distinction
that in 1900 a syndicate controlled several clubs in the same league,
whereas the Cardinals owned and operated so-called farms in
"double A" and minor leagues.

By offering contracts baited with large salaries and by staging
spectacular raids on the clubs of the old league, the American
League had by 1902 almost picked the rival circuit clean of stars.
The National League fought back and employed the weapon of
litigation. In 1902 the Philadelphia National Ball Club brought
a bill in equity for an injunction to restrain Napoleon Lajoie,
who had jumped his contract with that club, from playing with
the Philadelphia American League Club. Lajoie contended that
the so-called reserve clause in his contract was illegal in that at
the option of the club his contract could be renewed for two years
and he could be released on ten days' notice. In other words, the
contract was lacking in mutuality.

The Supreme Court of Pennsylvania upheld the mutuality of
the contract and ruled that Lajoie could be restrained from playing for another club in Pennsylvania during the time stipulated
in the contract. The victory for the National League, however,
was more apparent than real, because Lajoie was transferred to
another club in the American League. Within a few days the federal circuit court at St. Louis denied the application for an
injunction to restrain three contract-jumpers from playing with
the St. Louis Americans. The decision was based on the lack of
mutuality of contract, the abrogation of personal liberty, and a
combination in violation of anti-trust laws.

Finally, in 1903, after a series of events harmful to organized
baseball, the two leagues signed the National Agreement by which
a National Commission, composed of the presidents of the respective leagues and a third member to be chosen by them, was set up
as the supreme court of baseball to adjudicate disputes between

clubs of the same league, between clubs of different leagues, and between players and clubs. Most of the minor leagues were included within the scope of the National Agreement, and thereafter the reserve clause was enforced with a vengeance.

During the following ten years players and magnates made money; admission fees were raised; immense grandstands were erected; electric scoreboards attracted large crowds in front of newspaper offices; and the number of pages devoted to baseball in the press steadily increased. In 1913, however, a new outlaw claiming to be a major league arose to test the stamina of the National Commission. This was the Federal League, which was conceived in the lust for publicity and money in the persons of two or three prominent men in the financial world. Unable to purchase stock in existing big league clubs, they organized a league of their own. This inaugurated a baseball war of three years' duration—the most disastrous in the history of the sport. Again the reserve clause in players' contracts was under fire; and in a suit brought by the Federal League against the National and American Leagues in January, 1915, the contracts of ten thousand ball players were involved. The plaintiff sought to show that the National Agreement was illegal; that the defendants constituted a combination, conspiracy, and monopoly in contravention of anti-trust laws; and that the players' contracts were null and void.

Obviously organized baseball could not risk a decision that would put the National Agreement and the National Commission out of business. At the close of the year 1915 a treaty of peace was negotiated, which satisfied the ambitious Federal League magnates and safeguarded organized baseball.

The scandal connected with the World's Series of 1919 gave baseball a black eye. It was proved that certain players on the Chicago White Sox Club sold out to gamblers and threw the series to Cincinnati. The guilty players were blacklisted; but the scandal left such a bad taste in the public mouth that the moguls resorted to a radical measure to win back public confidence in the game. Finally, Judge Kenesaw Mountain Landis was named baseball commissioner. Thus a supreme judge succeeded a supreme court of baseball.

The World War, the World's Series scandal, the automobile, the moving picture theater, golf, and the radio seriously threatened to reduce the large attendance at baseball games, although since the World War the drawing power of certain clubs and the World's Series games continued to bring large sums into the coffers of magnates. At the beginning of the 1930's night baseball was introduced in order to recruit spectators from factories and offices to fill grandstands and bleachers deserted by men and women who found better recreation elsewhere.

After 1900 intercollegiate football vied with baseball as a public spectacle; and huge crowds and high admission fees made possible mammoth stadiums that exceeded the seating capacity of baseball parks. Harvard's stadium was the first to be erected, but after the World War it was only one of many similar structures. Overemphasis on football, proselyting of players who were reimbursed for their services in various and devious ways, unseemly conduct by students and others following victories, gambling, and the mounting injuries on the gridiron brought a wave of reform in 1905-06. Even President Theodore Roosevelt lent his powerful influence to the cause. The number of games on the schedule was reduced, the training table was abolished, proselyting was frowned upon, and some institutions even abolished the game.

However, the tremendous increase in the enrollment of colleges and universities, the rivalry for students, the tempting admission fees, the pressure of alumni who motored to homecoming games, the propaganda fostered by highly paid coaches and newspaper reporters, and the greed of hotels, restaurants, and other business establishments nullified the efforts of faculties to "place first things first"; and after the World War the evils that had brought the reform wave existed in exaggerated form, to the dismay of courageous and level-headed university and college presidents and the Carnegie Foundation, which published a scathing indictment of the game. With the repeal of the Eighteenth Amendment in 1933, drinking during and after games increased to an alarming degree.

Attendance at football games suffered less than that at baseball during the depression years that followed the crash of 1929.

Professional football made a bid for public favor after the World War, but the nature of the game, the short season, and the absence of loyalty to Alma Mater made the experiment for a time somewhat dubious.

The low estate of performers and spectators made the lot of promoters of professional boxing and prize fighting difficult at the close of the nineteenth century and at the beginning of the twentieth. The brutality of the fighters and the dishonesty of many fights caused many states to prohibit exhibitions within their borders. After the Corbett-Fitzsimmons heavyweight championship battle in 1897, cartoons and editorials pointed the finger of shame at Carson City, Nevada, for permitting the affair. The clergy were most positive in condemnation. However, with the fading influence of the puritan tradition, the complacency of public officials, and better rules governing the sport, the bars were let down, and promoters and champions received purses that would have seemed fabulous to the previous generation.

The first decade of the century brought prosperity to the theater. The musical comedy was the most popular stage performance, but managers also booked distinguished Shakespearian actors and other finished tragedians and comedians. Although "reformers" lamented the baneful influence of the theater, it was lily white in contrast with the performances on stage and screen in the twenties and thirties. Moreover, the theater-goers who could afford to pay the prices for theater tickets in the earlier period were few in contrast with the men, women, and children who were admitted to cinema theaters for as little as five cents.

At the close of the first decade the Shuberts were in opposition to a "theater trust" or syndicate owned by Klaw and Erlanger, and established competing theaters in a number of cities. Erlanger not only produced tawdry shows, but he himself was crude, rough, and boorish, and compelled playwrights, managers, and actors to bow to him and to meet his terms on penalty of having most of the cities closed to them. After 1920 the legitimate stage was eclipsed by the cinema, and old-style theaters were dark except for a few evenings in cities as large as Minneapolis. The little theater movement and stock companies, however, kept the spoken drama alive. Practically the same fate that overtook the old-style theaters befell the vaudeville stage. In 1927-28 the "talkies" succeeded the silent pictures.

Temperance crusades brought ordinances and laws that greatly restricted the areas in states and cities where liquor could be legitimately sold; but at the beginning of the century and down to the ratification of the Eighteenth Amendment in 1918, in many towns and cities the saloon remained the "poor man's club." Card tables and slot machines furnished amusement and fellowship, and free lunches satisfied many hungry mouths. Some saloon-keepers took a certain pride in running respectable places; but many saloons were owned by breweries and were affiliated with vice and gambling rings. In large cities like New York and Chicago, and even in cities with smaller populations, saloons sold drinks all day Sunday. Entrance was through a side door. For this illegal practice saloon-keepers made monthly payments to police, sometimes directly to policemen and sometimes through Retail Liquor Dealers' Associations.

Vice was openly flaunted in segregated districts, in spite of moral crusades, some of them sensational in that prominent men and women marched into "levees" to sing hymns and pray with the inmates. Wholesale "clean-ups" were forced on mayors and chiefs of police by campaigns conducted by newspapers, evangelists, and irate citizens. After the "lid" had been on for a longer or shorter period, and the crusading zeal had subsided, police usually relaxed their vigilance, and the last state of the city was as bad as the first.

At the beginning of the century every city had several newspapers competing for subscribers and advertisers; but through consolidation the number was greatly reduced within the next fifteen years. Compared with the newspapers in 1915, the make-up and contents of the papers fifteen years earlier were sober, dignified, and conservative. Except for a few sensational sheets, the heavy leaded headline that extended across the first page was missing. The Sunday comic section made its appearance before 1900, but it was not until ten years later that an increasing number of papers contained comic strips in their weekday issues. From

1890 to 1910 the cartoonist was in his glory; after that time many papers ceased to have this feature. Though traditionally conservative along social, economic, and political lines, during the first decade many large dailies were sympathetic with reform and progressive ideas and were even critical of big business and its exponents; after the World War, however, perhaps because reformers and agitators attacked the structure of society instead of individuals who abused its privileges, very few editorials contained even a grain of comfort for the exponents of liberal thought. Liberals in later years had no faith in the "kept press." The waning influence of the newspapers was strikingly demonstrated in 1936, when Franklin D. Roosevelt was elected by an unprecedented popular and electoral vote over the opposition of probably 85 per cent of the newspapers.

In the nineteenth century men like Horace Greeley, James Gordon Bennett, E. L. Godkin, and Joseph Medill exercised their personal influence through their newspapers; the editorials in the twentieth-century newspapers were as impersonal and lacking in warmth as the corporations that owned the newspapers. In the nineteenth century individuals and groups of individuals with limited capital could start a daily paper; but in the next century the cost of a building and equipment plus an Associated Press or a United Press franchise—if one could be purchased—ran the cost up to a million dollars. The number of franchises of these world-wide news-gathering agencies were limited for each city and thus became a monopoly of a relatively few corporations which owned the metropolitan press and the associations.

The popular magazines followed the traditions of the earlier century, and never before had the public been served by so many high-class monthlies and weeklies. The *Century, Harper's, Scribner's*, the *Atlantic Monthly*, the *North American Review*, and the *Review of Reviews* maintained their high standards and traditions. *Harper's Weekly* and *Collier's Weekly* had a brilliant array of talent among authors and artists. The *Outlook* and the *Independent* catered to a select clientele of readers of weekly periodicals, and the *Literary Digest* continued to be a well-edited survey of current events in various fields of human endeavor. Women's maga-

Brown Brothers

The Poor Man's Club

Paul Thompson Collection

zines like the *Ladies' Home Journal*, the *Woman's Home Companion*, and the *Delineator* broadened the scope of their contents and greatly improved their format. Of the ten-cent monthlies, *McClure's, Munsey's,* the *American*, and the *Cosmopolitan* were leaders and excelled in quality popular magazines of that character published before or since. After the World War there was no ten-cent monthly that even approached them.

It is a far cry—and significant of great changes—from the magazines of 1910 to the array of popular literature on newsstands at the beginning of the fourth decade, with "detective stories," "snappy stories," and suggestive titles and cover designs predominating. In 1907 the *Atlantic* ran serially a novel by May Sinclair which in 1930 would have been thought innocuous, but because of a bedroom scene cost the magazine many subscribers. About 1909 *Life* published an "improper number" which in 1930 would have been highly proper.

The same contrast is found in popular novels. Without cataloguing a formidable list of books of fiction that had their day on either side of the "great divide" of the World War, it may be suggested that a fair measure of that contrast may be obtained by reading Owen Wister's *The Virginian*, Winston Churchill's *The Crossing*, and George Barr McCutcheon's *Graustark*, which appeared in the first decade, and Sinclair Lewis's *Main Street*, Hervey Allen's *Anthony Adverse*, and Margaret Mitchell's *Gone With the Wind*, which were best sellers in the later period. A similar measuring rod with respect to the popular magazines may be used by going through the files of *Judge, Puck,* and *Life* or any other periodical published between 1900 and 1914, and of *Esquire* and *Life* for the decade of the thirties. The mortality of the popular monthlies and weeklies that were in vogue in 1910 was high after the World War; and some of them like the *Cosmopolitan* and the *American* entirely changed their character and format. The passing of the *Youth's Companion, Harper's Young People,* the *Outlook*, and the *Independent*—with their wholesome influence and dignified contents—was lamented by "old-fashioned" parents, teachers, and clergymen.

Comparisons like these are, of course, subject to the limitations of and objections to any attempts to sense the *Zeitgeist* of a given time. The *Saturday Evening Post*, for example, kept its pages clean and maintained its relatively large circulation throughout the years; and the *Readers' Digest* immediately found a receptive public in the post-war years. Certainly the historian would be chary of accepting the judgments of their generation by the evangelist Billy Sunday and by the inspirer and founder of the Watch and Ward Society in Boston in 1876, Anthony Comstock, who for almost a half-century waged war against the obscene in art and literature and other forces which he believed were undermining American youth.

During the twentieth century—and even during the last quarter of the previous century—individuals and organizations who strove to preserve the puritanical Sabbath fought a losing battle against baseball, bicycling, automobiling, golfing, and the immigrants who brought with them the continental Sabbath. In 1905 for the first time the number of immigrants arriving within a twelve-month reached the million mark, and in 1907 the number was 1,285,349, the peak for all the years before and after that date. After 1914 the numbers declined sharply. Whereas the ranking five countries in immigration to the United States in the eighties were Germany, Ireland, England, Canada, and Sweden, in the next decade the countries were Italy, Germany, Austria-Hungary, Russia, and Ireland; and from 1900 to 1914 the order was Austria-Hungary, Italy, Russia, England, and Ireland.

As in the case of the old immigration, which predominated from 1840 to 1885, the new immigration from southern and eastern Europe was the product of the impact of America on the changing environments in those countries. In the case of the old immigration, it was largely the impact of rural America; in the case of the later movement, it was the impact of industrial America. Many immigrants from Italy, Greece, the Balkan States, and Austria-Hungary were "birds of passage," seasonal employees who remained in the United States for a few months or years until they had earned sufficient money in factories and mines and on the city streets to enable them to return to their native parishes to advertise the riches of the western republic. As in the case of the Japanese and Chinese, there was a large proportion of single men among the new immigrants.

In the closing years of the nineteenth century Europe took alarm at the "American invasion" in the form of a heavy increase in the importation of the products of American industry. From 1893 to 1899 the export of American manufactures doubled, and it grew in volume in the next century. One result of this was the invasion of the countries of southern and eastern Europe by an army of emigration agents representing steamship and railroad companies and industrial establishments.

Some countries attempted to curb the activities of these agents by law, but the printed page and the spoken word could not be outlawed. Italy, Greece, and certain Balkan States actually encouraged emigration as a means of alleviating the problems of a congested and rapidly increasing population. Italian emigration legislation was, therefore, designed to protect and encourage emigrants, rather than to place obstacles in their way or to copy the example of Sweden who tried to stem the tide by counter-propaganda and by social, economic, and political reforms.

The volume of Italian immigration is indicated by the fact that in 1890 there were only 182,580 foreign-born from Italy in the United States as compared with 1,343,125 in 1910, and these figures take no account of "birds of passage." Prior to 1900 more than two-thirds of the Italian immigrants came from northern Italy, but after that date the southern Italians greatly predominated. In the southern provinces the percentage of illiteracy was high and the standard of living very low.

The Slavic immigrants—Poles, Slovaks, Croatians or Slovenians, Ruthenians, Moravians, Bohemians, Bulgarians, Serbians, Montenegrins, Russians, Dalmatians, Bosnians, and Herzegovinians—were exceeded only by the Italians. Over 90 per cent of the Slavs came from the old Austro-Hungarian Monarchy and the old Russian Empire, with the former far in the lead. In these political divisions excessive subdivisions of land, low wages, heavy taxation, military service, political unrest, "America letters," returned emigrants, and emigration agents explain why "going to America" became a new *Völkerwanderung*.

One of the most remarkable migrations of modern times is that of the Jews, who found in the United States not only a haven from oppression and persecution but also a country where their commercial instincts and ambitions could be satisfied. From 1881 to 1910 there entered the United States 1,562,800 Jews: 1,119,059 came from Russia, 281,150 from Austria-Hungary, and 67,057 from Rumania. In those countries the Jews did not enter the fabric of society, and the conditions under which they lived were strikingly similar.

The Jewry of America is the product of three successive waves of migration. First in point of time are the Spanish Jews, who came by way of Central and South America and were the descendants of exiles from the Iberian Peninsula. The second wave came from Germany from 1830 to 1870. The third and by far the most important in numbers took its beginning in 1881 and drew on a population of some eight million residing in that part of Russia which had been incorporated after the partition of Poland in the last quarter of the eighteenth century and known as the Jewish Pale.

The Jews in the Pale were distinguished from the Christian population by a distinctive dress, by speaking a jargon known as Yiddish, by the ritual and rites of their orthodox religion, by their residence in restricted areas, by their mercantile and commercial pursuits in a predominantly agricultural country, by restrictions on their business activities, by limitations on their admission into educational institutions and into professions, by onerous laws requiring military service in the army of a government that oppressed them, and the like. Certain holidays and festivals and untoward incidents occasioned pogroms or massacres in which hundreds and even thousands were killed. At the beginning of the eighties anti-Semitism was rising in Europe.

The American people and government were sincerely interested in and sympathetic with the Jews in Russia, not only because American-born or naturalized Jews felt the sting of persecution when they visited Russia, but also because of the humanitarian ideals of the American people. Protests from American Secretaries of State and resolutions adopted by Congress and at mass

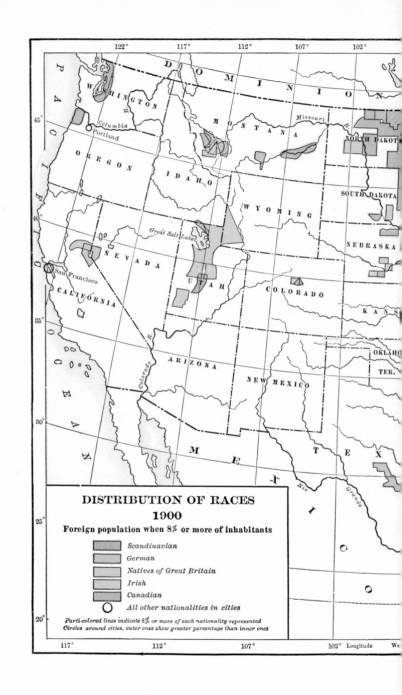

DISTRIBUTION OF RACES
1900
Foreign population when 8% or more of inhabitants

Scandinavian
German
Natives of Great Britain
Irish
Canadian
All other nationalities in cities

Parti-colored lines indicate 8% or more of each nationality represented
Circles around cities, outer ones show greater percentage than inner ones

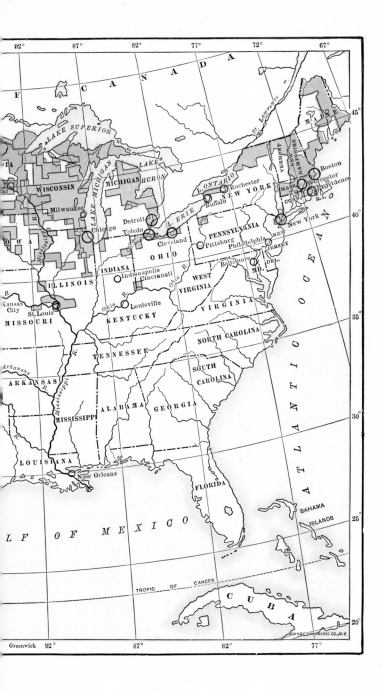

GUHMAY ENGRAVING CO., N.Y.

meetings expressed sympathy for the Jews; and in 1910 Congress voted to abrogate a treaty with Russia out of protest against the treatment Jews of American citizenship were accorded in Russia. Before all the world the American government was acclaimed as the champion of the oppressed, and this did not fall on deaf Jewish ears. Following a series of repressive measures, the Jewish exodus to the United States began in the early eighties. Prior to 1899 about 500,000 Jews entered this country, and from that date down to 1930 almost four times that number were admitted.

The Jews, like the other new immigrants, settled in cities, and New York became the largest Jewish city in the world. In spite of their orthodox religion, which set them apart from the gentile population, they became active and prosperous. They flocked to colleges and universities and very soon became influential politically.

As in the days when the Germans, Irish, Scandinavians, and Dutch were thronging the gates of the "Promised Land," there were individuals and organizations that were concerned about the capacity of the country to absorb and assimilate these strangers. It was pointed out that whereas the old immigrants were akin to the native population in race, language, religion, and institutions, the immigrants from southern and eastern Europe were high in illiteracy, low in standards of living, and unfamiliar with American ideals and ways of life. The Haymarket riot of 1886, the Homestead strike of 1892, the Pullman strike of 1894, and the anthracite coal strike of 1902 were said to furnish proof that dangerous agitators and radicals were coming through the portal of Castle Garden and, after 1892, through Ellis Island.

After 1890 there was an increasing number of articles bearing such titles as "Our Changing Immigration," "The Transformation of Our Cities," "The Roman Catholic Church as a Factor in Politics," "Government by Aliens," "Dangers of Unrestricted Immigration," and the like. Whereas the older immigrants found work on farms and gravitated to the Middle West where facilities for assimilation were easier, industrial America offered greater opportunities to the new immigrants in cities. The establishment of "Little Italys," "Little Polands," and "ghettoes" in large cities like New York, Chicago, and Boston was said to be incompatible with the general welfare.

The heavy increase in the membership and power of the Roman Catholic church through the immigration of hundreds of thousands professing that faith brought a revival of Know-nothingism in the form of the American Protective Association, popularly known as the A.P.A. This organization made large claims with respect to its membership and political influence, but its real significance lies in the fact that it reflected the fear, on the part of a considerable number of citizens, of the political power of the Catholic church. A.P.A. orators and publicists insisted that Romanism and republicanism could not live together. The president of the organization, W. J. H. Traynor, stated that the reason for its existence was the active and aggressive application of the temporal claims of the papacy by its subjects in the United States. He attributed utterances to Pius IX and Leo XIII in order to show that "the papal hierarchy declares its complete sovereignty over the state, and in utter disregard of the constitution and laws of the land decrees that the papal fiat is superior to the voice of the people."

The creed adopted by the supreme council of the A.P.A. in 1894 contained the following: Prohibition of pauper labor and the restriction of all immigration to persons who could show their intention of becoming self-supporting citizens. Stricter naturalization laws, including the requirement of the ability to speak English. Exclusion from the public schools of teachers who were subjects of an "un-American ecclesiastical institution." Opposition to state aid to parochial schools.

One of the fruits of the anti-foreign agitation was the enactment of the Bennett Law in Wisconsin in 1889. This was a compulsory education law designed to prevent non-attendance and truancy in schools and to compel all schools to teach reading, writing, United States history, and the English language. This law drew the fire of the large German Lutheran and Catholic population of the state, who believed that it was directed against the parochial schools maintained by their churches. The whole force of the Catholic hierarchy, in alliance with the German Lutherans, was enlisted in a campaign to repeal the law. During the campaign it was revealed that there were thousands of German children who were unable to speak English. It was charged that the parochial schools retarded assimilation by fostering racial exclusiveness.

The alarmists who feared the "Europeanization" of America were supported in their efforts to obtain legislation to restrict immigration by organized labor, the Farmers' Alliance, and similar organizations. In 1888 a committee of the House of Representatives reported that the time had come to draw the line, to select the good from the bad, to sift the wheat from the chaff; and in 1892 the Republican, Democratic, and Populist platforms favored restriction. In 1894 the Immigration Restriction League was organized to collect data and to disseminate it among members of Congress and their constituents. The principal methods of restricting immigration proposed in Congress were (1) a head tax; (2) consular inspection; (3) a literacy test.

In the short session of Congress following the election of 1896 a bill embodying a literacy test passed both houses by large majorities, the negative votes being largely Democratic and from Senators and Representatives from industrial states and districts where the Irish, Germans, and the new immigrants were strong and where industrialists wanted a reservoir of cheap labor. President Cleveland, who had been repudiated by his own party, submitted his veto message on March 3, 1897, the day before he vacated the White House in favor of William McKinley. His objections to the bill were grounded in the conviction that it proposed a radical departure from the generous and free-handed policy of the past; that the objections to the new immigrants were not well taken; that the prevailing unemployment was temporary; and that the congestion of population in cities was neither serious nor permanent.

There is some evidence that in the campaign of 1892 Cleveland had pledged himself to certain interests that he would veto a literacy test bill. Be that as it may, it was not until 1917, a few weeks before the entrance of the United States into the World War, that a bill embodying a literacy test became a law over President Wilson's veto. Previously, in 1913 and 1915, Taft and Wilson had vetoed similar bills.

It is a curious fact that the Republican Senators who voted for the restriction of immigration in 1897 and for a similar bill in 1898 because of opposition to the coming of "ignorant and inferior" races voted to annex the Philippines and Hawaii with their large Oriental populations.

From 1900 to 1917 immigration legislation was concerned mainly with providing better machinery for enforcing existing laws and with adding to the list of excluded undesirables, including anarchists, the insane and the feeble-minded, persons suffering from dangerous contagious and loathsome diseases, and prostitutes. In 1903 the office of commissioner-general of immigration, which had been created in 1894, was transferred to the jurisdiction of the newly created Department of Commerce and Labor; and in 1913 it was assigned to the Department of Labor, which was established that year.

In 1906 the need for a more effective and searching naturalization law was satisfied. Prior to 1870 naturalization laws applied to "free white persons," and excluded Indians and Negroes, who were considered unsuitable material for American citizenship. After the ratification of the Thirteenth, Fourteenth, and Fifteenth Amendments, the right of naturalization was extended to Africans and persons of African descent, but Orientals were not included. The Supreme Court construed the Fourteenth Amendment as conferring the right of naturalization on Negroes and Caucasians in such a restricted sense that Hindus were excluded.

The liberal naturalization policy probably facilitated assimilation; but it was also taken advantage of by unscrupulous native and foreign-born politicians to obtain by fraud citizenship papers for men who could satisfy neither the five-year period of residence nor other elementary tests of character or capacity to exercise the right of suffrage. A number of states conferred the right of suffrage on persons who had taken out only their first papers. Countless others, perhaps either through ignorance of the law or by deliberate violation, voted in local, state, and national elections.

Immigration restriction would have been adopted sooner or

later, but the progress toward that end was hastened by the catastrophic events of the World War and the years immediately following. The enactment of the literacy test marked the end of the period of regulation and the beginning of restriction. The drastic law of 1924 went far beyond the demands of the restrictionists who advocated a literacy test.

In an earlier page of this chapter it has been stated that in perspective it appears that from 1900 to 1917 America was a fool's paradise; but that the perspective only magnifies the chaos, misery, and disillusionment of the years of the World War and after. Nevertheless, there were forward-looking men and women who discerned, perhaps dimly, the signs of the times, and there were Presidents like Theodore Roosevelt, Woodrow Wilson, and Taft who saw that individualism unrestrained was heading for disaster and tried to put into action the aspirations to a better life, some of which are considered in the following chapter.

The World War unsettled the economic, social, and political structure of the world, including the United States; but even before this catastrophic event the twentieth century was "filled with epoch-making events and crowded with problems of great variety and complexity." We do but quote from *A Review of the Findings by the President's Research Committee on Social Trends,* published in 1933.[1]

The World War, the inflation and deflation of agriculture and business, our emergence as a creditor nation, the spectacular increase in efficiency and productivity and the tragic spread of unemployment and business distress, the experiment of prohibition, birth control, race riots, stoppage of immigration, women's suffrage, the struggles of the Progressive and Farmer-Labor parties, governmental corruption, crime and racketeering, the sprawl of great cities, the decadence of rural government, the birth of the League of Nations, the expansion of education, the rise and weakening of organized labor, the growth of spectacular fortunes, the advance of medical science, the emphasis on sports and recreation, the renewed interest in child welfare—these

[1] From *Recent Social Trends in the United States,* Report of the President's Research Committee on Social Trends; by permission of the publishers, McGraw-Hill Book Company, Inc.

are a few of the many happenings which have marked one of the most
eventful periods of our history.

With these events have come national problems urgently demanding
attention on many fronts. Even a glance at some of these points of
tension in our national life reveals a wide range of puzzling questions.
Imperialism, peace or war, international relations, urbanism, trusts
and mergers, crime and its prevention, taxation, social insurance, the
plight of agriculture, foreign and domestic markets, governmental regulation of industry, shifting moral standards, new leadership in business and government, the status of womankind, labor, child training,
mental hygiene, the future of democracy and capitalism, the reorganization of our governmental units, the use of leisure time, public and
private medicine, better homes and standards of living—all of these
and many others, for these are only samples taken from a long series
of grave questions, demand attention if we are not to drift into zones
of danger. . . .

Modern life is everywhere complicated, but especially so in the
United States, where immigration from many lands, rapid mobility
within the country itself, the lack of established classes or castes to act
as a brake on social changes, the tendency to seize upon new types of
machines, rich natural resources and vast driving power, have hurried
us dizzily away from the days of the frontier into a whirl of modern-
isms which almost passes belief. . . .

The result has been that astonishing contrasts in organization and
disorganization are to be found side by side in American life: splendid
technical proficiency in some incredible skyscraper and monstrous
backwardness in some equally incredible slum.

Thus in a few paragraphs have the men and women called by
President Hoover into public service summarized an avalanche of
events and developments that affected the life of the American
people in the twentieth century and charted the course of study
of the student who seeks to understand the political, economic,
and social history of the United States since 1900. They found
that the shifting of economic activities had brought innumerable
problems to the government and had forced an expansion of
governmental functions. The American people were confronted
with the problems of husbanding their political, economic, social,
and spiritual heritage that had taken root and flourished in frontier soil and had been transplanted.

Moreover, a considerable portion of the population itself had been transplanted from a European environment, which in itself produced problems for the individual and for society. Although successive censuses revealed large increases in the population of the country, the rate of population increase showed a decline in the twentieth century. The increase from 1920 to 1930 was 17,000,-000 as compared with 14,000,000 from 1910 to 1920; but from 1920 to 1930 the rate of increase was only 16 per cent as compared with about 35 per cent a decade before the Civil War.

A large chapter in the life of the American people after 1900 has for its theme the shifting of the population from the country to the city, the changing character caused by the invasion of millions of Europeans, the different attitude of the electorate caused by the enfranchisement of women and liberal naturalization laws, and the declining rate of population growth caused by a falling birth rate and drastic immigration restriction.

CHAPTER XVIII

ASPIRATIONS TO A BETTER LIFE, 1900-1917

THE NINETEENTH CENTURY BEQUEATHED TO THE TWENTIETH not only wealth and material possessions but also individuals and organizations dedicated to the achievement of a richer life for the high and the lowly. A new leaven was leavening American society. The conservative leaders were in retreat from advancing progressive Republicanism and Democracy. The apostles of social justice had their day in the first two decades of the new century.

Nowhere was this seen more strikingly than in the churches. In the free religious atmosphere of America, unencumbered by the trammels and traditions of a state-church system, the last quarter of the nineteenth century was most prolific in giving birth to sects and ecclesiastical organizations. This free religious atmosphere worked like an elixir on the religious leaders among the immigrants. In their native lands they had looked upon America as a land of ideals, where religion was democratized, where the clergy were not lords in their profession, where the common man could "witness for the truth," where rich and poor taught in Sunday schools and took part in services, and where there were no laws prescribing what men should believe in order to obtain salvation. The infinite variety of religious affiliations open to immigrants is revealed by the church census of 1916, which showed that not less than 132 of the 202 church organizations employed foreign languages to some extent and forty-one different languages were used.

Notwithstanding the fact that the churches of the immigrants for one or two generations retained their foreign languages and established their own educational institutions, newspapers, periodicals, and publication houses, they became parts of the unique

American pattern. One wonders at the speed with which they were transformed into organizations with the polity, spirit, and outlook of the adopted country. The American Sunday school was adopted; methods of recruiting members were copied from American churches; churches became "meetinghouses," from which social activity radiated; and in many cases the ritual and the liturgy were modified.

Most of the immigrants came from the humble classes in Europe, and their churches joined forces with the conservative elements in the American churches. Education for their children was almost a passion with many immigrants, but their educational institutions were hampered by meager financial resources, with the result that their pastors were ordained without adequate formal education. The need for ministers was urgent, and it would have been neither possible nor wise to detain men preparing for the ministry in colleges and seminaries for seven or eight years. However, as the churches crossed the threshold of the twentieth century to approach new problems that rushed in with the mingling of the second generation with the first, some of their educational institutions had already made necessary adjustments in the curricula.

By the time the churches had become bilingual, many members of the second and third generations had deserted the "faith of the fathers" in favor of "American" churches, partly because of the traditional conservatism of the immigrant churches, partly because of the inability of many pastors to use fluent idiomatic English, partly because of intermarriage, and partly because the leaven of Americanism had made them uncomfortable in organizations associated with anything "foreign." This constant leakage into the American churches left the older and more conservative elements in control of the immigrant churches.

The churches that profited most by immigration were the Roman Catholic and the Lutheran, because so many immigrants were Catholics and Lutherans. However, once free from the Old World environment of their native parishes, many immigrants also severed the ties that had bound them to churches. Membership in the established churches of Europe was either compulsory or traditional, and in the United States, where membership was optional, many elected to hold aloof.

At the opening of the century the Roman Catholic population was largely urban, whereas the Lutheran population, which was German and Scandinavian, was largely rural, although the urban population was increasing, partly because of the migration from farm to city and partly because the immigrants who came in the later years of the previous century found employment in factories. The influx of German and Scandinavian immigrants spelled victory for conservative and symbolical Lutheranism over the aggressive liberal and "loose" element which was in the ascendancy before the Civil War and remained a factor for some years after.

However, just as Lutheranism in the various countries of Europe had acquired a distinctive flavor, possessing characteristics arising from different civil governments and from the divergent views of founders, so did American Lutheranism adapt itself to the genius of American institutions and society. The twentieth century witnessed the drawing together of various Lutheran synods, which had been fenced off from one another by racial and linguistic barriers, into larger units. This was an inevitable consummation in the process of Americanization.

The hierarchical organization of the Roman Catholic church enabled it to deal effectively with the efforts of certain leaders to foster racial and nationalistic particularism. The early and heavy Irish immigration gave to this racial group a large proportion of priests and bishops, which brought criticism from the Germans, who also exhibited solidarity. The German Catholic parochial schools sought to perpetuate German as a spoken language, to the neglect of the language of the country. This was opposed by the Irish, who accused the German priests of lack of loyalty to the adopted country. In the early nineties this controversy centered around what was known as "Cahenslyism," which had its origin in a plan proposed to the pope by P. P. Cahensly, a member of the German Imperial Reichstag, to appoint bishops and priests in the United States on the basis of the strength of the various racial groups. This proposal was defeated by the opposition of Cardinal James Gibbons of Baltimore, Archbishop John Ireland of St. Paul, and Archbishop Keane, head of the Catholic University of America at Washington. These prelates were intensely American and insisted that the parochial schools should teach English. Their liberal and tolerant attitude won the respect and confidence of tolerant non-Catholics not only for themselves but also for the church they represented.

The twentieth century brought a tremendous increase in the membership, power, and wealth of the Roman Catholic church due to the heavy emigration from the Catholic countries of Europe, the large birth rate of the Catholic population, and the rise in the economic status of its members. Just as the immigration of conservatives stemmed the tide of liberalism in the Lutheran church, so did immigration overwhelm the liberal Catholic tradition handed down from the Colonial period and the early years of the nineteenth century, when the ties between Rome and the American church were very loose. After the death of the liberal Pope Leo XIII in 1903, who consulted frequently with the liberal Archbishop Ireland, the conservative trend in the church was unmistakable. On his visit to Rome in 1899, Archbishop Ireland found himself and the cause he represented attacked most bitterly within certain Catholic circles, but he gave to the press an interview in which he belittled the attacks of his enemies and declared unfounded the rumors that Leo XIII was opposed to Americanism.

The development of the Catholic parochial school system was phenomenal. The concentration of the Catholic population in cities and in certain sections of cities, together with the hierarchical policy of the church, made this achievement possible. Although prelates like Cardinal Gibbons and Archbishop Ireland spoke well of the public schools, in certain cities like New York, Chicago, and Boston, where the Catholic population was large, friction and rivalry between the two school systems gave school boards and teaching staffs complexions that perhaps otherwise would not have been developed. Efforts in some states to obtain appropriations for parochial schools also had political repercussions.

While the immigrant churches were tending toward doctrinal

conservatism, liberalism and modernism were making inroads on the American churches, except in the South. Prominent churchmen in the pulpit and in professorial chairs publicly proclaimed adherence to the theory of evolution and accepted the conclusions of higher critics. Unitarianism, which had dismayed conservatives in the Congregational church in the first half of the nineteenth century and had carried off the victory, made inroads on Trinitarian churches in the last quarter of the century. High-powered evangelists with their hell-fire preaching were losing their appeal in favor of preachers who expounded the social gospel and the doctrines of good works and brotherly love. Prominent clergymen questioned the divinity of Christ, and in some instances they were tried and convicted of heresy.

Clergymen, professors, novelists, and publicists attacked traditional Christianity and censured the churches for failing to emphasize the application of Christian principles to social problems. Andrew D. White's *History of the Warfare of Science with Theology in Christendom*, published in 1896, was a popular work of erudition that challenged a generation exposed to books popularizing the results of Biblical criticism and modern theological views. Colleges and universities were under fire as exponents of doctrines that caused young men and women to lose the faith of their fathers.

In a series of widely read articles that ran in the *Cosmopolitan Magazine* in 1909, Harold Bolce asserted that in his visits to classrooms in universities from Cambridge to California he found that "There is a scholarly repudiation of all solemn authority. The decalogue is no more sacred than a syllabus. Every thing is subject to searching analysis. The past has lost its grip on the professor. The ancient prophet is less potent than the new political economy."

We may make allowance for the sensationalism of articles that bore such titles as "Blasting at the Rock of Ages," "Polyglots in the Temples of Babel," and "Christianity in the Crucible," but the fact remains that the author set down on the printed page the fears of many who could not make the adjustment to the results of investigation and research in laboratories, libraries, and excavations.

Among the books that approached Christianity from the historical and critical point of view was *The Finality of the Christian Religion* by George Burman Foster, a professor in the Divinity School of the University of Chicago, published in 1906. The president of this Baptist institution, notable for its interest in the higher Biblical criticism, was William Rainey Harper, a brilliant Hebrew scholar who gave free rein to the members of his faculty in publishing the fruits of their research. Harvard's distinguished president, Charles W. Eliot, was no less advanced in his position, as were a number of other distinguished educators. Shailer Mathews of the University of Chicago and Walter Rauschenbusch of Rochester Theological Seminary were prominent and influential among the men who felt that the church was static in a changing order.

One of the best-known pioneers of the social gospel was Washington Gladden, pastor of the First Congregational Church at Columbus, Ohio. He popularized the results of Biblical criticism by writing *Who Wrote the Bible?* and *Seven Puzzling Books of the Bible* and espoused such radical ideas as government ownership of public utilities, though he rejected socialism as a system. He saw the danger to the church in an industrial society if it could be accused of making friends with mammon. He was aware of the growing hostility or indifference of the wage earners and he wished to spare the American churches from the fate of the established churches in Europe, where ministers preached to empty pews. He sounded a new note in American Christendom by condemning the American Board of Commissioners for Foreign Missions for soliciting from the president of the Standard Oil Company a gift of one hundred thousand dollars, which he said was "tainted money."

With the fading of sectarianism based on strict orthodoxy, churches tended to emphasize the things they had in common and to minimize differences. The way for this had been paved by great pulpit orators of the last quarter of the nineteenth century. The best-known and most influential preacher in the annals of the

American pulpit is undoubtedly Henry Ward Beecher, who in 1847 began his work as pastor of the Plymouth Congregational Church in Brooklyn. For thirty years his work as preacher and editor was preeminent. He accepted the evolutionary hypothesis and abandoned the hell-fire preaching of his generation. Phillips Brooks, an Episcopalian, who began his ministry in Trinity Church, Boston, was a great liberal-minded pulpit orator.

Lyman Abbott, who in 1888 succeeded Beecher in the pulpit of Plymouth Church and had been associated with him in the editorship of the *Christian Union*, was a leader of liberal thought in the field of religion down to the year of his death in 1922. He was often heard in the chapels of universities and colleges, and his tolerance and sweet reasonableness must have left an impression on a host of young men and women. As editor of the *Outlook*, which succeeded the *Christian Union*, he was the exponent of the social gospel and progressive politics.

Indicative of the growing activity and influence of laymen that characterized the closing years of the nineteenth century was the remarkable work of Dwight L. Moody. In 1860 he gave up a successful career as a business man to devote his abundant energies until the close of the century to promoting missionary work among unfortunates and in connection with the Y.M.C.A., Bible institutes, and foreign missionary projects. This great evangelist preached the gospel of the love of a Heavenly Father—not the terrifying wrath of a terrible and righteous God. Moody's practical preaching did not produce the excesses among his followers such as characterized the revival meetings of some of his contemporaries. Those who heard Moody preach and Ira D. Sankey, his organist, sing and play, carried with them lifelong memories. Their sermons and songs were translated into many languages. The example of a practical business man devoting his life to the cause of Christianity inspired many men of wealth to make large contributions to the church.

With the death of Moody in 1899, the period of revivalism in American religion may be said to have closed, but for some years old-fashioned exhorters like Sam P. Jones, Billy Sunday, and Gipsy Smith continued to sway large audiences and to attract throngs to their "after meetings," where converts confessed their sins and made their vows to lead better lives. Billy Sunday's protracted meetings were sometimes followed by "clean-up campaigns" in cities which struck terror, for a time at least, in the hearts of saloon-keepers and the population of the underworld.

The power of religion went deeper and wider in the years from 1900 to 1917 than during any other period of American history, partly because of the influence of great preachers, partly because of the increasing material resources of the church, and partly because of the awakening social and political consciousness of the people, which accompanied and was influenced by the larger and more intensive activity of the church. "The evangelization of the world in this generation" was the slogan.

What is said to have been one of the most effective and famous pulpit utterances in American history was a sermon preached in 1892 by Charles Henry Parkhurst, pastor of the Madison Square Presbyterian Church of New York. It was a clarion call to people throughout the land to wage a crusade against saloons, dance halls, gambling dens, and houses of prostitution, although his sermon was directed against those forces of evil in his own city. Out of his courageous attack came an official investigation, the defeat of Tammany Hall, and the sweeping reforms of a new city administration.

The marshaling of the forces of the churches through laymen's organizations is indicated by the founding, as the century was drawing to a close, of such societies as the Epworth League, the Luther League, the Baptist Young People's Union, the Westminster League, and the Christian Endeavor Society. The Young Men's Christian Association and the Young Women's Christian Association continued to be powerful agencies for lay influences in the churches, though some of the conservative churches looked askance at them on account of their emphasis on "good works" and lack of emphasis on doctrine. Never before had the churches bent such intensive efforts to propagate the gospel in foreign lands.

Indicative of the trend toward "unionism" and the leveling of doctrinal barriers was the organization in 1905 of the Federal Council of the Churches of Christ in America in order "(1) To express the fellowship and catholic unity of the Christian Church; (2) To bring the Christian bodies of America into united service for Christ and the world." Under the auspices of this organization the united churches brought their influence to bear in furthering large projects looking toward a more healthy body politic, a more efficient administration of foreign missions, and better relations between capital and labor, between the various racial groups in the United States, and between the nations of the world. Reports prepared by committees of this organization drew the fire of individuals who detected sympathy with "radicalism." Moreover, ecclesiastical bodies that lay great stress on doctrine held aloof on account of the unsafe "unionism" of the Federal Council.

The great revival that swept over the country in 1857 and 1858 gave a great impulse to the Sunday school. At the close of the century the enrollment in Sunday schools was over 12,000,000; and when it is remembered that among these were adults enrolled in Bible classes, the importance of the movement is still more impressive. Ecclesiastical organizations, either individually or cooperatively, published better textbooks, lesson leaflets, and weekly papers, and teachers became progressively better prepared for their work, although many churchmen were justly critical of this branch of the activity of their church.

In the sixties John Heyl Vincent, a Methodist clergyman and later bishop, became the outstanding leader of the Sunday school movement. In 1874 he inaugurated a summer school for Sunday school teachers at Lake Chautauqua, New York. Out of this developed the Chautauqua movement, which with all its ramifications became an educational project that included popular lectures throughout the country, correspondence study and extension divisions in connection with educational institutions, and summer sessions in practically every university and in many colleges. The Chautauqua was a typical American institution. It published its own textbooks and attracted able and popular lecturers and teachers. In the first decade of the present century the local Chautauquas held greater attractions than the county fairs; and their educational features were immeasurably greater. The programs included lectures, concerts, and varied forms of entertainment. Bryan and

La Follette, for example, used this forum. On hot and sultry July and August afternoons, these popular speakers, in shirt sleeves and wet with perspiration, expounded their reforms to farmers who crowded into the stifling tents.

The fact that at the close of the century the United States had almost one-half of the Sunday school population of the world is one obvious result of a free-church system in which the survival of churches hinged upon their success in attracting to their folds the youth of the land, whereas in the countries of Europe children were born into membership of the established churches. Statistics of church membership had more significance in the United States, where membership was voluntary, than in Europe, where membership was compulsory.

In spite of the democracy of the American churches, in the twentieth century they were losing influence with the working classes. Huge donations by captains of industry to the churches and their agencies, including educational institutions, enabled them to extend and promote their activity; but an increasing number of laborers, whether rightly or wrongly, believed that they were handmaidens of predatory wealth and out of sympathy with their hopes and aspirations. The urbanization of the country brought problems that usually accompany periods of transition. Churches had to adjust their agencies to minister to people in cities. The growth of the Salvation Army, an importation from England, showed the need for religious work among the unchurched and in the slums. The Salvation Army worked among the poor and uneducated on the city streets. On the other hand, Christian Science, a cult founded by Mary Baker Eddy, appealed to the well-to-do in the larger cities of the Middle West. Christian Science churches were impressive in architecture and revealed the economic status and loyalty of their members.

Among the problems connected with rural life, one of the most serious was the decline of the country church. In the nineteenth century the church occupied a large place in the rural community; and it was a cause for alarm among religious leaders in the following century to see the increasing numbers of dilapidated structures, shutters awry, window panes broken, surrounded by towering weeds and uncut grass. Students of the problem reported that attendance was declining; that the church was losing its prestige and influence; and that the persons identified with it constituted a less influential part of the population, compared with former days. Perhaps the fundamental reason for this was the migration of vigorous and ambitious young men and women from rural districts to cities. This entailed obvious consequences, including the loss of initiative, the difficulty of securing competent ministers, vacant parsonages, poor attendance, and inadequate financial support.

The more orthodox religious leaders were disposed to emphasize the devitalizing effect of the so-called new theology, with its diluted doctrinal content and the preaching on secular subjects, such as good roads, better markets, more favorable shipping facilities, and the best method of fighting the corn aphis or the wheat rust or the cattle tick or the foot and mouth disease. In the remote days when the man who held the plowhandle discoursed on abstruse points of doctrine and argued religion with his neighbors, the rivalry of sects brought more churches to a community than its people could properly support. In the course of years a number of congregations gave up the fight, and others merged with sister or rival congregations. The more conservative and liturgical churches like the Catholic, Episcopal, and Lutheran rejected proposals for mergers with congregations of other synods and conferences. The "community church" is a product of the twentieth century. Likewise the "institutional" city church with dance hall, gymnasium, bowling alley, and pool table.

At the time of the ratification of the Fifteenth Amendment in 1865, the great mass of the Negroes were in the rural districts of the South. The Negro churches were therefore rural in their inception. They became a part of the program to lead the freedmen into better and useful lives and functioned as social institutions as well as places of worship. The Sunday schools were instrumental in teaching the youth to read and write and thereby opened to them the literary and historical treasures of the Bible. The churches were also mediums through which educators and lecturers and entertainers reached this large element of the population. The last decade of the nineteenth century and the first third of the twentieth brought a remarkable increase in the number of members and congregations, the Baptist church showing the largest increase, with the Methodist second. The formal and liturgical churches—the Episcopal, Lutheran, and Catholic—made the least appeal to the emotional Negro. The publication activities of the Negro churches also made great progress.

The student of American history who overlooks the religious press falls short of understanding an important influence in molding public opinion with respect to religious, political, and social development. No country in the world had such a large number of religious periodicals. This is, of course, explained in part by the multitude of sects and ecclesiastical organizations, each one of which had one or more publications devoted to its interests. The sectarian nature of many publications brought to their columns polemical editorials and articles that often fell short of Christian tolerance and forbearance, but with the waning influence of doctrine and the fusion of the population into a more homogeneous body, acrid controversies became less pronounced.

The practical nature of American Christianity was reflected in the religious press by comments on politics and current problems, not least with respect to the cause of temperance and racial brotherhood. Moreover, the religious press was an important factor in acquainting the immigrants with the institutions and ideals of their adopted country; and many of the foreign-language periodicals were sponsored and financed, wholly or in part, by the larger denominations of which the immigrant churches were parts. For example, in 1895 fifty of the eight hundred German periodicals were religious, eleven of the sixty-eight Swedish, five of the seventy-two Norwegian-Danish and three of the thirty-three Bohemian.

The cause of temperance was promoted through organizations dedicated to that purpose; but their influence was measurably increased by the backing of churches, for the puritanical strain in American Christianity was carried on through the years. Through the exhortations of clergymen and laymen hundreds of thousands signed temperance pledges and joined the ranks of the marching hosts against the liquor traffic. The National Woman's Christian Temperance Union was founded in 1874, and the Anti-Saloon League of America in 1895; and through the influence of these organizations and others, like the Independent Order of Good Templars which was founded in 1851, virtually every state passed laws making instruction in the harmful effects of alcohol compulsory. Most of the Protestant churches opened their pulpits to representatives of the Anti-Saloon League, who distributed to their members pledge cards to aid in financing the war against King Alcohol. Certain German synods of the Lutheran church and the Catholic church did not cooperate. Cardinal Gibbons, for example, was opposed to prohibition.

Frances E. Willard, at one time president of the W.C.T.U., stressed the moral and religious appeal and denounced the liquor traffic as a menace to the Christian home and to the Christian life. She joined with other women in singing and praying on streets and even in saloons. She was one of the organizers of the Prohibition party in 1882.

According to the *Anti-Saloon League Yearbook of 1909*, the only licensing states (where the entire state was wet) were Washington, Montana, Idaho, Wyoming, Maryland, Utah, Arizona, New Mexico, Pennsylvania, New Jersey, and Missouri. For this sweeping series of victories for temperance no small measure of credit was due to the public school instruction in the hygienic effects of alcohol and narcotics. Normal schools drilled students in the technique of teaching this subject. Thus in their formative years the children of black and white, the foreign-born and the native, were taught in school the deleterious effects of indulgence in alcohol and tobacco. "Show me a drunkard who does not use tobacco and I will show you a white black bird," was a quotation from Horace Greeley in the pages of a widely used textbook on hygiene.

During the years under review the number of newspapers and periodicals that refused to publish liquor advertisements steadily increased. *Collier's Weekly* and other "muckraking" magazines were merciless in exposing profit-hunting brewers, manufacturers of aphrodisiacal gin, patent medicine makers, and purchasable politicians. William J. Bryan was the most prominent of many political leaders who espoused the cause of temperance and prohibition, and President Eliot of Harvard was the most prominent of many educators who enlisted in the same cause.

There were among the temperance crusaders individuals who brought discredit on the cause by their extreme statements and ill-advised actions. Of these perhaps the most famous or notorious was Mrs. Carry Nation of Kansas. Kansas was one of the original prohibition states, a constitutional amendment having been adopted in 1880. There were, however, a number of localities in the state where liquor was sold more or less openly; and Mrs. Nation, a woman nearly six feet tall, weighing 175 pounds, and with muscular arms, conceived it to be her duty and right to destroy liquor and the property of saloon-keepers, since their business was illegal. In 1900 she began her campaign of terror by wielding a hatchet to smash mirrors, bars, and pornographic pictures, besides finding time for lecture tours and stage performances. She even slapped cigarettes from the lips of young men. Her notoriety was so widespread that over the bars of some legal saloons were suspended signs reading: "All Nations welcome but Carry."

In the later stages of the prohibition movement the economic aspects of the consumption of liquor were stressed. It was argued that men who indulged were less efficient and reliable than total abstainers; and after the entrance of the United States into the World War the necessity of conserving grain in order to feed the men in the armies and navies was a "clincher" to the moral argument. The World War was a potent reason for the ratification of the Eighteenth Amendment in 1918, but the way had been prepared by the systematic education of a generation of voters in the evil effects of the use of alcohol. Moreover, the alliance between politicians and the disreputable element among brewers, distillers, and saloon-keepers repelled the decent element in the population. Every reform movement sooner or later found the saloon and its ally, the corrupt politician, in the way of progress and social decency, with rival breweries multiplying saloon-keepers and corrupting policemen, aldermen, mayors, and members of legislatures. The prohibition movement was more anti-saloon than pro-prohibition.

As evidence of this may be cited the activity of Archbishop Ireland of St. Paul, one of the powerful prelates in the Roman Catholic church. He waged campaigns against political corruption and the liquor interests, in spite of the fact, which he pointed out, that a large proportion of the intemperate and of the liquor dealers and saloon-keepers professed membership in his church. He stated that the peculiar circumstances into which the Catholic church in America had been thrown, by virtue of the fact that its membership was in large measure recruited from the immigrants, created a special obligation on the church to make the country understand that it was opposed to the saloon. To the united efforts of the churches, more than to any other single factor, may be attributed the victory for prohibition in 1918. It must not be forgotten that prohibition was an accomplished fact in most of the states before the Eighteenth Amendment was ratified.

Another cause that enlisted the efforts of reformers was the crusade against corruption in city, state, and federal politics. So intensive was the campaign that the first decade of the twentieth century is known as the "era of the muckrakers." Never before had the people been so conscious of the betrayal of their interests by corrupt politicians, whose nefarious transactions were uncovered by an army of vigorous writers for popular magazines and newspapers. In a series of articles published in *McClure's Magazine* in 1902, Lincoln Steffens laid bare "The Shame of the Cities." The revelations in these articles, as well as in others, presented the government of cities as the most conspicuous failure of the people to govern themselves.

Back in the seventies fearless newspaper publishers, uninfluenced by intimidation and proffered bribes, exposed the corruption of the Tweed Ring in New York City. William Marcy Tweed, the grand sachem of Tammany, was proved to have filched millions— some estimates are as high as two hundred millions—from New York City. He bribed the New York legislature to grant a new charter to New York City, which fastened his control over the city more securely than before. He maintained himself in power by shameless bribery, by obtaining fraudulent naturalization of aliens, and by voting repeaters.

Some years after the conviction of Tweed in 1885, Richard Croker succeeded him as the leader of Tammany. For sixteen years his word was law; and his financial manipulations were concealed because as chairman of the Tammany Finance Committee he kept no books. Throughout the years the friends of good government in New York City tried to get honest administrations by nominating men of proved integrity and ability for mayor and other offices, and sometimes their candidates were elected.

Chicago, with its composite population and mushroom growth, was likewise a feeding ground for self-seeking politicians who played the game of appealing to racial and religious prejudice in order to conceal their corruption and maintain themselves in power. "Gray wolves," one of the newspapers called these looters.

The career of Charles T. Yerkes is illustrative of the machinations of men who did not scruple to use money to line the pockets of legislators, aldermen, and mayors. In 1882 this traction king moved to Chicago and over a period of years obtained control of the street railways of Chicago by spinning a web of construction companies, holding companies, interlocking directorates, financial juggling, bribers, and court injunctions. In 1895 he bribed the Illinois legislature to pass bills which extended the renewal of his franchises for a century without paying a cent to the City of Chicago. Governor Altgeld, the incorruptible man who had braved the blasts of the newspapers by pardoning the Haymarket "anarchists" and who had acted courageously in the Pullman strike, vetoed the bills. In revenge, Yerkes used his money and influence to discredit the "radical" governor; and in 1897, after Altgeld's defeat for reelection, another corrupt legislature and a pliant governor responded by giving him a law that authorized the city council to do what the vetoed bills would have accomplished. An aroused public, however, intimidated the "boodle" aldermen, and the legislature repealed the law. For many years Chicago was deprived of adequate street car service by the manipulations of Yerkes and his henchmen. There was even demand for municipal ownership to rescue the city from an intolerable situation.

Similar conditions existed in many cities, notably in San Francisco in 1907-08, where the newspaper fairly reeked with revelations of graft, in which labor leaders joined to milk the public. Many solutions for the creaking machinery of municipal government were proposed, including the "city-manager" or commission form of government.

The remarkable career of Tom L. Johnson in Cleveland, Ohio, illuminates the problems of the cities and the efforts of public-spirited citizens to curb corrupt public utilities that fattened on a helpless public. After a successful career as a business man interested in street railway franchises, Johnson sold out and devoted himself to public life. He was profoundly influenced by the writings of Henry George and became converted to the principle of the single tax.

Beginning in 1901 he was four times elected mayor of Cleveland and attracted the attention of the country as an outstanding city executive. Under his administrations Cleveland was the best-governed city in the country. He carried his program directly to the people. In numerous addresses he insisted on honesty in government and explained the advantages of municipal ownership. The power of the vested interests was so great, however, that even a man of Johnson's ability was defeated in the end. His experiment in municipal ownership was wrecked by the traction magnates, and the property of the city was thrown into receivership. But he did succeed in giving Cleveland and other Ohio municipalities larger immunity from the control of the state legislature, and in compelling street railway companies to lower fares and to pay taxes that more nearly represented their just obligations.

The commission form of government instituted by Des Moines and other cities represented the efforts of reformers to free officials from control by individuals and corporations who cared nothing about the cities except to see that their investments paid excessive dividends. The rôle of public utilities in politics and the pyramiding of holding companies is a dark chapter in American history. After 1920 their piratical practices were even more ruthless and bold; and with few exceptions the newspapers were either silent or outright defenders of the men who defrauded the public.

In state, city, and national politics the direct primary was heralded as a measure that would restore government to the people by reducing the power of machine politicians to control parties by manipulating conventions. Many states enacted direct primary laws. After the fiasco of the Republican national convention of 1912, it was even said that the convention system of nominating candidates for the Presidency would be abolished before the next election. In his message to Congress on December 2, 1913, President Wilson stated that he felt confident that he did not misinterpret the wishes or expectations of the country when he urged prompt enactment of legislation that would provide for primary elections throughout the country at which voters might choose nominees for the Presidency without the intervention of nominating conventions. Party conventions, he said, should be retained only for the purpose of declaring the verdict of the primaries and formulating platforms.

In spite of the optimism of the President, Congress was cold to his suggestion; and Wilson lived to see the manipulation of the Republican national convention in 1920 by men whose one purpose was to nominate a successor who would banish from the White House his ideals of government and public service. After 1928, when the radio carried the proceedings of conventions into homes from coast to coast, these conclaves lost whatever of dignity and parliamentary procedure that had remained. They became carnivals of bombastic oratory, pipe organ and band music, and applause, jeers, and hisses from packed galleries, spectacles of emotion and display for which convention cities bid higher than ever before.

The proposal to nominate and elect candidates for municipal offices and state legislatures without party designation was advanced in order to reduce the influence of party loyalty and party machinery in matters pertaining to public policy that had little or no relation to politics. The experiment was tried in some states, but not with entire success.

The direct primary elections law in Oregon was used to circumvent the provision in the Constitution pertaining to the election of United States Senators. The candidate for the Senate who received the highest number of votes at the general election was to be elected by the legislature regardless of the political complexion of its members. In the June, 1908, election George E. Chamberlain, a Democrat, defeated his Republican opponent, and in 1909 a Republican legislature ratified the will of the people.

The conviction in the public mind that the Senate was the citadel of intrenched wealth grew increasingly strong in the early years of the twentieth century. During the year 1906 the *Cosmopolitan Magazine* published a series of articles by David Graham Phillips entitled "The Treason of the Senate," in which he reviewed the records of Senators who were notoriously out of step with the progressive movement. It was alleged that many of them could not have been elected but for the lavish use of money to bribe or influence members of state legislatures.

For example, Montana was represented in the Senate from 1901 to 1907 by William A. Clark, a millionaire who was said to have bribed his way to his high office. In a long-drawn-out fight that lasted for over a month Isaac Stephenson, a millionaire lumberman, was in 1908 reelected by the Wisconsin legislature. It was revealed that the aged millionaire had spent over one hundred thousand dollars, which inspired the comment from one of his adversaries that rich old men bought the Senatorship as a sort of floral tribute to themselves. A prominent Senator from New York, Chauncey M. Depew, whose intimate associations with the Morgan and Vanderbilt interests were well known, was caricatured by Homer Davenport, the well-known cartoonist, with the caption: "Chauncey Depew! Oh you mean the man that Vanderbilt sends to Albany every winter to say 'haw' and 'gee' to his cattle up there."

The most notorious senatorial election and one which stirred the country as no previous election had done was that of William Lorimer, who in 1909 was elected by the Illinois legislature after a long deadlock. After investigations conducted by committees of the United States Senate, Lorimer was acquitted and allowed to retain his seat. Criticisms and protests were sounded in all parts of the country; and Theodore Roosevelt refused to attend a banquet in his honor if Lorimer was present. Goaded to action by this storm, the Senate voted to reopen the case; and in July, 1912, on the eve of a presidential campaign, the Senate by a large majority adopted a resolution declaring that corrupt methods and practices had been employed and that the election was invalid.

Between the first vote in 1911 and the second in 1912 a number of old-line Republicans and Democrats had been retired in favor of progressives. This change in the membership of the Senate also expressed itself in the adoption in 1912, for submission to the states, of the Seventeenth Amendment providing for the direct election of Senators. The year before, the Senate had defeated a similar amendment. Of the thirty-three votes cast against the resolution to permit the amendment, New England contributed ten and the South eleven. The southern Senators opposed it on the ground that it called for the federal control of the election of Senators—always a sensitive point with the South, which was frightened by the bugaboo of another "Force bill." The New England Senators frankly stated that they did not wish to allow the people to have this power. In 1911 a change of four votes would have changed the result; and after March 4, 1911, six "lame-duck" New England Senators who had voted in the negative were retired. The Seventeenth Amendment was declared in force May 31, 1913.

On February 25, 1913, the Sixteenth Amendment giving to Congress power to lay and collect taxes on incomes was declared in force, Congress having adopted the resolution in July, 1909. This terminated a battle that took on momentum after the Supreme Court in 1895 had invalidated the income tax provision of the Wilson-Gorman Tariff Act of 1894.

Within about seven years two further amendments were ratified. The Eighteenth Amendment which prohibited the sale and manufacture of intoxicating liquor was ratified in 1918 and became effective in January, 1920. The Nineteenth Amendment

which had the effect of conferring suffrage on women was ratified in 1920, in time to permit the newly enfranchised to vote
in the presidential election of that year.

For many years before the ratification of the Nineteenth
Amendment women were becoming increasingly prominent in public life and in pursuits that had been closed to them. They were
especially interested in educational, temperance, and humanitarian
reforms and in promoting legislation granting equality between
the sexes in matters of property and civic rights and duties.
Frances E. Willard, Susan B. Anthony, and Elizabeth Cady Stanton were among the pioneers in these movements. In 1869 the
National American Woman Suffrage Association was formed,
with Miss Anthony as vice-president. From 1892 to 1900 she
served as president. Belva Ann Lockwood, the first woman admitted to practice before the United States Supreme Court, was
also the first woman candidate for President of the United States,
twice receiving the nomination of the National Equal Rights party
of the Pacific coast, in 1884 and 1888. In 1916 the people of
Montana elected the first woman to Congress, Jeannette Rankin.
Before the ratification of the Nineteenth Amendment a number
of states, especially in the trans-Mississippi region, had conferred
suffrage on women, and in many more states women had participated in school and local elections. In fact, the woman suffrage
states had no small part in reelecting Woodrow Wilson in 1916.

The General Federation of Women's Clubs, which originated
in the desire of women to continue and to improve their education, greatly increased its membership in the twentieth century.
At first these clubs were in reality classes for study. At the turn
of the century they were in transition from social and literary
activities to more practical activities, such as furthering legislation
in behalf of women and children. Significant developments of the
present century are the development of women's colleges like
Wellesley, Vassar, Smith, Mt. Holyoke, and Bryn Mawr, the increasing enrollment of women in state universities and colleges,
and their admission to graduate study in universities that had been
closed to them. Nor should the great work of women like Jane
Addams in settlement work in the slums be omitted. Hull House

Paul Thompson Collection

CAMPAIGNING FOR VOTES FOR WOMEN

in Chicago was peculiarly the creation of Miss Addams and became the model for settlement houses in many cities—institutions that ministered to the needy, inspired hopes and fostered self-respect in dwellers in the slums, gave instruction and advice to immigrants, and provided wholesome entertainment and amusement.

In summary, during the years under review in this chapter there was a remarkable increase of faith in the ability of the common man and woman to participate intelligently in affairs of government, as witnessed by the agitation for the initiative and the referendum, the extension of the franchise to women, and the direct election of Senators. There was also a disposition to distrust the men elected to make the laws and administer them. Events that revealed that Congress, legislatures, and city councils were boss-ridden and influenced by corruption drove the country to devise machinery which enabled the people themselves to act upon questions of importance and limited the power of legislative bodies by constitutional provisions. There was still abounding faith in American institutions and traditions. The objective of the reformer was to dethrone the bosses who sought their own, and to build a social structure that would promote the general welfare and establish justice.

CHAPTER XIX

THEODORE ROOSEVELT

ON SEPTEMBER 14, 1901, OCCURRED THE DEATH OF THE AMIABLE and well-beloved William McKinley, who eight days before had been felled by the bullet of an anarchist while attending the Pan-American Exposition at Buffalo. A united nation mourned the death of the third chief executive to fall by the hand of an assassin. McKinley had been triumphantly reelected over his Democratic opponent Bryan in 1900, and the country looked forward to four years of prosperity so auspiciously inaugurated with the beginning of the century.

McKinley's successor, Theodore Roosevelt, had achieved great popularity during the Spanish-American War; and as the vice-presidential candidate in 1900 he had proved himself to be a most effective and popular campaigner. In fact, the Democratic cartoonists pictured him as overshadowing McKinley; and it was alleged that Mark Hanna had arranged his itinerary so as to keep him from speaking in the conservative East, where his record as governor of New York was obnoxious to the financial and industrial interests. By nominating Bryan, who insisted that the "paramount" issue of the campaign was imperialism and militarism, the Democrats virtually assured a Republican victory; but Roosevelt's nomination undoubtedly strengthened the ticket, especially in the West. Bryan insisted that free silver was still an issue, but events proved that it had lost the potency it had had in 1896, when idle factory hands and bankrupt farmers gladly heard the "silver-tongued orator" expound his remedy for the ills that beset them.

During the seven and one-half years that Roosevelt occupied the White House it was fashionable to refer to the "Roosevelt luck." Certain it is that the circumstances of his nomination for the Vice-Presidency were unusual and that his accession to the high office of President was accidental. Both events struck consternation among old-line Republican leaders, including Mark Hanna. Roosevelt's gift for phrase-making, his outspokenness, his unconventionality, his belligerency, and his impulsiveness boded no good for the country, in the judgment of conventional politicians and conservative citizens.

Roosevelt entered upon his duties as President with a background and equipment that excelled all his predecessors since Abraham Lincoln, and this estimate takes into account moral integrity and political strategy and acumen. Of an old and distinguished New York family, a graduate of Harvard, with wide interests, a contributor to popular magazines on political and social subjects, a student and writer of history, he was in 1881 elected to the New York legislature. After serving one term he became a ranchman in "Cowboy Land," where he acquired a western veneer that concealed from the eyes of Westerners the New York politician who later appealed to them for votes. It has been said that Roosevelt wrote *The Winning of the West* before he won the West.

In 1889 he was appointed civil service commissioner by President Harrison. Three years before, he had been defeated for the mayoralty of New York. In 1895 he became president of the police commission of New York City. By that time, as he later said, he "was getting our social, industrial, and political needs into pretty fair perspective." In 1897 President McKinley appointed him Assistant Secretary of the Navy, where he improved his time in preparing the navy for the war with Spain, which he devoutly wished for and helped to bring on. After war was declared, he became lieutenant-colonel of the Rough Riders and a national hero, thanks to good fortune, commendable courage, great energy, and friendly war correspondents. "Teddy" became a household word, and his picture in the uniform of a cavalry officer hung in many homes.

Shortly after his regiment had been disbanded in September, 1898, his popularity was capitalized by machine politicians who nominated him for the governorship of New York. Despite their distrust of the strenuous reformer, he was, they felt, the only

Republican candidate who could win. One term in the governor-ship convinced Senator Thomas C. Platt that Roosevelt was not a safe man; he had antagonized big business and did not play the game according to the Albany rules. Platt resolved to remove him from the political arena by shelving him for four years in the Vice-Presidency. This scheme was not to the taste of either Mc-Kinley or Mark Hanna, who opposed it, as did Roosevelt himself. However, the "We want Teddy" sentiment of the delegates to the Republican national convention in Philadelphia was so strong that Hanna chose the lesser of evils by acquiescing in their wishes, at the same time breathing the prayer that McKinley would have a long life.

Upon succeeding to the Presidency Roosevelt made the usual announcement that he would continue the policies of his prede-cessor and requested the members of the cabinet to retain their posts. It was not long, however, before the country became aware of the vast differences between the personalities and mental proc-esses of McKinley and Roosevelt. McKinley had been schooled in the politics of a middle-western state; and after Mark Hanna became his mentor, one looks in vain for any serious departure in McKinley's course from the straight and narrow path that shunned Populism and other "heresies."

Roosevelt was an elemental man who knew the technique of making deals and striking compromises, but who also possessed the necessary moral indignation and stamina to throw down the gauntlet to individuals and organizations that sought to thwart his ambition and egotism or block his plans for effective and honest government. He lashed out with equal fury against "malefactors of great wealth" and the "mammon of unrighteousness" when dressed in the armor of big business, against "undesirable citizens" in the livery of political and economic radicalism, and against "mollycoddles" who preached uncompromising pacifism. In the midst of a crowded day at the White House he found time to write to a Harvard football player in praise of his spirit of sacrifice that made it possible for his Alma Mater to win over Yale by a field goal. It was just such things that kept the "strenuous Teddy" on the front page.

The keynote of Roosevelt's administration was loose construction of the Constitution. Under him the President assumed large powers. "I declined to adopt the view that what was imperatively necessary for the nation could not be done by the President unless he could find some specific authorization to do it," he said. "My belief was that it was not only his right but his duty to do anything that the needs of the nation demanded unless such action was forbidden by the Constitution or by the laws. Under this interpretation of executive power I did and caused to be done many things not previously done by Presidents and heads of departments. I did not usurp power, but I did greatly broaden the use of executive power." He was also the exponent of the theory that national resources should be preserved for public purposes.

When Roosevelt attempted to put his policies into practice, it was inevitable that he should meet with bitter opposition from the dominant leadership of his own party; that he should be hamstrung by the heritage of the individualistic and exploitive nineteenth century; that a century of inertia should slumber on in spite of thunder from the White House; that Wall Street should appeal to "government according to law and the Constitution." Faced with adverse decisions by conservative judges, the impatient President raised his voice against them, with the usual reaction from enemies that his fulminations were incitements to revolution.

History has not yet evaluated the Roosevelt administration; it has ventured to pronounce judgment on his predecessors—and even on three of his successors. This in itself is significant. His contemporaries were either hotly for or hotly against him. They were not lukewarm. It was said of Roosevelt that his "bark was worse than his bite." It is true that the legislative achievements of his administration are not especially impressive; but in the light of previous administrations they are both impressive and prophetic. Moreover, many of the substantial measures of his administration were achieved over the opposition of leaders of his own party. It was necessary to effect a political revolution in order to overthrow the Republican oligarchy, and this accomplishment must be credited in no small measure to Roosevelt, whether inadvertently or otherwise.

Bryan found the remedy for the evils of his time in reforming the currency. Roosevelt, who was in a sense heavily indebted to Bryan, sought reform by governmental regulation effected through the instrumentality of men who approached government from the point of view of trained men.

Roosevelt's place in history was tentatively fixed by his adversaries who compared him with Andrew Jackson, another vigorous President who was charged with usurpation. In a speech delivered in 1907, two years before Roosevelt left the White House, George Harvey, a defender of extreme property rights, who in 1904 doubted the wisdom of Roosevelt's announcement that he would not accept another nomination, referred to him as "Bombastes Furioso" and likened him unto Jackson. The speech embodied the accusation of Wall Street that Roosevelt was a dangerous oppressor, an enemy of industry and progress, an agitator against law and order who had done an enormous amount of harm by inspiring disrespect for the courts and who had fostered labor union tyranny, a usurper who had wielded the power of a dictator. It is the Roosevelt who preached a crusade against the unholy alliance between the predatory interests and the government who will probably be remembered after his intense hatred of men in other parties has been forgotten—men with the same objectives but with different methods.

During the Roosevelt era the Democratic party was an ineffective opposition party, torn with factional strife and divided between East and West. There were the idealistic Bryan Democrats who read Bryan's *Commoner*, which began publication in 1901. Bryan wrote its leading articles until he entered Wilson's cabinet in 1913. Then there were the old-line Democrats who either used Bryan's name to conjure with or fought him openly and secretly. Never acceptable to the eastern Democrats and anathema to Tammany Hall, Bryan sought to cement an alliance between the South and the West. George Harvey, the editor of the conservative *Harper's Weekly*, was the spokesman of the Democratic *émigrés* who tried to read Bryan out of the party. The same publication, which was owned by the Morgan interests, also reflected the conservative hostility against Roosevelt. With the rank and file of their respective parties both Roosevelt and Bryan were popular, and many Democrats even supported Roosevelt's policies.

When Roosevelt succeeded McKinley, he inherited the leadership of a party dominated by seasoned politicians who represented big business and who under Hanna's leadership had stemmed the tide of western revolt.

From 1903 to 1911 Joseph G. Cannon of Illinois was the speaker of the House of Representatives. A man of personal popularity with members on both sides of the aisle, he wielded greater power than any speaker before him. "Cannonism" became the symbol of the tyrannical rule of the majority and a synonym for "standpat" Republicanism. "Uncle Joe's" committee assignments placed the "standpatters" in strategic positions. It was not until the administration of Roosevelt's successor that the dissatisfaction of the progressives with their lot flamed into open revolt against "Cannonism."

The Senate was under the iron-clad control of bred-in-the-bone conservatives, an inner ring of four able men whose power was such that any one of them could dispose of bills by a wave of the hand. They were Nelson W. Aldrich of Rhode Island, William B. Allison of Iowa, Orville H. Platt of Connecticut, and John C. Spooner of Wisconsin. The strength of this cabal was such that Senators cultivated their approval, without which committee assignments and favors such as Senators covet would have been few and barren. Aldrich was the dominating personality on the powerful Committee on Finance. Allison was from 1881 to 1908 the chairman of the Committee on Appropriations and for thirty years a member of the Committee on Finance.

After Matthew S. Quay's death in 1904, Senator Boies Penrose succeeded to the leadership of the Republican organization in Pennsylvania. There was little idealism about him; and when his huge bulk arose in the Senate there was never any anxiety among the members of the cabal, who knew him as a brother in the faith. Senator Joseph B. Foraker of Ohio became a bitter antagonist of Roosevelt until he lost his influence in 1908, when the publication of the correspondence of John D. Archbold of the Standard Oil Company revealed that Foraker had been in the company's employ

while a member of the Senate and had received the sum of $29,-
500. The Archbold letters were purchased by Hearst from men
in the employ of the Standard Oil Company.

The opposition of these Senators and their satellites to Roosevelt's attempts to regulate the railroads and curb the power of
corporations contributed to the growing number of Senators who
in the Taft administration became known as "western insurgents."
The most prominent insurgents were Robert M. La Follette of
Wisconsin, Albert J. Beveridge of Indiana, Joseph L. Bristow of
Kansas, and Jonathan P. Dolliver of Iowa. Others joined their
group later. Roosevelt did not always satisfy the progressive instincts of these men, but as between the President and his adversaries they gave him their support. Unquestionably Roosevelt's
immense popularity the country over and with the Washington
correspondents was a strong asset to the incipient insurgent movement.

Roosevelt's popularity was abundantly demonstrated in the presidential election of 1904. The untimely death of McKinley upset
the plans of Roosevelt's adversaries to remove him from political
influence; and as President he proved to be as obnoxious to big
business as he had been in the governor's office at Albany. The
hope of preventing his nomination to succeed himself faded as his
popularity increased; and when Senator Hanna died in February,
1904, the Old Guard was resigned to the inevitable. The Republican national convention at Chicago was a Roosevelt "circus." The
proceedings were cut and dried. About the only consolation the
standpat element brought home was the nomination for the Vice-
Presidency of Charles W. Fairbanks of Indiana, whose frigid
personality was matched only by the cold shoulder he turned
against progressive policies. Roosevelt was a host in himself and
would have brought victory to his party regardless of platform or
running mate.

The proceedings and outcome of the Democratic national convention at St. Louis made assurance doubly sure. The defeat of
Bryan in two successive elections left him out of the picture. The
conservative Democrats in the East preferred Cleveland as the
one candidate who might possibly defeat Roosevelt, but he de-

clined to allow his name to be used. There was an active element among the Bryanites who attempted to inflate a boom for William Randolph Hearst who was conducting a spirited campaign in his newspapers against trusts and imperialism; but the more level-headed followers of the "peerless leader" preferred even a conservative to the self-seeking journalist. By the middle of April the nomination of Alton B. Parker of New York was practically assured. Bryan kept out of the platform what was objectionable to him.

Judge Parker was not the man to appeal to the progressive West. As soon as his nomination was announced, he dispatched a telegram to a delegate to the convention which stated that he regarded the gold standard "as firmly and irrevocably established" and requested that another candidate be nominated in case his position was not acceptable. Bryan left a sick bed in order to defend his pet issue, but by an overwhelming vote the convention indorsed Parker's position.

The position of the opposing parties was thus changed. In 1896 and in 1900 the Democratic party was the vehicle of liberalism and radicalism, with Bryan sitting securely in the driver's seat. The Republican party was dominated by Mark Hanna, the exponent of big business. But by 1904 Roosevelt had qualified for the position of distrust and hatred which Bryan had occupied.

Notwithstanding, Parker attracted badly needed attention to himself during the closing days of the campaign by charging that through the instrumentality of Roosevelt's Secretary of Commerce and Labor the Republican campaign chest had been generously filled by contributions from large corporations. Roosevelt had already become known as the founder of the "Ananias Club," to which he named for membership individuals who made objectional assertions about him. In this case he stigmatized Parker's allegation as "unqualifiedly and atrociously false." The Democratic candidate was unable to substantiate his charges; and Roosevelt's vigorous denial added to his own popularity. Subsequent investigations revealed that both parties were the beneficiaries of the good will of corporations, and that Roosevelt, either deliberately or out of ignorance, was too positive and sweeping in his denial.

The results of the election proved that the voters approved of
"T. R." He rolled up large majorities in western states where
Bryan and Weaver had had strong support, and won the electoral
votes of every state except the Solid South. He even carried Missouri. Parker's strength, such as it was, showed itself in the East.
Roosevelt's popular majority was the greatest in history up to that
time. In the flush of victory on election night, November 8, 1904,
Roosevelt gave out the following statement: "On the fourth of
March next I shall have served three and one-half years, and these
three and one-half years constitute my first term. The wise custom
which limits the President by two terms regards the substance and
not the form. Under no circumstances will I be a candidate for or
accept another nomination."

Many years later, in 1913, Roosevelt gave in his *Autobiography*
the reason for his choice of phraseology in his post-election statement. He believed then, and continued to believe, that the third-
term tradition was wholesome; but he did not wish to say specifically that he would not be a candidate for the nomination in 1908
because it would have been widely accepted as meaning that he
intended to be a candidate some other year, and he had no idea
that he would ever be a candidate again. "On the other hand, it
had no application whatever to any human being save where it was
invoked in the case of a man desiring a third consecutive term,"
he said. He amplified his statement still further by expressing the
opinion that if a tremendous crisis occurred at the end of the
second term of a man like Lincoln, "it would be a veritable
calamity if the American people were forbidden to continue to use
the services of the one man whom they knew could carry them
through the crisis."

What prompted Roosevelt's explanation was his acceptance of
the nomination for the Presidency by the Progressive party in
1912; and it will perhaps continue to be a topic of debate as to
whether Roosevelt in 1908 and in 1912 regretted having made
the statement in 1904.

The opening years of the twentieth century brought the consolidation of industries and railroads on a scale that even the Populists
had not predicted. At the close of the previous century the New

York Central absorbed the Lake Shore and Michigan Southern and thus made a single system between New York and Chicago. This striking example of railroad consolidation came within a generation that remembered when a traveler from New York to Albany changed cars five times and bought tickets from five different railroad companies. Within ten years after the opening of the century, out of some 225,000 miles of railroad there remained only a handful of independent units. Five great systems, integrated by interlocking directorates and community of interest, were controlled respectively by five groups of financiers. Certain benefits to the public from railroad consolidation were obvious. The essential ground for complaint was that too many benefits went to the men who controlled the systems.

The remarkable career of Edwin H. Harriman is illustrative of the methods of railroad consolidation and financing that ran afoul of an indignant public and the law. In 1897 Harriman became a member of the board of directors of the company that took over the bankrupt Union Pacific Railway, and within a few months he made himself the virtual dictator of its policies. It required courage and vision to take over and rehabilitate a railroad in the condition of the Union Pacific. Harriman not only succeeded, but also got control of the Southern Pacific and the Central Pacific. In fact, he used the credit and the resources of the Union Pacific for speculative purposes and as a holding company for securities of other transportation companies. His attempt to obtain control of the Chicago, Burlington, and Quincy in order to establish connections with Chicago conflicted with the plan of James J. Hill to attain the same objective for his railroads: the Great Northern and the Northern Pacific. Hill outgeneraled his rival, but Harriman bought stock in the Northern Pacific which owned half-interest in the Burlington. The upshot of the spectacular battle, which brought on a panic in May, 1901, was the organization of the Northern Securities Company as a holding company for the Great Northern and the Northern Pacific, in 1902. The Harriman interests were given representation on the governing board of the Northern Securities Company.

The State of Minnesota brought suit against the Northern

Securities Company, but the United States district judge decided that the holding company was not a railroad company and therefore was not in violation of the Minnesota statute forbidding the consolidation of parallel or competing railroads within the state. The state appealed to the United States Supreme Court. Finally a separate suit was brought by the Attorney-General of the United States which came up on appeal to the Supreme Court. By a five to four decision the highest tribunal ordered the dissolution of the Northern Securities Company because it violated the Sherman Anti-Trust Act by effecting a combination in restraint of trade. This decision was hailed as a great victory for the Roosevelt administration. Notwithstanding, Hill retained control of both roads.

Harriman sold his holdings in the Hill railroads and increased his interests in other roads, which brought an investigation by the Interstate Commerce Commission in 1906-07, under the increased power granted to it by the Hepburn Act. The investigation revealed the devious ways of Harriman. It was at this time that Roosevelt, in referring to his squabble with the prominent railroad man, said: "My spear shall know no brother."

The successful outcome of the Northern Securities case gave renewed impetus to the "trust-busting" policies of the Roosevelt administration. Suits were instituted against a number of trusts, including the Standard Oil Company, the American Tobacco Company, and the Beef Trust; in 1903 the Department of Commerce and Labor was established, and legislation aimed to protect the public from the practices of railroads and other corporations was enacted. The Elkins Act of 1903 prohibited secret rebates and discriminations, and the corporation as well as the guilty official was liable to fines for each offense. By the Hepburn Act of 1906 the Interstate Commerce Commission was authorized to prescribe just and reasonable rates. And in 1908 railroad passes to all except clergymen and employees were forbidden.

In 1907 Judge Kenesaw Mountain Landis of the United States District Court at Chicago assessed fines totaling $29,240,000 against the Standard Oil Company for receiving rebates from the Chicago and Alton Railroad; but a year later the United States Circuit Court of Appeals reversed the decision on technicalities that were hardly convincing to the public, unschooled in the ways of corporation lawyers. The suit against the same company under the Sherman Anti-Trust Act was not decided until 1911. This was the most notable decision rendered down to that time.

The Supreme Court ordered the dissolution of the Standard Oil Company of New Jersey. The attorneys for the company argued that there was no rule of fairness or reasonableness which regulated competition. "Price-cutting and rebating, collecting information on the trade of competitors, the operation of companies under other names to obviate prejudice or secure an advantage or for whatever reason, are all legal methods whatever moral criticism they may justify," ran the argument. The court did not make a clear distinction between fair and unfair methods of competition. If the decision did nothing else, however, it contributed to the enactment of legislation designed to clarify issues involved in similar cases. So far as the Standard Oil Company was concerned, the effect of the decision was merely to break up the trust into a number of smaller companies, each controlled by the Rockefeller interests.

Two weeks later the Supreme Court ordered the dissolution of the American Tobacco Company in a suit which had also been instituted by the Roosevelt administration. The court followed the reasoning in the oil case. The effect of the latter decision was more decisive, however, in that the various tobacco companies after the dissolution did not have the proportions of the Standard Oil Company and were not powerful enough to dominate the industry.

In any event, the voluminous testimony accumulated in the anti-trust cases was disconcerting to the men of big business, and awakened the public to the menace of unscrupulous practices, even though the mills of justice ground slowly. Further disillusionment did not overtake the public until an almost complete collapse of the economic structure of the nation was threatened at the time when another President bearing the Roosevelt name took the helm.

The dance of high finance grew dizzier and dizzier in spite of the hysterical articles on "Frenzied Finance" by Thomas W. Lawson, which jumped the circulation of *Everybody's Magazine* from 197,000 in 1903 to 735,000 in 1904. Ida M. Tarbell's "History of the Standard Oil Company," which ran serially in *McClure's Magazine* from 1902 to 1904, was more restrained but still sufficiently sensational to class the author with the muckrakers. In a generation when the great middle class reaped rich rewards, the best argument to confound prophets like Theodore Roosevelt, William J. Bryan, Robert M. La Follette, and Woodrow Wilson was to complain that they were conducting a "raid on prosperity" and were "unsettling business." It was a generation in which responsible people took seriously a book by the chancellor of Syracuse University, James R. Day, entitled *The Raid on Prosperity*. Day alleged that the people were not oppressed by the corporations but the corporations were oppressed by the people. The Standard Oil Company, he wrote, was one of the greatest benefactors the country had ever known.

One of the muckrakers had the unusual satisfaction of seeing immediate results of his novel portraying the sickening details of conditions in the packing houses of Chicago and the loathsome moral and physical conditions that surrounded the lives of their employees. This realistic bit of fiction was *The Jungle* by Upton Sinclair, who lived to write many more indictments of big business in *The Brass Check, The Goose Step, The Goslings,* and *The Profits of Religion. The Jungle* mightily stirred President Roosevelt and Senator Beveridge and inspired a bill to provide meat inspection by the federal government.

The beneficiaries of existing conditions unloosed a barrage of propaganda against the bill and succeeded in emasculating it by amendments until Roosevelt struck consternation in their camps by submitting to Congress the report of a government investigating committee. With great skill, enforced by righteous indignation, Beveridge steered his bill through the Senate, although he was unsuccessful in restoring certain provisions that have since been enacted into law.

The Meat Inspection Act of 1906 marked progress toward enlarged federal power in dealing with social problems and marked the partial fulfillment of the Populist demand for pure food legislation. It was followed by the enactment in the same session of Congress of the Pure Food and Drugs Act and the Employers'

Liability Act, both of which were forcefully advocated by Roosevelt. The latter law, which made employers engaged in interstate commerce responsible for injuries to their workmen, was declared unconstitutional by the Supreme Court in 1908 on the ground that it granted power to the federal government to interfere with matters outside the scope of interstate commerce. Congress immediately enacted a new law that omitted the objectionable provisions. Another measure quite as much in the interest of the safety of travelers as in the interest of labor was the law of March 4, 1908, which limited the hours of trainmen and telegraph operators.

Two executive acts of Roosevelt called down upon him the condemnation of widely different critics, namely, his interference in the anthracite coal strike of 1902 and his acquiescence in the absorption of the Tennessee Coal and Iron Company by the United States Steel Corporation in 1907.

The circumstances attending the latter transaction were as follows. At the beginning of the year 1907, and even before, there were indications of an impending panic. Unsettled conditions abroad and the speculative mania in the United States were the warning signs. In October the failure of the Knickerbocker Trust Company of New York precipitated the panic of 1907, which speedily spread to all parts of the country. Banks refused to honor checks of their depositors, and clearing house certificates were issued in order to alleviate the financial stringency. The "bankers' panic," as it was called, extended into the year of the presidential election and called forth the enactment of the Aldrich-Vreeland Act of 1908, which was intended to relieve periods of financial stringency by authorizing national banks to issue notes with approved securities as collateral, in addition to United States bonds. This effort to provide an "elastic currency" was far from satisfactory; but the act also provided for the appointment of a National Monetary Commission to make a thorough study of money and banking.

President Roosevelt and the Secretary of the Treasury kept in close touch with the situation during the panic and took what measures they could to prevent the depression from taking on even more serious proportions. In the early part of November two representatives of the United States Steel Corporation, Henry C. Frick and E. H. Gary, called on Roosevelt, to acquaint him with the dangerous condition of a certain business firm whose assets were largely in the form of securities of the Tennessee Coal and Iron Company, whose officials had urged upon Frick and Gary the urgent necessity for the Steel Corporation to purchase that stock. Frick and Gary stated that they desired to absorb the Tennessee Coal and Iron Company not for business advantages but solely to alleviate the dangerous financial situation. Roosevelt replied that although he could not advise them to take the action they proposed, he would not interpose any objections.

Roosevelt later expressed satisfaction with his policy in this matter and insisted that business was vitally helped by it; but during the presidential campaign of 1908 and the years following, when he was once more a candidate for the Presidency, Democrats and old-line Republicans cited the incident as proof that the crusader against big business had violated the Sherman Anti-Trust Act and was not sincere in professing sympathy with the progressive cause.

Roosevelt's part in the anthracite coal strike was an extraordinary interference of the federal government in the increasing tension in the relations between capital and labor, and won for him high praise and much criticism.

In the course of years the coal-carrying railroads had obtained a virtual monopoly of the anthracite coal mines in Pennsylvania and had thereby eliminated from this important industry the independent producers. For many years conditions in the coal fields had been unsatisfactory and dangerous for the men who mined the coal and for the operators as well. Union organizers had met with little success in their efforts to organize the thirty-five thousand soft coal miners in West Virginia and the one hundred and fifty thousand hard coal miners in Pennsylvania. The great immigration of the last quarter century had had the effect of dividing the miners among themselves along nationalistic and racial lines.

When in the fall of 1899 John Mitchell, president of the United Mine Workers of America, entered the anthracite area to organ-

Edwin Levick

ize the miners, he undertook what appeared to be a hopeless task. Wages were unbelievably low; the hazards of underground work were appalling; the system of weighing and measuring coal was unjust; hours were long and miners were idle for many days of the year; and through a system of company-owned houses and stores the miners were in a state of servitude to the corporations that owned them. In spite of these heavy obstacles, Mitchell, a conservative young man who had just turned thirty, became the first successful organizer of immigrant labor from southern and eastern Europe, won the support of public opinion for his cause, and successfully conducted a strike of five months' duration.

Mitchell's conservative and peaceful disposition caused him to exhaust every effort to prevent a strike, because he knew the terrible suffering of families that prolonged idleness would bring; but the operators were adamant in refusing to recognize the union. On May 15, 1902, Mitchell became the leader of a strike which he, together with other public-spirited citizens in various walks of life, had tried in vain to avoid. As the weeks dragged on, an appalling situation developed in the regions directly affected by the strike, and the nation was brought face to face with a fuel shortage.

It was fortunate for the strikers that a number of able writers and students of social problems invaded the strike area and presented to the public a picture of conditions that most of the newspapers ignored. It was still more fortunate for the strikers and for the country that President Roosevelt had the initiative and courage to use the power of his position and the prestige of his own popularity to force a settlement. Equally fortunate were the tactical errors of the men who were determined at all costs to resist the demands of the strikers. In reply to a correspondent who appealed to him to make concessions, George F. Baer, president of the Philadelphia and Reading Railway Company, made public his social philosophy. "The rights and interests of the laboring man will be protected and cared for—not by the labor agitators, but by the Christian men to whom God has given control of the property rights of the country, and upon the successful management of which so much depends."

In August Roosevelt directed the commissioner of labor to conduct an investigation into the issues at stake. His report suggested certain concessions and the appointment of a joint committee of conciliation. Baer, the spokesman for the operators, refused to consider compromise. In October Roosevelt summoned Mitchell and representatives of the operators to a conference in the White House, when he urged them to settle their differences. Mitchell came to the conference in a conciliatory mood, but the operators were in an insolent frame of mind, used insulting language, and declined to listen to suggestions of arbitration. Roosevelt later said: "There was only one man in that conference who behaved like a gentleman and that man was not I."

Roosevelt realized that he had no legal right to interfere, but the clamor of public opinion in the face of a fuel famine and the insolence of the operators aroused his fighting instincts. He resolved to act. Some years later, in 1909, Speaker Cannon told Archie Butt, military aide to President Taft, that in reply to his query as to what would have happened if the miners and operators had refused to compromise, Roosevelt said: "I would have seized the mines and the roads and would have given the freezing people coal, and Congress could have impeached and be damned."

The President's threat had the desired effect, and the operators agreed to arbitrate. The decision of the commission of arbitration appointed by Roosevelt was not a clean-cut victory for the strikers, but important concessions were made to them. The strike is important historically not because it is one of the greatest in the annals of American labor but because under Roosevelt's leadership the federal government took on a new function, namely, that of intervention in affairs that had previously been regarded as entirely private.

CHAPTER XX

THE INSURGENTS

THE PRESIDENTIAL CAMPAIGN OF 1908 WAS MILD AND UNINTER-
esting, but it was the calm that preceded the storm that broke
immediately after the inauguration of the new administration and
did not abate until the divided Republican party met disaster in
the election of 1912.

Before the opening of the year 1908 it was obvious that Roosevelt would honor his pledge not to seek or accept another nomination, notwithstanding the popular demand, and that he would be
able to dictate the nomination of his successor. His control of
the patronage and the demand of the rank and file of the party for
a candidate in sympathy with Rooseveltian policies made it easy
for the strenuous "Teddy" to accomplish his purpose, in spite of
the strategy of his opponents to sponsor "favorite sons" in order
to divide the Roosevelt strength.

The ablest man in Roosevelt's cabinet was Elihu Root of New
York, the Secretary of State, for whom the President had high
admiration and affection; but his record as a corporation lawyer
would have made him a vulnerable candidate against Bryan, who
was expected to be the Democratic standard bearer. William H.
Taft of Ohio, the Secretary of War, was crown prince. In the
words of a hostile editor, the Republican national convention at
Chicago was really not a convention. "The accredited representatives of the Republican party simply met to ratify President Roosevelt's choice of a successor and squabble a little over the platform."

On the first ballot Taft received 702 votes out of a total of
980. The nomination of James S. Sherman of New York for the
Vice-Presidency was the only consolation the conservatives, or
standpatters, derived from the convention. Taft had served with
distinction as governor-general of the Philippines before he became

a member of Roosevelt's cabinet in 1903. Roosevelt's offer to appoint him to the Supreme Court the year before was tempting and by accepting the proffered appointment his lifetime ambition would have been satisfied; but his obligations to the Filipinos and his popularity with them weighed more heavily.

Immediately after becoming a member of the cabinet Taft's relations with the President became intimate and cordial; and Roosevelt intrusted him with assignments that enabled him to render important public services and brought his name favorably before the public. He made speeches in various parts of the country, and his infectious chuckle, unfailing good humor, and loyalty to his chief made for him a host of friends. The only vulnerable part of his record was the fact that as a federal judge he had issued injunctions against labor. The Democrats made much of this, and Samuel Gompers, president of the American Federation of Labor, supported his Democratic opponent but made no serious effort to swing the labor vote.

In anticipation of the nomination of a man of Roosevelt's choice, the conservative Democrats as early as 1907 began a concerted effort to head off Bryan's nomination and to name a candidate in sympathy with Cleveland Democracy. On January 3, 1908, the *New York World* presented John A. Johnson of Minnesota as an available candidate for the Democratic nomination; and two weeks later George Harvey, the editor of *Harper's Weekly*, proposed Woodrow Wilson of New Jersey for the presidential nomination, and Johnson for the Vice-Presidency. *Harper's Weekly* was owned by the Morgan interests, and *Leslie's Weekly* and *Judge* were owned by the Standard Oil interests. These publications defended big business against the assaults of muckraking magazines like *Collier's Weekly* and *McClure's Magazine.*

Johnson was serving his second term as a Democratic governor of the rock-ribbed Republican State of Minnesota and was the most popular chief executive the state had ever had. He had been elected on the Democratic ticket as a protest against the machine domination of the Republican party; but he was an independent rather than a Democrat and was as popular with Republicans as with Democrats. Moreover, there was nothing in his record that made him obnoxious to James J. Hill and the powerful steel companies in the northern part of the state. Johnson had not built up a nation-wide organization, however, and he was opposed in his own state by the idealistic Bryan Democrats.

Bryan still remained the idol of the progressive element in the Democratic party. By 1908 the youthful face of the crusader of 1896 had grown more rugged and bore the stamp of maturity. In spite of the fact that under Roosevelt's leadership the country had moved forward in the direction pointed by the Populists and Bryanites, the Democratic party under Bryan or any other leader had small chance of success against a popular candidate who had the stamp of Roosevelt's approval.

After the Democratic national convention at Denver had nominated the Great Commoner in a frenzy of enthusiasm, *Harper's Weekly* commented that "the Democrats are now at liberty to resume their accustomed occupation of electing a Republican President." The Democratic platform included such progressive planks as tariff revision, guarantee of bank deposits, postal savings banks, exemption of labor unions from the anti-trust law, an income tax, and direct election of Senators. Toward the close of the campaign Bryan featured the guarantee of bank deposits. Curiously enough, this proposed measure did not become a law until twenty-five years later—and then under a Democratic President whose first official act was to close every national bank in the United States as a precaution against even greater disaster than had already overtaken them.

The election was an emphatic indorsement of Roosevelt's policies. Taft carried every state Roosevelt had carried in 1904, with the exception of Nebraska, Nevada, and Colorado. The South remained solid. Taft's assurance of loyalty to Roosevelt's policies kept the western states in line, but with pluralities greatly reduced over those of 1904. Taft's plurality throughout the country was considerably less than Roosevelt's. It is significant, however, that in spite of hard times, over a million out of employment, unsettled business conditions, and dissatisfaction of labor leaders with Taft's record and that of his party, the country not only gave Taft 321 electoral votes as against 162 for Bryan but also only slightly smaller Republican majorities in both houses of Congress than in the previous Congress.

The election statistics in 1908 are misleading, however. President Taft inherited the leadership of a party divided against itself. After the disappearance from the political stage of the dominating personality of Roosevelt, the cleavage in the Republican party which had been concealed, or at least partially concealed, under Roosevelt became apparent and grew wider and wider.

Fundamentally, Roosevelt and Taft were different in temperament, in political philosophy, and in political methods. Even before Taft's inauguration there were indications that all was not well, that the "close and sweet" intimacy between "Theodore" and "Will" had already been ruffled. Within a few days after Taft's inauguration, Roosevelt departed on an African hunting trip, to be absent for over a year. From the day of his departure on March 24, 1909, until his return on June 18, 1910, "T. R." was in the headlines. New York was as excited over the departure of the big game hunter as it would have been over his inauguration as President; and when he returned the city was a pandemonium. His drive up Broadway was a continuous ovation. It was most unusual, to say the least, for an ex-President to furnish better "copy" than the occupant of the White House.

From the very first days of his administration it was plain that Taft did not have the faculty of winning the good will of the Washington correspondents. Roosevelt was his own press agent, and between him and the newspaper men there was a perfect understanding. During the Taft administration, however, there were many "leaks" about the White House, and there was no one who knew how to control the news.

Roosevelt prided himself on the high caliber of the men in his cabinet and on their popularity with the country. Taft's cabinet, on the contrary, made little appeal; and there were at least three members who were unpopular from the start: Secretary of State Knox, Attorney-General Wickersham, and Secretary of the Interior Ballinger. Ballinger's appointment was especially unfortunate, partly because his administration soon came under fire and partly because Roosevelt was disappointed that Taft did not appoint James R. Garfield, the retiring Secretary and a member of Roosevelt's famous "tennis cabinet."

The chief usher of the White House, "Ike" Hoover, in his book *Forty-Two Years in the White House*, immediately sensed the change that came with Taft's inauguration. "Probably no administration has ever taken such a hold upon the people as that of Theodore Roosevelt," he wrote. "Every little event concerning any member of the family from the highest to the lowest . . . was broadcast through the newspapers." During the presidential campaign, he says, Roosevelt's every move was made with a view of promoting Taft's election. After Taft's election, however, almost immediately there seemed to spring from some unknown source the coolness that was so often noticed later. "There has seldom been such bitterness between an incoming and an outgoing administration," he continues. When Taft came to the White House on March 4, the employees noticed what a great change had come over him. "He had lost much of his good nature and seemed cross and uncomfortable—very different from his former self."

The testimony of Archie Butt, Taft's military aide who had also been closely associated with Roosevelt, substantiates that of the chief usher. Roosevelt visited the White House in Taft's absence on November, 1910, and in telling Major Butt about it Hoover said, with tears in his eyes: "It's the only happy day we have had in nearly two years, and not one of us would exchange it for a hundred-dollar bill." With such gossip floating about Washington, little wonder that the newspapers spoke of the prospective return of Roosevelt from Africa as "Back from Elba."

That all was not well with the new administration was revealed in March, 1909, when Congress convened in extraordinary session to revise the tariff. Twelve western insurgents—from Wisconsin, Iowa, Minnesota, Nebraska, Kansas, and Washington—voted against the election of Cannon for speaker. "Cannonism" had been an issue in 1908. Some candidates for Congress had pledged themselves not to vote for the tyrannical speaker. Taft did not like Cannon any better than the insurgents, but this open revolt against party regularity boded no good for the administration.

The Republican platform pledged the party to a revision of the tariff in rather ambiguous terms; but during the campaign Republican speakers in the West, including Taft, left the definite impression that revision would be downward. It was also pointed out that it would be better for the tariff to be revised by its friends than by its enemies in the Democratic party, who would not approach the task with proper reverence for the protective principle. By convening Congress on March 15, President Taft redeemed the promise in the Republican platform that the tariff would be revised in a special session.

The Payne Tariff Bill which passed the House of Representatives provided for downward revision of certain schedules of the existing Dingley Tariff, but it was leagues removed from genuine revision. When the bill came to the Senate it encountered bitter opposition from two sources: the standpat Republicans led by Aldrich of Rhode Island, and the Republican insurgents from the West. The Senate Finance Committee reported the Aldrich bill as a substitute. This bill and the Payne-Aldrich Tariff Act which finally emerged from the conference committee reduced duties on more articles than it raised them, but by means of reclassifying schedules and "jokers," the increases were more important than the reductions. In other words, the bill as proposed and as finally approved did not represent an honest reduction of the tariff and violated promises made by Republican speakers in the campaign. For this the Senate Committee on Finance was largely responsible. However, the bill did not come to a final vote before the western insurgents had exposed the inequalities and iniquities of the schedules; and on the final passage six insurgents and Senator Knute Nelson of Minnesota voted against it.

Having the assurance of President Taft that he would support them in their efforts to obtain a bill that complied with the Republican platform, the insurgents girded themselves for a battle against the resourceful Aldrich. Two of the insurgents—Albert J. Beveridge of Indiana and Jonathan P. Dolliver of Iowa—had rendered indispensable services by extended campaign tours in which they had assured their audiences that Taft was pledged to downward revision. Beveridge was the parliamentary leader of the insurgents on the floor of the Senate. Dolliver was conservative by instinct and loyal to his party, but he was outraged by the betrayal of the people in favor of the "interests" and enlisted his great oratorical power, flashing wit, and moral strength in the cause.

For years Robert M. La Follette had been recognized as the foremost of the progressives. Under his leadership Wisconsin blazed the way for other states in the matter of progressive legislation. As governor of the state from 1901 to 1906 he carried through a program of reform that came to be known as the "Wisconsin idea." In order to break down the control of the corporations and the railroads, he established the direct primary which made it possible for him to appeal directly to the people for his nomination and for support of his principles. The railroads and the corporations had retained control of the parties by means of the corrupt and unrepresentative convention system.

A man of superb moral courage, great energy, and belligerency, La Follette talked for hours at county fairs and Chautauquas and exposed the devious ways of the enemies he hoped to drive from their strategic positions. He believed that the government should be placed in the hands of experts for the accomplishment of equitable taxation of corporations and for the regulation of railroad rates according to the physical valuation of their property. He made use of the University of Wisconsin, in which he took great pride, for consultation and cooperation.

In 1906 he became a member of the Senate, where he served with great distinction and high purpose until his death in 1925. His fearless independence and record made him obnoxious to the standpat Republicans who, failing in their efforts to curb his course, tried to break his spirit by discourtesies and other means. Early in his senatorial career, observing that all but a few of his colleagues had "walked out" on him, he remarked: "I see a great many vacant seats in the Senate today. Many of the seats now temporarily vacant will be permanently so after a while."

La Follette's rectitude in private and public life and his carefully prepared and erudite speeches foiled the efforts of his adversaries and the newspapers to drive him out of public life. During the wartime hysteria, when the Senator's courage was put to the supreme test, it appeared for a time that they would succeed. That even the cloak of "loyalty" that was used to camouflage their sinister purpose did not succeed is the best possible proof of La Follette's stamina and his hold on the people of his own state. Like Bryan, the Wisconsin Senator established his own magazine which appeared in January, 1909, as *La Follette's Weekly Magazine*.

Allison's successor in the Senate was Albert B. Cummins, whose career as governor of Iowa, which began the same year La Follette assumed the reins in Wisconsin, paralleled that of the Wisconsin progressive. His exposition of an equitable revision of the tariff was known as the "Iowa idea." He was elected to the Senate in 1909, after the death of the veteran Allison, and joined his colleague Dolliver in the fight for tariff reform.

Joseph L. Bristow, the "countrified" Senator from Kansas, and Moses E. Clapp, the rugged Senator from Minnesota, were the other members of the insurgent group who for weeks applied themselves to the study of certain schedules of the Aldrich bill and sounded a new note in the Senate by propounding embarrassing questions to Aldrich and his cohorts. Working far into the night over reams of statistics and documents in the heat of a Washington summer, every day these men came to the Senate chamber primed with material and arguments that either drove Aldrich from the chamber or caused him to resort to the last refuge of a man unequal to his adversary—personalities. But the insurgents could give as well as take; and the swelling tide of public indignation, as day by day the iniquities of the tariff bill were exposed, buoyed their flagging spirits.

The most disheartening development of the situation was the desertion of the insurgents by President Taft, who had assured them that he was with them and would veto a bill that failed to conform to the Republican platform. In vain did the insurgents quote from Taft's campaign speeches to show that they, not Aldrich, were the spokesmen of the party. The tactics of the insurgents repelled rather than pleased the President, and there was a noticeable coolness in his attitude toward them. In fact, it was Aldrich and the standpat Senators who received the favors and the confidences of the White House.

The House having refused to pass the Aldrich bill with its some eight hundred amendments over the House bill, the two bills went to a committee of conference. While the committee was engaged in framing its report, the President made some efforts to obtain reductions, but with scant success. The bill as reported, known as the Payne-Aldrich Tariff Act, passed the House by a vote of 195 to 183, with twenty Republicans voting in the negative. Six insurgents were from Minnesota, four from Wisconsin, four from Iowa, and one each from Kansas, Illinois, North Dakota, Washington, New York, and Ohio. The Senate vote was 47 to 31, with six insurgent Republicans and Knute Nelson of Minnesota voting in the negative. Nelson, though a party regular, had been a consistent low tariff man. When he began his public career in the eighties, he was a tariff-for-revenue advocate.

The angry blasts of public opinion against the Payne-Aldrich Tariff were not unlike those that greeted the McKinley Tariff in 1890. Taft showed himself singularly inept in defending his approval of the bill. In September, 1909, following the enactment of the law, he started on a journey of almost thirteen thousand miles, stopping at many places to explain the issues before the country. His initial blunder was made in Boston when he praised Senator Aldrich; but the colossal mistake was reserved until he invaded the enemy country, the hotbed of insurgency in the Northwest.

Six of the eight Representatives and both Senators from Minnesota had voted against the Payne-Aldrich Tariff Bill, and there had been talk of staging a reception for them at the State Capitol upon their return from Washington; and yet in that state, in Winona, the home of James A. Tawney, a notorious reactionary and one of the two Minnesota Representatives who had voted for the tariff bill, Taft paid his cordial respects to him and then crowned his blunder by stating: "When I would say without hesitation that this is the best tariff bill that the Republican party has ever passed, and therefore the best tariff bill that has been passed at all, I do not feel that I could have reconciled any other course to my conscience than that of signing the bill."

On the morning of his arrival in Minneapolis following his Winona speech delivered the day before, there was barely a thin line of people along Nicollet Avenue to greet the President of the

United States. The coolness of the reception was painful to his adversaries as well as to his supporters.

The Payne-Aldrich Tariff was no more the sole cause of the disaster that overtook the Republican party in the congressional elections in 1910 and in the presidential election in 1912 than the McKinley Tariff was the sole cause of Republican defeat in 1890 and in 1892, but it was an important factor. In the next session of Congress the insurgents continued their effective guerilla warfare against the tariff bill and "Cannonism" and "Aldrichism." The tactics of the President and his advisers to read them out of the party were less effective than a policy of conciliation would have been. The insurgent Senators were more than a match for their opponents in oratorical skill, and they had the support of the enlightened public opinion of their own constituencies and of the entire country.

On the Senate floor on January 13, 1910, in a brilliant defense of the insurgents and an attack on the standpatters, Dolliver showed how Taft in the Winona speech had misrepresented the tariff and the insurgents. He analyzed certain schedules and showed how meaningless the reductions were. "The past year witnessed two events of unusual interest—the discovery of the North Pole by Doctor Cook and the revision of the tariff downward by the Senator from Rhode Island—each in its way a unique hoax, and both promptly presented to the favorable notice of the public by the highest official congratulations."

Taft was easily upset by criticism and could be exceedingly disagreeable to people he did not like. He read only the newspapers that praised him—like the *New York Sun*—and had among his chief advisers Senator W. Murray Crane of Massachusetts and Senator Boies Penrose of Pennsylvania, both of whom were anathema to the liberals. Among the members of the cabinet his closest advisers were Secretary of State Knox, Attorney-General Wickersham, and Secretary of Commerce Nagel—not a strong group from the standpoint of political strategy.

In the second Congress under Taft's administration, when the Democrats had a majority in the House and a coalition of Democrats and insurgents in the Senate passed a free wool bill and a farmers' free list bill, Taft imposed his veto. The veto of the latter bill was bad politically, but by that time the President knew that the insurgents were irrevocably lost to him.

Simultaneously with the assault of the insurgents on the tariff was waged a battle against the administration of the Department of the Interior under Secretary Ballinger. Taft had the disagreeable duty of defending a very unpopular member of his cabinet or else admitting that he had erred by appointing him.

It is the conclusion of a competent student of the forestry policy in the United States, John Ise, that it is a "story of reckless and wasteful destruction of magnificent forests, and of flagrant and notorious theft of valuable lands—a story that Americans will follow with little pride."

With the disappearance of the frontier and the end of free and cheap lands in sight, farsighted men began to take stock of the resources of the nation. Individualism unrestrained was seen to work out to the detriment of society. Great corporations were gaining control of the remaining lands and natural resources such as mines, forests, and water power. As early as the seventies scientists had begun to agitate for a conservation policy, and even earlier several states had taken action. Congress showed little interest. In 1873, however, it passed the Timber Culture Act which provided that settlers planting and maintaining forty acres of timber on any quarter section of land might receive a patent for the claim. This law is indicative of some interest in conservation, but the results were disappointing.

In 1878 the Timber and Stone Act provided that under certain restrictions and within certain regions public lands which were valuable chiefly for timber and stone and unfit for cultivation might be sold for their appraised value, with a minimum price of $2.50 per acre. Under this law large areas of timber were secured by corporations through collusion with individual applicants. Similar frauds were perpetrated under the Desert Land Acts of 1877 and 1879, by which land not sufficiently watered might be taken at a price of $1.25 per acre on condition that a certain amount of money be expended on irrigation. Good land that required no irrigation was fraudulently taken under these acts.

Definite progress toward conservation was marked by the Forest Reserve Act of 1891 which authorized the President of the United States to set aside forest reservations from time to time. Under this first important forest conservation measure successive Presidents—Harrison, Cleveland, McKinley, and Roosevelt—withdrew millions of acres for reserves, with Roosevelt adding more than four times as many acres as the combined total of his predecessors.

It was largely through the influence and activity of President Roosevelt and Gifford Pinchot, chief of the Division of Forestry, that interest in conservation developed rapidly during the opening years of the twentieth century. Pinchot, who had been trained under the best forestry experts in Europe, impressed Roosevelt by his zeal, knowledge, and unselfish devotion to the cause. Pinchot was not satisfied merely with a reserve policy; he believed that cleared land should be replanted, according to the policy of the advanced governments of Germany and Sweden.

In his first annual message Roosevelt made recommendations in line with Pinchot's policy and also made a plea for the reclamation of arid lands. In 1894 the Carey Act marked the beginning of reclamation, but the Newlands Act of 1902 is a landmark of great importance. It provided for the construction of irrigation works by the United States government, the cost of the works to be paid by settlers who used the water. The special problems of the New West were teaching the country the needs and uses of collectivism.

In 1903 President Roosevelt appointed the Public Lands Commission to report on the status and operation of land laws and to recommend such laws as might contribute to the most effective use of the public lands; and in 1907 he created the Inland Waterways Commission to study means of improving navigation, of developing water power and irrigation, and of preventing soil erosion. Of great national interest was the invitation extended in 1908 to the governors of states to a conference to be held in the White House to consider the whole question of conservation. The conference was suggested by Pinchot. Members of Congress and of the cabinet, Supreme Court justices, scientists, publicists, and prominent citi-

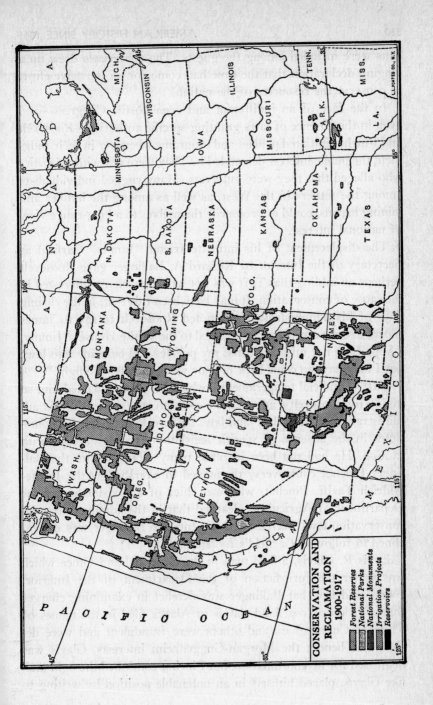

CONSERVATION AND
RECLAMATION
1900-1917

Forest Reserves
National Parks
National Monuments
Irrigation Projects
Reservoirs

L.L. POATES CO., N.Y.

PACIFIC OCEAN

zens were included among the guests. The conference drew up a
ringing declaration that the time had come for an intensive effort
to conserve the resources of the nation.

In the face of an indifferent and even hostile Congress—and
even in the absence of laws granting specific authority—Roosevelt
and Pinchot initiated policies and programs whenever in their judgment the public interest demanded it. They were not without critics
who alleged that they were autocrats. Many rugged individualists
among the settlers in the West, as well as among the lumber and
mining barons, could not reconcile themselves to a long-range view
of national interest.

The displacement of his intimate friend "Jimmy" Garfield as
Secretary of the Interior by Richard A. Ballinger gave Roosevelt
perhaps an inkling that Taft was not whole-heartedly interested in
the cause of conservation. It may have been this that, in the closing
days of his administration, prompted Roosevelt to say to James
Sloan, a secret service agent attached to the White House: "Jimmy,
I hope I am not mistaken: that my policies will be made into law;
but I may have to come back in four years to enter the fight."

Taft's "judicial temperament," which had recommended him so
highly to Roosevelt's adversaries, soon became evident in his administration of the public land laws. Where Roosevelt acted sometimes in the absence of specific legislation, Taft proceeded with
caution. He had not been in office many weeks before the Ballinger-Pinchot controversy threatened to overshadow the Payne-
Aldrich Tariff. Pinchot, who was chief of a division under the
Department of Agriculture, learned that in the administration of
conservation laws Secretary of the Interior Ballinger was not in-
clined to follow in Garfield's footsteps.

Louis R. Glavis, a field man in the General Land Office which
was under the jurisdiction of the Department of the Interior,
found evidence that Ballinger was derelict in examining charges
that a group of coal land claims in Alaska filed in the names of
Clarence Cunningham and others were fraudulent and were designed to benefit the Morgan-Guggenheim interests. Glavis was
dismissed for insubordination, but Pinchot continued the fight and,
like Glavis, placed himself in an untenable position by writing to

Senator Dolliver about it. This he did over his administrative chief.

Knowing the intimate relations between Roosevelt and Pinchot, Taft feared the consequences to himself if he dismissed Pinchot for insubordination. If a rupture between the President and the former President was to come, Taft preferred that it should not come through any action of his; but Pinchot's letter to Dolliver left him no alternative but to dismiss him. In fact, Pinchot courted dismissal. In the light of events that followed, Pinchot's dismissal was probably the decisive event in the growing estrangement between "Theodore" and "Will." So impatient was Pinchot to pour into the ears of Roosevelt the details of the "iniquities" of the Taft administration that he could not await the return of the African hunter but crossed the ocean to meet him.

Ballinger was a heavy load for the Taft administration to carry, in spite of his vindication by a congressional investigation committee. This committee report, which was prepared by the Republican majority, was regarded by the public as a "whitewashing document." *Collier's Weekly,* which from the beginning had been hostile to Taft, in spite of having supported him in 1908, was relentless in pursuing Ballinger. With the prospect of a Democratic House of Representatives after the congressional elections of 1910, Ballinger resigned in 1911 in the face of certain impeachment.

The Cunningham claims were later held by the courts to be fraudulent. The Ballinger-Pinchot controversy was a "bad break" for the Taft administration. It is not necessary to believe that Taft was entirely in sympathy with Ballinger or out of sympathy with conservation. It is necessary to believe, however, that Taft allowed himself to be maneuvered by Pinchot into a position that misrepresented his motives in dismissing him. As one of Taft's friends in the profession of journalism stated, Taft needed a "brutal friend"—somebody who could and would advise him with better judgment than those who enjoyed the President's confidence.

In the matter of the insurgent war against Speaker Cannon, the President was equally unfortunate. Taft stated frankly to his intimate friends that Cannon was the heaviest burden the administration had to carry, but he did not feel strong enough to defeat him.

Nevertheless, he went out of his way to court unpopularity by speaking well of him in public. By giving the impression that he approved of Cannon, the President made it possible for the insurgents and the Democrats to get under his guard by making "Cannonism" synonymous with the Republican party. Taft felt under obligations to Cannon because of his cooperation in putting measures through Congress, whereas the insurgents were becoming increasingly belligerent and were harassing the President at every stage. For this reason Taft solicited advice from Aldrich and Cannon and their associates on how to defeat the insurgents in the coming elections.

Another major battle between the standpatters and the insurgents began on March 16, 1910, when George W. Norris, a Republican from Nebraska, introduced a resolution creating a new committee on rules and making the speaker ineligible to membership. The resolution was intended to shear Cannon of his great power to crack the whip over members who kicked over the traces of the majority and to dictate what bills should or should not go through the legislative mill. The Democratic minority was entirely willing to give aid and comfort to the enemies of a Republican administration; and by a coalition of Democrats and insurgents the Norris resolution passed.

Cannon put up a magnificent fight against his adversaries; but having been beaten by a test vote, he could hardly do otherwise than resign. Accordingly, the veteran speaker announced that he would entertain a motion to declare the chair vacant, and a motion to that effect was made by Albert S. Burleson, a Democrat from Texas. Most of the insurgents, including Norris, were unwilling to go that far. Indeed, the passage of the original resolution had accomplished everything essential, and nothing was to be gained for the insurgents by electing a Democratic speaker.

By making the committee on rules elective instead of appointive, the party caucus became the instrument to enforce party regularity, so the defeat of Cannon was not as important as the public at the time supposed it to be. However, the insurgents had demonstrated their strength; and the overthrow of "Cannonism" was a major defeat for the administration.

The proverbial bad fortune that dogged Taft's footsteps was also manifest in his efforts to obtain a reciprocity agreement with Canada. Republican Presidents—Arthur, Harrison, McKinley, and Roosevelt—had recommended the principle of reciprocity. It was written into the McKinley Tariff Act, and the Republican platforms of 1896 and 1900 had indorsed it. Moreover, the American Protective Tariff League had broadcast propaganda in favor of reciprocal agreements with foreign governments. There was therefore nothing inconsistent with protection in advocating reciprocity with the neighbor to the north. The Democratic minority had assailed the Roosevelt administration for failing to revise the tariff downward and had also advocated reciprocity with Canada.

In a sense, therefore, Taft's espousal of the measure was good political strategy. On the other hand, his policy met with bitter opposition from the insurgents, who represented the agricultural states of the West where there was fear of competition with products raised on the cheaper lands of Canada. They raised the objection that the measure was another proof that the Taft administration was dominated by the industrial East which sought in Canada a market for its products and was willing to sacrifice the interests of the West.

In the short session of Congress which adjourned *sine die* on March 4, 1911, Canadian reciprocity passed the House but did not pass the Senate. The next Congress, which Taft convened in extraordinary session a month later, offered the strange spectacle of a House of Representatives with a heavy Democratic majority elected in the landslide of 1910 cooperating with a Republican President in passing a tariff measure.

In the Senate, however, it encountered opposition from the insurgents and from regulars from western states, and it passed only with Democratic support. What appeared to be a victory for Taft proved to be of no advantage when a political victory in Canada was won with the slogan "No trade or traffic with the Yankees." After the defeat of the Liberal party in the fall of 1911, Canada rejected reciprocity with the United States. Thus neither Taft nor the Republican party reaped the anticipated political benefits from the measure; instead, it was used to good advantage against the administration in the West in the primary campaigns which preceded the national convention of 1912.

Substantial achievements of the Taft administration were largely overlooked in the turmoil of politics which became increasingly tense with the approach of the presidential campaign. In 1910 the Interstate Commerce Act was amended by giving the Interstate Commerce Commission jurisdiction over telephone, telegraph, cable, and wireless companies. The Commission was given power to take the initiative in fixing rates, and it could suspend proposed changes in rates pending an investigation. In 1910 a system of postal savings banks was established, and in 1912 a parcels post service was added, thus bringing to realization measures advocated by Populists and other "liberals" as a means of breaking the alleged monopoly of banks and reducing excessive rates charged by express companies.

At a great conservation congress held in St. Paul, Minnesota, in September, 1910, Taft and Roosevelt spoke on successive days and indorsed the objectives of the conservationists. In spite of the unfavorable publicity of the Ballinger-Pinchot controversy, the Taft administration made commendable progress toward the goal set by its predecessor.

CHAPTER XXI

FOREIGN RELATIONS UNDER ROOSEVELT AND TAFT

THE PERSONALITY OF THEODORE ROOSEVELT IMPRESSED ITSELF ON the foreign policy of the United States no less than on its domestic policies. He was eminently the practical man, the man of action, of strong impulses, of sharp instincts, and of intense Americanism. He knew men and took their measure. His almost superhuman energy, amazing versatility, and interest in people enlisted many loyal friends and a wide acquaintance of which he took advantage. Certain aspects of his foreign policy were condemned by his contemporaries and have been condemned in the pages of history; but Roosevelt saw into the future further than most of his critics. He was compelled to deal with certain difficult situations that were not of his own making, and he acquitted himself with credit. Never had the prestige of the United States stood higher than it did when Roosevelt left the White House.

Roosevelt inherited from the McKinley administration the task of setting up governments in the newly acquired colonial possessions and of putting the Cuban house in order preliminary to redeeming the pledge to withdraw, embodied in the Teller resolution. This was a large assignment, but he was also confronted with the task of steering the diplomatic ship in a sea agitated by extraordinary events and developments in the Western Hemisphere, in Europe, in the Far East, and in Africa. He was fortunate in having two able Secretaries of State, John Hay (1898-1905) and Elihu Root (1905-08), but there were few men of first-rate ability in the diplomatic service, which was crippled by a niggardly and indifferent Congress and by a vicious spoils system. Events of catastrophic proportions and a President of unusual force did not arouse the American people from their indifferent attitude toward the world around them.

Despite McKinley's prayerful consideration of the question of the Philippine Islands, it is the verdict of history that by the annexation of this remote possession the United States headed into a succession of diplomatic blunders. By virtue of the possession of the Philippine Islands the United States was obliged to "sit in" at the diplomatic poker table, where the stakes were high and the cards were stacked. Events in the Far East were so kaleidoscopic that diplomats could not fathom them and committed blunders that only the next event could reveal. Territorial and commercial concessions in China were only portions of the stakes of world diplomacy, and the United States was inevitably drawn into affairs that a previous generation would have regarded as outside the scope of American interest.

After the Sino-Japanese War of 1894-95, Russia, Germany, and France compelled Japan to give up the major portion of the territory she had taken from China. Then followed a scramble among the European powers for territorial concessions. Great Britain, while not unsuccessful in obtaining a portion of the spoils, favored the maintenance of the integrity of China. The Spanish-American War occurred just at the time of the threatened breaking-up of China; and the annexation of Hawaii and the Philippines, together with the expansion of American export trade, made the United States a Pacific power with far-reaching interests.

It will be recalled that on the eve of the Spanish-American War the aged John Sherman was succeeded in the Department of State by William R. Day. When Day was appointed a member of the peace commission, John Hay became Secretary of State. Hay was the American minister to Great Britain during the Spanish war and won the good will of the British people and government. His cordial relations with Her Majesty's government caused him to be caricatured in the Hearst papers as an Anglophile. With Great Britain on the brink of war with France over rivalry for territory in Africa and with relations between her and Russia tense over ambitions in the Far East, Great Britain assumed a very friendly attitude toward the United States. She hoped to persuade the American government to cooperate with her in maintaining the "Open Door" in China, that is, territorial integrity for China and equality of opportunity for all.

Secretary Hay knew that the American people would not sanction a war to sustain his Far Eastern policy, nor would the Senate ratify a treaty of alliance with Great Britain. For these reasons he formulated on his own responsibility the "Open Door" policy in 1899. Although the powers, including Japan, responded to Hay's proposals with varying degrees of assent and cordiality, he was at the time acclaimed as a very successful diplomat. In the long run, however, the "Open Door" policy could not be maintained. The weakness of China, the deceitful policies of Russia and Japan, the Boxer rebellion of 1900, the Russo-Japanese War of 1904-05, and the World War played into the hands of Japan, who became dominant in the Far East.

In 1900 headlines in the American papers acquainted their readers with a rebellion in China fomented by a secret patriotic society known as the Boxers. One of the objectives of the Boxers was to expel from their country the hated foreign "devils," which included missionaries as well as business men and diplomats. Missionaries and their families were massacred, and several hundred foreigners, including Americans, were besieged in their legations in Peking. For over a month the world was in suspense while an army composed of European, American, and Japanese troops fought their way to rescue them. The foreigners were saved, but China was compelled to pay heavily for damages to lives, property, and national dignity. Hay succeeded in ameliorating somewhat the severe terms. In common with other governments, the United States demanded and received an indemnity, which proved to be in excess of the claims presented by American citizens; and several millions were returned to the Chinese government, which expressed its gratitude by investing the money in a trust fund for the education of Chinese in the United States.

Secretary Hay watched with concern the Russian advance toward the Far East and its threat against the "Open Door" policy. Under the constant prodding from Hay, Russia made promises that were not intended to be kept. Knowing that the American people would not go to war to maintain the "Open Door," Hay pretended to accept the Russian assurances at face value. It was not the United States that checked the Russian advance, however. That fell to the lot of Japan, who with startling suddenness broke off diplomatic relations and without warning attacked the Russian naval forces. Not only Russia but the diplomats of other countries were taken by surprise by the action of Japan.

Japan was fortified by the Anglo-Japanese Alliance which had been concluded in 1902 (and was superseded in 1921) and by the warm sympathy of the American people, who forgot the cordial relations that were supposed to have existed between the United States and Russia during the Civil War. The American newspapers reported with approval the series of Japanese victories and thrilled their readers by reporting the capture of Port Arthur on January 1, 1905, after a long siege and desperate fighting. Before the conclusion of hostilities, however, there was a noticeable cooling off toward Japan and a corresponding friendliness toward Russia. The great Japanese victories threatened to elevate Japan to a position of dominance in the Far East; and the alleged menace of the "yellow peril" seemed real, especially to people who had watched with alarm the growing Japanese immigration to the Pacific coast and Hawaii.

In perspective the Russo-Japanese War appears to be a prelude to the World War that came ten years later. The immediate cause of the war in the Far East was the clash of the nationalistic and imperialistic ambitions of Russia and Japan; but the roots of the conflict extended to Europe.

Roosevelt harbored a profound admiration for Japan, and his sympathies were with her in the titanic contest with Russia. Even before hostilities began he had given Japan assurance that his government would be more than neutral; and he politely informed both Germany and France that in the event of their interference in behalf of Russia, he would furnish aid to Japan. Roosevelt believed that Japan was fighting for the interests of the United States by challenging Russia's determination to dominate the Far East. He knew that the success or defeat of Russia would profoundly affect the balance of power in Europe; and for this reason he was wary of traps that might be, and were, set for him by the diplomats of Europe. He knew also that they would bend their efforts to effect a settlement at the close of the war that would favor their own governments. He was likewise concerned about the effect of the outcome of the war on the possessions of the United States in the Pacific.

Having won a series of major victories over Russia, Japan desired to bring the war to an end. In fact, it was imperative that she do so because her financial condition was precarious and Russia had the men and resources to conduct a long war. Accordingly, Japan requested Roosevelt to use his good offices to invite the belligerents to negotiate a peace. Before complying with the urgent request of Japan, Roosevelt exacted from her a promise that she would respect the "Open Door" in Manchuria; and before the commissioners of the respective governments met at Portsmouth, New Hampshire, he had obtained Japan's disavowal of aggressive designs on the Philippines.

Roosevelt's services in bringing about the peace conference at Portsmouth and in rescuing Japan from an embarrassing predicament which threatened to disrupt the conference were never appreciated by the Japanese people. Indeed, the people of Japan, who did not know that Roosevelt had intervened at the urgent request of their own government, turned against him and the United States because they believed that the President had robbed them of a more favorable settlement. Roosevelt was convinced that the treaty "was for the interest of Japan; it was for the interest of Russia; it was for the interest of the World." He firmly believed also that it would have been foolish for Japan to insist upon more than she obtained. He magnanimously refused to complain when he was so savagely criticized and never hinted that his action was prompted by the Japanese statesmen themselves.

An able student of Roosevelt's part in the Russo-Japanese War, Tyler Dennett, concludes that the result was a "commercial and political benefit to the United States"; that Japan had in reality accomplished what Roosevelt wanted to have accomplished, namely, the checking of the Russian advance, the prevention of the partition of China, and the prevention of the interference by Europe—all without the expenditure of a single life or cent by the United States. On the other hand, notwithstanding the fact that Roosevelt was awarded the Nobel prize and world-wide recognition for his services, it is the opinion of a competent scholar, Samuel Flagg Bemis, that "they did some harm and no good to the United States."

Be that as it may, the growing estrangement between the United States and Japan after 1905 was accelerated by an imbroglio for which Roosevelt was not in the least responsible and for the happy termination of which he deserves the gratitude of both the American and the Japanese people. A President with less understanding of Japan, without the prestige of having played the rôle of peacemaker, and without his boldness and initiative might not have averted the catastrophe of war between the two great powers of the Pacific. It is possible that some future historian will censure Roosevelt for not risking a war with a nation that in 1907 was less powerful than it came to be a generation later. The problem we are approaching concerns the treatment of Japanese in California and Japanese immigration to the United States.

After the inauguration of the permanent exclusion of Chinese immigrants in 1882, Japanese immigrants supplied the kind of labor which had been performed by Chinese. At first the Japanese, like the Chinese, were welcomed. They were said to be more desirable than other Orientals; but as their numbers increased, friction between the races also increased. In 1880, two years before Chinese exclusion became effective, there were probably less than two hundred Japanese in the country, but in 1899 as many as twelve thousand were admitted.

When the Japanese government became aware of the increasing anti-Japanese sentiment on the Pacific coast, it announced in 1900 that in the future no passports would be issued to Japanese who desired to immigrate to continental United States. After a sharp decline in 1900, the number of arrivals steadily mounted until in 1903 the figure reached twenty thousand and in 1907 thirty thousand. Moreover, the annexation of the Hawaiian Islands in 1898 made it possible for the immigrants to use them as a halfway house on their journey to the mainland.

In the early stages of the movement Japanese immigration was a local problem peculiar to the Pacific coast, with Congress showing little interest in it. The objections raised against the Japanese were similar to those raised against the Chinese, with organized labor demanding that the American standard of living be protected. Unlike the Chinese, however, the Japanese were aggressive. They were unwilling to live in segregated districts; they became competitors in business; they purchased property in business and residential districts; and they resented evidences of discrimination against them. Moreover, after the Russo-Japanese War the Japanese government reflected the belligerency and self-confidence of its people and showed a disposition to resent the hostility manifested in California against its subjects.

Then occurred something similar to the "sand lot agitation" against the Chinese in the seventies, when public sentiment was aroused by agitators who for political reasons or otherwise capitalized a local situation. In February, 1905, the *San Francisco Chronicle* launched a campaign against the Japanese; this played into the hands of organized labor which had already demonstrated its strong influence in politics. In May, 1906, the San Francisco Board of Education affirmed a policy of segregating Chinese and Japanese in separate schools. Hard upon this followed the organization of the Asiatic Exclusion League.

After the havoc in April, 1906, wrought by the terrible San Francisco earthquake and the fire that followed, irresponsible members of society took advantage of the catastrophe by looting and pillaging. A number of Japanese were attacked by these lawless individuals. An already dangerous situation was still further complicated by the circumstance that the government of San Francisco was controlled by a corrupt ring, whose shamelessness was later exposed. Fuel was added to the fire by intemperate comments and threats published in the newspapers of Japan, which found their way to the United States.

Fortunately, statesmen in both countries were anxious to avoid what might easily have become an armed conflict. The Japanese statesmen could not ignore the appeals of the Japanese in California to protect their rights, but they also remembered the historic friendship between the two countries. They were not concerned about the right of a few thousand of their countrymen to migrate to the United States; in fact, they preferred that they should go to Formosa, Korea, or Manchuria. But the resolutions from the California legislature calling on Congress to exclude Japanese by statute were irritating and insulting to the pride and honor of Japan. In common with other governments, Japan admitted the American claim that immigration was a domestic question, that it was the right of Congress to legislate on this subject as it saw fit. But her statesmen could not afford to yield complacently to a policy that singled the Japanese out for discrimination because they happened to belong to a certain race.

Under instructions from his government the Japanese ambassador to the United States protested the segregation of Japanese children in the schools and the boycotting of Japanese restaurants.

The dual nature of the American government made it difficult for the Department of State to handle the situation. The Japanese government could make representations only to the government at Washington, whereas the acts complained of were those of irresponsible individuals and of the City of San Francisco. The Japanese statesmen were fully aware of the dilemma that confronted President Roosevelt and Secretary of State Root; but they had to take action that would satisfy their people, who perhaps were not familiar with the American system of government. Moreover, demagogues in both countries could obscure the real issues at stake and make the path of any government thorny.

In a message to Congress and in public utterances Roosevelt denounced discrimination against the Japanese and sent a member of his cabinet, Victor H. Metcalf, to California on October 26, 1906, the day after the Japanese ambassador had lodged his protest. Metcalf was instructed to find the facts in the situation and to induce the local authorities to repeal the obnoxious school segregation order. At the same time, Roosevelt made it plain that he would not be intimidated by either party. His words and acts were not without effect on Californians and Japanese alike. It was fortunate that responsible persons in Japan believed in Roosevelt's friendliness toward Japan and were convinced of his good intentions. His vigorous language pointed to the San Francisco situation was as cordially received in Japan as it was denounced in California.

The Japanese having been mollified by the President, it remained for him to persuade the Board of Education to rescind the segregation order. This was accomplished by the assurance of the President that the immigration of coolies would be stopped. The administration succeeded in having the pending general immigration bill amended by a provision empowering the President to take action that would exclude from continental United States Japanese coolies who sought to enter through the Canal Zone, Mexico, and Hawaii, although neither Japan, Mexico nor Hawaii was specifically mentioned in the law. The exclusion of coolies migrating directly from Japan was effected by the Root-Takahira Agreement, commonly known as the Gentlemen's Agreement of 1907.

Although the details of this agreement were not made public at the time, the essentials were publicly stated by the Japanese ambassador to the United States in 1924, when the "menace" of Japanese immigration had again become acute. It was an understanding—not a treaty—by which the Japanese government voluntarily undertook to adopt administrative measures to check the immigration of Japanese laborers to the United States. It was not intended to restrict the sovereign right of the United States to regulate immigration. "It was because of the fact that discriminatory immigration legislation on the part of the United States would, naturally, wound the national susceptibilities of the Japanese people that, after thorough but most friendly and frank discussions between the two governments, the Gentlemen's Agreement was made for the purpose of relieving the United States from the possible unfortunate necessity of offending the national pride of a friendly nation." Although the Hawaiian Islands were not originally included in the agreement, the Japanese government, according to the statement of the ambassador, enforced practically the same procedure in that case.

It will be noted that the Root-Takahira Agreement was not a treaty but an unwritten and informal understanding by which the Japanese government pledged itself not to issue passports good for continental United States to laborers, skilled or unskilled, or their parents, their wives, or their children under twenty years of age. The opponents of the Gentlemen's Agreement questioned its wisdom and also the right of the government under the Constitution to subscribe to it. It was pointed out that it was in the nature of a treaty and that a treaty must be ratified by the Senate.

In the temper of public opinion in both countries it would have been exceedingly dangerous to run the risk of stirring up public discussion of the question which a debate over the ratification of a treaty would have undoubtedly produced. It is doubtful whether or not the necessary two-thirds majority in the Senate could have been mustered. Roosevelt deserves high praise for his vigorous as well as clever handling of a problem that under an inept and more conventional President might have produced war.

Events determined that the question was not permanently settled, however, though for some years the Gentlemen's Agreement smoothed the troubled waters, in spite of anti-alien land laws directed at the Japanese passed by the California legislature in 1913 and 1920 and the introduction of bills in Congress to exclude Japanese by law. The race question persisted because of the birth of Japanese children, though authorities and propagandists differ as to the increase of the Japanese population in the United States. Others questioned the good faith of the Japanese government in enforcing the terms of the Gentlemen's Agreement. The immigration of picture brides who came to their husbands in America after a marriage ceremony had been performed in Japan, with the groom present only by the proxy of his photograph, was alleged to be in violation of the Gentlemen's Agreement.

In season and out of season, the Westerners demanded the abrogation of the agreement and the exclusion of Japanese by law, until Congress satisfied them in 1924. This unfortunate event is reserved for later discussion. Let it suffice in this place to say that after 1905 the relations between the United States and Japan became increasingly troubled, although representatives of both nations constantly expressed friendly sentiments and deprecated the danger, or even possibility, of war—an ominous sign. In a sense the immigration problem was secondary, because it would not have assumed such serious proportions without the conjunction of events of still greater proportions.

Before the feeling between the United States and Japan had cooled off—indeed, while it was still warm—President Roosevelt made public an amazing bit of "diplomacy," which, like so many of his actions that appeared dubious at first, ended in a blaze of glory. Roosevelt himself later declared that it was the most important service that he had rendered to peace.

On December 16, 1907, a fleet of sixteen battleships, representing collectively the greatest tonnage and weight of armament that had ever undertaken so long a voyage, sailed from Hampton Roads under the command of "Fighting Bob" Evans on a cruise around the world. President Roosevelt went to Hampton Roads to bid the fleet godspeed. The English papers thought that the sailing of this extraordinary fleet, prepared for war, was most untimely because it excited the jingo spirit. Although the cruise was obviously intended to impress upon the Japanese people that the United States was prepared for war, Japanese statesmen hastened to declare that the fleet would receive a cordial welcome in Nippon and that they were confident that no hostile intent inspired the undertaking.

The reception of the fleet at the ports where it stopped was extraordinary. The South American countries vied with one another to pay their respects to the North American sister republic and to ratify the results of the good-will tour of Secretary Root in 1906. Perhaps the most remarkable demonstrations were staged in Australia. At Sydney nine thousand school children were grouped so as to form the words "Hail Columbia" and to trace the pattern in colors of the American and the Australian flags. The Australians were anxious to show their appreciation of the courtesy of the visit of the fleet, but they also looked upon it as in a sense their own, for, in spite of the Anglo-Japanese Alliance, they were alarmed over the possibility of a Japanese invasion of their own continent, just as were the people of California. In a conflict between the brown and white races they felt that they could claim the resources of the United States as their own.

In Japan the entertainment provided for the men of the fleet was carried out faultlessly, and what might have proved to be a most unfortunate venture was turned into a triumph. Extreme precautions were taken to prevent the occurrence of any untoward incident, and both entertainers and visitors acquitted themselves with the utmost credit. With due allowance for the enthusiasm of the moment, it appears that the visit of the fleet to Japan cleared the air, as it were, although it would be straining the truth to say that in the long run cordial relations between nations are promoted by a display of military and naval forces.

When the fleet steamed into Hampton Roads on February 22, 1909, ten days before his term expired, President Roosevelt was there to greet the officers and men as the "best of all possible ambassadors and heralds of peace." The strenuous President, whose succession to the Presidency raised apprehensions lest his impulsiveness would inaugurate a jingoistic foreign policy, had the satisfaction of writing in his *Autobiography*: "When I left the Presidency I finished seven and a half years of administration, during which not one shot had been fired against a foreign foe."

Roosevelt had the satisfaction also of inaugurating a great enterprise which marked the fulfillment of a national dream, though it fell to the lot of his successor to carry it to completion. This was the construction of the Panama Canal. In paving the way for this great national undertaking, Roosevelt's diplomacy laid him open to savage criticism at home and grave distrust in Latin America, although he has not been without staunch defenders from that day to this. In the diplomacy that preceded the acquisition of the Panama Canal Zone, Roosevelt showed the same impatience with shilly-shally and pretense that characterized his career.

This exaltation of the "Square Deal" sometimes brought strange results; but any effort to reduce Theodore Roosevelt to a formula is doomed to disappointment. He was not a reed shaken by the wind; he was a wind that shook the reed. His predilection for meddling could on occasion furnish amusement to friend and foe. In the case of the Panama Canal the chief indictment against Roosevelt is that he needlessly offended a weak power and thereby offended the people of an entire continent.

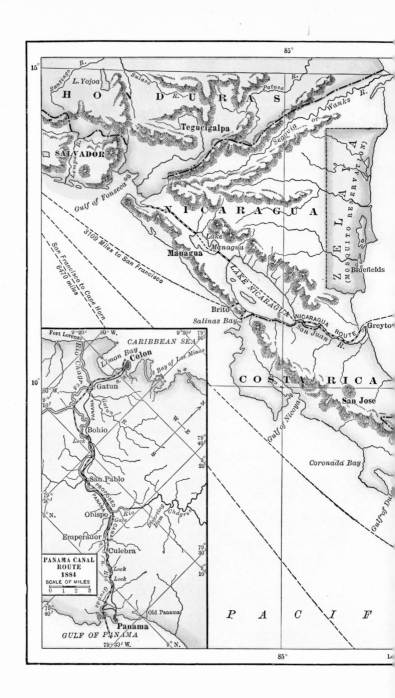

15°

H O N D U R A S

Santiago R.

L. Yojoa

Sulaco

Patuca

R.

Tegucigalpa

Segovia or Wanks R.

SALVADOR

Gulf of Fonseca

3109 Miles to San Francisco

San Francisco to Cape Horn

6470 miles

N I C A R A G U A

Lake Managua

Managua

LAKE NICARAGUA

Bluefields

(MOSQUITO RESERVE)

Z E L A Y A

Brito

Salinas Bay

San Juan R.

NICARAGUA ROUTE

Greyto

C O S T A   R I C A

San Jose

Gulf of Nicoya

Coronada Bay

Gulf of Dulce

P A C I F

Fort Lorenzo 9°20′ 80°W.

Rio Chagres

CARIBBEAN SEA

Limon Bay **Colon**

9°30′ 79° 50′

10°

80°W.

9° 10′

Gatun

R.

Bay of Las Minas

PANAMA

Gatun R.

N

W — E

79° 40′

Bohio

20′

Lock

79° 50′

79° 40′ N.

San Pablo

PROPOSED

Obispo

Rio Gato

PANAMA CANAL

Diverting Dam

Chagre

79° 30′

Emperador

Culebra

Rio Grande R.

10′

Lock

Lock

79° 40′

Old Panama

**PANAMA CANAL
ROUTE
1884**
SCALE OF MILES
0   1   2   3

Panama

GULF OF PANAMA

79°30′W.

9°N.

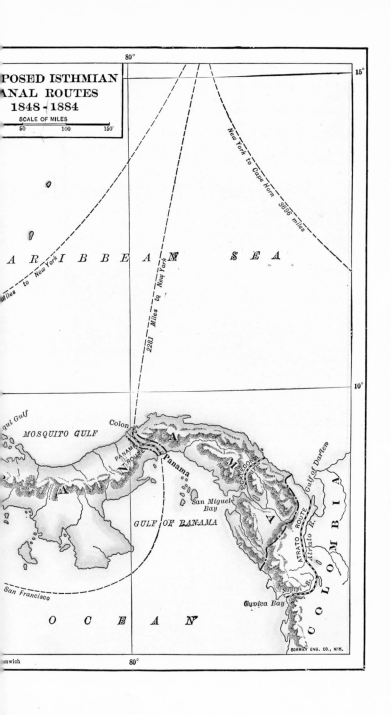

Ever since the ratification of the Clayton-Bulwer Treaty of 1850, the hands of the United States had been tied by an agreement with Great Britain that stipulated that neither the one government nor the other would ever obtain or maintain for itself exclusive control over an isthmian canal and that neither would ever maintain any fortifications commanding it. So long as this treaty remained in force, the United States could hardly undertake to invest millions in a waterway that it could neither control, defend, nor obtain benefits from, commensurate with the magnitude of the undertaking. Even before the Spanish-American War and the annexation of Hawaii and the Philippines, the United States was a Pacific power; but these events emphasized the necessity for an interoceanic canal for strategic purposes, no less than for commercial advantages.

Fortunately, the "splendid isolation" of Great Britain caused her to turn to the United States as a friend in need; and one method of cultivating the good will of the United States was to consent to the modification of the Clayton-Bulwer Treaty. After an abortive attempt to this end had been nullified by the refusal of the Senate to ratify the treaty, the Hay-Pauncefote Treaty was ratified on February 21, 1902. This conceded to the United States the right to construct the canal and omitted any prohibition to fortify it. It remained to select a route for the canal and to obtain sovereignty over it through the channels of negotiation with the government having jurisdiction over the territory through which the waterway would be constructed.

The advantages of a route through Nicaragua or Panama were debated in Congress and by engineers. The House of Representatives passed a bill for the construction of a Nicaraguan canal; but the Senate—possibly influenced by a speech by Senator Hanna —voted in favor of the Panama route, and the House concurred in the amendment. By this act President Roosevelt was instructed to negotiate with Colombia for the cession of a six-mile strip from ocean to ocean and to purchase for a sum not to exceed $40,000,000 the property of a bankrupt French company, which had begun excavation in the eighties. If satisfactory terms could

not be arranged, the President was authorized to negotiate with
Nicaragua.

Without entering into the difficulties that preceded the Hay-
Herran Convention of January, 1903, it is sufficient to say that
Colombia agreed by this treaty to grant to the United States full
control over a six-mile strip in return for the payment by the
United States of $10,000,000 in cash and an annuity of $250,000.
Unfortunately, the men in control of the unstable Colombian
government were not sufficiently aware of the impatience of
Roosevelt to proceed with the construction of the canal. Dissatisfaction with the amount of compensation and certain other stipulations caused the Colombian congress to reject the treaty. That
the Colombian congress acted entirely within its rights in so doing
is undisputed; that it was wise and prudent to do so is another
matter, because the compensation stipulated in the treaty was but
one of the advantages that the heavy commerce through the canal
would bring.

In any event, Colombia's dissatisfaction proved to be a golden
opportunity for schemers and intriguers. Philippe Bunau-Varilla
and a lawyer who were interested in the French Panama Canal
Company did not propose to lose the forty or less million dollars
that the abandonment of the Panama route would entail; they
speedily executed a revolution in true Central American style and
set up the independent Republic of Panama. President Roosevelt
ordered the commanders of American warships, which were conveniently within striking distance, to prevent the landing of Colombian troops to put down the revolt. The revolution occurred on
November 3, 1903; three days later the United States recognized
the independence of the Republic of Panama; and fifteen days after
that a treaty with the new government was an accomplished fact.

It was under these extraordinary circumstances that a new republic was born into the family of Latin American states. Panama
reaped the benefits of the Hay-Herran Convention and got the
assurance of the big brother to the north that her independence
would be maintained. Other stipulations made the Republic of
Panama a protectorate of the United States, a relationship that
remained in force until it was modified by the "good neighbor"

policy of a President bearing the Roosevelt name but whose methods were somewhat different from those of his distant cousin.

If one may judge by his vigorous defense of his canal diplomacy, Roosevelt's conscience never accused him of wrongdoing. "I deeply regretted, and I now deeply regret, the fact that the Colombian Government rendered it imperative for me to take the action I took; but I had no alternative, consistent with the full performance of my duty to my own people, and to the nations of mankind," he wrote in his *Autobiography*. "The good people of Colombia apparently made no effort, certainly no successful effort, to cause the government to act with reasonable good faith toward the United States; and Colombia had to take the consequences." He cited as proof of the justice of the Hay-Herran Convention the alleged acknowledgment of Colombia's guilt by her prompt offer to accede to its terms after Panama had been recognized. In an address delivered in 1911 Roosevelt said: "I took the Canal Zone and let Congress debate and while the debate goes on the canal does too."

Roosevelt's defense is not convincing to students who have studied the various treaties that bore on the status of what became the Canal Zone, and who have examined other pertinent documents. Although they have found no documentary proof that the revolution was fomented by agents of the United States or that the government knew beforehand of the intentions of the conspirators, they are convinced that Colombia's rejection of the treaty need not have seriously delayed the construction of the canal and that a more creditable way of obtaining the route might have been employed. Even admitting that a certain element in Colombia was bent on "holding up Uncle Sam," the effect of Roosevelt's action was to antagonize Latin America and to delay the dawn of a day when a better understanding between the guardian of the Monroe Doctrine and its supposed beneficiaries would prevail.

In line with Woodrow Wilson's idealistic Mexican policy and his efforts to instill in the people of Latin America confidence in the purity of its intentions, under his administration, in 1914, a treaty was negotiated with Colombia by which the American government apologized for the action of the Roosevelt administration and agreed to pay Colombia $30,000,000. The treaty failed of ratification partly because Roosevelt denounced it as a "blackmail treaty." Senator Lodge, an intimate friend of Roosevelt, led the fight against ratification. In 1921, as chairman of the Committee on Foreign Relations under a Republican administration, the same Senator reversed his position, and under his leadership a similar treaty was ratified. It provided for the payment of $25,000,000, but omitted the apology. This remarkable conversion may be attributed to the desire for commercial concessions in Colombia by American capital, the difficulty of dealing with Latin American states so long as the "wrong" against Colombia was unrequited, and the death of Roosevelt in 1919.

In the international anarchy that prevailed during the twentieth century the Monroe Doctrine saddled upon the United States the disagreeable duty of enforcing it and of assuming obligations that caused it to take on a new meaning. Moreover, it behooved the government at Washington to take practical measures to protect the Panama Canal. Roosevelt's vigorous Panama policy came to be known as the "big stick." In pursuing this policy Roosevelt and his successors—Taft, Wilson, Harding, Coolidge, and Hoover—were obliged to intervene in the affairs of the republics of Latin America in order to prevent the governments of Europe from taking action that would have greatly complicated the affairs of the New World and would have embroiled them and the United States still further in the tangled diplomacy of Europe.

In the early years of the century, when Germany was looking for a place in the sun, Roosevelt intervened in the affairs of Venezuela in order to forestall a possible menace to the control of the Panama Canal. Venezuela was in the unfortunate condition of being saddled with debts to foreign creditors and of having a dictator, Cipriano Castro, who played fast and loose with the credit of the government. In December, 1902, Great Britain, Germany, and Italy blockaded the ports of Venezuela and bombarded forts as a demonstration against the policy of the dictator. The governments of Great Britain and Germany, however, disclaimed any intention to occupy Venezuelan territory. Castro became alarmed at this turn of events and sought the good office of the Washington government to propose arbitration, which Great Britain promptly and Germany hesitatingly accepted. Italy fell into line as a matter of course.

A powerful fleet under the command of Admiral Dewey was stationed in Caribbean waters; and although historians are of different minds as to Roosevelt's intentions in case Germany refused to arbitrate and as to what he intimated to the German ambassador, it may be assumed that the fleet was not there wholly by chance and that its potentiality was not unknown in Potsdam.

In the light of present knowledge about German diplomacy between 1900 and 1914, it appears that Germany used the Venezuelan affair to test the mettle and intentions of Roosevelt. It also prompted the formulation of what became known as the Drago Doctrine. Luis M. Drago, the Argentinian minister of foreign affairs, submitted to Secretary of State Hay the proposition that public debt cannot justify armed intervention or occupation of the territory of American countries by a European power. A modified form of this proposition was written into international law at the Hague Conference in 1907.

The financial embarrassment of Haiti, Santo Domingo, and Nicaragua proved to be even more troublesome for the United States. In these republics the interests of foreign governments were menaced by wars, revolutions, dictatorships, and irresponsibility. In order to prevent the intervention by European governments in behalf of their citizens, a treaty with Santo Domingo was negotiated by which the United States in effect became the financial guardian of the republic. Pending the ratification of the treaty by the Senate, which was accomplished in 1907, agents of the Washington government administered and collected the customs of Santo Domingo. In his message to the Senate in 1905, Roosevelt disclaimed the slightest desire for territorial aggrandizement at the expense of Latin America, but affirmed that it was incompatible with international equity for the United States to refuse to allow other governments to take the only means at their disposal for satisfying the claims of creditors and at the same time to refuse to take steps necessary to obtain a fair settlement. This statement of policy is known as the "Roosevelt corollary" to the Monroe Doctrine.

This "protectorate" over Santo Domingo has continued down to the present time. In 1916 President Wilson was compelled to use armed intervention in order to put down rebellion. This lasted until 1924, when under the guidance of the United States a new constitution was adopted and elections were held.

Roosevelt's policy with reference to collecting debts was followed by the Taft administration, when in 1911 Secretary of State Knox negotiated treaties with Honduras and Nicaragua. In spite of his repudiation of the "dollar diplomacy" of Secretary Knox, President Wilson was obliged to deal with Central America after the fashion of Roosevelt and Taft. In 1914 Haiti was on the brink of anarchy, and Germany was ready to land marines, when the World War intervened. In July, 1915, Wilson inaugurated supervision of the affairs of this republic which continued until 1934, when under the terms of an executive agreement negotiated under Franklin D. Roosevelt the American military forces were withdrawn.

The disturbed conditions in Central America, including Mexico, and the tense relations betwen the United States and Japan prompted another adaptation of the Monroe Doctrine. The doctrine was extended to any power, whether European or Asiatic. It was suspected that Japan had designs on a tract of land in Magdalena Bay in Lower California; that the negotiation of a Japanese fishing company with the Mexican government cloaked the purpose of the Japanese government to obtain a naval base. The Senate in 1912 by a unanimous vote adopted the Lodge Resolution which affirmed that the government of the United States "could not see without grave concern" the possession by any corporation or association which "has such relation to another government, not American, as to give that government practical power of control for national purposes" of territory that might threaten the communications or safety of the United States.

The overthrow of the Diaz régime in Mexico which had held that country in an iron grip for some thirty years in the closing months of the Taft administration threatened to create a problem for the American government. It was feared that it would cause the revolutionary disturbances in other parts of Latin America to pale into insignificance. Inasmuch as it fell to the lot of Taft's successor, Woodrow Wilson, to find a solution for the Mexican imbroglio, it will be reserved for discussion in a later chapter.

The Magdalena Bay incident occurred when Mexico was drifting into chaos and newspapers were broadcasting rumors about Japanese designs in Lower California. With the American ambassador in Mexico City warning Taft of the seriousness of the situation and American investors in agony over the prospect of the eruption of the Mexican volcano, Taft in the early months of 1911 ordered the mobilization of troops on the Mexican border. As a part of the operations along the border a fleet was mobilized at Guantanamo, Cuba. On March 4, 1913, Taft bequeathed the Mexican "nightmare" to Woodrow Wilson.

CHAPTER XXII

THE BULL MOOSE CAMPAIGN

AT THE OPENING OF THE YEAR 1912 THE OUTLOOK FOR A REPUB-
lican victory in the coming presidential election was anything but
hopeful. The unpopularity of the Taft administration had been
demonstrated by the fiasco of promised downward revision of
the tariff in the Payne-Aldrich Act, by the Ballinger-Pinchot controversy, by the overthrow of "Cannonism" by a coalition of
Democrats and western insurgents, by the defeat of Republican
standpatters in the primaries, and by the election of a large Democratic majority in the House of Representatives. There were even
grave doubts if Taft could be renominated. The question most
widely discussed was, "What will Roosevelt do?" Would he openly
repudiate the candidate he had forced upon the Republican convention in 1908? Would he support La Follette or some other
insurgent? Or would he seek the nomination for himself?

Long before the pre-convention campaign it was evident that
there would be no reconciliation between Taft and the insurgents.
The President had read them out of the party. On January 21,
1911, leading insurgent Senators and Representatives met at La
Follette's home in Washington to organize the National Progressive Republican League. The objectives of this organization
were to promote such measures as the direct primary, direct election of Senators, a corrupt practices act, a lower tariff, conservation, and an income tax, and to bring about the nomination of a
progressive candidate to succeed Taft. At a meeting of the group
in Chicago in the following October La Follette was indorsed
for the Presidency. He was the logical candidate. His record of
progressive achievements excelled that of any man who was likely
to obtain the nomination.

La Follette, like his insurgent colleagues, was a man of moderate means and represented the great middle class. He was not a Socialist, but he had seen at close range the greed of big business and the tremendous power it exercised. He had dedicated himself to the task of devising governmental machinery to control this menace which threatened to destroy American institutions. His fearless and uncompromising position made his name anathema to the eastern wing of the Republican party, and made it unlikely that he would be able to break down the machine control of the party. In spite of the popularity and prestige of Roosevelt and his successful nomination of his successor, the Old Guard remained in control in strategic places.

Although Roosevelt had not committed himself to the support of any candidate, some of his close friends, like Pinchot, encouraged La Follette to contest the nomination with Taft. For example, on December 16, 1911, at a mass meeting of progressive Republicans in Tremont Temple, Boston, Pinchot stated that for the time being at least he was supporting La Follette's candidacy. The announcement was not greeted with enthusiasm. It is significant, however, that at this time the confidant of Roosevelt and the archenemy of Taft expressed approval of the Wisconsin progressive.

It soon became obvious that the La Follette boom would not soar very high; and when the newspapers on February 3, 1912, reported that on the previous evening La Follette had suffered a physical and nervous collapse while addressing the members of the Periodical Publishers' Association at Philadelphia, his star set rapidly. La Follette ever after maintained that the press reports were grossly misleading, and believed that he had been the victim of a well-planned campaign to kill his candidacy. He believed that he had been used as a stalking horse for Roosevelt. He pointed to Roosevelt's record as proof that he was not a sincere progressive and further cited his refusal to accept membership in the National Progressive League in 1911. It must be admitted that in his *Autobiography* La Follette makes out a good case against Roosevelt and had good reason for believing that he had been unjustly treated. In any event, the fact that La Follette did lose control of himself cost him his chance even with the friendly element.

In the meantime, Roosevelt was receiving the major attention of political prognosticators and politicians. The most interested man of all was President Taft. From the beginning of his administration he was grieved over Roosevelt's attitude toward him; and even before the end of the first year of his term his associates warned him that Roosevelt would contest the nomination with him. With the approaching return of the mighty hunter after his triumphant tour of Europe, in June, 1910, Taft more than ever occupied a secondary position. The President greeted Roosevelt with a letter intrusted to his military aide inviting him to visit the White House.

With the congressional elections approaching, Roosevelt was provokingly silent about commending his successor's administration. In fact, the colonel's victory over the regular organization in the New York Republican convention in the fall was not calculated to reassure the President, nor was the smashing defeat of the Republicans in the fall elections any more hopeful.

In the light of subsequent events, it seems certain that in the closing months of 1911 Roosevelt had determined to become a candidate, if his prospects of obtaining the Republican nomination were reasonably good. Following a conference held at Chicago on February 10, 1912, seven progressive Republican governors addressed a letter to Roosevelt urging him to declare whether, if the nomination for the Presidency came to him unsolicited, he would accept. The governors appealed to the former President to surrender his personal interests in the cause of good government and avowed that a large number of Republican voters favored his nomination. Within a few days Roosevelt announced that his hat was in the ring and that his formal answer would be forthcoming. On February 26 headlines from coast to coast blazed forth his announcement that he would accept the nomination. He expressed the hope that the people might be given the chance through direct primaries to express their preference for a candidate.

The primary campaigns and the elections in March, April, and

May were the most sensational, personal, and bitterly fought in the history of the country. The country became the arena of a political contest in which the major actors—erstwhile intimate friends converted into personal and political enemies, the one a former President and the other the President—hurled charges and denials at each other. In his falsetto voice when stung to anger and irony, Roosevelt referred to Taft as one who "means well, but means well feebly." Taft referred to the progressives as "neurotics." Certain newspapers refused to print Roosevelt's name and always called him the "third-term candidate" in order to emphasize his alleged betrayal of his election night pledge in 1904. He was said to be a bogus progressive who had joined the progressive forces to satisfy his colossal ambition and his insane jealousy of Taft.

In a speech delivered at Columbus, Ohio, on February 21, Roosevelt leaped ahead of the more radical progressives by advocating the recall of judicial decisions when it was evident that no other course would achieve the desired result. "But either the recall will have to be adopted or else it will have to be made much easier than it now is to get rid not merely of a bad judge who, however virtuous, has grown so out of touch with social needs and facts that he is unfit longer to render good service on the bench." In addressing the Massachusetts Assembly on February 26, he discoursed further on this radical measure. "I am advocating the recall of legalism to justice," he said. "My proposal applies only to the legislative acts which the courts declare unconstitutional."

Roosevelt's advocacy of the recall of judicial decisions drew the fire of conservatives and squarely joined the issue with Taft, who had blocked the admission of Arizona because the constitution of the new state contained a provision for the recall of judges. It was not received with enthusiasm by some of Roosevelt's ardent supporters, like Beveridge of Indiana, and it probably weakened his chances of obtaining the nomination by the Republican party. Rumors were even circulated—and many people credited them— that Roosevelt was losing his mind. Nevertheless, so great was the popularity of the former President that as soon as he had

announced that "My hat is in the ring," it was confidently predicted that he would win the nomination; and his enemies showed
their alarm by straining all their resources to prevent it. Even
Taft had a strong presentiment that Roosevelt would defeat him.

However, Taft had the advantage of controlling the patronage
and could count on a block of delegates from the states of the
Solid South, which were recruited and held in line by patronage.

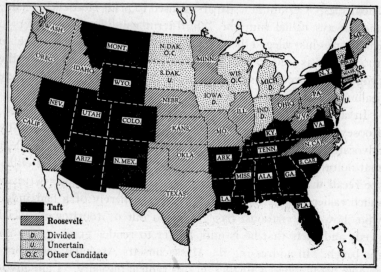

MAP SHOWING THE ROOSEVELT STRENGTH IN THE PRIMARY ELECTIONS PREVIOUS
TO THE ASSEMBLING OF THE REPUBLICAN NATIONAL CONVENTION IN JUNE, 1912

Roosevelt hoped to demonstrate his strength with the rank and
file of the party in the primaries, to get a number of contesting
delegations, and to stampede the convention. If the southern
delegates became convinced that the Republican party would go
down to defeat with Taft the nominee, they might desert him in
favor of "Teddy."

The trend of events was not encouraging to the Taft cohorts.
The President was decisively defeated in the Oklahoma, North
Dakota, and Wisconsin primaries; and the Roosevelt victory in
Illinois on April 9 by over 100,000 votes was regarded as a death-
blow to Taft's fortunes. Even more disastrous was the rout of

the Taft forces in Pennsylvania on April 14, when Roosevelt made an almost clean sweep of the delegates. Especially heavy was the Roosevelt vote in the mining regions.

The Roosevelt victories caused Taft to enter the primary campaign personally. On April 25 he delivered an address in Boston in which he charged Roosevelt with a breach of faith and read a private letter to him from Roosevelt in which the latter had indorsed Canadian reciprocity, whereas in the primary campaign he was denouncing it. Two days later at a meeting in Boston, when the enthusiasm greatly exceeded that of the Taft meeting, Roosevelt replied. He also paid his respects to the "silk stockings" of the Back Bay. The primary election in Massachusetts on April 30 was a drawn battle, with the popular vote slightly in Taft's favor and the delegates evenly divided.

The religious issue probably played a part in the Massachusetts election, as it did in other states. At the time of his visit to Rome following his African hunting trip, Roosevelt refused to pay a call on the pope, who insisted that the colonel should not speak at the Methodist Mission in Rome. Roosevelt declined to assent to any conditions. When the Methodists capitalized their "victory," Roosevelt promptly canceled his engagement with them. From Rome he wrote to Senator Lodge: "The only satisfaction I had out of the affair, and it was a very great satisfaction, was that on the one hand I administered a needed lesson to the Vatican, and on the other hand I made it understood that I feared the most powerful Protestant Church just as little as I feared the Catholics. If I were in politics, or intended to run for public office, I should regard the incident as gravely compromising my usefulness as a candidate."

The alleged "snub" of the pope was first-page news in the American papers. Taft, on the other hand, had cultivated the good will of the Catholics; and after the incident at Rome he expressed to Catholic prelates his deep regret over it and contrasted his own deep affection for their church. So persistent were the rumors of Taft's partiality to the Catholics that on May 13, on the eve of the Ohio primaries, he gave out a statement denying that he had favored the Roman church. About a week later Roosevelt carried

Taft's own state and received more than three times as many delegates. In the other primary states, including California and New Jersey, Taft was equally unfortunate.

At the beginning of June the political scene shifted to Chicago, where the Republican National Committee held its hearings on the Roosevelt contesting delegates. Here the fortunes of the rival candidates were reversed. One by one the Roosevelt delegations were denied seats in the convention. The claims of a number of these delegations were flimsy, but it was the strategy of the Roosevelt forces to present as many contesting delegations as possible. When their claims were rejected, the Rooseveltians raised the cry of "fraud" and "brigandage."

The temporary roll of delegates to the convention having been made up by the National Committee, it was a foregone conclusion that Elihu Root, the candidate of the Taft forces, would be elected temporary chairman of the convention over Francis E. McGovern of Wisconsin, who had been selected by the Rooseveltians. With the Taft delegates voting on their own cases, the seventy-two contesting Roosevelt delegates met the same fate at the hands of the convention as they had received before the National Committee. Under the masterly direction of Root, who was also elected permanent chairman of the convention, every effort to start a stampede for Roosevelt was promptly checked. There were catcalls and hisses from Roosevelt delegates and from Roosevelt partisans in the galleries, but Root never lost his composure. The Taft "steam-roller," as the Roosevelt partisans called it, was steered by a master hand.

When it became evident that the "steam-roller" would crush the contesting Roosevelt delegates, Roosevelt rushed to Chicago where he could be in close touch with his managers and lieutenants. Upon his arrival he was greeted by a tremendous crowd. On the evening of June 17 the colonel addressed a meeting in the Auditorium in which he asserted that the Republican party belonged to the rank and file, not "to the handful of politicians who have assumed fraudulently to upset the will of the rank and file." In his peroration he said: "We fight in honorable fashion for the good of mankind; fearless of the future, unheeding of our individual fates, with unflinching hearts and undimmed eyes; we stand at Armageddon, and we battle for the Lord."

The seasoned politicians who directed the Taft campaign were not to be swerved from their determination to prevent the nomination of Roosevelt. Overtures were made from the Taft camp to agree on a candidate other than either Taft or Roosevelt, but Roosevelt refused to listen to compromises unless the convention would purge the roll of Taft delegates which he claimed had been fraudulently seated. Had Roosevelt withdrawn his name it is probable that a compromise candidate would have been named, because it was certain that Taft could not be elected if nominated over the opposition from Roosevelt.

The Roosevelt leaders fought their adversaries at every turn until it became evident that the Taft organization could not be broken. Taft was nominated on the first ballot, with most of the Roosevelt delegates refusing to vote. Some of the delegates bolted the convention before the roll was called. On the same day that Taft and Sherman were nominated, the bolting Roosevelt delegates assembled in Orchestra Hall and nominated their idol. Roosevelt, however, would not accept this nomination and advised his followers to sound the sentiment of their respective states preliminary to a mass convention to be held later.

After a suitable interval, a committee which had been elected for that purpose issued a call for a convention to meet in Chicago on August 5, to which progressives of whatever political affiliation were invited to send delegates. This convention of the Progressive party was one of the most extraordinary political conventions in American history. The delegates came with the fervor of crusaders, and veterans of political campaigns listened with amazement when the vast assembly sang "Onward Christian Soldiers." It was a motley gathering. There were women like Jane Addams who had devoted their lives to the cause of social justice and the amelioration of poverty; there were college professors, farmers, and business men; there were Socialists and other "radicals"; and there were hard-faced professional politicians who seized the opportunity to turn idealism into possible political dividends.

The keynote speech was delivered by Beveridge of Indiana, who with epigrammatic conciseness indicted the "invisible government" and made a plea for social justice. Replying to the charge that many of the reforms proposed by the Progressives were unconstitutional, he asserted: "The Progressive party believes that the Constitution is a living thing, growing with the people's growth . . . permitting the people to meet all their needs as conditions change."

Roosevelt and Hiram Johnson of California were nominated respectively for the Presidency and the Vice-Presidency, and addressed the convention. The platform was "socialistic" and bears comparison with the Populist platform of twenty years earlier. It contained planks demanding equal suffrage for men and women, popular review of judicial decisions on laws for securing social justice, review by the Supreme Court of the United States of decisions of state courts declaring legislative acts unconstitutional, prohibition of injunctions in labor disputes when such injunctions would not apply if no labor dispute existed, prohibition of child labor, the minimum wage, the eight-hour day, a system of social insurance, rural credits, a national health service, conservation of natural resources, and a graduated inheritance tax.

The Bull Moose campaign—so called because in reply to an inquiry Roosevelt said he felt like a bull moose—was launched as a protest against what was alleged to be the "stolen nomination" of Taft, and as an expression of the ideals of men and women who had been active in promoting reforms which had received little sympathy from either of the major parties. But there were other idealists who doubted the sincerity of Roosevelt's tribute to the Progressive platform, which was the handiwork of men and women for whom some of the men who had managed Roosevelt's primary campaign had hitherto shown no favor.

There was, for example, "Boss" William Flinn of Pennsylvania, whose interest in the Roosevelt cause was inspired by his ambition to dethrone his enemies in the Republican party in his own state. There was also George W. Perkins, whose connections with the Morgan interests made his professions in favor of an equitable tariff seem doubtful. There were also newspapers like the *Chicago*

RECEIPT FOR CONTRIBUTION TO BULL MOOSE PARTY

Tribune, whose espousal of the Progressive cause seemed like mockery in the light of their former editorial policy.

When Roosevelt denounced the "bosses," his adversaries replied that his wrath was directed only against the bosses who remained in the other camps. It is also true that the large sums contributed to finance the Roosevelt primary campaigns in Illinois, Pennsylvania, and Massachusetts created doubts about the zeal of some of his supporters for legislation directed against big business. Moreover, during the seven years of his administration Roosevelt had not raised his voice publicly against the inequalities of the Republican protective tariff. His denunciation of the Payne-Aldrich Tariff, therefore, appeared to be dictated by opportunism.

Roosevelt explained his changed attitude toward Canadian reciprocity by stating that when he wrote his letter to Taft indorsing the measure, he did not know, as he later learned, that it was a "jug-handled" proposition, framed in the interest of the industrial East. La Follette, embittered by the collapse of his own campaign and remembering Roosevelt's coolness toward him, supported Taft, as did a number of other progressives like William E. Borah of Idaho. Others like Albert B. Cummins came out for Roosevelt without affiliating with the Progressive party.

With the Republican party split from stem to stern and with Roosevelt and Taft certain to divide the Republican vote, the election of the Democratic candidate was certain. The only question in the early stages of the campaign was whether the Democrats would nominate a progressive or an old-line Democrat. As in previous pre-convention campaigns, Bryan's enemies hoped to wrest the control of the party from him. His decisive defeats in three elections made him an unlikely candidate in 1912; but his followers were legion and he was a force to be reckoned with.

The anti-Bryan faction won the first battle at the Baltimore convention when Alton B. Parker, the Democratic standard bearer in 1904 and the author of the famous gold telegram, was elected temporary chairman. Champ Clark of Missouri, the speaker of the House of Representatives, on the first ballots led his rivals for the presidential nomination, with Woodrow Wilson second; Oscar

WILL MR. BRYAN ENJOY BALTIMORE AS MUCH AS CHICAGO?

[Copyright: 1912: By John T. McCutcheon.]

The Chicago Tribune

W. Underwood of Alabama and Judson Harmon of Ohio were also in the running.

Clark's chances appeared to be the best. He was a popular speaker of the House, was regarded as a moderate liberal, or at least not reactionary, and had fared better than his competitors in the primaries. Underwood, though definitely associated with the conservative Democracy of the South, commanded respect as a man of outstanding ability. Harmon, who had served in Cleveland's cabinet, had made a notable record as governor of Ohio. The pre-convention campaign on behalf of Wilson had been largely directed by the astute Colonel Edward M. House of Texas, who recognized in the Princeton man a brilliant student of government in sympathy with progressive Democracy.

Woodrow Wilson, who had won for himself the title, the "scholar in politics," had made a record as governor of New Jersey that attracted the attention of the country. Elected as a foe of machine politics, he proved to be more than the equal of the bosses who had controlled the politics of that state. As a professor of history and jurisprudence at Wesleyan, Bryn Mawr, and Princeton, he made a brilliant record in the classroom, and his clearly written and scholarly contributions to learned and popular periodicals attracted high recognition. His book, *Congressional Government,* written as a graduate student at Johns Hopkins University, revealed a mind of unusual power.

In 1902 Wilson became president of Princeton University. One of his close associates on the Princeton faculty, Bliss Perry, records that when he made the acquaintance of the thirty-six-year-old professor, there was little that was youthful in him except high spirits, energy, and self-confidence. "The son was a true child of the manse where religion, wit, and political theorizing went hand in hand. Both father and son were idealists, phrase-lovers, and critics." Perry found him open-minded and approachable.

As president of Princeton, Wilson conceived it to be his function to transform the institution from a haven where young men of wealth and aristocratic families assumed a cavalier attitude toward education, into a college where scholarship was exalted above membership in exclusive clubs and where the "side shows" on the campus would have less drawing power than libraries and laboratories. After eight years of conflict with faculty complacency, a stubborn Board of Trustees, and alumni and student politics, he found it more congenial to transfer his activities to the political arena in the capital of New Jersey.

In the meantime, George Harvey, editor of *Harper's Weekly*, who in 1908 had proposed the Princeton educator for the Democratic nomination for the Presidency as a relief from Bryanism and from Rooseveltian policies, was using the columns of his publication to set forth Wilson's qualifications for the Presidency. Unfortunately, Harvey's support was embarrassing to Wilson in the Middle West, where his weekly was unpopular as the exponent of the Wall Street point of view. Rumors having reached him that Wilson was not happy over his support, Harvey inquired of him if his activity was injurious. After a rather brusque affirmative reply, Harvey dropped his erstwhile *protégé* and entered the lists in behalf of Clark.

As between Clark and Wilson, Bryan was neutral, thanks to the skillful diplomacy of Colonel House. In order to prevent Bryan from indorsing Wilson, the governor's opponents published a letter that Wilson had written in 1904 in which he expressed the wish that "something at once dignified and effective" could be done "to knock Mr. Bryan once for all into a cocked hat." Wilson's break with Harvey and the transfer of the latter's political affections to Clark did much to counteract the effect of this unfortunate letter; but Colonel House took advantage of his long friendship with Bryan to win him over to Wilson, whose chances of obtaining the nomination and carrying the Democratic party to victory were dubious without the support of the Great Commoner.

As it fell out, Wilson owed his nomination to Bryan, whose wisdom and courage at the Baltimore convention will probably be remembered after many of his other achievements have been forgotten. The opportunity for Bryan's *coup* was prepared by Colonel House. As the time for the assembling of the delegates to the convention drew near, it was certain that Clark would have a majority of delegates pledged to him, but the two-thirds rule which had prevailed in Democratic conventions might be used to prevent his nomination. By capitalizing the jealousies of delegates pledged to candidates other than Clark, the Wilson cohorts made agreements with a sufficient number of them to stand firm until Clark was eliminated. This agreement deadlocked the convention, and time played into the hands of Wilson.

In the early stages of the convention Bryan presented a resolution regretting the presence at the convention of August Belmont of New York and Thomas F. Ryan of Virginia, both men representative of the kind of politics which Bryan had fought during his entire career. This resolution was passed by an overwhelming vote. His most dramatic and effective stroke, however, was executed after the tenth ballot when the New York delegation, dominated by Tammany Hall and bitterly opposed to Wilson, transferred its ninety votes from Harmon to Clark. This convinced Bryan that Wilson—not Clark—was his man, and he announced on the floor of the convention that he would not vote for any man whose nomination depended on New York. Clark had reached the zenith of his strength; on subsequent ballots his vote and that of the other candidates fell off, and on the forty-sixth ballot Wilson was nominated. His running mate was Thomas R. Marshall of Indiana.

The Democratic platform was not impressive; it was certainly innocuous in contrast with the Progressive platform. But with Wilson the nominee, the Democrats presented to the country their ablest candidate, although his speeches during the campaign did not evoke much enthusiasm. However, with the Republican vote split between Roosevelt and Taft, Wilson's part in the campaign was conducted with dignity and without rancor in the expectation that if he polled the normal Democratic vote, he would have a majority in the electoral college.

The acrimony of the Republican attacks on Roosevelt abated for a time after he had been shot by a demented man just as he had seated himself in an automobile after leaving his hotel in Milwaukee to address a meeting on October 14. Fortunately, the bullet struck the manuscript of his speech, making the wound superficial. Although he knew he had been wounded, Roosevelt insisted, over the protests of his physician and friends, on keeping his appointment at the Auditorium, where he spoke for an hour. His marvelous physique assured early recovery, and on October 31 he addressed an audience of twenty-five thousand wildly cheering people at Madison Square Garden, New York.

The Republican press and speakers directed their irony at Wilson's college training and pointed to the danger of a "free trade" tariff under Democratic rule. The Progressives stressed Wilson's failure as governor of New Jersey to curb the trusts, to which Wilson replied that his hands were tied by a Republican legislature. The Democrats appealed to the Republicans to vote for Wilson in order to defeat the Roosevelt "menace." The Progressives, on the other hand, advised the Republicans to vote for Roosevelt because a vote for Taft would give the advantage to Wilson, whose election would mean another "low tariff panic" according to the pattern of 1893. They also alleged that by accepting the "steam-roller" nomination, Taft had degraded his high office and was a receiver of "stolen goods."

Roosevelt was attacked as a revolutionist, anarchist, Socialist, drunkard, and a purveyor of profanity and platitudes. The New York papers, especially the *Times* and the *Sun*, were the most extreme. In the *Times* Roosevelt was always the "third-term candidate." His record on the trusts and the tariff was the subject of biting editorials. The Progressive party was said to be a "one-man party," and Roosevelt's election would place in the White House a man who would override all constitutional restraints. After the conventions had done their work, however, the third-term bogey lost its potency. The heavy Roosevelt vote in the primaries may have convinced the strategists that the people were not afraid of breaking the third-term tradition. After the first weeks of the primary campaign, the issue faded out of the picture, although after election many papers attributed Roosevelt's defeat to the third-term tradition.

The election returns vindicated the New York gamblers who offered five to one odds on Wilson. Wilson polled the normal Democratic vote, but the distribution of the vote was such that he received the largest electoral vote in history up to that time, a total of 435 out of 531. Taft carried only two states, Utah and

Vermont, giving him eight electoral votes and making him the worst-defeated Republican candidate in history down to 1936, when Landon's electoral vote equaled it. Taft was third in both popular and electoral votes.

Roosevelt's eighty-eight electoral votes were distributed in Pennsylvania, Michigan, Minnesota, South Dakota, Washington, and all but two in California. The Democratic majority in the House of Representatives was so large as to be unwieldy. The large Progressive vote was obviously intended for Roosevelt, in the light of the small delegation of Progressives elected to Congress. The Democratic majority in the Senate was close but ample, as it proved.

A combination of circumstances—the feud between Roosevelt and Taft and the effective tactics of Bryan—conspired to elect the first Democratic President since 1892, with Democratic majorities in both houses of Congress. Would the "professor in politics" prove equal to the task of maintaining the necessary discipline within the ranks of a party that had shown little coherency since the fatal days of Cleveland, when the Democratic convention repudiated a Democratic administration and entered every subsequent presidential campaign divided against itself? Would the Bull Moose party, with its great leader, succeed the Republican party, the "party of yesterday," as the Bull Moose himself was fond of calling it? These questions were answered during the next four years.

CHAPTER XXIII

WOODROW WILSON AND REFORM

ON MARCH 4, 1913, WOODROW WILSON AND THOMAS R. MARSHALL were sworn into their high offices, and for the first time in twenty years the federal government was Democratic in all its branches. Wilson's inaugural address was one of the ablest that has been delivered on these historic occasions and was the text of favorable editorial comments throughout the country. It was lofty in sentiment and set the standard of literary excellence that characterized Wilson's state papers. The closing words were especially fine: "This is not a day of triumph; it is a day of dedication. Here muster, not the forces of party, but the forces of humanity. Men's hearts wait upon us; men's lives hang in the balance; men's hopes call upon us to say what we will do. Who shall live up to the great trust? Who dares fail to try? I summon all honest men, all patriotic, all forward-looking men to my side. God helping me, I will not fail them, if they will but counsel and sustain me!"

In graceful but challenging sentences the "schoolmaster" paid tribute to the noble men and women who had exhibited in striking forms "the beauty and the energy of sympathy and helpfulness and counsel in their efforts to rectify wrong, alleviate suffering, and set the weak in the way of strength and hope." In congratulating the nation on its great achievements, the accumulation of great wealth and the abundance of life, he deplored the inexcusable waste that had accompanied it, and the cost in lives snuffed out, in overtaxed and broken energies, in blighted and stunted spiritual growth. "The great Government we loved has too often been made use of for private and selfish purposes, and those who used it had forgotten the people. . . . Our thought has been 'Let every man look out for himself, let every generation look out for itself,' while we reared giant machinery which made it impossible that any but those who stood at the levers of control should have a chance to look out for themselves."

The inaugural address was a call to national and individual repentance. The author was the preacher of righteousness, but he was much more than a prophet who believed that righteousness exalteth a nation; he was a scholar steeped in history and the science of government, who saw the havoc that had been wrought by unrestrained individualism, and the infinitely greater disasters that would overtake the nation unless his generation would take thought for the morrow. Wilson brought to the White House a great intellect, but his leadership was more than intellectual. It was intelligence with a burning moral fervor. To those whose eyes were blinded by the "scales of heedlessness" Wilson's words were hypocritical cant. In his own party were men who followed him without knowing whither they were going, and there were others who sighed for the days of orthodoxy and turned to other leaders.

Before his plunge into the agitated waters of the political sea, Wilson's writings and speeches revealed him as an admirer of Grover Cleveland; but the exigencies of politics confirmed what he already knew, namely, that a political system cannot be confined in a strait-jacket of theory. In the White House he matured into what he called himself, in a Jackson Day address on January 8, 1915, an "animated conservative." In the same notable address he avowed that "The trouble with the Republican party is that it has not had a new idea for thirty years." History taught Wilson that in the long run the living adapt their institutions to their needs and that a charter of government is valid only as it is a garment that can be adjusted to changing conditions.

Wilson's inaugural dream of a civilization sustained by happy men tilling their own soil and by men and women in factories, mines, and offices free in spirit was shattered by cataclysmic events on another continent; and after eight years he left the White House broken in health and spirit, repudiated by those who misunderstood him and hated by others who understood him all too well.

Between election and inauguration Wilson took counsel of

others, but he kept their counsel and his own so well that newspapers cartooned him as the "Sphinx." It was not until the day
of inauguration that the members of the cabinet were made public.
By appointing Bryan to the State portfolio, Wilson acknowledged
his indebtedness to the Great Commoner for his nomination. The
appointment was also an admission that the administration stood
in need of his unreserved support.

In the campaign of 1916 the Republicans made much of the
mediocrity of the cabinet; but it measures up with cabinets that
had been constructed before and that have been constructed since.
New England was unrepresented. It would have been represented
by the brilliant Louis D. Brandeis of Boston but for the strenuous
opposition of men in his own party who feared the attorney who
had fearlessly exposed the frenzied financial exploits of Charles
Mellen of the New York, New Haven, and Hartford Railroad.
Brandeis had made it plain that Mellen had employed the methods
of Jay Gould to monopolize the transportation facilities, including interurban lines, of New England.

Wilson's partiality to this brilliant lawyer and student of
government was indicative of his sympathy for the progressive
cause. It was reserved for him to flout his adversaries and to
hearten his admirers in 1916 by appointing the author of *Other
People's Money* to the Supreme Court over the frantic and bitter
opposition of men like Taft and President A. Lawrence Lowell
of Harvard, who aligned themselves with men who had better reasons for opposing Brandeis's elevation to the high office. Over a
long period of years Brandeis distinguished himself by writing
dissenting opinions that prevented this body from falling into still
lower esteem than that in which it was held, even by President Taft.

Wilson's official advisers were much less influential in shaping
the policies of the administration than was Colonel House, whose
close relations with the President won for him the designation of
the "Third House" and years later inspired a book by George
Sylvester Viereck entitled *The Strangest Friendship in History*.
In the summer of 1915 Wilson wrote to the mysterious adviser:
"You are the only person in the world with whom I can discuss
everything." House not only had a personal affection for the Presi-

dent which grew with the years of their close association, but he placed a high estimate upon his intellect. "I have come in contact with minds of greater initiative and imagination," he said, "but never one that had more analytical power and comprehension."

On April 8, 1913, Congress convened in extraordinary session to revise the tariff. By appearing in person to read his message in the presence of members of the Senate and House of Representatives and a large and distinguished audience, Wilson broke a custom that dated back to 1801, when Jefferson departed from the practice of Washington and Adams by sending his message in writing. This abrupt violation of a custom which had been regarded as irrevocably established better became the unconventional and strenuous Theodore Roosevelt—and Wilson himself was happy over having executed a *coup* that "T. R." had not thought of—but it was received with favor by the public and the press. William Randolph Hearst, however, published a long letter in which he attacked the President as a Federalist who was trying to introduce the English system of government.

Presidents since Wilson have consulted their own preferences in communicating with Congress. Harding followed Wilson's example, and so did Coolidge until after his election in 1924. Hoover communicated in writing. Franklin D. Roosevelt went back to the Wilsonian method in 1934, on January 3, when Congress convened in regular session under the amendment which eliminated the "lame-duck" session. This was the first presidential message ever to be broadcast via radio. Two years later two extraordinary features attended the delivery of the same President's message. For the first time in history a President deliberately chose to deliver his annual message in the evening, if exception is made of Wilson's war message in April, 1917, when the emergency was too great to delay it until the following day. The second extraordinary feature about Franklin Roosevelt's message is that it was not a "report on the state of the Union," but a political speech in which the President attacked his opponents and defended his administration on the eve of a presidential campaign. The Republicans attacked the President's course as a "political stunt," but it is evident that the radio furnishes opportunities that future Presidents will not overlook.

The first Democratic Senate to assemble since 1893 was living proof of the great change that had come over the Democratic party within twenty years, and indeed over the country. Of the Democratic majority when Cleveland was President, not one remained in the Senate in 1913; and of the Republican minority, only Henry Cabot Lodge of Massachusetts and Jacob H. Gallinger of New Hampshire survived the senatorial mortality of two decades. The progressive Democratic Senators passed over such veterans as Augustus O. Bacon of Georgia and Thomas P. Martin of Virginia, southern conservatives, and elected a Senator serving his first term, John W. Kern of Indiana, Bryan's running mate in 1908, as chairman of the caucus and floor leader. There was no coterie to succeed to the autocratic rule of the Aldrich régime. The small Democratic majority was in no danger of breaking on the rocks of a Gorman conspiracy such as wrecked Cleveland's efforts to revise the tariff downward, for there were enough progressive Republican Senators to unite with the progressive Democrats to defeat a coalition of conservative Democrats and Republicans. The votes on major items of progressive legislation during the administrations of Roosevelt and Taft gave ample assurance. On numerous occasions during Wilson's administration the Democrats received La Follette's support in return for favors to the Wisconsin progressive.

The speaker of the House was Champ Clark, who but for the tactics of the new Secretary of State might have made the inaugural address on March 4. Clark had not forgiven Bryan and perhaps never did forgive him. However, Speaker Clark did not wield the power over legislation commensurate with that of his predecessor, whose wings had been clipped by a coalition of Republican insurgents and Democrats. Oscar W. Underwood was the leader of the majority; and in spite of his conservative instincts, he was an able lieutenant in the service of a liberal President. Under the new administration Bryan and Bryanism came into their own, but the products of the legislative mill bore the stamp of the master in the White House.

On May 8, 1913, a month after Congress convened, the Underwood Tariff Bill passed the House by a vote of 281 to 139, with party lines closely adhered to. Three progressive Republicans voted with the majority. The party discipline administered by the caucus and by the "schoolmaster" in the White House was well-nigh perfect. When the bill came to the Senate, there were fears that the stories of 1894 and 1909 would be repeated—and it is true that many amendments were added—but some of them represented downward revision over the House schedules. The concentrated power of special interests to defeat the purpose of the administration was quickly shattered by Wilson's bold exposure of their lobby. In a public statement Wilson said: "Washington has seldom seen so numerous, so industrious, or so insidious a lobby."

Throughout the hot summer months the Senate debated the measure, but the Republicans could not break down the caucus rule. Progressive Republican Senators like William S. Kenyon of Iowa, successor to the late Senator Dolliver, commended many features of the bill and praised Wilson for his efforts to carry out the platform pledges of his party. Kenyon denounced the betrayal of the people by the Republican party in passing the Payne-Aldrich Bill and said that if Taft had vetoed it, he would have been reelected. The main contention of the progressive Republicans was that the Underwood bill ought to contain a provision for a tariff commission, which was one of the pet measures of this group and had been indorsed in the Bull Moose platform. On September 10 the amended bill passed the Senate by a vote of 44 to 37, with La Follette and Poindexter of Washington voting for it and two "sugarcrats" from Louisiana voting in the negative. The bill reported by the conference committee received the approval of the President on October 3.

The Underwood Tariff had the distinction of being the only law enacted since the Civil War that represented consistent downward revision and was free from the "jokers" and specific and *ad valorem* combinations of Republican tariffs. There were errors and inconsistencies, but they were not there by design to deceive the public. There were many additions to the free list, including articles of daily necessity. Wool and sugar were on the free list, but the provision with reference to sugar was not effective until after two and a half years. By insisting on free wool, which had made the Wilson-Gorman Tariff so obnoxious to certain interests, Wilson showed courage and convinced even his opponents of the sincerity of his purposes. A number of the reductions were nominal; but in the opinion of the most competent student of American tariff history, Frank W. Taussig, they were worth while, if for no other reason, because the bill might fairly be expected to put an end to the superstition that all prosperity was dependent on the maintenance of a rigid protective tariff.

The expected reduction of revenue from the operation of the tariff was one reason for the inclusion of a graduated income tax, another feature of the Democratic tariff of 1894 that was so hotly opposed by conservatives and was declared unconstitutional by the Supreme Court. The ratification of the Sixteenth Amendment in February, 1913, removed the constitutional objection. Compared with income tax legislation during and after the World War, the income tax rates of the Underwood Tariff Act were extremely moderate.

The practical working of the Democratic tariff was never fully demonstrated, because less than a year after it became a law the World War deranged the foreign trade of all countries and made it necessary to resort to other means of raising revenue. The panic predicted by the Republicans while the bill was pending did not materialize except for the continuation of the depression from the previous administration, which Wilson pronounced "psychological."

The most frequent indictment of the Underwood Tariff, which was also made against Wilsonian anti-trust legislation, the Federal Reserve Act, and rural credits, was that it was the child of an administration headed by a southern-born President and a Congress whose committee chairmanships were largely held by Southerners. The editorial reaction of the *Boston Herald* of January 30, 1914, was as follows: "Every man who votes for the maintenance of the present division of the Republican party, votes for the ascendancy of the South, which is traditionally 'solid,' and sure to remain undivided by Progressivism or any other of the fads and frills of the hour. If we do not like the sort of legislation pertaining to the tariff, and the trusts and the finances, which the southern statesmen give us, we can do what similarly circumstanced people everywhere would do, and that is to get together in furtherance of the interests of our section. . . . We are thus far pretty well satisfied with the leadership which the South is now giving the nation and so long as we are the South itself is likely to be."

If the Underwood Tariff Act was a triumph for Wilson's leadership, the Federal Reserve Act was an even greater test. In spite of the prolonged debates on the tariff which had sorely taxed the patience and strength of Senators and Representatives, Wilson gave them no respite and called upon them to grapple with a problem which had failed of solution in the Roosevelt and Taft administrations. Wilson knew the advantage of disposing of major items of legislation while the Democrats were still under the spell of victory and before the appetite of the legislators for patronage had been satisfied.

It will be recalled that the Aldrich-Vreeland Act of 1908 was passed in order to relieve the money stringency that accompanied the so-called "bankers' panic" of 1907. This act contained a provision for a monetary commission. In 1911 the National Monetary Commission of which Senator Aldrich was chairman, after intensive study, recommended the establishment of a central reserve bank, with branch banks throughout the country. A bill embodying these recommendations was introduced in the Taft administration, but there was so much opposition to a system that would enable the large banks to control the banking system of the country that the bill failed to pass.

In the meantime, a congressional committee—the so-called Pujo Committee—had uncovered some of the operations of the "Money Trust," which Woodrow Wilson in a speech during the campaign of 1912 pronounced the greatest monopoly in the country. On December 4, 1911, Congressman Charles A. Lindbergh of Minnesota, a progressive Republican, introduced a bill "authorizing the appointment of a committee to investigate as to whether there are not combinations of financial and other concerns who control money and credits and operate in restraint of trade through that control." Lindbergh stated to the House that an emissary of the "Money Trust" had warned him that unless he stopped his attacks a worse panic than the country had ever known would be brought about. Lindbergh's well-known courage and independence made it inadvisable to intrust the investigation to him, in the opinion of conservatives, but they were unable to prevent some sort of investigation. The upshot was the adoption on February 24, 1912, of the Pujo resolution.

Fortunately, the Pujo Committee secured the services of able counsel in Samuel Untermyer, who handled the inquiry with skill and success. Through searching examinations of such witnesses as J. Pierpont Morgan, George F. Baker, and other prominent financiers, Untermyer developed an amazing story that commanded front pages in the newspapers. The country learned of operations that netted millions to a favored few. The Pujo investigation turned out to be anything but a "whitewashing" affair.

It was found that there was "an established and well-defined identity and community of interest between a few leaders of finance which has been created and held together through stock holdings, interlocking directorates, and other forms of domination over banks, trust companies, public service and industrial corporations, and which has resulted in a vast and growing concentration of control of money and credit in the hands of a comparatively few men." Eighteen banks and trust companies were named in the report; but six were singled out as the most powerful which had directors in banks, insurance companies, transportation systems, public utility corporations, and trading corporations. It became known that dominant banking interests controlled the policies of mining, manufacturing, and transportation industries through their control of credit, and that their power extended to the executive and legislative branches of government. The "invisible government" about which the Progressives had complained became a reality.

The report of the Pujo Committee (1912) shattered whatever prospects there may have been for the enactment of a banking bill recommended by the Aldrich Committee; but it did more than that. It made it possible for the Wilson administration, over the opposition of the "Money Trust" itself, allied with bankers and a certain type of business man, to enact a law that established a system quite different, though the power of the "Money Trust" was such that disillusionment was in store for many who hoped for better days.

When Wilson wrote his book, *The New Freedom,* he undoubtedly had before him the Pujo report. "Don't deceive yourselves for a moment as to the power of the great interests which now dominate our developments," he wrote. "They are so great that it is almost an open question whether the government of the United States can dominate them or not. Go one step further, make their organized power permanent, and it may be too late to turn them back. . . . If there are men in this country big enough to own the government of the United States, they are going to own it; what we have to determine now is whether we are big enough, whether we are men enough, whether we are free enough, to take possession again of the government which is our own."

It was in this spirit that President Wilson undertook to obtain legislation to restore the government to the people. It demanded intelligence, moral integrity, and leadership, all of which Wilson possessed in high degree. These qualities raised the prestige of his administration to a point where it attracted the support and admiration of men and women without respect to party affiliation.

The President consulted with economists, bankers, and men of varied interests, in addition to reading a vast amount of literature on the subject of money and banking. The result was that he was fortified with a body of knowledge that confounded his adversaries. The President was fortunate in having a man of the ability of Carter Glass of Virginia in charge of the bill in the House. Colonel House, who took an active part in driving the bill through Congress, wrote: "The bankers, sad to relate, know next to nothing about it, and none of them agrees as to what is best. The only unanimity of opinion amongst them is that the bill should be made for them and be operated for them, and they cannot understand that the manufacturers, merchants, railroads, farmers, and others have any rights in the premises."

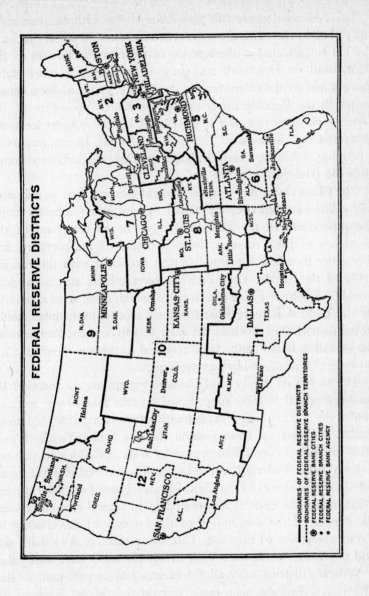

FEDERAL RESERVE DISTRICTS

BOUNDARIES OF FEDERAL RESERVE DISTRICTS
BOUNDARIES OF FEDERAL RESERVE BRANCH TERRITORIES
⊕ FEDERAL RESERVE BANK CITIES
• FEDERAL RESERVE BRANCH CITIES
○ FEDERAL RESERVE BANK AGENCY

The Federal Reserve Bill passed the House without great difficulty; but in the Senate weeks were consumed in efforts to have the bill emasculated in the interest of the financial powers of the East, until on December 20, 1913, it passed by a comfortable margin and went to a conference committee. After a sharp debate in which the Republicans criticized the caucus procedure of the Democratic majority, the bill reported by the conference committee passed the Senate. The majority in the House was overwhelming. Thus the President had scored an even greater triumph than the Underwood Tariff Act.

The Glass-Owen Act—or the Federal Reserve Act, as it is usually called—created twelve regional Federal Reserve banks under the supervision of the Federal Reserve Board composed of the Secretary of the Treasury, the comptroller of the currency, and five other members appointed by the President with the concurrence of the Senate. Each Federal Reserve bank was to be governed by a board of nine directors, of whom three were appointed by the Federal Reserve Board and six elected by member banks in the district. The stock of the bank was to be owned by member banks. All national banks were required to become members; for other banks, membership was optional.

The merits of the Federal Reserve system are as follows: By issuing Federal Reserve notes based on bills taken from member banks, the country was provided with an elastic currency. Member banks could borrow from Federal Reserve banks. To check possible inflation Federal Reserve banks were forbidden to pay out notes of other Federal Reserve banks. The Federal Reserve banks acted as fiscal agents of the United States, instead of subtreasuries. Distributing the Federal Reserve banks in several regions reduced the danger of the domination of the finances of the country by the money power of the East. This was a concession to the South and the West, where the "Wall Street bankers" were unpopular.

Wilson's distrust of Wall Street was just as profound as that of Andrew Jackson, who made war on the Second Bank of the United States; but Wilson conducted his warfare with a finesse that was anything but suggestive of the methods of the frontier President. That events proved that neither Jackson nor Wilson nor the country reaped the full measure of benefits from their efforts does not detract from their courage and ability. It merely proves the insuperable difficulty of the problems they tried to solve. Even the selection of the personnel of the Federal Reserve Boards proved to be difficult. Nevertheless, the Wilson administration succeeded where others had failed.

With two major accomplishments to his credit, Wilson set himself to the task of grappling with the trusts, which had been the text of campaign speeches and party platforms since the eighties. In his annual message of December 2, 1913, the President said: "I think it will be easily agreed that we should let the Sherman Anti-Trust Law stand, unaltered as it is, with its debatable ground about it, but that we should as much as possible reduce the area of that debatable ground by further and more explicit legislation; and should also supplement that great act by legislation which will not only clarify it but also facilitate its administration and make it fairer to all concerned."

On January 20, 1914, he addressed Congress with more specific proposals for the attainment of these objectives. He proposed legislation to prevent interlockings of the personnel of the directorates of great corporations—banks and railroads, industrial, commercial, and public service bodies—"as in effect result in making those who borrow and those who lend practically one and the same, those who sell and those who buy but the same persons trading with one another under different names and in different combinations." Holding companies were to be prohibited. The Interstate Commerce Commission was to be given power to superintend and regulate the financial operations by which railroads could be supplied with money necessary for their development.

Congress responded to the President's message by enacting the Clayton Anti-Trust Act and the Federal Trade Commission Act in 1914. By the Clayton Act certain business practices and relationships were made illegal, such as price discrimination, exclusive dealer agreements, tying contracts, and interlocking directorates. The provisions pertaining to labor will be discussed in another connection.

The Federal Trade Commission Act went much further than

the Clayton Act. The Federal Trade Commission of five members was clothed with power to investigate violations of the anti-trust acts, to require reports from corporations, to collect information about foreign trade, and in general to function with reference to organized trade in somewhat the same way that the Interstate Commerce Commission functioned with reference to common carriers. Unfortunately, the effectiveness of the Federal Trade Commission was hampered by decisions of the Supreme Court; but on the whole the work of the commission represented substantial progress in governmental regulation of business by protecting legitimate interests and by interfering with monopolistic practices. In a country as large as the United States, with huge and various enterprises, the matters that came before the Federal Trade Commission were numerous and highly complicated.

Wilson continued the "trust-busting" activities of Roosevelt and Taft, and some of the titanic battles brought victory to the government, as in the cases of the International Harvester Company, the Chicago meat packers, and the Corn Products Company. But the "rule of reason" laid down in the Standard Oil case of 1911 made it possible for the Supreme Court to hold that the mammoth United States Steel Corporation was not a monopoly and was innocent of unfair methods of competition. By the close of the Wilson administration it was plain that something more fundamental than "anti-trust legislation" was required to curb the concentration of industry into gigantic corporations; and the cataclysmic years from 1921 to 1933 emphasized the contention that the competitive idea of Wilson's "New Freedom" was largely a dream.

The enactment of the Underwood Tariff, the Federal Reserve Act, the Clayton Anti-Trust Act, and the Federal Trade Commission Act was evidence to conservatives that Wilson was "unsettling business"; but his concessions to labor were even more convincing proof that he was a dangerous "theorist."

In a previous chapter it was pointed out that it is the conclusion of students of the Sherman Anti-Trust Act that it was not intended to apply to labor organizations, although Senator Edmunds, one of the framers of the law, declared that it was so intended. Be that as it may, one of the grievances of labor was the use of the injunction in labor disputes; and in the campaign of 1908 Taft was criticized in labor circles because of his decisions when he was a federal judge. In 1912 the Democratic and Progressive platforms favored the exemption of labor unions from the scope of the Sherman Anti-Trust Act.

Certain court cases pending and decided were also disturbing to labor. The decision of the Supreme Court in the Danbury Hatters' case was a heavy blow to the efforts of the United Hatters of America to secure the closed shop. In 1902 the refusal of the firm of Loewe and Company of Danbury, Connecticut, to accede to the demand for a closed shop precipitated a strike. In cooperation with the American Federation of Labor a secondary boycott was initiated against the firm's products. Wholesalers and retailers were threatened with loss of business if they bought and sold Loewe goods. The losses to the Loewe Company were so serious that in 1903 a suit for damages under the Sherman Anti-Trust Act was filed against the members of the United Hatters' Union.

The case was in the courts until January 5, 1915, when the Supreme Court affirmed the decisions of the lower courts and held that the boycott violated the Sherman Act. By this decision it was established that the Sherman Act applied to labor combinations; that secondary boycotts affecting interstate commerce were illegal; and that suits for damages might be brought against individual members of unions. Loewe and Company eventually collected over $250,000 in damages from members of the United Hatters' Union.

In a similar attempt to boycott the Bucks Stove and Range Company, which began in 1907, the company obtained an injunction against the American Federation of Labor and its officers and the molders' union. The American Federation of Labor defied the court order; and its officers, Samuel Gompers, John Mitchell, and Frank Morrison, were sentenced to jail for contempt of court. Both contempt and injunction cases came up to the Supreme Court. The injunction proceedings were dismissed at the request of the firm after it had made peace with the union; and in 1911 the Supreme Court dismissed the contempt case on technical grounds. The court held, however, that if a strike violated the Sherman Act, the methods used to carry it out could be enjoined.

In the case of the Hitchman Coal and Coke Company *v.* Mitchell, which after years of litigation was decided by the Supreme Court in 1917, the legality of the so-called "yellow-dog contract" was upheld. After a strike conducted by the United Mine Workers in 1906, the company hired individual workers who bound themselves not to join a union so long as they remained in the employ of the company. When the United Mine Workers sent organizers into the territory of the Hitchman Company, the court granted an injunction to restrain attempts to organize the employees of the company without the latter's consent. The Supreme Court upheld the contention of the company, namely, that contracts whereby workers agreed with their employers not to join a union while in their employ were valid and that the activity of agents of unions to induce men to break their contracts could be enjoined. The decisions of J. J. Parker of North Carolina, a federal judge who had upheld "yellow-dog contracts," were instrumental in defeating the confirmation of his appointment to the Supreme Court in Hoover's administration.

The labor provisions of the Clayton Anti-Trust Act were intended to answer the prayers of labor for relief from injunctions under the Sherman Act. Samuel Gompers even wrote an article for the *American Federationist* in which he praised the Clayton Act as the "charter of industrial freedom."

The act stated that the labor of a human being is not a commodity or article of commerce; and the wording of the statute indicated that it was the intention to exempt unions from such legal actions as those that have just been cited. However, the decision of the Supreme Court in the case of the Duplex Printing Press Company *v.* Deering, on January 3, 1921, a few weeks before the termination of the Wilson administration, deprived labor of the benefits it had supposed the Clayton Act guaranteed. The court held that the Clayton Act had not changed the legal status of union activities under the Sherman Act and that Congress did not intend that secondary boycotts should be legalized.

By a narrow interpretation of the language of the act, the majority of the justices declared that it applied to disputes respecting terms or conditions of employment between employees and employers, whereas in the Duplex case thousands of machinists who had never worked in the factory of the company were involved in the boycott. In the words of the court, "Congress had in mind particular industrial controversies, not a general class war."

During the heat of the presidential campaign of 1916 a substantial victory for labor was gained largely by the vigorous and prompt action of President Wilson, and it undoubtedly contributed in some measure to his reelection, partly through the bungling of his Republican opponent.

The railroad employees threatened to tie up traffic unless they were granted an eight-hour day as the standard for computing wages. On August 15 Wilson called a conference of leaders on both sides of the controversy. The President astonished the union officials by his intimate knowledge of the issues at stake. After two weeks of uncertainty and threats, he issued an ultimatum to the railroad heads and demanded an immediate answer. No satisfactory answer having come, and with railroads running extra trains to clear their lines in anticipation of a strike, Wilson on August 29 addressed a joint session of Congress in which he stated that his failure to bring the parties to "this critical controversy to an accommodation" made it necessary to turn to Congress.

The President's recommendations included, among other things, the establishment of the eight-hour day, the appointment by the President of a body of men to observe the working of the eight-hour day, the possible increase in freight rates to meet additional expenditures, and adequate power for the President to act in similar emergencies that might arise in the future.

With unusual despatch Congress passed a bill embodying the first two recommendations, and the President signed it on September 3, 1916. In the Senate only one Republican (La Follette) voted for this so-called Adamson Act, and only two Democrats voted in the negative. In the House fifty Republicans and only two Democrats voted against the bill. Wilson was severely criticized by the Republicans for yielding to the threat of a group to cripple the nation's transportation facilities. It was alleged that the railroad men were in reality contending not for an eight-hour day but for higher wages. The reaction throughout the country, however, was divided but probably favorable to Wilson, who had averted a crisis by a remarkable exercise of leadership.

During Taft's and Wilson's administrations the American Federation of Labor was challenged by the more radical element in the ranks of labor, perhaps greatly to the detriment to the cause of organized labor.

The revelations in the McNamara case in 1911-12 were even more sensational than were those in connection with the assassination of former Governor Steunenberg of Idaho in 1905, when the excesses of the Western Federation of Miners were played up in the newspapers from coast to coast. The confessions of Harry Orchard implicated "Big Bill" Haywood and two other officials of the Western Federation of Miners, who were alleged to have employed Orchard to murder mining bosses and other enemies of the Federation. The trial at Boise, Idaho, in the summer of 1907 attracted feature writers and photographers from all parts of the country. The defendants were not without staunch defenders in the midst of clamor that short shrift should be made of these "undesirable citizens," as President Roosevelt called them. In a sense, the Western Federation of Miners was on trial. The jury brought in a verdict of acquittal, but it was strongly suspected that the jurors were afraid to bring in any other verdict for fear of their own lives and those of their families.

In the McNamara case, two brothers of that name confessed that they had dynamited the Los Angeles Times Building, causing the loss of twenty-one lives. This crime was one of a series in the conflict between the American Bridge Company and the Bridge and Structural Iron Workers' Union. John J. McNamara, the secretary of the union, and his brother dynamited structures in the process of construction by the American Bridge Company. They were employed by somebody, whose identity was never revealed, to dynamite the Los Angeles Times Building, whose owner,

Harrison G. Otis, was an uncompromising enemy of organized labor.

The American Federation of Labor came to the defense of the McNamaras in the belief that they were victims of a campaign of espionage and terror designed to discredit organized labor; and when they confessed their guilt, a heavy blow was struck against the prestige of the American Federation of Labor. This case, together with general labor unrest, was responsible for the creation of the Industrial Relations Commission by Congress in 1912. After extensive hearings, the reports of this commission were favorable to the American Federation of Labor.

One of the most savage conflicts between capital and labor was the strike in the mills of the American Woolen Company at Lawrence, Massachusetts, in 1912. Here twenty thousand unskilled workers representing a babel of nationalities were mobilized and held in line by agents of the Industrial Workers of the World, a rival of the American Federation of Labor. This militant organization grew out of the Western Labor Union, which had been organized in 1898 with the purpose of keeping the A. F. of L. out of the mining regions in the Far West. In 1905 the name Industrial Workers of the World was adopted. This organization represented industrial unionism as opposed to the craft unions of the A. F. of L. The preamble to its constitution affirmed that the working class and the employing class have nothing in common and that it is the historic mission of the working class to abolish capitalism. Whereas the A. F. of L. made contracts and agreements with employers, the motto of the I.W.W. was "Abolition of the wage system." Its weapons were the general strike and sabotage.

The seriousness of the Lawrence strike was in part due to the fact that practically the entire population of the city was dependent upon the earnings of men and women employed in the textile mills. The American Federation of Labor had made little or no attempt to organize the mass of these employees, who were either unskilled or semi-skilled. This was the opportunity for the I.W.W.

Much excitement was aroused by the discovery of dynamite in sections of the city, which the strikers claimed had been planted by persons connected with the mill owners in order to discredit them. The feeling was so intense that rioting and demonstrations made it necessary to declare martial law. Joseph Ettor and Arturo Giovanetti, I.W.W. leaders, were arrested as accessories to the murder of a striker. A novel development in the conduct of strikes was the sending of a number of children away from Lawrence to be cared for in the homes of strike sympathizers. The authorities attempted to interfere with this plan, but their efforts resulted in such brutality that it raised a storm of protests from many sources, including demands for a federal investigation by a Socialist Congressman.

The strike resulted in a remarkable victory for the employees. The fact that a major strike had been won under the leadership of the I.W.W., in which "Big Bill" Haywood had taken part, was alarming and portended the waning prestige of the conservative leadership of the A. F. of L. Still more alarming was the demand from the workers that Ettor and Giovanetti be released from custody. A defense committee was organized, with Haywood as chairman, and a publicity campaign was launched. Parades and demonstrations were staged in several cities, and on the opening day of the trial some fifteen thousand workers staged a twenty-four-hour demonstration, one of the first "political strikes" in the history of the country.

After six hundred veniremen had been examined, the trial began and lasted fifty-eight days. As in the Haymarket trial of 1886, the prosecution played up the dangerous principles harbored in the minds of the defendants. Ettor and Giovanetti delivered closing speeches to the jury in which they stated: "We shall return again to our humble efforts, obscure, unknown, misunderstood soldiers of this mighty army of the working class of the world, which, out of the shadows and darkness of the past, is striving towards the destined goal, which is the emancipation of human kind, which is the establishment of love and brotherhood and justice for every man and every woman on this earth."

The outcome of the trial was quite different from that of the Haymarket battle. The jury returned a verdict of not guilty; and the defendants, after ten months in jail, were cheered as they left the courthouse.

Another serious labor war occurred in Colorado in September, 1913, when some nineteen thousand miners and their families deserted their homes and established tent colonies in preparation for a strike that lasted fifteen months. The scene of this conflict was in the foothills of the Rocky Mountains, where some thirty thousand coal miners, mostly Greeks, Italians, Slavs, and Mexicans, were employed by the Colorado Fuel and Iron Company, the Rocky Mountain Fuel Company, and the Victor-American Fuel Company. The mining camps were practically owned by the companies. The houses in which the miners lived, the churches in which they worshiped, the schools in which their children were educated, and the stores from which they purchased their supplies were virtually owned or controlled by the companies. The camps were infested with spies whose vigilance quickly sought out men who might cause trouble between miners and employers.

John D. Rockefeller, Jr., who controlled the Colorado Fuel and Iron Company, admitted before the Commission on Industrial Relations that he had not visited Colorado for ten years and had no knowledge about the rents, wages, and living conditions of the workers. In his testimony before the House Committee on Mines and Mining, after the strike had been in progress for over six months, Rockefeller defended the principle of the open shop and declared that it was a national issue whether workers should be allowed to work under such conditions as they might choose. Rather than allow outside people to interfere with employees who were satisfied with labor conditions, he stated that his company would go to great lengths to prevent them.

Strike breakers escorted by militia and protected by gunmen in the employ of the companies brought bloodshed, the most serious of which was the so-called Ludlow massacre, when the militia fired with rifles and machine guns on men, women, and children in one of the largest tent colonies. A considerable portion of the press of the country denounced the slaughter and fixed the responsibility for it on the companies and on the authorities of Colorado.

President Wilson used his efforts to bring peace to the afflicted region, but without success. In the end the companies prevailed, and a convention of the United Mine Workers voted to terminate the strike. Through the Industrial Representation Plan, Rockefeller strove to bring about amicable relations between operators and workmen and to improve the conditions of the laborers and their families. An investigation conducted by the Russell Sage Foundation from 1919 to 1921 found that there had been many improvements in housing conditions, schools, and other aspects of community life.

During these years the membership and resources of the American Federation of Labor increased, but it afforded little assistance in the conduct of strikes. It played a more important rôle as a lobbying organization. The opposition to Gompers from Socialists and persons with a more comprehensive program for social justice had the effect of spurring him and his associates to greater activity. The World War, however, which diverted the energies and attention of the nation to the objective of overcoming the ambitions of German militarism and imperialism changed the outlook and the program of labor leaders. This period marked losses as well as gains for the wage earners, but in the post-war years heavy losses were sustained.

An important gain for labor was the Furuseth Seamen's Act of 1915, which provided a nine-hour day for seamen and gave them the right to leave their jobs while ships were in port on the forfeiture of one-half of the wages earned. It also limited to some extent the authority of sea captains and made improvements in the physical care of sailors. The bill was sponsored by Senator La Follette, who received the support of the Democratic majority for it in return for the Senator's friendly attitude toward certain measures sponsored by the Wilson administration.

On July 17, 1916, Wilson signed the Federal Farm Loan Act which enabled farmers to secure long-time loans at low rates of interest. This measure made real another of the planks of the Populist platform and also furnished an effective appeal for the support of the agrarian West in the presidential campaign of that year.

Wilson's proposal to create a United States Shipping Board to provide a naval auxiliary and to encourage the development of a merchant marine met with a determined opposition from the Republicans and a small group of Democratic Senators who conducted one of the most prolonged filibusters in congressional history down to that time (1915). The bill might have passed if Wilson had agreed to an amendment making the ownership of the vessels temporary and making it obligatory for the government to withdraw from the field after the close of the World War. The Democrats refused to adjourn and held the Senate in continuous session for over fifty hours. The majority also threatened the filibusterers with a cloture rule. However, the opponents of the bill won out. The bill signed by Wilson on September 7, 1916, was quite different from the original measure. After the United States became a belligerent power a few months later, the wisdom of the act was justified.

In reviewing the legislative achievements of his first term in his speech of acceptance delivered on September 2, 1916, Wilson could say with truth: "This extraordinary recital must sound like a platform, a list of sanguine promises; but it is not so. It is a record of promises made four years ago and now actually redeemed in constructive legislation. . . . We have in four years come very near to carrying out the platform of the Progressive party as well as our own; for we also are progressives."

Unfortunately, Wilson's hopes for reelection could not be based exclusively on this record. The World War, which by 1916 had resolved itself into a life and death struggle for survival between the nations of Europe, had injected some of its bitterness and deadly propaganda into the composite population of America. It was just there that Wilson's record was politically vulnerable, as would have been the record of any man who might have occupied his appallingly responsible position, which carried with it power over the lives of thousands of his fellow citizens.

CHAPTER XXIV

FOREIGN AFFAIRS IN A WAR-TORN WORLD

WHEN WOODROW WILSON WAS INAUGURATED PRESIDENT OF THE United States, little did he realize that within four years fate would call on him to play a leading part in international affairs; that the United States and Mexico would come to the brink of war; that a Democratic Senate traditionally opposed to "imperialism" would ratify a treaty with Denmark for the purchase of the Virgin Islands (1916); that the relations between the United States and Germany would several times be strained to the breaking point; that the country would drift into war with Germany; that Japan would protest vigorously against proposed legislation to exclude Japanese immigrants and to deny them the right to own land in California; and that in his campaign for reelection his opponents would make greater capital of his foreign policy than of his domestic program.

For many years to come historians will probably disagree among themselves as to the causes of the World War and the wisdom and justice of Wilson's attitude toward the belligerent powers. At every crisis he was savagely criticized by individuals and groups having widely divergent points of view: by pacifists, by jingoes, by pro-Germans, by pro-Allies; but throughout, a substantial portion of the American people believed in the sincerity of his professed desire to avoid war without sacrificing the honor and dignity of their country. It will always be easy to draw up an indictment of his foreign policy, and it will always be easy to defend it, so complicated and kaleidoscopic were the events that overwhelmed the world. Wilson's sense of justice, his insight into the consequences of war, his understanding of the composite population of the country, his consciousness that he was President of the United States—not of a racial or religious group or of a section—kept the nation on an even keel. He was remarkably successful in restraining the hot-heads within his own party and without; and he counted on the inherent sense of justice in the American people, their traditional aloofness from the age-long feuds, hatreds, and rivalries of Europe, as well as the healing influence of the lapse of time.

For over two years—until June, 1915—William Jennings Bryan was Secretary of State. For years he had preached the gospel of peace and good will. In his lecture "The Prince of Peace," which he had delivered from coast to coast, he had deprecated military preparedness and had exhorted his hearers to support policies that would cause the American flag to be loved and not feared. He was perhaps the foremost advocate of arbitration to settle controversies between nations; and during his brief tenure as Secretary of State he negotiated "cooling-off" treaties with leading governments, by which a period of negotiation should precede possible resort to arms. His adversaries ridiculed his policy as "grape-juice diplomacy," scoffed at his alleged naïveté, and demanded the resignation of this amateur in favor of a Secretary who conformed to the requirements of traditional diplomacy; but the trend of events since those fateful years seems to presage that in the dispassionate pages of history Bryan's name will shine with greater luster than historians a few years ago expected.

After Bryan's dramatic resignation as Secretary of State when it appeared that diplomatic relations with Germany would be severed, he was succeeded by Robert Lansing, a diplomat of the old school, who but for the master in the White House would have proceeded along traditional lines. There was little of idealism in his make-up. But whether Bryan or Lansing occupied the State portfolio, the notes that appeared over their signatures bore the unmistakable literary touches of Woodrow Wilson. The President was his own Secretary of State, and his policy was much more akin to the idealism of Bryan than to the conventionalism of Lansing. Moreover, Wilson and Bryan reflected the thought of the Middle West, where progressive ideas were in the ascendancy.

The nightmare of the Wilson administration was the Mexican imbroglio which taxed the patience of the idealistic President and on several occasions threatened to force upon him intervention in the affairs of that distracted country in order to protect the lives and property of American citizens, as well as to satisfy the demands of European governments that the United States guarantee a government stable and powerful enough to protect their interests. Wilson had to formulate a policy that would not increase the distrust of Latin America which had risen to a high pitch as a result of the Panama policy of the Roosevelt administration and the dollar diplomacy of the Taft administration.

Wilson's desire to avoid intervention and to allow the Mexican people to work out their own political, economic, social, and religious problems was several times almost frustrated by demands for intervention from heavy investors in oil, mines, and rubber and from prelates of the Roman Catholic church who believed that their church was the victim of persecution at the hands of men who had no interest in religion. For eight years Wilson stood firm in the face of jingoism, political opportunism, racial and religious antagonism, and distrust and hostility from Mexican statesmen who remembered all too well the war between the two countries which resulted in the cession to the United States of a large portion of Mexican territory. Certainly the provocation for war was much greater than in the case of the Spanish-American War and even in the case of the War with Mexico in 1846.

Fortunately, Wilson's firmness against war was strengthened by the experience of the American people after the war with Spain. The President counted on the support of his countrymen who had no desire to add to the problems of the country by annexing territory inhabited by millions of people, vastly different in race, religion, institutions, and language, only a small percentage of whom could read and write. Moreover, after the outbreak of the war in Europe in August, 1914, the pressure from the governments of Europe was relaxed; and the nation that had the largest interests in Mexico—Great Britain—gave the United States a free hand in working out a solution.

It will be recalled that in the closing months of 1910, a revolution that overthrew the régime of Porfirio Diaz took its inception. For thirty years this strong man had maintained what amounted to a military dictatorship, during which Mexico made great material progress at the expense of the great mass of its people who continued to be landless, illiterate, superstitious, and poverty-ridden. Diaz was very cordial to foreign capitalists who paid liberally to the clique in control for oil, mining, and rubber concessions. Only a small minority in the United States understood the basis of the Diaz supremacy, its ruthless disregard for the welfare of peons who lived in virtual slavery on haciendas— large plantations which under Diaz had increased in number and in acreage. Only occasional articles published in American periodicals set forth the plight of the victims of peonage.

In 1910 the combination of army, church, and capital, the pillars of the Diaz structure, were in danger of being pulled down by the arms of youth, democracy, labor, and a down-trodden landless people rising to self-consciousness. The man whose name is associated with the greatest social and economic upheaval in Mexico's history is Francisco I. Madero, who was the victim of the most savage and unscrupulous abuse from a press largely controlled by the interests allied with Diaz. The City of Mexico, always hostile to reform, and the foreigners in the capital, many of whom were representatives of mining and oil interests, were determined to destroy the apostle of reform and to reestablish the supremacy of the old clique in order to assure returns on their investments. American capital invested in mines, smelters, oil, and rubber totaled several hundreds of millions—more than that of all other foreigners combined and even more than that of the Mexicans themselves.

After the overthrow of the Diaz oligarchy in 1910-11, President Taft was confronted with the problem of protecting the lives and property of American citizens; and public opinion was stirred by the inevitable reports of outrages upon men, women, and children. Taft ordered the mobilization of several thousand troops on the Mexican border, which evoked severe criticism not only in Mexico but in the United States as well, although enthusiastic approval came from those who saw Mexico only in terms of dividends.

During the closing days of the Taft administration, in February, 1913, Madero was deserted by General Victoriano Huerta, who was proclaimed provisional president. On the night of February 22 the deposed Madero was killed in cold blood while he was being transported from the National Palace to the penitentiary. Huerta's part in the crime is not entirely clear; but there is little doubt that he was privy to the plans for the murder and did nothing to prevent it.

Unfortunately, the American ambassador to Mexico, Henry Lane Wilson of Indiana, played a part during these tragic days that reflected discredit on the government he represented as well as on himself. From that day to this it has been charged that Madero was murdered with the knowledge, if not the consent, of Henry Lane Wilson. This has never been proved; but it is beyond dispute that the ambassador never raised a finger to save Madero's life, and steadily bombarded the Department of State with misleading dispatches designed to discredit Madero and to effect the speedy recognition of the government set up by the assassins who had betrayed the principles of the revolution. Despite the incessant prompting of his ambassador, Taft refused to recognize the Huerta government and on March 4, 1913, bequeathed to his successor what became the nightmare of the Wilson administration.

Through eight stormy years Wilson's Mexican policy was the text of acrimonious editorials and political speeches designed to discredit his idealistic and disinterested attitude and to pave the way for intervention. Misunderstood and all too well understood by widely divergent interests in both countries—and in Europe as well—Wilson held to his determination to allow the Mexican people to work out their own salvation, though more than once it appeared that partisan politics in his own country and blundering and ingratitude in the other would plunge the two peoples into a war which neither could afford from the standpoint of either self-interest or altruism.

If the student of American history seeks proof of Woodrow Wilson's moral stamina, a study of the relations between the United States and Mexico from 1913 to 1921 will yield rich returns. In fact, the succeeding Harding administration, which was dominated by the interests Wilson loathed in the person of Albert B. Fall, Secretary of the Interior—later to be sentenced to the penitentiary for participation in one of the most scandalous of the many scandals that disgraced that administration—did not dare to reverse Wilson's "watchful waiting" Mexican policy. Senator Fall was one of the most persistent and unscrupulous assailants of Wilson's policy, and the world knows that he was the mouthpiece of the oil interests whose successful corruption of Harding's cabinet officer sent him to the penitentiary.

In the deposition and murder of Madero, Henry Lane Wilson and men of his kind saw only another incident in the long procession of Mexican revolutions; Woodrow Wilson saw beneath the contest between ambitious and selfish men the smoldering embers of a revolt against oppression. From the beginning the President set himself firmly against recognizing the drunken, brutal, "unspeakable Huerta," who within a few months brought Mexico to the brink of anarchy and the United States and Mexico to the brink of war.

Mistrusting reports that came to him from the embassy in Mexico City, Wilson sent special agents to report on conditions in Mexico; and on August 4, 1913, he recalled Henry Lane Wilson as ambassador and appointed John Lind of Minnesota as his personal representative and to act as adviser to the American embassy in Mexico. In intrusting this delicate and extraordinary mission to the rugged and plain-spoken Minnesotan, the President had the assurance of Secretary Bryan that he would have the services of an incorruptible man who had won his spurs as a crusader under the Populist and Democratic banners against big business and imperialism in his own state. In 1896 and 1900

Bryan and Lind had stood shoulder to shoulder and had inspired mutual respect and affection.

Lind, however, had no diplomatic experience, had only a superficial knowledge of Mexico, and was unfamiliar with the language and character of the people. These serious limitations were more than counterbalanced by his rugged honesty and by his ability to keep silent. At first he entirely misjudged the character of the Mexican statesmen with whom he was compelled to deal; but after he had taken their measure he was under no illusions as to the gigantic problems that confronted Mexico and the part the neighbor to the north ought to play in permitting the prophets of a new day to cope with them. He learned to admire the strong qualities of the Mexican people, and to despise the men, whether Mexicans or Americans, who were wedded to the old order. No diplomatic agent was more loyal to his government and to its chief executive.

Lind conceived it to be the sole object of his mission to secure peace under a constitutional, orderly form of government. He was instructed to demand an immediate cessation of fighting throughout Mexico, to obtain assurance of an early and free election in which all factions would agree to take part, to exact from Huerta a promise not to be a candidate for the presidency in the election, and to secure an agreement from all parties to abide by the results of the election.

Lind failed to accomplish any one of these objectives. Through the wily minister of foreign affairs, Huerta informed Lind that "Mexico cannot for one moment take into consideration the four conditions which His Excellency Mr. Wilson has been pleased to propose through your honorable and worthy channel."

Further attempts to negotiate with Huerta brought no results; and Lind departed for Vera Cruz, where he remained for seven months—until April, 1914—and functioned as chief watchman of Wilson's "watchful waiting" policy. As the mouthpiece of Wilson's proposals his words fell on the deaf ears of Huerta, who knew nothing of democracy and constitutional government; Huerta had been trained in the army, which in Mexico offered the most lucrative rewards and was beyond the control of the civil authorities. He was an unscrupulous military dictator who was free to choose weapons that Wilson would not deign to employ. At first neither Wilson nor Lind understood that political democracy was nonexistent in Mexico.

Wilson was faced with the further handicap of having men in the Department of State who were not in sympathy with his policy. The *chargé d'affaires* in Mexico City, Nelson O'Shaughnessy, was on intimate and cordial terms with Huerta and at every point sought to checkmate Lind's efforts. Moreover, the Americans resident in Mexico hoped and worked for military intervention by the United States. These conditions, coupled with the hostile attitude of many leading American newspapers, made it impossible for Lind to convince Huerta and his clique that public sentiment was back of Wilson.

Huerta, however, had his own troubles. Shortly after his *coup d'état,* sporadic revolutions against the usurper sprang up in various parts of the country. Lind finally prevailed upon Wilson to give aid and comfort to the revolutionists by lifting the embargo on arms and munitions. Lind also selected Venustiano Carranza from among the revolutionary leaders as the one man who might overthrow Huerta and set up a constitutional government strong enough to put in motion reforms that would eventually give the people of Mexico the measure of material progress and self-respect necessary to the establishment of a stable and democratic government. Early in November, Lind had reached the conclusion that it was a choice between the recognition of Carranza or military intervention and occupation by the United States. From that time on he kept up a steady bombardment of the State Department with dispatches recommending that aid be granted to the Carranzistas in their march on Mexico City.

A combination of events finally eliminated Huerta, who resigned and fled the country on July 15, 1914, about three months after Lind had departed from Vera Cruz. On April 14, 1914, about a week after Lind had left Mexico, the arrest of the paymaster and seven sailors from the United States gunboat *Dolphin* by Mexican soldiers at Tampico started a chain of events that made it possible for Wilson to eliminate Huerta indirectly by force.

Huerta refused to comply unconditionally with the demand that he salute the United States flag by firing twenty-one guns, and Wilson ordered Admiral Frank F. Fletcher to seize the custom house at Vera Cruz. With the shedding of blood it was inevitable that jingoistic papers in the United States should demand a declaration of war. Some papers—the Hearst publications in particular—declared that the time was ripe for the United States to seize and occupy Mexico for the mutual benefit of both countries. While the excitement was intense, Wilson promptly accepted the proffered good offices of the plenipotentiaries of Argentina, Brazil, and Chile to effect an amicable settlement of the imbroglio. The Carranzista representatives at the so-called A.B.C. conference were chary of committing themselves to any agreement that might divide the forces that were fighting against the Huerta régime or make it possible for the forces of reaction to get back into the saddle.

Aside from the resignation of Huerta, who felt things getting too hot for him, the chief accomplishment of the A.B.C. mediation was to extricate the American government from a difficult position and to postpone the probability of war. The Carranzistas refused to have anything to do with anyone friendly to, or previously connected with, the Huerta government. It was war to the knife between them and Huerta and anybody associated with him.

The events of the next twelve months or more were bewildering to readers of American newspapers. With Mexico in a state bordering on anarchy, with several revolutionary chieftains contending for the control of the government, with newspapers publishing reports of the destruction of American lives and property, with demands for intervention from influential individuals and groups, Wilson was sorely perplexed as to what course to pursue. Which party or faction offered the best hope for the triumph of constitutional government in Mexico?

Carranza had the advantage of having a number of able men in both countries who argued that he had the best claim for recognition; but Carranza himself was stubborn, pig-headed, lacking in diplomacy, and jealous and suspicious of his associates as well as of the sincerity of Wilson and his advisers. Moreover, some of Carranza's proposed reforms were opposed by the Catholic church in Mexico and by powerful Catholic prelates in the United States. In formulating policies both Wilson and Carranza had to take account of their respective constituencies. In view of the approaching presidential campaign, Wilson had to play a game that would leave the impression on the public mind that his hand was forced and that the recognition of Carranza was the only way out. Carranza could not divest himself of the suspicion that the occupation of Vera Cruz by American troops was not devised solely for the good of his cause. Moreover, the war between the two countries was too recent to have been forgotten. It was difficult for him to credit the humanitarian professions of the United States, even though spoken by so high-minded a man as Woodrow Wilson.

Fortunately, the United States and Great Britain were no longer at odds over Mexico, as they had been during Lind's sojourn at Vera Cruz. The World War made it necessary for British statesmen to remove every cause of friction between the two governments. Lind was instrumental in having Sir Lionel Carden, the British minister to Mexico who was closely allied with the British oil interests, recalled. Thereafter the United States had virtually a free hand in dealing with Mexico.

After weeks and months of uncertainty, during which the newspapers had printed contradictory and highly sensational stories about the state of affairs in Mexico, Secretary Lansing called an informal conference of the diplomatic representatives of Argentina, Brazil, Chile, Guatemala, Bolivia, and Uruguay to confer with him with reference to an opportune time to recognize a responsible government in Mexico; and on October 19, 1915, formal recognition was given to the Carranza government.

The recognition of Carranza was in a way a triumph or vindication for the Wilson administration, and it paved the way for a revolution in Mexico as profound as any that has taken place in modern times. Unfortunately, within a few months a series of events threatened to undo everything that had been accomplished by it, and to bring the two countries to the verge of war. During the presidential campaign of 1916 the Republicans seized upon the Mexican problem to make an issue that might contribute to the healing of the schism in their party that had given Wilson the largest electoral vote in history down to that time. The press teemed with dispatches and editorials breathing hostility against Mexico. Theodore Roosevelt in particular was unmerciful and uncharitable in flaying what he called the "weak" policy of Wilson.

General Pancho Villa, one of the leaders who had fought to overthrow Huerta, was disappointed that Carranza and not he had been recognized as the head of the *de facto* government, and he made common cause with the forces of reaction to overthrow Carranza and to complicate the relations between the United States and Mexico. A series of crimes perpetrated in the early weeks of 1916 against Americans in Mexico and raids across the border which resulted in the death of civilians and soldiers caused Wilson to order Brigadier-General John J. Pershing to pursue Villa and his bandits across the border to capture them dead or alive.

The penetration of an American army into Mexican territory was embarrassing to Carranza, who had to frame his policy with respect to public opinion. Throughout the winter and spring glaring headlines played up skirmishes and raids until on May 31, 1916, the American government received a long note from the Mexican government, questioning the good faith of the United States and threatening war. This insulting note was made public on the eve of the assembling of the Republican national convention and furnished the occasion for savage attacks on Wilson and for demands for the complete occupation of Mexico. To make matters worse, on June 16 Carranza notified General Pershing that any movement of his troops east, west, or south would be met with bullets. The reply of the American government to this was an order from the War Department mobilizing the militia on the border, and a stiff note from the State Department accusing Carranza of bad faith and warning him that if

American troops were attacked, the United States would not be responsible for the consequences. Carranza was told that American troops would remain in Mexico until the government had assurance that its citizens would be protected.

The afternoon papers of June 20 published Lansing's note; and two days later headlines reported a battle between American troops and Carranza forces near Carrizal. In this serious crisis, with public sentiment aroused to a high pitch of indignation, Wilson on June 25 sent a circular to the Latin American governments stating that the United States had no intention of intervening; and to Carranza he addressed a note demanding the release of American prisoners and an early statement of his intentions. Evidently Wilson wanted to make it plain to the world that the United States did not desire war and that if it came, it would be at the choice of Carranza.

Wilson's level head, the well-used influence of certain individuals in both countries, the release by Carranza of the American prisoners, and a remarkably conciliatory note from the Mexican government paved the way for the appointment by the respective governments of representatives to a joint commission which held its first meeting at New London, Connecticut, on September 6, 1916. A protocol was signed on November 26, providing for the eventual withdrawal of American troops and for an arrangement by which the forces of both countries should patrol the border.

The withdrawal of the last American soldier from Mexico on February 5, 1917, the presentation by the American ambassador of his credentials to Carranza on March 3, and the election of Carranza as president eight days later augured well for the future. But events since those auspicious days proved that it was a gigantic task to set the Mexican house in order; and succeeding administrations were perplexed by problems that more than once threatened to precipitate war or intervention.

When Wilson's Mexican policy is seen in retrospect, it appears that in spite of the fact that the idealistic President did not understand Mexico or the Mexicans, in the long run his policy worked out as well as any other would. The cause of liberal government is heavily indebted to him. Moreover, Wilson's policy of enlightened self-interest, though thwarted to some degree by the Mexicans themselves and by partisan politics in his own country (as in the case of the proposed treaty with Colombia), heralded a time of better understanding between the United States and the republics of Latin America. His refusal to take forcible occupation of Mexico, his willingness to call their diplomatic representatives into consultation, and his memorable address before the Southern Commercial Congress at Mobile, Alabama, on October 27, 1913, were all most favorable factors. Wilson spoke to Latin America when he "took this occasion to say that the United States will never seek one additional foot of territory by conquest." "It is a very perilous thing," he said, "to determine the foreign policy of a nation in the terms of material interest." Wilson's words were intended to dispel the conviction in the Latin American mind that the Monroe Doctrine was a shield for the imperialistic ambitions of the United States. His acts were intended to make the Latin American states partners in shaping the destiny of the Western Hemisphere.

By means of an agreement effected in Washington, the British government promised not to interfere with the American policy in Mexico, and President Wilson promised to urge upon Congress the repeal of the provision in the Panama Canal Act of August 24, 1912, exempting American ships engaged in coastwise shipping from paying tolls through the Panama Canal. The British claimed that the exemption violated the spirit of the Hay-Pauncefote Treaty of 1902, as interpreted in the light of the Clayton-Bulwer Treaty of 1850.

Although the Democratic platform of 1912 favored the exemption of ships engaged in coastwise trade, Wilson in a brief and strong message read to a joint session of Congress recommended repeal of the provision in the existing law. "Whatever may be our own differences of opinion concerning this much-debated measure, its meaning is not debated outside the United States," he said. "The large thing to do is the only thing we can afford to do, a voluntary withdrawal from a position everywhere questioned and misunderstood." He closed the address with these pregnant words: "I ask this of you in support of the foreign policy of the administration. I shall not know how to deal with other matters of even greater delicacy and nearer consequences if you do not grant it to me in ungrudging measure."

At the time there was some speculation as to the meaning of the "other matters," but it was strongly suspected that this referred to Mexico. Be that as it may, Congress was immediately deluged with telegrams and petitions, many of them coming from Irish-American and German-American societies, declaring for an "American as against a British interpretation of the treaty." On the whole, the message was well received by the American press, with the natural exception of the anti-British Hearst publications; but it precipitated a spectacular debate in Congress.

The Democratic speaker of the House, Champ Clark, made the effort of his life to defeat the President's proposal. The leader of the Republican minority, James R. Mann of Illinois, and the leader of the small Progressive group, Victor Murdock of Kansas, also opposed repeal; but it passed by a vote of 247 to 161. In the Senate the fight against the bill was led by James A. O'Gorman, a Democrat of New York; but, curiously enough, one of the strongest speeches in support of the President was made by a prominent Republican and later the archenemy of Wilson, Henry Cabot Lodge of Massachusetts. The vote in the Senate was 50 yeas to 35 nays.

This was a brilliant victory for Wilson; but to some it seemed to presage the beginning of the end of the harmony in the Democratic party which had made possible the enactment of such far-reaching legislation as the Underwood Tariff and the Federal Reserve Act. Moreover, Wilson's courageous stand branded him as pro-British in the judgment of German sympathizers after the outbreak of the World War in the following summer.

On Monday, June 29, 1914, the papers carried the news of the assassination of the archduke and heir to the Austrian throne; and a month later, on Tuesday, July 28, they reported that Austria had declared war on Serbia and that the danger of a European conflagration was great. On the following day the stock exchanges of the world, including New York and Chicago, were

closed. Almost overnight Europe became an armed camp and international communications were almost entirely suspended. On
Sunday morning, August 2, the papers brought the news that
Germany had declared war against Russia and that the general
European war, which had been predicted for years, was a step
nearer. Before the end of the week Great Britain, France, Russia, Belgium, Serbia, Germany, and Austria-Hungary were engaged in what became the greatest war in history; and Americans were eagerly buying papers telling about the preparations
for a gigantic battle in Belgium in order to prevent the invasion
of France by the Germans.

During the early days of the war public sentiment in the
United States appeared to be hostile to Germany, although the
press was guarded in its statements. About the middle of the
month the papers took note of Japan's ultimatum to Germany
demanding that she withdraw from the Shantung Peninsula and
that she keep her warships out of Far Eastern waters. At the
same time Japan assured the United States that the integrity of
China must be maintained. On August 18 President Wilson stated
that the United States was not affected by the Far Eastern situation, and at the same time he issued an address to the American
people counseling them to refrain from taking sides and from
discussing the war from partisan angles. "The people of the
United States are drawn from many nations, and chiefly from
the nations now at war," he said. "It will be easy to excite passion
and difficult to allay it. Those responsible for exciting it will assume a heavy responsibility, responsibility for no less a thing than
that the people of the United States, whose love of their country and whose loyalty to its government should unite them as
Americans all, bound in honor and affection to think first of
her and her interests, may be divided into camps of hostile opinion, hot against each other, involved in the war itself in impulse
and opinion if not in action."

The President's statement was bitterly assailed, but under the
circumstances then existing it was the height of wisdom. Although
Wilson could have had no inkling of the increasing magnitude
and bitterness of the war and of the infinitely complicated prob-

lems it would create for his own government, he was aware of the composite composition of the American population and of the inevitable cleavages of public opinion with respect to any action that he might be compelled to take in order to maintain neutrality and protect the rights of American citizens. Wilson knew that individuals and groups of individuals would take sides in a titanic conflict that not only involved the honor and safety of the country but also aroused age-long sympathies and hatreds within the hearts of individuals.

The difficulty of Wilson's position was greatly augmented by the intensive propaganda to enlist American sympathy conducted by both sets of belligerents. Only after the war was over did the American people become aware of the insidious and unscrupulous propaganda that permeated the press, the schoolroom, the pulpit, and even the officials of the American government itself. Much that was written and said by eminent men during the war was not pleasant reading to them in after years. A whole library of books and pamphlets was written in all countries to supply the social psychologist with a mountain of evidence on the instability of the human mind. In the avalanche of propaganda that overwhelmed the world, it was impossible to maintain perspective. The historian who sits in judgment on the men who played their parts during the holocaust is prone to forget that they were mere pawns moved hither and yon by forces that were seen and unseen.

The most vocal and acrimonious criticism of Wilson came from the German-Americans and Irish-Americans and those who sympathized with their points of view. To them it seemed that Germany had been grossly misrepresented; that Germany was fighting a defensive war; that in Germany's position every nation would do what Germany was doing; and that there was no essential difference between German militarism and British navalism. On the other hand, Wilson was savagely attacked by Theodore Roosevelt for his alleged failure to discern the clear-cut contest between the high moral principles for which the Allies were fighting and the barbarism of the Germans.

Wilson has been criticized for failing to recognize that the blame for the ferocious warfare which violated international law and flouted the rights of neutrals rested not only on one set of belligerents but that both were guilty to a degree; that he countenanced the sale of munitions to the belligerents and thereby offended those who could not profit by it; that by permitting huge loans to the Allies he thereby involved the government; and that he was misled by the American ambassador to Great Britain, Walter Hines Page and by his closest adviser, Edward M. House, both of whom were ardently pro-British and amateurs in diplomacy. Every one of these indictments could be, and has been, refuted by Wilson's defenders, who contended that he did make protests to both sets of belligerents; that he could not have made new international law at that time; and that Ambassador Page had not the slightest influence over him, except to confirm his distrust of the British government.

It was recognized that the great natural resources and wealth of the United States could be drawn upon to furnish materials for war and loans to finance the war. In this the advantage lay with Great Britain and France, partly because of sentimental reasons, but chiefly because the British navy controlled the sea. In wars that assume the proportions of life and death struggles between nations, belligerents restrict the rights of neutrals as far as it is deemed safe to go. In the World War Great Britain sought to prevent the importation into Germany of food and all other commodities that would prolong the conflict. Her navy was strong enough to compel the German navy to stay within the shelter of her own harbors and to make it difficult for neutrals to trade directly with Germany; but according to international law Great Britain had no right to seize ships carrying cargoes to Dutch or Scandinavian ports from which they could be transported to Germany.

Without entering into the technicalities of international law and without attempting to assess the blame for the "first" violation of the rights of neutrals, let it suffice to say that before the war had been in progress many weeks the belligerents were at the old game of hurling charges of atrocities at one another and of accusing one another of violating international law. The student of history knows that it is a part of the grim business of war for governments to vie in attempting to fasten unworthy motives and charges of excessive cruelty upon their enemies. Even the dispatches of generals in the field to their respective war departments cannot be taken at face value. The World War assumed such a character that it invaded the domain of science and letters. The intellectual world was divided in twain. Great libraries ceased to receive the books and reviews of enemy countries.

Great Britain on her part, alleging that Germany was planting mines "of the prohibited class" in the open waters of the North Sea, claimed the right of taking retaliatory measures. She laid mines in designated areas and notified neutrals that it would be dangerous for their ships to enter them. She maintained a long-range blockade of German ports by declaring the North Sea to be a military area. She steadily increased the list of contraband articles and brought neutral ships into British ports for search, instead of searching them at sea. She opened and censored mail with a ruthless disregard for neutral rights.

At the beginning of the war Germany was inferior to Great Britain on the sea, but she employed submarines on a large scale not only for the purpose of sinking warships but also for sinking merchantmen, without providing for the safety of passengers and crew. It was her intention to whittle down the British merchant marine by this illegal use of submarines. At the beginning of February, 1915, she announced her intention to torpedo merchant ships bound for the British Isles, without warning and without regard for the safety of passengers and crew.

By the middle of February the United States protested Britain's use of the American flag for merchantmen, and Germany's announced intention of enforcing a submarine blockade of the British Isles. Both protests were friendly but firm. Germany was informed that she would be held to "strict accountability" for the destruction of American lives and property.

Despite this protest, Germany put her blockade into operation and sank merchantmen without warning; and Great Britain declared that she would shut off all food supplies for Germany. By this time the American press was overwhelmingly on the side of Great Britain and supported the position of the American government. In order to counteract this, German sympathizers held mass meetings all over the country demanding that the United States place an embargo on arms and munitions. This would have injured Great Britain, whose control of the sea made it possible for her to purchase munitions in the United States. At a "peace meeting" in Chicago on February 7, 1915, German-Americans hissed the name of Secretary of State Bryan. On the other hand, several periodicals like the *Nation,* the *New Republic,* the *Outlook, Harper's Weekly,* and *Collier's Weekly* were fearless in denouncing the activities of the German-Americans and the Irish-Americans. They were stigmatized as "hyphenated citizens," whose allegiance was divided between their adopted country and their native lands.

The war zone had been established for about ten weeks when the world was horrified to learn that on the afternoon of May 7, 1915, a German submarine had sent a torpedo crashing into the side of the Cunarder *Lusitania* off the Old Head of Kinsale, Ireland, causing the death of 1,195, of whom 128 were Americans. Previous to the sailing of the *Lusitania* the German embassy in Washington had inserted advertisements in American newspapers warning travelers against taking passage for the British Isles because vessels flying the British flag or the flag of any of her allies were liable to destruction; but few believed that the threat would be carried out.

The press was filled with stories of the tragedy, and papers that had previously only whispered hostility against Germany now thundered in unmistakable language that American honor and dignity could no longer be silent. The people trusted Wilson, although some maintained that the *Lusitania* would not have been sunk if the government had pursued a firmer policy. Theodore Roosevelt denounced the Germans as "barbarians" and "pirates" and scathingly criticized the Wilson administration, which he accused of inconsistency in its dealings with Germany and Mexico. The administration, he said, had refused to go into Mexico because it would be acting in the interest of American dollars, and now it refused to act in the name of humanity for the sake of

American dollars. German sympathizers, on the other hand, pointed to the inconsistency of the administration which had served notice that Americans remained in Mexico at their own risk and then insisted on protecting citizens who risked their own lives and jeopardized the peace of their country by traveling in the German war zone.

For a week the American nation was tense with anxiety and expectation as to the character of the note that would be forthcoming from their government. On May 10 Wilson addressed a meeting of newly naturalized citizens in Philadelphia and threw out certain statements that were taken as indications of his action or as "feelers" of public opinion. Conscious of the fact that the eyes of millions of naturalized citizens were upon him, he made an appeal for their confidence in the government. He counseled naturalized citizens to be thorough Americans and not to think of themselves in groups. "A man who thinks of himself as belonging to a particular national group in America has not yet become an American, and the man who goes among you to trade upon your nationality is no worthy son to live under the Stars and Stripes," he said.

The President made no direct reference to the *Lusitania* or to the Imperial German government, but he knew the thought that was uppermost in the minds of his countrymen—the possibility of war. He delivered himself of a statement that was as much attacked as it was misunderstood and misrepresented. "The example of America must be a special example," he said. "The example of America must be the example not merely of peace because it will not fight, but of peace because peace is the healing and elevating influence of the world and strife is not. There is such a thing as a man being too proud to fight. There is such a thing as a nation being so right that it does not need to convince others by force that it is right."

The first *Lusitania* note was made public on May 14. In effect it informed the German government that the American people could not bring themselves to believe that an enlightened nation like Germany would countenance such a dastardly crime as the slaughter of innocent non-combatants. It expected Germany to cease her unrestricted submarine warfare against merchantmen. It closed with these ominous words: "The Imperial German government will not expect the government of the United States to omit any word or act necessary to the performance of its sacred duty of maintaining the rights of the United States and its citizens and safeguarding their free exercise and enjoyment."

With the exception of the German-American press, the newspaper comments on the note were highly laudatory. They agreed that the President had been tried and found equal to the occasion and should therefore be backed up in the present crisis, especially in view of the excellent poise he had shown in the preparation of the note. Wilson understood that a nation may be carried away by the passions of the moment, and he took time to allow the points of view of the German and American people to sink into his mind. He left open a door through which Germany might retire with honor and still satisfy the demands of an indignant people.

Wilson's insistence that merchantmen should not be sunk without warning and without providing for the safety of passengers and crew eventually brought the United States into the war; and he has been criticized for insisting on the letter of the law in a war-torn world in which Germany's enemies were guilty of outrages on American rights. His critics argued that it was no worse for Germany to suffocate thousands in the waters of the war zone than it was for Great Britain by means of an illegal blockade to starve a whole nation, including women and children. But Wilson probably felt at the time of the *Lusitania* crisis that for the great and powerful neutral nation which he represented to condone the kind of warfare practiced by Germany would be to surrender whatever safeguards for neutrals had been won in the slow process of abolishing international anarchy. As he later said, Germany was making war on mankind.

On Memorial Day the newspapers published the text of the German reply to Wilson's note. It was an evasive document which quibbled over matters which Wilson regarded as non-essential. Then followed more than a week of suspense and speculation as to the contents of the forthcoming American note, an interval

that furnished another sensation. On June 9 heavily leaded headlines announced the resignation of Secretary of State Bryan because he could not approve of the forthcoming reply to Germany.
He was fearful that it would lead to war. Bryan's resignation
won for him the warm applause of German sympathizers and
opponents of war.

Two days later, on June 11, the text of Wilson's reply was
made public. It was firm but courteous, and not nearly as stiff
as the world had been led to expect because of Bryan's resignation.
The note reiterated the stand taken in the first note and swept
aside technicalities in the German note. It asked for assurance
that citizens of the United States be allowed the freedom of the
seas. The reasonableness of the note robbed Bryan of any advantage he may have expected, and it left the door open for
further negotiation. Bryan issued an address to German-Americans exhorting them to use their efforts to maintain peace between
the two nations. The former Secretary also defended Wilson's
refusal to lay an embargo on arms and munitions.

The German reply to Wilson's second note was delayed until
July 11, and again the American demand was evaded. It promised
protection to American vessels and safety to Americans traveling
on other vessels provided the American government guaranteed
that such ships carried no contraband of war.

In his reply, about two weeks later, the President adroitly put
an end to Germany's stalling by serving notice that the United
States stood by its original principles and expected the German
government to respect them. Failure to do so would be regarded
as "deliberately unfriendly." Though not an ultimatum, in effect
it was exactly that.

During July, August, and September, 1915, the problems of
the Wilson administration were further complicated by the seriousness of the Mexican situation; by the sinking of the White Star
liner *Arabic* by a German submarine, with the loss of two American citizens; and by the revelation that the Austrian ambassador,
Constantine Dumba, had fomented trouble and strikes in American industrial plants and had violated diplomatic usage by employing an American citizen traveling under an American passport

to carry messages to his government. The ambassador was recalled at the demand of the United States.

The year 1915 ended without Germany having disavowed the
sinking of the *Lusitania* and without her having given unconditional compliance with Wilson's demands in his notes. The year
also closed in gloom for the Allies; and but for the ill-advised
submarine campaign and the bungling secret service system of
the Central Powers, public sentiment in the United States might
have veered in favor of Germany. Notwithstanding acrimonious
criticism of Wilson's "weak" foreign policy emanating from certain quarters—notably from Republican leaders—the country as
a whole approved of his efforts to avoid intervention in Mexico
and to keep out of the war in Europe.

The first six months of the following year—the presidential
election year—provided an even greater test for Wilson's diplomacy. Villa's raids across the border were followed by General
Pershing's pursuit of the bandit deep into Mexican territory
and by Carranza's vigorous protest. The sinking of the French
channel steamer *Sussex* on March 24 brought the relations between the United States and Germany once more to the breaking
point. There were also ominous signs of revolt in Congress against
Wilson's diplomacy. With the approach of the pre-convention
campaign, a number of Senators and Representatives were fearful of their political lives because of threats from Germans and
Irish and those who sympathized with their point of view.

There were heated debates in Congress over the advisability
and the right of American citizens to take passage on armed merchantmen flying the flags of belligerents, and over the proposition
to lay an embargo on arms and munitions. Resolutions were introduced warning citizens against traveling on armed merchantmen. The situation came to a head during the closing days of
February and the early days of March, when Wilson wrote a
letter to the ranking member of the Committee on Foreign Relations in the House requesting an early vote on the resolutions
warning American citizens against taking passage on armed merchantmen flying the flags of the belligerents, because the uncertain

attitude of Congress hampered his conduct of foreign relations. The President demanded a "showdown."

John Sharp Williams, one of the ablest debaters in the Senate and trained in German universities, defended the President's course and said it was a "case of America first or Deutschland über alles." On March 4, 1916, the Senate voted to table the Gore resolution, with 47 Democrats and 21 Republicans sustaining the President and 12 Republicans and 2 Democrats in opposition. On March 7 the House tabled the similar McLemore resolution by a decisive vote, with prominent Democrats in opposition to the President and the rank and file supporting him. Most of the votes cast against Wilson's policy were Republican. This triumph for the President immeasurably strengthened his hand in dealing with the new crisis that had developed with Germany.

On February 10, 1916, Germany announced that after February 29 armed merchant vessels would be treated as warships by German submarines. Against the advice of some of his closest counselors, who believed that Germany was justified in making a distinction between armed and unarmed merchantmen, Wilson refused to accept a "single abatement of right"; and after the *Sussex* had been torpedoed, he addressed Congress on April 19, reviewed briefly the history of the submarine controversy and conveyed the information that he had issued an ultimatum to Germany. He had notified the German government that unless it should immediately declare and effect an abandonment of its present methods of submarine warfare, the United States would sever diplomatic relations.

Germany took her own good time to reply to the ultimatum; and when the note was made public on May 5, the newspaper comments, except those in the German-American press, were mainly hostile. After insinuations about the insincerity of the sentiments of humanity which the American government "extends with such fervor to the unhappy victims of submarine warfare," the note stated that German commanders had been notified to conduct warfare according to the American demands. The promise was conditional, however, upon the success of the United

States in obtaining Great Britain's promise to abandon her illegal trade restrictions. Failing to do so, the German government reserved to itself complete liberty of action.

The American reply to this note was an exceedingly clever "last word." The United States accepted the assurance that Germany would conduct submarine warfare with due respect for the rights of neutrals, but added that it could not entertain, much less discuss, the suggestion that respect for the rights of citizens of the United States by German naval authorities should be made contingent upon the conduct of any other government. "Responsibility in such matters is single, not joint; absolute, not relative," said the President.

This was the state of affairs that continued through the presidential campaign. Germany's compliance with the ultimatum was conditional, although Wilson refused to recognize the validity of the condition.

In spite of what at times appeared to be insuperable obstacles, Wilson had through two years maintained peace with both sets of belligerents. The chief indictment of his policy at the time, and it has since been maintained, was that it did not take sufficient account of the fact that Germany's submarine warfare was in the nature of a reprisal for the illegal blockade maintained by Great Britain. It was alleged that America's neutrality was technical and that the language of the notes to Germany was sharp and threatening, whereas the protests against Britain's interference with the mails and with American shipping were unusually polite and friendly. In the *New York Times* of May 21, 1916, a well-known professor of history and government, Albert Bushnell Hart of Harvard, used caustic language in contrasting Wilson's insistence that Germany should conduct warfare with due respect for humanitarian principles and then rapping her over the knuckles for suggesting that Great Britain be compelled to do likewise.

During the presidential campaign Wilson avowed that he was playing for the verdict of mankind; but events proved that he was unusually skillful in playing for the verdict at the polls in November. His opponent was as politically inept as he was capable.

CHAPTER XXV

THE PRESIDENTIAL CAMPAIGN OF 1916

WHEN THE DEMOCRATIC NATIONAL CONVENTION ASSEMBLED AT St. Louis on June 14, 1916, any serious opposition to the re-nomination of Woodrow Wilson had vanished. The man who had succeeded to the leadership of a badly divided Democratic party which had come into power largely as a result of the split in the Republican party had proved himself to be a masterly leader of men and had been instrumental in having enacted the most far-reaching legislative program since the administration of Lincoln. At the end of the first year of his term the news-papers, regardless of party, praised his administration and paid tribute to his ability and sincerity. The only vulnerable part of his record was his handling of the Mexican situation; but even there it was recognized that if he succeeded in eliminating Huerta, his policy would meet with approval. After the injection of prob-lems of diplomacy connected with the World War, criticism of the President became increasingly partisan; and at the opening of the year 1916 there were grave doubts as to whether or not he could be reelected. Much depended on the success of the Re-publican leaders in healing the schism in their party.

In shaping the strategy of the campaign Wilson had the advice of the astute Colonel House; but Wilson himself was no amateur in the political game. Both men realized that the election of Wilson hinged upon the success of the Democratic efforts to at-tract the votes of the Progressives who had deserted the Republican party to support Theodore Roosevelt. For this reason Wilson stu-diously avoided any direct answer to the bitter attacks launched against him by the Bull Moose; he understood that Roosevelt still had a large personal following that would resent personal at-tacks upon their hero in the previous campaign. In fact, Wilson was so careful to avoid mention of Roosevelt's name during the campaign that the latter could not restrain his feeling and publicly said, "Why doesn't Wilson mention my name? Is he afraid of me?" Roosevelt had met his match. His hatred of Wilson knew no bounds. Against Wilson's finesse Roosevelt thundered in vain.

HIS FIRST YEAR'S REPORT.

The Chicago Tribune

In 1916 it was not the Roosevelt of 1904 and 1908 who appealed to the electorate. Approaching age, failing health, and bitterness engendered by his disappointment in 1912 congealed into such fanatical hatred of Wilson that even many of his staunch admirers could not understand his opposition to a President who had thrown his influence with the progressive elements of both parties. Roosevelt was undoubtedly sincere in believing that Wilson had failed to pursue a foreign policy that carried respect. In his correspondence with Senator Lodge he classed Wilson with the "Jefferson and Buchanan type." He believed that if Wilson had used his influence to strengthen the army and navy of the United States, his notes to Mexico and Germany would have brought those governments to respectful consideration of the rights of American citizens. He even went so far as to denounce Wilson as a "Byzantine logothete" and compared his alleged betrayal of the rights of humanity with that of Pontius Pilate.

In reviewing the record of his administration, the historian finds inconsistencies with and lapses from the idealism of Wilson's public utterances. However, in the avalanche of events that descended upon the country, no President could have anticipated the situations that arose. Moreover, Wilson was conscious of the fine traditions of his office, and his very position precluded the frankness of his adversaries. Rather should the historian censure a former President who above everyone else ought to have been charitable in his judgments of the man who faced infinitely more difficult situations than he had confronted himself.

In his message to Congress in December, 1914, Wilson expressed strong disapproval of further increases in the regular army and declared that a militia and a strong navy for defense were all the country needed. Increased armament, he said, would injure the country's rôle as a disinterested and peaceful nation. In his annual message delivered a year later, everything was subordinated to national defense. It declared for the maintenance of the Monroe Doctrine and adopted an optimistic tone about the future relations between the United States and Latin America. The message concluded with a stinging rebuke to Americans who put the interests of their native country above loyalty to their adopted land. He asked for legislation to stamp out this dangerous element. "Such creatures of passion, disloyalty, and anarchy must be crushed out. They are not many, but they are infinitely malignant, and the hand of our power should close over them."

In the early weeks of 1916 the President made a series of "preparedness" speeches in several cities, partly to counteract the criticism of his failure to secure a satisfactory settlement of the *Lusitania* controversy, and partly to win the confidence of the country in his peaceful intentions and at the same time to prepare it for a spontaneous and effective response if it became necessary to resort to warlike measures. The Pershing expedition into Mexico and the seriousness of the relations with Germany reinforced the attacks of his adversaries who said he was negligent in preparing for national defense. The resignation of Secretary of War Lindley M. Garrison in February, 1916, over a disagreement with the President as to the reorganization of the army was also seized upon to embarrass the administration.

Wilson also reversed himself on women's suffrage and a tariff commission, both of which were indorsed in the Progressive platform of 1912. The South was opposed to women's suffrage, and Wilson had taken the position that this was a matter for the individual states to decide; but on the eve of the presidential campaign he came out definitely for a suffrage amendment to the Constitution and in favor of a tariff commission, which he had formerly opposed.

Perhaps the most brilliant appeal to the progressive West was the nomination of Louis D. Brandeis to the Supreme Court. This Boston attorney had taken a leading part in exposing the corrupt financing of railroads and insurance companies, had fought for the interests of organized labor, and had delivered telling blows in favor of conservation in the famous Ballinger-Pinchot controversy in the Taft administration.

The nomination of Brandeis was sent to the Senate during the closing days of January, 1916, and from then until June 1, the united forces of the American Bar Association, representatives of big business, the metropolitan newspapers, fanatical haters of Jews, and individuals like William H. Taft, Elihu Root, Henry Cabot Lodge, and A. Lawrence Lowell fought to defeat the confirmation of a great liberal and the first Jew to sit on the Supreme

Court. Again Wilson won a spectacular victory. Only one Democratic Senator voted against confirmation, and only four Republicans voted in favor. The Brandeis appointment was an important factor in swinging the labor vote to Wilson and in cementing the political solidarity of the South and the West, which, as it proved, elected Wilson. By transforming the Democratic party into an exponent of progressive measures, Wilson alienated the industrial and financial East; but in so doing, he won the West.

We have seen that the most outspoken and bitter opponent of Wilson was Theodore Roosevelt; and there were many voters who wished that the wielder of the "big stick" and the exponent of the "Square Deal" was in the White House to deal with the "barbarous" Germans and the exasperating Mexicans. Instead of writing notes, they argued, Roosevelt would command respect by action. However, the wounds that had been inflicted by the strenuous "Teddy" in the campaign of 1912 were still smarting in the Republican camp; and by his bitter denunciation of Germany and those who sympathized with her, he had overshot the mark. His name was anathema to German-Americans and to Irish-Americans.

Roosevelt's part in the history of the United States during the campaign of 1916 and during the two years that remained to him are the least satisfactory in his entire career. His one ambition—at least, the one that overshadowed all others—was to accomplish the defeat of Wilson. In the early weeks of the World War, in an article in the *Outlook* for September 23, 1914, apropos of the violation of the neutrality of Belgium by the German military forces he said: "We have not the smallest responsibility for what has befallen her." But less than two months later, in his *Fear God and Take Your Own Part*, he wrote: "When Germany thus broke her promises, we broke our promise by failing at once to call her into account." From that time on he was an uncompromising critic of the President.

As a practical politician Roosevelt knew that the only hope of defeating Wilson was by uniting the Republican party. There are indications that even during the first year of the Wilson administration he was preparing for a graceful leap back into the Republican fold. His article in the *Century Magazine* for October, 1913, on "The Progressive Party" was interpreted by some Republican papers, like the *Boston Herald*, as a preliminary step to placing himself in a position where he could accept the Republican nomination in 1916. However, in a speech at a banquet in honor of his departure for South America in the first week of October, 1913, he declared that he would never desert the Progressive party; and in the following May he gave out an interview in which he denied that he intended to join the Republican party.

The results of the elections in November, 1914, indicated that the Progressive party had few, if any, hopes for the future. On April 15, 1915, headlines announced that Roosevelt was ready to return to the Republican fold and intended to make national defense the issue in the next presidential campaign. During the following months "T. R." made speeches denouncing Germany and criticizing the "flabbiness" of Wilson's policy.

At a meeting of Progressive leaders in Chicago on January 11, 1916, an address was drawn up in which it was stated that they would support the Republican nominee if he was in sympathy with progressive principles and ran on such a platform. Several leaders expressed a preference for Roosevelt. Wilson was said to have failed to uphold American honor.

Of extraordinary significance was the meeting of Roosevelt and Elihu Root in New York on March 31, at which Senator Lodge and General Leonard Wood were also present. This was the first meeting of the former President and his Secretary of State since their break in 1912, when they bitterly attacked each other. Almost every day the newspapers reported visits of individuals and delegations to Oyster Bay to consult with Roosevelt; and in Chicago, Kansas City, and St. Louis in the latter part of May he received receptions that recalled the huge demonstrations of 1912.

On the eve of the assembling of the Republican and Progressive conventions at Chicago in June, George W. Perkins, who had assumed charge of what was left of the Progressive party, bought up the most desirable hotel space and sought to restrain the Progressives from nominating Roosevelt until a deal had been struck with the Republicans.

In the meantime the seasoned politicians who controlled the G.O.P. were playing their own game and had decided on the candidate who appeared to have the best prospects of defeating Wilson. Instead of nominating the hard-hitting Roosevelt, who had made his name anathema to the German-American Alliance and similar organizations enlisted in the cause of defending Germany, they groomed a man whose position on the Supreme Court had shielded him from current political controversies and prevented him from expressing himself on vital issues. This man was Charles Evans Hughes, who had an excellent record as a "reform" governor of New York and was recognized as one of the ablest men in the Republican party. In answer to queries as to whether or not he was a candidate for the nomination, the justice refrained from making any commitment, except to deny that he was a candidate. When the Republican national convention was called to order, however, the prospects of "favorite sons" had faded and it was a question of Roosevelt or Hughes, with a heavy advantage in favor of the latter. A stampede on the third ballot gave the honor to Hughes.

The Progressive convention nominated Roosevelt, but he declined to accept the honor until he had ascertained how Hughes stood on certain issues. After an interval of two weeks, Roosevelt gave out a letter in which he declined the nomination and indorsed Hughes. He made the extraordinary suggestion that the Progressives should nominate Senator Lodge!

By nominating Wilson the Democratic party had both the advantage and the disadvantage of presenting a candidate whose foreign policy was clean cut and public property and who adroitly took advantages of the mistakes of his opponent. Hughes violated the first principles of salesmanship by running down his competitor's goods. Neither Hughes nor his supporters developed any kind of positive appeal to the intelligent voter. In his speech of acceptance the Republican candidate waxed critical of Wilson's Mexican and European policy, but failed to outline one of his own. He was obviously playing both ends against the middle and angling for the German-American and Irish-American vote. His speeches featured Wilson's Mexican policy and his appointments, giving special emphasis to the alleged mediocrity of his cabinet. In an article in the *Independent* Hughes did nothing but castigate the Adamson law, which had the approval of organized labor.

In his references to Wilson's foreign policy, Hughes played up his failure to bring Great Britain to terms. He was often heckled and asked what he would have done when the *Lusitania* was sunk. He evaded a definite reply until at Louisville on October 12 he said that he would have severed diplomatic relations; and in reply to a heckler at Evansville, Indiana, on October 31, he avowed that he was opposed to an embargo on arms and munitions and against warning Americans off armed merchantmen. His speeches in the Northwest were coldly received. The Republican newspapers were obviously disappointed in their candidate. This was revealed unconsciously during the last weeks of the campaign when Hughes became more definite and they referred to him as the "new Hughes."

Roosevelt's part in the campaign was probably detrimental to Hughes. It was even said that Roosevelt's disappointment in the Republican candidate was so great that he deliberately made speeches to embarrass him. Be that as it may, nobody accused the strenuous "Teddy" of "pussyfooting." He not only delivered sledgehammer blows against Wilson's foreign policy but he unmercifully flayed the "hyphenated citizens." His blistering speech at Battle Creek, Michigan, on September 30 was called the "skin 'em alive speech" by the newspapers. It was difficult, if not impossible, for many voters to reconcile Roosevelt's speeches with those of Hughes. It gave Wilson the opportunity to refer to the "vocal and equivocal" wings of the Republican party.

The campaign had not progressed very far before Wilson had demonstrated his immense intellectual superiority and great generalship. His speech of acceptance was dignified, calm, and convincing. He set forth the reactionary character of the Republican party and recited a formidable list of progressive measures enacted during his administration. After enumerating such laws as the Underwood Tariff, the Federal Reserve Act, the Rural Credits

Act, the Clayton Anti-Trust Act, the income tax, the child labor law, the Federal Trade Commission, and conservation, he said: "We have in four years come very near to carrying out the platform of the Progressive party as well as our own; for we also are progressives."

Devoting a large portion of his address to foreign affairs, he avowed that his guiding principle was that property rights could be vindicated by claims for damages, but the fundamental rights of humanity could not be. "The loss of life is irreparable. Neither can direct violations of a nation's sovereignty await vindication in suits for damages," he said. "I neither seek the favor nor fear the displeasure of that small alien element amongst us which puts loyalty to any foreign power before loyalty to the United States."

In defending his Mexican policy, he admitted that he had no doubt made mistakes, but not in purpose or object. He also admitted that serious wrongs against the property and persons of Americans had been committed within the territory of Mexico. But he had heard no friend of Mexico propose interference by the United States with the internal affairs of Mexico. The Mexican people were entitled to their own country and to direct their own institutions, without interference by men of other nations and with interests alien to those of the Mexican people. "The Mexican people are entitled to attempt their liberty from such influences; and so long as I have anything to do with the action of our great government I shall do everything in my power to prevent anyone standing in their way. . . . I am more interested in the fortunes of oppressed men and pitiful women and children than in any property rights whatever."

The concluding paragraphs of the address which set forth a policy and program for justice and peace within the United States and its insular possessions and for righteousness among nations thrilled men and women who sensed the moral fervor of his words.

Wilson took advantage of the efforts of Hughes to play up to the German-American and Irish-American vote. The German-language papers and the *Fatherland*, established and edited by George Sylvester Viereck in the interest of "fair play for Germany and Austria," and such pro-German societies as the German-

American Alliance and the American Truth Society were unmistakably for Hughes. Sensing that he had no hope of attracting the votes of men who held their point of view, Wilson made an effective appeal for the votes of those who were opposed to war and also opposed to a "disgraceful" peace by sending a telegram to Jeremiah O'Leary, the president of the American Truth Society, who had addressed an insulting telegram to the President of the United States. Wilson's telegram of September 30 had the sting of an adder: "I would be deeply mortified to have you or anybody like you vote for me. Since you have access to many disloyal Americans, and I have not, I will ask you to convey this message to them."

This telegram cleared the air, as it were, and it became even more significant some days later when it came to public notice that at a meeting of some two hundred German Lutheran clergymen in Chicago assurance was given that Hughes would bring Great Britain to terms. The Democrats followed this up with the charge that Hughes himself had had a meeting with O'Leary, which the Republican candidate admitted, claiming, however, that at the time he did not know what O'Leary represented—a damaging confession in the judgment of discerning people.

During the closing weeks of the campaign Hughes apparently realized that he had overplayed his hand, and he tried to dispel the growing conviction throughout the country that he was playing both ends against the middle. After Roosevelt had made a most intemperate speech denouncing everything German in Rooseveltian fashion, Hughes sent him a congratulatory telegram. This telegram did not cause the German-language press to cease supporting Hughes, but it did disillusion certain German leaders who alleged that the Republican party intended to use the German vote merely as a catspaw in the "anything to beat Wilson" campaign. However, others continued to believe that Roosevelt was disloyal to Hughes and was deliberately trying to defeat him. There were even rumors in the press that the Republicans were seriously thinking of "muzzling" the outspoken "Teddy."

Undoubtedly, the religious issue played a part in the campaign. The World War, the Mexican imbroglio, and certain other issues and events raised what at the time was called the "anti-papal panic." The recognition of Carranza was bitterly opposed by certain Roman Catholic prelates. It was alleged that Carranza and his advisers were fanatically opposed to the Catholic church, and reports of the persecution of nuns and priests and of the desecration of churches were broadcast. The Catholic press was openly hostile to John Lind, Wilson's personal representative in Mexico, who was said to be violently anti-Catholic.

The Republicans made good use of the Mexican situation, even in the pre-convention campaign, when Elihu Root, Secretary of State under Roosevelt, delivered a scathing philippic against Wilson's policy. This line was also pursued by Hughes, whose speeches on Mexico were probably inspired by Henry Lane Wilson, ambassador to Mexico under Taft and bitterly opposed to the recognition of Carranza. In a speech at Fort Wayne, Indiana, the home of Henry Lane Wilson, Hughes asserted that President Wilson had given Lind instructions when he left for Mexico to say that "Huerta will be put out if he does not get out."

Fortunately, after the two countries had been on the brink of war in the spring and summer, their difficulties were amicably settled, and the Republican attacks lost much of their force. However, the reduced Democratic vote in certain strongly Catholic cities like New York, Chicago, and Detroit may be indicative of dissatisfaction with Wilson's Mexican policy, although, of course, the heavy Irish vote in those cities may have been more concerned about Wilson's alleged "pro-British" policy. On the other hand, Wilson's Mexican policy was heartily approved by others who resented the bases chosen for criticism.

Contrasted with Wilson's methods, the efforts of a number of Democratic campaigners to smear the issues are not at all impressive; but in comparison with the inept Republican campaign the strategy of the Democratic leaders is most impressive.

The three days following election day, November 7, were more exciting than the closing days of the campaign, and the final result was most extraordinary. The crowds that intently watched the bulletin boards on election night returned to their homes believing that Charles Evans Hughes was the next President of the United

States, although a close scrutiny of the trend of the returns gave some reason for thinking that the morning papers might show that Wilson had a majority in the electoral college. The extras issued in the forenoon carried headlines: "Wilson or Hughes—in Doubt." Both parties claimed victory. The evening extras reported Wilson in the lead with 256 electoral votes, and some 20 votes in doubt. On Thursday and Friday the result was still in doubt, with

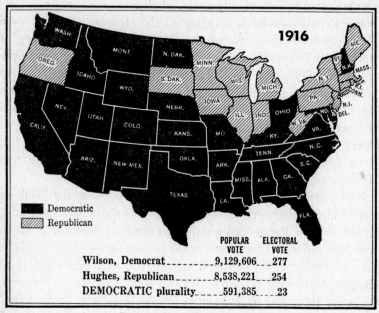

	POPULAR VOTE	ELECTORAL VOTE
Wilson, Democrat	9,129,606	277
Hughes, Republican	8,538,221	254
DEMOCRATIC plurality	591,385	23

PRESIDENTIAL ELECTION, 1916

the probability that Wilson was elected; and the Saturday morning papers were all but unanimous that Wilson was the victor. The Republicans, however, demanded recounts in several states.

It was not until November 22, after the recount in California had been completed, that Hughes wired his congratulations to Wilson, although the country for some time had accepted the fact of a Democratic victory. Wilson had 277 electoral votes, to 254 for Hughes. Wilson's plurality of popular votes was in excess of 450,000 and about 2,400,000 more votes than he had polled in 1912. He was the first Democratic President to serve two successive terms since Andrew Jackson.

Still more noteworthy is the fact that Wilson was reelected by the voters of the South and the states west of the Mississippi. East of the Mississippi, excluding the South, he carried only Ohio and New Hampshire, thus disproving the contention that a President could not be elected without the electoral vote of New York. "The scepter of power is passing to the West in conjunction with the South and Southwest," commented the *New York Evening Post*.

It was said at the time, and it has since been repeated, that the election hinged upon California, where Hughes was alleged to have made one of the most serious of his many mistakes by ignoring Hiram Johnson, Roosevelt's running mate on the Progressive ticket in 1912. In 1916 Johnson was the Republican candidate for the Senate, but his spectacular fight against the domination of his state by the Southern Pacific Railroad made him odious to the standpatters in his own party. For example, Harrison Gray Otis and his newspaper, the *Los Angeles Times*, in the interest of regular Republicanism supported the Democratic candidate and refused to print Johnson's speeches for Hughes. Hughes was the victim of the split between the Progressive and Old Guard factions in the Republican party. Johnson carried his state by 300,000 votes, and Hughes lost it by 3,800 votes.

This view, however, leaves out of account the fact that if Wilson had not carried the twenty-four electoral votes of Ohio, he would have been defeated regardless of the California vote.

It was the irony of fate that the strongholds of the Progressive movement—the states west of the Mississippi which Roosevelt had carried in the primaries of 1912—showed great Wilson strength. For example, the rock-ribbed Republican State of Minnesota, apostate only once before in a presidential election when the Progressive candidate wooed and won it in 1912, went for Hughes by only a few hundred votes. In this state, as well as others, the western Progressives were convinced that Wilson was more of their kind of progressive than Hughes. In the words of one of the most distinguished Progressive leaders, William Allen White of Kansas, "The Progressives . . . found nothing in the Hughes speeches in which to set their teeth. He talked tariff like

Mark Hanna; he talked of industrial affairs in the McKinley tongue. . . . To get the loyalty of the Progressives, Mr. Hughes had to convince them. He took them for granted and failed. . . . Naturally they turned to Wilson. He at least had Progressive achievement; not what they had hoped for, but something upon which to build."

With the exception of Illinois and Oregon, Wilson carried the states which had woman suffrage. The Democratic slogan "He kept us out of war" made an appeal to the women, as it did to the men in the former Roosevelt strongholds in the West, where peace was a passion. This slogan also appealed to the labor vote in the country at large.

Perhaps the best campaign asset the Democrats had was the prosperity of the western farmer. In spite of Republican predictions that the enactment of the Underwood Tariff would be followed by a "Democratic panic," the demands of the warring countries of Europe gave the farmers two dollars a bushel for their wheat and ten dollars a hundred for their hogs.

Relying on the unpopularity of Wilson in the East and the intense hatred of him by industrial magnates who sensed his distrust of them by his exposure of the tariff lobby, by his astute handling of the Federal Reserve Act, and by his insistence on legislation in the interest of labor, like the Clayton Act and the Adamson Act, the Republicans adopted the strategy of avoiding issues that might disturb this solidarity. It was the failure of the Republican campaign to develop any kind of positive appeal that cost Hughes the electoral vote of the trans-Mississippi region. After Hughes' visit to the Northwest, the Republican papers were critical of his superficial speeches and stated that if that was all he had to say to the voters, he had better remained at home. In contrast with Roosevelt's brutal straightforwardness, Hughes' "pussyfooting" was too obvious.

In spite of the fact that the Democrats lost their absolute majority in the House of Representatives, making the membership 213 Democrats, 212 Republicans, 3 Progressives, 3 Independents, 1 Prohibitionist, and 1 Socialist, the election was a defeat for Old Guard Republicanism and a victory for the progressive policies of

Wilson, in which younger, idealistic, and experimental men were instruments. This was revealed by the Republicans themselves after the election when their newspapers wailed over the domination by the Old Guard.

The second inauguration of Woodrow Wilson on Monday, March 5, 1917, presented a very different spectacle from that of four years before. Little of the fuss and feathers of the usual inauguration attended this one. Secret service men took utmost precautions. The inaugural address was devoted almost entirely to the new responsibilities of the American people and portended grave events. The gravity of the situation was emphasized four days later when Wilson called Congress to meet in extraordinary session on April 14. Momentous events rushed in with such torrential force that on March 21 the date for convening Congress was advanced to April 2. When that day dawned, there were few American citizens who did not know that before many days their country would be at war with Germany.

On the evening of April 3, 1917, Woodrow Wilson delivered before a joint session of Congress one of the most momentous, eloquent, and forceful messages in history. His message satisfied the most belligerent of the critics of his former policy. In the following chapter we shall give a rapid survey of events that convinced the President that it was his "distressing and oppressive duty . . . to lead this great peaceful people into war, into the most terrible and disastrous of all wars, civilization itself seeming to be in the balance."

CHAPTER XXVI

THE GREAT CRUSADE

WHILE THE POLITICIANS IN THE UNITED STATES WERE HURLING charges and countercharges and the people were enjoying prosperity, the nations of Europe were sinking into the depths of despair. Before the end of the year, on December 21, 1916, Secretary Lansing gave out an interview in which he said that the United States was in danger of being dragged into the war. Within a few hours the Secretary tried to explain away what he had said, but he made a poor fist of it. Faced with food shortages and prospects of famines, it was obvious that the belligerents would employ every available weapon and means to strangle their enemies. In the case of Germany this meant that at the propitious moment she would launch a submarine campaign of renewed intensity which would draw the United States into the terrible vortex.

As early as February, 1916, President Wilson had probably made up his mind that if the war continued for a greater length of time, the United States would be compelled to enter the conflict on the side of the Allies. Not that the President wanted war—he exasperated some of his advisers by hoping to avert it even to the last—but the trend of events across the water was too obvious to be misunderstood.

As the year 1916 drew to a close Great Britain and France were faced with a food shortage, and Germany had failed in her gigantic effort to capture Verdun. Her people were war-weary, but she had not yet shot her strongest bolt—the supreme energy of her people. Germany did not desire war with the United States; but in the death grapple that was hers, she felt obliged to do what any nation in her circumstances would have done. In the meantime deadly propaganda was doing its work. The execution of the English nurse, Edith Cavell, on October 12, 1915, by the Germans and the deportation of Belgian civilians during the later months of 1916 counted heavily against the German cause in the United States. In the closing months of 1916 there were rumors of peace; but the reorganization of the British cabinet, with David Lloyd George succeeding Herbert Asquith as prime minister, indicated that the British were determined to make no peace until the military prestige of Germany had been shattered.

In spite of the strenuous objection of his closest adviser, Colonel House, after his reelection Wilson believed that the time was propitious for him to make a move for peace. House was strongly of the opinion that any such move at the time would play into the hands of Germany and would be resented by the Allies. Wilson had made up his mind, however, when a diplomatic bombshell hurled by Germany ruined whatever chances he might have had of bringing the belligerents together at a peace conference.

On December 12, 1916, Germany made a clever move to place the responsibility for continuing the war on her enemies. In rather ambiguous language and accompanied by boasting about her prowess and invincibility, Germany proposed to make peace. On December 21, two days after Lloyd George had spurned the German proposals, Wilson's peace note was made public. In making his overture the President delivered himself of a statement that was seriously criticized at home and resented by the Allies. "The objects which the statesmen of the belligerent powers on both sides have in mind in this war are virtually the same, as stated in general terms to their own peoples and to the world," he said.

In the light of events that followed, it seems reasonable to conclude that Wilson's note was prepared to warn the American people of the crisis he knew was approaching. In a courteous and frank note dated January 10, 1917, the Allied governments replied to Wilson's note. They questioned the good faith of Germany and mildly rebuked Wilson for insinuating that the aims of both sets of belligerents were the same.

The reply of the Allies stiffened Wilson's resistance to the clamor for war, by arousing suspicions that they were not without nationalistic ambitions. Moreover, he knew that his reelection was a mandate from the people to keep the country out of war; and he knew the consequences of war and the long aftermath of problems. On January 22, 1917, Wilson broke a precedent of a century's standing by appearing in the Senate to discuss foreign policy. Comments on the address by members of Congress, by prominent individuals, and by newspapers varied from extreme praise to sarcasm. To some it was an epoch-making paper, and others ridiculed its idealism. Roosevelt attacked it on the ground that anything the government of the United States might say had no weight because of the weak policy of the administration. Bryan objected that it would not do to make the United States a party to enforcing the peace of Europe.

After positing the premise that "No covenant of cooperative peace that does not include the peoples of the New World can suffice to keep the future safe against war" and that "Only a peace between equals can last," Wilson proposed that no nation should seek to extend its polity over any other nation or people; that henceforth all nations should avoid entangling alliances; that the seas should be free; that armies and navies should be limited; and that government should be by the consent of the governed. His crowning proposal was that the nations of the world should enter a league of nations.

In a world deafened by the din of battle, there were few ears to hear the idealism of the President. Before the end of the month, on January 31, 1917, Ambassador von Bernstorff notified the United States that at midnight Germany would begin unrestricted submarine warfare.

When this announcement was made public, the tone of the press was decidedly warlike, but it counseled the people to trust the President, just as it had at the time of the *Lusitania* crisis. On Saturday, February 3, Wilson addressed Congress and, after reviewing the diplomatic correspondence between the United States and Germany, made the momentous announcement that diplomatic relations between the two governments had been severed. He expressed the hope that Germany would not carry out her threat; but in the event that his hope proved unfounded, he stated that it was his purpose to ask Congress for authority to use any means that might be necessary to protect American rights.

This action of the President was the signal for loyalty demonstrations and pledges and for federal and state governments to guard arsenals, public buildings, and bridges. Pacifists and opponents of the entrance of the country into the war also staged meetings. The submarine menace threatened to tie up the railroads because ships did not dare to venture from ports. Prices of foodstuffs soared, and there were reports of food riots in several cities. The German announcement of war zones and directions as to camouflage or the painting of ships permitted to enter the zones under very restricted conditions made the Middle West bristle over the arrogance of the war lords—and the attitude of the Middle West was decisive.

On February 26 Wilson again addressed Congress. He admitted that Germany had not as yet committed an overt act, but by tying up shipping in American ports she might accomplish what the submarine orders were meant to accomplish. He therefore asked Congress to grant authority to arm merchantmen and to authorize him to employ other means that might be necessary to protect shipping.

The message precipitated a most acrimonious debate in Congress. Certain Republican Senators out of partisan motives, and others because of opposition to warlike measures, took advantage of the expiration of Congress by constitutional limitation on March 4 to prevent a vote on the armed merchantmen bill by a determined filibuster. Of the eleven Senators who blocked the passage of the bill, eight were from the Middle West and Far West and one each from Arkansas, Mississippi, and New York. On the evening of March 4 Wilson issued a statement in which he excoriated "a little group of willful men, representing no opinion but their own," who had made the great government of the United States helpless and contemptible; and on March 9 he gave orders to the Navy Department to assist in arming merchantmen, without the specific authority of Congress.

While the Senate was deadlocked by the filibuster, the Department of State made public on March 4 the text of a note from the German Foreign Office, which, with comments, occupied the entire first page of American newspapers. The so-called "German plot" consisted of a note from Alfred Zimmermann, German foreign minister, to Count von Bernstorff, German ambassador to the United States, instructing him to inform the president of Mexico that, as soon as it was certain that there would be war between the United States and Germany, he should propose an alliance with Mexico and promise financial support in a campaign to reconquer New Mexico, Texas, and Arizona. The president of Mexico should make overtures to Japan to join forces. Two days later Zimmermann admitted the authenticity of the note, much to the discomfiture of German propagandists who had pronounced it a "stupid forgery."

Events marched through the month of March. On March 16 America was startled by huge headlines announcing that Nicholas II had abdicated and that within a week Russia had passed through a successful revolution. For some time the character of news, or the absence of news, from Russia portended some strange turn of events. There had been rumors of a separate peace with Germany, but these had always been denied by the Allies. Events proved that there was a basis for these rumors. The pro-German party was overthrown, and the army in Leningrad refused to fire on the hungry people and went over to the revolutionists. At the same time the newspapers were speculating as to the meaning of the voluntary withdrawal from a large area in France by the Germans, who with ruthless thoroughness devastated the country, even to cutting down fruit trees.

Prominent men like Theodore Roosevelt, Elihu Root, Joseph Choate, former ambassador to Great Britain, and George W. Wickersham, Attorney-General under Taft, and the newspapers bent their efforts to raise the war spirit and advocated that the country should go into the war "to the hilt." The President called out the National Guard in the Atlantic coast states, increased the number of divisions in the regular army, and ordered the navy to be recruited to its maximum strength. Military preparedness meetings were held, and college and university faculties voted to give full credit to students who enlisted. On Palm Sunday, April 1, from pulpits throughout the land allusions were made to the impending war, and flags were displayed in many sanctuaries.

When Congress assembled on April 2, Washington was over-run by propagandists, but meetings of pacifists were broken up by mobs. The venerable Senator Lodge even resorted to the use of his fists to prove his patriotism before a delegation of pacifists and received the plaudits of the newspapers.

At eight-thirty that evening President Wilson delivered his war message. He declared that the German submarine warfare was a war against mankind, a war against all nations. Armed neutrality, he said, had proved to be impracticable. After recommending that Congress declare the recent course of the Imperial German government nothing less than war against the government and people of the United States and that it formally accept the status of belligerent that had been thrust upon it and that it employ all its resources to bring the war to a successful termination, he exposed the illegitimate ambitions of Prussian autocracy. "We are now about to accept the gauge of battle with this natural foe to liberty and shall, if necessary, spend the whole force of the nation to check and nullify its pretensions and its power. We are glad, now that we see the facts with no veil of pretense about them, to fight thus for the ultimate peace of the world and for the liberation of its peoples, the German peoples included: for the rights of nations great and small and the privileges of men everywhere to choose their way of life and of obedience. The world must be made safe for democracy."

Immediately after the President had concluded, the war resolution was introduced in the Senate. La Follette objected to immediate consideration, as he had a right to do under the rules. When the majority leader, Martin of Virginia, attempted to impress upon the Senator from Wisconsin the "momentous consequences" and to lecture him for objecting to immediate consideration, La Follette replied: "Mr. President, it is quite unnecessary for the Senator to call my attention to the momentous consequences of this joint revolution. I think I realize them quite as fully as he does."

The passage of the resolution was a foregone conclusion. In the Senate the vote was 82 to 6. The negative votes were cast by three Democrats—Stone of Missouri, Vardaman of Mississippi, and Lane of Oregon—and a like number of Republicans—La Follette of Wisconsin, Norris of Nebraska, and Gronna of North Dakota.

In a speech of three hours' duration La Follette reviewed the diplomatic relations between the United States and Germany and Great Britain. The burden of his argument was that Wilson's policy was not neutral and that Germany's warfare was contingent upon the illegal mining of the North Sea and the illegal blockade of Germany. He maintained that the rights of the United States on the seas were "relative" because the government had not insisted on maintaining its rights against Great Britain. "The present administration has assumed and acted upon the policy that it could enforce to the letter of the law the principles of international law against one belligerent and relax them as to the other," he said. Williams of Mississippi immediately attacked the patriotism of La Follette and ridiculed his reasoning. He said that a man who made no distinction between the violations of international law by Great Britain and by Germany "did not know the difference between a prize court and a torpedo." With reference to Norris' allegation that by passing the war resolution "we are about to put the dollar sign upon the American flag," Williams declared: "If it be not treason it grazes the edge of treason."

The vote in the House of Representatives was as overwhelming as the Senate vote, with 373 ayes and 50 nays; and on April 6, 1917, the wireless at Arlington sputtered the news to American vessels in all parts of the world that the United States was at war with Germany.

The six Senators and many Representatives who voted against the war resolution were the victims of most bitter attacks from the press, organizations, and individuals; and efforts were made to drive them out of public life. The brunt of the attacks fell upon La Follette. War furnishes excellent opportunites for individuals of a certain type to pay off old scores by bringing charges of disloyalty and alleged disloyalty against past and present enemies. La Follette was a shining target because he had exposed the conspiracy of big business to force intervention in Mexico and, in common with other progressive Republicans, had charged that there was a conspiracy of the money power to force the United States into the World War. In his own state members of the faculty of the University of Wisconsin adopted resolutions of censure, and petitions and telegrams poured into Washington demanding that he be expelled from the Senate. On September 20, 1917, La Follette made a speech in St. Paul, Minnesota, which was grossly misquoted in the newspapers; and this precipitated another campaign to have him ousted. A week later Theodore Roosevelt delivered a speech in the same city, when his falsetto voice betrayed his hatred of the Wisconsin Senator and his "shadow Huns."

La Follette loyally supported the war measures of the government, but made no apology for his vote on the war resolution in subsequent campaigns for reelection. He did not live to accept the invitation to a public meeting, twenty years later, to honor the small group of survivors of the fifty-five men and one woman for their courage in facing the angry blasts of propaganda. A perspective of twenty years brought editorials of praise for these victims of war hysteria in newspapers whose editorials and cartoons had portrayed them as traitors.

The opponents of the war claimed that the people were opposed to it, and demanded a popular referendum. It is probably true that, the country over, the people were lukewarm and many were even opposed to it. Not only were the foreign-born divided in their sympathies for the belligerent nations, but among the native-born as well many had difficulty in reconciling themselves to a war waged beyond the seas. They argued that the roots of the war were in European soil and did not concern the people of the United States. However, as the war spirit increased, fanned as it was by high-powered propaganda and by the steadily increasing numbers of parents, brothers, and sisters who had men and women dear to them in the various services of the government, the country became a very uncomfortable place for people who did not give unstinted support to the war.

The declaration of war enabled federal and state governments to take strong measures to stamp out disloyalty and to intimidate shirkers. Very shortly Congress passed the most drastic espionage

WANT TO FEEL LIKE THIS? : : : By Briggs

The Minneapolis Journal

(From F. F. Holbrook and Livia Appel, *Minnesota in the War with Germany.*
By courtesy of the Minnesota Historical Society)

law in its history, and legislatures took similar action. In many communities citizens appointed themselves guardians of the patriotism of their neighbors; and strong-arm methods were employed to coerce people to subscribe to Liberty Loans and to give financial support to other patriotic activities.

The Committee on Public Information under competent leadership promptly assembled a staff; and within a few weeks through bulletins, pamphlets, films, and four-minute-men it acquainted the public with the war aims of the government and the issues at stake. The tone and content of the publications of this branch of public service were in striking contrast with the activities of many individuals and other "patriotic" organizations.

In his war message President Wilson made it clear that the entrance of the United States in the war would involve the "utmost practicable cooperation in counsel and action with the governments now at war with Germany, and, as incident to that, the extension to those governments of the most liberal credits, in order that our resources may so far as possible be added to theirs." It would also involve the mobilization of the material resources of the country; the full equipment of the navy; immediate additions to the armed forces, who should be chosen upon the principle of universal liability to service; and the granting of adequate credits to the government.

Promptly and without opposition Congress authorized the first Liberty Loan and voted the largest appropriation in the history of the country. It also increased import duties and taxes on incomes and profits, and raised the rates on first-class postage from two cents to three.

More opposition was encountered by the Selective Service Bill. It was objected that compulsory military service ran counter to American traditions. However, on April 29 the bill passed both houses by large majorities, but it was held up in the conference committee because of disagreement over the age limits and over the proposition to permit Theodore Roosevelt to raise an army of volunteers. As finally approved, the bill included within the scope of the draft men between the ages of twenty-one to thirty, both inclusive, and left it to the option of the President to accept Roosevelt's offer to recruit an army for overseas service.

On May 18, six weeks after the declaration of war, the President signed the Selective Service Act and issued a proclamation directing all men between the stipulated ages to register on June 5. In a separate statement he announced that a division of regulars would be sent to France as soon as possible. He added that at the present stage he would not avail himself of the authorization conferred by the act to organize volunteer divisions. To do so, he said, would be to interfere with the purpose of the conscription act. This decision was criticized in some quarters and was attributed to the President's hostility to Roosevelt; but it was in accordance with the advice of army officers, and reduced to a minimum the scramble for military appointments on the part of politicians and others who were neither prepared nor competent to discharge such duties. The President's courageous decision saved the country from a repetition of the scandals and inefficiency of the Civil War and the Spanish-American War. The appointment of General Pershing rather than General Leonard Wood, whose political activity was well known, brought severe criticism from Theodore Roosevelt and his supporters; but the President held firmly to his courageous and wise course.

The majesty of American citizenship was demonstrated on June 5, when some ten million men registered under the terms of the Selective Service Act, with little disorder. This is all the more extraordinary when one remembers that conscription was not resorted to until after the Civil War had been in progress for two years. It is true that there were many in the North who sympathized with the southern cause and were opposed to the policy of the Lincoln administration, but divisions were probably not so violent or fundamental as they were during the World War.

As in the Civil War, there was impatience with the slow progress of placing an army in the field, and there was much criticism of Secretary of War Baker and Secretary of the Navy Daniels for their alleged failure to "speed up" the war program. In view of the traditional unpreparedness of the country and the extraordinary demands on the resourcefulness of the government to transport troops overseas, it was probably more than "politeness" on the part of Arthur J. Balfour, a member of the British commission to the United States, when in a speech before the National Press Club in the latter part of May he said that American progress was "remarkable" and deprecated the charges of tardiness. It was natural, however, for the people of Great Britain and France to show impatience and to expect large contingents of American troops, in view of the fiery ordeal of three years and the seriousness of the military situation.

On June 10, 1917, the papers reported the arrival of General Pershing and staff in England; and on June 28 headlines reported that American troops had landed in France, although how many or where they had landed was naturally not indicated. One of Pershing's first recommendations from France was that a force of at least one million men be sent over as soon as possible, and a few days later he cabled that the goal should be three million. A year elapsed, however, before Pershing's estimates could be met and the American forces became an important force on the western front.

Before that time the armies of the Allies faced disaster on several fronts. In October, 1917, the defeat of General Cadorna's Italian army threatened to become a debacle. The collapse of Russia became more significant as the year drew to a close. The overthrow of the Kerensky government by the Bolsheviki brought the triumph of the peace party, and on March 3, 1918, the withdrawal of Russia from the war was confirmed by the Treaty of Brest-Litovsk.

On Palm Sunday, March 24, 1918, the minds of the American people were centered on the long-expected German drive on the western front; and their anxiety was not unlike that of the days when events appeared to be in the balance on the battlefield of Gettysburg in the first days of July, 1863. The world stood aghast at the terrific onslaughts of the "Huns" and the terrible consequences that might follow the smashing the French and British lines. After the drive had been in progress for a month, the Allies faced the probability of a retirement along the whole Ypres salient, which would necessitate the evacuation of the Channel ports. While the British army was standing at bay, literally with its back to the wall, the reports of American casualties emphasized the seriousness of the situation.

The supreme effort of the Germans to win the war before the full force of America's power could be exerted ended in failure; and if pride in achievement begets patriotism, the Fourth of July celebrations throughout the land must have radiated optimism. In a statement making public a letter addressed to him by the Secretary of War, Wilson declared that the information was so satisfactory that its publication would be welcomed and would give additional zest to the national celebration of Independence Day.

The Secretary of War reported that on July 1 there were 1,019,115 American troops overseas, of which 276,372 had been added in June alone. The United States was six months ahead of its original program of shipping overseas, said the Secretary.

Independence Day was celebrated in England, France, and Italy as though it were the natal day of those countries; and the whole world listened to the eloquent, concise, and deeply spiritual address of the President of the United States delivered at the tomb of Washington. "There can be but one issue," he said. "The settlement must be final. There can be no compromise. No half-way decision is conceivable."

With the world shrouded in gloom, and peace seemingly far away, the nations pinned their hopes on the United States. Woodrow Wilson had risen to the heights of world statesmanship. In the meantime, despite impatience, criticism, and inevitable miscalculations, American food and money sustained the Allies while every American was exhorted, encouraged, and coerced to "do his bit" to bring the war to a successful termination.

On April 15, 1917, Wilson appealed to the farmers to increase production of their land and to bring about the most effectual cooperation in the sale and distribution of their products. "The world's food reserves are low," he said. "Not only during the present emergency, but for some time after peace shall have come, both our own people and a large proportion of the people of Europe must rely on the harvests in America."

A DEPARTMENT STORE WINDOW DISPLAY

(From *Minnesota in the War with Germany*. By courtesy of the Minnesota Historical Society)

Congress gave to the President large powers over the food supply. Herbert Hoover, who had been in charge of Belgian relief, was appointed "food dictator," and "Hooverize" promptly became a word in the American vocabulary. In cities vacant lots and lawns were spaded or plowed and soon took on the appearance of vegetable gardens. Prices of food and grain soared. On May 11, 1917, the price of May wheat rose to $3.25 per bushel. In August Wilson fixed the price of wheat at Chicago at $2.20 per bushel, over the protest of farmers who wanted $2.50 and of labor delegates who held out for $1.80. Early in the war a prohibitive tax was placed on grain to be used in the manufacture of distilled spirits for beverages; and the President proclaimed an embargo on coal, gasoline, and foodstuffs.

During the war period there was grumbling among farmers who said that it was unfair to fix the price of wheat when corn, rye, and barley sold for unheard-of prices. In July, 1918, Wilson vetoed the annual agricultural appropriation bill because it fixed the guaranteed minimum price of wheat at $2.40 per bushel. The President stated that the farmers were patriotic and needed no such spur. By approving the bill, he said, the price of flour and the cost of living would be greatly increased.

State and local governments cooperated in the conservation program, and many reported instances of hoarding sugar and flour were investigated. Undoubtedly the drive for efficiency and frugality played a part in inducing Congress in December, 1917, to submit to the states for ratification a constitutional amendment providing for national prohibition. War-time economy cut down Christmas purchases, and department stores reported reduced volumes of business. Grocery stores limited the amount of sugar that could be purchased, but in spite of this speculators reaped heavy profits from steadily mounting prices.

Some regimentation was voluntary, or at least the observance of laws, ordinances, and recommendations was sometimes left to the discretion of the individual. People observed "meatless" and "wheatless" days and used a certain proportion of other cereals in making bread. More serious was the order of the fuel administrator, Harry Garfield, in January, 1918, compelling cessation of

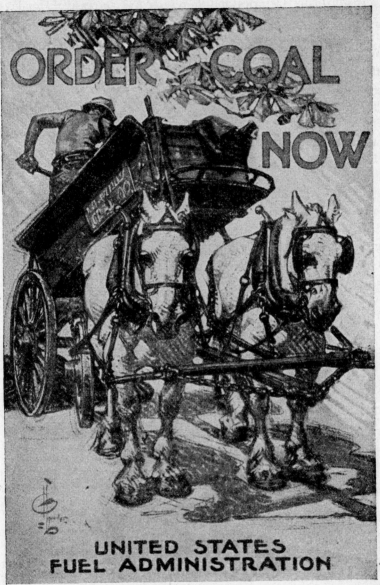

(From *Minnesota in the War with Germany*. By courtesy of the Minnesota Historical Society)

work in many factories and stores on five successive Mondays. Scarcity of fuel caused by lack of production and by congested traffic necessitated this drastic action. Floods of protests poured into Washington, and the Senate by a large majority asked that the order be delayed, but to no avail. On "heatless" Mondays grocery stores closed at noon; and drug stores and similar establishments were not allowed to sell tobacco and other non-essentials, in order not to do injustice to tobacconists and other merchants whose chief profits were derived from articles that were not deemed necessities.

In August, 1918, the fuel administrator forbade pleasure automobiling on Sundays, a measure designed to replenish the gasoline supply.

In spite of unusual cooperation and of the vigilance of the government, the Federal Trade Commission in reporting the results of its investigations charged that profiteering on a large scale was practiced in almost every necessity of life. The millers and packers came in for the most severe censure. In August, 1918, the Federal Trade Commission recommended that the government assume control of all the principal stockyards, cold storage plants, and refrigerator and livestock cars in order to destroy the monopoly of the five big firms.

Along the same line of effort to win the war, in May, 1918, the government announced a policy of making all men of draft age work or fight. All men in non-essential industries between the ages of twenty-one and thirty were to be compelled to fight or to be drafted into useful employment. This policy, together with waning interest in the game, played havoc with professional baseball, and some clubs and leagues closed their seasons early or disbanded.

The paramount necessity of transporting troops and supplies to the eastern seaboard and overseas taxed the resources and ingenuity of the government, and the administration could not hope to escape criticism. The lack of cooperation between the different railroad systems and the difficulties inherent in the operation of transportation facilities under several managements impelled President Wilson, on December 28, 1917, to take possession and assume control of the railroad lines and the systems of water transportation under their control. The President stated that the common administration would be carried out with as little disturbance of the present operating organizations and personnel of the railroads as possible; but some months later (in May, 1918) he removed the presidents of the roads. Under the director-general of railroads economies were introduced, although freight and passenger rates and the wages of employees were increased. On May 28, 1918, the four principal express companies were placed under federal control. In the face of an impending strike of union operators employed by the Western Union Telegraph Company in June, the President asked authority to take over the telegraph lines; and on July 22, 1918, he issued a proclamation designating the Post-master-General to act as supervisor.

The rising cost of living increased unrest and dissatisfaction within the ranks of labor. In certain industries wages rose to fabulous heights; but the high cost of rentals, clothing, and food made the lot of many wage earners and salaried people exceedingly difficult. Serious strikes broke out all over the country, and some of them—especially in the shipyards—threatened to disrupt the war program. In January, 1918, the Secretary of Labor, upon the nomination by the president of the American Federation of Labor and of the National Industrial Conference Board, appointed a War Labor Board for the purpose of devising a method of labor adjustment.

This body recommended the creation of a National War Labor Board to be composed of distinguished disinterested citizens and representatives of employers and employees. President Wilson appointed ten umpires on the National War Labor Board to officiate in matters pertaining to its jurisdiction. In certain situations the government was prepared to use strong measures. For example, in September, 1918, striking machinists at Bridgeport, Connecticut, were notified by Wilson that unless they returned to work and agreed to abide by the award of the National War Labor Board, they would be barred from employment for a year and draft boards would be instructed to reject any claim for exemption from military service based upon usefulness in war production. Other federal boards were charged with administrative, legislative,

MAKE EVERY MINUTE COUNT for PERSHING

UNITED STATES SHIPPING BOARD
EMERGENCY FLEET CORPORATION

(From *Minnesota in the War with Germany.* By courtesy of the Minnesota
Historical Society)

and judicial powers pertaining to labor; and state Commissions of Public Safety often intervened to iron out difficulties.

Among the important agencies of the government was the United States Shipping Board, which incorporated the Emergency Fleet Corporation to purchase, construct, equip, lease, and operate merchant ships. The work of this board was delayed by a long and tedious quarrel between the chairman of the Shipping Board and the head of the Fleet Corporation as to whether steel or wooden ships should be constructed, until President Wilson took a hand in July, 1917. Under the direction of their successors construction proceeded at such a pace that in September, 1918, the Emergency Fleet Corporation had under its jurisdiction more than ten million tons of shipping.

Perhaps the greatest disappointment was the failure of the War Department to manufacture and deliver to American aviators a sufficient number of airplanes. While a resolution proposing an inquiry into the conduct of the war was pending in the Senate in May, 1918, Wilson directed Attorney-General Gregory to investigate charges of dishonesty and malversation in regard to the production of aircraft; and he surprised the country by appointing his opponent in the campaign of 1916, Charles E. Hughes, to act with the Attorney-General in making the investigation. The Hughes report was not placed in the hands of the Attorney-General until the last days of October—a few days before the congressional elections—and thus had little influence on the conduct of the war but probably some influence on the outcome of the elections. It revealed incompetency and corruption and singled out certain individuals.

Dissatisfaction with the conduct of the war threatened to bring a congressional inquiry. In January, 1918, the newspapers severely criticized Secretary of War Baker, and there were rumors that he might be forced to retire. Wilson, however, staunchly defended the able Secretary; and when Baker appeared before a Senate committee, he declined to assume an apologetic tone and insisted that the government was doing great things. He admitted certain errors, but stated that there was a "substantial army" in France. On his appearance before a committee of the House of Representatives some days later, even the newspapers admitted that he made a fine impression.

Senator Chamberlain of Oregon, chairman of the Committee on Military Affairs, launched a severe attack on the administration, alleging inefficiency and demanding a reorganization of the administrative machinery. Roosevelt entered the lists against Wilson and sustained Chamberlain's charges. Republican Senators also joined forces with the Democratic Senator from Oregon. Defenders of the administration alleged that the movers of the investigation were actuated by motives of partisanship.

Wilson's answer to the "meddling" by Congress was a bill making him virtually a dictator. He demanded that the resolution of inquiry be voted down. If it passed, he said, it would be tantamount to a vote of lack of confidence in the administration. The President won a significant victory when the Senate by a heavy majority passed the Overman Bill, which practically gave him blanket power to effect reorganization and provided "scissors" with which to cut red tape. The House of Representatives fell in line. The Overman Act (approved May 20, 1918) was speedily followed by recommendations, legislation, and administrative orders which satisfied all but the most carping critics of the administration. The appointment of Hughes to investigate aircraft production was a shrewd strategical move and did much to disarm criticism and to obtain the passage of the Overman Act.

A chapter on the World War would not be complete without reserving a place of honor for the women. It was not only that Red Cross nurses ministered to the sick and wounded in France, on transports, and in base hospitals; but their sisters at home organized Red Cross chapters and units, spent days with needle and thread, made house-to-house canvasses, and contributed of their means. Some of the most efficient units were made up of immigrants.

No less patriotic were the women in the five Liberty Loan campaigns which were spread from June, 1917, to April, 1919, the last being called the Victory Loan. The opening of each campaign was signalized by blowing whistles and ringing bells. Merchants,

manufacturers, financiers, and other public-spirited citizens de-
frayed the cost of full-page advertisements in newspapers and of
posters exhibited in street cars and public places, even in churches.
Artists vied in producing attractive and appealing posters. Business
houses, factories, and homes were canvassed, and in not a few
cases individuals were arbitrarily assigned to purchase a certain
number of bonds. Subscribers were given buttons to display on
their persons and posters to display in windows of their homes.
War Savings Stamps in smaller denominations than Liberty
Bonds were offered to people who preferred them. The temper of
solicitors and of many leading citizens was such that if individuals did not subscribe to the amount expected of them, their
houses were painted yellow and charges of disloyalty were whispered and even shouted from the housetops.

A study of the Liberty Loan posters from the first campaign to
the last reveals what usually happens to a people engaged in a
great war. The posters of the first interpreted the idealism of crusaders against the enemies of liberty and democracy; the posters
of the last exhorted subscribers to "Keep the Hun on the Run."
As the war lengthened into months, editorials and news stories
grew increasingly bitter; and during the closing weeks it appeared
that Wilson would have greater difficulty in getting the people to
accept peace than he had had in inspiring them to support the
declaration of war. The press was almost unanimously opposed
to an armistice. "Unconditional surrender" or "On to Berlin"
was the cry. Months of propaganda and the presence of two
million American soldiers in France in part explain the belligerency
of the press and a vocal element of the people.

It will be recalled that in the winter of 1917-18 the fortunes
of the Allies were at low ebb; all they could reasonably hope to
do was to hold out on the defensive until the American forces
arrived in such numbers as to make victory possible in 1919.

Against strong pressure from the Allies, General Pershing insisted that the American army must be brought over in complete
divisions and must form a unit holding its own sector of the front
line. He refused to allow his men to fight as replacements under

foreign flags or under foreign leadership. He believed that it would imperil the morale of the fresh American soldiers to feed them into the ranks of the weakened armies of the Allies. At the beginning the Americans were sent to quiet sectors in order to release units of the armies of the Allies for active duty. After further training under their own officers, they were ready for the baptism of fire.

At the beginning of May, 1918, after the first force of the German drive had spent itself, Secretary Baker announced that there were more than 500,000 American troops in France and that by July 1 the number would be doubled. By that time the officers' training camps had turned out enough men to increase the thousands who were in training in cantonments. At the end of May, Prime Minister Lloyd George stated that for the next few weeks there would be a race between President Wilson and General Hindenburg. Wilson won the race.

After their drive toward Compiègne had been halted, the Germans waited about thirty days before launching a new offensive over a front of about sixty-five miles, on July 15. Reports from the battle front indicated that the Germans had made important gains; but America's glow of enthusiasm and pride over the achievements of her sons on the firing line raised high hopes. On July 18 the Franco-Americans made a surprise counter-attack on the confident enemy. About 85,000 American troops took part in this engagement at Château-Thierry. In some American cities bells rang and business was suspended for a time in honor of local boys who were in the battle.

While the battle of the Aisne-Marne was in progress from July 18 to August 6 the exuberancy of the American people rose to such a high pitch that rumors flew thick and fast that the kaiser was captured, that Hindenburg was dead, and that the end of the war was imminent. Some draftees lamented that they would not arrive in France in time to take part in the triumphant advance. Certain it is that the infusion of a larger number of fresh troops, unwearied by four years of war, revived the drooping spirits of the Allies and took the initiative from the enemy. Had it not been for America's decision, Italy would probably have made a separate peace with Germany after the rout of Cadorna's army in October, 1917.

On the fourth anniversary of the declaration of war on Serbia by Austria, July 28, 1918, the Sunday papers featured articles in retrospect and prospect. A syndicated writer, Frank Simonds, who had been fairly level-headed during the years he had been writing on the war, believed that the chances for the defeat of the Allies were past, or nearly past. "America, like Blücher, has come," he wrote. "And a long and bitter year is having a glorious ending." Not only had 300,000 men been sent over in July, but thousands of men in the national army cantonments were ready to go, and the tonnage necessary to transport them was there.

At the same time the food administrator issued an order to permit restaurants to serve wheat and to relax certain restrictions on housewives. The chief of staff, General P. C. March, announced that there was no danger of lack of man power to keep the armies filled up; and during the first week of August he appeared before a Senate committee to urge the enactment of a law extending the draft ages from eighteen to forty-five. Pending the disposition of the bill, voluntary enlistments in the army and navy were suspended in order to prevent disruption in industry.

On September 12, the day men between the ages of eighteen and forty-five registered, the American forces began their first great offensive. The attack was carried out by the First Army under the direct command of General Pershing. In a brilliant offensive an army of nearly 600,000 cleared the St. Mihiel salient which for four years had been held by the enemy.

On September 26 began the forty-seven-day battle of the Meuse-Argonne, in which 1,200,000 Americans were engaged—the greatest battle in American history. The British and French attacked simultaneously. In spite of stubborn resistance, the German lines were broken in several places; and at the time of the signing of the armistice, the rout was rapidly becoming a debacle.

After weeks of negotiations, which will be detailed in the following chapter, Germany accepted the harsh terms of the armistice on November 11, 1918. The day before newsboys hawked extras with monstrous headlines: "Germany in Revolution." The kaiser abdicated and fled to Holland. On armistice night American cities were riots of humanity, with streets strewn with confetti and made hideous by the blowing of horns, the ringing of bells, and the beating of pans. In truth it was a day of triumph, not of consecration to the ideals to which Wilson had dedicated the wealth and man power of the country.

In the midst of this bedlam many homes were in sadness over the loss of sons in France, and many more were in mourning over parents, brothers, and sisters who had been cut down by the deadly Spanish influenza which ravaged the country from coast to coast. Authorities closed churches, schools, theaters, and department stores; political and other meetings were suspended; and passengers in street cars sat in alternate seats. Visitors to hospitals were provided with masks after their throats had been sprayed, barbers wore the same protection, and some even wore masks on the streets. Platforms at railroad stations were piled high with coffins of the victims of the scourge.

The sudden ending of the war caught universities and colleges unprepared for the inevitable disbanding of the Students' Army Training Corps and for the invasion of a host of young men released from military service. With the opening of colleges and universities in the fall of 1918, campuses took on the appearance of military camps. Men were quartered in barracks and were expected to pursue studies in addition to intensive military training. A whole army of instructors was assigned to classes in "war aims," which were intended to acquaint the youth with the issues involved in the conflict and with the idealistic peace program of the President. Before the end of the academic year, the syllabus and lectures appeared to be hollow mockery.

Unfortunately, it was not only young men who had worn the uniform overseas, in cantonments, and in the S.A.T.C. who were disillusioned. From the wail of Lloyd George in the early part of the year that America's effort was a disappointment, to the triumphal tour of Europe by the President of the United States, the year 1918 witnessed a marvelous transformation. During the coming months observers were to focus their attention on the great drama that was about to be acted in Europe. America relaxed after a strain of two years and had no inkling of the social aftermath of the carnival of blood and hatred. Bolshevism, revolution, famine, and the revival of old hatreds and rivalries were the next acts in the drama.

CHAPTER XXVII

THE COLLAPSE OF WILSONISM

"THE PASSING OF WOODROW WILSON" WAS THE CAPTION OF MANY editorials published on March 4, 1921. Perhaps almost everyone was surprised and shocked to read about the sad physical condition of the war President on the day he was succeeded by Warren G. Harding. When he ascended the steps of the automobile, attendants placed his feet; and when he walked through a Capitol corridor to the President's room, there were murmurs of sympathy. Woodrow Wilson broken in health and spirit on that day symbolized the tragic collapse of idealism that had sustained him and millions of his countrymen. This tragic story and the story of the President's fight for a peace of justice and righteousness are the theme of this chapter.

The greatest handicap that beset Wilson was the conviction of the common man that the war was unnecessary and would not have come but for Wilson's mistaken policy of insisting on the rights of neutrals on the high seas in a war-mad world. It would not down that it was a "millionaire's war." Men who had condemned Bryan without measure a few years before called him the greatest statesman of the day because of his efforts to keep the country out of war. The disillusionment of the American doughboy after a few days of service in France was only a reflection of his reluctance to don the uniform in what he and his parents conceived to be an unnecessary war.

Nothing could give the historian a more false understanding of the temper of the mass of the American people than the press from 1917 to 1918. And even the press revealed its hypocrisy immediately after the armistice when it engaged in propaganda against the President of the United States as unscrupulous and unfair as that against Germany had been.

It has been said that Wilson was an amateur in diplomacy and the dupe of the experienced statesmen of Europe. It is true that his methods and words were strangely unfamiliar in the capitals of Europe, but they were also so straightforward and brutally true and just that during the conflict nobody in high positions dared publicly refute them. It is just as plausible to argue on the basis of the available documents that Wilson was aware of the inherent difficulties of obtaining a satisfactory peace and for that reason asserted the great moral force of the United States through a series of public addresses and statements which were designed to commit the Allies to a world settlement that would inaugurate a new day. In the early stages of the war Wilson's efforts were bent to prevent a premature peace—a peace that would continue the *status quo* and ratify the principle of the balance of power which had brought the catastrophe.

On August 27, 1917, Wilson rejected the peace proposal addressed to the belligerents by the pope because "It is manifest that no part of this program can be successfully carried out unless the restitution of the *status quo ante* furnishes a firm and satisfactory basis for it." In substance, the President said that it was useless to negotiate with the present German government because it could not be trusted. In a single paragraph there was a concise and sweeping indictment of the infamy of the autocracy of Germany and a statement of the object of the war: "To deliver the free peoples of the world from the menace and the actual power of a vast military establishment controlled by an irresponsible government." Wilson's reply was greeted by a chorus of praise from the press.

The President's annual message to Congress of December 3, 1917, was addressed to public opinion in all countries rather than to the body before which it was read. It was an answer to pacifists and other dissatisfied elements. "I hear men debate peace, who neither understand its nature nor the way in which we may attain it with uplifted eyes and unbroken spirits. . . . They may be safely left to strut their uneasy hour and be forgotten." He asked for a declaration of war against Austria-Hungary, but not against Turkey or Bulgaria.

Again the press praised the lofty eloquence of the document, and Congress responded by declaring war on Austria, with only one dissenting vote in both houses, that of Meyer London, a Socialist Representative from a district in New York City. La Follette did not vote, but stated that he would have voted against it without an amendment specifying that the United States did not indorse Italy's demands on Austria.

On January 8, 1918, the President laid down the conditions of peace—a program of world peace—in an address before a joint session of Congress. The occasion for the address was the parley at Brest-Litovsk between the representatives of the Central Powers and of Russia. A few days before, Lloyd George had answered the German peace proposals and had laid down the terms upon which the Allies would make peace.

Wilson's address was in line with his previous statements, but he went further and specified fourteen points for a peace acceptable to the United States. Omitting the details pertaining to the adjustments of boundaries, the evacuation of Belgium, and the recognition of the aspirations of races to independence, we are concerned with the general principles enunciated. Open diplomacy—no private international understandings of any kind; absolute freedom of navigation on the seas; the removal, so far as possible, of all economic barriers and the establishment of an equality of trade conditions among nations; the reduction of national armaments to the lowest point consistent with domestic safety; a free, open-minded, and absolutely impartial adjustment of all colonial claims, with the interests of the populations concerned having equal weight with the claims of the government whose title was to be determined; a general association of nations formed under specific covenants for the purpose of affording mutual guarantees of political independence and territorial integrity to great and small states alike.

In line with his war message, the President tried to drive a further wedge between the German people and the "military party and the men whose creed is imperial domination." In other words, Wilson insisted that before the military foes of Germany could discuss terms of peace, it was necessary to know whom her spokesmen represented.

This notable pronouncement called forth a chorus of praise from the newspapers and from Senators and Representatives, though some Republicans took exception to the proposal to remove economic barriers. On February 11 the President delivered another unexpected address to Congress in which he discussed the answers of Germany and Austria to his "fourteen points." By praising the speech of the Austrian foreign minister and exposing the "hollowness" of the speech of the German chancellor, he probably sought to sow dissension between the Central Powers. The President stated that the only obstacle to peace was the military party in Germany, which alone refused to indorse the principles laid down in his address of January 8. The German chancellor's reply to this address included a concession that Wilson's proposals might mean "a small step toward a mutual rapprochement"; but he insisted that so long as Great Britain retained her imperialistic ambitions and refused to apply the Wilsonian proposals to Ireland, India, and Egypt, there was little hope for immediate peace.

This long-range discussion between Wilson and the spokesmen for the Central Powers was carried on on the eve of the great German drive on the western front and while certain periodicals in the United States were outspoken in their criticisms of Japan's intentions in Siberia. It was said that the Allies were afraid to express themselves and that Wilson was alone in having the courage to speak out boldly. Wilson even sent a message of encouragement to the Russian people through the congress of the Soviets, which assembled in March.

After this exchange of speeches, Wilson's resistance to peace feelers and peace talk stiffened. In a speech delivered at Baltimore on April 6, he said that the answer of the military masters of Germany to his proposals by their conduct in Russia, in Rumania, and in the Ukraine left but one response possible from America: "Force to the utmost, force without stint or limit."

By the middle of July, 1918, the Germans had shot their bolt in their supreme effort and the Allies had begun a steady advance. The chances of a German victory were gone. Rumors that peace feelers from the Central Powers might be expected were verified on September 14, when Austria-Hungary invited the belligerents to send delegates to a confidential and unbinding discussion of the basic principles for the conclusion of peace. Wilson directed Secretary Lansing to reject the suggestion. In a curt and telling paragraph the President stated that the American government had made the terms upon which it would make peace so plain that it would entertain no proposal for a conference. And in a speech opening the fourth Liberty Loan campaign on September 27, he avowed that there must be no dickering for peace; a league of nations was the only possible condition.

With the Germans staggering on the western front, with Bulgaria surrendering, and with Turkey in a state of collapse, Germany prepared the way for formally suing for peace by the resignation of Chancellor von Hertling in favor of Prince Maximilian of Baden. On October 5, the new German chancellor addressed the Reichstag and announced that a note had been sent to President Wilson asking for a peace parley. The change in the political leadership of the German Empire was a move to comply with the oft-repeated declaration by Wilson that there could be no discussion of peace so long as Germany was dominated by her military masters. The German chancellor accepted the program set forth in Wilson's address of January 8 and in his later pronouncements as the basis for peace negotiations.

The American newspapers received the German overture with sarcastic coldness. They stated that Germany could not be trusted so long as she held Belgium and French territory. They called for a defeated and humiliated Germany. Even the captions interspersed in Prince Maximilian's address to the Reichstag were sarcastic.

Wilson replied to the German note by positing two adroit and well-phrased questions. He asked whether the German government accepted his peace terms as laid down in his speeches, leaving only the arrangement of the practical details for negotiation, and whether Prince Maximilian represented the authorities which had so far conducted the war. The President further stipulated that the Central Powers must evacuate invaded territory in order to prove their sincerity. Wilson's reply disarmed the German leaders, if they intended to make use of a brusque reply to bolster German morale by playing up the determination of the Allies to crush Germany without regard to her intentions.

With some exceptions, the American newspapers reacted favorably to Wilson's note, although some editors lamented that it opened the way for future negotiations and also that at this late stage the President should have entered into a discussion with Germany. Both Roosevelt and Taft expressed disapproval.

The German reply, dated October 12, complied in all respects with the conditions and queries of Wilson's note, even to the evacuation of invaded territory. The reaction in the press was the cry of "unconditional surrender." Two days later Wilson rejected the proposed armistice. The process of evacuation and the conditions of an armistice were matters which must be left to the judgment of the military advisers, he said. The President also observed that the inhumanities of the Germans in evacuating Belgian and French territory did not portend a change of heart. He also took occasion to say that according to his Mount Vernon speech no peace could be made with the arbitrary German government.

The reply to this note, dated October 22, revealed a meek, chastened, and submissive Germany. It agreed to every proposition of the President. Wilson replied promptly that in view of the promises of the German chancellor, he had submitted to the governments associated with the United States the proposal for an armistice, but he again expressed skepticism as to the changes in the German government, and fear that the power of the king of Prussia to control the policy of the empire was unimpaired. The concluding paragraph was one of the stiffest in diplomatic annals : If the government of the United States "must deal with the military masters and the monarchical autocrats of Germany now, or is likely to have to deal with them later in regard to international obligations of the German Empire, it must demand, not peace negotiations, but surrender. Nothing can be gained by leaving this essential thing unsaid."

Before the Allied Council had submitted its terms, Turkey had accepted the terms of an armistice; the crumbling Austria-

Hungary, with its armies fleeing on a hundred-mile front and its emperor in flight, had surrendered unconditionally; the kaiser had abdicated; and Germany was seething with revolution. On November 11, 1918, the morning papers appeared with huge headlines: "World War Ends." The Germans had accepted the harsh terms of the armistice.

During the days of suspense, when peace hung in the balance, the "bitter-enders" and the shriekers for a ruined and humiliated Germany almost succeeded in causing America to fling to the winds the idealistic and humanitarian principles upon which she had entered the war. The liberal weeklies, the *Nation* and the *New Republic*, were almost alone among their contemporaries in counseling moderation and in crediting Germany with harboring a sincere desire for peace. In perspective, it appears that Wilson was already a defeated man. The torrent of reaction was already tearing away the foundation he had laid for a peace of righteousness.

The outcome of the elections that were held on November 5, six days before Armistice Day, revealed the beginning of the end of Wilson's superb leadership and furnished the opportunity for his unrelenting enemies to work his downfall.

We have seen that Wilson's graceful gesture of appointing his opponent in the election of 1916 to investigate aircraft production was turned to partisan purposes by submitting it to the President on the eve of the election. The Republicans, seeking advantage, demanded that it be made public before election day. We have also seen that the Republicans in Congress harassed the administration by proposing investigations into the conduct of the war and by proposing the creation of a nonpartisan war cabinet. The relentless Roosevelt kept up a steady fire of criticism of the President. In August he declared in a speech at Springfield, Illinois, that it was sheer nonsense or rank hypocrisy to think that a league of nations or any other machinery would definitely do away with war. His remedy was universal military service. In a syndicated article published in a number of newspapers in October and entitled "High-Sounding Phrases of Muddy Meaning," the former President attacked Wilson's proposal to reduce armaments.

He said that Wilson's attempted negotiations with Germany made him need watching and that he had no right to commit the nation to the fourteen points.

In the campaign preceding the state and congressional elections of November, the Republicans capitalized what at the time was thought to be the immense popularity of Wilson by stressing the loyal support the Republicans in Congress had given to the war policy of the administration. They argued that in certain states the election of Republican candidates would deal a heavy blow against disloyalty and check the rising tide of radicalism.

Wilson sought to unmask the hypocrisy of the Republican campaign by staking what he thought was his invincible popularity with the masses against the tactics of his adversaries. He issued an appeal to "my fellow countrymen" to cast a vote of confidence in his leadership by electing a Democratic majority in Congress. The Republicans, he said, had been pro-war but anti-administration and had tried to control the President. The Republicans attacked the President's appeal as a repudiation of his "politics is adjourned" statement, which he had made in May after he had defeated his adversaries by obtaining the enactment of the Overman Act. Roosevelt and Taft, who had had a meeting of reconciliation earlier in the year—their first since the Bull Moose campaign of 1912—issued a joint reply to Wilson's appeal.

The adverse election returns proved that Wilson's appeal was a tactical mistake because it afforded his opponents the opportunity to claim that the President's leadership had been repudiated. In the light of events that followed, however, it appears that Wilson's idealistic peace program was already doomed to defeat. Even before the election, the President had been obliged to notify the German government that the Allied governments reserved complete freedom on the clause pertaining to the freedom of the seas and that they would demand compensation for all damage done by Germany on land and sea and in the air. The Allies themselves had thus already repudiated two of the most important of the fourteen points: the freedom of the seas and the pledge not to demand indemnities. Wilson was confronted by a hostile Republican Congress and the traditions and intrigues of Old World diplomacy. The seating of Senator Newberry, a Republican whose election was dubious, made possible the organization of the Senate Committee on Foreign Relations by Wilson's adversaries.

The Republicans lost no time in launching their campaign against the President. His decision to take active part in the peace conference at Versailles furnished the first target. They insinuated that he was actuated by personal ambition and was about to entangle the United States in matters that did not concern its own interests. Republican Senators assailed the seizure of the cables as proof that Wilson intended to enforce a censorship of newspapers; and some even proposed that a delegation should go to Europe to keep watch on the course of events.

The President's appointments to the peace delegation were bitterly assailed. In addition to the President himself, they were Edward M. House, Henry White, Secretary Lansing, and General Tasker H. Bliss. It was said that the only Republican member was Henry White, and that he was only a nominal Republican. It was also argued that Wilson ought to have followed the example of McKinley, who appointed two United States Senators to the commission to negotiate the treaty with Spain.

Wilson's address to Congress of December 2, 1918, was somewhat disappointing to his liberal supporters. After paying eloquent tribute to soldiers, sailors, and civilians, he recommended that a program of internal improvements should be inaugurated in order to furnish employment during the months of transition; that the three-year naval building program should be continued on account of the unsettled international situation; that the railroads should not be returned to private operation unmodified—to do so would be unjust to the railroads as well as to the public. In view of the fact that the Allies and the Central Powers had accepted his fourteen points, he said that it was his duty to be present at the peace conference to interpret them, but he promised to keep in touch with Congress and to keep the country informed. Two days later he sailed for France on the *George Washington*.

While wireless reports from the liner assured the people that all was well, the press broadcast reports about the chaotic condition of Europe and the menace of Bolshevism. During the following months systematic propaganda was spread over the pages of the newspapers in order to reduce the influence of the President. Reaction was riding high. Propaganda fell on fertile soil. The labor situation was exceedingly dangerous, with strikes in progress throughout the country. Seattle was in the grip of a general strike which practically tied up the entire city. The cost of living was steadily mounting, and people were paying fabulous prices for milk, butter, flour, sugar, and clothing—so fabulous that buyers' strikes were in force in many cities. The farmers in the Northwest were clamoring for the early return of the soldiers. The Senate inaugurated an investigation of radical propaganda in the country.

The newspapers used their best efforts to keep alive the hatred of Germany and deplored the friendly attitude toward the German civilians on the part of the American soldiers in the army of occupation. The editors called this attitude "lack of perspective" and alleged that the friendliness of the Germans was all for effect. "Huns Playing on Yank Sympathy" was the headline of a middle-western paper.

The state of affairs in Ireland and Russia also profoundly affected public opinion in the United States. The demand for an Irish republic met with sympathy among certain elements; and the propaganda sponsored by Irish-Americans did much to discredit the League of Nations as a "triumph of British diplomacy."

The Russian situation was ominous. During the summer of 1918 the United States and the Allies agreed upon a plan of intervention in Russia, with the United States furnishing troops to form an army also consisting of Japanese, British, and French. In the closing days of July, American troops landed at Archangel, and in the early days of September, another detachment under the command of Major General William S. Graves landed at Vladivostok. After the armistice the Americans continued to fight in the arctic cold of Russia, and some of the soldiers were mutinous. In January, 1919, Senators regardless of party assailed the intervention in Russia and demanded that the administration either make public its Russian policy or else withdraw the troops. Pressure became so strong that in the middle of February, Secretary Baker announced that the troops would be withdrawn at the earliest possible moment. This military episode is far from creditable to the United States and was used with good effect to embarrass the administration.

The chaotic condition in Russia, with the Red Army in deadly combat with the White Army, also reacted in the United States. The United States Senate and state legislatures pursued investigations into the activities of "Reds" and German agents. Newspapers published sensational stories about their subversive activities and proposed radical measures. An anti-immigration hysteria was also sweeping over the country and gave rise to ridiculous prophecies about the threatened invasion from Europe, which would make the unemployment situation even worse. It was said that immigrants who had evaded military service were depriving the American-born of employment and were undermining American institutions by their alien sympathies and activities. The Americanization movement and the "one hundred per cent American" spirit were manifestations of nativism and hostility toward anything that smacked of Europe.

With this background we shall have a better understanding of the difficulties that beset Wilson in Europe and of the reception of his handiwork in America. The President landed at Brest on December 13 and received an ovation worthy of the occasion. On the following day he made a carefully phrased address in reply to the words of welcome from President Poincaré. For the first time in history a President of the United States made an address on European soil. For weeks the eyes of the world were fixed on him. Wherever he went, whether in France, England, Italy, or Belgium, the crowds were immense, cannons boomed, whistles shrieked, bells rang, and flags waved. Peasants burned candles before his picture and removed their hats when his name was spoken.

These demonstrations and gestures were expressions of gratitude for deliverance from the horrors of war rather than favorable omens for the success of his mission. When the peace conference opened on January 18, 1919, Wilson had already lost the opening battle when it was decided that newspaper reporters were to be admitted to the sessions of the full peace conference but excluded from the preliminary sessions, which were to be held in secret. The major provisions of the treaty were agreed upon in conferences attended only by President Wilson, Premier Clemenceau of France, and Prime Minister Lloyd George of Great Britain, though for some weeks Premier Orlando of Italy was a member of this select group.

Inasmuch as the United States did not ratify the treaty that was drawn up at Versailles, we are not primarily concerned with the territorial and political adjustments embodied in the text. Secret treaties between the Allied governments, nationalistic and imperialistic rivalries and ambitions, age-long hatreds, and diplomacy steeped in conventions, red tape, and ineptitude defeated the grandest mission ever undertaken by a President of the United States.

His efforts to draw up a treaty based on the Christian conception of justice and liberty were defeated not only by compromises and deals but by the combined efforts of newspapers and politicians to discredit his motives, to impugn his honesty, and to keep alive the mythical isolation of the United States. It was a most extraordinary situation. Congress in the short session from December, 1918, to March 4, 1919, not only marked time, but leaders of both parties engaged in bitter partisanship and bent their efforts to discredit and repudiate the President of the United States.

Wilson's dream of a League of Nations, that grandiose conception that had fascinated idealists for centuries, was woven into the texture of the treaty; but the exponents of the principle of the balance of power like Clemenceau and the isolationists in the United States, who continued to pin their faith on the Monroe Doctrine and on Washington's Farewell Address, nullified its force from the beginning. The world was in the throes of a political and spiritual crisis, and few there were who could discern the signs of the times.

On February 14, 1919, Wilson read the provisions of the constitution of the League of Nations to the conference and on the following day sailed from Brest to return to the United States to be present during the closing days of Congress. Previously, in a cablegram to his secretary, Joseph P. Tumulty, he had requested Congress to defer debate on the League Covenant until he might have the opportunity to explain the meaning and reasons for the phraseology and substance of each article. This request was flouted by Senators in both parties. Senator Lawrence Y. Sherman of Illinois, a Republican, pronounced the League of Nations a "Pandora's box of evils which would empty upon the American people the aggravated calamities of the world."

In order to force Wilson to call a special session of Congress which would enable them to checkmate the President, the irreconcilables in the Senate conducted a successful filibuster to prevent the passage of important appropriation bills. Senator Lodge, the leader of the Republicans, read into the *Congressional Record* the names of thirty-nine Senators who were opposed to the constitution of the League of Nations as it was written.

On the eve of his second departure for France on March 4, the newspapers praised the courage of the thirty-nine Senators and demanded that a special session of Congress be called in order that the new Congress elected in November might be allowed to transact the business of the government. The line of editorial attack at this stage was that although the principle of a league of nations was a good thing, the wisdom of Wilson's plan was open to question. Some of the papers took up with Senator Borah's suggestion that the League of Nations be submitted to a popular referendum. Others harped on the necessity of an immediate treaty of peace in order to stabilize conditions, leaving the League of Nations for later consideration. Few newspapers protested the harsh terms that were imposed on Germany.

Upon his return to France, Wilson refused to recede from his position that the League Covenant should be an integral part of the treaty. For a time it appeared that the entire Wilsonian program would be wrecked by Italy's demand that Fiume be awarded to her, by France's insistence that she be assured protection in the future against aggressions from Germany, by Japan's claim for racial equality and for recognition of her conquest of the German colonies in the Far East, and by a number of demands that Bolshevism in Russia be put down by intervention.

In this crisis in the first week of April, Wilson ordered the *George Washington* to proceed from an American to a French port, which was taken to mean that the President's patience was exhausted and that he was about to withdraw from the conference. It was not until June 28, 1919, on the fifth anniversary of the assassination of the Austrian archduke, that the treaty was signed. In an address to his countrymen Wilson hailed the treaty as the charter of a new order, in spite of the severe terms imposed on the Central Powers and the wide gulf between its provisions and the fourteen points.

Wilson's compromises at Versailles lost him the support of many liberals. Some of them could forgive him for failing to beat down the formidable opposition to his program, but they could not forgive him for defending and even praising the treaty. The tripartite alliance signed by Wilson, Lloyd George, and Clemenceau pledging the United States and Great Britain to come to the aid of France in case of an attack by Germany was singled out as a gross betrayal of Wilson's principles.

The harassed President, already weakened in physical stamina by the severe ordeal of the peace conference, appeared before the Senate on July 10 and with fine phrases smoothed over the conflicting interests which had torn his fourteen points into shreds. It was necessary, he said, to take into account the previous agreements between the Allied governments and the historical backgrounds of the provisions of the treaty. There were significant omissions in the President's address. There was no mention of two of the most mooted provisions in the treaty: the cession of the Shantung Peninsula to Japan, and Article X.

Senator Norris of Nebraska, one of the ablest and best known among the progressive Republicans, read into the *Congressional Record* the correspondence between Great Britain, France, and Japan in 1917, which proved that the two European powers had pledged themselves to support Japan's claim to Shantung. Norris charged that while the Allies were inducing China to go into the war, they were also secretly plotting to destroy her. "In all the annals of history," he said, "I do not believe there is recorded an

instance of a more disgraceful and dishonorable agreement to
carve up the territory not of an enemy but of an allied friend."

This was a telling blow to Wilson's cause. This provision alone
was sufficient to discredit the treaty in the judgment of many
people. Senators minced no words in denouncing Japan's unfaith-
fulness as an ally. Serious race riots in Washington, D. C.,
Norfolk, Virginia, Chicago, and other cities that occurred simultaneously with the debate on the provision were symptoms of the
temper of the country. Wilson tried to minimize its importance
by pointing out that the provision applied only to rights of citizenship and economic concessions.

Conditions could hardly have been less favorable when Wilson
set out on a speaking tour to appeal for popular support in his
fight for the ratification of the treaty. The Senate was debating
various propositions to modify the treaty, including reservations;
strikes were unsettling the economic life of the people; investigations into the high cost of living were uncovering shameless
profiteering in food and clothing; the strained relations between
the United States and Mexico were again in the headlines; and
raids against the "Reds" were the order of the day.

The keynote speech of the President's campaign was delivered
at Columbus, Ohio, on September 4. He admitted that the terms
of the treaty were severe, but denied that they were unjust. The
treaty was intended to punish one of the "greatest wrongs ever
done in history" and to prevent any similar war. It was unique
in the history of mankind because the center of it was the redemption of weak nations. In similar vein the President went on to
explain and defend the important provisions.

In his speech at Indianapolis he declared that Article X of the
Covenant of the League of Nations, which had been so bitterly
attacked, spoke the conscience of the world by enlisting all members of the League to resist and preserve against external aggression the integrity and independence of the nations concerned. In
answer to objections that by ratifying the Covenant the United
States would be robbed of some degree of sovereign independence,
he stated that any action taken would have to have the unanimous

approval of members of the council, of which the United States was a member.

The President's tour brought him to the Pacific coast, and everywhere large and enthusiastic crowds heard him defend the League of Nations. He denounced the proposed reservations that were designed to relieve the United States of the obligation to preserve the territorial integrity and political independence of any country, to exclude domestic questions (such as immigration) from consideration by the council or by the assembly of the League, to make it clear that the Monroe Doctrine was "wholly outside the jurisdiction of the League," to protect the United States against an unequal vote, and to withhold the assent of the United States to the Shantung settlement.

The size and enthusiasm of the crowds were so noticeable that the newspapers made it appear that they were not a personal tribute to the President or to the cause he represented but solely to the dignity of the office he held. Simultaneously he was "trailed" by Senators Hiram Johnson and William E. Borah, who also attracted large crowds to hear them refute the President's arguments.

Whether or not Wilson "lost ground" on his tour, as it was alleged at the time, cannot be determined, because on September 26 illness resulting from physical exhaustion compelled him to cancel the remaining engagements. "Ike" Hoover, who was with the President on his two trips abroad, noticed the effect of the strain of his duties. He said that Wilson had the appearance of a tired old man. "He is feeling the strain and seems to realize the enormousness of the proposition he is up against. . . . Just on the surface it looks like the statesmen of the more important countries of Europe, especially, have the cards stacked against the President." Hoover marveled that the President was able to keep his poise and to bear up as well as he did. "If he does not break down when it is all over, he will be a wonder indeed."

These fears of the chief usher of the White House, who to the last was a great admirer of Wilson, came true with startling suddenness when on the morning of October 2, 1919, Mrs. Wilson hurriedly called Hoover by telephone and told him to summon a physician to the White House. From that fatal hour to the end of his life Wilson was only a wreck of his former self. "I was with him at some time every day and saw him, even up to the end, at his private residence," wrote Hoover. "There was never a moment during all that time when he was more than a shadow of his former self. He had changed from a giant to a pygmy in every wise. He was physically almost incapacitated. . . . It was so sad that those of us about him, who almost without exception admired him, would turn our heads away when he came along or we went near him."

During the following fateful months the country was without a leader. The masterly skill of the "schoolmaster" in the White House was no more. The vigorous mind that had worked like a steel trap could no longer give direction to the affairs of state. Perhaps the cards were stacked against the President in his own country as they were in Europe. Perhaps the fate of the treaty would have been the same if Wilson had been spared to do battle to the end. Be that as it may, the uncompromising stand of the President against any fundamental reservations and the opposition of Senators, some of whom desired nothing better than the scrapping of the entire treaty and others who were sincerely desirous of making what they conceived to be a better treaty, nullified the herculean efforts of Woodrow Wilson.

Disillusionment that followed an unpopular war and the abnormal psychology of the American people played into the hands of Senator Lodge, whose methods were none too scrupulous and whose chief ambition was to wreak vengeance on Wilson. The President's politics, policies, and methods were entirely foreign to the Senator who had come to Washington as "the scholar in politics."

The fight in behalf of the ratification of the treaty was led by Senator Gilbert M. Hitchcock of Nebraska, who was no match for such debaters and strategists as Lodge, Borah, and Reed of Missouri. The most brilliant debater and staunchest supporter was John Sharp Williams of Mississippi, who loosed his sarcasm on Lodge.

As the time for the final vote on the ratification of the treaty drew near, Wilson wrote a letter to Hitchcock advising the friends of the treaty to vote against the Lodge reservations. On November 19, 1919, a combination of Democrats and irreconcilables defeated the Lodge reservations; the milder reservations proposed by Hitchcock were likewise voted down; and finally the reservationists and the irreconcilables joined forces in defeating the treaty without reservations by a vote of 52 to 38.

In the session of Congress that convened in the following month, the treaty was reconsidered, and again with the Lodge reservations it was defeated. In a letter read to a Jackson Day banquet on January 8, 1920, Wilson declared that the treaty must go before the people at the election in November. At the same meeting Bryan spoke and insisted that the treaty with reservations should be ratified as soon as possible. To bring the issue before the people, he said, would mean a delay of fourteen months, and success could be obtained only if a two-thirds majority in the Senate was secured.

The Democratic candidate for the Presidency, James S. Cox, indorsed the treaty and the League; but it fell to the lot of a Republican President, Warren G. Harding, to sign a resolution passed by a Republican Congress on July 2, 1921, which terminated a technical state of war with Germany. It remained for the Senate in the following months to ratify treaties with Germany, Austria, and Hungary.

For this anti-climactic termination of the great adventure that entailed the loss of thousands of lives, thousands of wrecked homes, the expenditure of billions of dollars, and a national debt of twenty-four billions, and eventually dragged the nation perilously near to the level of a disheveled Europe, partisan politics, whether played by Republicans or Democrats, bears a portion of the blame. In the years that followed, three Republican Presidents —Harding, Coolidge, and Hoover—made no effort to revive the League of Nations issue; and even the Democrats were chary of praising the first Democratic President to win two successive victories at the polls since 1832. The catastrophic events on the continent of Europe and in the Far East disillusioned the American people even further and caused them to congratulate themselves that their government did not join the League.

CHAPTER XXVIII

THE AFTERMATH OF WAR

WE HAVE SEEN THAT THE DECLARATION OF WAR ENABLED THE federal and state governments to take strong measures to stamp out the activities of secret agents of the enemy governments and to silence those who had difficulty in reconciling themselves to the war. Some of these measures were objectionable and unnecessary and defeated the purposes for which they were intended. A loyalty campaign is as successful as its leaders are judicious and tactful. Great injustice was done to individuals and groups of individuals by government officials and by self-appointed patriots who spied on neighbors or joined with others to terrorize persons who in reality were as loyal to the government as they were.

The very fact that an individual's name was of German, Irish, or Scandinavian origin made him suspect and prevented him from expressing himself as frankly and honestly as others. Level-headed agents of the government were reluctant to make arrests, because they knew that the temper of the community was such that arrest was equivalent to conviction; but there were all too many who did not exercise such caution. Not infrequently pressure was applied by federal and local officials to induce certain groups—and this was especially true where the foreign-born were numerous—to hold "loyalty meetings" at which patriotic speeches were made and patriotic resolutions were adopted—always by a unanimous vote.

The full force of the war psychology—which speedily became hysteria—descended on individuals who before the entrance of the United States into the war had been pro-German, and upon Socialists and other "radicals" who had loudly proclaimed that there was a conspiracy of the money power to have the United States step in to protect its interests. Teachers in primary and secondary schools, in colleges and universities, were summarily dismissed; the teaching of German was discontinued in many schools; enrollment in German classes dwindled almost to the vanishing point; German books in school and city libraries were burned; symphony orchestras were forbidden to play the masterpieces of German composers; and even sauerkraut was transformed into "liberty cabbage."

During the war and in the year following the armistice, over a score of states made English the only medium of instruction in public and private schools; and about the same number of states prohibited the teaching of foreign languages in schools under the eighth grade. In certain communities placards were posted exhorting people to speak only the "American language"; and churches in which services were conducted in foreign languages were under suspicion.

The governor of Iowa on his own responsibility issued a proclamation forbidding public worship in a foreign tongue; in Missouri services in German were prohibited by law; and the Oregon legislature, over a year after the armistice, made it unlawful for any person, firm, corporation, or association of persons to print, publish, circulate, exhibit, sell, or offer for sale any paper, treatise, pamphlet, or circular in any other language than English, unless those prints included translations. By act of Congress approved October 6, 1917, no foreign-language publication could print matter pertaining to the war without filing a translation with the postmaster, unless the loyalty of the paper was unquestioned. Editors of foreign-language papers were arrested, their offices were attacked by mobs, editions of their papers were confiscated or torn to shreds by excited citizens, and firms advertising in these papers were boycotted.

Churches became agents for and disseminators of war propaganda; and no clergyman would be tolerated who did not allow his pulpit and auditorium to be used for patriotic purposes. Four-minute men, speakers in behalf of the Red Cross, and representatives of other causes and organizations were permitted to appear at the hours of worship. Service flags studded with stars for members of congregations who wore the uniform were prominently displayed in churches. Congregations and clergymen whose doctrine or conscientious scruples did not permit the intrusion of "secular" things during the hours of worship felt the heavy hand of laws, ordinances, and public sentiment.

Parochial schools conducted by Catholic, Lutheran, and other ecclesiastical organizations were also under suspicion, largely because of prejudice against anything remotely connected with foreign origin, many such schools being supported by immigrant churches. In Oregon the so-called compulsory education law was adopted by a popular referendum on November 11, 1922. This law, which was to become effective in 1926, compelled children between the ages of six and sixteen to attend the state schools. It was declared unconstitutional by the United States Supreme Court on June, 1925. Two years previously the same tribunal had declared unconstitutional laws prohibiting the teaching of foreign languages in schools.

For the most part the press of the country acquiesced in these repressive measures; indeed, the propaganda that appeared in the news and editorial columns fanned the fury. It was only the exceptional editor who ventured to express the opinion that these measures were contrary to the spirit of American institutions; and they, together with individuals who harbored like opinions, were sometimes threatened with similar treatment.

The Espionage Act (June 15, 1917), the Trading-with-the-Enemy Act (October 6, 1917), and the Sedition Act (May 6, 1918) were so inclusive as to make almost any form of dissent disloyal in the ears of a jury. The foreign-born were singled out in a separate law of October 16, 1918, which rendered liable to deportation aliens who advocated the overthrow of the government by force or violence or who were members of, or affiliated with, any organization which advocated the use of violence.

In the deportation raids in January, 1920, about ten thousand arrests were made. The accused were brought before an inspector in the Department of Labor, the final decision resting with the Secretary of Labor. The accused were deprived of the right of trial by jury and were compelled to testify against themselves. These raids were inspired by Attorney-General A. Mitchell Palmer, who became exceedingly active after the armistice. For a time Louis F. Post, Assistant Secretary of Labor, was Acting Secretary and drew the fire of newspapers for his alleged failure to act promptly and firmly in the cases that came before him. Post was not carried away by the hysteria, and he proceeded carefully before making decisions that would tear families asunder or work grave injustice to individuals. The press and certain members of Congress detected in Post sympathy with radicalism and proposed impeachment. Three years later Post defended his policy in a book which Senator Thomas F. Walsh of Montana pronounced "a ringing indictment of both the American government and the American people—the former for acts of heartless oppression . . . and the latter for the indifference with which the most hideous injustices perpetrated by high officials in perfect contempt of constitutional guarantees were regarded."

The opposite view was expressed by the newspapers in the last days of 1919, when the army transport *Buford* sailed out of New York Harbor with two hundred and forty-nine deportees, among whom Emma Goldman and Alexander Berkman were the most conspicuous. A Boston newspaper expressed the opinion that the sailing of the "Soviet Ark," as the newspapers called the transport, "with its cargo of undesirables" may prove to be "as epoch-making as the immortal voyage of Columbus."

It was not only men and women of foreign birth who ran afoul of sedition acts, committees of public safety, and vigilantes; anybody suspected of sympathy with radicalism might be called upon to defend his loyalty. While the war resolution was pending, Socialists and pacifists staged meetings of protest, and Washington was deluged with petitions and telegrams that emanated from such meetings. After a few weeks or months Socialists like Bouck White and John Spargo fell in line and demanded that the war against Prussian militarism should continue until the world was free from this menace. Other Socialists, however, could see nothing but the cold steel of capitalism in the world conflagration in which the American people were but pawns. They, too, were enemies of Prussian militarism, but, like the pacifists, they could not convince themselves that darkness could be dispelled with darkness.

The most conspicuous victim of the Espionage Act was Eugene V. Debs, who had four times been honored by the Socialist party as their candidate for the Presidency. In a speech full of irony delivered at Canton, Ohio, on June 16, 1918, Debs avowed that the Socialist movement was conceived in opposition to militarism and lauded the pioneer exponents; but he was very caustic in dealing with individuals who had been recently converted to the crusade against militarism and autocracy. He waxed sarcastic over Theodore Roosevelt's visit to the kaiser after his return from the African hunting expedition. "And, while Roosevelt was being entertained royally by the German kaiser, that same kaiser was putting the leaders of the Socialist party in jail for fighting the kaiser and the Junkers of Germany. Roosevelt was the guest of honor in the white house of the kaiser, while the Socialists were in the jails of the kaiser, for fighting the kaiser."

In the federal court at Cleveland, Ohio, Debs was tried for inciting mutiny in the United States army, for stirring up disloyalty in his countrymen, for encouraging resistance to the United States, and for promoting the cause of the enemy. He was convicted and sentenced to serve ten years in the penitentiary. The Supreme Court upheld the decision. In a message to the Socialist monthly, the *Liberator*, Debs stated that the "cabal of begowned corporation lawyers at Washington have decided better than they knew. They have added a million fresh recruits to the ranks of Bolshevism in the United States."

While Debs was serving his sentence in the federal penitentiary at Atlanta in 1920, he polled nearly a million votes as the presidential candidate of the Socialist party. Early in 1921 the Department of Justice recommended that his sentence be commuted, but Wilson refused to act on the grounds that Debs had sought to handicap the Selective Service Act and that if clemency were extended it might induce contempt for the law in future wars. Shortly after Harding's inauguration, however, Debs was summoned to Washington by Attorney-General Daugherty. He made the trip unattended, after having promised not to make a statement

"Are you a Socialist?"
"Certainly."
"Show your indictment."

(From *The Liberator*)

for publication until after the application for pardon had been acted upon. He left Washington with his sentence commuted and declared himself still a "flaming radical."

Among the famous cases prosecuted under the Sedition Act was that of Victor Berger of Milwaukee, a former Socialist Congressman, who was indicted, together with other prominent Socialists, on February 2, 1918. Several months elapsed before Berger was brought to trial, and in the meantime he was elected to Congress. In January, 1919, Berger and four other Socialists were convicted. Berger was denied his seat in Congress, with only one vote in the negative. This was followed by the demand from the American Legion, then in session, that he be deported. In December, 1919, when the "Red" hysteria was running high, Berger was reelected to Congress, and again the House denied him the right to his seat, this time with six votes in the negative. James R. Mann of Illinois, a Republican, led the fight to seat the Socialist leader, on the ground that people who desired changes in the law of the land had the right to be represented in Congress. Mann's espousal of Berger's cause came a few days after five Socialists had been denied seats in the New York legislature and after Maartens, the "ambassador" of Soviet Russia to the United States, had been arrested. Maartens was subsequently deported. The high-handed action of the New York legislature was denounced by Charles E. Hughes, a former justice of the United States Supreme Court, who stated that it was un-American and calculated to breed Socialism.

The effort to convict the editors of the Socialist monthly, the *Masses*, ended in a disagreement of the jury. The editors and publishers of this periodical, of whom Max Eastman, Art Young, and Jack Reed were the most prominent, were literary men and artists in a state of revolt from the commercial magazines and were also dissatisfied with the present state of affairs in politics and society. Their magazine was excluded from the mails by Postmaster-General Burleson; and the editors were indicted for conspiracy to promote mutiny or disloyalty or refusal of duty in the army and to obstruct recruiting and enlistment. Eastman addressed the jury and denied that there was any intent to obstruct the military enterprises of the United States, nor did he deny the right of a state to pass extraordinary laws in an emergency. "I do not ignore the right of the government to defend its armies with a military and war-time censorship. I am not a bigoted or fanatical advocate of the mere abstract principle of free speech. I simply say that if a government avails itself of this right of war-time censorship, in order to suppress and whip into jails as criminals the candid and sincere spokesmen of a political minority which is opposed to its policies, then that government is violating not only the principles of the United States Constitution, but the spirit and principles of free government as they have existed in the earth from the beginning." Referring to the St. Louis resolution opposing the entrance of the United States into the war adopted by the Socialist party, Eastman avowed that the principles proclaimed in it were his principles.

Members of the I.W.W. also felt the heavy hand of the law when some ninety leaders, including "Big Bill" Haywood, were found guilty of a conspiracy to disrupt the nation's war program. On August 30, 1918, Haywood was sentenced to serve thirty years in the penitentiary and to pay a fine of twenty thousand dollars. He escaped imprisonment by fleeing to Russia, where he remained to the end of his life.

Regimentation during the war, bitter and grossly unfair propaganda broadcast by newspapers, motives of revenge, wars and rumors of wars, nation rising against nation, class rising against class, pillars of government and society falling under the weight of famine, pestilence, and poverty or torn down by the strong arms of prophets of a new order or of selfish and ambitious men, and the tremors of an uneasy civilization inspired legislation designed to protect society against real and imaginary dangers. It was easy to read into events that transpired in the United States the influence of events abroad, just as it was in the United States and England at the time of the Reign of Terror in France. The wild stories about the Bolshevik régime in Russia and the fear of the spread of Bolshevism in the United States brought charges of Bolshevism against individuals in the United States. In Minnesota and North Dakota the adherents of the Nonpartisan League, which represented a revolt against the domination of those states by what they conceived to be the reactionary and plutocratic Republican party, were attacked as Bolsheviks who were contaminating the youth of the land with the doctrine of free love. Nonpartisan meetings were broken up by mobs, speakers were escorted out of town by self-appointed patriots, and a reign of terror was launched against men who in reality were as hostile to the war profiteers as they were to the military foes of their country.

Sensational extracts from investigating committees of the New York legislature (the Lusk Committee) and of the United States Senate aroused citizens to the supposed conspiracy of Communists and other radicals to inject their teachings into the public schools and to poison the very arteries of the body politic. Textbooks in American history were scrutinized by organizations for evidences of unsound Americanism.

A widely used high school textbook written by a distinguished student of American history was singled out by a certain citizens' association as a book that "by innuendo, distortion, modification, and suppression of undoubted historical facts, falsifies American history, robs it of patriotic inspiration, and obscures the great principles upon which our Republic is founded." Historians of international reputation found their names included among dangerous radicals. In 1923 the legislature of Wisconsin enacted a law which prohibited the adoption for school use of any history or other textbook "which falsifies the facts regarding the War of Independence, or the War of 1812, or which defames our nation's founders or misrepresents the ideals and causes for which they struggled and sacrificed, or which contains propaganda favorable to any foreign government."

This law substituted the prejudices of individuals, of minorities, and of majorities for the erudition and interpretation of seasoned historians and experienced teachers. It reflected the reaction of the population of a strongly German state against the pro-British propaganda of the days when the United States and Great Britain were associated in the herculean task of defeating Germany. It also illustrates the words of a distinguished student of history: "The average person welcomes an invention that enables his children to fly where he walked, he is even getting wonted to the strange things the biologist and chemist tell him about his body, but let a historian give his children a new conception of American history or a founding father, something different from what he was told in the country school forty years ago, and he is sure the fabric of national life is being disintegrated."

Beginning in 1917 many states passed laws requiring teachers to take oaths of loyalty to the Constitution of the United States and to the constitution of the state. In the abstract, there was little that was objectional in these oaths, but the animus back of them was obvious. The oaths were designed to furnish handles to those interests who desired to have teachers discharged because their principles were obnoxious to them. The example of teachers and professors who had lost positions and influence was menacing to the principles of academic freedom and sound educational policy.

One group of constitutional literalists took a curious position. They contended for the literal interpretation of Holy Writ and rejected *in toto* the researches of Biblical scholars and their colleagues in other fields; and in their zeal to defend their faith, they tortured the meaning and interpretation of the bill of rights in the federal and state constitutions. In some states these fundamentalists joined with others of more liberal views in persuading legislatures to compel Bible reading in the public schools—over the opposition of Catholics, Jews, agnostics, and others who feared that such laws would promote dissension and intolerance rather than Christian patience and forbearance.

In other states, notably in the South, fundamentalism took the form of legislation to prohibit the teaching of the theory of evolution in tax-supported schools. The advocates of this measure reversed the argument of those who opposed religious instruction in the schools, by arguing that the exponents of the evolution theory rejected the fundamental teachings of the Bible and thereby taught anti-Christian doctrines.

William Jennings Bryan was the foremost of the fundamentalists. His crusades against the *status quo* in politics and economics, his denunciation of the Supreme Court for its dogmatism, his quest for social justice did not run counter to his conviction that modern science with its scientific theories and hypotheses sinned against the Bible and the Constitution. Large and enthusiastic audiences listened to his attacks against "little men with big degrees" whose speculations about the creation of life and the origin of species contradicted the First Book of Moses, commonly called Genesis. Advocates for and against anti-evolution laws appeared before legislative committees and were alternately hissed and cheered by excited citizens; synods and conferences adopted anti-evolution resolutions; and teachers were summoned before school boards.

The height of the fundamentalist movement was reached in the summer of 1925 in the famous trial of John T. Scopes, a high school teacher in Dayton, Tennessee, who voluntarily made a test of the law that forbade the teaching of any theory that denied the story of creation as recorded in the Bible.

The trial assumed the character of a circus, with a swarm of newspaper reporters dispatching sensational stories about the principals in the legal battle. To accommodate the curious, the trial was held in the open. Bryan was there to testify; and Clarence Darrow, the famous attorney who had figured in many battles, was a member of Scopes' counsel. Bryan's smiling countenance was conspicuous in the news reels; and *Judge*, a comic weekly, had a special "Fundamentalist Number." The newspapers gave the impression that the trial would decide the truth or falsity of the evolution theory, whereas obviously it would decide only whether the state had the right to enact the law that Scopes had violated. The frivolous publicity boded no good for either church or state.

A sad and strange interlude was injected in the proceedings by the sudden death of Bryan on July 26. In retrospect, Darrow's relentless cross examination of the Great Commoner seemed still more brutal, and Bryan's rôle even more pathetic. Scopes was convicted, and the Tennessee Supreme Court sustained the constitutionality of the statute which he had violated. The ridicule heaped on Bryan and the Tennessee legislature undoubtedly discredited the fundamentalist movement and played into the hands of the more sober fundamentalists and the exponents of academic freedom who were in agreement that such legislation was unwise.

Other by-products of war were the Ku Klux Klan and the Americanization movement, widely apart in objectives, but born of the fear that American institutions were in danger from the importation of foreign ideas in the souls of immigrants. In the South the Negro population was included in the list of the proscribed. Fear of the Negro was not entirely negligible in the North, where the unprecedented migration of Negroes to the industrial centers like Chicago and Detroit was not unnoticed.

The Ku Klux Klan was organized in 1915, and its membership mounted until it reached its peak in 1925. This organization, a lineal descendant of Know-nothingism and A.P.A.-ism, took strong hold in the South and in the Middle West, where it recruited its members from the descendants of the old American stock and of the Protestant "old immigration." The organizers of the Know Nothing party of the fifties and of the American Protective Association of the nineties professed alarm at the increasing political influence of the Roman Catholic church and advocated political proscription of its members. In the increasing immigration from the Roman Catholic countries of Europe they saw grave danger to American institutions, especially to the public schools. The organizers of the Ku Klux Klan directed their propaganda against Catholics, Jews, and Negroes.

The Jews were under fire because of their alleged radicalism, their clannishness, their financial power, and their growing political influence. Henry Ford's *Dearborn Independent* published a series of anti-Semitic articles purporting to lay bare the insidious international activity of Jewish leaders. The anti-Catholic movement had gained momentum even before the outbreak of the World War. The activity of "hyphenated Americans" stimulated "one hundred per cent Americanism." After the war the fear of radicalism was fanned by sensational articles in newspapers and periodicals, some of which were established in order to profit by the rising intolerance. In 1924 the *American Standard*, published in New York, advocated an "uprising of genuine Americanism, which is preparing to eject from our land anti-Christian Judaism, whether from Soviet Russia, Poland or elsewhere, and Roman

Catholic subjects of a foreign government, the Vatican, who owe first allegiance to a foreign potentate, the pope."

The strength of the Ku Klux Klan is not to be judged by its membership of five million in 1925. There were scores of other organizations whose members were animated by the same spirit, and there were thousands of individuals who held aloof from membership in these societies who were openly or secretly in sympathy with them. In fact, many newspapers whose editorial pages bristled with denunciations of the Ku Klux Klan betrayed their real sentiments by printing grossly untrue news stories and editorials that did grave injustice to individuals, groups, and communities. The war and post-war years furnished golden opportunities for newspapers to pin the stigma of disloyalty on men and women whose principles clashed with those of the dominant elements in the Republican and Democratic parties. Mob rule, lynchings, raids on the headquarters of Communists and Socialists took the place of orderly discussion. In certain states of the South it is doubtful if a man could have been elected to public office without joining the Klan.

A benevolent form of nativism manifested itself in the Americanization movement which got under way during the war years and rode high for a few years after the armistice. Prominent citizens who conceived it to be their duty to assist the immigrants to prepare themselves for effective citizenship were joined by others who judged the patriotism of individuals by the naturalization statistics pertaining to their respective national groups. Classes were organized to instruct them in English and to acquaint them with the spirit and workings of the American system of government. Colleges and universities established Americanization courses and even departments of Americanization for the purpose of training "Americanization workers."

Conceived in the spirit of service to fellow men, the Americanization movement was overwhelmed by the tide of intolerance. Immigrants looked with suspicion on those who knocked at their doors in order to help them. Moreover, they resented the insinuation that inability to speak fluent English implied lack of loyalty to their adopted country. In all too many instances the

Americanization worker did not know how envious the average immigrant was of the prosperity, the language, and the manners of his American neighbor, nor did he know the aching immigrant hearts who felt the pangs of children looking down on their "foreign" parents, refusing to speak their native tongue, resenting any suggestion of foreign parentage, and in one gulp swallowing "Americanization."

They did not know that the finest emotions cannot be nurtured by a hothouse system; that the flower of patriotism and loyalty can be blighted by bungling gardeners; that love for country cannot be learned like the multiplication table; that the kingdom of heaven cannot be taken by violence and that it cometh not with observation. Moreover, a few—but entirely too many—took up "Americanization work" as a fad; and when they tried to instruct women of foreign birth, they merely revealed their ignorance of methods of frugality and efficiency which had been practiced in their homes since childhood. Sensing the unfortunate connotation of the name, the social workers among the immigrants later took for their enduring program the name of "adult education" and continued and augmented work that for years had been pursued by settlement houses, of which Hull House in Chicago was the most famous. In promoting this activity federal, state, and local governments cooperated with churches, schools, employers of labor, the Y.M.C.A., the Knights of Columbus, the American Legion, the World War Veterans, fraternal organizations, organizations sponsored by immigrant groups, and the like.

In spite of some misguided leaders and the existence of congested districts which were designated as "ghettos," "little Italys," "little Polands," and "little Germanys," the magic of America worked through the public schools, the parochial schools, the printed page, tolerant neighbors and employers, zealous priests, pastors, and rabbis, and philanthropic individuals. The box scores of professional baseball games and the roster of college and university football squads in the fourth decade of the century prove that the process of Americanization was not seriously checked by war, depression, or political tumult and strife.

The drastic immigration laws of 1921, 1924, and 1929 were

perhaps inevitable in a topsy-turvy world and salutary to the United States as well as to Europe, in spite of the fact that they were fostered by unintelligent propaganda. These legislative enactments are reserved for discussion in a later chapter.

Four years of war all but dried up the stream of immigration. This, together with the extraordinary demand on the man power of the nation, created a labor shortage. "Non-essential" industries curtailed their output, and wages in certain industries and on farms were excessively high. Women stepped into places formerly occupied by men; and at the time of the armistice it was not an unusual sight to see women dressed in overalls on their way to work. In some occupations women permanently displaced men, as for instance operating passenger elevators in department stores and office buildings. After the armistice prosperity ebbed rapidly and thousands sought employment in vain.

In an earlier chapter we have seen that serious strikes threatened to disrupt the war program and that the National War Labor Board was created to adjust disputes. The extraordinary powers of federal and state governments enabled officials to take arbitrary measures; but after the armistice an epidemic of strikes broke out, accompanied by a wave of lawlessness. In January, 1919, some fifteen thousand marine workers in New York Harbor went on strike, and a serious food shortage was threatened. In June a nation-wide strike of telegraph operators was threatened. In August railroad shopmen struck. Wilson notified them that they must return to work before the government would act on their demands for wage increases; and at the same time he sent a message to Congress in which he bore down on the profiteers and recommended measures to reduce the cost of living. A few days later the President refused to grant the wage increases, and the director-general of the railroads ordered the employees to return to work under threat that the government would run the railroads.

A sensational manifestation of the prevailing unrest was the strike of the police in Boston in September, 1919, which was accompanied by violence and rioting. According to the newspapers, crooks and gamblers flocked into the city and the state troops were attacked by mobs.

The most decisive battle in the industrial war was the steel strike which was called in September, 1919. After the organization of the United States Steel Corporation in 1901, union organizers were confronted with the opposition of this industrial mammoth. In 1901 and 1909 the Amalgamated Association of Iron, Steel, and Tin Workers met disastrous defeats in strikes. The immigrants who made up the bulk of common and semi-skilled laborers worked long hours at low pay. The Steel Corporation defended its labor policy by explaining that the labor shortage made long hours necessary and that the workingmen themselves coveted the increased earnings which long hours brought them. It also cited the immense sums appropriated for welfare work, such as accident prevention, care for the injured, its housing program and recreational facilities.

The extraordinary activity of the steel industry during the war years convinced leaders of the American Federation of Labor that the time was propitious for organizing the steel workers. Under the direction of William Z. Foster the drive for unionization got under way. The Steel Corporation made certain concessions; but the president, Elbert H. Gary, in a letter to Samuel Gompers, the president of the Federation, stated that the policy of his organization was to maintain the open shop. "In view of the well-known attitude . . . the officers of the corporation respectfully decline to discuss with you, as representatives of a labor union, any matters relating to employees."

President Wilson requested the union leaders to postpone action until after the Industrial Conference which had been called to meet on October 6, 1919. In the meantime strong pressure for immediate action came from the rank and file, workers were discharged from the mills for membership in unions, and special deputies prohibited meetings. By the end of the month over 300,000 men were on strike, the largest number in the history of the industry up to that time.

The large number of immigrants employed in the steel industry furnished an opportunity for the officials of the Steel Corporation and the newspapers to capitalize the anti-red hysteria. The strike was said to be a conspiracy hatched by Communists and Bolsheviks who were infected with un-American ideas. Foster was singled out as a fomenter of "this un-American strike" because of a pamphlet on "Syndicalism" which he had written some eight years before.

FULL-PAGE ADVERTISEMENT IN THE PITTSBURGH PRESS, OCTOBER 3
(From *The Liberator*)

Just as the strike was getting under way, President Wilson was stricken while he was on his speaking tour in behalf of the ratification of the Versailles Treaty. A committee of the Senate immediately inaugurated an investigation of the strike and poured oil on the fire by reporting that by means of the strike I.W.W.'s, anarchists, Bolsheviks, and revolutionaries were attempting to elevate themselves to power in the conservative American Federation of Labor. The Interchurch Commission of Inquiry, however, was unable to find evidence to substantiate the Senate report, in spite of many efforts to induce the several steel companies to produce it. Martial law was declared in Indiana Harbor, East Chicago, and Gary. In the latter city army intelligence officers raided radical headquarters. These and similar events were reported in the newspapers, alongside of lurid and grossly exaggerated stories about Russia and the predicted imminent collapse of the Bolshevik régime.

After the strike had been in progress for a month, Gompers and the labor group quit the Industrial Conference, in spite of Wilson's appeal from his sick bed. Gompers issued a warning that labor would meet in a future labor conference, when the other side would be glad to talk collective bargaining. Hard upon this came the threat of a strike by the bituminous coal miners. Again Wilson wrote a strong letter demanding that the strike order be rescinded in order to avert a calamity. In plain language the President announced that the government would maintain order and would operate the mines. As the strike drew near in the closing days of October, the government planned to use every resource to prevent famine, and railroads were instructed to seize coal in transit to enable them to keep traffic open. Fuel director Garfield stood ready to take charge.

On November 1, 1919, nearly 400,000 men went out, a day or two after a federal district judge in Indianapolis had issued a temporary restraining order against eighty-four officials of the United Mine Workers of America. (This order was later made permanent.) In this strike, as well as in the steel strike, public opinion was intensely hostile to the strikers. The miners wanted the government to intervene, but Attorney-General Palmer insisted that the injunction would stand and that there would be no parleying until the men returned to work. A hostile government, a hostile court, and an unsympathetic public were more than the strikers could overcome; and on November 11 the strike was called off. In spite of its brief duration, however, coal shipments to non-essential industries were curtailed, railroad passenger service was cut down, department stores and banks restricted hours, and schools, colleges, and universities closed their doors. It was not until December 10 that the strikers accepted Wilson's proposals and danger of further strike was allayed, although both sides were dissatisfied with the terms of settlement.

In the meantime, the forces of the strikers in the steel industry were torn with discord and open dissatisfaction on the part of several of the federated unions. In the first days of January, 1920, the remaining strikers capitulated without having gained a single concession, after three and one-half months of bitterness and at great cost to labor and to the industry.

Having maintained a stone wall opposition to organized labor, the Steel Corporation voluntarily granted an increase of 10 per cent in the wages of common laborers and announced its intention to grant shorter hours. It was not until seventeen years later that the steel workers under leadership other than that of the American Federation of Labor again challenged the steel companies, this time under the dynamic and bold John L. Lewis, the organizer of the Committee for Industrial Organization.

It would be difficult to exaggerate the intensity of the "red panic" of 1919, which cast long shadows into the future. Millions were in a state of hysteria; cities prepared in anticipation of raids by the I.W.W.; returning service men raided radical headquarters; and the American Legion in convention in Minneapolis in November, 1919, denounced radicals and demanded their deportation. A proposed drastic sedition act called forth a stinging denunciation from Gompers, who said that the entire A. F. of L. would oppose an enactment that would clamp an autocratic censorship over the American press.

The famous case of Sacco and Vanzetti is illustrative of the temper of the people. In the afternoon of April 15, 1920, two men carrying the payroll of a factory in South Braintree, Massachusetts, were killed by two bandits who escaped in an automobile containing several other men. On May 5 Nicola Sacco, a factory worker, and Bartolomeo Vanzetti, a fish peddler, were arrested and on September 14 were indicted for murder. The case was brought to trial on May 31, 1921, and after nearly seven weeks the jury brought in a verdict of guilty. For more than six years the case was before the courts of Massachusetts and became a topic not only of national but also of international interest.

Liberals and labor leaders in the United States and in other countries and prominent lawyers believed in the innocence of these two men, and exposed the "grave breach of official decorum" on the part of the trial judge and the composition of the jury, the contradictory and obviously inspired testimony of witnesses, and the hostile atmosphere of the courtroom. As in the Haymarket case, it developed that the defendants were on trial for their social and political beliefs. Both Sacco and Vanzetti were radicals and pacifists who had fled to Mexico to escape the Selective Service Act. Moreover, they were foreign-born Italians—all of which was played up by the prosecution in taking testimony and in addressing the jury, without interference or reproof from the trial judge. In his last statement to the court on April 9, 1927, Vanzetti said: "We were tried during a time that has now passed into history. I mean by that, a time when there was hysteria of resentment and hate against the people of our principles, against the foreigner, against slackers, and it seems to me—rather I am positive, that both you and Mr. Katzmann [the prosecuting attorney] has done all what it were in your power in order to work out, in order to agitate still more the passion of the juror, the prejudice of the juror, against us."

The courageous stand of the *Boston Herald* enlisted the support of some of the most distinguished citizens of Massachusetts—clergymen, professors, lawyers, and business men—in behalf of the doomed men, but to no avail. The men were electrocuted on August 23, 1927.

It is ironical that individuals and organizations that had opposed the principles and policies that brought the world catastrophe should have suffered bitter persecution after German militarism was crushed; but it is still more ironical that a war which was popularly supposed to wipe out militarism should have been followed by an agitation in favor of compulsory military training. The National Security League and the Universal Military Training League, with prominent business men, statesmen, judges, clergymen, and educators as directors and advisers, and certain patriotic organizations launched a campaign to expand the Reserve Officers' Training Corps and to introduce compulsory military training in high schools and colleges. Among the benefits universal military training was said to bring were the reduction of crime, physical benefits, higher sense of responsibility in citizenship, reverence for authority, and the leveling of class distinctions.

Labor and liberals detected in this proposal the spirit of those who were inimical to organized labor and liberalism in politics. For a few years after the armistice there appeared to be some prospects of success, but the tide turned. Some state universities where the administration was in the hands of liberals, like Wisconsin and Minnesota, made military training optional, much to the dismay of the army officers and conservative elements in the population.

The slump in the idealism and morale of the nation from the somewhat artificial level of 1917 and 1918 may be partially attributed to the disillusionment that inevitably follows a great war. Moreover, within a surprisingly short time after the armistice the publication of secret documents by the government of Soviet Russia and the researches of scholars revealed that the public had been grossly deceived by propaganda. Within six years the courageous and forceful writings of Harry Elmer Barnes shattered the belief that the World War was a deliberate German plot against the peace of the world and a bid for world supremacy, which had been set forth in popular form by William Stearns Davis in a book entitled *The Roots of the War*, published in the spring of 1918.

This book, which was widely read and used as a text in War Aims courses in universities and colleges, attempted to outline the circumstances that "came to play simultaneously into the hands of the Pan-German schemers, master-financiers and manufacturers, doctrinaire professors, irresponsible journalists, highly titled officers, princely and royal 'Serenities' and 'Highnesses' and above these finally, it would seem, the 'All-Highest' himself, in their deliberate conspiracy to achieve at one or, at most, two or three ruthless and gigantic strokes of the sword, the establishment of a world empire, an Empire of Teutonia, indescribably vaster, richer, and more irresistible, more universal than that of imperial Rome."

Professor Barnes' article in the *New Republic* for March 19, 1924, entitled "Seven Books of History against the Germans," was a savage attack on a well-known American professor of history for having failed to make use of recently published material that would have modified his pages on the causes of the war in his recently published book. Editorials in the daily press quoted with approval Barnes' article. The researches of other American historians, notably Sidney B. Fay and Charles A. Beard, likewise had a sobering effect on the historical and teaching profession and trickled down to the plain people.

It required more than one decade, however, before historians regained their vaunted historical-mindedness, which they had lost in the orgy of national and racial hatreds and slaughter. Teachers, professors, and textbooks continued for some time to expound the 1917-18 version of the causes of the war; but many of their contemporaries had taken to heart the words of Henry Morse Stephens, president of the American Historical Association: "Woe unto us, professional historians, professional teachers of history, if we cannot see, written in blood, in the dying civilization of Europe, the dreadful result of exaggerated nationalism as set forth in the patriotic histories of some of the eloquent historians of the Nineteenth Century."

With the return of prosperity, or the fiction of prosperity, in the third decade of the century and a more settled state of affairs abroad, the war hysteria subsided; but when the presidential campaign of 1920 approached, the public mind was in anything but a healthy condition to evaluate the fundamental and vital issues that were crying for solution. Statesmen had drawn up peace treaties, and governments had ratified them, but mankind craved the peace and security that were lost to the post-war generation.

CHAPTER XXIX

POLITICS, 1920-1928

BEFORE THE ASSEMBLING OF THE NATIONAL CONVENTIONS IN 1920, the temper of the country and the trend of events presaged the triumph of reactionary Republicanism. "Progressive" was no longer a word to conjure with. Woodrow Wilson was a tragic figure, repudiated by liberals, radicals, and leaders in his own party. In his keynote address before the Republican national convention Senator Lodge probably sounded a popular note when he exhorted the country to repudiate Wilsonism, Wilson, and all his assigns. The men who in 1912 had sought to save the Republican party from the Lodges, Smoots, and Penroses had only a feeble voice in the convention.

The lingering hope of the remaining progressives in all parties that a third party might furnish a vehicle of political expression brought a meeting of men and women interested in public affairs in New York City in January, 1919. The Committee of Forty-Eight was the result of this gathering. This committee issued a call for a national conference to be held in St. Louis in December, 1919. The three hundred delegates who attended the St. Louis meeting represented a wide variety of interests and opinions. When they assembled, it appeared for a time that the stage was set for another exhibition of lawlessness and suppression of free speech and that the meeting would not be permitted. However, on the very afternoon that the conference was scheduled to begin, the court sustained the injunction which made it possible to hold the meeting.

The brief platform was redolent of similar declarations from the Grangers, the Populists, and the Progressives. It favored public ownership of transportation facilities, public utilities, and the principal natural resources; revision of tax laws; equal economic, political, and legal rights for all; the restoration of free speech, free press, peaceable assembly, and all civil rights guaranteed by the Constitution; the abolition of injunctions in labor cases; and the right of collective bargaining. The following resolutions were adopted: It opposed the immediate return of the railroads to private control; Congress should not declare war without a popular referendum; it opposed the fostering of militarism by military training; the economic blockade of Russia should be lifted immediately; political prisoners should be immediately released; the American government should make every effort to secure universal disarmament by international agreement.

The national convention of the Committee of Forty-Eight which grew out of this conference was held at Chicago in July, 1920. It proved to be impossible to reconcile the individualistic delegates to this assembly. The laborites bolted, organized the Farmer-Labor party, and nominated Parley P. Christensen, a Utah attorney. The Committee of Forty-Eight did not place a ticket in the field. The Socialist party had already nominated Eugene V. Debs, who has the unique distinction of being the only presidential candidate to conduct his campaign from behind the walls of a penitentiary. The Prohibition party had the satisfaction of expressing "its thanks to Almighty God for the victory over the beverage traffic which crowns fifty years of consecrated effort." It rejoiced that the traffic and manufacture of intoxicating drink "have been forever prohibited in the fundamental law of the land"; that Congress had enacted laws for the enforcement of the Eighteenth Amendment; and that the Supreme Court had upheld both the amendment and the law.

The public was in the dark as to the identity of the Republican nominee until after the national convention had convened; but that the candidate would have to be acceptable to the old standpat leaders was a foregone conclusion. At a "love feast" held in Chicago in the early days of January, 1920, the Republican leaders vied with one another in denouncing radicals. At that time Frank O. Lowden of Illinois was prominently mentioned for the nomination. Herbert Hoover, whose position as food administrator had made his name a household word, was also a possible nominee.

He was definitely classed among the liberals. In an editorial on January 21, 1920, the *New York World*, which had been a consistent Wilson supporter, declared that the old parties were bankrupt in principles and that their prospective candidates for the Presidency were unacceptable. It announced that it would support Hoover on any ticket, even the Republican. This suggestion, however, did not meet with favorable response from the politicians, who made the objection that he was not "regular" enough. At first Hoover stated that he was not a candidate and declared himself in favor of the League of Nations with certain changes; but during the last days of March he declared himself to be a receptive candidate for the Republican nomination. He labeled himself an independent Republican in favor of a "forward-looking platform."

When the delegates to the Republican national convention assembled at Chicago in June, Governor Frank O. Lowden, Senator Hiram Johnson, and General Leonard Wood were the most prominent of the presidential possibilities. Johnson had made a surprisingly good showing in the primaries, but he was obnoxious to the old-line leaders because of his Progressive bolt in 1912. Wood had the largest number of delegates pledged to him. There was little enthusiasm either in the convention or in the country at large; and when it was learned that Warren G. Harding of Ohio and Calvin Coolidge of Massachusetts had been chosen to be the standard bearers, the public was not only surprised but astounded.

Harding was not an unknown man. He had carried the Ohio primary election in April, but his vote was less than 50 per cent, and it was conceded that he had been eliminated from any chance of obtaining the nomination. He had been a member of the Ohio legislature, attorney-general of Ohio, and at the time of his nomination was a United States Senator. He had been a henchman of Joseph B. Foraker of Standard Oil fame. His political associates, soon to become infamous as the "Ohio gang," were bad. This newspaper editor was the beneficiary of political methods and policies that had been condemned by liberals, progressives, and reformers ever since the days of the Populists. In 1912 Harding trailed Theodore Roosevelt on his campaign tours and sought by reactionary speeches to stem the tide of progressive thought. As a Senator his speeches were rambling and diffuse and revealed the man portrayed in an editorial in the *New Republic* of August 14, 1920: "Not in this generation has a more illiterate mind and a feebler intelligence reached so exalted a place. . . . The Republican papers know that to be the truth. Because they can think of nothing else to praise, they are praising Mr. Harding's 'character.' . . . Should they elect him, a regency would be necessary almost immediately, if America is to preserve any dignity in the eyes of the world."

The nomination of this man who had some of the virtues and all the faults of a typical "good fellow" in politics—whose administration was so malodorous that for months an ex-President and a President of the United States belonging to his party could not be induced to deliver addresses at the dedication of a great memorial in his honor—was engineered by a coterie of politicians who summoned him to a room in a Chicago hotel to inquire if there was anything in his private life that would make him unavailable for the nomination. Upon being assured that there was nothing (later revelations proved that he was the father of an illegitimate child), Lodge of Massachusetts, Brandegee of Connecticut, Smoot of Utah, Wadsworth of New York, Harold F. McCormick of Illinois, and George Harvey, the persistent maligner of Wilson in his *Weekly*, accomplished their purpose.

Calvin Coolidge, a tight-lipped machine politician who was the direct opposite of Harding in personality, was nominated for the Vice-Presidency because of the newspaper publicity he had received at the time of the Boston police strike in September, 1919. In November Coolidge was reelected governor of Massachusetts by a huge majority over his Democratic opponent, who had expressed sympathy with the policemen. President Wilson telegraphed his congratulations on the victory for law and order. That Coolidge's courage in the crisis was proved to be greatly inflated did not dim his luster in the pages of the Republican newspapers. In the popular mind Coolidge was thought of as a "bigger man" than his running mate.

Harding's speech of acceptance was a commonplace effort expressed in clumsy style. He began by paying his respects to the autocratic rule of the past years. "No man is big enough to run this great republic. There never has been one," he said. He condemned the League of Nations, but declared for "an association of nations." He catalogued the problems that confronted the country and promised to solve them without committing himself to specific measures.

After the Republican convention had done its work, the newspapers concerned themselves about speculations as to the Democratic nominee. There was uncertainty about Wilson's position. Would he allow his name to go before the convention or would he get behind a certain candidate? There was little enthusiasm for Wilson and his policies among the delegates, but the convention could not repudiate the man who for eight years had been the titular head of the party. Bryan was present at the convention and made known his opposition to the League of Nations. To judge by the newspapers, William G. McAdoo, son-in-law of Wilson, and his war-time Secretary of the Treasury, appeared to be the favorite candidate, but his close association with the President was a liability. A. Mitchell Palmer, the red-baiting Attorney-General, James S. Cox, an Ohio newspaper publisher and machine politician, and Bainbridge Colby, Secretary of State, were also in the running, with some mention of Alfred E. Smith of New York. On the forty-fourth ballot Cox was nominated. Franklin Delano Roosevelt of New York, Assistant Secretary of the Navy, was nominated for the Vice-Presidency.

The keynote speech of Homer S. Cummings glorified the Wilson administration and portrayed Wilson as a martyr to blind partisanship and hatred; but the platform, though more liberal than the Republican, was not calculated to arouse enthusiasm among progressives. However, the character of the opposing candidates and their platforms signified little in the contest that followed; the issue was Wilsonism. The discontented factions—and they were legion—united to wreak vengeance on the party in power. Among the foreign-born voters each group had its own grievance in terms of the Treaty of Versailles, as well as propaganda directed against them while they were obliged to remain silent. The plight of farmers, whose farms were saddled with heavy mortgages, high prices and mounting rents, unemployment, and a host of other grievances—all spelled a Republican victory.

Harding conducted a "front-porch campaign" at his home in Marion; Cox made a stumping tour of the country. The Democratic candidate surprised the political commentators by coming out for the League of Nations and the ratification of the treaty in his speech of acceptance. Harding's statements on the League of Nations were equivocal; his advisers apparently were not certain how much strength there was for the League, in view of the declarations made by prominent Republicans that they would vote for Cox and the League of Nations. The straddling of the Republicans was even more obvious after election, when prominent men in the party like Elihu Root and leading Republican newspapers stated that under the Harding administration the United States would enter the League of Nations. When Harding said the League of Nations was dead, they claimed, he meant the League of Article X.

The Republican landslide was a victory for the Old Guard, which Theodore Roosevelt had fought and Woodrow Wilson had scornfully ignored. Perhaps Taft—destined to be appointed chief justice by Harding—wrote with prophetic insight in the *Yale Review* for October, 1920, when he said: "There is no greater domestic issue in this election than the maintenance of the Supreme Court as the bulwark to enforce the guarantee that no man shall be deprived of his property without due process of law." He criticized two of Wilson's three appointments to the Supreme Court, Louis D. Brandeis and John H. Clarke, who represented a new school of constitutional construction which if allowed to prevail, he said, would greatly imperil the fundamental law. The former President referred to the fact that four of the incumbent justices were over seventy years of age, and the next President would probably be called upon to appoint their successors.

Harding's inaugural address was a hodgepodge of involved sentences and platitudes. "We must strive for normalcy to reach stability," he said. In his quest for "normalcy" the President had the cooperation of a House and Senate under Old Guard leadership and of a cabinet that was a curious conglomerate of ability, mediocrity, and venality. Charles E. Hughes, Secretary of State, and Herbert Hoover, Secretary of Commerce, were outstanding. The Secretary of the Treasury was Andrew W. Mellon, a Pittsburgh millionaire, a director and stockholder in financial institutions and manufacturing corporations, who under three successive Presidents was acclaimed as the "greatest Secretary of the Treasury since Hamilton" until the debacle of 1929. The appointment of Albert B. Fall as Secretary of the Interior struck consternation in the hearts of liberals. A man of low instincts, in his career in the Senate he had been chiefly concerned to foment war with Mexico in order to force intervention to protect American oil and mining interests. During the Wilson administration his one obsession seems to have been to embarrass the President in his efforts to allow Mexico to work out her own problems and to maintain peace between the two neighbors. As late as December, 1919, he introduced a resolution to sever diplomatic relations with Mexico.

Harry M. Daugherty, one of the "Ohio gang" and mentor of Harding, was a rabid enemy of organized labor and the most dangerous man ever to occupy the important position of Attorney-General. For the wrecking of the Harding administration Fall and Daugherty must bear a major portion of the blame. They and their associates took Harding's measure and not only looted the government of millions of dollars but debauched their departments and besmirched the name of the government.

Under the leaderless Wilson administration and with the presidential election approaching, Congress marked time and bequeathed to the incoming administration a plethora of problems. Both the irreconcilables and the progressives showed impatience. In the special session Congress, on July 2, 1921, complied with Harding's recommendation for a resolution declaring the war with Germany ended. But the tariff was more difficult to handle. An emergency tariff was approved in May, 1921; but it was not until September 19, 1922, that the Fordney-McCumber Tariff Act went into effect. It was the highest tariff down to that time. A Tariff Commission was created, and the President was clothed with power to proclaim new rates recommended by the commission, but he could ignore recommendations if he so desired. The tariff act remained in force until it was superseded by the Smoot-Hawley Act of June 17, 1930.

Harding incurred the powerful opposition of the war veterans by opposing legislation granting them a fifty-dollar bonus for each month of service. Because of the condition of the treasury, the President opposed it unless a sales tax were levied. Congress, however, passed the bill, but it was vetoed on September 19, 1922.

In an effort to alleviate labor unrest, Harding called an unemployment conference at Washington in September, 1921, but he had no specific recommendations to make when it assembled. "It is fair to say that you are not asked to solve the long-controverted problems of our social system," he said. "We have builded the America of today on the fundamentals of economic, industrial, and political life which made us what we are, and the temple requires no remaking now. We are incontestably sound." The recommendations adopted by the conference were made on the assumption that unemployment was essentially a problem for each community to solve.

It was not many months before serious strikes of railroad shopmen and coal miners contradicted the President's assurance that the country was incontestably sound. It was a danger signal that was ignored, except for the realization of employers throughout the country that the time had come to deal a smashing blow to organized labor.

In July, 1920, the employees of the railroads were awarded a substantial increase in pay; and this was followed within a few days by an order from the Interstate Commerce Commission granting the greatest increase in railroad rates in history. On July 1, 1921, on recommendation of the Railway Labor Board, the wages of employees on practically every large railroad were reduced. The danger of an immediate strike was averted by divided counsels among labor leaders. A year later, however, the Railway Labor Board ordered a reduction of the wages of shopmen, and this precipitated a strike on July 1, 1922. Previously, on April 1, the coal miners had struck.

The railroads prepared for a fight to the finish; they immediately advertised for men to take the places vacated by the strikers and issued a warning that unless the men returned to work before a certain date, they would lose seniority rights and pensions. Injunctions against picketing were granted; and in September, shortly before the strike ended, Attorney-General Daugherty obtained in the United States District Court in Chicago an injunction applicable throughout the country against strikers and union officials. Previously, on July 11, Harding had issued a proclamation directing all persons to refrain from interference with lawful efforts to maintain interstate transportation and the carrying of mail.

In protest against the use of armed guards, trainmen on some railroads struck out of sympathy. In the face of severe criticism for his infirm grappling with the serious state of affairs, Harding addressed Congress on August 18. He reviewed the course of events pertaining to both strikes, condemned the lawless acts of the strikers, and censured those who waged war on labor unions. He made no important recommendations, but proclaimed that government by law must be maintained. After weeks and months of violence, the coal strike virtually ended on August 15, and the railroad strike in the middle of September. With the exception of minor concessions, labor met ignominious defeat. It was left in an ugly mood, and the administration had definitely lost ground.

Another grievance against the administration in the Northwest, where there were serious signs of revolt against the old parties, was the nomination of Pierce Butler of St. Paul to the Supreme Court on November 23, 1922. La Follette of Wisconsin blocked the immediate confirmation of this prominent railroad and corporation attorney, who had made himself obnoxious to liberals by his tactics in the courtroom and as a member of the Board of Regents of the University of Minnesota. After his nomination, the *Minneapolis Star*, the organ of the Farmer-Labor party, published extracts from Upton Sinclair's *The Goose Step* in which Butler's methods were exposed. A former professor in the University of Minnesota, who after many years of distinguished service had been summarily dismissed for disloyalty in 1917, was summoned to Washington to testify against the nominee. The appointment of John F. McGee of Minneapolis, who was of the Butler type, to a federal judgeship was also a political mistake.

The disasters that overtook the Republican party in Minnesota, North Dakota, and Wisconsin in 1922 and 1923, and the disaffection of Republicans like Senator Smith W. Brookhart of Iowa and Senator George W. Norris of Nebraska, were symptoms that were too plain to be misunderstood. In 1922 Senator Frank B. Kellogg of Minnesota, who had launched a bitter attack on La Follette by impugning his patriotism, was defeated by Henrik Shipstead, the candidate of the Farmer-Labor party. La Follette got sweet revenge when he spoke in behalf of Shipstead in St. Paul and Minneapolis and castigated the Twin City papers, which had maligned him after his St. Paul speech in 1917, and excoriated Kellogg as a cringing servant of predatory interests. The immense crowds and enthusiastic receptions that awaited the Wisconsin Senator not only revealed the unpopularity of the Republican party but also showed how sharply public opinion had reversed itself.

An even more vital blow was struck against the Harding régime when in a special election on July 17, 1923, Magnus Johnson, a "dirt farmer," was elected to succeed the late veteran Republican Senator Knute Nelson. The country watched the campaign in Minnesota and was astounded at the huge majority rolled up by the Farmer-Labor candidate, who in 1891 came as an immigrant to the United States and spoke with a pronounced Swedish "brogue." Harding was apprised of this blow to his party on his return trip from Alaska, which was cut short by his sudden death in San Francisco on August 2, 1923. Although at the time the country was not aware of the orgy of corruption in Washington, Harding knew enough to hasten his death. He knew that impeachment proceedings had been proposed against Attorney-General Daugherty.

In the Wisconsin primary elections of September, 1922, the La Follette slate won a decisive victory over the old-line faction, in spite of efforts to revive the war hysteria and discredit La

Follette as only a "voice of protest" in the Senate. La Follette made no apology for his vote against the war resolution and delivered telling blows against the Esch-Cummins Act (which will be discussed later), the pending Fordney-McCumber Tariff, and the Harding administration generally.

The elections of November, 1922, brought reproof to old-line leadership in both major parties. It was not only that the Republicans lost six Senators and that their number in the House was reduced from 299 to 222, but that such staunch Republican Senators as Townsend of Michigan, Calder of New York, and Kellogg of Minnesota went down to defeat. Even Senator Lodge was reelected by only a small margin.

Harding's tragic death probably saved him from impeachment —certainly from humiliation such as no President has experienced. His body had hardly been laid to rest in the temporary tomb in the cemetery near Marion, Ohio, before the storm broke. Although his successor, Calvin Coolidge, had sat with Harding's cabinet without any public sign of disapproval of what was going on, the country had confidence in his integrity. He had made himself ridiculous in the estimation of the critically minded by his platitudinous articles in popular magazines and by his speeches. The Republicans could retort that it was sacrilege to step on the dead body of Harding; and the apostles of the *status quo* did not propose to discredit his successor who would be just as innocuous and complacent. "Keep cool with Coolidge" was the campaign slogan in 1924, and that meant that the government should keep hands off business. Some years later the well-known humorist of his day, Will Rogers, said of Coolidge: "He didn't do anything, but that's what people wanted done."

During the storm that raged while the newspapers teemed with the scandals of the Harding administration, the Republican papers put the soft pedal on the editorial pages and thanked God that a calm man like Coolidge was in the White House. When the Democrats and insurgent Republicans in Congress tried to prod the President into action, the newspapers condemned them as demagogues. The same papers that had applauded Congress for opposing Wilson now accused Congress of usurping the prerogatives of the executive.

It was inevitable that in the Congress that convened in December, 1923, and continued until the presidential campaign was under way the Democrats and the insurgents should capitalize the scandals of the Republican administration and use every means of implicating Republicans in the systematic looting of the government. In syndicated articles the carelessness and dishonesty in the administration of the Veterans' Bureau were laid bare, and Charles R. Forbes, the head of the bureau, was sent to jail. It is estimated that more than two hundred million dollars in graft were collected by Forbes and his lieutenants.

Investigations into the affairs of the office of the Alien Property Custodian convicted T. W. Miller, the custodian, and implicated not only Mal S. Daugherty, brother of the Attorney-General, but the Attorney-General himself. Moreover, Jess Smith, who shared an apartment with Attorney-General Daugherty, collected millions of dollars from violators of the prohibition law, which he turned over to the "Ohio gang." Suicides, suspected murders, destruction of letters and ledgers, and refusals to testify before investigating committees saved individuals from prosecution. Daugherty was brought to trial, but two juries were unable to agree and the indictment was dismissed. Pressure was put on Daugherty to resign and on Coolidge to compel his resignation; but the Attorney-General stubbornly refused until finally Coolidge's embarrassment was so great that the President demanded his resignation on March 27, 1924, in a letter that left something to be desired in the way of moral indignation.

The scandal that rocked the country was revealed by the adoption of a resolution introduced in the Senate by La Follette instructing the Committee on Public Lands to investigate the subject of leases upon naval oil reserves. The investigation was conducted by Senator Thomas J. Walsh of Montana, a Democrat. This able, just, and skillful lawyer proceeded with such fact-finding deliberation that it was eighteen months before the stage was set for one of the most dramatic episodes in American history.

Unrelenting and skillful examination of witnesses, aided somewhat by the stupidity of the criminals themselves and "lucky breaks," proved that Albert B. Fall, Secretary of the Interior, had leased the naval oil reserves at Teapot Dome, Wyoming, and at Elk Hills, California, to Harry F. Sinclair and Edward F. Doheny, wealthy oil magnates. These oil reserves for the use of the navy were under the jurisdiction of the Secretary of the Navy. However, with the approval of the amiable and incompetent Secretary of the Navy, Edwin Denby, Secretary Fall induced President Harding to sign an executive order transferring the reserves to the Secretary of the Interior. In a communication to the Senate, Harding stated that the transfer of custody and the leases had at all times had his "entire approval." Senator Walsh's investigations, lawsuits, and criminal trials showed that Fall had received large sums of money from Doheny and Sinclair. Fall, shattered in health and spirit, was sentenced to serve a year in the penitentiary; Doheny and Sinclair were acquitted, though the latter served a double term in prison for contempt of the Senate in refusing to answer questions; and the Supreme Court voided the Doheny and Sinclair leases.

It was cruel irony that the morning papers of February 4, 1924, which reported the proceedings of the Senate committee in the Teapot Dome scandal, also reported the death of Woodrow Wilson. Still more ironical were editorial comments that the world was not ready for Wilson's idealism. "Humanity failed or was not equal to the faith he had in human nature," was the comment of a newspaper that had entirely failed to give its readers a sympathetic interpretation of his policies.

More cruel than ironical was the fate that befell Thomas J. Walsh and Burton K. Wheeler, whose courage and ability had exposed the orgy of corruption. Leading newspapers hurled at them such epithets as "Montana scandalmongers" and "assassins of character." In revenge, on April 8, 1924, Wheeler was indicted by a federal grand jury charged with unlawfully receiving money as a retainer fee to influence the issuance of oil- and gas-prospecting permits. The Senator was later exonerated.

The Republican party, no less than Harding himself, was fortunate in the time of the President's death. Long before the Republican national convention assembled at Cleveland, it was certain that Coolidge would be nominated to succeed himself. The progressives expected and received nothing but rebuffs. But for the refusal of the La Follette delegates from Wisconsin and South Dakota, Coolidge's nomination would have been unanimous. Charles G. Dawes of Illinois was nominated for the Vice-Presidency, after Frank O. Lowden had declined the proffered honor.

The unspeakable corruption of the Harding administration and the colorless administration of his successor warranted predictions that if the Democrats nominated an outstanding candidate from the Middle West or Far West, they would win. But the spirit and conduct of the delegates to the Democratic national convention were not calculated to promote harmony or to inspire confidence in the leadership of the party. Thomas J. Walsh presided over a noisy turmoil of name-calling and fist fights between the adherents of Alfred E. Smith, efficient governor of New York and a Roman Catholic, and William G. McAdoo, the choice of the Ku Klux Klan. The convention city, New York, was favorable to its son, Al Smith, and the galleries were filled with his enthusiastic supporters who booed Bryan and yelled "oil" at the mention of McAdoo's name. After two weeks of bedlam, John W. Davis of West Virginia was nominated on the one hundred and third ballot. Charles W. Bryan of Nebraska, a brother of the Great Commoner, was nominated for the Vice-Presidency, after Senator Walsh and E. T. Meredith of Iowa had declined the nomination.

Davis was a former ambassador to Great Britain and an able man, possessing all the qualifications of wealth and society; but he was a conservative and a corporation lawyer who made no appeal to the western farmer who had barely eked out his sustenance during four years of depression. In the ensuing campaign the Republican papers, confident that the schismatic Democratic party had no chance of success, praised Davis and conceded that he was the best possible candidate. This strategy was devised to keep the Democrats faithful to their own party and to prevent them from voting for La Follette, the candidate of the Progressive party, who had been nominated by the Conference for Progressive Political Action at Cleveland. In a letter to the convention La Follette accepted the nomination and declared himself opposed to placing in the field candidates for other offices against progressive Democrats and Republicans. Two weeks later the national committee nominated a Democrat, Senator Wheeler, for the Vice-Presidency.

The campaign was a drab affair, with two colorless and conservative candidates pitted against each other, and the third too radical to have even a faint chance in a year when people voted for the *status quo* rather than for principles, party, or men. Coolidge's popular and electoral vote was large. States in which La Follette was expected to have heavy support were comfortably in the Republican column; but there were indications that the unpopularity of the Democratic candidate and the fictitious prosperity of the country, which obviously brought the results, made the victory barren for the Republicans.

La Follette's popular vote was nearly five million; in twelve middle-western and far-western states it either exceeded or nearly approached that of Davis, an indication that some Republicans and many more sincere liberal Democrats did not want to see their states committed to Coolidge and what he stood for. It was a negative victory, giving a lease of life to a party which but for circumstances not to be credited to the foresight of its leaders would have gone down to defeat. Four years later a divided Democratic party, without even an auxiliary liberal third party, extended the Republican lease for another administration, perhaps fortunately for the Democratic party.

Intoxicated by their triumph, the Republican regulars proceeded to heat a furnace for their disloyal Republican colleagues when Congress convened in December, 1925; but an aggressive Democratic minority and an unruly agricultural and progressive bloc made it difficult for Coolidge to pursue anything but a negative course. The resignation of Charles E. Hughes from the State portfolio boded no good for the administration. Hughes gave as his reason for resigning the desire to retire from public life; but there was reason for suspecting that the succession of a western progressive and an irreconcilable on the League of Nations, Senator Borah, to the chairmanship of the Committee on Foreign Relations had some bearing on the Secretary's decision. The appointment of Frank B. Kellogg as Secretary of State neither strengthened the hand of the government in dealing with Mexico and Europe nor gave prestige to the administration at home.

Another manifestation of the strained relations between the President and Congress was the refusal of the Senate to confirm the appointment of Charles F. Warren as Attorney-General because of his unfortunate connection with certain business transactions. Under John Garibaldi Sargent the office of the Attorney-General was entirely passive and oblivious to the Sherman Anti-Trust Act and to the machinations of business, a fact that cannot be overlooked in searching for the causes of the debacle that overtook the country not long after Coolidge had left the White House.

The defeat in the Republican primary election in Pennsylvania of Senator George W. Pepper, an administration man, by William S. Vare in May, 1926, in a contest marked by the reckless and lavish use of money, was variously interpreted, but it certainly did not add to the prestige of the administration. In the following month Smith W. Brookhart, an insurgent Republican and a militant critic of Coolidge, defeated Senator Albert B. Cummins, a Coolidge regular, in the Iowa primary election. That Iowa, hitherto a rock-ribbed Republican state, cast its vote against the administration spoke loudly of the discontent in the agricultural West. In September of the same year John J. Blaine, a La Follette man, defeated Senator Irvine L. Lenroot, who belonged to the opposing faction. In the fall elections the Republicans lost such stalwarts in the Senate as William Butler of Massachusetts, Coolidge's right-hand man, and James W. Wadsworth of New York. In the new Senate there were 48 Republicans, 47 Democrats, and one Farmer-Laborite.

In spite of these and other "straws" which indicated the direction of the political breeze, it was a sensational surprise when on August 2, 1927, Coolidge summoned the newspaper reporters assigned to his summer camp in the Black Hills of South Dakota and handed them a mimeographed slip reading as follows: "I do not choose to run for President in 1928." For months political prognosticators speculated as to the meaning of this cryptic statement. It certainly left room for his nomination if the "public demanded it," and it was calculated to dispel the third-term objection. In the previous April Coolidge had refused to reply to an open letter to be published in the *Forum*, asking him to state his attitude toward a "third term." After the laconic statement had been made, the importunities of a steady procession of White House visitors in the succeeding months yielded no clarifying statement. Neither were there indications of preference for one of the numerous men in line for the succession. The chief usher of the White House and the employees who watched carefully for any change in the President's attitude or in his relations with his political advisers were forced to conclude that he hoped to the very last that the convention would "draft" him.

In the Republican national convention in Kansas City there was no audible sentiment in favor of Coolidge's nomination. Herbert Hoover was nominated on the first ballot; but he was not the choice of old-line Republicans like Andrew Mellon, James E. Watson of Indiana, and Charles Curtis of Kansas. However, Hoover's organizing ability, shrewd bargaining, and bungling opposition brought results. His loyalty to party was under suspicion, and he had none of the "graces" of the expert politician; but he was in the good graces of Lady Fortune. The fates were again unkind to the Democratic party.

Before the Democratic national convention assembled at Houston, Texas, it was certain that Alfred E. Smith would be the nominee. Why he should have won the nomination on the first ballot, with only a few scattering votes for favorite sons, is somewhat of a mystery, in view of the fact that he was bitterly opposed by prominent Democrats who could not reconcile themselves to having a Roman Catholic, a wet, and a Tammany man in the White House.

Al Smith, as he was popularly known, was a product of New York City and had come "up from the city streets." He had been a newsboy, a "truck chaser" for a truckman, an office boy, an assistant shipping clerk, a salesman and bookkeeper in a fish market, a common laborer handling steam pipes, and a subpoena server, before he was elected to the New York Assembly. He was a member of Tammany, and learned many valuable lessons from the politicians who frequented that club. He was an industrious and able member of the Assembly. As a member of the New York Constitutional Convention of 1915 he proved himself to be well informed about government. After filling other public offices with credit, he was four times elected governor of New York, made a brilliant record, and won the confidence of liberals and exponents of good government.

The prolonged conflict between the Smith and the McAdoo forces in the Democratic national convention of 1924 split the party wide open. It was recognized that the principal objection to Smith was his membership in the Roman Catholic church. Smith's growing strength alarmed his opponents, as witnessed by "An Open Letter" to Smith by Charles C. Marshall published in the *Atlantic Monthly* for April, 1927. In an able article Smith made it plain that in the event of a conflict between the Catholic church and the government, he would be for the government. Unfortunately, the activity of prominent Catholic prelates and laymen in condemning the church policy of the Mexican government was fresh in the memory of many Americans, and the spirit of the Ku Klux Klan was still abroad in the land.

For the first time the radio was an important medium of reaching the voters, and both Smith and Hoover were heard over national hookups. Hoover, though far from being an effective campaigner, had an advantage over his opponent, whose "radio voice" was far from agreeable. Moreover, Smith alienated rather than attracted votes by devoting portions of his addresses to replies to the effective speeches delivered by Senator Borah. These attacks were not calculated to strengthen the Democratic candidate in the West, where his support was weak. Replying to Smith's reference to Hoover's silence at the time of the Teapot Dome scandal, Borah inquired if Smith was willing to adopt the "rule of vicarious responsibility in his campaign." "Is the governor willing to try this campaign upon the question of associations? The governor has been a member of Tammany Hall for thirty odd years. Is he responsible for the stealings and extortions of Croker? . . . Let us not try candidates in this campaign by association. It would be too severe."

Prosperity, or at least the belief that the country was prosperous, was the best asset the Republican party had; and the Tammany millstone around the neck of the Democratic donkey was the worst liability of the opposition.

Herbert Hoover had 444 electoral votes, against 87 for his opponent. By carrying Virginia, North Carolina, Florida, Tennessee, and Texas—states of the "Solid South"—Hoover won the distinction of being the first Republican President since 1876 to make serious inroads on that bloc. Of the northern states, Smith carried only Massachusetts and Rhode Island, industrial states, with large foreign-born and Catholic populations. The Republicans gained several seats in the Senate, but it is significant that progressive Republican and Democratic Senators were re-elected.

Smith could congratulate himself that his popular vote exceeded that of any defeated presidential candidate; and within a few months he could congratulate his party as well as himself that Hoover was President of the United States.

CHAPTER XXX

FOREIGN RELATIONS SINCE THE WORLD WAR

THE TANGLED SKEIN OF POST-WAR DIPLOMACY BAFFLES SIMPLI-fication. The unsuccessful efforts of Wilson to obtain the ratification of the Treaty of Versailles and the overwhelming defeat of the Democratic party in 1920 made succeeding Presidents—Harding, Coolidge, and Hoover—chary of injecting the League of Nations into the public forum. Moreover, on more than one occasion the Senate refused to ratify unconditionally the protocol that would have made the United States a member of the Permanent Court of International Justice, usually called the World Court. On January 29, 1935, a Senate with a heavy Democratic majority rejected the resolution of adherence by a vote of 52 to 36, with 43 Democrats and 9 Republicans in favor, and 20 Democrats, 14 Republicans, one Progressive, and one Farmer-Laborite against. Public opinion seems to have been either lukewarm or hostile; and it was suspected that even Franklin Roosevelt himself was not enthusiastic.

In spite of the fear of "entangling alliances" ingrained in the American people, their government has been steadily drawn into the coils of world diplomacy. Within slightly more than two months after Harding's inauguration, Secretary Hughes accepted the invitation of the Allies to "sit in" with the Supreme Council when it considered the amount of the German reparations; but for about two years he showed little interest in the work of the League of Nations, except for the formal acknowledgment of certain communications. However, the United States was the greatest creditor in the world, and the government could not ignore the trend of events abroad if it was to protect its own interests and those of its citizens.

During the war the United States loaned to the Allies more

than seven billion dollars, and in addition more than three billion to relieve the civilian populations of these countries and to bolster the credit of their governments. Moreover, during the war and after, large sums in the form of voluntary contributions for the Red Cross and similar organizations crossed the Atlantic. At the peace conference the American delegates refused to entertain the proposition that the payment of the war debts be made dependent on the payment of huge reparations to be exacted from Germany. To have done so would have entangled the United States in the machinery for collecting the reparations.

In January, 1923, President Harding ordered the return of American troops who were occupying Coblenz as part of the army of occupation. This order was issued just at the time the French troops were ready to march into the Ruhr Valley to take possession of that rich industrial region, an act of coercion permitted by the treaty in the event that Germany failed to live up to its terms. Conditions in Europe were becoming worse. France's invasion of the Ruhr made it necessary for Germany to agree to a compromise in the matter of reparations.

At the suggestion of Secretary Hughes, the Reparations Commission invited Charles G. Dawes and Owen D. Young to preside over international commissions to work out a plan by which Germany could pay her obligations. The Dawes plan was in effect from 1924 to 1929, when it was superseded by the Young plan, both of which scaled down the bill for reparations. The Ruhr invasion turned American public opinion against France. Even the newspapers changed their tone and demanded that the United States make it plain that it did not approve of the French militaristic policy.

Meanwhile efforts were being made to bring about a settlement of the debts owed by the Allies to the United States. Over a period of seven years extending from 1923, agreements for funding these debts were made with the respective governments. Force of circumstances compelled Uncle Sam to be a generous creditor, but it was impossible to convince the peoples of Europe of that fact. In the aggregate, about 43 per cent of the total indebtedness was canceled, some countries getting more favorable settlements than others. Payments were made until 1931, when a financial crisis in Germany threatened to wreck the financial structure of Europe. With the approval of Republican and Democratic leaders in Congress, Hoover proposed a one-year moratorium. Except for Finland, the debtor nations have not paid a penny since; and soon even "token" payments were discontinued.

Prominent financiers, business men, and economists proposed the permanent cancellation of the debts as sound economic policy; but the refusal of leaders of both political parties to write the proposal into their platforms is indicative of a public opinion impatient with European statesmen who recommended large appropriations for armies and navies in preference to paying obligations to a government which extended liberal credits in time of dire need and whose citizens poured out their blood and substance without demanding anything in return except a righteous peace.

Harding made a magnificent gesture looking to international good will when he issued a call to an international conference on disarmament. What prompted the President was the adoption by the Senate of a resolution directing him to consult with Great Britain and Japan on the subject of disarmament.

On Armistice Day, 1921, Washington was the scene of impressive festivities over the burial of an unknown American soldier, whose remains had been brought from France to rest in a shrine at Arlington. The day before, thousands had filed past his coffin under the dome of the Capitol. On Armistice Day in the presence of delegates to the disarmament conference—a day marked by the first public appearance of Woodrow Wilson since his retirement from the Presidency—President Harding made a fine address; and on the following day he opened the conference with an address of welcome. After Secretary Hughes had been unanimously chosen presiding officer, he read an address which was an effective, practical, and bold proposal for a ten-year naval holiday and the scrapping of capital ships belonging to the United States, Great Britain, and Japan. It was finally agreed that the respective armaments of these nations should be reduced according to the ratio 5—5—3. This represented a greater sacrifice on the part of the United States than on the part of the other two powers, because the United States had many more new battleships completed or under construction. Unfortunately, the limitation did not include submarines and aircraft.

The conference was not without dramatic moments, which threatened to plunge it into the bargaining and compromises that made the Treaty of Versailles so odious. When the French delegates opposed the inclusion of airplanes, they were reminded of the huge debts owed to the United States and Great Britain and of the lavish preparations for war. The head of the delegation replied defiantly that France was as proud of that debt as a wounded man is proud of his scars and that she intended to pay it. When the same spokesman accepted America's proposal to outlaw submarine warfare against merchantmen "in principle," Secretary Hughes asked what that could mean with reference to such a broad proposal.

The most important thing that emerged from the Washington conference was the nine-power treaty by which the signatories agreed to respect the sovereignty, independence, and territorial integrity of China; to allow China to maintain an effective and stable government; to use their influence to establish and maintain the principle of equal opportunity for the commerce and industry of all nations throughout China; and to refrain from seeking special rights or privileges in China. According to Henry L. Stimson, Secretary of State in the Hoover administration, "this was one of the most admirable and far-sighted treaties in the history of modern civilization."

Another treaty, known as the four-power pact between the United States, Great Britain, France, and Japan, bound the signatories to respect the colonial possessions of the respective powers in the Pacific and to construct no new fortifications or naval bases in those possessions.

A distinguished student of diplomatic history, Samuel Flagg Bemis, concludes that the Washington conference amounted to a "face-saving retreat of the United States from active diplomacy in the Far East under cover of a multilateral international agreement for the observance of the traditional American policies for the Open Door and the administrative, political, and territorial integrity of China." This conclusion, however, represents the opinion of a scholar who is consistently critical of American post-war diplomacy.

Another achievement of American diplomacy, highly acclaimed at the time, was the Pact of Paris, usually known as the Kellogg-Briand Pact. This pact had its immediate origin in a suggestion from Aristide Briand, the French minister of foreign affairs, that the United States and France pledge themselves never to go to war with each other, although neither of these statesmen had much to do with the inception or extension of the principle. That distinction belongs to James T. Shotwell, professor of history in Columbia University. Secretary Kellogg formally suggested that other nations be invited to join in a pact of perpetual friendship. The upshot was a document pledging the high contracting parties to renounce war as an instrument of national policy in their relations with one another and to settle all disputes or conflicts by peaceful means. In August, 1928, Secretary Kellogg visited Paris, and he and Briand affixed their signatures to the document. All the great powers and all but a handful of the other nations of the world speedily ratified it.

The effectiveness of the pact was nullified by Kellogg's explanation that it did not outlaw wars of self-defense. Inasmuch as the United States regards an infringement of the Monroe Doctrine as a menace to its national security, and inasmuch as Japan invaded China and Italy sent an army against Ethiopia without a formal declaration of war, the Kellogg-Briand Pact may be cited as documentary evidence of the international anarchy that prevailed in the twentieth century.

Secretary Kellogg also negotiated a new series of arbitration treaties with about thirty nations, but many vital questions were excluded from their scope. Most alarming and significant was the omission of Japan from the list of arbitration and conciliation treaties to which the United States was a party, although both nations pledged perpetual peace by adherence to the Kellogg-Briand Pact.

In a previous chapter we have seen that after the Russo-Japanese War the relations between the United States and Japan grew increasingly strained, although both nations expressed friendly sentiments and deprecated the danger of war—an ominous sign. The Gentlemen's Agreement of 1907 was accepted as a satisfactory settlement of the problem of Japanese immigration except on the Pacific coast, where the good faith of Japan's enforcement of the terms of the agreement was questioned. During the first year of Wilson's administration the enactment of a California anti-alien land law, which was directed against the Japanese, created a serious situation; and by that time propaganda had created a Japanese bugaboo more terrifying than the figure of 1907. Reports of Japanese spies in the United States and of Japan's designs on Mexico at the time of the Magdalena Bay incident had done their deadly work.

During the World War, in 1915, the imperialistic ambitions of Japan were revealed in all their nakedness by the twenty-one demands made against China. Japan denied that she was acting contrary to American interests in the Far East, but her denial was not convincing to those who suspected that she was making the most of her opportunity while Europe was engaged in deadly combat. The Lansing-Ishii Agreement of November 2, 1917, was an effort to compromise the conflicting interests of the two powers; but it was so ambiguously worded that Japan could interpret it to suit her own wishes. This agreement was superseded by the nine-power treaty of 1922.

At the peace conference at Versailles, Japan insisted upon the formal recognition of racial equality; but the state of public opinion in the United States was such that the American recognition of the demand would have been fatal to the treaty. Moreover, the fear that immigration might come under the jurisdiction of the League of Nations was responsible for the vote of thirty-six Democratic Senators in favor of a reservation providing that the United States would not be obliged to submit to the League any matter, including immigration, which it regarded as a domestic question.

During the closing months of the Wilson administration (1920) the California legislature adopted an anti-alien land law more drastic than the measure that had been adopted in 1913.

It was carried by a decisive vote in a popular referendum; and the United States Supreme Court held that it was neither a violation of the treaty with Japan nor contrary to the Constitution.

From time to time, even as early as 1907, efforts had been made to incorporate into general immigration bills a provision for the exclusion of Japanese immigrants, but they had either been killed in committee or voted down on the floor of the House and Senate. In the campaign of 1920 both parties adopted planks to curry favor with the exclusionists on the Pacific coast. Numerous organizations, including the Veterans of Foreign Wars, adopted resolutions advocating the abrogation of the Gentlemen's Agreement and the adoption of a constitutional amendment withholding citizenship from American-born Japanese. The press in Japan boiled over in condemning these proposals, and stated that Japan could not silently endure insult and contempt from a nation which had not signed the League of Nations Pact.

In 1923-24, with anti-Japanese sentiment mounting and the presidential election approaching, the House of Representatives included a Japanese exclusion provision in the general immigration bill; but it was expected to be eliminated in the Senate. An amicable settlement of the question, however, was foiled by an indiscreet communication from the Japanese ambassador, Hanihara, in which he stated very candidly to Secretary Hughes that enactment of the proposed measure would inevitably bring "grave consequences." Senators on both sides of the aisle resented this statement as a "veiled threat" and announced that the ambassador's communication left them no alternative but to vote for the exclusion provision. Members of both houses objected emphatically to any recognition of immigration as a proper subject for international negotiation. "If we recognize the right of Japan to stipulate conditions upon which Japanese can come into the United States, we will be confronted immediately with the demand from other nations which have equal rights to the same recognition," was the assertion of Senator Joseph T. Robinson, the leader of the Democratic minority.

At the urgent request of President Coolidge and Secretary Hughes, the conference committee agreed to postpone the effective date of the exclusion provision, in order to afford the President time to negotiate with the Japanese government for the termination of the Gentlemen's Agreement; but this was voted down by large majorities in both houses. On July 1, 1924, the exclusion of Japanese immigrants by statute became effective.

There was considerable speculation as to the purpose of the Japanese ambassador in using the words "grave consequences." Why did a diplomat with his experience make such a serious blunder? It is true that Hanihara explained that the words were not intended to convey a "veiled threat," but this did not satisfy those who suspected that the ambassador deliberately played into the hands of the jingoes in his own country who needed anti-American propaganda to support their demands for larger appropriations for the land and naval forces.

On the other hand, it is equally difficult to fathom the action of Congress. If Japan had been included in the quota system that applied to the countries of Europe, not more than one hundred Japanese could have been admitted annually.

The Gentlemen's Agreement was accepted by Japan as a fairly satisfactory solution of a difficult problem; the abrogation of the agreement awakened suspicion and distrust of the United States. The conspicuous discrimination against her people, which implied racial inferiority, was a blow to Japan's prestige. She suspected that the United States had been working quietly to have all Central and South American countries exclude Japanese.

It was most unfortunate that the action of Congress came at a critical moment in the relations between the two countries. The American ambassador to Japan, Cyrus E. Woods, called the act "an international disaster of the first magnitude." The disaster, he said, fell upon every single interest of the United States in the Far East. It nullified the gratitude of the Japanese for the splendid response of the American people in alleviating the suffering and distress caused by the earthquake in September, 1923, one of the greatest disasters in history. Moreover, when the exclusion measure was pending, Secretary Hughes in a communication to the chairman of the House Committee on Immigration regretted that the legislation would largely undo the work of the Washington conference on the limitation of armament.

Without minimizing the sins of the United States, it would be unhistorical to overlook the shortcomings of Japan. The immigration question was a football of politics in both countries, and it was aggravated and magnified by growing estrangement over other matters of even greater moment. Students of diplomacy hint that Japan used the agitation over immigration as a "smoke screen" to conceal her ambitions in Manchuria and China.

The absorption of Korea by Japan coincided with the agitation that preceded the Gentlemen's Agreement; the Shantung aggression was pending when the issue of racial equality was raised at Versailles; and the opposition of Japanese militarists to the naval agreement of 1922 preceded the exclusion act of 1924. Whatever justification there may be for Japan's seizure of Manchuria, the setting up of the puppet state of Manchukuo in 1931, and the launching of her armies against Shanghai in 1932 and again in 1937, these were regarded as acts of aggression by the United States and the League of Nations. Japan's withdrawal from the League of Nations, her formal notice of the cessation of the 5—5—3 naval ratio in 1934, and her withdrawal from the naval conference in London in 1935—all contributed to the increasing suspicion of the good faith of Japan, whether it applied to the Gentlemen's Agreement or to treaty obligations. The fact remains, however, that the exigencies of politics in the United States and Japan brought a situation which tempts Japan to seize favorable opportunities to press for a satisfactory settlement of the immigration question.

While these and other questions taxed the resources of the Department of State, the nightmare of the Wilson administration continued to haunt the administrations that succeeded it. Even before the armistice, conditions and events in Mexico threatened to undo what had been accomplished by the elimination of Huerta and the recognition of Carranza. The infinite patience of Wilson, who dedicated his policy to the yearning of the Mexican people for political, social, and economic reform, was rewarded with niggardly gratitude from the Mexicans themselves and was misunderstood and turned to partisan advantage in the United States. Sporadic revolutions against the Carranza government affected American interests in Mexico and necessitated sending more troops to the border and battleships to Mexican waters. By the end of 1919 American papers were demanding "action" in Mexico.

In 1919-20 an investigation of Mexican affairs by a committee of the Senate was inspired by the later notorious Albert B. Fall in order to discredit the Wilson administration, to aggravate the religious controversy over the Mexican question, and to pave the way for intervention. While the committee was engaged in taking voluminous testimony, Carranza was killed in a mountain shack, a fugitive from the armies of General Obregon and General Adolfo de la Huerta. Thus once more Wilson was confronted with the question of recognizing a government that could command the support of the Mexican people and maintain order. Harding's campaign speeches gave hope to those interests that demanded a "vigorous" Mexican policy—one that would teach the Mexicans to respect their neighbor to the north.

The communications to the Mexican authorities that emanated from the State Department under Secretary Hughes (1921-25) and Secretary Kellogg (1925-29) breathed a different spirit from those Wilson directed Bryan and Lansing to send; but the issues that provoked them and the consequences that would follow intervention had been brought to the attention of the country by the forceful and courageous speeches and communications from Wilson. Limits to the bullying of Mexico had been set, notwithstanding the presence of Fall in Harding's cabinet.

Wilson was hampered in dealing with Mexico by a weak power's natural suspicion and fear of a powerful neighbor, by the attitude of big business and the jingo press, by the attitude of Catholic prelates in both countries, by the unfortunate reaction in Mexico to the seizure of Vera Cruz in 1914 and the Pershing expedition in 1916, by the instability of the Mexican government, and by the lack of mutual understanding between the Latin American and the American mind. During the administrations of Harding and Coolidge, these formidable obstacles were augmented by the efforts of the Mexican government to put into effect one of the profoundest revolutions that has taken place in modern times. The recognition of Carranza paved the way for the adoption of the Mexican Constitution of 1917, which a competent student of the Mexican revolution pronounces "one of the most significant and influential documents of the present century."

During the long dictatorship of Porfirio Diaz, the Mexican people were gradually dispossessed of their land, which was incorporated into haciendas; and foreign capitalists obtained control of much of the wealth of the country in the form of oil and mining concessions, usually by lining the pockets of the Diaz clique but without giving adequate returns to the mass of the people. Under the new Constitution Mexican statesmen inaugurated a program to effect a more equitable distribution of land and to reserve for the public welfare the rich natural resources beneath the soil. However, "Mexico for the Mexicans" conflicted with the interests of the landholding aristocracy in Mexico and of American and foreign capitalists. Moreover, American citizens pressed their government for a settlement of claims against Mexico for destruction of property during the revolution and for the payment of the principal and interest on bonds which the Mexican government was unable to meet. Secretary Hughes was disposed to take a legalistic attitude toward these matters. A basis for an understanding, in which both governments made concessions, preceded formal recognition of the Obregon government on August 31, 1923.

Under the presidency of Plutarco Calles who, in 1924, succeeded Obregon, further steps in the progress of social reform were taken, and the Mexican Congress enacted legislation contrary to the promises of the Obregon government. Secretary Kellogg provoked much criticism in the United States, and fear and hatred in Mexico, by his belligerent notes to Mexico. He even appropriated the anti-red hysteria by making charges of Bolshevism and international intrigue in Nicaragua against the Mexican government. The "smoke screen" of Bolshevism was used by numerous organizations, and it was made even more dangerous by injecting the religious issue. Pamphlets "exposing" the menace of Bolshevism and atheism in Mexico were published in the United States.

Beginning with Henry Lane Wilson, Taft's ambassador, the United States was unfortunate in the selection of ambassadors to Mexico; but both countries are indebted to Coolidge for the happy appointment of Dwight W. Morrow in October, 1927. The new ambassador not only proved to Mexico that he did not underestimate the gigantic problems that confronted the government but his ingratiating personality and Chesterfieldian manners appealed to the Mexican statesmen. A decision of the Supreme Court of Mexico declaring unconstitutional certain provisions of a law relating to petroleum and new regulations pertaining to similar legislation satisfied the American government.

The famous aviator and lionized hero of the American people, Charles A. Lindbergh, accomplished more in a fortnight to gain the good will of the Mexican people than diplomats had accomplished in years. On the invitation of President Calles and Ambassador Morrow, "Lindy" flew from Washington to Mexico City in December, 1927, where he was officially greeted by the president of Mexico and the American ambassador. The day of his arrival was declared a national holiday, and a few days later school children were recalled from their holidays to greet him. All in all, the Mexican capital celebrated a fortnight of festivities, banquets, parades, and bull fights—all in honor of the daring young American. From Mexico City Lindbergh departed on a good-will tour of Latin America and at every stop proved by example to be the peer of accomplished diplomats in winning the hearts of statesmen and their countrymen.

Since those happy days the relations between the "Colossus of the North" and the other states of the Western Hemisphere have grown more cordial, although the expropriation by the Mexican government of American and other foreign oil properties in March, 1938, threatened to renew anti-Mexican propaganda in the United States. Fortunately, the attitude of the Franklin Roosevelt administration was so reasonable that President Cardenas of Mexico made public a statement that the Roosevelt administration had "won the esteem of the people of Mexico" by admitting that Mexico was within her rights in seizing the oil properties, providing that fair payment was made. Roosevelt was also bent on scaling down drastically the claims presented by the American oil companies, whereas the demands of the British government by contrast were so severe that Mexico broke off diplomatic relations.

In the process of restoring the land to the people of Mexico, American-owned lands to the value of more than ten million dollars were confiscated. In reply to a note from President Cardenas rejecting arbitration of claims, Secretary of State Hull, in August, 1938, demanded that Mexico discontinue its seizure of American-owned lands unless accompanied by arrangement for adequate, prompt, and effective payment. Hull branded as "alien" to the Western Hemisphere the theories advanced by the Mexican government on its right to seize aliens' properties without compensation. "In the opinion of my government," said the Secretary, "the doctrine as proposed runs counter to the basic precepts of international law and of the law of every American republic, as well as to every principle of right and justice upon which the institutions of the American republics are founded."

At successive inter-American conferences progress has been made on the construction of a foundation for peace; and the patience and forbearance of the United States during the long years of the Mexican revolution, in spite of certain lapses, proved that idealism could triumph over dollar diplomacy. It is true that Woodrow Wilson's and Franklin Roosevelt's policy was enlightened self-interest; but it is a test of statesmanship to work out a policy of enlightened self-interest.

Between his election and inauguration Herbert Hoover made a good-will tour of South and Central America; and it remained for his successor, Franklin D. Roosevelt, and his able Secretary of State, Cordell Hull, to reap rewards in the cultivation of what Roosevelt called the "good neighbor policy." In an earlier chapter mention was made of Roosevelt's Cuban policy and of his efforts to remove from the Monroe Doctrine the connotation of economic exploitation.

In a world quaking with feverish preparations for war, and

with religious persecution tearing at the hearts of millions, President Roosevelt, with the prestige of having won at the ballot boxes the indorsement of forty-six states on November 17, 1936, set out on an errand of peace. After the greatest reception ever accorded a foreign visitor in Buenos Aires, Argentina, with streets lined with cheering Latin-Americans, the American President addressed the Latin American conference in that capital city. His speech was lofty in spirit and purpose and concluded with a plea for religious toleration and trust in God.

Referring to one of the major achievements of his administration, the President stated that the resolution adopted at the Inter-American Conference at Montevideo in 1933 indorsing the principle of liberal trade policies "has shone forth like a beacon in the storm of economic madness which has been sweeping over the entire world during these later years." He stated that he has done all in his power to sustain the efforts of Secretary Hull in negotiating agreements for reciprocal trade.

Twenty years after the entrance of the United States into the World War, when a new generation stood on the abyss of another war that would destroy the edifice raised during centuries of bloodshed, toil, sacrifice, faith, and hope, the American people were committed to peace. However, on October 6, 1937, there came with startling suddenness in an address delivered by President Roosevelt at Chicago the warning that the Western Hemisphere was not safe, that the United States might be forced to act. The President denounced the prevailing international anarchy and by indirection referred to Japanese aggression in China and the intervention of Italy and Germany in Spain.

The papers of the following day published the text of the State Department's condemnation of Japan's undeclared war on China : "In the light of the unfolding developments in the Far East, the government of the United States has been forced to the conclusion that the action of Japan in China is inconsistent with the principles which should govern the relationships between nations and is contrary to the provisions of the nine-power treaty of February 6, 1922, regarding principles and policies to be followed in matters concerning China, and to those of the Kellogg-Briand Pact of

August 22, 1928." These conclusions, according to the statement, were in general accord with those of the Assembly of the League of Nations.

The unqualified condemnation of Japan's course from the pen of former Secretary of State Stimson was published in many papers the day following Roosevelt's Chicago address and was timed to strengthen the hand of the government.

The conference at Brussels, which met on November 3, 1937, was called under the nine-power treaty to consider the Sino-Japanese undeclared war. Japan declined to attend; and the delegates were unable to come to agreement on a policy of economic sanctions, an instrument of coercion that had a double edge. Moreover, a tripartite treaty between Japan, Italy, and Germany against Communism was made public in time to counteract the possible influence of the Brussels meeting. Russia, a power which had been excluded from the nine-power pact, withdrew from the Brussels meeting because of her feeling that she would not have a part in possible mediation between the two Far Eastern governments.

Hard upon these events occurred a series of occurrences that magnified the seriousness of the situation in the Far East. In December, 1937, Japanese airplanes bombed an American gunboat, the *Panay*, above Nanking. President Roosevelt instructed Secretary Hull to inform the Japanese ambassador "that the President is deeply shocked and concerned by the news of indiscriminate bombing of American and other non-Chinese vessels on the Yangtse, and that he requests that the emperor be so advised." Roosevelt expected from the Japanese government "full expression of regret and proffer of full compensation" and methods guaranteeing against a repetition of any similar attack in the future. The Japanese government speedily complied with these requests.

A profuse apology did not allay the suspicions of Japan. In the first week of February, 1938, the United States, joined by Great Britain and France, warned Japan that unless these powers received positive assurances by February 20 that Japan was not building battleships exceeding 35,000 tons in size, they would consider themselves released from the battleship limitations stipulated in the London Naval Treaty.

To this Japan replied that in view of the fact that there was as yet no fair disarmament treaty to which Japan was a party, "the Japanese government is of the opinion that mere communication of information concerning the construction of vessels will, in the absence of quantitative limitation, not contribute to any fair and equitable measures of disarmament and regret that they are unable to comply with your government on this point."

This exchange of notes only increased the tension in a "jittery" world. There were rumors that Japan was seeking a submarine base in Mexico to threaten the Panama Canal; and the newspapers and the air were filled with stories about Hitler's seizure of the control of the German army and his designs on Austria (which were shortly to be realized) and on Czechoslovakia. With Great Britain obviously unprepared for war and with the American people unwilling to sanction an alliance with Great Britain, the balance of power swung to Italy, Germany, and Japan, with Nippon exercising the controlling influence. Britain's willingness to negotiate and compromise with the two dictators, Hitler and Mussolini, was patent proof that Britannia was no longer mistress of the seas: that the danger of war in Europe was too great to risk a conflict with Japan. It was also proof that the British navy could not be relied upon to maintain the Monroe Doctrine.

Roosevelt's answer was a request for a billion-dollar appropriation for the navy, which Congress speedily voted. And in an address to the National Press Club Secretary Hull stated that the United States must arm for protection against international lawlessness.

The reactions in the press to Roosevelt's addresses and to the statements and notes from the Secretary of State revealed a state of mind quite different from that of 1914-17. Perhaps the efforts of organizations to acquaint the country with the horror and futility of war, the outspoken condemnation of war by college and university students, and the fuller knowledge of the responsible members of society as to the inevitable doom of the existing system that another great war would bring, prompted the cautious editorials.

Moreover, the revelations by the Nye Munitions Committee of inquiry into the munitions industry in 1934 and 1935 acquainted the public with the enormous war profits of 1914-18 and the pro-Ally propaganda broadcast by the beneficiaries. It also stimulated demands that a declaration of war should be submitted to a popular referendum, and precipitated legislation that was designed to prevent the United States from being drawn into a war under circumstances similar to those that existed from 1914 to 1917. The neutrality resolution of August 31, 1936, which was later extended and modified by the Neutrality Act of May, 1937, prohibited, in time of war between foreign nations, the exportation from the United States of arms, ammunition, and implements of war for the use of a belligerent country, except in the case of an American republic engaged in war with a country outside the Western Hemisphere. The making of loans and extending of credit by an American national, with the same exemption, were also prohibited. The legislation also included provisions intended to control the munitions industry in time of peace and of war. Thus Congress in a sense admitted the validity of the contentions of those who in 1914-17 stigmatized the Wilsonian foreign policy as technical as against a frank recognition of existing conditions, that at a time when chaos reigned in a certain part of the world, it might have been advisable and prudent not to insist on rights of American citizens that were undoubtedly legal.

On the other hand, in the case of the undeclared Japanese war in China in 1937 and the civil war in Spain, it was pointed out that the legislation worked to the advantage of the aggressors— Japan and the Spanish rebel Franco to whom the Italian dictator Mussolini furnished troops and munitions—whereas the removal of the American embargo would have enabled the United States to pursue a policy that would have more nearly approached the spirit of neutrality and been less likely to lead to war. While the so-called Ludlow Resolution proposing a constitutional amendment for a national referendum on war was pending in Congress (1937-38), President Roosevelt and Secretary Hull stemmed the tide of tele-

grams and petitions that poured into Washington by statements
that the enactment of the resolution would greatly hamper the
President and Congress in the conduct of foreign relations. In
this the President and the Secretary were supported by Alfred M.
Landon, the defeated Republican candidate for the Presidency in
1936.

It is significant that after the refusal of the Wilson, Harding,
Coolidge, and Hoover administrations to recognize Soviet Russia,
diplomatic relations with that great and powerful people were
resumed not long after Roosevelt took office. Hope of trade was,
of course, a factor; but it was a very different situation in the
Far East that confronted Franklin Roosevelt from that of the
years of the first Roosevelt. Revealing documents are not open to
the perusal of historians; but they can surmise that the recognition
of Russia by the United States may prove to be highly significant
in the years to come.

CHAPTER XXXI

CONSERVATIVE REPUBLICANISM

ALTHOUGH THE DEMOCRATIC PARTY SUFFERED A SUCCESSION OF defeats from 1918 to 1928, the Old Guard leadership in the Republican party was deprived of the full fruits of victory by the insurgent bloc in the Senate. This agricultural group held the balance of power from 1919 to 1925 and by combining with the Democratic minority made the conservative leaders uncomfortable. After the election of Coolidge insurgent Republicans were removed from important committee assignments; and some of them, like Norris of Nebraska, of their own accord broke with the party.

Republican traditions under Harding were coined into high protective tariffs: the emergency tariff of 1921 and the Fordney-McCumber Act of 1922. Under three successive Republican administrations the tariff wall was the highest in history.

One of the most difficult problems that cried for immediate solution was that of the railroads. In 1917 the executives of the railroads admitted that they were unequal to the exigencies of providing adequate transportation, and the government assumed control and operation. Under the director-general of railroads, William G. McAdoo, the chaos of the fall and early winter of 1917-18 yielded to better coordination, and economies were introduced. Money was saved by discontinuing advertising, by publishing consolidated time tables, and by merging pretentious ticket offices into one for each city. The advocates of government ownership were hopeful that the war-time experiment would prove to be permanent; but the railroad magnates and business men generally were hotly opposed and broadcast propaganda that the government had made a miserable failure. The time was not ripe for a project that could be labeled "socialistic."

In his annual message of December 2, 1918, Wilson disap-

pointed liberals and many labor leaders by making no recommendations with reference to the railroads, except for a statement
that it would be unjust to both the railroads and the public to
revert to the old system unmodified. However, in his message
cabled from Paris to the special session that convened on May
19, 1919, he announced that the railroads would be returned to
their owners at the end of the calendar year. It fell to the lot of
a Republican Congress to work out the details of the transfer.

It was an exceedingly difficult task to reconcile the conflicting
interests of the railroads, the public, and the employees; and for a
time it appeared that a bill would be passed in such a form that
Wilson would veto it. The employees pressed Director-General
Hines, who had succeeded McAdoo, to work out a solution of
their demand for better compensation before the lines were returned to private operation. Glenn E. Plumb, who spoke for the
organized employees, proposed a solution which attracted considerable attention. The Plumb plan called for government ownership under tri-party control, shared equally by the public, the
management, and the classified employees. It provided for the
incorporation of the roads under one charter, and their operation
as a single system. The corporation was to be governed by a board
of directors, one-third to be named by the President of the United
States to represent the public, one-third by the employees in
managerial and executive positions, and one-third by the wage
earners.

Under this proposed plan the railroads would cease to be private properties operated primarily for profit. They would be purchased by the government by issuing securities, the interest of
which would be guaranteed and the principal ultimately retired by
earnings from operation. The government would lease the lines
to the corporation for operating purposes. The valuation of the
roads would be based on the amount of money that had actually
been invested, thereby eliminating fictitious securities and improvements paid for out of surplus. In other words, the government would purchase the roads according to their physical valuation, with the watered stock squeezed out.

The Esch-Cummins Act of February 28, 1920, finally emerged

after months of committee hearings and debate. It was bitterly opposed by progressives, but it marked a radical departure from existing railroad legislation. It provided for the reorganization and enlargement of the Interstate Commerce Commission, for a Railway Labor Board to deal with questions pertaining to wages and labor disputes, for financial rehabilitation of the roads, and for the termination of federal control on March 1, 1920. The act guaranteed earnings to the roads and provided that earnings over a certain percentage should be placed at the disposal of the government for the use of lines not so fortunate. The Interstate Commerce Commission was clothed with power to permit the consolidation of the express companies into what eventually became the Railway Express Company.

In spite of changes effected through the Interstate Commerce Commission and through the railroads themselves, the lines had fallen on evil days. The Panama Canal seriously reduced traffic on certain transcontinental roads; buses, trucks, private automobiles, and trailers operating on cement roads reduced the volume of freight traffic and compelled the abandonment of passenger trains; coal was shipped on barges operating on rivers whose channels had been deepened; and pipe lines transported crude and refined oil and gasoline. Farmers and commission men "trucked" cattle, hogs, and sheep to the packing houses, and on the return trip the trucks brought to the country merchants crates and boxes to replenish their stocks. In fact, so serious was the situation brought about by this development that, in fear that certain railroads would be abandoned, merchants in some towns agreed to ship by rail.

It is a far cry from the independent and haughty railroad executives in the days of the Grangers and the Populists and the humble men who, like Oliver Twist, "begged for more" legislation to protect them from competition, and for governmental assistance to save them from their own folly in forming holding companies and in watering stock far beyond the ability of the roads to carry. This made it difficult to replace equipment, to keep roadbeds in repair, and to pay adequate wages to their employees.

The reduction of rates—especially on western roads—round-trip fares, increased speed, and streamlined trains driven by Diesel engines reduced somewhat the losses in traffic that went to buses and air lines; but more heroic measures were needed. In 1937 the Interstate Commerce Commission granted increased freight rates on certain commodities, but the railroads were disappointed in the conservative increases, and certain business interests were disappointed that they had been granted at all.

The business recession of 1937-38, however, threw more railroad mileage into receivership, and by the summer of 1938 the railroad situation was acute. The average share of railroad stock had declined more than 40 per cent in value; more than 30 per cent of the mileage was in receivership; the number of railroad employees had dropped to a forty-year low—913,070; within a twelve-month the net operating income had fallen off more than 50 per cent; and nearly one-half of the Class I railroads did not make their running expenses and taxes in the first months of 1938.

On March 8, 1938, the Interstate Commerce Commission allowed a 5 per cent increase in rates on farm and forest products, and a 10 per cent increase on virtually everything else, which included raises already granted on steel, coke, and many other "heavy" commodities. Bituminous coal, lignite, and iron were specifically excluded from further increases.

These remedies, however, did not get to the roots of the railroad problem; the railroads clamored for substantial financial assistance from the government, and ran full-page advertisements designed to counteract demands that the roads be "put through the wringer" to squeeze out the watered stock before applying for assistance such as had been given through the Reconstruction Finance Corporation under Hoover and Roosevelt.

The plight of the farmers was as serious as that of their ancient enemies the railroads. The rocketing prices of farm products during the war boosted the values of land beyond the dreams of earlier generations. Illinois and Iowa farmers, for example, not only invested their rapidly accumulating surpluses in stocks of doubtful lineage but bought cheaper land, though at inflated prices, in Minnesota, the Dakotas, and other western states. Some sold their homesteads at soaring figures and bought more land at lower prices. When the bottom fell out of the prices of grain, cotton, and livestock not long after the armistice, mortgagors and mortgagees alike were caught; and in the ensuing months and years bankers saw thousands of men in tears imploring them to do something to rescue them from foreclosure proceedings.

The day of the Republican spellbinder who told the farmers that under a protective tariff the "foreigner pays the tax" and the farmer receives only the benefits was gone; and Harding, Coolidge, and Hoover were sorely distressed as to the means of fulfilling the promises of their party that the farmer would soon be on his way to prosperity. The farmer's traditional individualism stood in the way of developing cooperation, although the Farmers' Alliance of the latter part of the nineteenth century and organizations like the Farmers' Union in the next century made some progress along that line. But after the World War the high tariff barriers abroad, the disturbed state of Europe, unfavorable rates of exchange, the introduction of improved agricultural methods, and changes in the diet of many consumers created a heavy surplus of farm products.

Under Harding the agricultural bloc was instrumental in obtaining legislation designed to aid the exportation of surpluses, to prevent abuses in manipulating prices, and to extend credits. Under Coolidge the McNary-Haugen Bill was passed only to meet the veto of the President, who believed the bill was impractical, that it would harm, not benefit, the farmer; and that in the long run the law of supply and demand would govern prices. A similar bill by the same name was vetoed in 1928. Without entering into the details of these complicated bills, we may say that an equalization fee was to be paid by the grower of each staple in order to extend the benefits of a protective tariff to agriculture. A federal farm board was to collect this fee, which was to cover losses in marketing the surplus abroad at a lower price than that obtained in the domestic market. The board was also empowered to make loans to cooperative associations.

In the Hoover administration efforts were made to pass a similar bill with a debenture provision for exports of farm products;

but the certainty of a presidential veto caused its advocates to abandon it. Instead, on June 15, 1929, Hoover signed the Agricultural Marketing Act with the object of encouraging cooperation among farmers and of establishing corporations to buy and

Copyrighted by George Matthew Adams.

PRIVATE BROWN—"Who's been here while I've been away?"

sell in the open market. A Federal Farm Board was created to stabilize prices and reduce overproduction. In the dismal depression years after 1929 Congress passed other laws to rescue the farmers; but it was not until Roosevelt became President that the government took action that, for a time at least, gave them a new lease on life.

While some four million men were dressed in military and naval uniforms, profiteers waxed fat off the public, and the wages of artisans who remained in civil pursuits steadily increased, although the purchasing power of the salaries of clerks, teachers, and clergymen steadily decreased. Returning service men naturally resented the rise of their friends and associates in the economic scale while they were deprived of such opportunities, and not a few of them found their former jobs filled by others. The veterans pressed state and federal governments for adjusted compensation, and a number of states provided bonuses according to length of service. In May, 1920, the House of Representatives passed a soldiers' bonus bill by a heavy majority. It was not until 1922, however, that Congress passed a bonus bill, which Harding vetoed. The veto message stressed the heavy burden that would be laid on the government and stated that it would but mark the beginning of additional demands in the form of pensions.

The powerful veterans' lobby could not for long be denied, and on May 5, 1924, the Adjusted Compensation Act became a law over President Coolidge's veto. By this act some three and a half million service men received certificates to the aggregate amount of $3,500,000,000. The next stage in the battle was the drive to obtain immediate payment of the certificates, instead of awaiting the date of maturity, which was 1946. After the country had plunged into the depression, service men felt the pinch of poverty and financial embarrassment; and it was argued that immediate payment of the bonus would not only aid them but would also indirectly promote prosperity by increasing the purchasing power of a large number of citizens. A long step in that direction was taken when on February 27, 1931, Congress over Hoover's veto passed an act permitting holders of certificates to borrow from the government, with interest, a sum not to exceed one-half of the face value. The final chapter was written on January 27, 1936, when over Roosevelt's veto Congress made provision for immediate payment in the form of bonds redeemable at post offices after June 15, 1936.

In addition to bonuses paid by federal and state governments, lavish appropriations were made for the construction and maintenance of veterans' hospitals, for disabilities, for education, for special pensions, and for dependents. Nor were veterans of the

Spanish-American War slighted in the matter of increased pensions.

Meanwhile Secretary of the Treasury Mellon was prodding Congress to reduce taxes. Against the opposition of Republican progressives and some Democrats, Congress continued to reduce rates on incomes, corporations, excess profits, inheritances, and excises. Simultaneously, Secretary Mellon was receiving the congratulations of the country over reducing the public debt from its peak of $24,061,000,000 on June 30, 1920, to $16,185,000,000 on June 30, 1930, little realizing that shifting the burden of taxation from the wealthy to the moderate-salaried and wage-earning classes stimulated speculation and hastened the day of reckoning. It was only the unpopular few who ventured to suggest that the country could not prosper with a large part of its capital tied up in speculative enterprises.

One legislative achievement of the Harding and Coolidge régime stood the test of time. At least, there has been no serious demand for revision. It will be recalled that the Immigration Act of 1917 which contained a literacy test registered the demand for immigration restriction in anticipation of a deluge of immigrants after the war. Although the shortage of labor and the high wages that prevailed during the months of America's participation in the war brought forth an agitation for the repeal of this restrictive measure, the tide was running strongly in the opposite direction; and with the mounting unemployment that followed demobilization and depression, the anti-immigration sentiment became hysteria. Newspapers and periodicals literally teemed with editorials, feature articles, and news stories pertaining to immigration. Predictions were made that more than ten millions in war-stricken Europe were ready to swarm to the United States as soon as transportation could be provided. Those were the days when the "Soviet Ark" sailed with its cargo of radicals and "undesirables"; when raids on "Reds" were almost daily occurrences; when alarmists feared for the safety of American institutions; when Ku Klux Klan organizers were abroad in the land to stimulate the fear of Catholicism and to fan anti-Semitism.

Bills were introduced to suspend immigration from one to fifty years. The Senate substituted for a House bill to suspend immigration for fourteen months a bill to restrict immigration on a percentage basis. It was frankly stated that the Senate bill was intended to reduce the immigration from southeastern Europe. This bill, however, was killed in the closing days of Wilson's administration by a pocket veto.

In the special session which Harding convened in April, 1921, Congress speedily enacted a law which was practically identical with the one that met with Wilson's disapproval. This was a temporary measure, to remain in force until June 20, 1922, while Congress formulated a more comprehensive measure. Congress needed more time, so the law, with minor changes, was extended until June 30, 1924. Up to that time the number of immigrants admissible from any European country was 3 per cent of the foreign-born from that country resident in the United States, according to the Census of 1910.

The administrative features of this law were faulty. The regulation that not more than 20 per cent of a country's quota could enter the United States in any one month brought steamships racing into New York Harbor in order to land their passengers and relieve transportation companies of the expense of carrying them back to Europe.

The practical operation of the law did not satisfy the exponents of the theory of Nordic superiority: those who believed that the Germanic peoples of Great Britain, the Netherlands, Germany, and the Scandinavian countries were superior to the Italians, Slavs, Jews, and the peoples of the Balkan countries. Numerous popular articles which set forth the claim of Nordic superiority took their cue from such books as C. S. Burr's *America's Race Heritage* (1922), Lothrop Stoddard's *The Revolt Against Civilization* (1922), and Madison Grant's *The Passing of a Great Race* (1921).

It was pointed out that the Nordic peoples were more akin to Americans in appearance, in spirit, and in their attitude toward American institutions; that their superior education and training in self-government made them useful and intelligent citizens; that they established permanent homes and remained with their earnings in the country of adoption, instead of working for a season, living like church mice, and returning to their native lands with their accumulated money.

By reason of the fact that the bulk of the so-called new immigrants came after 1890, and the number of old immigrants declined, the quota base of the law of 1921 gave a preference to the former. Moreover, in the years immediately after the armistice, immigration from England, Germany, Norway, Sweden, and Denmark was slight and their quotas were not filled. However, for the years from 1921 to 1924 the net immigration from the countries of southeastern Europe was small.

As the time for the expiration of the existing law approached, the House Committee on Immigration reported the most comprehensive and drastic immigration bill ever reported, and it undoubtedly registered the wishes of the vast majority of the people, although the minority was hotly opposed and threatened reprisals on Senators and Representatives who voted for it. The vital point in the House bill was the reduction of the percentage from three to two, and the change in the quota base from the Census of 1910 to that of 1890, obviously intended to reduce immigration from southern and eastern Europe. For example, there were only 182,-580 foreign-born Italians in the United States in 1890 as compared with 1,343,125 in 1910; 182,644 from Russia in 1890 as compared with 1,184,412 in 1910.

This discrimination offended the new immigrants; and there were even formal protests registered in the Department of State by certain governments of Europe. For example, Italy, while expressly disclaiming the intention of questioning the right of the United States to dispose of internal affairs as best suited to its national interests, protested the discrimination against its citizens in changing the quota base.

Senator James T. Heflin of Alabama voiced the sentiment of the South and of vast numbers in other sections when he said:

Mr. President, we have now reached the time in the life of the Nation when those who are for America must stand out on the one side and those who are willing to throw the gates of our country open to an indiscriminate horde of unfit foreigners must stand on the other. . . . .

IMMIGRATION

UNITED STATES - FISCAL YEARS, 1820-1931

TOTAL IMMIGRATION

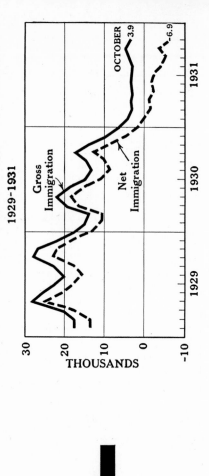

GROSS IMMIGRATION, THOUSANDS
1820-1931

ANNUAL AVERAGE	YEAR
1820-49	70
1850-74	271
1875-99	392
1900-09	820
1910-14	1,035
1915-19	235
1920-29	430
1930	242
1931	97

GROSS AND NET IMMIGRATION BY MONTHS
1929-1931

Gross Immigration
Net Immigration
OCTOBER 3.9
-6.9

THOUSANDS
30
20
10
0
-10

1929   1930   1931

GROSS IMMIGRATION BY COUNTRY OF ORIGIN

Great Britain and Ireland
Germany
Scandinavia
Austria, Hungary, and Balkan States
Russia, Poland, and Baltic States
Italy
Other European
Canada, Mexico, and Other Non-European

FROM ALL COUNTRIES, 1820-1931 – PER CENT DISTRIBUTION

1820-1874   1875-1899   1900-1914   1915-1931

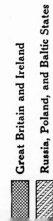

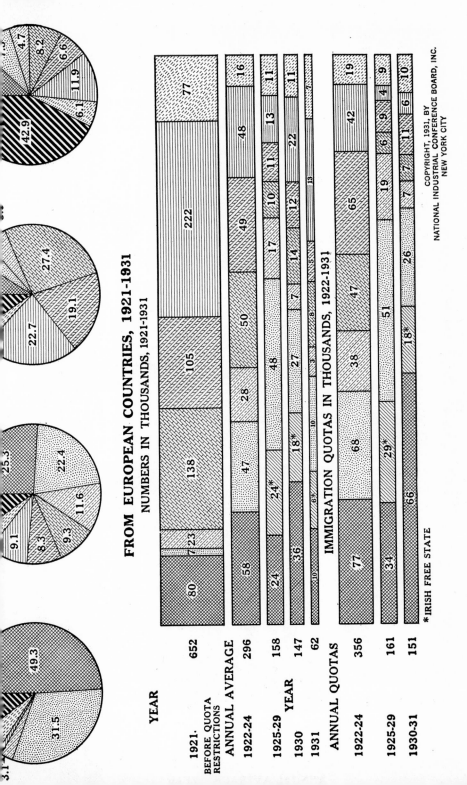

FROM EUROPEAN COUNTRIES, 1921-1931

NUMBERS IN THOUSANDS, 1921-1931

YEAR						
1921. BEFORE QUOTA RESTRICTIONS	652	80	7	23	138	222	77
ANNUAL AVERAGE						
1922-24	296	58	47	28	105	50	49	48	16
1925-29	158	24*	17	48	10	11	13	11
1930	147	18*	27	14	7	12	22	11
1931	62	10*	6*	3	8	5	13	7

IMMIGRATION QUOTAS IN THOUSANDS, 1922-1931

ANNUAL QUOTAS					
1922-24	356	77	68	38	47	65	42	19
1925-29	161	34	29*	51	19	6	9	4	9
1930-31	151	66	18*	26	7	7	11	6	10

*IRISH FREE STATE

COPYRIGHT, 1931, BY
NATIONAL INDUSTRIAL CONFERENCE BOARD, INC.
NEW YORK CITY

I want to do, in this legislation, what is the highest and best interest of my own country. I am not legislating for Italy or for any other foreign country. . . . My good friend who has just spoken is from Rhode Island, a splendid state in our sisterhood, but there are over 60 per cent of foreign-born and their offspring in his state. Have we enough Americans here to speak the American spirit, to talk the American language, to vote for the benefit of America, to take a positive American stand on this question now? If not, Mr. President, the day is coming when we cannot take it. . . . We are told that New England is against this measure; that New England does not want restricted immigration. Why? Because more than 50 per cent of the population of some of their states is foreign-born and the offspring of foreigners.

The bill passed the House by an overwhelming vote which clearly revealed the distribution of the immigrants. Of the seventy-one negative votes, only three came from states west of the Mississippi River, the remainder being from New York, New Jersey, Massachusetts, Connecticut, Rhode Island, Pennsylvania, Illinois, Michigan, Wisconsin, and Maryland, where the new immigrants and the Irish were concentrated in industrial centers. The old American stock and the old immigration, with the exception of the Irish, were strongly in favor of the bill. The Senate vote was less one-sided and less sectional.

The immigration law of 1924 provided that the annual quota for any country should be 2 per cent of the number of individuals born in that country resident in continental United States as determined by the Census of 1890, the minimum quota being 100. Asiatics, Canadians, and the people of Latin American countries were not included in the quotas. All immigrants were required to pass the literacy test, this being the sole restrictive method applied to Latin America. It was feared that if the countries of Latin America were included within the quota system, it would be interpreted as a violation of the spirit of Pan-America. It is true that the proposal to include them called forth sharp criticism in the Latin American press. Consular inspection, which had been proposed in the nineties, was written into the act of 1924.

The percentage basis for determining quotas remained in operation until July 1, 1929, when the national origins provision became effective. This scheme had been inserted in the act of 1924 in the form of an amendment introduced by Senator David A. Reed of Pennsylvania. Under the 1890 quota base the number of immigrants admissible annually totaled about 162,000, whereas under the national origins provision the maximum was arbitrarily fixed at 150,000. With the minimum quota of any nationality fixed at 100 (Canadians and Latin Americans and Asiatics always being excepted), the annual quota of each nationality was a number that bore the same ratio to 150,000 as the number of inhabitants in continental United States in 1920 having that national origin bore to the number of inhabitants in continental United States in 1920.

The fundamental difference between the national origins provision and the percentage plan lies in the fact that in determining the quotas the entire population of continental United States— native and foreign-born—is taken into account, instead of only those born abroad. In theory it is a more equitable and reasonable system, although it is open to objection because of the difficulty of determining the numbers of the respective "nationals" in the United States. Intermarriage has so fused the population that in the case of millions of individuals it was difficult, if not impossible, to determine their "national origin."

The effective date of the national origins provision was postponed until 1929 in order to allow sufficient time to determine the quotas. In the meantime petitions and memorials poured into Congress asking the repeal of the provision. These came mainly from Germans, Scandinavians, and Irish because it reduced their quotas from the percentage basis. The new system increased the quotas for Great Britain and northern Ireland and decreased them for the Irish Free State, Germany, and the Scandinavian countries. It also decreased some of the quotas from the countries of the new immigration, but it increased others, with the result that it did not materially affect the number of immigrants admissible from southern and eastern Europe.

Since the beginning of the depression in 1929, the number of immigrants has been small, the net immigration from 1930 to

1935 being only 229,363. The number dropped from 241,700 in 1930 to 23,068 in 1933. The depression itself and executive orders and stringent regulations made necessary by the depression explain these figures.

Down to the depression it was commonly asserted that the prosperity of the country was stimulated by immigration restriction, just as it was believed by some that national prohibition had contributed to the same result. Be that as it may, the law of 1924 closed a unique and important chapter in the history of the United States. For better or worse, a heavy majority of the American people believed that the time had come to close the doors and discontinue the free-handed, *laissez-faire* policy of the nineteenth century. In finding a solution for the immigration problem, the pride of certain countries was injured, and Uncle Sam's generous and free-handed policy was quickly forgotten.

After the World War applicants for naturalization were scrutinized more carefully, and the Supreme Court interpreted legislation to exclude all but Caucasians and Negroes from the right of naturalization. In the case of Ozawa *v.* the United States (1923), the Supreme Court admitted that the plaintiff, who was a Japanese and had resided in the United States for twenty years, was by character and education well qualified for citizenship, but held that only persons popularly understood to be Caucasians and Negroes were eligible. In the case of Thind (1923), a high-caste Hindu of full blood was declared ineligible because his physical characteristics and background did not conform to the popular conception of a "white person."

During the World War a resident of the United States within the draft age who refused to renounce his allegiance to a foreign government waived all claims to American citizenship in the future. On the other hand, the government was generous in granting citizenship to aliens who entered the military and naval service. In their cases the five-year period of residence was waived and they became citizens upon honorable discharge from service, except in the case of Chinese and Japanese who the Supreme Court in 1922 declared were not entitled to this recognition.

In spite of the Kellogg-Briand Pact outlawing war, the Supreme

Court in 1931, by a five to four decision, denied the right of naturalization to Professor Douglas MacIntosh of Yale University because his pacifistic convictions did not permit him to bear arms under certain conditions. Similar applicants were denied citizenship, one of the most famous being Rosika Schwimmer.

Another aftermath of war was the proposal to require aliens to register with county clerks or police officers once a year, or more frequently if they moved from place to place. Perhaps the best argument in favor of this proposed regulation was that it would be an effective method of enforcing the immigration law. If an alien could not produce a registration certificate, it would be evidence that he had entered the country unlawfully. It was also argued that it would be good protection for the law-abiding immigrant and enable him to make contacts with organizations interested in his welfare. On the other hand, it was objected that the regulation would lower the standard of citizenship by unduly stimulating naturalization as a means of escaping the trouble of registration, that it would furnish a basis for action against political refugees, and that it violated the spirit of the freedom of the individual from government surveillance.

CHAPTER XXXII

DISILLUSIONMENT

FROM 1921 TO 1929 THE UNITED STATES WAS PERHAPS THE most self-satisfied country in the world. On March 4, 1929, millions heard with approval the optimistic words of Herbert Hoover's inaugural address which was broadcast from coast to coast. "In the large view, we have reached a higher degree of comfort and security than ever existed before in the history of the world," said the new President. "Through liberation from widespread poverty we have reached a higher degree of individual freedom than ever before. . . . For wise guidance in this great period of recovery the nation is deeply indebted to Calvin Coolidge."

Before the end of Hoover's first year in the White House, these words seemed like hollow mockery. The bubble of fictitious prosperity had burst; and the problem of the President and Congress was how to deal with a depression that had turned millions into the streets or reduced their incomes to the level below subsistence.

Although the two preceding administrations had not been without problems of unemployment, wages compared with those in the pre-war period were high and people lived in what that generation would have called luxury. Merchants, manufacturers, and bankers—at least most of them—were happy over dividends, profits, and booming stocks, rejoiced that the country had entered an era of permanent prosperity, and predicted that wages would never fall below the present level. People in almost every walk of life bought stocks on margins with their savings; and on his next visit the salesman had no difficulty in persuading them to increase their purchases. The "up market" made previous promises seem true; and many thought they were on easy street or were soon to be there. Their increased wealth was in unrealized paper profits.

Then, on Thursday, October 24, the talk of the country was the great crash in the stock market—much more serious than the slump of the day before. Business was frightened, as evidenced by "reassuring" statements made by business men. The following Monday, October 28, was even more disastrous, the sales on the stock market reaching the huge total of 12,800,000. This was but the prelude to a debacle such as the world had never seen on the fatal Tuesday of October 29, 1929, when the sales mounted to 16,400,000. Thousands were "cleaned." Men and women with drawn faces visited brokers' offices only to learn that investments which a few days before had promised so much had been wiped out.

For four years following the tragic and exciting October days the country sank deeper and deeper into the mire of a depression such as it had never before experienced, with an occasional revival which swiftly ran its course. So complicated was the commercial and economic structure of the country—and, indeed, of the world—that stocks, bonds, and other securities declined much after the fashion of a row of dominoes falling before each other. The blind optimism of the years of Coolidge prosperity vanished like a rainbow before gloom and pessimism.

To explain the causes of the depression would tax the resources of a host of specialists in the field of economics—and there would be disagreement among them. However, there is general agreement that the roots extend back to the World War, when millions of lives were destroyed, other millions incapacitated, billions of dollars' worth of property destroyed, and stupendous debt structures set up. The regular channels of trade and commerce were shut off and governments resorted to inflation in order to liquidate their debts.

Moreover, business fell victim to overproduction, just as farming had after the armistice. During the war farmers had been urged to make every acre count; and land that had lain idle was placed under cultivation. Improved farm machinery, including tractors and combines, made it possible for farmers to augment their crops in spite of a labor shortage. Similarly, in the years preceding the depression industry was speeded up to a remarkable pace by the introduction of improved machinery which increased the output of factories and threw men and women out of employment. Extensive advertising, high-pressure salesmanship, and installment-buying made it possible to purchase automobiles, electric refrigerators, radios, furniture, vacuum cleaners, oil burners, fur coats, and what not.

Economists and others had speculated as to the time when the American people would reach the "saturation point" in the purchase of automobiles; but the Ford assembly line showed no signs of slowing up. Indeed, several other automobiles in the "low price field" shared streets and highways with the Ford. People mortgaged homes in order to invest in stocks; but they also found it possible to make monthly payments on automobiles. In fact, thousands derived more satisfaction from driving automobiles than from owning and improving homes.

In 1921 the radio boom was on, and within a few years "broadcast" became a household word. In 1920 the Westinghouse Company established the first permanent radio broadcasting system; and shortly every city of importance had not one but several stations, some of them locally owned and others owned by or affiliated with broadcasting systems. This cheapest and speediest mode of communication became an effective advertising medium. Symphony concerts, baseball games, football games, wrestling and boxing matches, comedians, and almost every conceivable form of entertainment were sponsored by almost every conceivable form of commercial enterprise.

The psychology of the American people during the years of Coolidge prosperity has been designated as "stadium-thinking." It was a time of slogans and special days: Mother's Day, Safety First Day, Mobilization Day, Navy Day, Go to Church Sunday, Eat More Cheese Week, Tag Day, and the like. The "drive method" of raising money probably originated during the war, when newspapers, billboards, and house-to-house canvassers were used to put Liberty Loan campaigns over the top. "War chests" for the benefit of charitable organizations and institutions became permanent

Community Funds. Experts in mob psychology made use of the "drive" to raise large sums for hospitals, colleges, and universities, whether the purpose was to obtain money for endowments, buildings, or stadiums. In every "drive" the methods were similar: advertisements, speeches, committees, banquets, posters, and buttons reading "I gave" to be displayed in windows or on coat lapels. Banks, department stores, and factories practically dragooned employees into making contributions, and in some instances the amount of the contributions was deducted from pay checks. These concerted efforts brought results and were symptoms of the trend toward consolidation in many lines. It was the day of big undertakings. Small enterprises were swallowed up, just as the voices of individuals were drowned out in the stadium.

Mass education was the order of the day. The small colleges found competition with the junior colleges and universities difficult, just as private academies were driven out by consolidated high schools. State universities with impressive physical plants, student bodies mounting into the five and ten or more thousands, and unprecedentedly large appropriations expanded their curricula. Not only state universities but educational institutions supported by churches reflected the materialism of the time, with the emphasis on the building program and on quantity rather than quality. The invasion of high school students into colleges and universities, which was made possible by the prosperity of their parents, was partly responsible for the problems of mass education at the college level; and the tremendous growth of high schools was chiefly due to child labor laws and compulsory school laws. Moreover, parents believed that a high school and college education was an *entrée* to social distinction, white-collar jobs, and a higher standard of living.

Under these circumstances high schools and colleges and universities ceased to be what they were originally intended to be. Cultural pursuits yielded to courses in advertising, home economics, manual training, physical education, child welfare, and similar subjects, valuable in themselves but entirely absent in the older curricula. The weeks before commencement brought swarms of recruiting agents to high schools to offer inducements of one kind or another to students to enroll in the institutions they represented, regardless of the aptitude of individuals for work at the college level. Indeed, many of them had been promoted in high school not because of intellectual curiosity, originality, or achievement, but because educational experts had accepted the theory that failure to promote would make for inferiority complexes. Universities and colleges were swamped with men and women who had not acquired habits of study and application and whose ambition was to "get by." This resulted either in the lowering of standards or in the failure of a large number of students.

What of the churches? During the war the voice of peace and good will to men was stilled by the raucous shout of the propagandist, who invaded the sanctuary and occupied the pulpit to breathe defiance and death to the military foes of the country. Preachers who had discarded belief in the devil found a good substitute in Nietzsche or in the kaiser. The minister of the gospel who tried to shut out from the house of worship the din of battle was under the surveillance of secret service men or of self-appointed patriots.

After the war the churches prospered, but the Christian religion had lost much of its radiancy. Pulpit, pew, and professorial chairs profited by the profits of a materialistic age. It is true that there were occasional pastors and bishops who protested burning incense before the altar of Mammon, that the Federal Council of Churches published a book entitled *Christianity and Economic Problems,* edited by Kirby Page, that Upton Sinclair drew up a formidable indictment in *The Profits of Religion;* but the church did not begin to reckon its war-time and prosperity losses until after the depression had revealed the flaws in the economic and political structure.

In response to a questionnaire sent to Protestant ministers and Jewish rabbis, nearly 13,000 clergymen declared their determination not to sanction or participate in any future war, and more than 18,000 repudiated capitalism as it prevailed in 1929. In reply to the question: "Which economic system appears to you to be less antagonistic to and more consistent with the ideals and methods of Jesus and the noblest of the Hebrew prophets?" about eighteen times as many chose a cooperative commonwealth as capitalism. Questionnaires have serious limitations; but the responses to this one revealed unmistakable disillusionment with the old order. And this disillusionment afflicted millions who had been lulled either to complacency or to enthusiasm by the false prosperity of the twenties.

In an age of supposed "rugged individualism" the individual was in retreat before the advance of mergers, consolidations, and corporations. The independent banker was frozen out by chain banks controlled by giant holding companies. Notwithstanding "friendly" advertisements of branch banks, the personal element in banking was passing out of the picture for better or worse—not infrequently for the better. The friendly local banker who called his customers by their first names, made loans without collateral or other securities, and made no charge for checking accounts—who in some cases was ignorant of the fundamentals of banking—was displaced, after he went to the wall and after the bank became a link in a chain, by an individual under orders.

The "community" drug store had hard sledding in competition with "cut-rate" stores or with nationally owned stores with their "loss leaders." The corner grocery, which extended liberal credits and carried the family over the period when the wage earner was out of a job, either failed, sold out to a "cash and carry" chain, or affiliated with other independent retailers. The general merchandise store in the country town and the "notion store" in the suburbs were overshadowed by five and ten cent stores in the chains of Woolworth, Penney, Kresge, and Neisner, and by the auxiliaries of the great mail-order houses of Montgomery Ward and Sears, Roebuck.

The Harding and Coolidge administrations watched with utmost complacency the building up of vast consolidated structures and mammoth pyramids of holding companies. Especially was this true of public utilities. Power companies, electric companies, gas companies, and street railway companies were so inextricably laced together that municipalities and states were baffled in efforts to regulate them or to levy taxes in proportion to their earnings or some other equitable valuation. Public service companies obtained through commissions or through the courts increased fares and rates on the ground that higher wages, higher taxes, higher costs of material, and, in some cases, reduced income required them. Before the war street railway companies charged a five-cent fare, though in many cities a three-cent fare would have been adequate. Having taken no thought for the morrow but having watered their stocks in the days of prosperity, the companies sent their attorneys to appear before committees of city councils and state commissions and, perchance failing there, into the courts to obtain permission to increase rates. Not infrequently citizens who opposed these petitions were discredited by paid propagandists who branded them dangerous radicals in sympathy with Communism or even Red Russia. Some members of university faculties teaching classes in corporations and public utilities received retainers from public service companies.

Promoters issued large blocks of common stock and sold it to unwary speculators on the stock exchange. Financial jugglers, manipulators, and evangelistic salesmen persuaded thousands of people that they were doing them a favor by allowing them to purchase these "securities" which could not fail to soar to fabulous heights. Even the very "elect"—members of the banking fraternity—played fast and loose with other people's money. For months and perhaps years the ticker and the financial page seemed to testify that these financial wizards and their agents had preached the true gospel. Computing in terms of the latest quotations, thousands believed themselves wealthy or on the high road to wealth, until the inevitable crash not only wiped out the savings that had been invested but in many cases deprived them of the automobile which had been purchased through finance companies. Worst of all, the home that had been mortgaged in order to buy stocks went under the sheriff's hammer. In some instances salesmen exacted promises from purchasers that they would not dispose of their stocks within a stipulated time, hoping in that way to keep the bubble inflated.

As the depression deepened, liquidation proceeded. When stocks went down, banks demanded more collateral; when farmers were unable to pay interest on their mortgages, banks foreclosed; when homeowners could not meet monthly payments, foreclosure proceedings were instituted; when people with charge accounts or under contract to make monthly or weekly payments on furniture and clothing lost their jobs, merchants could not meet their bills; when taxes were not paid, sheriffs tacked up notices of sales for taxes; when salaries and wages were reduced or ceased entirely, the bottom fell out of prices. From 1930 to 1933 the United States furnished the paradox of a country with millions haunted by the specter of poverty and starvation, and with granaries bursting with grain and warehouses choked with food and garments that could not be sold because they could not be bought.

In spite of President Hoover's plea that American standards must be maintained, factories and stores reduced wages; schools, colleges, and universities cut salaries, and in some instances paid them in kind or not at all; cities like Chicago paid school teachers and employees in scrip; some congregations were unable to pay pastors, and appropriations for missions, hospitals, and education remained unpaid; prices sank so low that farmers struck, refused to deliver to market non-perishable products, and even left their crops unharvested; banks failed right and left; and all the while the stock market kept hitting "new lows."

During the campaign of 1920 the Republicans portrayed Harding as a man of the plain people—"one of us"—who would be a welcome relief from Wilson—the superman, the "highbrow" in the White House. During the campaign of 1928, however, Hoover was lauded as a superman, a great engineer, who had worked wonders in bringing relief to Belgium during the World War and had worked miracles as food administrator in his own country. The man who as Secretary of Commerce under Harding and Coolidge had had a large part in pulling the country out of the post-war depression was the Moses to lead the farmers out of the wilderness of low prices.

As an administrator Hoover's place in history is probably secure; but he was no leader of men. As a speaker he was heavy and uninteresting, and as President he was irritated by criticism and often petty in his likes and dislikes. His associates respected his ability; but he had none of the magnetism of Theodore Roosevelt to draw men unto him. It was his misfortune to be President of the United States during a depression which made a mockery of his party's claim to have a copyright on prosperity and of his own childish statements about the future under continued Republican rule. Nevertheless, he was a far abler man than his two predecessors. His cabinet was perhaps above the average in ability; but his advisers and chief strategists were mediocre, and he was hamstrung by such Old Guard leaders as James E. Watson of Indiana, George H. Moses of New Hampshire, David A. Reed of Pennsylvania, Reed Smoot of Utah, and Hiram Bingham of Connecticut.

Moreover, the attempt of the Old Guard in the previous administration to reduce the progressive Republicans to "innocuous desuetude"—and Hoover's open hostility toward them, in spite of his desire to be known as a "middle-of-the-road liberal"—boded no good for his administration. The President informed these obstreperous individuals that "we cannot legislate ourselves out of this depression."

In his message of April 16, 1929, to the special session of Congress, Hoover centered his attention on farm relief and limited changes in the tariff. "An effective tariff upon agricultural products . . . has a dual purpose," he said. "Such a tariff not only protects the farmer in our domestic market, but it also stimulates him to diversify his crops and to grow products that he could not otherwise produce, and thus lessen his dependence upon exports to foreign markets." The President thought that there had been economic shifts necessitating a readjustment of some tariff schedules.

The Smoot-Hawley Tariff Act was finally approved by Hoover in June, 1930, after months of debate, and was as odious to certain interests in the West as the Payne-Aldrich Tariff of 1909. Hoover, unlike Taft, escaped the bitter attacks of newspapers. This law not only raised duties on agricultural products to the highest point in history but it also raised them on manufactured articles. An incident in the legislative progress of the bill which illustrates the tactics of its proponents made it even more odious

to friends of scientific revision. In November, 1929, the Senate
voted to censure Senator Bingham for employing as his secretary
a man loaned to him by New England manufacturers. As secretary to a Senator this man had *entrée* to committee hearings
and even to the floor of the Senate.

The Smoot-Hawley Tariff passed over the negative votes of
eleven Republican Senators, and Hoover signed it against the
advice of more than one thousand economists, who pointed out
the disastrous consequences that would follow. Their prediction
that it would bring retaliatory high tariffs by foreign governments was speedily realized. Not only did foreign trade decline
still further at a time when means were sought to provide a market for surplus agricultural products, but American manufacturers were driven to establish branch factories in other countries. The depression that preceded the Smoot-Hawley Tariff, and
the tobogganing prices and increasing unemployment that followed, gave the lie, in the judgment of many, to the Republican
claims that protection spelled prosperity. Neither the Smoot-Hawley Tariff nor the Agricultural Marketing Act of 1929 answered
the prayers of farmers in the South and West.

For years students of economic and social problems had exposed major defects in the system, and progressives like Norris,
Borah, and La Follette had warned the people of calamities ahead;
but Hoover and his advisers and the spokesmen of big business
reiterated that the fundamental business of the country was on
a sound basis. In the first two years of the depression statements
emanated from the White House to assure the public that the
worst was over, that "prosperity was just around the corner,"
that signs were hopeful.

Of course, these statements were partly designed to stiffen the
morale of the people and to inject optimism into the arteries of
the system; but critics of the administration believed that the
crisis called for measures more fundamental than exhortations
to employers to maintain the old level of wages; than the maintenance of planned construction work by industry; than each
industry's care of distress among its own employees; than the
shortening of hours of work; than the speeding up, by govern-

mental agencies, of construction on public works. In an address to the United States Chamber of Commerce on May 1, 1930, the President was convinced that "with unity of effort we shall rapidly recover." And on October 30, 1930, in addressing the American Bankers Association, he was "completely confident of the future of the United States. . . . This is no time . . . to talk of any surrender. . . . The spirit of this people will never brook defeat." Hoover's successor said much the same thing, but they did not mean the same solution or strategy.

In response to members of Congress who demanded larger appropriations and direct organization of relief by the federal government instead of by states and communities, the President charged them "with playing politics at the expense of human misery." In 1931, at a time when local relief was showing unmistakable signs of breaking down under the great burden imposed upon it, Hoover set his face against abandoning voluntary agencies in favor of federal action. The mobilization of agencies of self-help in communities was the "American way" of relieving distress, he said. "The moment that responsibilities of any community, particularly in economic and social questions, are shifted to Washington, then that community has subjected itself to a remote bureaucracy."

The President's scheme to keep public finance on a sound basis rested on economy, opposition to the enlargement of federal expenditures, and temporary increase in taxation. However, pressure from the distressed, high and low, became so great that he was driven to recommend drastic measures—entirely out of line with Republican philosophy—to save the crashing banking structure and to make credits available to tottering industries and limping railroads.

In January, 1932, Congress accepted the President's proposal to set up the Reconstruction Finance Corporation. Leaders in his own party, like James E. Watson, urged Hoover to arm the Corporation with authority to lend money directly to industry, but without success. Most of the money lent by the RFC went to banks and railroads on the theory that banks would lend money to industry and thereby create employment. In the uncertain condition of industry, however, the banks refused to lend. Fortunately, the RFC did make loans through banks and other agencies in order to rescue agricultural and urban homeowners from foreclosure. The railroads borrowed large sums to bolster their sadly depleted finances.

This achievement of the Hoover administration stands out as the most effective. By lending money to self-liquidating projects, it stimulated employment and assured eventual repayment. Its full measure of usefulness, however, was thwarted by the President's determination to keep the government out of private business. One of the most effective attacks directed against Hoover in the presidential campaign was the charge that the appropriations by the government went directly to the men at the top, with the expectation that benefits would trickle down to the common man in the form of employment and higher prices for agricultural and industrial products. Whether rightly or wrongly, it created suspicion that the government played favorites, as in the case of the ninety-million-dollar loan to a Chicago bank in which Charles G. Dawes, former Vice-President, was heavily interested. When this transaction became public property, the veil of secrecy was lifted from future loans.

Hoover's campaign for reelection in 1932 was waged under the most serious handicap that can beset a President, namely, hard times. Deserted by powerful leaders in his own party and having only the lukewarm support of many others, Hoover almost single-handed waged his battle before the public. The Democrats were not slow to capitalize the depression as a Republican achievement, after the fashion of the Republicans who had laid the depressions of 1893 and 1920 at the doors of Democratic administrations.

Hoover committed two political mistakes in the early part of 1930, when he nominated Charles E. Hughes to be chief justice of the Supreme Court and John J. Parker of North Carolina to be associate justice.

Twenty-six votes were cast against Hughes' confirmation after Republican insurgents and Democrats had opposed him because of his alleged conservative views on property and because of his resignation from the Supreme Court in 1916 to enter the political arena as a candidate for the Presidency. Senator Borah, whose masterly speeches in support of Hoover in 1928 had carried great weight in the West, was one of the group opposing Hughes because they believed that in deciding social and economic questions which would come before the Supreme Court, he would espouse the views of corporate wealth against the interests of the public. The large vote against confirmation was a blow to the prestige of both Hoover and the court.

The nomination of Parker, two months later, in April, 1930, was a major blunder and revealed the political obtuseness of the President. So odious was the nomination to labor and the Negroes that the Committee on the Judiciary returned an unfavorable report. Again Borah led the fight against confirmation, ably assisted by Norris, centering his fire on Parker's social and economic philosophy. He cited Parker's decision as a federal district judge when he had sustained a "yellow-dog" contract, by which an employee pledges himself not to join a labor union during the time of his employment. Borah exposed the absurdity of the claim that the Senate ought not to scrutinize the philosophy of nominees to the Supreme Court. Parker's confirmation was defeated by a vote of 39 to 41.

Borah's refusal to give public support to Hoover in 1932 was a severe blow; and hardly less serious was the defection of Norris, Hiram Johnson, and the younger La Follette, who had succeeded his father in the Senate.

Notwithstanding the unpopularity of Hoover with the politicians and the public, the Republican party could not refuse to renominate him. To have done so would have violated a tradition of the party and been tantamount to a confession that the party had been found wanting in a national crisis. There was little enthusiasm in the national convention. The keynote speech of Senator L. J. Dickinson of Iowa was an old-fashioned political blast. The only thing that stirred the convention was the adoption of a plank which in equivocal and clumsy language proposed that the repeal of the Eighteenth Amendment be submitted to the people. Hoover's speech of acceptance, while carefully worded and definitely conservative, favored modification of the amendment.

Perhaps no President in history has been subjected to the experiences that came to Hoover in the campaign. With farmers' strikes, with threatened strikes of taxpayers, with people deprived of homes and lifetime savings, the public was in an ugly mood; and there were individuals not above hurling insulting epithets at the President as he rode through city streets. In St. Paul, Minnesota, where he delivered the last important speech of the campaign, he saw posters and heard language that almost unnerved him when he arrived at the Auditorium to speak.

An unfortunate incident, which Hoover referred to in his St. Paul speech, was the dispersion of the so-called bonus army which in the summer of 1932 had taken possession of government property in Washington and built shacks for shelter while awaiting action by the government for relief. Advised by the commissioners of the District of Columbia that riots were imminent and that life and property were unsafe, Hoover called out troops to disperse what in his St. Paul speech he called a mob. He did so against the advice of Senator Watson, the Republican floor leader, who told him that the measure he proposed was a colossal political blunder and that neither the bonus-seekers nor their families and sympathizers, whose numbers ran into millions, would ever forgive him. In dispersing the veterans and their wives and children, cavalry, infantry, tanks, and machine gun units were used. From the temper of the public the President ought to have known that there was grave danger in taking such action.

For the first time since 1912 the Democrats could look forward with supreme confidence to victory, although at the opening of the year the identity of the candidate was unknown. Franklin D. Roosevelt's overwhelming reelection to the governorship of New York in 1930 marked him as a strong contender. After his unsuccessful candidacy for the Vice-Presidency in 1920, he was stricken with infantile paralysis, and it appeared that his public career was over. However, with a determination and cheerfulness characteristic of the victims of that dread disease, he made remarkable progress toward recovery, although he never regained the normal use of his legs. In the Democratic national conventions of 1924 and 1928 he nominated Alfred E. Smith and called his good friend the "happy warrior." At the urgent request of the presidential candidate, he ran for the governorship of New York. Roosevelt was elected, but Smith failed to carry the state.

During his convalescence Roosevelt built up a wide correspondence. A man of ingratiating personality, incisive and charming gifts of conversation, and uncanny political intuition, he gathered to himself a majority of delegates to the Democratic national convention in 1932. However, when in the first days of February Al Smith announced that he would accept the nomination, it was said that Roosevelt's chances were gone. It certainly improved the prospects of John N. Garner of Texas, himself no novice at the political game, as he had demonstrated in the capacity of floor leader in the House of Representatives.

In the pre-convention campaign Roosevelt's managers favored the repeal of the two-thirds rule; but in the convention they did not dare to ask for a test vote. The speech placing Smith in nomination was followed by a demonstration lasting an hour. The result was uncertain until the fourth ballot, when, as the outcome of a deal, Roosevelt was nominated and Garner was named as his running mate.

The following day Roosevelt threw tradition to the winds by traveling by air from Albany to Chicago to make his speech of acceptance before the convention. He praised the platform, which was brief and concise, and avowed that it was intended to be carried out, economy plank and all.

Smith's disappointment was bitter and intense, and he sulked in his tent until October 24, when he made his first "national" speech. He devoted the greater part of the address to a denunciation of prohibition and bigotry, and refrained from mentioning Roosevelt's name until the concluding sentence, which was scarcely audible to some radio listeners. The address left the decided impression that Smith's support of his old friend was not wholehearted and that he was thrown off balance by the memory of the whispering campaign which had been conducted against his religion in the previous campaign.

Roosevelt was an adroit campaigner; and his extensive speaking tours were in part designed to allay suspicion that his infirmity would hamper him in discharging the duties of the presidential office. Unlike his distant cousin Theodore Roosevelt, he radiated good humor and refrained from personalities. His speeches were heartening to liberals, who found little comfort in the speeches of the candidates of the major parties after 1916.

Roosevelt remembered the "forgotten man" and promised him a "new deal" under a Democratic administration. He attacked Hoover's policy of bestowing favors on big business in the hope that they would leak through to men and women in the lower strata of society. While Hoover was excoriating progressives like Norris and Johnson, his opponent was currying favor with them. Both candidates were opposed to the immediate payment of bonus certificates. Roosevelt advocated postponement until the budget had been balanced. He also praised the economy plank in his platform and denounced the accumulation of a heavy public debt under Hoover. He also promised more adequate revenue from a tax on beer, which he would propose to Congress.

It was said that one of Roosevelt's greatest assets in the campaign was a perfect "radio voice," whereas his opponent was at a disadvantage in speaking into a microphone. This was undoubtedly true, but both candidates might have refrained from speaking without affecting the outcome of the election, although perhaps Roosevelt's majorities would not have been so large. It was a Democratic year; it was a year of disillusionment; it was a year when a change was demanded. The Republican party had made its record, and it was read in the light of existing conditions.

By nine o'clock on election night Chicago knew that Roosevelt was elected; and at midnight it was known that he had been swept into office by the largest electoral and popular vote in history. He had 472 electoral votes against 59 for Hoover. Outside of New England (with the exception of Massachusetts and Rhode Island), Hoover carried only Delaware and Pennsylvania, with greatly reduced pluralities over previous elections. The Democratic majorities in both houses of Congress were overwhelming. Carried down to defeat in the landslide were such Republican stalwarts as Senators Watson, Smoot, Moses, and Bingham.

The meaning and magnitude of the Democratic victory may be indicated by the fact that Iowa went Democratic by 183,586; Minnesota, by 236,847; and Wisconsin by 359,889. Minnesota added insult to Republican injury by reelecting a Farmer-Labor governor, Floyd B. Olson, and five Farmer-Labor congressmen out of a total of nine. Only eight Republican governors were elected. It was a desperate nation that went to the polls on November 8, 1932. The election cleared the air, as it were; but it was an assignment too great for one administration to clear away the débris and to restore the full measure of American optimism.

CHAPTER XXXIII

THE NEW DEAL

THE HOOVER ADMINISTRATION EXPIRED AT A TIME WHEN MANY people—including business men—feared that the country was about to topple into an abyss. Certain it is that the country barely escaped an economic cataclysm. In the interval between the election and inauguration of Roosevelt, banks were closing all over the country. In some cities and towns no banks were open for business. Confidence in the banking structure was not improved when states declared moratoria and when it was learned that depositors were withdrawing deposits and hoarding gold. It was no more reassuring to learn that crooked banking transactions in cities like New York and Detroit had jeopardized financial structures with wide ramifications, and that nineteen officials of the Insull public utilities had been indicted and that Samuel Insull of Chicago was himself a fugitive from justice. The uncertainty of the moment was not alleviated when the radio flashed the news that at Miami, Florida, on February 15, an assassin fired several shots into President-elect Roosevelt's automobile, fatally wounding Mayor Anton Cermak of Chicago.

On the day of Roosevelt's inauguration the banks were in such distress that moratoria were in force in about three-fourths of the states; and on the following day the President by proclamation closed all banks in the United States from March 6 to 9, both inclusive. There were certain qualifications, but no ordinary banking could be transacted.

Not since 1913 had the American people heard or read an inaugural address that breathed the spirit of the one delivered by Franklin Delano Roosevelt on March 4, 1933. The gravity of the situation was evident from the content of it, and the threat of a substantial dictatorship was there. "Only a foolish optimist can deny the dark realities of the moment," he said. "Practices of the unscrupulous money changers stand indicted in the court of public opinion. . . . They know only the rules of a generation of self-seekers. They have no vision, and where there is no vision the people perish. The money changers have fled from their high seats in the temple of our civilization. We may now restore that temple to its ancient truths." The nation called for action, he said, and he proposed to act quickly.

The new cabinet conformed to the usual standard, with some members chosen for outstanding ability and others from the stand-point of political expediency. It was the first cabinet to include a woman, Frances Perkins of New York, Secretary of Labor. Cordell Hull of Tennessee, Secretary of State; Harold L. Ickes of Illinois, Secretary of the Interior; Henry A. Wallace of Iowa, Secretary of Agriculture; and James A. Farley of New York, Postmaster-General, were outstanding. William H. Woodin of New York, Secretary of the Treasury, resigned after a few months and was succeeded by Henry Morgenthau, Jr., of New York. The announcement that Thomas J. Walsh of Montana would be appointed Attorney-General was heartening to liberals. His con-sistent liberalism, his great ability, his courageous and brilliant in-vestigation of the Teapot Dome scandal were guarantees of a new deal in the Department of Justice, which sorely needed rehabilita-tion after twelve years of mediocrity or worse, beginning with the notorious Harry M. Daugherty. Walsh's sudden death two days before inauguration day deprived the government of his services. Homer S. Cummings of Connecticut, a Wilson Democrat, was appointed in his stead.

The new President was not an unknown man before his nomina-tion, but in the country at large little was known about his ability and philosophy of government. He speedily won the confidence of the country and proved himself to be a man of action, unafraid of flying in the face of tradition and precedent. His optimism was contagious; and the restoration of some measure of individual self-confidence and confidence in the government by his own ex-ample must be set down as not the least of his achievements. Con-fronted with problems that few of his predecessors had faced, he had the advantage of taking over the reins of government from a party that was entirely discredited and did not even function as a feeble opposition party. Moreover, the crisis was so acute that newspapers, regardless of political complexion and in great fear that the institutions which sustained them would collapse, refrained from criticism that would further shatter confidence, and ran editorials praising the President and exhorting their readers to support him.

The immediate tasks that confronted the administration were to restore confidence in the hearts of the people, to restore price levels that had sunk almost to the vanishing point, to put people back to work, to give relief to the destitute and the unemployed, and to rescue thousands from the perils of foreclosure. Spurred by the extraordinary initiative and leadership of the President, Congress which sat in special session from March 9 to June 6 passed with breath-taking speed a succession of laws to meet the emergency.

When Congress convened, it speedily effected its organization, received a brief message from the President recommending emergency banking legislation, and before the close of the day (March 9) passed the Emergency Banking Act. This act provided that additional Federal Reserve bank notes were to be issued to member banks; that Federal Reserve banks could make loans to persons and corporations on government bonds as security; that member banks of the Federal Reserve System could reopen under licenses issued by the Treasury; and that the Secretary of the Treasury could call in all gold certificates. On March 13 began the gradual process of reopening the banks. A more comprehensive measure designed to strengthen the Federal Reserve System and to correct weaknesses in the banking structure, known as the Glass-Steagall Banking Act of June 16, 1933, contained a provision for the guarantee of bank deposits, a measure Bryan had featured in the presidential campaign of 1908.

Although this banking legislation fell short of eliminating a number of defects in the system, at the close of his first term Roosevelt could point with pride to the unprecedentedly small number of bank failures.

During the presidential campaign the Republicans issued warn-ings that in the event of Roosevelt's election "tinkering with the currency" could be expected; and the banking and gold panic was cited by them as proof of their contentions. However, the financial chaos and the temper of the country made it imperative for the administration to take action. Moreover, inflationists—including many business men—advocated their remedy on the ground that almost anything was better than the slow death that was clamping down on them. In the last days of April their cause looked up when the Senate, with a few Democrats and most of the Republicans voting in the negative, passed a free coinage of silver bill. The upshot of the debates in both houses was the passage of the Gold Repeal Joint Resolution in the first days of June, a measure that eliminated the gold clause in all federal and private obligations and all other obligations that specified payments in gold. The majorities in both houses were large, with Democrats and western Republicans voting in the affirmative and Republicans in the negative.

This resolution and the Farm Relief and Inflation Act of May 12 paved the way for Roosevelt's policy of controlled inflation. In the fall and early winter of 1933 the government purchased domestic and foreign gold, and silver mined in the United States, at prices higher than the old legal price of gold and the market price of silver; and on January 15, 1934, Roosevelt asked Congress for authority to devalue the dollar, a measure that had been foreshadowed in a provision of the Farm Relief and Inflation Act. The bill passed Congress on January 27 over the opposition of conservatives and after a silver amendment had been defeated by a very close vote. By the Gold Revaluation Proclamation of January 31, the President reduced the value of the dollar to 59.06 per cent of its old value. All gold in the Treasury and in Federal Reserve banks was impounded. The profit made by the government from this transaction was set aside as a fund to stabilize the dollar. Thus the danger of uncontrolled inflation had been averted and the government returned to a modified gold standard. The devaluation of the dollar was expected to ease the problems of creditors and to raise prices in the interest of producers—farmers and manufacturers, who in turn could buy more and pay better wages. It was also pointed to the problem of foreign exchange.

During the presidential campaign Roosevelt had directed sharp criticism against the extravagance of the Hoover administration and promised to balance the budget. Within a few days after his inauguration he dispatched an economy message to Congress and immediately proceeded to carry out a program in accordance with it. Reductions were made in the salaries of federal employees, and over the opposition of the powerful veterans' lobby reduced compensation for war veterans was effected. This victory for the President proved to be short-lived, however, for within a few months the demands of the former service men were satisfied by Congress and pay cuts were restored. Moreover, in the light of Candidate Roosevelt's strictures on the heavy appropriations of the Hoover administration (during the last twenty months the national debt had increased by four billion), the unprecedentedly heavy peace-time appropriations and the mounting debt under President Roosevelt were ironical and eloquent of the tragically critical situation that confronted him.

Early in the special session Congress passed a law legalizing the sale of beer, and this in turn was followed by state laws and municipal ordinances regulating its sale. This measure was acclaimed as a means of bringing money to grain producers and revenue into the public coffers as well as of furnishing employment not only to dispensers of the beverage but also to men engaged in the manufacturing of fixtures for beer parlors and "taverns"—the saloon having odious connotations from pre-prohibition days.

President Hoover appointed a body of distinguished men and women—the so-called Wickersham Commission—to investigate and report on the advisability and enforcement of the Eighteenth Amendment. The members of this Commission were badly divided among themselves and rendered a report, together with dissenting reports, that bewildered rather than clarified the problem. The report, which was made public early in 1931, stated that settled habits and social customs did not readily yield to legislation, and that, taking the country as a whole, people of wealth, business men, professional men and their families, and perhaps the higher-paid workingmen and their families were drinking in large numbers. "Unless the number of speak-easies can be substantially and permanently diminished, enforcement cannot be held satisfactory," it was reported.

The Commission also learned that almost all the bodies seeking to repeal the amendment conceded that under no circumstances should the licensed saloon be restored, and it concluded that the great achievement of the amendment was the abolition of the saloon. Although there was disagreement as to what action should be taken with reference to repeal or enforcement, there was general agreement in opposing proposals to modify the Volstead Act in order to permit the sale of beer and light wines. Such action, it was reported, would be ineffectual in reaching the root of the problem. There was unanimous opposition to the return of the saloon in any form.

It was not until December 3, 1933, that the Eighteenth Amendment was officially repealed by the ratification of the Twenty-first, thus marking an astounding reversal of public opinion and ending the first effort to extend directly by constitutional provision the police control of the federal government to the personal habits and conduct of individuals. The government was without organization for or experience in enforcing a law of this nature. Moreover, states like New York, Massachusetts, Maryland, Wisconsin, Montana, and Nevada did not have enforcement acts and thus placed the entire burden of enforcement on the federal government.

It must be set down as most unfortunate that the legal sale of liquor returned without proper regulation and that the saloon came back in an even more vicious form. The mounting toll of deaths and injuries from accidents on streets and highways bears testimony to the hazards of allowing the promiscuous sale of liquor, although high-speed automobiles and lax and ineffective traffic laws and regulations must also be taken into account. Neither did the repeal of prohibition eliminate the bootlegger and hi-jacker, as was so confidently predicted by the advocates of repeal.

The plight of the farmers received immediate attention from the Roosevelt administration in the form of the Agricultural Adjustment Act of May 12, 1933, and the Farm Credit Act of June 16. Without entering into the details of the provisions of these epoch-making acts and the machinery set up for their enforcement, we may content ourselves by saying that by extending loans to farmers on their crops and by enabling them to refinance mortgages, money was made available to provide for the running expenses of farms and families, thereby saving thousands from foreclosures that would have deprived them of their property. In order to make money available to the farmers and to raise the level of prices, the government embarked on the experiment of reducing the surplus in the production of staple crops like cotton, wheat, corn, tobacco, rice, hogs, and dairy products by reducing acreage and by slaughtering hogs. Undoubtedly the farmers profited by these measures. On the other hand, many—including farmers—could not approve of a policy that destroyed millions of dollars' worth of food at a time when there were hundreds of thousands of hungry mouths to feed. As an emergency measure to alleviate the desperate condition of the farmers, this policy can probably be justified; but the quandary in which the President and Congress found themselves in 1937-38 in attempting to find a solution of the farm problem showed the ephemeral character of this emergency legislation.

In fact, in seeking to promote consumption more soundly, the New Deal frankly admitted the experimental character of this legislation. In the words of Secretary of Agriculture Wallace, "It should be recognized that our surplus here in the United States, and the resulting necessity of keeping parts of our factories idle and withdrawing acreage, or of widening foreign markets, or of doing these things in combination, is really part of a world surplus problem. The country has more industrial as well as more agricultural capacity than it needs for home consumption." During the World War, millions of acres in Europe were out of cultivation. Food prices in America soared to great heights, with the result, according to Secretary Wallace, that America added forty million acres to its tilled domain and threw its whole farm plant into high gear. After the war the tremendous export of American products was stimulated by lavish loans to foreign countries, in spite of the fact that the tariff was raised to new high levels. The end of this false prosperity was inevitable.

Pending the solution of the problem of surplus acreage which

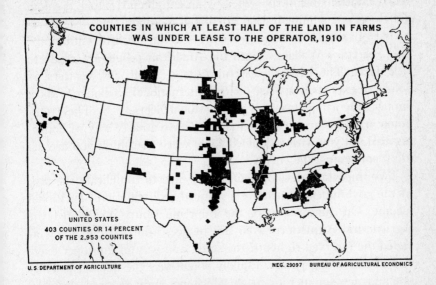

COUNTIES IN WHICH AT LEAST HALF OF THE LAND IN FARMS
WAS UNDER LEASE TO THE OPERATOR, 1910

UNITED STATES
403 COUNTIES OR 14 PERCENT
OF THE 2,953 COUNTIES

U.S. DEPARTMENT OF AGRICULTURE   NEG. 29097   BUREAU OF AGRICULTURAL ECONOMICS

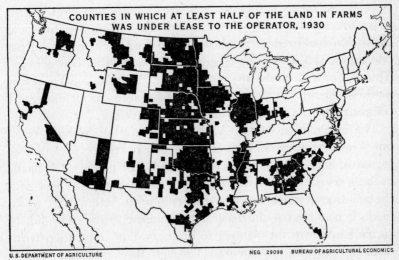

COUNTIES IN WHICH AT LEAST HALF OF THE LAND IN FARMS
WAS UNDER LEASE TO THE OPERATOR, 1930

U.S. DEPARTMENT OF AGRICULTURE   NEG. 29098   BUREAU OF AGRICULTURAL ECONOMICS

FARM LANDS UNDER LEASE TO THE OPERATOR, 1910 AND 1930

involved many factors, including tariff adjustments and bold and skillful statesmanship supported by an enlightened public opinion, the Roosevelt administration attempted to conduct an orderly retreat from surplus acreage. "We are sparring with the situation," said Secretary Wallace, "until the American people are ready to face facts. The bare, distasteful facts . . . on such matters of policy as exports, imports, tariffs, international exchange, export quotas, import quotas, and international debts. . . . These economic weapons are so subtle that they have a nasty way of bouncing back on you with redoubled force when you think you are using them against the enemy."

Two important developments intervened to complicate the task of the government to achieve a planned redistribution of national income. On June 6, 1936, the Supreme Court invalidated the Agricultural Adjustment Act. Six justices held that the AAA invaded the reserved rights of the states and was an improper exercise of the taxing power. Equally potent was the unprecedentedly hot and dry summer of 1934 which not only reduced the corn crop, but killed by starvation millions of cattle and hogs. Three years of experimenting demonstrated that although nature and legislation could reduce surpluses in the United States, it did not prevent the people of other countries from adding to their acreage. This not only deprived the cotton, corn, and tobacco farmers of markets abroad, but also raised apprehensions as to the danger of competition from abroad in the domestic market.

The invalidation of the AAA was a blow to "planned economy" for agriculture and threatened to plunge farmers into another period of unrestricted competition which had played such havoc in the years after the World War. Congress responded at once with the Soil Conservation and Domestic Allotment Act of 1936, which made it possible for the federal government to pay subsidies to farmers in return for planting soil conservation crops, thereby indirectly regulating production. Through the Commodity Credit Corporation the Reconstruction Finance Corporation continued to make loans on certain crops. For example, in 1933 the government loaned $120,000,000 on approximately 270,000,000 bushels of corn at forty-five cents a bushel, and in 1937 on corn at fifty cents a bushel. Beginning in 1935 the Resettlement Administration made rural life more attractive and aided farmers by building homes, making loans, adjusting mortgages, and withdrawing from cultivation and improving marginal lands. Despite failures and errors, in 1933 the Roosevelt administration inaugurated a program which did more for the rural population than any previous administration had done. It was achieved in spite of divided counsel among the farmers themselves, the refusal of many to cooperate, and the nullifying activities of "chiselers."

In his inaugural address the President stated that "our greatest primary task is to put people to work. . . . It can be accomplished in part by direct recruiting by the government itself, treating the task as we would treat the emergency of a war, but at the same time through this employment accomplishing greatly needed projects to stimulate and reorganize the use of our natural resources." It could also be helped, he said, by unifying relief activities. When these words were spoken, there were about 15,000,000 unemployed; a year later the number stood at over 12,000,000; and four years later there were almost 10,000,000. Obviously the stupendous burden of caring for this army was beyond the resources of local relief agencies. Thousands of men and women had reached the stage of life when the prospects of reemployment were slight, and other thousands were youths standing on the threshold of life gazing into black despair. It has been estimated that during the first three years of Roosevelt's administration one-fifth of the population received some form of public relief—federal, state, or local— and appropriations mounted into billions. Obviously there was much waste, extravagance, and corruption in which officials and beneficiaries participated; but, after all, this money was appropriated to save human life, not to destroy, as in the case of the huge appropriations in 1917-18.

Under the Federal Emergency Relief Administration, which was set up under the Federal Emergency Relief Act of May, 1933, money was doled out to the needy and used to make work for men and women who revolted against accepting doles or whose physical condition made it advisable for the government to furnish employment to them, in the absence of opportunities in private industry.

The largest number of workers employed by the several agencies of the federal government was 3,853,000 in February, 1936.

In 1933 the Civil Works Administration got under way. It was provided for by the National Industrial Recovery Act of June, 1933. Within a remarkably short time an organization was set up, and before the end of the year some four million men were at work. In the meantime young men were enrolled in Civilian Conservation Camps. This service not only furnished employment in reforestation, reclamation, fighting and preventing forest fires, building dams, eliminating insect pests, improving and beautifying highways and parks, and similar projects, but through an educational program taught illiterates to read and write and provided others with instruction and recreation in libraries and on the platform and stage. Moreover, federal aid afforded opportunities for thousands of graduates, undergraduates, and high school students to continue their studies. Merely to list the activities sponsored by the National Youth Administration and similar services would suggest the ingenuity of leaders in many walks of life.

In spite of the lack of perspective which alone enables the historian to evaluate events, the extraordinary departures from the procedure of previous administrations marked by such federal agencies as the Civilian Conservation Camps, the Resettlement Administration, the Public Works Administration, and the Works Progress Administration (which in 1935 succeeded the PWA) entitles him to say that Roosevelt led the American people in a revolutionary experiment in self-government. It implied that the government was obliged to create jobs in times when private industry was unequal to the task of providing work for the able-bodied. PWA and WPA projects added thousands of miles of improved roads, built or remodeled thousands of buildings for educational purposes, laid out and beautified parks and playgrounds, constructed thousands of public buildings and hundreds of airports, and contributed to the public welfare by improving and extending water and sewage systems.

The amazing prosperity of the United States during the nineteenth century and in the pre-war years of the twentieth and the youthful character of its population made it possible for private

charity and families to care for the aged and the infirm, just as
before the establishment of state hospitals for the care of the insane these unfortunates were cared for in homes and in semi-
private institutions or had been allowed to shift for themselves.
The platforms of third parties like the Socialist, Progressive, and
Farmer-Labor parties had demanded old age pensions and unemployment insurance; but these proposals were too radical for the
leaders of the Republican and Democratic parties. However, the
tragedies of the depression years and the growing complexity of
society, together with the increase of the urban population, revealed as never before in American history the need for social
security legislation. Many of these measures plus a good banking
system had been in use in Europe for a half-century.

The President's social security message of July, 1934, and the
appointment by him of a committee to formulate a program paved
the way for the Social Security Act of August 14, 1935. This
comprehensive and complicated law provided for cooperation between state and federal governments, and for contributions of employers and employees in order to pay pensions to indigent persons above the age of sixty-five and to beneficiaries of a system of
old age insurance and of unemployment insurance. The act also
made appropriations for blind and crippled children, maternity and
child welfare, and public health services. The attainment of the
objectives of this legislation would have been impossible without
cooperation between federal and state governments, far beyond
the dreams of earlier generations. According to the tenets of men
who had opposed income and inheritance taxes, railroad regulation, and rural credits, this was "class legislation" with a vengeance. However, Roosevelt's opponents continued to confuse class
privilege with individual opportunity. On May 24, 1937, when the
newspapers gave columns to obituaries of John D. Rockefeller, one
of the last survivors of the individualistic, exploitive nineteenth
century, who died at the age of ninety-seven, the Supreme Court
by a five to four decision upheld the unemployment insurance provision of the Social Security Act. It also sustained the old age pension provision.

In making war on unemployment the President and his advisers made a bold frontal attack on the abuses and practices of big business and labor organizations. Capital was primarily interested in profits; and the speed-up and stretch-out systems were employed when they were deemed profitable, and production was curtailed when that seemed to be profitable. Workingmen were hired and fired and wages were raised and lowered under an industrial system that knew no other procedures. Industrialists with a broader vision were at the mercy of competitors whose ethics were those of the jungle. Roosevelt knew that unrestricted competition was unworkable and that it benefited neither manufacturer, laborer, merchant, banker, nor consumer. It was in the spirit of reform and recovery that he set about to frame legislation that would reinforce the girders of the economic structure. He believed that the American people could pull themselves out of the depression if they wanted to be pulled out. His plan had its roots in the Hoover administration.

It was in this spirit that the National Industrial Recovery Act of June 16, 1933, was conceived and passed. It made the federal government at once monitor and umpire in the regimentation of industry and business, in the belief that the "Constitution is so simple and practical that it is possible always to meet extraordinary needs by changes in emphasis and arrangement without loss of essential form." It suspended the operation of anti-trust laws in favor of regimentation which would recognize the rights of labor, eliminate cutthroat competition, utilize the man power and physical equipment of the country to its fullest extent, raise wages and reduce hours, and regulate prices in the interest of the public. The blue eagle, the symbol of the NRA, represented an effort to control production and exchange. It was an admission that the country had emerged from the horse and buggy days; that the Industrial Revolution had already effected a social revolution; that competition among individuals was largely a myth; that huge collective enterprises were a reality and were recognized as such by industrialists themselves in the form of holding companies, trade agreements, and cartels. The NRA was an effort to extend to industry something similar to the efficient control and regulation of traffic on Broadway, New York, and Michigan Avenue, Chicago.

It fell to the directing genius of the dynamic and bluff General Hugh Johnson to set up codes for hundreds of industries and classes of business which included fixing minimum wages, hours of labor, ages of employees, and rules of trade. Thousands of blue eagles were displayed in factories, stores, offices, and homes to advertise that "We are doing our part." Outwardly at least, almost everybody seemed to be enthusiastic over the gigantic experiment. But it was inevitable that individuals and groups of individuals should feel that they had been singled out for special sacrifices in order to promote the general welfare, and that others should take secret advantage of individuals and corporations which made honest efforts to comply with the codes. The small merchant, the owner of an independent garage, the operator of an independent filling station, and the "little fellow" generally complained that the codes were drawn up in favor of the big concerns and monopolies. The consumer felt the pinch of higher prices. The employer who feared labor organizations rebelled at the provision for collective bargaining, and the laborer suspected that Regional Labor Boards were partial to the employers. All in all, enthusiasm was waning. There was wholesale violation of codes by industrialists. It was the Supreme Court, however, that put an end to the NRA.

The first legal blow was struck in the decision of the so-called "hot oil case" of January 7, 1935, which involved the validity of the petroleum code. The tremendous increase in the production of oil not only reduced the price of the product, but threatened to put the big companies out of business. In order to regulate production, the State of Texas attempted to limit the large oil wells to a fixed quota per month. Notwithstanding, hundreds of thousands of barrels of oil in excess of the quotas were shipped out of the state. In order to dam up the stream of this so-called "hot oil," a petroleum code was drafted under a provision of the National Industrial Recovery Act which authorized the President to prohibit the shipment of oil in interstate commerce which had been produced in violation of a state law.

This effort to eliminate wasteful competition in one of the most valuable natural resources resulted in higher prices for oil, but it threatened to wipe out the smaller independent producers. The large companies also resented government interference in their business. The Panama Refining Company brought suit against the government for unconstitutionally interfering with its oil production. The Supreme Court, with only one dissenting justice (Cardozo), held that Section 9c of the National Industrial Recovery Act went beyond the constitutional limits of the right of Congress to delegate its lawmaking functions.

The decision of the Supreme Court in the case of the Schechter Poultry Corporation v. the United States on May 27, 1935, gave the deathblow to the NRA. The poultry code outlawed the sale of diseased poultry, fixed hours of work and wages, and by other provisions protected farmers and consumers. The Schechter brothers violated the code in various ways, including the sale of diseased chickens, and were duly indicted. In a unanimous decision the court held that the National Industrial Recovery Act involved an illegal delegation of power and contained an invasion by the federal government of jurisdiction reserved to the states. Holding that the Schechters did not sell poultry in interstate commerce, the justices agreed that if the commerce clause of the Constitution were construed to extend indirectly to similar enterprises, "the federal authority would embrace practically all the activities of the people, and the authority of the state over its domestic concerns would exist only by sufferance."

The death of the NRA was unmourned by the people at large; and it was followed by price-cutting, wage reductions, and threats of strikes. Roosevelt, however, was bitterly disappointed and publicly attacked the reasoning of the court. "The gravest question," he said, "revolves around the court's interpretation of the government's power over interstate commerce. These powers constitute the only weapon we have to fight conditions not even dreamed of a hundred and fifty years ago." The decision, he said, threw the country back into the horse and buggy stage at the time of the adoption of the Constitution.

The chaotic conditions in the coal fields which had produced the savage strikes of 1919 and 1922 threatened to precipitate another fierce labor war and to demoralize the entire coal industry. Cutthroat competition threatened to wreck both operators and workers. John L. Lewis, president of the United Mine Workers, took advantage of the NRA by organizing the discouraged and underpaid miners, and for a time conditions were improved. But code violations threatened to bring back the old chaos. The Guffey Coal Act of August 30, 1935, permitted operators to set the price of coal at the mine and made it possible for them to pay better wages, fix shorter hours, and grant other concessions to the miners. It also provided for a 15 per cent tax on coal, 90 per cent of which would be rebated if the operator complied with the coal code.

On May 18, 1936, another New Deal measure went by the board, when the Supreme Court by a six to three decision invalidated the Guffey Coal Act. By throwing out the labor provisions, the court also invalidated the entire law, but not without a biting dissenting opinion concurred in by Justices Cardozo, Stone, and Brandeis (Carter *v.* Carter Coal Company).

Perhaps one of the most radical and soundest policies of the New Deal was the conservation of natural resources; but in the process of realizing it, the Roosevelt administration was the object of the same criticism that nullified efforts to attain similar ends during the administrations of Theodore Roosevelt and Woodrow Wilson. The hue and cry of socialism was raised. Thousands and thousands of dollars were spent by private power companies to discredit the policy of the Franklin Roosevelt administration to sell to municipal plants power generated at dams constructed by the federal government. These same interests saw no objection to the government's appropriating money for the generation of electricity so long as the power was sold to private companies who would retail it to the public at a profit to themselves.

The most interesting and far-reaching experiment in social service, which included providing urban water supply, irrigation, flood control, navigation, reforestation, soil conservation, and electric power, was the creation of the Tennessee Valley Authority on May 18, 1933. It was an experiment in socialism for the benefit of a vast region, including Tennessee, Virginia, Kentucky, North Carolina, Georgia, Alabama, and Mississippi. The funds were provided by the Public Works Administration. At the same time the PWA encouraged the public ownership and operation of public utilities by furnishing money to assist in financing such enterprises. In fact, the TVA was intended to serve as a "yardstick" to measure the cost of supplying the public with the conveniences and necessities that hitherto, with few exceptions, had been sold by private companies.

The man who waged an unceasing fight against the power companies in behalf of this project and finally won the battle against great odds and unscrupulous methods used to drive him from public life, is Senator George W. Norris of Nebraska, a man whom President Roosevelt described as obedient only to his own conscience. This project dates back to the World War, when the government constructed two nitrate plants at Muscle Shoals, Tennessee, and a dam to supply the electric power. After the war the nitrate plants were not operated, and the power generated by the dam was sold to a private company. Contending that electric energy could be produced at a cost much lower than power companies charged, Norris succeeded in having Congress pass resolutions in 1928 and 1930 providing for the completion and operation of the Muscle Shoals plant. The respective resolutions were vetoed by Coolidge and Hoover. Hoover was suspicious of the motives of Norris and others who sponsored the bill. He believed that it was a scheme to discredit the power companies. If they were guilty of abuses, the President considered that the remedy was regulation, not government competition with private enterprise.

Roosevelt was not so tender of property rights; and at the time he took the helm even the expensive propaganda of the public utility companies could not appease a public enraged by the exposure of the methods and practices of giant holding companies like the Insull system. The New Dealers and the Tennesseans were jubilant when on February 17, 1936, Chief Justice Hughes read the decision sustaining the right of the government to generate and sell power. In the words of Secretary of the Interior

Ickes, the indignation of the power companies was "very like that of the boy who finds that his mother has locked the door to the jam cupboard." The Secretary asserted that the administration was "dedicated to conservation for all our citizens and, regardless of misrepresentations and loud outcries from rugged individualists who would continue to exploit the people, it has no intention of lining the private pockets of the few with the money which properly belongs to all."

In March, 1938, President Roosevelt intervened in a dispute between Arthur E. Morgan, chairman of the TVA, and David Lilienthal, a member of the commission, over the objectives of the TVA, which precipitated an investigation by Congress. In the meantime Roosevelt dismissed Morgan, whom Lilienthal accused of being too tender with the power interests and of lack of sympathy with the broader aspects of social service.

The development of the Tennessee River Basin created demands for similar conservation programs on other rivers. In his message to Congress in 1937, Roosevelt said: "Experience has taught us that the prudent husbandry of our national estate requires far-sighted management. Floods, droughts, and dust storms are in a very real sense manifestations of nature's refusal to tolerate continued abuse of her bounties. Prudent management demands not merely works which will guard against these calamities, but carefully formulated plans to prevent their occurrence. Such plans require coordination of many related activities."

On his trip to the Pacific coast in the late summer of 1937, Roosevelt had the satisfaction of dedicating at Bonneville, Oregon, a battlement of steel and concrete that spans the Columbia River; and in the State of Washington he saw in the process of construction the Grand Coulee Dam, the largest structure ever built by man, the cost of which exceeds that of the Panama Canal. On this trip the enthusiastic President saw the greatest construction program ever undertaken by the federal government. It embraced flood control, navigation, irrigation, and power.

No less disturbing to the public utility companies was the Wheeler-Rayburn Act of August, 1935, which was pending while a Senate committee came forth with daily exposures of the lobby conducted by holding companies, together with the sordid business of huge profits and schemes. Congress did not go as far as the President had suggested; but the act gave the federal government power to regulate interstate power and gas, compelled lobbyists to register, and gave the Securities and Exchange Commission enlarged authority over public utilities, and also included the New York Stock Exchange. A drastic amendment introduced by Senator Borah was defeated in favor of a provision clothing the Securities and Exchange Commission with authority to liquidate holding companies deemed to be detrimental to the public interest.

The same Congress passed a "soak the rich" tax bill (1935). This much-criticized law was aimed directly at individuals and corporations that evaded taxes which would normally be payable by them. The methods used were devious and many. One device was to set up foreign holding companies in the Bahamas, Panama, Newfoundland, and other places where taxes were low and corporation laws were lax. Another was to organize insurance companies in the Bahamas under a plan by which individuals paid large single premiums for their policies and immediately borrowed back practically the entire sum. Personal holding companies made it possible to conceal incomes by failing to distribute incomes or by complicating the task of the Treasury Department in auditing transactions or by shifting income from one member of a family subject to higher surtax rates to another member of the family subject to lower rates. Splitting incomes two ways between husband and wife or into still smaller fractions among children through the device of multiple trusts left the money actually in the same hands but evaded taxes. In some instances yachts and country estates were incorporated and the owners rented them from their personal holding companies.

The law of 1935 increased corporation income taxes and provided for a graduated tax on undivided profits. The undivided profit tax was denounced as a heavy handicap to the small business man and a deterrent to business expansion. The real purpose of the tax, however, was to prevent evasion of the income tax by individuals who concealed their dividends by keeping them in the business, which in turn often resulted in overexpanding the business.

In May, 1938, a new tax bill went into effect, which reduced the undistributed profits tax by exempting from it corporations with incomes of less than $25,000. Smaller corporations were required to pay a flat income tax of 12½ to 16 per cent, graduated according to profits. The tax on capital gains was also drastically revised. Roosevelt allowed the bill to become a law without his signature and called attention to what he considered two vital defects. He said the measure might restore "certain forms of tax avoidance," because it retained but a remnant of the old tax on profits which corporations held in their treasuries instead of disbursing as dividends upon which stockholders had to pay an income tax. He also stated that the bill abandoned the principle of dividing the costs of government among those best able to pay. "Taxes, local and state and federal combined, are nowhere as high in this country as they are in any other great nation that pretends to be up to date," he said.

When the Seventy-fourth Congress adjourned on June 20, 1936, the record of the Roosevelt administration had been written in a formidable list of laws and executive orders and proclamations. The Republican national convention had done its work and the Democratic national convention was about to meet. It is significant that on the eve of the assembling of the Democratic convention, the papers on June 22 published an appeal to the delegates to defeat the renomination of Roosevelt. The signers of this document—Alfred E. Smith, Bainbridge Colby, James A. Reed, Joseph B. Ely, and Daniel F. Colahan—appealed to the ideals of Jefferson, Jackson, and Cleveland, and significantly omitted Woodrow Wilson, who blazed trails followed by Roosevelt. The concluding statement read as follows: "If you fail, then patriotic voters of all parties will know unhesitatingly to what standard they must rally in order to preserve the America of the great leaders of the past."

CHAPTER XXXIV

THE ELECTION OF 1936

IT WOULD BE AN EXAGGERATION TO SAY THAT DURING THE FIRST three years of Roosevelt's administration the Republican party functioned even as a feeble opposition party. It was torn by dissension and was without a constructive program. The anti-New Dealers presented the spectacle of a group of malcontents arrogating to themselves all the virtues of Americanism and appointing themselves the guardians of the Constitution and of liberty, shouting loudly about the sacred Declaration of Independence and bemoaning the threat of Communism. They alleged that the Roosevelt administration had departed from the principles of constitutional government; that Roosevelt was seeking to make himself a dictator; that "government in business" had retarded recovery; that huge expenditures would be followed by unbearable tax burdens; and that the country was under a bureaucracy. Business men who had praised the recovery measures enacted during the first months of the New Deal, including the NRA, after three years condemned the "reform" measures that followed, and acclaimed the Supreme Court as the bulwark against the madness of the "Brain Trust," as the advisers of the President were stigmatized.

Within the Democratic party there were signs of revolt against the President's bold and aggressive leadership from conservatives who could not reconcile certain items in the New Deal with what they conceived to be sound Democracy. Alfred E. Smith, who, together with other conservative Democrats, had joined forces with prominent Republicans in an organization called the American Liberty League, was exceedingly bitter against Roosevelt and served notice that he would "take a walk" if Roosevelt were renominated.

If Roosevelt had alienated those who were pleased to call themselves "Jeffersonian Democrats," he had also won the support of prominent Republicans who had been virtually read out of their party by the Old Guard. The result of the election on November 6, 1934, showed the direction of the political breeze. Not only did the Democrats increase their already large majorities in both houses of Congress and make almost a clean sweep of the governors, but even Pennsylvania elected a Democratic governor and a United States Senator. Very significant was the outcome of the election in Wisconsin, where the La Follette brothers, Robert and Phillip, cutting loose from the Republican party, were elected on their own Progressive ticket to the Senate and the governorship, respectively. In Minnesota the Farmer-Labor party reelected the brilliant and courageous Governor Floyd B. Olson and made great inroads on the Republicans. In both states the La Follettes and the Farmer-Laborites indorsed the Roosevelt administration.

In the months preceding the Republican national convention at Cleveland, the newspapers indulged in the usual pre-convention speculations about the candidates for the nomination for the Presidency. Herbert Hoover, Senator Borah, Colonel Frank Knox of Illinois, and Governor Alfred M. Landon of Kansas were the most prominent candidates. Hoover departed from the heavy style of his earlier addresses and indulged in a liberal application of humor and sarcasm in attacking the New Deal. Borah, whose prospects were dim, assumed the rôle of a gadfly by alleging that the Republican party was controlled by monopolies and by threatening to bolt unless the party purged itself of this influence. His independent record did not recommend him to party leaders. Knox, the publisher of the *Chicago Daily News*, was regarded as a satellite of William Randolph Hearst because for some years he had been the general manager for the wealthy publisher. His vituperative speeches were strongly suggestive of Hearstian journalism.

Some weeks before the convention met, the prospects of these three men had faded before the rising sun of Landon, whose fortunes were underwritten by John M. Hamilton, his chief strategist, and by the Hearst newspapers. Born in Pennsylvania and graduated from the University of Kansas, Landon soon made a substantial fortune in oil. He came into some prominence by virtue of the fact that he was one of the few Republicans to be elected to the governorship of a state in the Democratic landslide of 1932; and he rose to greater prominence when the report was broadcast that under his administration Kansas, unlike other states that had accumulated heavy deficits in their accounts, had a balanced budget. Quite naturally, the Republicans made no mention of the fact that balancing the budget was mandatory under legislation passed before Landon became governor, and that it had been achieved by unwise economies and by the use of large sums of money made available by agencies of the federal government. Landon's pre-convention speeches dealt in generalities and vague promises.

The Republican convention produced the mock heroics expected of it by the radio public, but it fell far short as a theatrical entertainment, in spite of strained efforts to ridicule the Roosevelt administration by interspersing in the proceedings a parody on "Three Blind Mice" in the form of "Three Long Years." Confident that Landon had the nomination "in the bag," his managers were not disturbed when Hoover was cheered for fifteen minutes before he made his speech excoriating the New Deal, which was punctuated by enthusiastic applause. The keynote speech of the temporary chairman, Senator Steiwer of Oregon, stressed the iniquities of the New Deal and extolled the "American System."

Before John Hamilton made his speech nominating Landon, the other candidates had withdrawn; and the Kansas governor was nominated on the first ballot. Hamilton prefaced his speech by reading a telegram from Landon in which he stated that he would accept the nomination with the understanding that he favored a constitutional amendment which would permit states "to adopt such legislation as may be necessary adequately to protect women and children in the matter of maximum hours, minimum wages, and working conditions." With reference to the plank pledging the party to preserve a sound currency, the telegram placed the governor on record as favoring a currency expressed in terms of gold and convertible into gold. The first statement conceded too much to the New Dealers' criticism of the Supreme Court; and the second alienated Borah and hosts of others, like the followers of the radio priest, Father Coughlin.

By nominating Knox for the Vice-Presidency the Republicans presented a ticket headed by men from the Middle West. By nominating Landon the Republicans could emulate the tactics of the Whigs in 1840 and the Republicans in 1920; but it was an insuperable task for spellbinders and newspapers to attain the success that attended those campaigns. Issues were too vital to be obscured; and the Democrats had too many assets, the major ones being the superb equipment of Roosevelt as a campaigner and the unbeatable strategy of James A. Farley. Al Smith's cynical remark that you can't vote against Santa Claus never touched the millions who did not understand individual measures of the New Deal and might even disapprove some, but felt that the man who sponsored them was headed in the right direction and had the well-being of the common man at heart.

The Democratic national convention which met at Philadelphia in the last week of June was a Roosevelt circus, with the Postmaster-General the ringmaster. Al Smith's "stop Roosevelt" telegram fell flat and, if anything, solidified the ranks of the New Dealers. The convention had no more respect for the traditions and rules of the twenty-five previous national conventions of the party than the New Dealers had for Jeffersonian democracy. When the Philadelphia convention repealed by acclamation the two-thirds rule, it scrapped a method of nominating candidates that had been in force since 1836 and had played havoc with the political ambitions of many worthy Democrats. The only serious objection to the repeal was from the South; but a sop was thrown to the delegates from that section by a promise that a readjustment of representation in the convention would be considered at the next convention. The party violated another tradition and made a bid for the Negro vote when it chose a Negro chaplain to invoke divine blessing and permitted a delegate of that race to speak on the floor. To make it a revolutionary convention in all respects,

it smashed another precedent by nominating Roosevelt by acclamation and adopting the most straightforward platform ever
adopted by a major party. Social justice was woven into its
texture.

In 1932 Roosevelt flew in the face of political conventionality
by flying to Chicago to make his acceptance speech before the convention; and in 1936, on the last day of the convention, he and
Vice-President Garner delivered their acceptance speeches before
115,000 people in Franklin Field, Philadelphia. The President
was in fine form and sounded a trumpet call for war against
"economic royalists" who "seek to hide behind the flag and the
Constitution." By coining that term, the popular President added
another to the long list of reasons for the intense hatred toward
him of the interests and individuals who saw themselves mirrored
in that designation.

The campaign of 1936 was a contest—if it can be dignified
by that name—between Roosevelt and Landon; but there was the
usual number of minor parties. The Socialist party nominated
Norman Thomas, a Presbyterian minister who had led the party
in 1928 and 1932. Earl Browder and James W. Ford, a Negro,
were the standard bearers of the Communist party. Browder's
arrest in Terre Haute, Indiana, on September 30, as he stepped
off the train to fulfill a radio engagement, evoked a chorus of
protests and demands for respect of the right of free speech from
the newspapers, very different from the tone of the press during
the years of red-baiting that followed the armistice. While appealing for votes in their own behalf, the speeches of the Communist
candidates left no doubt as to their preference for Roosevelt over
Landon. "Today, the Republicans, sponsored by the Liberty
Leaguers, are in alliance with the most bitter enemies of the
Negro people. . . . The Democratic administration has been a
little more favorable to Negroes," said Ford. "Copy all the most
hysterical Hearst editorials of today against Moscow, Lenin,
Stalin; substitute the words, America, Washington, Jefferson;
and the result is an almost verbatim copy of the diatribes of English and European reactionary politicians in the closing years of
the eighteenth century against our American founding fathers,"

said Browder. "Revolution was then 'an alien doctrine imported from America' as now it is 'imported from Moscow.' "

A movement that gave promise of considerable strength culminated in the organization of the Union party on June 19, 1937, which adopted a platform favoring a central bank of issue and the retirement of all tax-exempt interest-bearing bonds and the refinancing by Congress of all present agricultural mortgage indebtedness. Other planks declared for legislation insuring a living wage, assurance of production at a profit for the farmer, security for the aged and the unfortunate, public works, and the limitation of income. The candidates were William Lemke of North Dakota, co-author of the Frazier-Lemke Farm Mortgage Bill and active in farmers' movements, and Thomas Charles O'Brien of Massachusetts, lawyer and humanitarian.

Father Charles E. Coughlin, the Detroit radio priest, announced his support of the Union party, and to him perhaps may be attributed the impulse back of its organization. The militant priest had a large radio audience who heard his Sunday afternoon broadcasts in which he had denounced the Coolidge and Hoover administrations and had been correspondingly laudatory of Roosevelt in the early months of his administration. However, he developed into a caustic critic of the New Deal and its monetary policies; and over the air he traded epithets with General Hugh Johnson, who had branded the priest as a demagogue. During the presidential campaign Coughlin accused Roosevelt of playing into the hands of the Communists.

One of the most bitter and dangerous critics of the New Deal was Senator Huey P. Long of Louisiana, whose domination of the state was so complete that it won for him the sobriquet of "kingfish." He was the champion of the underprivileged—white and colored—and he filled hundreds of pages of the *Congressional Record* with stories and wit that grew out of his backwoods environment. He had no inhibitions and ruffled the dignity of his colleagues in the Senate with a recklessness that exceeded the best efforts of "Pitchfork Ben" Tillman in the nineties—a man who also rose to political power over the Bourbons in South Carolina. Long's career was cut short on September 8, 1935, by an assassin who shot him down in the Capitol at Baton Rouge after the adjournment of the legislature, which he dominated as completely as he did the governor of the state.

Long and his political heir, the Reverend Gerald L. K. Smith, popularized the Share-the-Wealth program which proposed to limit incomes and the amount of inheritances, to assure to every family an income of not less than $5,000, to limit hours of employment and agricultural production, to reduce large fortunes by taxation, and to guarantee a homestead to every family. Long and Smith claimed to have several million people enlisted in their cause; but how seriously it was taken it is difficult to say. Certain it is that in his own state Long proved himself to be a masterly and ruthless leader who was feared by vested interests and worshiped by the downtrodden.

Somewhat akin to Coughlin's National Union for Social Justice and Long's Share-the-Wealth program was the Townsend Old Age Pension Plan, which was promoted by Dr. Francis E. Townsend through clubs and a weekly publication. Townsend proposed that every citizen over sixty years of age who had retired from productive employment should receive from the federal government $200 a month which was to be spent within thirty days. Townsend made the religious appeal, as did also Coughlin and Long. In the spring the Townsend plan was much in the headlines, partly because of its large following and partly because of Dr. Townsend's action in defying a committee of the House of Representatives investigating the methods of his organization. In July, 1936, the Townsend group held a convention at Cleveland at which the presidential candidates were invited to make addresses, but only Lemke and Thomas accepted. Although the Townsendites could not agree over the proposed indorsement of Lemke, it was expected that they would support him in preference to his competitors.

It was predicted that Lemke's candidacy would cut in on Roosevelt's vote and work to the advantage of Landon; but Lemke's vote was very disappointing, failing to reach 700,000. In fact, the combined popular vote of the candidates of five minor parties failed to reach the million mark, which may be an indication of the popularity of Roosevelt.

The situation in Wisconsin and Minnesota was indicative of Roosevelt's success in enlisting the support of the individualistic and monopoly-baiting farmers and laborers who followed the La Follettes and the leaders of the Farmer-Labor party. On his deathbed the Farmer-Labor governor of Minnesota, Floyd B. Olson, issued a statement in support of Roosevelt. He praised Lemke and his movement, but stated that the fight was between Roosevelt and Landon.

In order to cement the merger of the Farmer-Labor and Democratic parties in Minnesota, by which the Democratic candidates for the Senate and the governorship withdrew in favor of Farmer-Laborites, Roosevelt on October 9 spoke in St. Paul, paid tribute to the late Governor Olson, praised cooperative enterprises, and defended reciprocal tariff agreements. The following day at Omaha he urged the reelection of Senator Norris who was running as an independent. Similar alliances and friendly gestures were made between the La Follette brothers and the liberal Mayor LaGuardia of New York. Norris's speeches were fervent pleas for the election of a President who had done more for the people than any President since Lincoln. At a meeting of Progressives in Chicago on September 11, at which Senator La Follette presided, Roosevelt was indorsed.

Before the campaign had progressed very far, it was evident that the Republican cause was lost. Landon was a poor campaigner; there was little consistency in the plan of campaign; the leaders were at odds among themselves; and the support of the American Liberty League and of the Hearst publications was detrimental. At the opening of the campaign the Republicans laid down a barrage of criticism of the New Deal, but before election day those guns had been silenced in favor of promises to exceed the generosity of the administration in furnishing relief and employment on public works, without repudiating Landon's earlier promise to balance the budget. Moreover, it did not ring true to hear Alfred E. Smith and James A. Reed, self-styled Jeffersonian Democrats, excoriate liberals like Norris, denounce Roosevelt as

a traitor to the Democratic party, warn intelligent voters against
an impending invasion from Moscow, and make tearful eulogies
of the flag. Too many remembered Reed's Des Moines speech
four years earlier in which he flayed Hoover and advocated the
election of a "real American" in the person of Roosevelt; and
many more remembered Smith as a renegade who could not forgive his erstwhile friend for winning the nomination in 1932.

Before a crowd estimated at 100,000, Landon delivered his acceptance speech at the Capitol in Topeka. In a faltering voice he
began by telling his hearers that he was of the plain people and
craved the gift of plain, simple speech. The editorial comments
in the Republican papers admitted that the Kansan was no match
for Roosevelt in speech and personality; but these qualities, they
said, were not essential in a President. Throughout the campaign
the Republican eulogies of the candidate were labored. From
Secretary of the Interior Ickes the Topeka speech evoked a telling
contrast, based on official correspondence, between the attitude toward the New Deal on the part of "Governor" Landon and "Candidate" Landon.

In an excellent speech delivered at Chautauqua, New York,
Landon in effect admitted the liability of Hearst's support by devoting his entire address to education and making a bold appeal
for academic freedom. It was obviously an effort to counteract
charges that he was a puppet of Hearst who had advocated loyalty
oaths for teachers and had baited "reds" on college faculties.
Prominent educators like Charles A. Beard had condemned
Hearst in no uncertain language.

Hoping to capitalize the traditional hostility of the Northwest
against Canadian reciprocity—and probably having in mind the
fate of the Taft administration which had favored such a measure—Landon, in a speech delivered at Minneapolis, attacked the
reciprocal agreements sponsored by the Roosevelt administration.
The praise bestowed on the Kansan's "clear-cut solution" of the
farm problem by the Republican papers was quickly nullified by
Secretary of State Hull in the same auditorium when he ridiculed the "incoherent" utterances of the previous speech and
proved that Landon's statistics were far out of line chronologically.

In summary, the chief articles in the indictment of the New Deal by the Republicans were as follows: The accumulation of a huge public debt; the erection of a bureaucracy based on the spoils system and graft; centralization at the expense of the Constitution; undermining the morale of the people by making them wards of the government; hostility toward private business; mounting and unfair taxes; an unsound fiscal policy which had jeopardized investments and repudiated the obligations of the government; reciprocal trade agreements which favored foreign countries at the expense of the American farmer, wage earner, and manufacturer; truckling to irresponsible and racketeering labor leaders; executive usurpation looking toward a dictatorship; the importation of un-American ideas and practices; and class legislation.

In the closing days of the campaign an effort to discredit the Social Security Act took the form of inserting slips in pay envelopes warning workers of the amounts to be deducted from their pay checks after January 1. This was a desperate move to alienate the labor vote from Roosevelt. Prominent labor leaders like William Green, John L. Lewis, and Daniel Tobin had unqualifiedly indorsed the Democratic ticket. The desperate plight of the Republican strategists who resorted to this trick is indicated by the fact that the Social Security Act by tacit agreement among party leaders in Congress was advertised as a non-partisan measure not to be used for partisan advantage. Moreover, it was regarded as a partial, though imperfect, answer to the prayers of humanitarians and laboring men and women.

Republicans as well as Democrats understood that the best campaign asset of the Democrats was Roosevelt himself. The Republicans paid tribute to the President's incomparable "radio voice" by referring to him as a "radio crooner"; and they sought to swing the spotlight away from him by exhibiting the bugaboo twins of Communism and Fascism. The other villains in the piece were Chairman Farley and the members of the "Brain Trust."

When the lapse of time makes it possible to write the history of the election of 1936, honorable mention will be made of the strategy of Farley and of Charles Michelson, publicity director for the Democratic National Committee; but the superb show-

manship of Roosevelt that scintillated against the drab background of his colorless opponent will probably carry off the
honors. Moreover, the intense hatred for the President that was
whispered in drawing rooms and counting houses could not fail
to register itself in the press and less suspected places, and undoubtedly worked to the advantage of the object of their venom.
Also, the President maintained a most irritating silence in the
face of allegations that he was a "President without a conscience,"
and never attacked his opponents in public by name. The only
public mention he made of Alfred E. Smith was a complimentary
reference to his early association with him when he was a liberal.
Perhaps it was his confidence that the "game was in the bag"
that caused him to mention by name prominent political opponents
in his audiences and to request them to come forward to grasp
his hand, as he did when he spied the nationally known Kansas
editor and pioneer liberal, William Allen White. He invited Landon as one of several governors of western states to confer with
him on drought relief at Des Moines on September 3, when the
two candidates dined together. Ostensibly to get a close-up view
of conditions in the drought-stricken area, the President made a
tour of inspection and upon his return to Washington used the
radio to report his findings and to outline plans to absorb into
private employment men and women on relief.

The opening gun of the President's campaign was a fighting
speech delivered before the Democratic convention at Syracuse,
New York, on September 29, in which he sought to disprove the
allegations of his opponents that he was controlled by Communist
and foreign influence. In subsequent speeches he cultivated the
good will of business men by declaring himself in favor of private
enterprise, at the same time taking a fling at disgruntled business
men who in the early weeks of his administration flocked into
Washington beseeching him to rescue them from ruin. The President said that he had their "fever charts." At Madison Square
Garden, New York, he stated that he alone carried the pass-key
to the White House, unlike his three immediate predecessors who
admitted representatives of interests that were consumed by hatred

of him. He promised that the policies that he had inaugurated would be harbingers of even more fundamental reforms.

The night before election was cloudy with political broadcasts. The Republican National Committee put on a show which included an invocation and a benediction, the singing of "Onward Christian Soldiers," and brief addresses by Landon, Chairman Hamilton, and others. This was followed by a similar show, minus the religious aspects, sponsored by the Democratic National Committee, featuring addresses by Roosevelt, Farley, and others.

Early in the evening of election day Roosevelt's opponents were stunned by the magnitude of his victory. Roosevelt carried forty-six states, and Landon two, thus ratifying Farley's prediction that the Republican candidate would win the electoral votes of only Maine and Vermont. In the next Congress the Democratic majorities were larger than ever, and the remnants of the Old Guard fell right and left. Liberals like Norris and Borah were elected to the Senate; and in Minnesota, in the eyes of conservatives one of the "plague spots" of the nation, the Farmer-Labor party rolled up the largest majorities in the history of the state. In other states anti-New Deal Democrats felt the displeasure of the voters.

In retrospect, it seemed to Charles Michelson that the Democratic campaigners and field marshals were frequently "fighting shadows; that the people's faith in Roosevelt had not waned and they had decided long ago that they wanted and would have him again as President. Probably the result of the election would have been just the same had neither the Democratic nor the Republican National Committee functioned at all." Perhaps the approval of Roosevelt would not have been so vociferous if several millions had not seen reflected in their own budgets the Roosevelt boast that his administration had "rolled up its sleeves," contrasted with the alleged "do-nothing" previous administration. In barber shops, in baseball grandstands, in movie houses, in beer taverns, in garages, in grocery stores, in CCC camps, among WPA workers, at educational conventions, at ministerial associations, and among social welfare workers Roosevelt was idolized as a "prosperity bringer." The specter of starvation, lost homes, and a government fettered by fine-spun constitutional interpretations had vanished before returning security and awakening ambition. The men and women who voted for Roosevelt were interested in their own budgets far more than they were in a balanced federal budget. Whether or not their instincts were sound must be left to the sifting process of time. It may be that the prosperity they voted for was as deceptive as the prosperity that lulled the public into complacency in 1924 and 1928. On the other hand, the depression lasted long enough to make it possible for Roosevelt to effect reform while striving to bring back a measure of comfort to people easily swayed by false issues.

As the first Roosevelt term was drawing to a close, a spirit of optimism prevailed and many congratulated themselves that the depression was over. It is true that some lines of business were up to the pre-depression level, but others—building, for example— were far down. Millions were still getting support in one way or another from the government, and there was still the problem of how to reduce their numbers. It remained to be seen how social security legislation—unemployment insurance and old age pensions—sponsored jointly by federal and state governments would work out in practice. Minority groups were still making great demands on the government. The instability of the economic structure was manifest in widespread unrest and strikes which threatened to spread to other industries. The situation in Europe and in the Far East was so dangerous that war was more imminent than at any time since 1914.

CHAPTER XXXV

THE SECOND ROOSEVELT ADMINISTRATION

IT WAS EMINENTLY FITTING THAT IT FELL TO THE LOT OF A President who had broken with tradition and had led the nation far away from the rugged individualism of the frontier to be the first President to be inaugurated on January 20 instead of March 4. Under a pouring rain that converted the streets of Washington into rivers, a President and a Vice-President for the first time in history were inaugurated on the same platform; for the first time since 1917 a President and a Vice-President were reinaugurated; and for the first time in history a Vice-President made no inaugural address. It required but eighteen minutes for the President to deliver his inaugural address—the shortest ever to be made.

Washington rode into office with the unanimous vote of the electoral college, and in 1821 Monroe would have had a unanimous vote but for the desire of one elector to preserve this distinction for the Father of his Country; but in 1937 Franklin D. Roosevelt took the oath of office with the greatest popular indorsement that had ever come to a President. He had swept the opposition parties almost off the map. The Roosevelt tidal wave had inundated every state in the Union except remote Maine and Vermont.

After reminding his nation-wide audience of the conditions that obtained at the time of his first inauguration and referring to the achievements of the past four years, in calm and measured words Roosevelt served notice that returning prosperity would not swerve him from making further advances in the direction of social security. Although the term was not used, there were veiled threats against "economic royalists." In referring to the fact that the year 1937 marked the one hundred and fiftieth anniversary of the meeting of the Constitutional Convention, the President rejoiced that the Constitution was still adequate to meet the condi-

601

tions of the present, just as it had been framed to meet the conditions that obtained in 1787. In so saying, Roosevelt was but reiterating what he had stated in his address to the Congress that convened on January 6. On that occasion he praised Congress for cooperating with the executive department and suggested that the courts get in line and interpret the Constitution liberally, as the framers intended it should be interpreted.

In this Congress—the seventy-fifth—the leaderless and demoralized Republican minority was so small that it could hardly be dignified by the name. The collapse of the Republican party was more complete than the fate that overtook the Federalist party in 1800. Then, as in 1937, whatever effective opposition remained to the minority party was vested in the judiciary, which was packed with appointees of previous administrations. Since 1897—in spite of eight years when Woodrow Wilson was President and four years when Franklin Roosevelt presided—only three appointments had been made to the Supreme Court by a Democratic President.

In 1937 it was most extraordinary that six of the nine justices were past seventy years of age and five were past seventy-four, a circumstance that inspired a caustic and widely read book by Drew Pearson and Robert S. Allen entitled *The Nine Old Men.* The character of the decisions rendered by the Supreme Court invited suspicion that the justices clung to their judicial robes in order to nullify legislative items in the New Deal, just as it was rumored during Wilson's administration that justices past the allotted three score and ten withheld their resignations for fear that their successors would subscribe to the social and economic philosophy of Louis D. Brandeis. It will be recalled that during the campaign of 1920 former President Taft stated that there was no greater domestic issue in that election than the maintenance of the Supreme Court as a bulwark to enforce the guarantee that no man shall be deprived of his property without due process of law. This statement came from a man who had publicly opposed the confirmation of Justice Brandeis and who knew that Wilson's successor would probably be called upon to appoint successors to four justices who were over seventy years of age. It fell to Warren G. Harding to make those appointments, one of whom was Taft himself.

During the campaign of 1936, Roosevelt refrained from making a frontal attack on the Supreme Court; and after he had fired the opening gun, the Republican papers alleged that it was not an issue in the campaign. This contention can be disproved in the easiest possible manner by citing the dispatches and comments in the press on the meaning of the election in the days immediately following. For example, in a syndicated article that appeared on November 6, 1936, it was stated that "the biggest single question of the months ahead is what the President will do about the court." And on November 9, a prominent syndicated writer, Mark Sullivan, in discoursing on the feeble Republican minority in the next Congress, predicted that "in any struggle that may arise over the Constitution and the Supreme Court, Mr. Borah would quite certainly champion the Constitution."

Moreover, Roosevelt had made no effort to conceal his displeasure over the conservative majority of justices who had not only irritated the New Dealers but provoked caustic, ironic, and belligerent dissenting opinions from the liberal minority. In the early months of the New Deal the Supreme Court sustained certain items of legislation, but by majorities so narrow as to make the fate of other legislation dubious. For example, in January, 1934, it upheld the Minnesota Moratorium Act by a five to four decision, with Chief Justice Hughes voting with the majority; and in February, 1935, also by a five to four decision, it sustained the abrogation of the gold clause in contracts. However, the unanimous decision of the court on May 27, 1935, declaring the NRA unconstitutional was the first in a series of judicial blows directed against the New Deal. It was followed by the invalidation of the Agricultural Adjustment Act on January 6, 1936, and of the Guffey Coal Act on May 18.

The NRA decision drew the fire of the President, who said it threw the country back to the horse and buggy stage; and shortly before the meeting of the national conventions in 1936, in a speech at Little Rock, Arkansas, on the occasion of the opening exercises to commemorate the centennial of the State of Arkansas, he eulogized Jackson who defied the Supreme Court and praised Jefferson for assuming responsibility for the purchase of Louisiana without waiting for a constitutional amendment granting specific authority. In his keynote speech at the Democratic national convention, which was obviously submitted beforehand to Roosevelt, Senator Alben Barkley did not mince matters in dealing with the Supreme Court; and in his acceptance speech the President's meaning was not obscure when he referred to "economic royalists" who hid behind the flag and the Constitution.

It was in his concluding speech of the campaign, however, that Roosevelt betrayed his knowledge that members of the legal profession hoped for and expected Supreme Court decisions that would nullify the Wagner Labor Relations Act and the Social Security Act. In the Madison Square Garden speech he made it plain that he would continue to fight for the federal control of relations between employers and employees, for reduction of hours of labor, for the elimination of unfair competition, for the establishment of collective bargaining, and for the return of crop control—all of which had been written into the NRA and the AAA.

Moreover, labor was in an ugly mood, and its whole-hearted support of the President for reelection left him no alternative but to achieve those ends. It was no less a matter of life or death for the New Deal than it was for the peace and safety of the country that the Supreme Court should not be permitted to reduce the Constitution to a state of *rigor mortis*. Bourbons in every age are oblivious to the fact that revolutions, including the American Revolution, are caused by failures to adjust constitutions and laws to changing conditions.

Yet the country was taken by surprise by the President's bold and adroit attack on the Supreme Court, even though it had been recognized that his message to Congress had been fashioned for the edification of the conservatives on the bench. In his message of February 5, 1937, Roosevelt discoursed on the necessity of infusing new blood into the courts in order to expedite and cheapen legislation and to bring the judiciary abreast of the times. In substance he proposed to empower the President to appoint an additional justice of the Supreme Court when a sitting justice reached the age of seventy and continued to sit on the bench. There could be no more than fifteen justices at any one time. It was also proposed to empower the President to appoint a certain number of judges of inferior courts under similar circumstances.

Even hostile newspapers admitted that Roosevelt had prepared a document that crackled with irony and adroit reasoning; but, in the words of the *New York Times*, "Cleverness and adroitness in dealing with the Supreme Court are not qualities which sober-minded citizens will approve." The President enumerated instances when Congress had changed the number of Supreme Court justices and had altered their duties. He then referred to delays in litigation caused by an insufficient number of judges and by the aged and infirm character of many of them who "cling to their posts, in many instances far beyond their years of physical and mental capacity." "A lowered mental or physical vigor leads men to avoid an examination of complicated and changed conditions. Little by little, new facts become blurred through old glasses fitted, as it were, for the needs of another generation." With no small degree of playfulness the President quoted what Chief Justice Hughes, six years earlier, had said of these men: "They seem to be tenacious of the appearance of adequacy"; and equally playful was his citation of a recommendation made by Justice McReynolds, one of the staunch conservatives, as Attorney-General in Wilson's cabinet, that when a district or circuit judge failed to retire at the age of seventy, an additional judge might be appointed.

At the "Victory Dinner" on March 4, 1937, Roosevelt again loosed his shafts at "defeatist lawyers" and defied anyone to read the opinions concerning the AAA, the NRA, the Railroad Retirement Act, the Guffey Coal Act, and the New York Minimum Wage Law, "and tell us exactly what, if anything, we can do for the industrial worker . . . with any reasonable certainty that what we do will not be nullified as unconstitutional." He said that it had pleased the "personal economic predilections" of a majority of the court that "we live in a nation where there is no legal power anywhere to deal with its most difficult practical problems—a no-man's land of final futility." He stated that he did not want to leave the nation to his successor in the condition in which Buchanan left it to Lincoln. "Economic freedom for the wage earner and the farmer and the small business man will not wait, like emancipation, for forty years," he said. "It will not wait at all."

In a "Fireside Chat" on the Supreme Court on March 10, the President described the American form of government as a three-horse team: the Congress, the executive, and the courts, with the people in the driver's seat expecting the third horse to pull in unison with the other two. He lamented the increasing tendency of the Supreme Court to act not as a judicial body but as a policy-making body and to cast aside the sound rule of giving statutes the benefit of reasonable doubt. He said that the exercise by the majority of the Supreme Court of the power to pass on the wisdom of certain New Deal laws had been stigmatized by dissenting justices as "tortured construction of the Constitution," "an unwarranted limitation upon the commerce clause," and the like. He accused the conservative majority of setting up the Supreme Court as a third house of Congress. His proposed reform bill was designed to establish an independent judiciary as intended by the framers of the Constitution—a Supreme Court that would enforce the Constitution as written. "Fundamentally, if, in the future, America cannot trust the Congress it elects to refrain from abuse of our constitutional usages," he said, "democracy will have failed far beyond the importance to it of any kind of precedent concerning the judiciary."

Roosevelt's adversaries were gleeful at the unexpectedly inviting opportunity to deal a telling blow to his prestige. Despite the fact that the Supreme Court had repeatedly been under fire—sometimes from Democrats, sometimes from Republicans, and sometimes from third parties like the Grangers, the Populists, and the Progressives—Presidents and candidates for the Presidency—Jefferson, Jackson, Lincoln, Bryan, Theodore Roosevelt, and La Follette—who criticized the court for its philosophy of extreme property rights to the detriment of human rights were accused of demagoguery and incitements to revolution. Franklin Roosevelt went to bat with the Supreme Court in a way that left no doubt about what he wanted done and why he wanted it done. He felt that unless the reactionary decisions of the court were curbed, not only would the structure of the New Deal be destroyed, but serious labor disturbances might get beyond the control of the government. His enormous prestige following the overwhelming indorsement at the polls made him confident that he could accomplish what Presidents before him would not have dared to undertake.

For over six months the country watched one of the most sensational and spectacular political and legislative battles in the annals of Congress—a contest that produced tragedy and comedy and furnished Roosevelt's adversaries, the first favorable opportunity to discredit him before the electorate.

Fully aware of the unpopularity of their own party and of its leaders, the Republicans in Congress did not dare to challenge Roosevelt openly even on such a controversial issue as the reform of the Supreme Court, for fear that as between them and the President the popular verdict would be against them. They were content to have Senator Burton K. Wheeler, a Democrat from Montana, lead the opposition. This man who in 1924 was the running mate of La Follette on the Progressive platform, which favored submitting to the people a constitutional amendment providing that Congress might by enacting a statute make it effective over a judicial veto, became the champion of the conservatives. Senators Copeland of New York, Walsh of Massachusetts, and Burke of Nebraska, all Democrats, spoke against the President's proposal under the auspices of the League for the Protection of the Constitution; and Senator Glass of Virginia, a persistent foe of New Deal measures, in another broadcast flayed the bill.

Justices of the Supreme Court themselves entered the political arena, directly and indirectly. Chief Justice Hughes wrote a letter to the Senate Committee on the Judiciary in which he denied that the Supreme Court was behind in its work and argued that an enlarged court would be less efficient; but much more effective were the resignation of Justice Willis Van Devanter, seventy-eight years of age, one of the consistently conservative justices, and an amazing succession of decisions upholding the constitutionality of important New Deal measures in which the court ignominiously reversed itself.

On March 30, 1937, by a five to four decision the Supreme
Court upheld the constitutionality of the Washington State Minimum Wage Law and thereby reversed a previous decision in a case
involving a New York statute. Similarly, it sustained the revised
Frazier-Lemke Act designed to aid farmers whose mortgages had
been foreclosed, and thereby reversed a decision in a previous
act of that name. On May 24, by five to four decisions the unemployment and old age pension provisions of the Social Security
Act were approved.

The most sweeping victory for the New Deal since February,
1935, when the gold invalidation clause was upheld, was a series
of vital decisions on April 12, 1937, when the general constitutionality of the Wagner Labor Relations Act was sustained and
the interpretation of the interstate commerce clause was broadened. Although the court was bitterly divided—in four of the five
test cases Van Devanter, Sutherland, McReynolds, and Butler
dissented—the opinions of the majority left conservatives wonder-
ing if, as a result of the President's attack, the court had not
given him a free hand—if Hughes and Roberts, moderates, were
not aware of the disastrous consequences to the court if the acts
were not sustained. It was also suspected that the seriousness of
the labor situation as revealed in sit-down strikes had registered
itself in the minds of the "open-minded" justices.

It was also a great victory for organized labor in that the Wagner Act assured workers of the right to organize into unions for
the purpose of collective bargaining, free from interference by
employers. The act also forbade the fostering of company unions
and employers' participation in union activities, outlawed "yellow-
dog" contracts, and compelled employers to bargain collectively
with representatives chosen by a majority of their employees.

While the newspapers and prominent members of the American
Bar Association and their allies busied themselves with attacks on
the attempt of the "dictator" in the White House to "pack" the
Supreme Court, the Senate Committee on the Judiciary on May 18,
1937, after conducting hearings, reported adversely on the bill by
a vote of ten to eight, with seven Republicans and three Democrats against seven Democrats and Norris, an Independent.

The debate in the Senate began on July 6, 1937, with Joseph T. Robinson, the leader of the Democratic majority, firing the opening gun, and Burton K. Wheeler the floor leader of the opposition. As reported to the Senate, the compromise bill called for the appointment of an additional justice for every incumbent who continued to serve beyond the age of seventy-five, with such additional appointments limited to one each year. Both leaders expressed confidence in the ultimate success of their cause. Roosevelt himself, misled perhaps by the succession of victories that had crowned his leadership, appeared to have no doubt of the passage of the bill.

However, an unexpected event, which climaxed a series of events that spelled defeat, further disorganized the administration forces. On July 14 Senator Robinson was found dead in the bathroom of his apartment, a victim of the extraordinary demands on his strength made by the court bill and the heat of the summer. This tragic event not only deprived the administration of an able and popular leader but precipitated a contest between Alben W. Barkley of Kentucky and Pat Harrison of Mississippi for the position of majority leader. Barkley, with the support of Roosevelt, defeated his rival by the slim margin of 38 to 37. On the same day (July 24) the bill was recommitted to the Committee on the Judiciary, which ended the battle, although a bill was finally enacted that provided for certain changes in the lower courts in line with the President's proposals.

But the fight was not over. The one objective of President Roosevelt in proposing changes in the personnel of the Supreme Court was to appoint liberals to outvote the uncompromising conservatives. His purpose was to "unpack" the court, whereas his opponents charged that he intended to "pack" it. With the prospect of five new justices, it was expected that Robinson would be one of the appointees; but under the terms of the compromise bill, the President could appoint only one justice to succeed Van Devanter. Robinson was fundamentally conservative; and the President could hardly appoint him, if he wanted a liberal majority.

In this dilemma Roosevelt made an adroit maneuver by appointing, on August 11, 1937, Senator Hugo Black of Alabama, a consistent and aggressive supporter of the New Deal. This appointment disarmed the President's enemies who could be expected to embarrass him by attempting to block the confirmation of a liberal. The Black nomination, however, capitalized "senatorial courtesy" and also made it embarrassing for southern conservatives to oppose the confirmation of a man from their own section. Within a week the nomination was confirmed by a vote of 63 to 16, with a few Democrats voting in the negative.

But Roosevelt's enemies were not to be silenced by "senatorial courtesy." The "economic royalists," whose political influence had been reduced far below that in previous administrations, spared neither President Roosevelt nor Justice Black. A new offensive was launched when newspapers from coast to coast published six syndicated articles revealing that Black had been a member of the Ku Klux Klan in Alabama—a very effective method of discrediting a liberal justice. While Black's confirmation was pending, the Klan issue had been raised; and after the articles appeared, several Senators hastened to say that had they known that he was a Klansman they would not have voted to confirm him. It is inconceivable, however, that the Senators were ignorant of that fact. At the time when Black was initiated into the mysteries of the hooded order, the Klan spirit in the South was so strong that aspirants to political office had no alternative but to join. Moreover, millions in the North were Klansmen in spirit. However, the press throbbed with denunciations of intolerance as exemplified in Justice Black, and with eulogies on the perfection of the other justices of the Court. "Tolerance" implied race and religion, with no economic implications in the word. Economic organization did not deal in public branding, lynching, and the fiery cross; it was much more refined in promoting sweatshop suicide and slow demoralization and death.

When the storm broke, Justice Black was in England and refused to see the swarm of newspaper reporters who besieged him. After his return to the United States, he shattered precedent on October 1, 1937, by making a radio address over a nation-wide hookup, an address that had been awaited with intense interest.

The justice admitted that he had joined the Klan, but had left it before he became a Senator. He referred to the intolerance in the presidential campaign of 1928 and deplored efforts to infuse religious and racial animosity in politics and in the life of the people. He cited his record in the Senate to free him from charges of racial and religious intolerance. The Bill of Rights, he said, was the heart of the Constitution.

The reaction to the address in the press was hostile. The *New York Herald Tribune* headed its editorial "A Humbug and a Coward." The *New York World-Telegram* admitted that the address was clever, "but like too many happenings in the region of the Supreme Court, 'too damned clever.'" And the *New York Times* commented: "The nomination was a tragic blunder: a case of acting without adequate consultation and an example of political adroitness which overreached itself. At every session of the court the presence on the bench of a justice who has worn the white robe of the Ku Klux Klan will stand as a living symbol of the fact that here the cause of liberalism was unwittingly betrayed."

Who won the court battle? If the question refers to the fate of the bill sponsored by the administration, then the President met inglorious defeat. If, however, the larger aspects of the controversy are considered, Roosevelt was correct in referring to it on June 24, 1938, a year later, as a lost battle which won a war. "The attitude of the Supreme Court toward constitutional questions is entirely changed," he said. "Its recent decisions are eloquent testimony of a willingness to collaborate with the two other branches of government to make democracy work."

When the court bill was pending, Roosevelt in a public address cited the gloomy predictions about the future of democracy in America from the pen of the historian Macaulay and compared his lack of faith in democracy with that of the Liberty League, the United States Chamber of Commerce, and the newspapers. And after the attack on Justice Black had been launched, the President spoke of the Constitution as a "layman's document" rather than a "lawyer's contract." He asserted that eminent lawyers at all times had sought to prove that forward-looking laws were unconstitutional. He also alluded to "twenty-year lags" and to the reversal by the Supreme Court of laws that later generations demanded and got.

The attacks on Justice Black were somewhat similar to those directed against Justice Brandeis, with the important exception that many of the latter's opponents were as hostile to Jews as were the knights of the Ku Klux Klan. The minority report of the Senate Committee of which one of the signers was George Sutherland, who was later appointed to the Supreme Court, said of Brandeis that it was a "great misfortune and a distinct lowering of the standards heretofore maintained for making appointments to the Supreme Court."

On the other hand, those who supported Black could, within a few months, congratulate themselves that his opinions sustained their faith that he would bring to the Supreme Court a new economic realism, just as Brandeis heartened liberals by his brilliant dissenting opinions. Both men were appointed by liberal Presidents for their "personal economic predilections." Both men were instrumental in removing inhibitions to the growth of governmental competence to deal with critical problems that faced the nation.

The prestige of the Supreme Court received a heavy blow not only from the attacks that emanated from the White House but likewise from men who posed as its defenders. In their zeal to discredit the President by discrediting Black, they contributed to the sum total of indictments of the Supreme Court. They charged that the President's appointee was guilty of what the court's critics said the conservative justices were guilty of, only in a different way.

The retirement of Justice Sutherland on January 5, 1938, a Harding appointee and one of the four justices who almost invariably opposed the movement for the government control of business, paved the way for the second Roosevelt appointment to the Supreme Court. The choice fell upon Stanley High, the Solicitor-General who had successfully handled New Deal cases before the Supreme Court and had won the respect of the legal profession. The nomination was unanimously confirmed—with the approval of the press.

During the first eighteen months of Roosevelt's second term it appeared that the President had definitely lost ground—not necessarily with the people but with Congress. Although the Democratic majorities in both houses were unprecedentedly heavy, there was a considerable element among them, especially from the South, who were not in sympathy with the social objectives of the New Deal and would have followed more willingly a President who used the language of Calvin Coolidge.

In the turmoil of the first session of the Congress which adjourned on August 21, 1937, Roosevelt's major bills were either killed or emasculated by rebelling conservatives, who took advantage of parliamentary rules to delay or prevent votes while awaiting favorable events, such as the retirement of Justice Van Devanter and decisions of the Supreme Court. The President lashed out at this minority in a speech at the Virginia Dare celebration on Roanoke Island on August 18, 1937, when he referred to Tories who prevented majorities from expressing their will.

The President's troubles were further complicated by the business recession which came in the fall of 1937. Big Business seized the opportunity to discredit New Deal legislation by charging that it was hamstringing business. For a time it appeared that Roosevelt was cultivating the good will of the men whom he had designated as "economic royalists"; but he was stung to fury when he became convinced that they would be satisfied with nothing less than complete surrender.

At the close of the year the administration struck back. William O. Douglas, chairman of the Security and Exchange Commission, in a speech on November 24, 1937, "cracked down" on Wall Street and notified those concerned that the New York Stock Exchange must reorganize or else be more drastically regulated. Douglas said that the recent stock market slumps "serve only to fortify further the conclusion . . . that members of the exchange trading for their own account either create daily price fluctuations or else contribute materially to their severity." Following a sensational scandal which sent the chairman of the board to the penitentiary, the New York Stock Exchange in the summer of 1938 made a bid for favor by electing a successor whose record was clear.

The Douglas speech was followed within a few weeks by two bold attacks on Big Business by Robert Jackson, the Assistant Attorney-General, and by a withering blast from Secretary of the Interior Ickes. The Secretary placed the blame for the recession squarely on the "economic royalists." He avowed that Big Business had gone on a sit-down strike, and he singled out certain men who had openly or secretly defied labor laws and had hired lawyers to keep the government in trouble but who were not wise enough to get business out of trouble. "Big Business should wash in strong disinfectants so that it can come into the court of public opinion with clean hands," he said.

Following the reverberations of these thunderbolts, the mild language of Roosevelt's message to Congress on January 3, 1938, was rather surprising, although the document had the flavor of certain speeches that emanated from Theodore Roosevelt and Woodrow Wilson. It brought assurance that the government was not falling into the control of the interests that sat in the saddle during the years of Harding, Coolidge, and Hoover.

This assurance was confirmed by Roosevelt's Jackson Day speech of January 8, when he served notice that there would be no compromise with economic autocrats and that he was working "to restore and to uphold the integrity of the morals of democracy— our heritage from the long line of national leadership—from Jefferson to Wilson—and preeminently from Andrew Jackson." In the heat of the battle with what he called the "small minority which claimed vested rights to power," the President became an ardent admirer of Andrew Jackson. Perhaps it was the depression of 1937-38 that reminded Roosevelt of the business stringency that followed Jackson's war on the Bank of the United States and which the admirers of "Old Hickory" laid at the door of Nicholas Biddle, the president of the bank, who used this method of intimidating the frontier President. With the bank, said Roosevelt, were "aligned all of the nationally owned press of the day, with the exception of three newspapers. The bank sought to array all the money in the country against him." He praised Jackson for refusing to compromise with the forces of evil, whether in Congress or in the cabinet or in the country as a whole. The compromisers of his own day Roosevelt later compared with the Copperheads who in Lincoln's day wanted peace at any price. "Never before have we had so many Copperheads," he said.

The Seventy-fifth Congress revealed a decided cleavage in the Democratic party, with southern members resting uncomfortably under the leadership of a militant champion of measures that would satisfy the clamor of labor in the industrial centers of the North. Moreover, on April 15, 1937, the House of Representatives by a vote of 216 to 119 passed an anti-lynching bill, after southern Democrats had strained every effort to defeat it. In the special session which convened on November 15, 1937, and in the regular session which began on January 3, 1938, the Senate for a time was tied up by the anti-lynching filibuster, while the proponents of legislation to alleviate the serious business recession were growing restless, and conferences between Roosevelt and business leaders were in progress. Possibly the administration forces were merely making a stage play for Negro votes and the favor of the National Association for the Advancement of Colored People. In any event, once more the South, aided by a number of Republicans, defeated what was branded as an effort to deal with a local problem in a way that violated the Fourteenth Amendment.

Smarting under southern opposition to his policies, in a speech at Gainesville, Georgia, Roosevelt breathed defiance in hostile territory by asserting that wages in the South were too low. It was southern opposition to the wages and hours bill, which was obnoxious to employers of labor in southern factories, that prompted the President's statement.

A major defeat comparable to that on the court bill was suffered by the administration on the Government Reorganization Bill, which clothed the President with power to revamp the executive branch of the government. The bill passed the Senate by a vote of 49 to 42; but before it reached a vote in the House, the methods employed to defeat the court bill were resorted to. Again the hue and cry was raised that Roosevelt was seeking to make himself a dictator. Father Coughlin was especially active in broadcasting this charge over nation-wide hookups. Representative John O'Connor of New York, who was aided by Republicans and a few Farmer-Laborites, led the revolt of the Democrats. Smoke screens raised by various minority groups obscured the merits of the bill and defeated another effort of Presidents since the days of Taft to provide more businesslike machinery for running the executive department of the government. Back of the defeat were the greed of Congressmen for patronage and the fear of governmental interference on the part of several interests.

The business recession which deepened as the session dragged on brought additional demands on the treasury and shattered vague promises and faint hopes that the budget would be balanced. According to the preliminary report of the unemployment census undertaken at the suggestion of Roosevelt, the total number of unemployed as of November 20, 1937, was estimated between 7,822,912 and 10,870,000, and the number increased during the following months. On April 14, 1938, the President recommended huge appropriations for relief, public works, and credits to business. He stated that he had waited to see whether the forces of business itself would counteract the depression; but he had come to the conclusion that the government could no longer safely delay taking aggressive steps to meet the situation.

This "pump-priming" involved a turnover of more than $6,500,-000,000 for relief and public works, lendable funds for banks, and reducing bank reserve requirements. This legislation, together with an enactment that increased the loan powers of the Reconstruction Finance Corporation, passed Congress by huge majorities. The RFC was authorized to grant long-term loans which banks could not take, and to make loans to states and municipalities.

Simultaneously the President called for legislation to place limits on wages and hours and demanded action against "business monopoly," lest a "concentration of private power without equal in history" grow greater than the government itself and engulf the nation in Fascism—a statement similar to that of Woodrow Wilson in referring to the power of the "Money Trust," whose machinations were revealed by the Pujo investigation in 1912. Roosevelt persuaded Congress to authorize an inquiry to be conducted by the Federal Trade Commission, the Securities and Exchange Commission, the Department of Justice, and other agencies, into "collectivism in business." The investigation was to include such subjects as improved procedure in enforcing anti-trust statutes, mergers and interlocking directorates, financial controls, activities of trade associations, patent laws, and tax laws. "That heavy hand of integrated financial management and control lies upon large and strategic areas of American industry. The small business man is unfortunately being driven into a less and less independent position in American life. That you and I must admit," said the President.

The Seventy-fifth Congress also amended the Federal Housing Act by making it easier for private capital to build modest homes and low-rental dwellings; and it also set up the United States Housing Administration to help finance large-scale slum clearance and to provide low-rental housing in cities.

The invalidation of the AAA by the Supreme Court was a blow to planned economy for the farm; and the Soil Conservation Act was a hasty effort to meet the emergency. In February, 1938, however, the President approved a bill establishing a system under which the Secretary of Agriculture, in cooperation with farmer committees, could prescribe limitations upon the quantity of wheat, corn, cotton, rice, and tobacco that could be grown or marketed.

In general, the law directed the Secretary of Agriculture to make an estimate of the expected supply and to set this figure against expected demand in order that production might be adjusted accordingly. Benefits would be paid to farmers who planted no more than a specified acreage. In years of bumper crops the Secretary of Agriculture would be empowered to fix marketing quotas, limiting the quantities that could be sold. In the words of the President, the law was designed to give the farmer a fairer share of the national income, to preserve the soil, to provide an all-weather granary, to help the tenant farmer toward independence, to find new uses for farm products, and to begin crop insurance.

No administration in history made such bold and consistent appeals for the support of labor as did the Roosevelt administration; and in 1936 they were rewarded with enthusiastic indorsement from labor leaders. Not only was legislation enacted to relieve labor from legal and other restrictions on collective bargaining and on the conduct of strikes, but free rein was given to the investigations conducted by the Committee on Education and Labor, of which Senator La Follette was chairman. In a preliminary report submitted by this committee in February, 1938, it was revealed that detectives had been employed as spies on labor and as strike breakers and that laborers had been bribed and employed as stool pigeons. It was also revealed that detective agencies had destroyed documents in order to prevent the committee from obtaining evidence against them. During the strikes of 1937-38 the committee was active in collecting data and information about the tactics and strategy of the opposing forces.

The knowledge that the administration was in sympathy with the aspirations of labor, and the memory of the ruthless suppression of strikes during the post-war years, brought to the fore militant leaders who challenged the powerful steel and automotive industries and resorted to sit-down strikes to make the challenge even more formidable. At the opening of the year 1937, in addition to the strikes in these key industries, the costliest maritime strike in American history tied up shipping on the Pacific coast.

The situation was complicated by a serious split in the ranks of organized labor. When in 1924 the death of Samuel Gompers brought to the presidency of the American Federation of Labor William Green, the conservative and traditional policies of that organization were continued. Eleven years later, however, John L. Lewis, the president of the powerful United Mine Workers, challenged craft unionism by attempting to organize the basic industries into industrial unions, thus reverting to the principle on which the Knights of Labor had been organized. The bluff, dynamic Lewis formed the Committee for Industrial Organization and defied the American Federation of Labor, which under Green's direction suspended Lewis and the C.I.O.

Within two years the C.I.O. passed the older organization in membership, partly because the aggressive leadership of Lewis overshadowed the conservative and complacent policies of the A. F. of L., which had brought shorter working hours, better wages, and improved working conditions for a relatively small group of skilled laborers. Lewis brought into the fold the unskilled and the semi-skilled. In a radio report on the progress of the C.I.O. in September, 1937, Lewis claimed an enrollment of almost three and three-quarter millions. Although Lewis was branded by his opponents as a radical and a Communist, he accepted the capitalistic system. He was primarily interested in effecting an organization that would protect the workingman who was a part of that system. Lewis speedily tested the stamina of the C.I.O. by invading the hostile territory of automobile factories and steel mills.

The NRA, after having been hailed as a means of pulling the country out of the depression, fell victim to a hostile and indifferent public and finally to a decision of the Supreme Court on May 27, 1935. Employers had scented danger in the labor provisions of the NRA which strengthened organized labor by sanctioning collective bargaining free from interference, restraint, or coercion by employers. The year 1934 produced an epidemic of strikes, in spite of a number of successful efforts to adjust differences by the National Labor Board and the National Labor Relations Board, both of which were established in the summer of that year.

A few weeks after the invalidation of the NRA, labor gained a great victory on July 5, 1935, by the enactment of the Wagner Labor Relations Act, which successfully passed the scrutiny of the Supreme Court after Roosevelt had launched his attack on that body. As has been stated, this act, in addition to providing agencies to effect peaceful settlements of labor disputes, compelled employers to bargain collectively with representatives chosen by a majority of employees, outlawed "yellow-dog" contracts, and forbade the fostering of company unions and the participation of employers in union activities. The Supreme Court handed down its epochal decisions on the Wagner Labor Relations Act in April, 1937, when sit-down strikes in the General Motors and Chrysler motor plants and other industrial centers were attracting the attention of the country.

Governor Murphy of Michigan attempted to mediate and succeeded in postponing the execution of a court order to evict sit-down strikers in a plant at Flint. After weeks of negotiations and acts of defiance on both sides, the controversy in the automotive industry was settled by compromise; but the fact that the powerful General Motors Corporation negotiated at all was a victory for the C.I.O. and inspired Lewis to further conquests.

On the other hand, Lewis found an implacable foe in Henry Ford who, in the words of the *New York Times*, ruled a "world of machinery and men such as no civilization other than ours has ever seen before." This resourceful leader, who could be equally critical of stock jobbers and financiers, set his face firmly against collective bargaining. He clung to the belief that workingmen fared better at the hands of fair-minded industrialists than under the leadership of labor agitators. He took pride in the fact that the minimum wage in his colossal plants on the River Rouge and in other cities was equal to or higher than that exacted from his competitors by the United Automobile Workers of America after costly strikes.

The warfare in the steel districts of Pennsylvania, Ohio, Illinois, and Michigan in the spring and early summer of 1937 brought bloody encounters between deputies and pickets and clashes between strikers and vigilantes. In Pennsylvania the governor declared martial law and closed a steel mill while the C.I.O. was threatening to march on a city. The mediation board publicly censured the steel companies for refusing to confer with strike leaders.

The upshot of the long and costly battles on the labor front was the negotiation of contracts between the C.I.O. and the United States Steel Corporation; but "Little Steel"—that is, the independent companies—refused to yield.

In the face of hostile criticism from his consistent adversaries, Roosevelt maintained a neutral position. He breathed a "plague on both your houses," appointed a mediation board, and recommended a law fixing wages and hours, which was not enacted until a year later.

The victories for labor in many industries in many parts of the country may be attributed to enlarged powers granted to unions by federal and state legislation, to more sympathetic attitudes on the part of federal, state, and municipal governments, to court decisions that made it impossible for employers to defy laws, and to highly developed techniques and strategy in conducting strikes.

Greater financial resources enabled strike leaders to counteract hostile propaganda by publishing daily bulletins of their own. Moreover, the strike mechanism functioned with military precision. From strike headquarters, where hundreds and perhaps thousands of men ate and slept, picket squads were dispatched which kept in touch with captains through telephone service. In some instances strike headquarters were equipped with hospital service to care for the sick and for comrades wounded in battles with police or with deputies hired by employers. During the vigil strikers and pickets and their wives and children were entertained by speakers and musicians. Mechanics stood ready to repair automobiles and motorcycles belonging to individuals and unions to be used in transporting pickets to spots where conditions were menacing.

These strikes were visible evidences of the dilemma of the machine age. The modern factory, with its mass production, speed and efficiency, demands stamina, skill, and alertness, takes the joy out of many jobs, and makes dubious the outlook for the future of the man of middle age. WPA records reveal the discrimination against the man whose step is not so elastic, whose hands are not so deft, and whose temples are tinged with gray. Moreover, in many factories and mills, in spite of the noise and hum of looms, forging presses, millstones, riveting machines, and the like, the small number of men and women employed is noticeable. Automatic machinery does the work of men. Steam shovels, cranes, and concrete mixers have reduced the number of unskilled laborers in employment where these machines are used. Monstrous high-powered locomotives haul long freight trains that eliminate enginemen, brakemen, and conductors who would be required to operate a larger number of trains were it not for the ingenuity of mechanical engineers and the uses of natural forces that were unsuspected a generation ago.

Naturally the Wagner Labor Relations Act was not entirely satisfactory either to labor or to industry. For one thing, it contained no provision that made it possible to compel labor to comply with the decisions of the National Labor Relations Board; and after strikes had apparently been settled, so-called "outlaw" strikes broke out anew. It was inevitable that both parties to a controversy should accuse the Board of partiality. For example, on May 4, 1938, the United States Chamber of Commerce, which was intensely hostile to the C.I.O. and was opposed to government encroachment on business, adopted a resolution urging repeal of the Wagner Labor Relations Act. About ten days later the United States Circuit Court of Appeals at Covington, Kentucky, held that the employer cannot be accused of "discrimination when his repeated and sincere attempts have failed to produce agreement on a labor policy." The court held that the findings of the NLRB against the Sands Manufacturing Company were not substantiated by the facts. "The statute . . . merely requires the employer to negotiate sincerely," said the court. On the other hand, in the case of the Republic Steel Company the Supreme Court leaned heavily in the direction of labor.

The Roosevelt administration won a telling victory over southern opposition on May 24, 1938, when the House of Representatives by a vote of 314 to 97 passed the Wages and Hours Bill. Southern Democrats fought to force the adoption of amendments giving the South a lower wage minimum than the North. Northern and eastern Republicans and conservative northern Democrats lined up with liberal Democrats in favor of the bill because they believed that the manufacturers in their sections would fare better if their southern competitors were forced to pay the same minimum wage.

As approved by the President, the Wages and Hours Act represented a compromise between the North and the South, but it also represented a broad extension of federal control of industry. There was no recognition of regional differentials in wages and hours, which the South wanted; but the South got a concession in the form of a provision that allowed the various committees to fix wage scales with due regard for "competitive conditions as affected by transportation, living, and production costs."

The committees were to be appointed by the administrator, who in turn was under the Secretary of Labor. The administrator was directed to set up "industry committees" for each industry. Each committee was to consist of three groups—"distinguished persons representing the public; a like number of persons representing employees; and a like number of persons representing employers." In a sense, the act was designed to accomplish some of the fundamentals of the NRA; in effect, it gave the country a federal child labor law. The enforcement of the law is attained through prohibition against shipment of articles in interstate commerce if made in violation of the standards fixed in the act.

The minimum wage starts at twenty-five cents an hour for the first year and increases five cents an hour each year until it reaches forty cents. The maximum weekly hours drop from forty-four the first year to forty after the second. The fishing industry, newspapers of less than three thousand circulation, child moving picture actors, and canneries under certain conditions are exempted from the application of the law.

President Roosevelt pronounced the Wages and Hours Act the "most far-sighted program for the benefit of workers ever adopted," except perhaps for the Social Security Act. "Do not let any calamity-howling executive with an income of $1,000 a day, who has been turning his employees over to the government relief rolls in order to preserve his company's undistributed reserves, tell you—using his stockholders' money to pay the postage for his personal opinions—that a wage of $11 a week is going to have a disastrous effect on all American industry," said the President.

In reviewing the record of the Congress which adjourned on June 16, 1938, Roosevelt expressed the opinion that it "achieved more for the future good of the country than any Congress between the end of the World War and the spring of 1933."

Although this Congress dealt major defeats to the President when it rejected the bills proposing to reform the Supreme Court and to reorganize the executive branch of the government, the resourceful leader was prepared to appeal to the country for the election of "liberals" in the primaries. In order to prevent the return to the kind of government "we had in twenties," the President took the stump to urge the election of Democrats who were committed to his liberal program against those who misused his own name. "We are opposed," he said, "to the kind of moratorium on reform which, in effect, is reaction itself."

In spite of intense opposition—and hatred that exceeded that directed against Theodore Roosevelt and Woodrow Wilson—in spite of serious mistakes committed by the government and by labor, which had perhaps benefited most by New Deal legislation, in spite of self-seeking men and women who traded in the political market and capitalized Roosevelt's name, the President maintained his poise and good nature and at every critical situation brought into play his understanding of the popular mind, his superb self-confidence, and his uncanny political intuition. He could be depended on to give the liberals in his own party a slogan or a phrase that confounded adversaries—as, for example, "economic royalists" and "Copperheads" who cried out for compromise and "breathing spells."

Perhaps hated more violently in conservative circles than any American liberal since Governor John P. Altgeld, the fearless opponent of extreme property rights in the last decade of the nineteenth century, Roosevelt won and retained the admiration of an overwhelming majority of his countrymen. Attempts to magnify opposition to certain items in the New Deal program into mistrust of the President invariably failed. He dominated politics more completely than any President before him. His "Fireside Chats to the Nation" were so personal and pleasing that millions retired with thankful hearts that their happiness and well-being were in the care of "Our President."

BIBLIOGRAPHY

FOR THE STUDY OF THE HISTORY OF THE UNITED STATES SINCE 1865 the student must rely on a mass of monographic and biographic material, much of which is not definitive. This is especially true of material pertaining to the later years of the period. The following bibliography is selective. It is intended to suggest some of the more important books, selected on the dual basis of quality and accessibility, with the interests of the undergraduate student and the general reader in mind. Authors and titles are grouped under the titles of the respective chapters, but for convenience works of a more general nature and usually covering a longer period of time are listed as follows:

The *Dictionary of American Biography* (20 volumes and an index volume) contains excellent brief biographical sketches of men and women of achievement in various fields of endeavor. A brief bibliographical note is appended to each article. Valuable works of reference are the *Cyclopedia of American Government* (3 volumes) and *Encyclopedia of the Social Sciences* (15 volumes), also with bibliographical notes appended to each article.

The American Nation: a History, edited by Albert Bushnell Hart (27 volumes and an index volume), is a cooperative work. Each volume is a mine of facts, with a critical essay on authorities. The following volumes fit into a chronological sequence for the years from 1865 to 1917: William A. Dunning, *Reconstruction, Political and Economic, 1865-1877*; Edwin E. Sparks, *National Development, 1877-1885*; Davis R. Dewey, *National Problems, 1885-1897*; John H. Latané, *America as a World Power, 1897-1907*; Frederick A. Ogg, *National Progress, 1907-1917.*

The fifty volumes of the *Chronicles of America*, edited by Allen Johnson, which cover the period from 1492 to 1920, were not designed to meet the requirements of a chronological scheme. Such topics as "Our Foreigners" (S. P. Orth), "The Railroad Builders" (John Moody), "The Agrarian Crusade" (S. J. Buck), and the like are titles of separate volumes.

Ellis P. Oberholtzer, *A History of the United States Since the Civil War* (5 volumes), brings the story down to 1901. Oberholtzer wrote history after the fashion of the nineteenth century.

The Pageant of America, edited by Ralph H. Gabriel (15 volumes), is a pictorial history of the United States. Each volume contains about six hundred pictures and a text of some sixty thousand words. Four volumes deal with material progress, exploration, the frontier, and industry; six volumes are given to social history, including religion, education, literature, the fine arts, the stage, and sports; two volumes are on political history, and a like number on the army and the navy.

James Ford Rhodes, *A History of the United States from the Compromise of 1850 to the Final Restoration of Home Rule at the South in 1877* (7 volumes), *History of the United States from Hayes to McKinley, 1877-1896,* and *The McKinley and Roosevelt Administrations, 1897-1909.* The last two volumes from the pen of Rhodes are greatly inferior to the larger and earlier work. The seven-volume work maintains its place among the "classics" because of the personal touch of the author, its style, its absorbing interest, and its colorful presentation of personalities and events that played in an era big with fate. It relates the story of the emancipation of the slave and the efforts to give the freedman rights equal to those of the white man. Politics all but crowds out the social, economic, and religious aspects of the period.

Woodrow Wilson, *History of the American People* (5 volumes), brings the story down to 1900. Wilson's graceful pen was more at home in characterizing political leaders than in analyzing the forces of which they were instruments. The future President was the first southern scholar of adequate training and power to deal with American history as a whole and in a continental spirit.

A History of American Life, edited by Dixon R. Fox and Arthur M. Schlesinger, in twelve volumes, presents cross-section pictures of American life at different periods. The volumes dealing with the period after 1865 are: Allan Nevins, *The Emergence of Modern America, 1865-1878;* Ida M. Tarbell, *The Nationalizing of Business, 1878-1898;* Arthur M. Schlesinger, *The Rise of the City, 1878-1898;* Harold U. Faulkner, *The Quest for Social Justice, 1898-1914;* Preston W. Slosson, *The Great Crusade and After, 1914-1928.*

Recent Social Trends in the United States. Report of the President's Research Committee on Social Trends (2 volumes, 1933). The scope and quality of this work justify its inclusion in this list.

Documentary Source Book of American History, edited with notes by William MacDonald, is a useful compilation of laws and state papers. *Documents of American History,* edited by Henry S. Commager, is more inclusive and broader in scope. Felix Flügel and Harold U. Faulkner, *Readings in the Economic and Social History of the United States,* presents a judicious selection. The texts of national party platforms since 1840 are printed in *National Party Platforms,* compiled by Kirk H. Porter.

Charles O. Paullin, *Atlas of the Historical Geography of the United States* (1932), Albert B. Hart, *American History Atlas* (3rd edition revised, 1930), and Dixon Ryan Fox, *Harper's Atlas of American History* (1920), should be in every college and university library.

SELECTED READINGS FOR EACH CHAPTER

I. A PRESIDENT WITHOUT A PARTY

GENERAL HISTORY.

J. F. Rhodes, *History of the United States,* Vols. V-VII, presents an unfavorable interpretation of Johnson, but achieves objectivity in dealing with the period of reconstruction. James Schouler, *History of the United States Under the Constitution,* Vol. VII, is pro-Johnson. W. A. Dunning, *Reconstruction, Political and Economic,* is a concise model of factual selection and judicious interpretation. E. P. Oberholtzer, *History of the United States,* Vol. I and following, and J. G. Randall, *The Civil War and Reconstruction,* reflect the results of recent scholarship.

MONOGRAPHS AND BIOGRAPHIES.

Claude G. Bowers, *The Tragic Era,* portrays Johnson against a lurid background. Howard K. Beale, *The Critical Year: A Study of Andrew Johnson and Reconstruction,* relates the events of the eighteen months between the death of Lincoln and the congressional elections of 1866. George F. Milton, *The Age of Hate: Andrew Johnson and the Radicals,* represents the revisionist point of view. Walter L. Fleming, *The Sequel of Appomattox,* is the work of an able southern scholar. Lloyd P. Stryker, *Andrew Johnson: A Study in Courage,* and Robert W. Winston, *Andrew Johnson: Plebeian and Patriot,* are recent biographies. David M. De Witt, *The Impeach-*

ment and Trial of Andrew Johnson, is a vindication of the President. Horace White, *The Life of Lyman Trumbull*; J. A. Woodburn, *The Life of Thaddeus Stevens*; and G. H. Haynes, *Charles Sumner,* are studies of congressional leaders. For the legal aspects of reconstruction, see Charles Warren, *The Supreme Court in American History,* Vol. III; Ambrose Doskow, *Historic Opinions of the United States Supreme Court*; and H. S. Commager, *Documents of American History.*

II. RADICAL RECONSTRUCTION AND ITS UNDOING
The Practical Working of Reconstruction.

Rhodes, Dunning, Oberholtzer, and Randall, previously cited. J. R. Lynch, *Some Historical Errors of James Ford Rhodes,* is an attempt by a colored man to refute facts and interpretations in the larger work. William B. Hesseltine, *A History of the South, 1607-1936,* and Emory Q. Hawk, *Economic History of the South,* contain chapters on conditions in the South. Robert S. Henry, *The Story of Reconstruction,* relates the story of the rebuilding of the industry and society of the South. Paul H. Buck, *The Road to Reunion, 1865-1900,* is a scholarly development of the central theme: national integration. Walter P. Webb, *Divided We Stand: the Crisis of Frontierless Democracy,* is a controversial book about the encroachment of the North on the South since the Civil War. W. E. Burghardt Du Bois, *Black Reconstruction. An Essay toward a History of the Part which Black Folk Played in the Attempt to Reconstruct Democracy in America, 1860-1880,* is written by a chauvinistic champion of the Negro race, who purports to show "how the facts of American history have in the last half century been falsified because the nation was ashamed." Paul Lewinson, *Race, Class, and Party: a History of Negro Suffrage and White Politics in the South,* and Horace M. Bond, *The Education of the Negro in the American Social Order,* are useful recent studies. Among the numerous special studies of states the following may be cited: Francis B. Simkins, *South Carolina During Reconstruction*; James W. Garner, *Reconstruction in Mississippi*; James W. Patton, *Unionism and Reconstruction in Tennessee, 1860-1869*; W. L. Fleming, *Reconstruction in Alabama*; C. Mildred Thompson, *Reconstruction in Georgia.* H. J. Pearce, *Benjamin H. Hill: Secession and Reconstruction*; Wirt A. Cate, *Lucius Q. C. Lamar: Secession and Reunion*; and E. Merton Coulter, *William G. Brownlow, Fighting Parson of the Southern Highlands,* are studies of prominent southern leaders. On the election of 1868, see Charles H. Coleman, *The Election of 1868: the Democratic Effort to Regain Control*; W. B. Hesseltine, *Ulysses S. Grant: Politician*; Stewart Mitchell, *Horatio Seymour of New York*. The Supreme Court and reconstruction: Warren, *The Supreme Court in American History,* Vol. III; Doskow, *Historic Opinions of the United States Supreme Court*; Commager, *Documents of American History*; Allen Johnson, *Cases in Constitutional Law*; A. C. McLaughlin, *Constitutional History of the United States*; J. M. Matthews, *Legislative and Judicial History of the Fifteenth Amendment*. Gilbert T. Stephenson, *Race Distinctions in American Law,* is a scholarly dissertation.

III. WAVING THE BLOODY SHIRT
The Liberal Republican Movement.

E. D. Ross, *The Liberal Republican Movement,* is an excellent account. In addition to the general works by Rhodes, Oberholtzer, and Dunning, considerable material is found in Hesseltine, *U. S. Grant*; Don C. Seitz, *Horace Greeley*; Claude M. Fuess, *Carl Schurz*; Henry Watterson, *Marse Henry*; Royal Cortissoz, *Whitelaw Reid* (2 vols.). Allan Nevins, *Hamilton Fish and the Grant Administration,* supersedes all other books on the eight years of Grantism. The bulky Vol. II of James G. Blaine, *Twenty Years of Congress: From Lincoln to Garfield,* is an interesting narrative by a Republican leader.

The Election of 1876.

Paul L. Haworth, *The Disputed Election of 1876,* is the standard work. The opposing candidates have satisfactory biographies in C. R. Williams, *The Life of Rutherford Birchard Hayes* (2 vols.); H. J. Eckenrode, *Rutherford B. Hayes: Statesman of Reunion*; and John Bigelow, *Life of Samuel J. Tilden* (2 vols.). Carl Schurz, *Speeches, Correspondence, and Political Papers* (6 vols.), illuminates many aspects of political history from 1865 to 1904.

IV. POST-BELLUM DIPLOMACY AND FINANCE
Diplomacy.

The best one-volume work is Samuel Flagg Bemis, *A Diplomatic History of the United States*. There is no bibliography, but there are judicious citations to authorities. Other satisfactory books are R. G. Adams, *History of the Foreign Policy of the United States*; C. R.

Fish, *American Diplomacy*; Louis M. Sears, *History of American Foreign Relations*; John H. Latané, *History of American Foreign Policy*; J. F. Rhodes, *History of the United States,* Vol. VI; C. F. Adams, *The Life of Charles Francis Adams.* The best treatment of the diplomacy of the Grant administration is found in Allan Nevins, *Hamilton Fish and the Grant Administration.* For the Alaska Purchase, see Frederic Bancroft, *Life of William H. Seward* (2 vols.) ; Victor Farrar, *The Annexation of Russian America*; Jeannette P. Nichols, *Alaska.* The Mexican episode is discussed in Dexter Perkins, *The Monroe Doctrine, 1867-1907.* The author is the leading authority on the Monroe Doctrine. See also James M. Callahan, *American Foreign Policy in Mexican Relations.*

FINANCE.

A standard work is Davis R. Dewey, *Financial History of the United States.* The following texts on the economic history of the United States are valuable: Harold U. Faulkner, *American Economic History*; E. L. Bogart, *An Economic History of the United States*; Fred A. Shannon, *Economic History of the People of the United States*; W. W. Jennings, *History of Economic Progress in the United States.* Especially pointed to the subjects treated in this chapter are Don C. Barrett, *The Greenbacks and the Resumption of Specie Payments, 1862-78*; Alexander D. Noyes, *Forty Years of American Finance*; Wesley C. Mitchell, *History of the Greenbacks*; Murray S. Wildman, *Money Inflation in the United States*; Albert B. Hepburn, *History of Coinage and Currency in the United States*; J. Laurence Laughlin, *History of Bimetallism in the United States*; Theodore E. Burton, *John Sherman*; Henrietta M. Larson, *Jay Cooke: Private Banker*; Ellis P. Oberholtzer, *Jay Cooke: Financier of the Civil War* (2 vols.).

V. THE POST-WAR GENERATION

The volumes in *A History of American Life* are the most satisfactory for the portrayal of the life of the people: Allan Nevins, *The Emergence of Modern America*; Arthur M. Schlesinger, *The Rise of the City*; Ida M. Tarbell, *The Nationalizing of Business.* Each volume contains a bibliography for the reader who desires to pursue further investigation. The fifteen volumes of *The Pageant of America*, edited by Ralph H. Gabriel, are colorful. A recent study is Henry C. Hubbart, *The Older Middle West, 1840-80:Its Social,*

Economic, and Political Life and Sectional Tendencies Before, During, and After the Civil War. Edwin V. Mitchell, *American Village,* is an attempt to describe the nineteenth-century village. A stimulating, comprehensive, and scholarly volume that contains considerable social history is H. L. Mencken, *The American Language. An Inquiry into the Development of English in the United States* (4th edition, 1936). In the absence of a satisfactory history of agriculture, the reader may consult the *Encyclopedia of the Social Sciences,* the economic histories (cited under the previous chapter), *The Pageant of America* (Vol. III), Louis B. Schmidt and Earle D. Ross, *Readings in the Economic History of American History of American Agriculture,* and William T. Hutchinson, *Cyrus Hall Mc-Cormick* (2 vols.). In Wayne C. Neely, *The Agricultural Fair,* the approach is that of the sociologist and social historian. Harry C. Minnich, *William Holmes McGuffey and His Readers,* sets forth the work and influence of a unique figure in American education.

There is a vast literature on immigration, but only a few volumes measure up to the standard of historical scholarship. The volumes listed here are intended to be suggestive. Maurice R. Davie, *World Immigration with Special Reference to the United States,* and George M. Stephenson, *A History of American Immigration, 1820-1924,* have classified bibliographies. The latter book makes the historical approach and deals especially with the political and legislative aspects, with a brief section on the European background. The following general works are among the best: Richmond Mayo Smith, *Emigration and Immigration*; J. W. Jenks and W. J. Lauck, *The Immigration Problem*; H. P. Fairchild, *Immigration*; Edith Abbott, *Historical Aspects of the Immigration Problem.* For brief explanatory statements and valuable statistics, with graphs and charts, see Imre Ferenczi, *International Migrations,* Vol. I (National Bureau of Economic Research, 1929). Vol. II (1931) of this work presents "interpretations." A. M. Carr-Saunders, *World Population. Past Growth and Present Trends,* has statistics, tables, graphs, and interpretations. The following studies pertaining to the old immigration are recommended: Albert B. Faust, *The German Element in the United States, with Special Reference to Its Political, Moral, Social, and Educational Influence* (2 vols.); Stanley C. Johnson, *A History of Emigration from the United Kingdom to North America, 1763-1912.* William A. Carothers, *Emigration from the British Isles,* is valuable for the background. Theodore C. Blegen, *Norwegian Migration to*

America, 1825-1860, is the best study of the Norwegians. It stops at 1860, but it is indispensable for the background of the entire period. Carlton C. Qualey, *Norwegian Settlement in the United States,* is a factual survey. T. C. Blegen and Martin B. Ruud, *Norwegian Emigrant Songs and Ballads,* is appetizing. George M. Stephenson, *The Religious Aspects of Swedish Immigration,* is a study of social and religious life in the United States and of its heritage from Sweden, John S. Lindberg, *The Background of Swedish Emigration to the United States,* is based on official documents. Jacob Van Der Zee, *The Hollanders of Iowa,* gives a good background. Edward F. Roberts, *Ireland in America,* sets forth the political and social influence of the Irish. William F. Adams, *Ireland and Irish Immigration to the New World from 1815 to the Famine,* is scholarly but is confined to the early years.

VI. INDIANS, COWBOYS, AND RAILROADS

GENERAL.

Frederick Jackson Turner, *The Frontier in American History,* consists of a series of essays written by the pioneer and foremost interpreter of the influence of the frontier and of the "West" on American history. Walter P. Webb, *The Great Plains,* is a brilliant contribution to institutional history. Two books by Frederic L. Paxson, *History of the American Frontier, 1763-1893,* and *The Last American Frontier,* bristle with facts. Books similar in content are Robert E. Riegel, *America Moves West,* and Dan E. Clark, *The West in American History.* Everett Dick, *The Sod-House Frontier, 1854-1890,* is a sprightly narrative of railroads, wild-cat banks, mortgages, and domestic life. A gripping portrayal of pioneer life in Nebraska is Mari Sandoz, *Old Jules* (1935).

INDIANS.

Francis E. Leupp, *The Indian and His Problem,* and G. B. Grinnell, *The Story of the Indian,* are useful but not entirely satisfactory. Stanley Vestal, *Sitting Bull,* is by a professor of literature who has lived and talked with Indians. Martin S. Garretson, *The American Bison,* is a recent work on a colorful chapter in western history.

THE CATTLE COUNTRY.

Ernest S. Osgood, *The Day of the Cattleman,* is from the pen of a man who knows the spirit of the West. Edward E. Dale, *The Cattle*

Range Industry, is also the work of a specialist who has lived in the Southwest. Louis Pelzer, *The Cattlemen's Frontier: A Record of the Trans-Mississippi Cattle Industry from Oxen Trains to Pooling Companies, 1850-1890;* Andy Adams, *The Log of a Cowboy,* and John A. Lomax, *Cowboy Songs,* afford entertaining reading.

RAILROADS.

John Moody, *The Railroad Builders,* and Robert E. Riegel, *The Story of Western Railroads,* are brief and good. Lewis H. Haney, *A Congressional History of Railways in the United States, 1850-1877,* is a legislative history concerned mainly with land grants. On the Pacific railways see E. L. Sabin, *Building the Pacific Railway,* and J. B. Crawford, *The Crédit Mobilier of America.* Paul W. Gates, *The Illinois Central Railroad and Its Colonization Work,* is a model for similar studies of other railroads. Biographies of railroad promoters are James G. Pyle, *James J. Hill* (2 vols.) ; James B. Hedges, *Henry Villard and the Railways of the Northwest;* E. P. Oberholtzer, *Jay Cooke: Financier of the Civil War* (2 vols.) ; Henrietta Larson, *Jay Cooke: Private Banker.* Oscar Lewis, *The Big Four,* is a colorful account of Huntington, Stanford, Hopkins, and Crocker and the building of the Central Pacific and the Southern Pacific. The author presents the "big four" as typical of their time.

RIVER TRANSPORTATION.

Mildred L. Hartsough, *From Canoe to Steel Barge on the Upper Mississippi,* is excellent. William J. Peterson, *Steamboating on the Upper Mississippi: The Water Way to Iowa. Some River History,* is an episodic account confined chiefly to the years before the Civil War.

VII. DISCONTENT ON FARMS

The standard works are Solon J. Buck, *The Granger Movement,* and *The Agrarian Crusade,* and John D. Hicks, *The Populist Revolt: A History of the Farmers' Alliance and the People's Party.* There are ample bibliographies for further study. F. E. Haynes, *Third Party Movements Since the Civil War, with Special Reference to Iowa,* is fair. A. B. Paine, *The Granger Movement in Illinois,* is an excellent study of an important state. Satisfactory chapters are found in E. E. Sparks, *National Development, 1887-1885;* D. R. Dewey, *National Problems, 1885-1897;* E. P. Oberholtzer, *A History of the United States Since the Civil War;* and M. S. Wildman, *Money In-*

flation in the United States. Material is also found in the following biographical studies: C. Vann Woodward, *Tom Watson: Agrarian Rebel;* Fred E. Haynes, *James Baird Weaver;* George M. Stephenson, *John Lind of Minnesota*; F. B. Simkins, *The Tillman Movement in South Carolina*; Allan Nevins, *Grover Cleveland: A Study in Courage*. Munn *v.* Illinois is No. 294 in Commager, *Documents of American History*.

VIII. DISCONTENT IN CITIES

John R. Commons and associates, *History of Labour in the United States* (2 vols.), is the best single work. Among the better books, the following are suggested: Frank T. Carlton, *History and Problems of Organized Labor*; Norman J. Ware, *The Labor Movement in the United States, 1860-1895: A Study in Democracy*; Leo Wolman, *The Growth of American Trade Unions, 1880-1923*; Frank T. Carlton, *Organized Labor in American History*. Marjorie R. Clark and Fanny S. Simon, *The Labor Movement in America* (1938), is a brief survey. Samuel Yellen, *American Labor Struggles,* has interesting chapters on the railroad strikes of 1877 and on the Haymarket affair. Terence V. Powderly, *Thirty Years of Labor* (1889), and Lewis L. Lorwin, *The American Federation of Labor* (1933), are accounts of the two great labor organizations discussed in this chapter. For the life and influence of a prominent leader, see Samuel Gompers, *Seventy Years of Life and Labor* (2 vols.) ; Louis S. Reed, *The Labor Philosophy of Samuel Gompers*; Rowland H. Harvey, *Samuel Gompers: Champion of the Toiling Masses*. The Haymarket affair is presented from several angles in Henry David, *The History of the Haymarket Affair: A Study in the American Social-Revolutionary and Labor Movements*; Alan Calmer, *Labor Agitator: The Story of Albert Parsons*; Waldo R. Browne, *Altgeld of Illinois: A Record of His Life and Work*; Harry Barnard, *Eagle Forgotten: The Life of John Peter Altgeld*; Samuel P. McConnell, "The Chicago Bomb Case," in *Harper's Magazine,* May, 1934. Brand Whitlock, *Forty Years of It,* has interesting sidelights on the Haymarket trial. Chauncey D. French, *Railroadman* (1938), is an autobiography of a railroadman.

IX. POLITICS, 1876-1884

In some respects the best single volume dealing with politics from 1884 to 1896 is Allan Nevins, *Grover Cleveland*. J. F. Rhodes, *History of the United States from Hayes to McKinley,* and E. P. Oberholtzer, *History of the United States Since the Civil War,* Vols. III and IV, are not satisfactory. Harry T. Peck, *Twenty Years of the Republic, 1885-1905,* is a chatty, gossipy, and interesting book, but superficial. E. E. Sparks, *National Development, 1877-1885,* is factual. Matthew Josephson, *The Politicos, 1865-1896,* is a lengthy survey of the politics of the period and a caustic appraisal of the leading actors. Satisfactory biographies in the *American Political Leaders Series* (edited by Allan Nevins) are H. J. Eckenrode, *Rutherford B. Hayes*; Robert G. Caldwell, *James A. Garfield*; George F. Howe, *Chester A. Arthur*; David S. Muzzey, *James G. Blaine*; Frederick H. Gillett, *George Frisbie Hoar*; Claude M. Fuess, *Carl Schurz.* Other good biographies are Charles R. Williams, *The Life of R. B. Hayes* (2 vols.); Theodore C. Smith, *James A. Garfield* (2 vols.); Theodore E. Burton, *John Sherman*; Donald B. Chidsey, *The Gentleman from New York: A Life of Roscoe Conkling*; Allan Nevins, *Abram Hewitt*; Joseph Schafer, *Carl Schurz.* One of the best autobiographies is George F. Hoar, *Autobiography of Seventy Years* (2 vols.). Carl Schurz's brilliant speeches are printed in his *Speeches, Correspondence, and Political Papers* (6 vols). Books dealing specifically with civil service reform are Carl R. Fish, *Civil Service and the Patronage*; Edward Cary, *George William Curtis*; James Bryce, *The American Commonwealth,* Vol. II. Frank W. Taussig, *Tariff History of the United States,* is standard. On Chinese immigration, see M. R. Davie, *World Immigration,* Chap. VII; James Bryce, *The American Commonwealth,* Vol. II, pp. 426-448; A. C. Coolidge, *The United States as a World Power,* pp. 313-340; M. R. Coolidge, *Chinese Immigration.*

X. DEMOCRATIC VICTORY AND DEFEAT, 1884-1888

POLITICS.

To the biographies listed in the previous chapter may be added: Robert McElroy, *Grover Cleveland: The Man and the Statesman,* and Richard W. Gilder, *Grover Cleveland: A Record of Friendship.* H. C. Thomas, *The Return of the Democratic Party to Power in 1884,* is excellent. Henry J. Ford, *The Cleveland Era,* is very brief. D. R. Dewey, *Financial History of the United States,* and A. D. Noyes, *Forty Years of American Finance,* contain material on pensions. On the politics of the tariff, consult F. W. Taussig, *Tariff History of the United States;* Edward Stanwood, *American Tariff Con-*

troversies in the Nineteenth Century (2 vols.) ; Ida M. Tarbell, *The Tariff in our Times.*

TRANSPORTATION AND THE INTERSTATE COMMERCE ACT.

Seymour Dunbar, *History of Travel in the United States* (4 vols.), is the most comprehensive study of this subject. E. R. Johnson, *American Railway Transportation,* is a good brief account. Special aspects, management, finance, and the like are discussed in W. Z. Ripley, *Railroads, Rates and Regulations* (2 vols.) ; A. T. Hadley, *Railroad Transportation*; W. C. Noyes, *American Railroad Rates*; F. A. Cleveland and F. W. Powell, *Railway Promotion and Capitalization*; B. H. Meyer, *Railway Legislation in the United States.* Matthew Josephson, *The Robber Barons,* is an "exposure." J. R. Dos Passos, *The Interstate Commerce Act: An Analysis of Its Provisions* (1887), is a valuable brief summary and explanation of the act. E. B. Peirce, *Digest of Decisions of the Courts and the Interstate Commerce Commission under the Act to Regulate Commerce from 1887 to 1908.* F. N. Judson, *The Law of Interstate Commerce and Its Federal Regulation* (1905). E. Watkins, *Shippers and Carriers of Interstate Freight* (1909), is a valuable compilation of cases and literature on the subject, with copious citations. F. H. Dixon, "Publicity for Express Companies," in the *Atlantic Monthly,* July, 1905, is the best single article on the subject. An article, "Renewed Activity of the Modern Dick Turpins," in the *Arena,* April, 1908, is intensely hostile to the express companies. There is no satisfactory single treatment of the express companies.

XI. THE REPUBLICANS IN CONTROL

POLITICS.

There is no satisfactory biography of Benjamin Harrison. To the biographies listed for Chapter IX may be added William A. Robinson, *Thomas B. Reed*; Royal Cortissoz, *Life of Whitelaw Reid* (2 vols.) ; C. S. Olcott, *William McKinley* (2 vols.). Mary P. Follett, *Speaker of the House of Representatives,* is a standard treatise.

TARIFF AND FINANCE.

F. W. Taussig, *Tariff History*; A. D. Noyes, *Forty Years of American Finance*; D. R. Dewey, *Financial History*; J. Laurence Laughlin, *The History of Bimetallism in the United States*; G. M.

Stephenson, *John Lind of Minnesota*; M. S. Wildman, *Money Inflation in the United States*; T. E. Burton, *John Sherman*.

TRUSTS AND ANTI-TRUST LEGISLATION.

Albert H. Walker, *History of the Sherman Law*; Myron W. Watkins, *Industrial Combinations and Public Policy*; Gustavus Myers, *History of the Great American Fortunes* (3 vols.); Matthew Josephson, *The Robber Barons; The Great American Capitalists, 1861-1901*; Ida M. Tarbell, *The History of the Standard Oil Company* (2 vols.); Ida M. Tarbell, *The Nationalizing of Business, 1878-1898*; Edward Berman, *Labor and the Sherman Act;* John W. Jenkins, *James B. Duke: Master Builder*; John K. Winkler, *Morgan the Magnificent: The Life of J. Pierpont Morgan*; Burton J. Hendrick, *Life of Andrew Carnegie* (2 vols.); Felix Frankfurter and N. V. Greene, *The Labor Injunction*.

XII. THE GATHERING STORM

GENERAL.

The three best books on the topics treated in this chapter are Allan Nevins, *Grover Cleveland*; James A. Barnes, *John G. Carlisle: Financial Statesman*; and John D. Hicks, *The Populist Revolt*. They may be supplemented by Fred E. Haynes, *James Baird Weaver*; C. Vann Woodward, *Tom Watson: Agrarian Rebel*; F. B. Simkins, *The Tillman Movement in South Carolina*; G. M. Stephenson, *John Lind of Minnesota*; S. J. Buck, *The Agrarian Crusade*; M. S. Wildman, *Money Inflation in the United States*; A. D. Noyes, *Forty Years of American Finance*; W. Jett Lauck, *The Causes of the Panic of 1893*; Allan Nevins, *Letters of Grover Cleveland, 1850-1908*; Charles B. Kuhlman, *The Development of the Flour-Milling Industry in the United States. With Special Reference to the Industry in Minnesota*; William C. Edgar, *The Medal of Gold: A Story of Industrial Achievement*.

THE PULLMAN STRIKE AND UNREST.

Donald R. McMurray, *Coxey's Army*; Harry Barnard, *Eagle Forgotten: The Life of John Peter Altgeld*; Waldo R. Browne, *Altgeld of Illinois*; Henry James, *Richard Olney and his Public Services*; Grover Cleveland, *The Government in the Chicago Strike of 1894*; James W. Linn, *Jane Addams*; Coleman McAlister, *Eugene V. Debs: A Man Unafraid*.

THE REFORMERS.

Joseph Dorfman, *Thorstein Veblen and His America,* is an excellent summary of the history of economic and social thought. Louis F. Post, *The Prophet of San Francisco: Personal Memoirs and Interpretations of Henry George*; George R. Geiger, *The Philosophy of Henry George*; Caroline A. Lloyd, *Henry Demarest Lloyd, 1847-1903* (2 vols.). The atmosphere of this period may be breathed by perusing the articles and cartoons in the *Review of Reviews,* 1892-1896, and by reading Bellamy's *Looking Backward,* Lloyd's *Wealth Against Commonwealth,* and George's *Progress and Poverty.*

XIII. THE BATTLE OF THE STANDARDS

The best accounts of the strategy and conduct of the presidential campaign are found in Herbert Croly, *Marcus Alonzo Hanna: His Life and Work,* and John D. Hicks, *The Populist Revolt.* G. M. Stephenson, *John Lind of Minnesota,* is pointed to the situation in the Northwest. There is no satisfactory biography of Bryan, but one is in preparation by Henry S. Commager. M. Werner, *Bryan,* is an attempt, but there is more profit in reading William J. Bryan, *The First Battle: A Story of the Campaign of 1896.* Mark Sullivan, *Our Times: The Turn of the Century* (Vol. I), and Henry T. Peck, *Twenty Years of the Republic,* are very readable. Edgar E. Robinson, *The Presidential Vote, 1896-1932,* is a compilation of election returns by counties for ten presidential elections. The maps present in graphic form the preponderant strength of the political parties. There are a number of articles of quality in the *Review of Reviews* for 1896. W. H. Harvey's *Coin's Financial School* can still be picked up in second-hand book stores.

XIV. FOREIGN AFFAIRS UNDER CLEVELAND AND HARRISON

The most satisfactory treatments are S. F. Bemis, *A Diplomatic History of the United States*; Allan Nevins, *Grover Cleveland*; D. S. Muzzey, *James G. Blaine.* The reader is also referred to the diplomatic histories listed for Chapter IV. Archibald C. Coolidge, *The United States as a World Power,* is objective and suggestive. Alice F. Tyler, *The Foreign Policy of James G. Blaine,* is friendly but critical. Julius W. Pratt, *Expansionists of 1898: The Acquisition of Hawaii and the Spanish Islands,* is a well-documented effort to sense public opinion and is readable. Dexter Perkins, *The Monroe Doctrine, 1867-*

1907, is by a foremost student of the subject. James M. Callahan, *American Foreign Policy in Canadian Relations,* is by a writer on several aspects of foreign relations. George H. Ryden, *The Foreign Policy of the United States in Relation to Samoa,* tells the whole story. Chapters on the Secretaries of State written by different authors are in S. F. Bemis (ed.), *The American Secretaries of State and their Diplomacy* (10 vols.).

XV. THE WAR WITH SPAIN

Walter Millis, *The Martial Spirit: A Study of Our War with Spain,* is intensely interesting. The author has sensed the psychology of the war. Biographies of leading exponents of "yellow journalism" are similar contributions: Don C. Seitz, *Joseph Pulitzer: His Life and Letters*; J. K. Winkler, *W. R. Hearst: An American Phenomenon.* See also Joseph Wisan, *The Cuban Crisis as Reflected in the New York Press*; Marcus Wilkerson, *Public Opinion and the Spanish-American War.* On the diplomacy of the war, see S. F. Bemis, *A Diplomatic History of the United States*; French E. Chadwick, *Relations of the United States and Spain: Diplomacy* (2 vols.); S. F. Bemis, *American Secretaries of State,* Vol. IX. Books dealing with military and naval operations: F. E. Chadwick, *Relations of the United States and Spain: The War* (2 vols.); Theodore Roosevelt, *Autobiography*; Henry F. Pringle, *Theodore Roosevelt: A Biography*; Herman Hagedorn, *Leonard Wood: A Biography* (2 vols.); Henry Cabot Lodge, *Selections from the Correspondence of Theodore Roosevelt and Henry Cabot Lodge, 1884-1918* (2 vols.); Lawrence S. Mayo, *America of Yesterday as Reflected in the Journal of John Davis Long*; George Dewey, *Autobiography*; W. S. Schley, *Forty-Five Years Under the Flag*; Robley D. Evans, *A Sailor's Log: Recollections of Forty Years of Naval Life*; Fletcher Pratt, *The Navy: A History* (1938); Richmond P. Hobson, *The Sinking of the Merrimac*; Nelson A. Miles, *Serving the Republic*; Joseph Wheeler, *Reminiscences of the Santiago Campaign.* There is a vast amount of material embedded in the two volumes entitled *Record of Proceedings of a Court of Inquiry in the Case of Rear-Admiral Winfield S. Schley, U. S. Navy. Convened at the Navy-Yard, Washington, D. C., September 12, 1901.* It is published as *House Document,* 57th Congress, 1st Session, No. 485. Serial numbers 4370, 4371. Schley's case is presented in James Parker, *Rear-Admirals Schley, Sampson, and Cervera* (1910). The illustrations, special articles, and editorials in the following periodicals supply excellent material: *Harper's Weekly, Collier's Weekly, Leslie's Weekly, Review of Reviews,* and *Literary Digest.* Finley P. Dunne, *Mr. Dooley in Peace and War* (1898), is priceless.

XVI. THE OBLIGATIONS OF A COLONIAL EMPIRE

The spirit of anti-imperialism can best be found in the writings and speeches of its exponents: William Graham Sumner, *War and Other Essays,* Chap. XV; Carl Schurz, *Speeches, Correspondence, and Political Papers,* Vols. V, VI; George F. Hoar, *Autobiography of Seventy Years,* Vol. II; Andrew Carnegie, *Autobiography.* Stimulating and objective are Chaps. IV to VIII in A. C. Coolidge, *The United States as a World Power.* Merle Curti, *Bryan and World Peace,* and M. A. De Wolfe Howe, *Portrait of an Independent: Moorfield Storey,* are biographical studies of anti-imperialists. On the Treaty of Paris, see the general diplomatic histories listed for Chapter IV, and the following: F. E. Chadwick, *Relations of the United States and Spain: Diplomacy;* Royal Cortissoz, *The Life of Whitelaw Reid* (2 vols.); Tyler Dennett, *John Hay: From Poetry to Politics;* William R. Thayer, *Life and Letters of John Hay* (2 vols.). The government of dependencies is discussed in John H. Latané, *America as a World Power;* F. A. Ogg, *National Progress, 1907-1917;* W. F. Willoughby, *Territories and Dependencies of the United States;* Herman Hagedorn, *Leonard Wood* (2 vols.); Theodore Roosevelt, Jr., *Colonial Policies of the United States;* Nicholas Roosevelt, *The Philippines: A Treasure and a Problem;* Leland H. Jenks, *Our Cuban Colony: A Study in Sugar;* A. G. Robinson, *Cuba and the Intervention;* Knowlton Mixer, *Porto Rico;* Dean C. Worcester, *The Philippines: Past and Present.* Grayson Kirk, *Philippine Independence,* analyzes the forces that led to the passage of the Philippine independence legislation. Two excellent articles are Lester B. Shippee, "Germany and the Spanish-American War," in the *American Historical Review,* July, 1925; and Stephen Duggan, "The Philippines Today and Tomorrow," in the *Yale Review,* Spring, 1937.

XVII. THE LIFE OF THE PEOPLE, 1900-1917

The two best single volumes are in *A History of American Life:* Harold U. Faulkner, *The Quest for Social Justice, 1898-1914;* and Preston W. Slosson, *The Great Crusade and After, 1914-1928.* Scattered through the fifteen volumes of *The Pageant of America* (edited by Ralph H. Gabriel) is a great deal of material. See especially Vol.

XV, J. A. Krout, *Annals of American Sport.* J. F. Steiner, "Recreation and Leisure Time Activities," in *Recent Social Trends in the United States,* Vol. II, pp. 912-957, is excellent. Mark Sullivan, *Our Times: The United States, 1900-1925* (6 vols.), is a scrapbook rather than a history; but the volumes contain a wide variety of interesting material. H. L. Mencken, *The American Language. An Inquiry into the Development of English in the United States* (4th edition, 1936), shows how the life of the people affected their speech. George M. Stephenson, *The Religious Aspects of Swedish Immigration,* presents the life and contributions of a single immigrant stock. From a number of books dealing with the press, literature, and the theater, the following are suggested: Alfred McC. Lee, *The Daily Newspaper in America: The Evolution of a Social Instrument* (1937); W. G. Bleyer, *Main Currents in the History of American Journalism*; C. H. Dennis, *Victor Lawson*; Allan Nevins, *The Evening Post: A Century of Idealism*; Oswald G. Villard, *Some Newspapers and Newspapermen*; Elmer Davis, *History of the New York Times*; Candace Stone, *Dana and the Sun*; Oliver Carlson and Ernest B. Sutherland, *Hearst: Lord of San Simeon*; Fred Lewis Pattee, *The New American Literature, 1890-1930*; Algernon Tassin, *The Magazine in America*; Benjamin Hampton, *A History of the Movies*; Maurice Bardeche and Robert Brasillach, *The History of Motion Pictures*; O. S. Coad and E. Mims, Jr., *The American Stage (Pageant of America,* Vol. XIV); C. B. Glasscock, *The Gasoline Age.* There is no satisfactory history of baseball.

THE SOUTH.

Howard W. Odum, *Southern Regions of the United States* (1936), is a valuable reference work, encyclopedic in content. John Dollard, *Caste and Class in a Southern Town,* is a psychological study of the Negro problem. Gerald W. Johnson, *The Wasted Land* (1938), discusses the decline of cotton farming: cotton raising abroad, synthetic products, the mechanical cotton picker, soil erosion, and the wearing out of soil. Harry H. Kroll, *I Was a Sharecropper,* is the life story of a man who emerged out of the class of southern poor whites to become an author and educator. C. B. Glasscock, *Then Came Oil,* is the story of oil and Oklahoma. W. B. Hesseltine, *A History of the South, 1607-1936,* presents a more general picture. Albert B. Hart, *The Southern South,* and Ray S. Baker, *Following the Color Line,* are earlier books written by northern observers. A. M. Sakolski, *The Great American Land Bubble,* has a chapter on the Florida boom.

IMMIGRATION.

General works are listed under Chapter V, to which may be added those especially pertaining to the new immigration: F. J. Warne, *The Immigrant Invasion* (1913); Annie M. MacLean, *Modern Immigration* (1925); and two monographs published by the Census Bureau: *A Century of Population Growth from the First Census of the United States to the Twelfth, 1790-1900*; and W. S. Rossiter, *Increase of Population in the United States, 1910-1920.* A journalistic account of the A. P. A. movement and nativism is John M. Mecklin, *The Ku Klux Klan: A Study of the American Mind.* The history of immigration legislation is told in George M. Stephenson, *A History of American Immigration*; Roy L. Garis, *Immigration Restriction*; and Maurice R. Davie, *World Immigration.* Harry Jerome, *Migrations and Business Cycles* (1926), is a detailed study of the relations between immigration and business conditions in America and in the mother country. M. K. Reely, *Selected Articles on Immigration* (1917), gives convenient summaries of important articles in periodicals. There is no satisfactory history of naturalization legislation. The best accounts are J. P. Gavit, *Americans by Choice,* and Darrell H. Smith, *The Bureau of Naturalization: Its History, Activities, and Organization.* There are many books on the individual groups of the new immigration. Most of them are eulogistic. Samuel Joseph, *Jewish Immigration to the United States from 1881 to 1910,* is concise and scholarly. Mary Antin, *The Promised Land*; Ludwig Lewisohn, *Up Stream*; and Michael I. Pupin, *From Immigrant to Inventor,* are personal narratives by gifted immigrants. Robert F. Foerster, *The Italian Emigration of Our Times,* is the best thing on the subject. A delightful personal account of an Italian immigrant is Constantine Panunzio, *The Soul of an Immigrant.* Emily G. Balch, *Our Slavic Fellow Citizens,* is largely a study of backgrounds. Thomas Capek, *The Czechs (Bohemians) in America,* is popular. Henry P. Fairchild, *Greek Immigration to the United States,* is a scholarly production. Louis Adamic, *The Native's Return: An American Immigrant Visits Yugoslavia and Discovers His Old Country,* is fascinating. For a digest of immigration legislation and information about administrative machinery, together with a working bibliography, consult Darrell H. Smith and H. G. Herring, *The Bureau of Immigration: Its History, Activities, and Organization.*

XVIII. ASPIRATIONS TO A BETTER LIFE, 1900-1917
RELIGION.

William W. Sweet, *The Story of Religions in America,* is all too brief on the period after 1865. Luther A. Weigle, *American Idealism (The Pageant of America,* Vol. X). C. Luther Fry, "Changes in Religious Organizations," in *Recent Social Trends in the United States,* Vol. II, pp. 1009-1060. There are many histories of the various churches. See P. G. Mode, *Source Book and Bibliographical Guide for American Church History* (1920). *The American Church History Series* consists of denominational histories published under the auspices of the American Society of Church History. The volumes are old but still useful for the period before 1900. Vol. XIII in this series is Leonard W. Bacon, *A History of American Christianity* (1897). A more recent book is Henry K. Rowe, *The History of Religion in the United States* (1924). H. K. Carroll, *The Religious Forces of the United States* (1893), is an older work giving brief histories of churches and statistics of membership. *Bureau of the Census: Religious Bodies* (1916) gives more recent figures. *Annual Reports of the Federal Council of the Churches of Christ,* beginning in 1909, are useful. E. B. Sanford, *Origin and History of the Federal Council of the Churches of Christ in America.* W. H. Lyon, *A Study of Christian Sects* (1926), is a handbook giving brief historical sketches, doctrinal position, and statistics. Alvin W. Johnson, *The Legal Status of Church-State Relationships in the United States* (1934), is excellent. Samuel W. Brown, *The Secularization of American Education as Shown by State Legislation, State Constitutional Provisions, and State Supreme Court Decisions* (1912). Carl Zollman, *American Civil Church Law* (1917). Gustavus Myers, *The History of American Idealism.* Herbert Croly, *The Promise of American Life,* is stimulating. Robert L. Kelly, *Theological Education in America,* is the best discussion of the subject. Henry F. Cope, *The Evolution of the Sunday School,* is not a history but contains historical data. Frank O. Erb, *The Development of the Young People's Movement.* Charles O. Gill and Gifford Pinchot, *The Country Church: The Decline of Its Influence and the Remedy* (1913). Carter G. Woodson, *The History of the Negro Church* (1921). Ephraim Emerton, *Unitarian Thought,* is an "authoritative" statement by a distinguished church historian.

Jesse L. Hulburt, *The Story of Chautauqua*. Studies of distinguished leaders: Henry H. Sanderson, *Charles W. Eliot: Puritan Liberal*, is a stimulating survey of the evolution of Congregationalism from Calvinistic orthodoxy to Unitarian liberalism. A. V. G. Allen, *Life and Letters of Phillips Brooks* (2 vols.). Lyman Abbott, *Henry Ward Beecher*, is eulogistic but not uncritical. Gamaliel Bradford, *D. L. Moody: A Worker in Souls*. Paul D. Moody, *My Father: An Intimate Portrait of Dwight Moody*. H. F. Rall, *Religion and Public Affairs*, is a symposium in honor of Bishop Francis G. McConnell. A. S. Will, *Life of Cardinal Gibbons, Archbishop of Baltimore* (2 vols.), is a biography of a great Catholic leader. William H. O'Connell, *Recollections of Seventy Years* (1934), is the work of a Catholic leader in New England.

EDUCATION.

Charles H. Judd, "Education," in *Recent Social Trends in the United States*, Vol. I, pp. 325-381. E. P. Cubberly, *Public Education in the United States*. Samuel E. Morison, *Three Centuries of Harvard, 1636-1936*. Bliss Perry, *And Gladly Teach: Reminiscences*, is a brilliant account of educational developments in the last decades of the nineteenth century and in the century following.

REFORMS AND REFORMERS.

James Bryce, *The American Commonwealth* (2 vols.), still holds its place as the best study. M. Ostrogorski, *Democracy and the Organization of Political Parties* (2 vols.). W. B. Munro, *Initiative, Referendum, and Recall*; E. P. Oberholtzer, *The Referendum in America*. F. C. Howe, *Wisconsin: An Experiment in Democracy*. Kirk H. Porter, *A History of Suffrage in the United States*. C. R. Woodruff, *City Government by Commission*. Harold Zink, *City Bosses in the United States*. William B. Munro, *Personality in Politics: Reformers, Bosses, and Leaders. What They Do and How They Do It*. Charles E. Merriam, *Chicago: A More Intimate View of Urban Politics*. Carter H. Harrison, *Stormy Years: An Autobiography*. Brand Whitlock, *Forty Years of It*. F. C. Howe, *Confessions of a Reformer*. Louise Ware, *Jacob A. Riis: Police Reporter, Reformer, Useful Citizen*. Lincoln Steffens, *The Shame of the Cities*, and *Autobiography*. Tom L. Johnson, *My Story*. James W. Linn, *Jane Addams*. Gustavus Myers, *History of Tammany Hall*. M. R. Werner, *Tammany Hall*. D. T. Lynch, *"Boss" Tweed*. Ernest R. Groves, *The*

American Woman (1937). Freda Kirchwey, *Our Changing Morality.* Anna Howard Shaw, *The Story of a Pioneer.* Ida H. Harper, *The Life and Work of Susan B. Anthony* (3 vols). Frances E. Willard, *Glimpses of Fifty Years: An Autobiography of an American Woman,* and *My Happy Half-Century.* George H. Palmer, *The Life of Alice Freeman Palmer.* E. H. Cherrington, *The Evolution of Prohibition in the United States of America.* J. A. Krout, *The Origins of Prohibition.* Peter Odegard, *Pressure Politics.* Joseph Rowntree and Arthur Sherwell, *The Temperance Problem and Social Reform.* Herbert Asbury, *Carry Nation.*

XIX. THEODORE ROOSEVELT

Claude G. Bowers, *Beveridge and the Progressive Era,* gives a good background for the events treated in this chapter, as does Harold U. Faulkner, *The Quest for Social Justice, 1898-1914.* Herman H. Kohlsaat, *From McKinley to Harding,* is journalistic. Harold Howland, *Theodore Roosevelt and his Time,* is another general treatment. There are several biographies of Roosevelt, of which Henry F. Pringle, *Theodore Roosevelt,* is the best. William R. Thayer, *Theodore Roosevelt: An Intimate Biography*; Lord Charnwood, *Theodore Roosevelt*; Owen Wister, *Roosevelt: The Story of a Friendship, 1880-1919.* Theodore Roosevelt, *Autobiography,* is interesting and colorful. The Northern Securities case is discussed in B. H. Meyer, *A History of the Northern Securities Case*; George Kennan, *E. H. Harriman: A Biography* (2 vols.) ; J. J. Pyle, *James J. Hill* (2 vols.). See also B. J. Hendrick, *The Age of Big Business.* Light on the coal strike is found in Elsie Glück, *John Mitchell: Miner-Labor's Bargain with the Gilded Age,* and in Roosevelt, *Autobiography.* Roosevelt's enemies are portrayed in Nathaniel W. Stephenson, *Nelson W. Aldrich: A Leader in American Politics*; Herbert Croly, *Marcus A. Hanna*; L. White Busbey, *Uncle Joe Cannon*; J. B. Foraker, *Notes of a Busy Life* (2 vols.) ; James E. Watson, *As I Knew Them*; Thomas C. Platt, *Autobiography*; Robert Douglas, *Boies Penrose: Symbol of an Era.* The story of the muckrakers can be read in Cornelius C. Regier, *The Era of the Muckrakers*; John H. Chamberlain, *Farewell to Reform*; Lincoln Steffens, *Autobiography.*

XX. THE INSURGENTS

There is no satisfactory biography of Taft. Herbert S. Duffy, *William Howard Taft,* is an attempt. Very enlightening and delightfully written is Archie Butt, *Taft and Roosevelt: The Intimate Letters of Archie Butt, Military Aide* (2 vols.). C. G. Bowers, *Beveridge and the Progressive Era,* is excellent. There are significant letters in Henry Cabot Lodge, *Selections from the Correspondence of Theodore Roosevelt and Henry Cabot Lodge, 1884-1918.* Roosevelt's speeches and writings show the reactions of the Taft administration: *Autobiography* (1913), *The New Nationalism* (1910), and *Progressive Principles* (1911). J. Hampton Moore, *Roosevelt and the Old Guard,* presents some interesting facts pertaining to the politics of the time and the break between Roosevelt and Taft. N. W. Stephenson, *Nelson W. Aldrich,* and L. White Busbey, *Uncle Joe Cannon,* present biographical data on two leaders of the Old Guard. Claudius O. Johnson, *Borah of Idaho,* is a study of the career of a prominent insurgent and progressive. B. P. De Witt, *The Progressive Movement,* and F. A. Ogg, *National Progress, 1907-1917,* are serviceable. For the Ballinger-Pinchot controversy, see Gifford Pinchot, *The Fight for Conservation*; John Ise, *The United States Forest Policy* (1924); Charles R. Van Hise and Richard Havemeyer, *The Conservation of Our Natural Resources* (1930); Rose M. Stahl, *The Ballinger-Pinchot Controversy*; *Collier's Weekly,* 1910-13. F. W. Taussig, *Tariff History,* discusses the Payne-Aldrich Tariff.

XXI. FOREIGN RELATIONS UNDER ROOSEVELT AND TAFT

The diplomatic histories are listed under Chapter IV. For a good survey of the American Far Eastern and Latin American policies, see Parker T. Moon, *Imperialism and World Politics,* Chaps. XIV-XVI. Tyler Dennett, *John Hay,* has an excellent account of the diplomacy of the first part of the Roosevelt administration. Scott Nearing and Joseph Freeman, *Dollar Diplomacy: A Study of American Imperialism,* is caustic.

JAPANESE-AMERICAN RELATIONS.

For the background: K. K. Kawakami, *American-Japanese Relations* (1912), *Japan in World Politics* (1917), and *What Japan Thinks* (1921), are by a Japanese-American who deplored the trend of events and employed his pen to bring about a better understanding. J. F. Steiner, *The Japanese Invasion* (1917), is a brief and readable account. H. A. Millis, *The Japanese Problem in the United States* (1915), is a thorough study. T. Iyenaga and K. Sato, *Japan and the*

California Problem (1921), has a bibliography, the text of anti-alien land laws, and a chapter on the background of emigration. S. L. Gulick, *The American Japanese Problem,* is a missionary's plea for a sympathetic attitude. Yamato Ichihashi, *Japanese in the United States: A Critical Study of the Japanese Immigrants and Their Children* (1932), is by a professor in Leland Stanford University. Eleanor Tupper and George E. McReynolds, *Japan in American Public Opinion* (1937), is a comprehensive study of the changing attitudes of the American public toward the Japanese people since 1900. For the diplomacy: Tyler Dennett, *Roosevelt and the Russo-Japanese War* (1924); Thomas A. Baily, *Roosevelt and the Japanese-American Crisis* (1934), an account of negotiations leading up to the Gentlemen's Agreement; Rodman W. Paul, *The Abrogation of the Gentlemen's Agreement* (1936). Payson J. Treat, *Diplomatic Relations between the United States and Japan* (2 vols.), is comprehensive.

THE PANAMA CANAL.

E. Taylor Parks, *Colombia and the United States* (1935); William L. McCain, *The United States and the Republic of Panama* (1937); H. C. Hill, *Roosevelt and the Caribbean* (1927); J. B. and F. Bishop, *Goethals: Genius of the Panama Canal*; M. C. Gorgas and B. J. Hendrick, *W. C. Gorgas: His Life and Work*; Theodore Roosevelt, *Autobiography.*

XXII. THE BULL MOOSE CAMPAIGN

Henry F. Pringle, *Theodore Roosevelt,* is objective. Claude G. Bowers, *Beveridge and the Progressive Era,* is mildly pro-Roosevelt. There is no biography of Robert M. LaFollette, but his *Autobiography* presents his side. James E. Watson, *As I Knew Them,* is by a Taft leader in the convention. Victor Rosewater, *Back Stage in 1912: The Inside Story of the Split Republican Convention,* is by the chairman of the Republican National Committee. Oscar K. Davis, *Released for Publication. Inside Political History of Theodore Roosevelt and His Times,* is by a Roosevelt partisan. William J. Bryan, *The Story of Two Conventions,* is by an observer at the Republican convention and a leader in the Democratic convention, who fails to do justice to his own decisive leadership. Bliss Perry, *And Gladly Teach: Reminiscences,* is an intimate portrayal of Woodrow Wilson as a professor and president at Princeton. Eleanor Wilson McAdoo, *The Woodrow Wilsons,* presents a charming account of the human side of her father.

William E. Dodd, *Woodrow Wilson and His Work,* is by a strong admirer of the man and presents a masterly survey of politics and events before and after Wilson's inauguration. George Sylvester Viereck, *The Strangest Friendship in History: Woodrow Wilson and Colonel House.* Charles Seymour, *The Intimate Papers of Colonel House* (4 vols.). Ray Stannard Baker, *Woodrow Wilson: Life and Letters,* is a comprehensive work, of which six volumes have appeared. Woodrow Wilson, *The New Freedom* (1913). Champ Clark, *My Quarter-Century of American Politics* (2 vols.), breathes hostility to Bryan. David Bryn-Jones, *Frank B. Kellogg,* throws some light on the campaign.

XXIII. WOODROW WILSON AND REFORM

Three general works furnish satisfactory reading on this period: Frederic L. Paxson, *Pre-War Years, 1913-1917*; Dwight L. Dumond, *Roosevelt to Roosevelt: The United States in the Twentieth Century*; F. A. Ogg, *National Progress, 1907-1917.* W. E. Dodd, *Woodrow Wilson and His Work,* gives a good account of the domestic achievements of the Wilson administration. Ray Stannard Baker, *Woodrow Wilson: Life and Letters.* The first six volumes cover the years before the entrance of the United States into the World War. R. S. Baker and W. E. Dodd, *The Public Papers of Woodrow Wilson* (6 vols.). George McLean Harper, *President Wilson's Addresses,* is a convenient compilation. Charles Seymour, *The Intimate Papers of Colonel House* (4 vols.), is very interesting and valuable. David F. Houston, *Eight Years with Wilson's Cabinet* (2 vols.), is mainly a record of the proceedings of cabinet meetings. Josephus Daniels, *Life of Woodrow Wilson,* is an entertaining book. William G. McAdoo, *Crowded Years,* presents the reminiscences of the Secretary of the Treasury. Franklin K. Lane, *Letters,* is delightful. Thomas R. Marshall, *Recollections.* W. C. Redfield, *With Congress and Cabinet.* For the history of the tariff, see F. W. Taussig, *Tariff History*; Ida M. Tarbell, *The Tariff in Our Times.* Books on the Federal Reserve Act: J. Laurence Laughlin, *The Federal Reserve Act: Its Origins and Problems*; Paul M. Warburg, *The Federal Reserve System* (2 vols.); E. W. Kemmerer, *The A. B. C. of the Federal Reserve System*; Lynn and Dora B. Haines, *The Lindberghs.* Labor and the Clayton Act: Edward Berman, *Labor and the Sherman Act*; Felix Frankfurter and N. V. Greene, *The Labor Injunction*; William H. Taft, *The Anti-Trust Act and the Supreme Court*; Alfred Lief, *The Dissenting Opinions of*

Mr. Justice Holmes; Alfred Lief, *The Social and Economic Views of Mr. Justice Brandeis*; Felix Frankfurter, *Mr. Justice Brandeis*; Louis Adamic, *Dynamite: The Story of Class Violence in America*; Samuel Yellen, *American Labor Struggles* ("The Lawrence Strike," "Bloody Ludlow") ; *Bill Haywood's Book: An Autobiography*; P. T. Brissenden, *The I. W. W.*; G. C. Henderson, *The Federal Trade Commission*; T. C. Blaisdell, *The Federal Trade Commission*.

XXIV. FOREIGN AFFAIRS IN A WAR-TORN WORLD
MEXICO.

Samuel F. Bemis, *A Diplomatic History of the United States,* pp. 539-564. James M. Callahan, *American Foreign Policy in Mexican Relations,* presents a brief summary. Robert D. Gregg, *The Influence of Border Troubles on Relations Between the United States and Mexico, 1876-1910.* George M. Stephenson, *John Lind of Minnesota,* tells the story from Lind's famous mission through 1916. Carleton Beals, *Porfirio Diaz: Dictator of Mexico,* and Frank Tannenbaum, *Peace by Revolution: An Interpretation,* give the Mexican background. Ray S. Baker, *Woodrow Wilson: Life and Letters,* Vol. IV, is a sympathetic interpretation of Wilson's policy. Edith O'Shaughnessy, *A Diplomat's Wife in Mexico,* is interesting and strongly anti-Wilson. Satisfactory books of a more general nature are Herbert I. Priestly, *The Mexican Nation: A History*; J. Fred Rippy, *The United States and Mexico*; Charles W. Hackett, *The Mexican Revolution and the United States.* A mine of highly colored material is found in *Investigation of Mexican Affairs* (Report of the Subcommittee on Foreign Relations of the United States Senate, Senate Document, 66th Congress, 2nd Session, No. 285. Serial nos. 7665, 7666. 2 vols. Washington 1920).

WORLD WAR.

The diplomatic histories listed under Chapter IV. Walter Millis, *Road to War: America, 1914-1917* (1935), is a stimulating but one-sided arraignment of Wilsonian diplomacy. Charles Seymour, *American Neutrality, 1914-1917: Essays on the Causes of American Intervention in the World War,* is a brief survey by a specialist in the field. Charles Seymour, *American Diplomacy During the World War,* is an earlier work based chiefly on the papers of Colonel House. Charles Seymour, *The Intimate Papers of Colonel House Arranged as a Narrative* (4 vols.) is more comprehensive than the two former books. In Charles C. Tansill, *America Goes to War* (1938), the author has made extensive use of documents gathered by the Nye Committee. He acquits Wilson of the charge that he did the bidding of big business. He praises Bryan and is hard on House and Lansing. Burton J. Hendrick, *The Life and Letters of Walter H. Page* (3 vols.), reveals the efforts of the American ambassador to Great Britain. Harley Notter, *The Origins of the Foreign Policy of Woodrow Wilson* (1937). Ray S. Baker, *Woodrow Wilson: Life and Letters,* Vols. V and VI. William E. Dodd, *Woodrow Wilson and His work.* Newton D. Baker, *Why We Went to War,* is a brief and careful survey by the Secretary of War. For the play of propaganda, see George S. Viereck, *Spreading Germs of Hate*; M. E. Spratt, *Survey of British War-Time Propaganda in the United States*; James D. Squires, *British Propaganda at Home and in the United States from 1914 to 1917*; Carl Wittke, *German-Americans and the World War*; Jeannette Keim, *Forty Years of German-American Political Relations*; Henry Landau, *The Enemy Within* (the story of German sabotage in the United States); John P. Jones and Paul M. Hollister, *German Secret Service in America.* Count von Bernstorff, *My Three Years in America,* and *Memoirs,* are by the German ambassador to the United States.

XXV. THE PRESIDENTIAL CAMPAIGN OF 1916

Of the histories and biographies dealing with the Wilson administration, the most satisfactory on the election of 1916 are Charles Seymour, *The Intimate Papers of Colonel House,* Vol. II; Frederic L. Paxson, *Pre-War Years;* F. A. Ogg, *National Progress, 1907-1917*; E. E. Robinson, *The Evolution of American Political Parties*; William E. Dodd, *Woodrow Wilson and His Work*; Henry F. Pringle, *Theodore Roosevelt;* Herman Hagedorn, *Leonard Wood* (2 vols.); Claude G. Bowers, *Beveridge and the Progressive Era*; Claudius O. Johnson, *Borah of Idaho*; Henry Cabot Lodge, *Selections from the Correspondence of Theodore Roosevelt and Henry Cabot Lodge, 1884-1918,* Vol. II; E. E. Robinson, *The Presidential Vote, 1896-1932.* Among the periodicals the most valuable are the *Outlook,* the *Independent,* the *Literary Digest,* the *Nation,* the *New Republic, Collier's Weekly,* and *Harper's Weekly.*

XXVI. THE GREAT CRUSADE

For a survey of the diplomacy that preceded the declaration of war and the political controversies, see the works listed under Chapter XXIV. To these may be added Alex M. Arnett, *Claude Kitchin and the Wilson War Policies* (1937), which is a biography of a Democratic leader in Congress who opposed the declaration of war, and the *Congressional Record* from December, 1916, to April, 1917. Two excellent accounts of America's part in the war written by participants are James G. Harbord, *The American Army in France, 1917-1918*; John J. Pershing, *My Experiences in the World War* (2 vols.). Frederick Palmer, *Newton D. Baker: America at War* (2 vols.). The Russian intervention is discussed in William S. Graves, *America's Siberian Adventure, 1918-1920,* and Leonid I. Strakhovsky, *The Origins of American Intervention in North Russia.* John B. McMaster, *The United States in the World War* (2 vols.), and John S. Bassett, *Our War with Germany,* are not very satisfactory. Various aspects of America's contributions are treated in Arthur Bullard, *Mobilizing America*; George Creel, *How We Advertised America*; Walker D. Hines, *War History of American Railroads*; Samuel Gompers, *American Labor and the War*; Edward Hurley, *The Bridge to France*; Thomas G. Frothingham, *American Reenforcement in the World War*; Frederick Palmer, *America in France*; Henry P. Davison, *The American Red Cross in the Great War*. Franklin F. Holbrook and Livia Appel, *Minnesota in the War with Germany* (2 vols.), is the story of a single state, which is fairly typical of others. Mark Sullivan, *Our Times,* Vol. V, is revealing. The publications of the Committee on Public Information are interesting. There are excellent chapters in Preston Slosson, *The Great Crusade and After.*

XXVII. THE COLLAPSE OF WILSONISM

Samuel F. Bemis, *A Diplomatic History of the United States,* pp. 611-664, is the best single brief account. James T. Shotwell, *At the Paris Peace Conference* (1937), is an intimate story of day-by-day happenings in the American peace delegation told by a distinguished professor of history. Robert Lansing, *The Peace Negotiations: A Personal Narrative* (1921), is an ill-fated attempt of the Secretary of State to justify himself. Robert Lansing, *War Memoirs* (1935), was published later. Ray S. Baker, *Woodrow Wilson and World Settlement* (3 vols.). The first two volumes contain a narrative of what happened at Paris, and the third is devoted to letters and memoranda referred to or quoted in the narrative. There is much valuable documentary material. Allan Nevins, *Henry White,* and Frederick Palmer, *Bliss: Peacemaker,* are biographies of two members of the American delegation. David Hunter Miller, *The Drafting of the Covenant* (2 vols.), is valuable. For the League of Nations and the debate on the ratification of the treaty, see Denna Frank Fleming, *The United States and the League of Nations, 1918-1920;* John S. Bassett, *The League of Nations;* T. H. Dickinson, *The United States and the League;* Henry C. Lodge, *The Senate and the League of Nations;* Claudius O. Johnson, *Borah of Idaho;* David Bryn-Jones, *Frank B. Kellogg;* W. F. Johnson, *George Harvey: "A Passionate Patriot."*

XXVIII. THE AFTERMATH OF WAR

Three general treatments set forth the war-time hysteria and the post-war reaction: Preston Slosson, *The Great Crusade and After;* Alvin W. Johnson, *The Legal Status of Church-State Relationships in the United States;* Dwight L. Dumond, *Roosevelt to Roosevelt.* Zechariah Chaffee, *Freedom of Speech,* is a scholarly lawyer's account of war legislation and its enforcement. E. B. Sutherland, *This Land of Liberty,* reviews some of the painful events during the war and after. John Chamberlain, *Farewell to Reform,* begins with the background of the nineties and carries the story through. Granville Hicks, *John Reed: The Making of a Revolutionary,* contains illuminating events and episodes pertaining to radical activities and persecution. Felix Frankfurter, *The Case of Sacco and Vanzetti,* is a brief masterly summary and evaluation of the evidence in this famous case. John M. Mecklin, *The Ku Klux Klan: A Study of the American Mind,* is popular and brief. Louis F. Post, *The Deportations Delirium of Nineteen-Twenty: A Personal Narrative of an Historic Official Experience,* and F. C. Howe, *Confessions of a Reformer,* were written to justify efforts to induce sanity in public administration. Norman Thomas, *The Conscientious Objector in America,* is by a Socialist candidate for the Presidency. Joseph Dorfman, *Thorstein Veblen and His America,* relates the war and post-war experiences of this brilliant writer and student of social and economic problems. The volumes in *Americanization Studies,* edited by Allen T. Burns (1920-1924), are special studies of immigration problems. Philip Davis, *Immigration and Americanization,* contains "selected readings" on Americanization and a digest of addresses made before a conference of Americanization specialists held in Washington in 1919. C. Aronovici, *Americanization,* is skeptical of the movement. *New York Legislature. Joint Committee Investigating Seditious Activities. Revolutionary Radicalism* (4 vols., 1920). This is the title of the so-called Lusk Committee Report, extracts of which were widely published in the press. Stewart G. Cole, *The History of Fundamentalism,* and Maynard Shipley, *The War on Modern Science,* are satisfactory accounts of this phase of reaction. Harry Elmer Barnes, *In Quest of Truth and Justice: Debunking the War Guilt Myth* (1928), is a militant and polemical attack on the author's adversaries. On labor and the steel strike, see William Z. Foster, *The Great Steel Strike* (1920); Samuel Yellen, *American Labor Struggles* (1936), pp. 251-91; Rose M. Stein, *M-Day: The First Day of War* (1936).

XXIX. POLITICS, 1920-1928

Informing and interesting are D. L. Dumond, *Roosevelt to Roosevelt*; Frederick L. Allen, *Only Yesterday: An Informal History of the Nineteen-Twenties* (1931); Mark Sullivan, *Our Times,* Vol. VI. Robert S. Allen, *Washington Merry-Go-Round,* is sensational. The scandals of the Harding administration are aired in M. E. Ravage, *Teapot Dome,* and Morris Werner, *Privileged Characters.* The spirit of the Middle West is reflected in G. M. Stephenson, *John Lind of Minnesota*; Charles E. Russell, *The Story of the Nonpartisan League: A Chapter in American Evolution* (1920); Herbert E. Gaston, *The Nonpartisan League.* The biographies and autobiographies must be used with caution. "Warren Gamaliel Harding," by Allan Nevins, in *Dictionary of American Biography*; *Mirrors of Washington*; William Allen White, *Masks in a Pageant*; W. A. White, *Calvin Coolidge*; Calvin Coolidge, *Autobiography*; James E. Watson, *As I Knew Them*; Henry F. Pringle, *Alfred E. Smith: A Critical Study*; Norman Hapgood and Henry Moskowitz, *Up from the City Streets: Alfred E. Smith* (1927); Irwin H. Hoover, *Forty-Two Years in the White House*; C. W. Thompson, *Presidents I've Known*; Alfred E. Smith, *Up to Now.* Herbert Hoover, *The New Day,* is a compilation of campaign speeches. For material on the political campaigns, see E. E. Robinson, *The Presidential Vote, 1896-1932;* Roy V. Peel and Thomas C. Donnelly, *The 1928 Campaign.*

XXX. FOREIGN RELATIONS SINCE THE WORLD WAR

Samuel F. Bemis, *A Diplomatic History of the United States,* is the best survey. Frank H. Simons, *American Foreign Policy in the*

Post-War Years, is a judicious treatment. Harold G. Moulton and Leo Pasvolsky, *War Debts and World Prosperity; The Inter-Ally Debts and the United States* (published by the National Industrial Conference Board). Yamato Ichihashi, *The Washington Conference and After,* is a scholarly treatment. David Bryn-Jones, *Frank B. Kellogg,* and Claudius O. Johnson, *Borah of Idaho,* are biographical studies of men who had a prominent part in foreign affairs. James T. Shotwell, *War as an Instrument of National Policy,* is by the man whose name figures prominently in the Kellogg-Briand Pact. For Mexico and Japan, see the works listed under Chapters XXI and XXIV. To these may be added Harold Nicolson, *Dwight Morrow,* and William C. Johnstone, *The Shanghai Problem.* Hubert Herring, *And So To War,* is a hostile treatment of Roosevelt's foreign policy and his "quarantine" speech at Chicago on October 5, 1937.

XXXI. CONSERVATIVE REPUBLICANISM

The economic histories listed under Chapter IV deal briefly with the topics treated in this chapter. More special treatments are Rogers MacVeagh, *The Transportation Act, 1920: Its Sources, History, and Text*; H. W. Laidler, *Concentration of Control in American Industry*; W. M. Splawn, *Government Ownership and Operation of Railroads; The Agricultural Problem in the United States* (published by the National Industrial Conference Board) ; Nathan Fine, *Labor and Farmer Parties in the United States*; Edwin G. Nourse, *American Agriculture and the European Market*; John D. Black, *Agricultural Reform in the United States*; Arthur Capper, *The Agricultural Bloc*; Wilson Gee, *The Place of Agriculture in American Life.* For the history of immigration restriction, see G. M. Stephenson, *A History of American Immigration*; Roy L. Garis, *Immigration Restriction*; Constantine Panunzio, *Immigration Crossroads*; Maurice R. Davie, *World Immigration*; J. P. Gavit, *Americans by Choice*; Luella Gettys, *The Law of Citizenship in the United States*; Sidney L. Gulick, *American Democracy and Asiatic Citizenship*; D. H. Smith and H. G. Herring, *The Bureau of Immigration: Its History, Activities, and Organization.* E. M. Phelps, *Selected Articles on Immigration* (1921), is a valuable bibliography.

XXXII. DISILLUSIONMENT

Frederick L. Allen, *Only Yesterday,* is a graphic story of the years of Coolidge prosperity and the stock market crash. William S.

Meyers and Walter H. Newton, *The Hoover Administration: A Documented Narrative* (1936), is Hoover's defense. D. L. Dumond, *Roosevelt to Roosevelt,* is packed with facts pointing the way to disaster. *Recent Social Trends in the United States* is a Report of the President's Committee on Recent Social Trends (2 vols.). Robert S. and Helen Merrell Lynd, *Middletown: A Study in Contemporary American Culture* (1929), and *Middletown in Transition* (1937), are interesting and penetrating sociological studies of many phases of life. Stuart Chase, *Prosperity, Fact or Myth?* is critical. Wallace B. Donham, *Business Adrift,* is by an economist. Sinclair Lewis, *The Man Who Knew Coolidge,* is a satire on complacent Americans. C. A. and Mary R. Beard, *The Rise of American Civilization,* Chap. XXX, "The Machine Age." R. C. Epstein, *The Automobile Industry*; T. F. McManus, *Men, Money, and Motors*; and W. M. Seabury, *The Public and the Motion Picture Industry,* are studies of recent industrial developments. There are several biographical studies of Henry Ford. Charles Merz, *The Dry Decade,* brings the story to 1929. Charles R. Walker, *American City: A Rank-and-File History* (1937), explains certain adjustments from the "Golden Age of Economic Empire" to class warfare in Minneapolis and St. Paul. J. V. Thompson, *Urbanization: Its Effects on Government and Society,* is a broader study. On the bonus, see Walter W. Waters. *B. E. F.: The Whole Story of the Bonus Army,* and Katherine Mayo, *Soldiers, What Next!* On the campaign of 1932, see Roy V. Peel and T. C. Donnelly, *The 1932 Campaign: An Analysis*; E. E. Robinson, *The Presidential Vote, 1896-1932*; Eleanor Roosevelt, *This Is My Story*; Franklin D. Roosevelt, *Public Papers and Addresses,* Vol. I, "The Genesis of the New Deal, 1928-1932"; W. F. Dexter, *Herbert Hoover and American Individualism*; Norman Thomas, *As I See It*; W. Z. Foster, *Toward Soviet America.*

XXXIII. THE NEW DEAL

Franklin D. Roosevelt, *Public Papers and Addresses,* Vols. II to V, tells the story through the election of 1936. Louis M. Hacker, *A Short History of the New Deal* (1934), is concise. D. L. Dumond, *Roosevelt to Roosevelt,* is sympathetic. Rexford G. Tugwell, *The Battle for Democracy* (1935), is a defense by one of the original "Brain Trusters." Charles A. Beard and George Smith, *The Future Comes: A Study of the New Deal* (1933), is a brief survey of the first months of the Roosevelt administration. Similar studies are

656 AMERICAN HISTORY SINCE 1865

Harold Ickes, *The New Democracy*; Henry A. Wallace, *New Frontiers*; A. A. Berle, *America's Recovery Program*; Ernest K. Lindley, *The Roosevelt Revolution: First Phase* (1933), and *Half Way with Roosevelt* (1936). Marie D. Lane and Francis Steigmuller, *America on Relief* (1938), is a brief and critical survey. Leverett S. Lyon, *The National Recovery Administration: An Analysis and Appraisal* (1935), renders an adverse verdict. H. L. Ickes, *Back to Work: The Story of PWA* (1935), is by the Secretary of the Interior. E. G. Nourse and others, *Three Years of the Agricultural Adjustment Administration,* and E. G. Nourse, *Marketing Agreements under the AAA,* are comprehensive treatments. On the TVA, see H. S. Raushenbush and H. W. Laidler, *Power Control,* and F. L. Bird and F. Ryan, *Public Ownership on Trial.* The case for social insurance is set forth in Abraham Epstein, *Insecurity: A Challenge to America,* and Paul Douglas, *Social Security in the United States.* J. P. Warburg, *Hell Bent for Election,* and *The New Dealers,* by Unofficial Observer, are caustic attacks on the New Deal. W. S. Meyers and W. H. Newton, *The Hoover Administration,* condemns Roosevelt's fiscal policy. The Supreme Court is excoriated in Drew Pearson and Robert S. Allen, *The Nine Old Men.* E. S. Corwin, *The Twilight of the Supreme Court: A History of Our Constitutional Theory,* and *The Supreme Court and the Commerce Power,* are scholarly treatises.

XXXIV. THE ELECTION OF 1936

Franklin D. Roosevelt, *Public Papers and Addresses,* Vol. V, "The People Approve," contains the candidate's speeches. Alfred M. Landon, *America at the Crossroads,* presents the Republican candidate's views. Biographical studies of the famous Louisana Senator are Thomas O. Harris, *The Kingfish*; Hermann Deutsch, *Huey Long*; Carleton Beals, *The Inside Story of Huey Long.* See also Huey Long, *My First Day in the White House.* Hearst, Long, Coughlin, Bilbo, and Townsend are dealt with in R. G. Swing, *Forerunners of American Fascism.* Charles E. Coughlin expounds his views in *A Series of Lectures on Social Justice.* The concluding chapter in Dumond, *Roosevelt to Roosevelt,* is on the election of 1936. Ferdinand Lundberg, *America's Sixty Families* (1937), is a bitter indictment of an alleged hierarchy of families who are said to dominate the United States and who hate Roosevelt as fiercely as Lundberg excoriates them. Raoul E. Desvernine, *Democratic Despotism*

(1936), was sent out with the compliments of the American Liberty League as part of the campaign to defeat Roosevelt.

XXXV. THE SECOND ROOSEVELT ADMINISTRATION

Stanley High, *Roosevelt—and Then?* brings the story into the second Roosevelt administration. The following are interesting contributions to the controversy over the Supreme Court: Joseph Alsop and Turner Catledge, *The 168 Days*; Homer Cummings and Carl McFarland, *Federal Justice*; Drew Pearson and Robert S. Allen, *The Nine Old Men*; Charles Fairman, "The Retirement of Federal Judges," in the *Harvard Law Review,* January, 1938. On labor: Edward Levinson, *Labor on the March,* is a discussion of recent issues and policies. J. Raymond Walsh, *C.I.O. Industrial Unionism in Action,* is an account of the history, aims, and leadership of the C.I.O. in relation to the American labor movement. Robert R. R. Brooks, *When Labor Organizes,* is a guide book to the facts behind the La Follette committee investigations and the split between the C.I.O. and the A. F. of L.

INDEX